Financing Growth in Canada

THE RESEARCH ASSEMBLED IN THIS VOLUME is mainly the product of work undertaken by academic researchers. Industry Canada staff, however, formulated and managed the project and provided constructive feedback throughout the process. Nevertheless, the papers ultimately remain the sole responsibility of the authors and do not necessarily reflect the policies or opinions of Industry Canada or the Government of Canada.

GENERAL EDITOR: PAUL J.N. HALPERN

Financing Growth in Canada

The Industry Canada Research Series

University of Calgary Press

ISBN 1-895176-95-6
ISSN 1188-0988

University of Calgary Press
2500 University Dr. N.W.
Calgary, Alberta, Canada T2N 1N4

Canadian Cataloguing in Publication Data
Main entry under title:
Financing Growth in Canada

(Industry Canada research series, ISSN 1188-0988; v. 8)
Issued also in French under title: Le financement de la croissance au Canada.
Includes bibliographical references.
ISBN 1-895176-95-6

Cat. No. Id53-11/8-1997E

1. Corporations — Canada — Finance.
2. Business enterprises — Canada — Finance.
I. Halpern, Paul J.N.
II. Series.

HG4090.F56 1997 658.15'0971 C97-910900-0

University of Calgary Press appreciates the assistance of the Alberta Foundation for the Arts (a beneficiary of Alberta Lotteries) for its 1997 publishing program.

EDITORIAL & TYPESETTING SERVICES: PMF Editorial Services Inc. and Allium Consulting Group Inc.
COVER DESIGN: Paul Payer/ArtPlus Limited.

Printed and bound in Canada

∞ This book is printed on acid-free paper.

Table of Contents

Preface

OVER THE LAST DECADE, ECONOMIC GROWTH RATES in the developed countries of the world have slowed. In an attempt to reverse this trend, many countries are exploring various economic policies which can be used to stimulate key sectors of the economy. One sector often considered vital for economic growth is the financial sector. An efficient financial sector minimizes the financing costs involved in the transfer of funds from savers to borrowers. This in turn encourages higher levels of savings by individuals and higher rates of investment by corporations. An efficient financial sector also ensures that savings are directed toward the most productive investments and that good projects do not go wanting because of a lack of funds. The end result is an economy that is able to grow more quickly, generating increasing employment opportunities and rising incomes for a nation's citizens.

Recognizing the need to examine fully the challenges and opportunities that exist for Canada in the area of capital markets, coupled with indications that the performance and quality of our financial services lagged many of our trading partners, the Micro-Economic Policy Analysis Branch of Industry Canada, in collaboration with the Financial Research Foundation of Canada, invited a group of experts in corporate finance, business and economics to explore various aspects of Canada's capital markets. Their research studies were presented and their findings discussed at a two-day conference, held in Toronto in January 1996 on *Capital Market Issues*. At the conference, the experts presented 13 research papers dealing with factors that influence investment and the operation of markets for both debt and equity capital. In the latter case, special attention was given to issues confronting firms that are in need of high-risk equity or venture capital financing. Various perspectives on the cost of capital were also addressed along with initiatives aimed at assisting firms to access capital markets. The papers were subsequently revised in light of comments received from academic, government and business experts who participated in the conference.

The final version of these studies appears in this, the eighth, volume of the Industry Canada Research Series. The research assembled here will contribute to government policy making by enhancing the understanding of various capital market issues and the challenges governments face when attempting to remedy capital market inefficiencies. In addition to the studies on specific aspects of Canada's capital market, the volume includes two overview papers summarizing the conference proceedings: one highlights the research findings while the other focuses on the policy implications.

Academic and private-sector organizations actively participate in the preparation of some of the Department's research documents. Occasionally, other organizations also contribute resources toward Industry Canada's research programs. For this volume, I would like to acknowledge the Financial Research Foundation of Canada which contributed both the time of its principals and financial support toward the successful completion of this project.

Professor Paul Halpern of the University of Toronto has overseen this project and served as General Editor for the research volume. I would like to thank Professor Halpern, as well as all of the authors and discussants for their valued role in this project.

JOHN MANLEY
MINISTER OF INDUSTRY

Paul J.N. Halpern
Faculty of Management
University of Toronto

1

Introduction and Overview

INTRODUCTION

INCREASINGLY, ECONOMIES ARE BECOMING GLOBAL. Not only are products and services being sold around the world and being produced in countries where it is most efficient to do so, but access to capital is becoming global as well. For Canada to compete effectively in this global context, Canadian capital markets must be effective and efficient in providing capital to firms. Funds are needed in the initial phases of growth, such as in venture capital, for succeeding phases in the growth of companies and for ongoing operations of more mature companies. Large and small firms, high-technology as well as the more conventional industries, are all crucially dependent on the effectiveness of Canadian capital markets. With effectively functioning capital markets, including the presence of global suppliers of capital, firms can access funds at costs reflecting the risk of their operations.

The field of inquiry in the area of capital markets is extremely wide. A list of topics in the capital markets section of the Financial Economists Network on the Internet includes research ranging from "rational herding" in capital markets to the existence of segmented capital markets, through to tests of capital market efficiency. These topics are all important since they have implications for the functioning of the capital markets, their price-setting capacity, the price discovery process, their use in allocating risk and, ultimately, the efficiency with which capital is allocated to competing uses in the economy. Identifying a set of research topics for this conference was very difficult since hard choices had to be made concerning which topics should be included. At first, the task appeared almost impossible.

To complicate the task even further, capital markets include a variety of securities of which bonds and stocks are the most basic; financial innovation has made the set of securities available in capital markets very rich and institutionally complex. In addition, there are markets which cater to different clienteles and currencies. These markets and financial securities are important for the management of risk, the financing of investment activities and the growth of the Canadian economy.

In fact, it was this latter issue – the importance of capital markets for economic growth in the Canadian economy – which provided the necessary focus to decide on the research papers. Each author was required not only to analyse the research question but also to address policy implications of the analysis. As expected, this task was more difficult for some topics and the policy implications are not equally drawn out for each paper. Two additional papers in this volume summarize the other papers and draw conclusions from the presentations and discussions. The first is by Donald Brean who acted as rapporteur for the conference. The second is by Jack Mintz whose focus is on the policy issues arising from the conference. His paper is unique in that it is intended to address the general use of economic and financial research in the policy area with specific issues from the conference papers as examples.

Access to capital markets is necessary to fund investment in plant and equipment and other assets. Otherwise, companies face liquidity or capital constraints when investments are limited to funding through retained earnings and restricted amounts of bank debt. This situation results in reduced economic wealth for shareholders and, ultimately, the economy. While there are many forces affecting investment decisions, one that is of concern in this research program is the cost of capital. The cost of capital is defined in different ways and the research papers in this volume reflect these different approaches. However, regardless of the measurement technique used, the underlying concept is the dependence on the cost of funds used in financing investment. When the cost of funds is high due to underlying imperfections in capital markets, risk characteristics of the Canadian economy or lack of competition, the cost of capital is high with a depressing impact on investment activity and economic growth. In the extreme, when a firm is denied access to capital, the cost of capital is infinite.

The research program includes inquiry into the financing of large and small companies and the importance of certain variables, such as cost of capital and marginal tax rates, on investment activity. In addition, the interaction of capital markets and costs of capital is investigated since it is fundamental in understanding investment behaviour. The research papers address the allocative efficiency of Canadian capital markets, potential problems in these capital markets, government involvement in the capital markets to address perceived problems and an evaluation of government initiatives in this area. As already noted, all research papers present suggestions arising from the research for appropriate policy initiatives. Many papers provide new empirical analyses on the functioning of both formal capital markets, such as stock exchanges, and informal markets, such as the venture capital market.

Competition is an overriding force in capital markets. In Canadian capital markets, competition is both domestic and global. There is one paper in the research program that is directly concerned with this international competition – the use of interlisting for equity securities. Moreover, competition is present in other areas in the capital markets. One of the new areas is the use of foreign "lending" markets for small to medium-sized firms – companies that, historically, were unable to access the cheaper foreign debt markets. With the fluidity of capital, competition should be sufficient to resolve problems of access to capital and the supply of capital to various markets and market participants.

However, even with competition, capital markets have frequently been accused of not working effectively, i.e., they exhibit market failure. In one way or another, market failures have been cited to justify intervention strategies by governments at the federal and provincial levels. Usually, the market failures have been identified with little, if any, reference to theory or empirical work. Most often, there is a reliance on someone's intuition or an affected party's self-interest. A number of the papers address the issues of market failure in a systematic way. The usual argument is that a market failure can arise in the context of a start-up company or a company in a later stage of development in which equity (venture) capital is needed. The source of the market failure can be asymmetries in information between the user of capital and the supplier leading to pre-contractual opportunistic behaviour by the user of capital (referred to as adverse selection) or post-contractual opportunistic behaviour on the part of the demander of capital (referred to as moral hazard) resulting from the inability of the supplier of the funds to monitor behaviour effectively. The presence of asymmetries of information, the significant cost of monitoring and the fact that the entrepreneur, who is the owner-manager of the firm, operates the firm as an agent for the minority owners, can generate wealth transfers from investors, both debt and equity, to the entrepreneur.

Even with the problems associated with asymmetric information and costly monitoring, there are responses undertaken by market participants, without government initiatives to mitigate their impact. These responses include contract provisions which reduce the incentive for the entrepreneur to behave in this manner and facilitate monitoring. In other situations, a market solution is identified. For example, consider the use of love capital provided to start-up ventures by relatives and friends of the entrepreneur. This approach reduces monitoring costs and, due to the close links of family, post-contractual opportunism is expected to be reduced. Alternatively, certain types of securities can be used in the financing of the enterprise; these securities have payoffs designed to reduce opportunistic behaviour. Convertible debt or convertible preferred equity provides an example of this type of security and is discussed in two papers in this volume.

However, there may be situations in which these solutions are not possible and a market failure continues to affect the flow of funds. A frequently cited example is the supply of debt capital to small high-risk companies. Having identified the market failure, the next step in the policy decision should be the evaluation of what institution, if any, is able to deal with these problems. Shifting the financing of these entities to institutions which have no better capacity to monitor owner-manager behaviour or remove the opportunistic behaviour than capital market participants, but have a comparative advantage in absorbing significant financial loses, is not efficiency enhancing for the economy. Thus, government programs based on the premise of market failure must be assessed on whether they provide more funds to the affected firms than provided before – they most likely, but not always, will – and on whether they can alleviate the problems so the resources dedicated to the enterprise are not wasted.

In today's economy, with the presence of substantial deficits at all levels of government, the capacity to lose money through financing of various programs designed to address these market failures has diminished dramatically. The rationale for, and the instruments to use in the event of, a true market failure have to be assessed carefully. It is from the analysis of research papers such as those prepared for this conference that policy makers can be informed of the existence of market failures and, if failures exist, whether or not intervention in the markets should be undertaken.

THE RESEARCH PROGRAM

THE FOLLOWING OUTLINE DESCRIBES THE RESEARCH PROGRAM and how the papers link together to address the purposes of the conference, as articulated by Denis Gauthier at the start of the conference. Primary among these are the identification of improvements in capital markets and whether existing programs have succeeded in meeting their mandates. The description of the research papers will be brief since Brean and Mintz highlight the analyses and conclusions of each paper.

Figure 1 presents a schematic representation of the conference papers and how they link together. The order of the papers in Figure 1 (and in this introduction) does not reflect the order in which the papers were presented at the conference.

The research papers have been combined into four major areas. (Of course, others could group the papers in different ways.)

- Influences on investment
- High-risk equity: venture capital financing
- Equity markets: non-venture capital financing
- Debt markets: small and large firms.

When there are multiple papers in an area, they have been grouped so the last paper in the section refers to a government initiative to address what has been perceived as a market failure.

Each area is considered in turn describing both the rationale for the inclusion of each paper and the issues each is intended to address.

INFLUENCES ON INVESTMENT

THE FIRST SECTION OF THE CONFERENCE PROVIDES A MACRO PERSPECTIVE of the forces affecting corporate investment decisions. Corporations grow through the application of funds to purchase productive assets to generate cash flows. To the extent that productive investment is undertaken, the economy grows and prospers. However, there should be no artificial stimulation of investment activity through specific policies of the government since this will result in a misallocation of resources and

FIGURE 1
RESEARCH PROGRAM

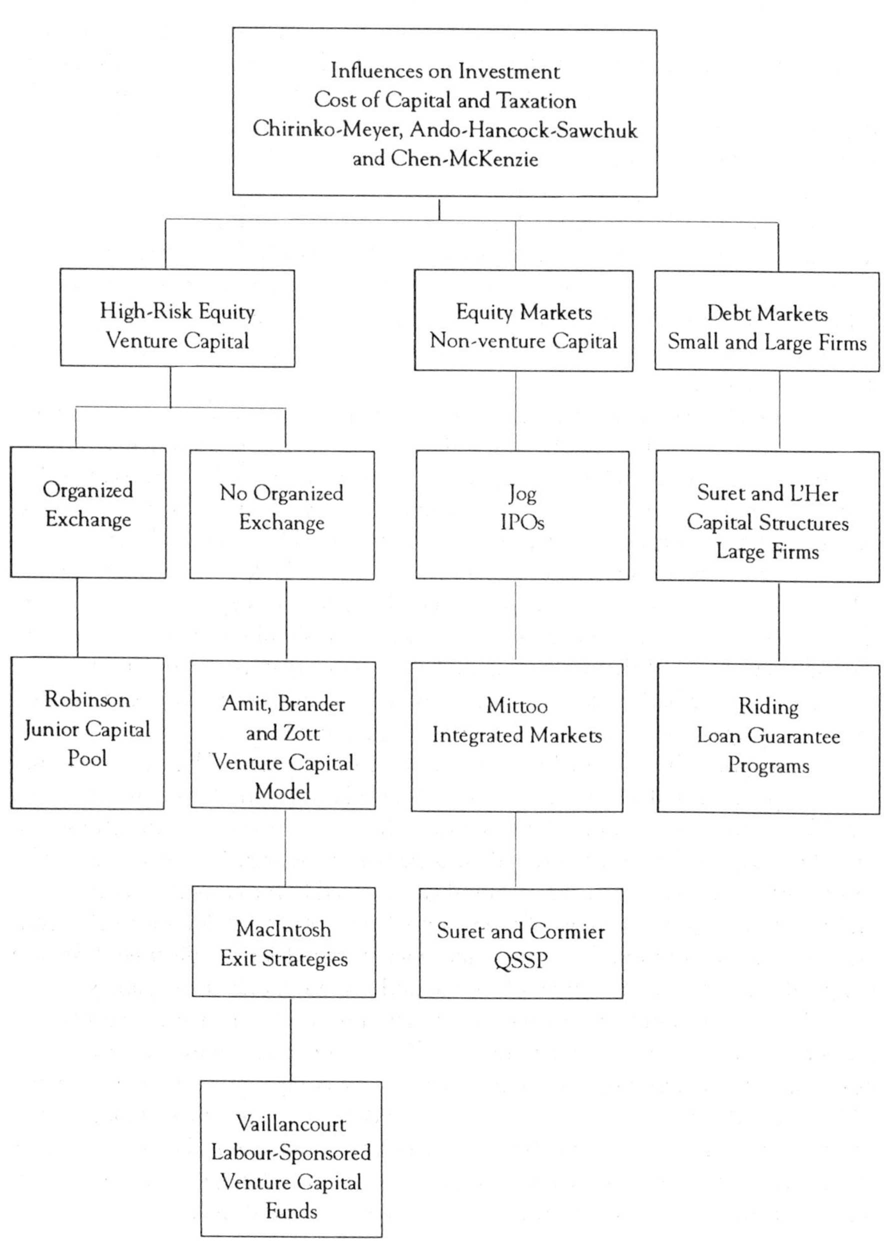

an arbitrary shift of growth from one area of the economy to another without an increase in aggregate economic growth. In fact, it is possible that overall growth may be negatively affected. Similarly, economic growth will be harmed if investment is artificially reduced by specific policies.

There are many influences on corporate real investment decision making. The two major forces highlighted in the papers found in this section are the cost of capital and taxation. For the cost of capital variable, the important issues are the impact of cost of capital on investment behaviour, the existence of a differential impact by industry sector, international differences and the measurement and use of the cost of capital by companies.

Underlying all cost of capital studies is the assumption that the cost of capital will have an impact on investment behaviour. Factors which increase the cost of funds to corporations will influence the cost of capital and, ultimately, the investment behaviour of firms. The elasticity of investment with respect to cost of capital by industry category will demonstrate the importance of the cost of capital factor to different industries.

In an open economy with global capital markets, there should be no differences in cost of capital among countries. However, while capital markets are becoming more global and their integration is moving forward through competition and the elimination of regulatory impediments, fully integrated capital markets may not yet be attained even in a small open economy like Canada. Therefore, the cost of capital may differ among countries potentially leading to competitive advantages for industries in one country over the same industry in another country. The observation that cost of capital differences exist should lead policy makers to identify the sources of the problem and, if they are regulatory, remove them. Note that there may be basic risk differences between countries which may lead to different costs of capital for similar industries over various periods.

Two approaches are used to measure the cost of capital. The first is the user cost of capital and reflects the financing costs faced by the firm (sometimes adjusted for risk), as well as economic depreciation. The user cost is the approach used in two of the papers although the actual measurement technique is very different. The second way to measure the cost of capital is employed in the corporate finance area and reflects a weighted average of the marginal costs of the specific sources of funds faced by the corporation. This approach always includes risk adjustment for the marginal costs of specific sources of capital and is used in one of the papers.

Taxation also influences investment. The tax system of each country has an impact on the taxes paid by domestic as well as foreign companies investing in the host country. A comparison of taxation of domestic companies in a set of countries will identify the relative burden of taxation to domestic companies. In addition, a comparison of taxation of domestic and foreign companies across different countries will provide an indication of the incentives provided to foreign investment – an important ingredient in generating economic growth for a country.

Cost of Capital Papers

There are three papers that address the cost of capital issue. Chirinko and Meyer in "The User Cost of Capital and Investment Spending: Implications for Canadian Firms" address the importance of costs of capital in investment decision making. The paper assesses the sensitivity of investment to changes in the cost of capital by estimating the elasticity of investment spending with respect to the cost of capital. The data used are "pseudo" Canadian, i.e., U.S. firm-specific data are grouped to match the industry characteristics of the Canadian economy. The empirical results are crucial to understanding the role cost of capital plays in investment spending and the relative sensitivity of the impact of the cost of capital in different industries. In addition, the paper provides a comparison of the elasticities for similar industries in both Canada and the United States.

With the importance of international growth, are Canadian companies facing similar costs of capital as their international competitors? The remaining two papers in this section address this issue. Ando, Hancock and Sawchuk in "Cost of Capital for the United States, Japan and Canada: An Attempt at Measurement Based on Individual Company Records and Aggregate National Accounts Data" utilize the user cost of capital framework to measure the cost of capital in three countries. This approach differs from that used in the Chirinko and Meyer. Ando, Hancock and Sawchuk measure the cost of capital as the sum of the returns to the capital employed (interest, dividends, retained earnings with the inventory valuation adjustment and capital consumption allowance) divided by an approximation of the market value of capital employed by a firm. By measuring this *ex post* cost of capital over a number of periods and firms, a good estimate of the cost of capital should result. This paper has to address some methodological and interpretation issues for the Japanese cost of capital estimates given the very different accounting practices and the fact that the cost of capital estimates are driven by the accounting numbers.

The final paper in this set by Jog, "Investing in Canada: Estimation of the Sectoral Cost of Capital in Canada and Case Studies for International Comparisons" differs from the previous two in its use of a corporate finance approach to measure the cost of capital for a number of Canadian sectors. He then applies the approach to three case studies to determine the cost of capital in the United States and Finland for specific industries. The paper applies two corporate finance methodologies to measure the cost of equity, an input in the cost of capital calculation, discusses the problems associated with each approach and presents a method to make international comparisons.

Taxation

The other influence on investment behaviour is taxation and this is assessed in a paper by Chen and McKenzie "The Impact of Taxation on Capital Markets: An International Comparison of Effective Tax Rates on Capital." The authors construct marginal effective tax rate (METR) estimates for a number of countries and assess the METR of a Canadian company investing in the United States. The purpose is to determine if the tax system in Canada creates any bias against investment activity. An interesting issue addressed in the paper is the relative size of the METR for the various provinces of Canada. Perhaps government policies should be directed at cleaning up our own house!

ACCESS TO HIGH-RISK EQUITY: VENTURE CAPITAL FINANCING

VENTURE CAPITAL PROVIDES A VERY INTERESTING LABORATORY to investigate issues that can cause capital markets either to operate ineffectively or, in the extreme, fail. As described in the introduction to this overview, two problems associated with differential information between participants in the market can lead to badly functioning capital markets: opportunistic behaviour and adverse selection. In the venture capital area, opportunistic behaviour is an important issue since it is very difficult and costly to monitor the entrepreneur once funding has been provided. While the entrepreneur can promise to use the funds provided for a particular purpose, once the funds are provided, there is no constraint on the actual use of the funds. Similarly, asymmetric information leading to adverse selection problems is rampant in this market since the entrepreneur has better information than the financier on whether he or she is of above, below or average quality. The adverse selection problem can also lead to restricted access to funds or, in the extreme, the disappearance of the market.

In the early stages of financing for the venture capital firm, there is an informal market in which the entrepreneur obtains funding from friends, relatives and/or business associates. These funds are called "love" capital and the individuals who provide this financing are called "angels." The moral hazard and adverse selection problems exist but the close ties of the entrepreneur and those providing capital will probably reduce their impact. However, as the firm grows, the need for larger amounts of capital arises. This capital is typically provided by specialized financing groups in the form of equity or a fixed claim with equity participation given to the financing group.

With the importance of the funding of these high-risk ventures to the growth of the economy, the papers found in this section consider the venture capital market. This market is described, some of the problems of the market identified and the resolution of these problems within the market context described. There is also an analysis of the attempts by government to address what is perceived as market failure. These failures are called "financing gaps" in the policy-related literature and refer to the inability of certain types or sizes of firms to obtain financing given their risk.

There are two subsections in this area. The first considers venture capital in which there is an organized capital market such as a stock exchange. The second considers the more frequent situation where there is no formal equity market for high-risk venture capital funds.

Organized Exchange

It is well known that listing requirements, issue costs and other informational and cost factors limit the use of equity markets for the financing of small firms, especially small high-risk firms. In "Raising Equity Capital for Small and Medium-Sized Enterprises Using Canada's Public Equity Markets," Robinson addresses the use of public equity markets for high-risk firms. He identifies the costs of raising equity on Canadian exchanges through an initial public offering (IPO) observing that there are differences among the equity exchanges in Canada. Robinson also considers the conditions under which an equity market for high-risk companies can exist by looking at the experience of such markets in Canada and Europe. A necessary condition for the continuation of these markets is the maintenance of liquidity in the market, and this may be hampered by informational problems.

An interesting part of the paper is the investigation of the Junior Capital Pool (JCP) on the Alberta Stock Exchange. In the JCP, companies raise equity through the stock market to finance the range of needs from seed capital to secondary issues. However, there is very little information provided on the use of the proceeds of the issue. Thus, moral hazard and adverse selection problems should be crucial in this market. Regulations, which require some information dissemination and impose a limit to the time elapsed from the raising of the funds to their use, may be useful mechanisms to control the asymmetric information and monitoring problems.

The JCP has been successful and a number of these companies have subsequently raised equity on senior exchanges such as the Alberta and Toronto stock exchanges. Even though companies are not subsequently listed on an exchange, they can still be profitable and may be taken over by another firm. The Robinson paper addresses the question of the success of the JCP given the moral hazard and adverse selection problems and whether it can be used as a model for other exchanges or is idiosyncratic to the Alberta context.

No Organized Exchange

The first paper in this section by Amit, Brander and Zott, "Venture Capital Financing of Entrepreneurship in Canada," provides some background on the venture capital industry in Canada, a general approach to viewing venture capital, its problems and the solutions to these problems. The authors identify three stylized observations.

- There is a specialized industry dedicated to venture capital.
- Very little of the funding is focused on start-up companies.
- The home run, i.e., the unusual occurrence of a company that generates a high rate of return is important.

To explain these observations, the authors provide a theory based on asymmetric information between the venture capitalist (supplier of capital) and the entrepreneur, and the existence of limited liability. The former leads to adverse selection problems whereas the latter leads to moral hazard. The authors also provide some indirect empirical support to their theory. They consider whether government intervention is needed in this market and identify the role of contracts in addressing the potential market failure. Note that this paper and the developed model are useful in explaining the problems of using organized stock exchanges to provide venture capital. This is the subject of the paper by Robinson.

When a venture capitalist provides funds to a high-risk entity, there is an expectation of a high rate of return. However, as noted in Amit, Brander and Zott, most of the investments are either failures or limp along. It is the home run that generates the high profits for the venture capitalist on average. When the venture capitalist invests the funds, he or she also considers the liquidity of the investment where liquidity reflects the ability of the venture capitalist to exit the investment. Exit strategies are very important to the success of this market. Without viable exit strategies, the average expected rates of return on the portfolio of investments would have to be even higher, and there would be a reduced supply of these projects. Thus, viable exit strategies will reduce the cost of capital for venture capital enterprises.

Exit strategies are analysed in depth in the paper by MacIntosh, "Venture Capital Exits in Canada and the United States." MacIntosh identifies exit strategies by referring to previous studies and by undertaking a questionnaire survey of U.S. and Canadian venture capitalists concerning the ways in which they exited their investments. The differences between the United States and Canada are assessed. With the importance of the IPO market in the exit decision, a well-functioning IPO market is crucial in reducing the cost of capital to venture capital enterprises.

The final paper in this section is by Vaillancourt, "Labour-Sponsored Venture Capital Funds in Canada: Institutional Aspects, Tax Expenditures and Employment Creation." The labour-sponsored venture capital fund (LSVCF) uses government tax policy to encourage financing to high-risk venture capital firms. While these funds are relatively new in most provinces, they have been in existence for many years in Quebec. Thus, the information from the Quebec-based funds is used to assess their benefits and costs. These funds represent a significant block of financing available to fund venture capital usually in the stages beyond seed capital requirements. The rationale for the introduction of the LSVCF is the belief that there is a financing gap for these high-risk firms which is not being satisfied by the conventional venture capital market. The Vaillancourt paper looks at the rationale for the provincial intervention, the success of these funds in meeting their mandate and the costs of these funds in terms of tax expenditures.

EQUITY MARKETS: NON-VENTURE CAPITAL FINANCING

THROUGHOUT THEIR ECONOMIC LIFE, FIRMS NEED ACCESS TO EQUITY CAPITAL. This equity refers not only to the initial start-up funds and continuing growth needs in the venture capital area but also to continuing equity needs to fund investments and restructure corporate balance sheets for more mature companies. In the previous section, the papers analysed access to equity for firms that needed venture capital and considered both formal exchanges and informal sources. In this section, the focus shifts to consider more formal equity markets in the context of non-venture capital needs.

One function of equity markets is to provide a market in which firms can raise publicly traded equity and thereby share risk among investors. This issue can be an IPO to finance a division of a company which has been removed from the corporate empire and will operate on its own with its own equity capital. At the other extreme, as noted in the previous section, the IPO provides an exit strategy for investors who have financed venture capital firms and for the entrepreneurs who started the firm. The effective functioning of these markets provides liquidity to investors and should ameliorate the concern of investing in venture capital which is typically illiquid.

With well-functioning liquid equity markets, the firm has access to equity – either IPO or seasoned equity issues – at low cost, given the risk of the entity and, hence, this component of the cost of capital is reduced. The result is a lower cost of capital, more investments and increases in wealth to existing shareholders due to the investments.

The papers in this section differ from those in the venture capital section since the former considered market failures in the source of equity capital for small (high-risk) firms. Here the papers consider raising funds in IPOs for larger firms, financing through secondary market offerings, and government policies to improve the flow of equity funds and reduce the cost of equity capital.

The first paper is by Jog, "The Climate for Canadian Initial Public Offerings." Jog's paper addresses three issues: short-term underpricing of a new equity issue, long-term performance of a new equity issue and a survey of users of the IPO market concerning issue costs and compensation paid to underwriters of the issue. The underpricing of new equity issues is a puzzle that has intrigued many finance scholars. A number of papers provide theoretical rationales for this underpricing; they are generally related to problems of asymmetric information. A review of these papers is presented in the Jog and Robinson papers. The Jog paper identifies the underpricing cost and compares it to the values in other countries. If the underpricing issue is a puzzle, the negative stock market performance of the new issue relative to the overall market after the new issue is completed is total confusion. Jog measures this performance for Canadian firms and relates it to the observed performance in other markets. In addition to looking at the stock market performance, the paper investigates the performance of the companies subsequent to the new issue by looking at accounting data. This provides an interesting complementary view of the post-issue performance of new-issue companies. The final section of Jog's paper is novel in corporate finance: ask the participants their views! The results provide some light on the theoretical contributions and empirical observations in the literature.

The second paper in this section, by Mittoo, "Seasoned Equity Offerings and the Cost of Equity in the Canadian Market," investigates the influence on the stock market performance of a secondary offering of common equity for firms that are listed on the Toronto Stock Exchange (TSE) and a U.S. exchange. The empirical evidence on secondary offerings – the issue of new common equity for securities that are already listed on an exchange – demonstrates that the announcement of a new secondary equity offering is associated with a reduction in share price. To the extent that the stock price decreases, the cost of equity capital is higher. This reduction in share price is found in all markets around the world. There are a number of theories which attempt to explain this observation; most of the arguments relate to the existence of asymmetric information between the management and the new shareholders.

If capital markets are fully integrated, then a secondary issue of equity by a company with equity traded only in Canada should have the same announcement price effect as observed for a Canadian company that has interlisted equity. Mittoo investigates whether capital markets are truly integrated and whether there is a differential impact on the share price on the announcement of a new equity issue if the security is interlisted. The size of the negative stock price movement can be related to a number of firm-specific variables including the interlisting status. To the extent that interlisted companies have a smaller negative price impact, they face a low cost of capital, and equity markets are segmented in some form.

As in the previous sections, the final paper in this section refers to government operations in the particular market of interest. In this instance, government tax policy is used to encourage ownership of equity and lower the cost of equity capital to certain companies. Suret and Cormier in "The Quebec Stock Savings Plan: Overview and Evaluation," investigate the Quebec Stock Savings Plan (QSSP) introduced in 1979. The QSSP has gone through a number of changes, all intended to focus the program's benefits on the companies that are purported to have troubles raising equity. The current program provides assistance to companies which are large enough to meet the Montreal exchange listing requirements; these requirements are less onerous than those found on the TSE. The paper evaluates how the plan has worked, the costs of the plan, the impact on the share prices of eligible companies and on the cost of equity capital, and the lessons to be learned in designing other plans of this type. The latter issue is very important in the policy context since the program, while generating some benefits, may distort markets or provide assistance to companies which do not need it, thereby resulting in windfall gains to existing shareholders.

Debt Markets: Small and Large Firms

Debt is an important source of funds to both large and small firms. For the former, the costs at which debt can be issued will affect the cost of capital and the amount of investment that will be undertaken. For the latter, there are situations where the cost and access to this form of capital are problematic. For small, high-risk companies, the use of debt introduces problems associated with moral hazard arising from the costs of monitoring, which can be substantial, and the limited liability for corporations. In this section, the papers investigate the use of debt for both large and small firms to determine if there are any access problems and, if so, how they can be addressed.

In "The Evolving Capital Structure of Large Canadian Firms" Suret and L'Her investigate the debt-equity choice of companies over time and explain why firms choose the capital structures that we observe. The authors consider a number of theories that have been presented in the literature to explain capital structure choice and look at unique characteristics of the Canadian market such as high ownership concentration and tax structure. This paper follows in the steps of a substantial literature found in other countries that addresses the determinants of capital structure choice including problems in the operation of debt markets.

The archetypal example of financing gaps has always been the availability of debt (loan) capital to small businesses. Many governments have established programs to improve the flow of funding to these companies. The programs normally use loan guarantees. In "On the Care and Nurture of Loan Guarantee Programs" Riding asks whether there is truly a market failure that requires such programs. A market failure is defined as a situation in which firms of identical risk have different borrowing costs. Riding, in looking for the existence of market failure, also identifies the success of these loan guarantee programs in terms of screening credit and finding viable companies which were incorrectly screened out of the market. The research also derives policy implications on access to loan guarantees and the use of user fees which reflect the risk of the borrower. The fees have to be viewed in the context of adverse selection where a poor quality borrower may pay a fee because of being placed in the wrong credit class. Finally, Riding compares the loan guarantee program in Canada with similar programs in other countries and draws conclusions on their design and effectiveness.

Conclusions

The effective functioning of capital markets is crucial to the growth of the Canadian economy. Capital markets affect both large and small firms along with high technology and the more traditional industries. Well-functioning capital markets provide for access to capital at yields which reflect risks of the cash flows associated with the financial instrument issued thereby minimizing the firms cost of capital. The papers in this volume address a number of important issues and provide us with a better understanding of the Canadian capital markets, their functioning and the potential problems which may require government intervention. The underlying concerns in a number of papers reflect imperfections in capital markets, and the problems associated with moral hazard and adverse selection. In addition, several papers evaluate existing government policies intended to correct for perceived market failures. The papers provide research on capital market issues to inform policy makers on the presence of market failures, to assess the success of existing policy initiatives and to provide an appreciation of the importance of the policy instrument used in the event that intervention is deemed necessary.

Finally, I want to thank a number of individuals who were very important to the evolution of the research program, to the care and nurturing of the financial resources and, of course, to ensuring that the conference and the subsequent research volume were kept on track. Denis Gauthier, Gerry Tapp, Bob Kunimoto and Gary Sawchuk, all from Industry Canada, deserve not only my gratitude but that of the authors, discussants and participants at the Capital Markets Issues conference.

Session I *Cost of Capital*

Robert S. Chirinko & *Andrew P. Meyer*
Department of Economics *Federal Reserve Bank of St. Louis*
Emory University

2

The User Cost of Capital and Investment Spending: Implications for Canadian Firms

ABSTRACT

PUBLIC POLICIES AIMED AT ENHANCING ECONOMIC PERFORMANCE through increases in business capital depend on two separate and quantitatively important channels – the response of investment incentives to changes in policy and the subsequent impact of these incentives on investment spending. Quantifying the latter channel is the task of this paper.

Unfortunately, Canadian time series data at the firm level are unavailable. The user cost elasticity is estimated with a panel data set containing 21,516 non-duplicative observations for 3,296 manufacturing and non-manufacturing U.S. firms for the period 1972 to 1991. Panel data permit us to control for several factors that may distort estimates of the user cost elasticity. The U.S. data are grouped into sectors comparable to those in Canada, thus enhancing the usefulness of the estimated user cost elasticities for assessing issues facing Canadian policy makers.

The paper reviews the strengths and weaknesses of several different investment models, and favours a modified Jorgenson neoclassical model to estimate the impact of the user cost. The estimated user cost elasticities vary widely across the 11 sectors studied here, and are sizable in several sectors. However, the elasticities are not precisely estimated. Our overall finding is that there is too much imprecision in these estimates to reach firm conclusions about sectoral user cost elasticities. We offer several suggestions for future research which should involve searching for better instrumental variables, defining the sectors more broadly and using estimators that avoid simultaneity problems efficiently. The collection of suitable Canadian firm-level data must be a high priority for future research.

INTRODUCTION

PUBLIC POLICIES AIMED AT ENHANCING ECONOMIC PERFORMANCE through increases in business capital depend on two separate and quantitatively important channels. The first channel is examined in several papers published in this volume that focus on how government policies can correct market failures and enhance economic performance by altering economic incentives for acquiring capital. These incentives have usually been stated in terms of the user cost of capital that constrains investment decisions.

Substantial changes in the user cost are necessary but not sufficient for effective policy. The second critical channel translates a given change in the user cost into a change in factors of production. Quantifying the sensitivity of investment spending to the user cost of capital is the task of this paper.

The structure of the Canadian economy makes this task quite difficult. The user cost of capital, which depends on relative prices and the rates of interest, depreciation and taxation, is a relatively restricted concept with which to capture the enormous complexity of the tax code. In simple tax systems, the user cost can only approximate the effects of the tax code on business investment decisions. In the case of Canada, however, the approximation is particularly poor because of the very liberal carry-back and carry-forward provisions that make the timing of tax payments largely discretionary. The openness of the Canadian economy and the tax rules governing foreign activities add additional complexities. Moreover, the tax depreciation rates, asset mixes and income tax rates are quite complicated, and vary substantially across firms. Care must be taken in incorporating these factors into the user cost in a reasonable manner. Unfortunately, time series data at the firm level that would reduce the approximation error to a tolerable level are unavailable.

This problem is circumvented by examining an economy with a simpler tax structure which also has market conditions and available technologies resembling those in Canada. These criteria are met by firms in the United States. However, useful comparisons between Canadian and U.S. firms are compromised by substantial differences in the composition of industrial and commercial activities in the two economies. The U.S. data become useful for issues facing Canadian policy makers when grouped into sectors comparable to those in Canada. For example, the Canadian health care sector comprises firms with Canadian Standard Industrial Classification (SIC) codes 3740, 3770 and 8600. These SICs are matched to comparable U.S. firms to form the health care sector used in this study. (Details of the SIC matches are provided in the third part of this paper and in Appendix A.) Based on these "Canadian sectors," estimates of the user cost elasticities are generated from the U.S. data that are relevant for understanding the responsiveness of Canadian firms to variations in the user cost of capital.

The second part of this paper provides a review of the investment literature with a particular focus on the sensitivity of investment spending to the user cost. Extant models are divided into two broad categories depending on whether dynamics are treated implicitly or explicitly. Models are included in the latter category if dynamic elements appear explicitly in the optimization problem and if the estimated coefficients are linked explicitly to the underlying technology and expectation parameters. The implicit category contains those investment models that do not meet these criteria. For each category, a benchmark model is developed and related to specific models appearing in the literature.

Readers who are acquainted with the Jorgenson neoclassical model used in this study and who have no immediate interest in modelling issues may wish to skip on to the next section which presents a self-contained development of the framework for estimating the responsiveness of investment. The strengths and weaknesses of the implicit and explicit models are highlighted, and it is concluded that neither category dominates in estimating user cost elasticities. The reasons for using the implicit Jorgenson neoclassical model are discussed. This section then identifies several factors that may distort elasticity estimates but that are avoided with the panel data used in this study. The data set contains 21,516 non-duplicative observations for 3,296 manufacturing and non-manufacturing firms for the period 1972 to 1991. These data, the mapping between Canadian sectors and U.S. firms, and the econometric equation that is the basis for all of the estimates reported in this study are discussed.

Empirical results are presented in the next section. Panel data permit several different estimation techniques to be employed, and four are used: pooled, mean-difference, first-difference and first-difference with instrumental variables. As emphasized in much recent work, the availability of internal finance may loom large in investment equations, and estimates with and without cash flow are presented for all four estimators. Hence, eight estimates of the user cost elasticity are computed for each of the 11 sectors.

The final section summarizes the results for the user cost elasticities and presents the preferred estimates.

A Review Of Investment Models[1]

This section presents an overview of the investment literature with an emphasis on issues pertaining to estimating the effects of taxes and other price variables on business investment spending. To place some structure on this vast literature, extant models are divided into two broad categories depending on whether dynamics are treated implicitly or explicitly. Models are included in the latter category if dynamic elements appear explicitly in the optimization problem and if the estimated coefficients are linked explicitly to the underlying technology and expectation parameters. The implicit category contains those investment models that do not meet these criteria.

Implicit Models

This section begins by sketching a benchmark model that serves as a basis for interpreting implicit models followed by an extensive discussion of the neoclassical model and criticisms thereof. Theory and key assumptions are reviewed. Other implicit models developed in the 1980s are discussed briefly.

The Benchmark Model

The benchmark model is based on a demand for capital and, with the addition of dynamics, a demand for investment. The demand for capital is derived from elementary economic principles and is determined by the equality between the expected marginal benefits and costs from an additional unit of capital. This equality can be transformed so that the desired (or optimal) capital stock (K^*_t) depends on price variables, quantity variables and autonomous shocks:

$$K^*_t = f\,[prices,\ quantities,\ shocks] \tag{1}$$

Equation (1) follows from well-known static theory and, in the absence of any dynamic considerations, the firm would achieve K^*_t instantaneously. Dynamics are introduced into the benchmark model when specifying the demand for the flow of investment, and are imposed implicitly, i.e., without reference to an explicit theory. The benchmark model depends on two types of dynamics. First, the translation from a stock demand to a flow demand is based on a series of maintained assumptions about delivery lags (as well as expenditure and gestation lags); adjustment costs; vintage effects, i.e., the putty and clay qualities of capital; and replacement investment. These dynamic elements may compel the firm to look deep into the future. The firm's expectations, however, are usually unobservable to the applied researcher. A second set of dynamics is introduced when these unobservable expectations are linked to observable variables through regressive or extrapolative schemes represented by distributed lags. Various combinations of assumptions concerning the desired capital stock (equation [1]), expectations, and the other dynamic elements listed above define the different implicit models appearing in the literature.

Neoclassical Models – Theory

By far, the most frequently used specification for the analysis of investment spending has been the neoclassical model pioneered by Dale Jorgenson and his numerous collaborators (Jorgenson, 1963, 1971). In this model, the firm maximizes the discounted flow of profits over an infinite horizon, delivery lags, adjustment costs and vintage effects are absent, and capital depreciates at a geometric rate. As a consequence, the firm can achieve any (K^*_t) instantaneously. Thus, the firm does not need to take a deep look into the future, and the multiperiod optimization problem becomes essentially static.[2] Maintaining that the production function has a constant elasticity of substitution (σ) between capital and variable inputs, we obtain the following well-known relation between the desired stock of capital, the level of output (Y_t), and the user cost (or rental price) of capital (U_t):

$$K^*_t = \xi\, Y_t\, U_t^{-\sigma} \tag{2a}$$

$$U_t = (p^I_t / p^Y_t)\,(r_t + \delta)\,(1 - m_t - z_t)/(1 - t_t) \tag{2b}$$

where ξ is the CES distribution parameter, p^I_t is the purchase price of new capital, p^Y_t is the price of output, r_t is the real financial cost of capital, δ is the geometric rate of capital depreciation, m_t is the rate of the investment tax credit, z_t is the discounted value of tax depreciation allowances and t_t is the rate of business income taxation at both the provincial/state and federal levels. The r_t variable is defined as a weighted average of the cost of equity (a dividend-price ratio cum real capital gains or an earnings-price ratio) and the cost of debt (average yield on new issues of high-grade corporate bonds). The cost of debt is lowered by its tax deductibility and expected inflation. The weights can vary from zero to one but, generally, equity receives a larger weight of approximately two thirds, reflecting the average share of retentions and new equity issues in financing investment.

To form an investment relation, divide total investment into net and replacement components. Capital is assumed to depreciate geometrically at a constant mechanistic rate (δ). Hence, replacement investment (I^r_t) is proportional to the capital stock available at the beginning of the period and, in contrast to net investment, adjusts instantaneously:

$$I^r_t = \delta K_{t-1} \tag{3}$$

Net investment (I^n_t) is the change in the capital stock between periods $t-1$ and t, and is scaled by the existing capital stock. This ratio (plus 1.0) equals K_t/K_{t-1}, which is assumed to adjust according to the weighted geometric mean of relative changes in the desired capital stock:

$$\begin{aligned} I^n_t/K_{t-1}+1.0 = K_t/K_{t-1} &= \prod_{h=0}^{H} [K^*_{t-h}/K^*_{t-h-1}]^{\mu_h} \\ &= \prod_{h=0}^{H} [\Delta K^*_{t-h}/K^*_{t-h-1}+1.0]^{\mu_h} \end{aligned} \tag{4}$$

where the μ represents the delivery lag distribution extending for $H+1$ periods.[3] Taking logs of equation (4), using the approximation $ln(1+x)\approx x$, differentiating the logarithm of equation (2a) and substituting for $\Delta K^*/K^*$, using equation (3) for replacement investment, and appending a stochastic error (ϵ_t) results in the following distributed lag investment equation:

$$\begin{aligned} I_t/K_{t-1} &= I^r_t/K_{t-1} + I^n_t/K_{t-1} \\ &= \delta - \sigma \sum_{h=0}^{H} \mu_h (\Delta U_{t-h}/U_{t-h-1}) \\ &\quad + \sum_{h=0}^{H} \mu_h (\Delta Y_{t-h}/Y_{t-h-1}) + \epsilon_t \end{aligned} \tag{5}$$

While the dynamics associated with replacement investment follow from explicit assumptions, theory has been relatively silent on the dynamics for net investment as represented by the distributed lag coefficients.

Neoclassical Models – Key Assumptions and Caveats

Estimated equations based on variants of equation (5) have appeared frequently and, as with any pioneering effort, have been subject to a number of criticisms. Three are reviewed here: consistency of the theoretical model, characteristics of the technology, and quantification of expectations.

The initial set of criticisms pertains to the consistency of the theoretical model. There have been three specific problems. First, the profit-maximizing firm chooses the capital stock, other factors of production and output simultaneously.[4] Equation (2) or (5) does not usually recognize these interactions nor the dependence of the optimal level of output on the user cost. Regarding the latter point, even if the endogeneity of output does not distort the estimated coefficients (discussed below), simulations based only on equation (5) may underestimate the effects of policies intended to stimulate capital formation.

Second, the development of equation (5) was based on an inharmonious treatment of delivery lags. The optimal capital stock defined by equation (2) was derived under the assumption that delivery of capital goods was immediate, but net investment defined by equation (4) was based on a delivery lag distribution. In this formulation, the investment path generated by the neoclassical model may not be optimal. However, under static expectations (as assumed by Jorgenson), the model is consistent because the benefits and costs of acquiring capital are expected to be the same at any point in time and, hence, independent of any delivery lag.

Third, the definition of K^*_t in equation (2) has been questioned. No problem arises if the production technology exhibits decreasing returns to scale but, when returns are constant (as assumed by Jorgenson), K^*_t is not well-defined. In this case, Jorgenson (1972, p. 246) has argued that "desired capital should be interpreted as a moving target rather than the long-run equilibrium value of capital.... This policy is identical to that appropriate for a description of technology with production and installation subject to constant returns to scale." As with the analysis of delivery lags, such an interpretation depends crucially on static expectations. Relaxing this assumption and specifying the theoretical model explicitly were items that remained on the investment research agenda.

The second set of criticisms concerns the characteristics of the technology, and three aspects have been discussed. First, vintage effects may influence the relation between past investments and the capital stock entering the production function. Under one specification, vintage effects are absent if capital is putty-putty, i.e., both before and after installation, capital can be combined with other inputs in any desired proportions. This assumption is used in most investment studies and implies that the period in which capital is purchased is of no particular importance. At the opposite extreme, vintages matter if capital is putty-clay, i.e., before installation, capital can be combined with inputs in any desired proportion, which depends on the path of input prices expected at the time of acquisition. However, after installation, the proportion is fixed until the capital good is retired. Consequently, output changes lead to more rapid investment than comparable (with respect to K^*_t) user cost changes, and equation (5) must contain separate distributed lags for the output and user cost terms.

Second, the neoclassical model assumes that capital depreciates at a constant geometric rate, thus justifying the treatment of replacement investment as a fixed proportion of the existing capital stock. The validity of constant geometric depreciation has been the subject of numerous empirical investigations providing mixed support for this assumption. Introspection suggests that, for many capital goods, depreciation rates can be altered by firms through variations in usage or maintenance. These choices represent additional margins through which economic factors, such as tax, interest and inflation rates, can affect the firm.

Third, an additional aspect of the technology that has generated significant controversy is the value of σ. This parameter is both the elasticity of substitution between labour and capital and the elasticity of K^*_t with respect to U_t which contains all the price terms. Thus, in the original version of the neoclassical model in equation (5), the potency of tax policies and interest rates, *ceteris paribus*, is closely linked to the value of σ. Direct estimates of σ are mixed, with cross-section studies finding values near unity (as assumed by Jorgenson) and time series analyses generating much lower estimates.

The third set of criticisms concerns expectations. For example, the above-noted role for σ depends heavily on static expectations. However, in the presence of non-static expectations and delivery lags, the terms in equation (2a) would be distributed over current and future periods and interpreted as expected values.[5] Approximating K^*_t linearly and assuming that expectations of the output and user cost terms are based on extrapolations of their past values, results in the following modified neoclassical model:

$$I_t/K_{t-1} = \delta - \sigma \sum_{h=0}^{H_U} a_h (\Delta U_{t-h}/U_{t-h-1})$$

$$+ \sum_{h=0}^{H_Y} b_h (\Delta Y_{t-h}/Y_{t-h-1}) + \epsilon_t \tag{6}$$

As shown by equation (6), knowledge of σ alone does not determine the response of investment to the user cost. Rather, the estimated distributed lag coefficients represent an amalgam of technology, delivery lag and expectation parameters, as represented by σ and the a_h coefficients.[6]

In the above discussion and elsewhere, expectations play a crucial role in investment decisions. Static or extrapolative expectations are assumed in versions of the neoclassical model, and unknown expectations are replaced by distributed lags of past observations. While easy to implement empirically, these expectation schemes are totally at odds with the fundamental forward-looking nature of capital accumulation. Four related concerns have arisen. First, such extrapolations treat all changes, perhaps brought about by tax policy, as though they were permanent. For example, the change in the investment tax credit in 1966 that was announced as temporary would have the same impact on the expected user cost as permanent changes.

Second, preannounced changes in tax parameters would have no immediate effect in the neoclassical model, yet firms would be expected to alter their plans to benefit from the anticipated future policy. Such a scenario was presented in the United States by the phase-in provisions for depreciation allowances in the 1981 10-5-3 program, where firms had an incentive to delay current investment in anticipation of more generous tax write-offs in later years (which were eventually rescinded). Similar incentives existed in the latter part of 1992 concerning an anticipated reinstatement of the investment tax credit under the Clinton administration.

Third, firms form their expectations based on whatever information is available, and the assumption that firms use a single lag with invariant parameters may be restrictive. These parameters reflect basic characteristics of the economy that may themselves be subject to change. For example, the forecasting rules for interest rates pre-1979, when they were targeted by the U.S. Federal Reserve, may have changed radically after the October 1979 policy switch to monetary aggregates and the reversal in October 1982.

A fourth and related point is that utilizing a univariate autoregression for the expected user cost constrains all the variables embedded in U_t to have the same set of expectation parameters. Yet it is doubtful that expected rates of interest and taxation possess similar time series properties. The ramification of unstable expectations from whatever source is that the estimated coefficients in the investment function will be unstable over time and unreliable in assessing alternative policies.

These four concerns about the modelling of expectations are usually referred to as the Lucas Critique.

Other Implicit Models

This review of the neoclassical model has highlighted three important criticisms: consistency of the theoretical model, characteristics of the technology and quantification of expectations. These unresolved issues have generated two contrasting responses: the introduction of *more* structure (following the pattern initiated in the neoclassical research program) or of *less* structure. While each strategy has its strengths and weaknesses, most research has pursued structural model building, and subsequent work has been based on explicit modelling of the firm's optimization problem with careful attention to dynamics and technology. While this line of research is examined in terms of the explicit models in the next section, this subsection describes briefly three models – vector autoregressive, effective tax rate and return over cost – that were introduced in the 1980s and use less structure than the neoclassical model.

Autonomous shocks may play an important role in assessing the determinants of investment. Reported empirical results could be affected seriously by a simultaneity problem induced by autonomous shocks contained in ϵ_t. For example, shocks could be correlated positively with both ΔY_t and ΔU_t in equation (5) or (6) because of technology shocks interacting with the joint endogeneity of firm decisions or because of links between aggregate saving and investment. The resulting distortion could account for the finding of significant output effects and insignificant user cost effects, even though the latter has a substantial negative impact on investment. Instrumental variables is the appropriate econometric technique for addressing this problem, but obtaining valid instruments is a difficult task, especially at the aggregate level.

In response to these potential problems, Sims (1980) argued for a relatively non-structural approach. Believing that the restrictions needed to identify the econometric structure were "incredible," Sims treated each variable in the system as endogenous, and regressed current values on their own lags and on those of all other variables in the system. In this vector autoregression, the dynamics are implicit. Only a few authors have applied this approach to investment spending: Gordon and Veitch (1986) and McMillin (1985) with U.S. data and Funke (1989) with West German data.

In his Fischer-Schultz Lecture, Martin Feldstein (1982) introduced two new investment models focused on quantifying the role of taxes.[7] His effective tax rate model relates net investment directly to a quantity and a price variable, and is of particular interest because it provides an alternative way of examining the effects of taxes on investment. The price variable (RN_t), the net real return to capital, is defined as the average yield to bondholders and equityholders net of depreciation and effective taxes. The latter is a comprehensive measure of taxes affecting the ultimate providers of funds, and incorporates taxes on corporate income, property, dividends, capital gains and interest income received by creditors. The quantity variable captures fluctuations in demand and is measured by an index of capacity utilization ($UCAP_t$). Dynamics enter by lagging both the price and quantity variables one period to reflect delays in decision making, production and deliveries, and to avoid simultaneity bias. (Since his investment equation is estimated with a generalized least squares [GLS] correction for autocorrelated residuals, the effective lag exceeds one period.) These considerations, coupled with a stochastic error term, lead to the following specification of the effective tax rate model:

$$I^n_t/Y_t = \gamma_0 + \gamma_1 RN_{t-1} + \gamma_2 UCAP_{t-1} + \epsilon_t \qquad (7)$$

where the dependent variable is scaled by output presumably to account for the trend component in the investment series and to place all variables in the same units.

An important difference between the neoclassical and effective tax rate models is that the price variable in the neoclassical model (U_t) is defined as a marginal concept, while RN_{t-1} is based on averages.[8] Neither would appear to be dominant in the analysis of capital formation incentives. Average returns are a deficient measure because they are not directly related to the marginal decisions at the core of economic theory. However, quantifying the marginal benefits and costs of capital can be achieved only by considering selected features of the tax code and by relying on a number of maintained assumptions – competitive markets, uniformly positive taxable profits and the maximization of a particular objective function constrained by a particular technology. Studies using average returns are best viewed as complementary to work with marginal concepts where, in the former, potentially restrictive assumptions are relaxed at the expense of a direct link to a well-specified model of capital accumulation.

The second new model presented by Feldstein quantifies marginal investment incentives by contrasting the maximum potential net return ($MPNR_t$) that firms can afford on a standard investment project with the cost of funds (COF_t). In this return over cost model, the following decision rule equates benefits and costs and determines the desired capital stock (cf. equation [1] or [2]):

$$MPNR_t = COF_t \tag{8}$$

$MPNR_t$ depends positively on a hypothetical marginal return inclusive of taxes. Dynamics enter in terms of a partial adjustment mechanism: whenever the benefits ($MPNR_t$) exceed the costs (COF_t), firms begin to acquire capital in order to re-establish equation (8). Assuming that net investment is positively affected by fluctuations in demand conditions, lagging the independent variables per the above discussion, and appending a stochastic error term results in the return over cost model:

$$I_t^n/Y_t = \gamma_0 + \gamma_1 (MPNR_{t-1} - COF_{t-1}) + \gamma_2 UCAP_{t-1} + \epsilon_t \tag{9}$$

Explicit Models

An alternative response to criticisms of the neoclassical model is to introduce more structure into the specification of the investment equation. This section presents models in which these dynamic elements appear explicitly in the optimization problem and the estimated coefficients are linked explicitly to the underlying technology and expectation parameters. The benchmark model is presented, and three solutions to the unobservable expectations problem are discussed. These solutions are related to the Brainard-Tobin Q, Euler equation and direct forecasting models. Before developing the benchmark model, it is important to first review the Lucas Critique of econometric models and practice.

The Lucas Critique of Econometric Models

A watershed in the modelling of investment behaviour occurred in the mid-1970s when Robert Lucas published his often-cited critique of the prevailing practice for quantifying the effects of alternative economic policies. He argued that, in formulating plans, economic agents necessarily look into the future and, thus, the decision rules guiding their actions depend on parameters describing the expectations of future variables, as well as parameters of taste and technology. Lucas viewed economic policy as the selection of rules that generate paths of policy variables, rather than the selection of arbitrary paths. Thus, "any change in policy will systematically alter the structure of econometric models" (Lucas, 1976, p. 126), and the estimated coefficients in (the then current) consumption, wage/price or investment models could not be considered structural, i.e, invariant to alternative policy regimes. The important and damning implication for policy analysis is that these econometric relations will prove unstable in precisely those situations in which they are called on to analyse proposed policies.

In light of this Lucas Critique, quantitative policy analysis can proceed only if the econometric specification permits the expectation parameters, which will vary with alternative policies, to be identified separately from technology parameters, which are invariant to policy changes. As noted earlier, especially in equation (6), the estimated coefficients in implicit models are generally an amalgam of expectation and technology parameters and, thus, are vulnerable to the Lucas Critique. Consequently, much subsequent work, to be reviewed in this section, has focused on the modelling and isolation of dynamics arising from expectations.

The Benchmark Model

In the benchmark model, dynamic aspects of the technology are captured by the assumption that, in varying its capital stock, the firm faces adjustment costs. These adjustment costs were introduced by Eisner and Strotz (1963) and may represent either external costs, due to an upward sloping supply curve for capital goods, or internal costs. Studies have generally focused on internal adjustment costs, which represent lost output from disruptions to the existing production process (as new capital goods are "broken in" and workers retrained), additional labour for "bolting down" new capital or a wedge between the quantities of purchased and installed capital. These costs increase at an increasing rate, an assumption that plays a crucial role in explicit models. With linear or concave adjustment costs, the firm would have an all-or-nothing investment policy. Convexity forces the firm to think seriously about the future, as too rapid accumulation of capital will prove costly. Alternatively, too little accumulation results in foregone profits.

For expositional purposes, it is useful to derive the benchmark model from an optimization problem. First, assume that the firm chooses inputs to maximize the discounted sum of expected cash flows, which is equivalent to maximizing its market value. The firm is a price taker in both its input and output markets, and is further constrained by production, adjustment cost and accumulation technologies.

Output (Y_t) is determined by labour (L_t), capital (K_t), and a stochastic technology shock (τ_t). The production technology is $Y_t=F[L_t,K_t:\tau_t]$.[9] An important element in the explicit models considered in this section is that, in contrast to variable labour input, capital is quasi-fixed, i.e., net increments to the capital stock are subject to adjustment costs. These are represented by $G[I_t,K_t:\tau_t]$, which is increasing in I_t, usually decreasing in K_t, and valued by the price of foregone output. The stock of existing capital is accumulated as a weighted sum of past investments. If the weights follow a declining geometric pattern, we obtain the familiar transition equation for capital, $K_t=I_t+(1-\delta)K_{t-1}$. The price of output is the numeraire, and the relative prices of labour and investment are represented by w_t and $p^{I'}{}_t$,[10] respectively, adjusted for taxes.[11] To emphasize the fundamentally forward-looking nature of the firm's decision problem, we introduce an expectations operator, $E_t\{.\}$, where the subscript indicates that expectations are based on information available to the firm at the beginning of period t. These considerations lead to the following equation for the firm's cash flow (CF_t) in period t:

$$E_t\{CF_t\} = E_t\{F[L_t,K_t:\tau_t] - G[I_t,K_t:\tau_t] - w_tL_t - p^{I'}{}_tI_t\} \tag{10}$$

With the restriction implied by the capital accumulation constraint, the firm has two margins along which to maximize the sum of expected cash flows discounted to the beginning of the planning period t at rate r, and faces the following optimization problem:

$$\underset{\{L_s,K_s\}}{MAX}\ E_t\{\sum_{s=t}^{\infty}\{(1+r)^{-(s-t)}\{F[L_s,K_s:\tau_s] - G[I_s,K_s:\tau_s] - w_sL_s - p^{I'}{}_sI_s\}\}\} \tag{11a}$$

subject to

$$I_s \equiv K_s - (1-\delta)\ K_{s-1} \tag{11b}$$

Using variational methods and differentiating equations (11a and b) with respect to labour and capital, results in the following conditions characterizing an optimum:

$$E_t\{F_L[L_t,K_t:\tau_t] - w_t\} = 0 \tag{12a}$$

$$E_t\{\lambda_t - \Delta^\rho\{G_I[I_t,K_t:\tau_t]\} - \Delta^\rho\{p^{I'}{}_t\}\} = 0 \tag{12b}$$

$$\lambda_t \equiv F_K[L_t,K_t:\tau_t] - G_K[I_t,K_t:\tau_t]$$

$$\Delta^\rho\{X_t\} \equiv X_t - \rho X_{t+1},\ X_t = \{G_I[t],p^{I'}{}_t\}$$

$$\rho \equiv (1-\delta)/(1+r) < 1$$

$$\lim_{s \to \infty} E_t \{(1+r)^{-(s-t)} \{\lambda_{t+s} - p^{I'}_{t+s} - G_I[t+s]\} K_{t+s}\} = 0 \qquad (12c)$$

These conditions have the following economic interpretations. Equation (12a) is the familiar marginal productivity condition for a variable input. Equation (12b) indicates that, along the optimal capital accumulation path, the firm will be indifferent to an increase in capital by one unit in period t and a decrease of $1\text{-}\delta$ units in $t+1$, thus leaving the capital stock unaffected from period $t+1$ onward. The benefit of this perturbation is represented by λ_t – the one-period marginal revenue product of capital net of the decrease in adjustment costs due to a higher level of capital. Perturbing the capital stock is costly, and the Euler equation (12b) sets λ_t equal to the marginal adjustment and purchase costs incurred in t and saved in $t+1$. These perturbations are represented by the $\Delta^{\rho}\{.\}$ operator in equation (12b), and the $t+1$ savings are adjusted for discounting and depreciation as represented by ρ.

The transversality condition is provided by equation (12c), and restricts the value of the firm and the value of the capital stock from exploding. Its importance in applied work arises as a boundary condition used in obtaining the following solution to the difference equation (12b) for capital:

$$E_t\{\Lambda_t - p^{I'}_t - G_I[I_t, K_t : \tau_t]\} = 0 \qquad (12d)$$

$$\Lambda_t \equiv \sum_{s=0}^{\infty} \rho^s \lambda_{t+s} \qquad (12e)$$

Equation (12d) is the dynamic equivalent of the simple decision rule for the optimal capital stock of equation (1) and equates the expected marginal benefits and costs of investing in period t. The marginal benefit is measured by the shadow price of capital Λ_t. Owing to capital's durability, Λ_t is the discounted sum of the "spot" marginal revenue products λ_{t+s}'s over the life of the capital good as evaluated with information available in period t. The marginal costs are the sum of purchase costs and the sunk adjustment costs associated with investing. Since the sunk costs cannot be recovered, they force the firm to look ahead when investing. Thus, the optimal investment policy can be characterized by two alternative formulations – a comparison of the net benefits of investing today vs. tomorrow (equation [12b]) or a comparison of the benefits over the life of the capital good to its costs (equation [12d]).

To obtain an investment equation to serve as a benchmark for the models found in the literature, it is assumed that adjustment costs are quadratic in gross investment, homogeneous of degree one in I_t and K_t, and affected by the technology shock (τ_t):

$$G[I_t, K_t : \tau_t] = (\alpha/2)[I_t/K_t - \tau_t]^2 * K_t \qquad (13)$$

With equation (13), the following benchmark model is obtained:

$$I_t/K_t = (1/\alpha)(E_t\{\Lambda_t\} - p^{I'}_t) + u_t \qquad (14)$$

where the error term (u_t) is identical with the technology shock. Whenever there is a discrepancy between $E_t\{\Lambda_t\}$ and $p^{I'}_t$, the firm has an incentive to change its capital stock, but its actions are tempered by the convex adjustment cost technology. The steeper the adjustment cost function, the larger α, and the more slowly investment responds.

In contrast to the implicit models, lag variables do not appear in equation (14). The latter is somewhat surprising given the dynamic adjustment costs faced by the firm. It must be realized, however, that equation (14) is not a closed-form decision rule for investment (since I_t affects the λ_{t+s}'s in Λ_t), but rather a consistency condition reflecting only part of the information from the optimization problem. If the other restrictions implied by optimal behaviour were considered simultaneously, then the paths of I_t and K_t would be "sluggish," and would depend on lagged variables.[12]

The benchmark model of equation (14) is the basis for all the models discussed in this section[13] and successfully addresses a number of the unresolved issues highlighted in the neoclassical research program. Since equation (14) is derived directly from an optimization problem, it is theoretically consistent, recognizes explicitly the dynamics due to expectations and technology, and isolates their separate influences. Furthermore, the error term follows explicitly from the theory. For empirical researchers, the critical problem with developing an estimable equation from equation (14) is relating the unobservable $E_t\{\Lambda_t\}$ to observable variables.

Three Solutions to the Unobservable Expectations Problem

There are three solutions to the unobservable expectations problem that exists with equation (14), and each solution is reviewed briefly.[14]

The Q theory of investment uses information in financial markets to relate $E_t\{\Lambda_t\}$ to observables. In this theory, investment expenditures are positively related to average Q, defined as the ratio of the financial value of the firm (V_t) to the replacement cost of its existing capital stock:

$$Q^A_t = V_t / p^{I'}_t K_t \tag{15}$$

The intuition underlying Q theory has been articulated vividly by Keynes (1936, p. 151):

> ...daily revaluations of the Stock Exchange...inevitably exert a decisive influence on the rate of current investment. For there is no sense in building up a new enterprise at a cost greater than that at which a similar existing enterprise can be purchased; whilst there is an inducement to spend on a new project what may seem an extravagant sum, if it can be floated off on the Stock Exchange at an immediate profit.

This intuitive notion has been validated in formal models in which the adjustment cost technology and optimizing behaviour lead to a relation between investment and marginal Q, the ratio of the discounted future revenues from an additional unit of capital to its purchase price: $E_t\{\Lambda_t\}/p^{I'}_t$. Since marginal Q is unobservable, empirical researchers have used observable average Q. The formal conditions under which this substitution is appropriate were established by Hayashi (1982): product and factor markets are competitive, production and adjustment cost technologies are linear homogeneous, capital is homogeneous, and investment decisions are largely separate from other real and financial decisions. Under these conditions, optimizing behaviour implies the following relation for the (constant dollar) value of the firm as evaluated on financial markets (V_t):

$$V_t = E_t\{\Lambda_t\} K_t \qquad (16)$$

In equation (16), the assumptions on market structure and technology ensure that the firm does not expect to earn any profits from actions taken in and beyond period t. Hence, the value of the firm equals the quasi-rents – the product of the expected shadow price of capital and K_t – from the existing capital stock.[15]

The Q investment model follows from equations (14) to (16), and relates the investment-to-capital ratio to observable Q.

$$I_t/K_t = (1/\alpha)Q_t + u_t \qquad (17)$$

$$Q_t \equiv (Q^A_t - 1)p^{I'}_t$$

where including $p^{I'}_t$ in the definition of Q_t reflects the valuation of adjustment costs.[16] Equation (17) solves the problem of unobservable expectations by equating a forward-looking variable to one that is readily observed. A particularly attractive aspect of equation (17) is that, unlike the neoclassical or other implicit models (cf. equations [6], [7] and [9]), the Q investment equation will not be affected by instability in expectation parameters because expectations enter equation (17) directly through Q^A_t. Q models provide a direct role for expectations in the econometric specification by relying on financial market data which, in principle, incorporates expectations of future variables relevant to the investment decision and, in practice, are readily available.

Euler equations provide a second solution to the problem of unobservable expectations, i.e., the unobservables contained in $E_t\{\Lambda_t\}$. In equation (12e), the bulk of the variables in $E_t\{\Lambda_t\}$ can be eliminated by a Koyck-lead transformation. An alternative and more direct approach combines the Euler equation (12b) and the adjustment cost technology equation (13). In either case, we obtain the following equation:

$$I_t/K_t = \rho E_t\{I_{t+1}/K_{t+1}\} - (1/\alpha)(p^{I'}_t - \rho E_t\{p^{I'}_{t+1}\}) + (1/\alpha)E_t\{\lambda_t\} + \tau_t \qquad (18)$$

The importance of equation (18) is that the infinite number of unknown λ_{t+s}'s ($s=0,\infty$) has been reduced dramatically to just λ_t.

Estimation proceeds by parametrizing λ_t in terms of the technology (cf. equation [12b]) and substituting actual for expected values in equation (18). Under rational expectations, the actual values represent the appropriate expectation up to an additive and orthogonal expectation error (McCallum, 1979), and thus equation (18) yields the following Euler equation model:

$$I_t/K_t = \rho(I_{t+1}/K_{t+1}) - (1/\alpha)(p^{I'}_t - \rho\, p^{I'}_{t+1}) + (1/\alpha)\,\lambda_t + u_t \tag{19}$$

$$u_t = \tau_t + e_t - \rho\, e_{t+1}$$

where the error term (u_t) is a combination of technology shocks and expectation errors (e_t's).[17]

A third solution to the unobservable expectations problem is to forecast directly the unknown λ_{t+s} terms in Λ_t. A key element in direct forecasting models is the assumed stochastic processes governing λ_t, which, for expositional convenience, can be specified as a first-order univariate autoregression:

$$\lambda_t = \mu\, \lambda_{t-1} + e_t \tag{20}$$

where μ is an expectation parameter and e_t is an expectation error. Under rational expectations e_t is orthogonal to all variables known to the firm in period t. Combining this assumption with equation (20), we compute the expected value of λ_{t+s} with information available at the beginning of period t with the following simple recursive relation:

$$E_t\{\lambda_{t+s}\} = \mu^{s+1}\lambda_{t-1} \tag{21}$$

The direct forecasting model has been implemented by estimating the equations describing forecasts and optimization either simultaneously or sequentially. In the former case, equation (21) is substituted repeatedly into the benchmark model of equation (14), thus replacing the unobserved $E_t\{\Lambda_t\}$ as follows:

$$E_t\{\Lambda_t\} = \sum_{s=0}^{\infty} \rho^s\, E_t\{\lambda_{t+s}\} = \lambda_{t-1} \sum_{s=0}^{\infty} \rho^s\, \mu^{s+1} = \lambda_{t-1}(\mu/(1-\rho\mu)) \tag{22}$$

and generating the following closed-form model:

$$I_t/K_t = (\mu/\alpha(1-\rho\,\mu))\lambda_{t-1} - (1/\alpha)p^{I'}_t + u_t \tag{23}$$

where u_t contains only τ_t and is orthogonal to λ_{t-1}. As with the implicit models, the estimated coefficients in equation (23) are an amalgam of the underlying expectation (μ) and technology (α,ρ) parameters. These are identified by estimating the stochastic forcing process (equation [20]) and the investment decision rule (equation [23]) simultaneously.

The sequential approach separates the forecasting of expected values from the estimation of technology parameters. In the first step, $E_t\{\Lambda_t\}$ is quantified in terms of parameters and variables known at time t by estimating the expectation parameter in equation (20) and then computing the $E_t\{\lambda_{t+s}\}$'s with equation (21) and $E_t\{\Lambda_t\}$ with equation (12e) and a preset ρ. In the second step, the constructed $E_t\{\Lambda_t\}$ is inserted as a regressor in the benchmark model, and equation (14) is estimated.

A Framework for Estimation[18]

Which Model?

From a theoretical perspective, explicit models clearly dominate implicit models, as the latter suffer from problems of model consistency and expectations. However, the above review did not mention the empirical performance of explicit models, a consideration that reverses the ranking.[19]

Implicit models perform well empirically. These models explain a reasonable amount of the variation in the aggregate data and, apart from the user cost, usually obtain coefficients that have the theoretically correct sign and are statistically and economically significant. Moreover, despite the availability of many alternative specifications, implicit models containing output, user cost and liquidity variables continue to be the model of choice among forecasters.

This favourable empirical performance is not enjoyed by explicit models. While explicit models provide attractive frameworks for ultimately understanding investment behaviour, their overall empirical performance has not been satisfactory. Thus, questions exist concerning the ability of the current generation of models to deliver empirical estimates that are useful in the analysis of public policies.

The applied econometrician is thus faced with the dilemma of choosing between implicit models that are dependable empirically but deficient conceptually or explicit models that have a solid theoretical foundation but a shaky empirical superstructure. Both approaches have strengths and weaknesses, and provide useful and complementary information. While some empirical successes have been achieved, explicit models are insufficiently "sturdy" to estimate price elasticities with panel data and draw inferences for tax policy. Furthermore, the implicit neoclassical model provides a direct estimate of the user cost elasticity of primary concern in this paper. Thus, we proceed with estimating a neoclassical model, though the concerns raised in the second part of this paper must temper our policy conclusions.

Specification, Estimation and Empirical Issues

The model to be used in this study follows from equation (6) with several modifications discussed in this subsection:

$$I_{i,t}/K_{i,t-1} = \phi_i + \sum_{h=0}^{6} \alpha_h(\Delta U_{i,t-h}/U_{i,t-h-1}) \quad (24a)$$

$$+ \sum_{h=0}^{4} \beta_h(\Delta S_{i,t-h}/S_{i,t-h-1})$$

$$+ \sum_{h=0}^{4} \gamma_h(CF_{i,t-h}/K_{i,t-h-1}) + \epsilon_{i,t}$$

$$U_{i,t} = (p_{i,t}^{I}/p_{i,t}^{y})(r_{i,t}+\delta)(1 - m_{i,t} - z_{i,t})/(1 - t_{i,t}) \quad (24b)$$

where the i subscript indexes firms, CF represents cash flow, and ϕ is a constant that represents δ_i as well as other firm-specific factors. Sales S replaces output as a measure of demand. An examination of alternative lag lengths indicated that lags of 0 to 6 for $\Delta U_{i,t}/U_{i,t-1}$ and lags of 0 to 4 for $\Delta S_{i,t}/S_{i,t-1}$ and $CF_{i,t}/K_{i,t-1}$ are adequate. The user cost formula is identical to equation (2a) except for the i subscripts, and is presented for expositional convenience. The elasticity of the long-run capital stock to changes in the user cost is captured by the sum of the α's (SUM(α)).[20]

There are five important empirical issues that may seriously affect the estimated α's and, hence, the implications for tax policy. First, critical to the empirical results is the manner in which ΔS_t and ΔU_t enter the regression. The version of the neoclassical model estimated by Jorgenson and his collaborators contains the composite term $\Delta(S_t/U_t)/(S_t/U_t)$ entered as a distributed lag. Such a specification is justified under the assumption that expectations are static and $\sigma=1$ (cf. equation [5]) or, under the alternative derivation based on non-static expectations of equation (6), that $\sigma=1$ and the expectation parameters for both sales and user cost are identical. In general, the estimated coefficients on the composite term will reflect a mixture of sales and user cost effects, and can generate misleading implications for policy evaluations.[21] Consider a situation where the relationship between investment and sales is stronger than that between investment and user cost. Estimated coefficients from a regression using $\Delta(S_t/U_t)/(S_t/U_t)$ will exceed coefficients on the user cost from a regression where $\Delta S_t/S_t$ and $\Delta U_t/U_t$ have been entered separately. Thus, the version of the neoclassical model with a composite term, often used in policy analysis, may overstate the effects of changes in fiscal and monetary policies, operating through U_t, on investment spending. This bias has been confirmed empirically in a number of studies,[22] and is avoided in the estimates reported in this paper by estimating separate distributed lags for sales and user cost variables.

Second, a firm's financial structure may matter for investment, and this issue has been investigated extensively. For example, with aggregate data, Sinai and

Eckstein (1983) found that an interest coverage variable is an important determinant of investment. However, in reviewing the results from a number of models, Jorgenson (1971, p. 1133) concluded that "variables associated with internal finance do not appear as significant determinants of desired capital in any model that also includes output as a significant determinant."

Recent work with panel data has found a more substantial role for financial variables, especially for firms which may face information problems in capital markets.[23] If a firm has access to internal sources of funds for investment, it need not resort to debt or new equity, which may involve higher costs due to capital market frictions. The financial variable used most often in this context is internal cash flow. The estimated α's will be affected by this financial variable if cash flow is significant, and cash flow and the user cost variables are correlated. To examine the impact of financial structure, cash flow, scaled by the beginning-of-period capital stock, is included in some of the regressions.

As an aside, this formulation of finance constraints does not follow directly from an economic model. In an explicit model, Chirinko and Schaller (1995) developed the theoretical conditions under which a liquidity variable enters a Q investment equation. Since implicit models are not as closely related to a formal optimizing framework, the approach in Chirinko and Schaller is not of immediate use. In the present study, we assume that internal funds enter the model only to account for short-term finance constraints and, thus, affect the timing of investment along the transition path between steady states (cf. Coen, 1971). Under these assumptions, cash flow does not affect K^* in equation (2a),[24] but enters the investment equation in levels scaled by the firm's capital stock.[25]

Third, an advantage of a panel data set is that it allows for different responses by firms. Ideally, both intercept and slope coefficients would be permitted to vary by firm. This more general model cannot be estimated because of too few degrees of freedom. We restrict the slope coefficients to be the same across firms, and this homogeneity restriction is evident in equation (24) by the absence of i subscripts on the α, β and γ coefficients. It is feasible, however, to allow each firm to have its own intercept, an important generalization because firm-specific depreciation rates entering the model of equation (24) generate an *a priori* reason to expect firm-specific fixed effects.[26] If variation in ϕ's across firms is not permitted, estimates of the α, β and γ coefficients can be distorted.

Equation (24) is estimated in three ways. We begin by maintaining that $\phi_i=\phi$ for all firms, and estimate a pooled model. This specification has the advantage that it uses all the variation in the data, but has the disadvantage that the ϕ's are forced to be equal. Fixed effects can be allowed for with either mean-difference or first-difference estimators. The mean-difference estimator subtracts the firm-specific means from all variables entering equation (24), and is equivalent to adding constants for each firm. The pooled model is nested within the mean-difference model, and an F-test can evaluate the restriction that $\phi_i=\phi$ for all i. An alternative method to deal with fixed effects eliminates the ϕ's directly by differencing the data by firms.[27]

Fourth, errors in measuring the regressors can lead to coefficient estimates that are too close to zero relative to their "true" values. As noted in the Introduction, user cost is a relatively simple concept with which to represent the complexities of the tax code and may not capture important features, e.g., tax loss carry forwards.[28] Ballentine (1986) reported that only 8.1 percent of the dollar volume of corporate tax increases (over a five-year period) in the 1986 tax act in the United States are reflected in the variables entering U_t. Further measurement error might enter because of margins along which firms optimize that are omitted in the neoclassical framework.[29]

We test for user cost measurement error by comparing estimates of the sums of the α's from mean-difference and first-difference models. The first-difference estimator generates coefficients that are asymptotically equivalent to those from the mean-difference estimator under the assumption that the model is correctly specified. If the regressors are measured with error, however, coefficients estimated using a first-difference estimator will be closer to zero (asymptotically) than those estimated using a mean-difference estimator.[30]

To understand the impact of heterogeneity and measurement error, pooled, mean-difference and first-difference estimates are presented for each sector.

Fifth, since the regressors are predetermined but not exogenous, coefficient estimates may be affected by a simultaneous equation bias due to correlations between $\epsilon_{i,t}$ and any of the regressors. As noted earlier, simultaneity could account for estimated user cost elasticities that are too close to zero relative to their "true" values. Instrumental variables is the appropriate econometric technique for addressing this problem, and the extensive variation in micro data may provide better instruments than can be obtained at the aggregate level.

When using instrumental variables, the choice between mean-difference and first-difference estimators is important. As with most studies, this paper uses lagged regressors as instruments. Lags should be valid instruments because they are likely to be correlated with the included predetermined variables and, under the assumption that $\epsilon_{i,t}$ is serially uncorrelated, uncorrelated with the error term. However, if mean-difference data are used, then the latter condition will not hold because of a correlation between the future values of the regressor used to compute its mean and the contemporaneous error term.[31] This problem does not arise when using first-differences to remove fixed effects. Thus, to account for simultaneity (as well as measurement error), we present first-difference estimates with instrumental variables.

The Data Set and the "Canadian Sectors"

To estimate equation (24), we linked two unique data sources that each provide information needed to estimate user cost elasticities. We obtained information on the user costs (maintained by Data Resources, Inc. [DRI]) for 26 different capital assets (24 types of equipment and two types of structures) and created industry-specific user costs as a weighted average of the asset user costs. The weights are the proportion of capital accounted for by each of these assets for 26 different industries.[32] This industry information is then merged with the firm-level Compustat data using each firm's SIC code.[33] These data provide important micro-level variation in user costs that should prove helpful in estimating the effects of tax and other policies.

The investment, sales and cash flow data come from the extensive Compustat "full coverage" files. Selecting usable data for regressions and computing the necessary lags resulted in a sample of 4,118 firms from all sectors of the economy that provide 26,227 usable annual observations for the regressions from 1972 to 1991.

These data are then grouped into 12 sectors for which Industry Canada has mandated responsibility for following ongoing developments. These 12 sectors were defined by the Canadian SIC categories listed in Appendix A. The sectors used in this study are constructed from the SIC codes in the corresponding U.S. industries (also listed in Appendix A). Note that this grouping is non-exclusive (as some U.S. firms are in several "Canadian sectors") and non-exhaustive (as 18 percent of the observations are not used in any of the sectors). Also, there are no U.S. data in the sample for the environmental affairs sector (No. 5). The total number of non-duplicative observations in the 11 sectors is 21,516.

Four variables enter the regression model. The variable I_t/K_{t-1} is the investment-capital ratio (firm and industry subscripts are suppressed for simplicity). Investment is Compustat's capital expenditure variable from the firm's uses of funds statements, and represents spending on plant and equipment.[34] Capital is the estimated constant dollar replacement value of plant and equipment. The t-1 subscript on the capital stock indicates that it is measured at the beginning of each accounting year. Sales is taken from the Compustat net sales figure, and is deflated by the appropriate industry output price deflator. The growth rate in real sales is represented by $\Delta S_t/S_{t-1}$. Cash flow (CF_t) which is scaled by the beginning-of-period capital stock is defined as net after-tax income plus non-cash charges, where the latter is primarily depreciation. The measure of cash flow is adjusted for deferred taxes and equity – corrected for net losses and earnings; dividend payments are not subtracted. The $\Delta U_t/U_{t-1}$ variable is the percentage change in the user cost defined in equation (24b).

Summary statistics for the 11 sectors are presented in Table 1 for the period 1972 to 1991, which is the full period over which lags are computed.[35] Two measures of standard deviation are reported: STD which measures all of the variation in a particular variable and WFSTD, the within-firm standard deviation computed by subtracting firm means from each variable before computing the standard deviation, i.e., the data are "mean-differenced" before computing the standard deviation. Thus, STD reflects both cross-section and time-series variation, while WFSTD reflects only the latter.

The investment-to-capital ratios (Panel 1) have mean values that range from 15 percent to 21 percent, and exhibit a great deal of variability, as the STDs are equal to or slightly greater than the means. The user costs average somewhat greater than 20 percent (Panel 2), and they generally fall during the sample period (Panel 3). For three model variables – I_t/K_{t-1}, $\Delta U_t/U_{t-1}$ and $\Delta S_t/S_{t-1}$ – differences between STD and WFSTD are modest. Thus, a great deal of variability remains even after the data are "mean-differenced." However, for CF_t/K_{t-1}, WFSTD is markedly lower than STD, and the differences vary across industries. These characteristics of the cash flow data reflect, *inter alia*, the positive impact of economic depreciation on cash flow and the dispersion of depreciation rates across industries.

Empirical Results

This section contains empirical results for the 11 sectors. Eight estimates are computed for each sector. For the model without cash flow, the least squares estimates are presented with the data pooled, mean-differenced and first-differenced, and instrumental variable estimates only with the data first-differenced. These four estimators are recomputed with a model that includes a distributed lag of cash flow. The focus is on a discussion of the coefficient sums in Table 2 with a particular emphasis on the user cost elasticities, i.e., the sum of the α's. (Estimates of individual coefficients are available from the authors on request.)

To begin, a model without cash flow and with pooled data is examined utilizing all the variation in the panel data set. The elasticities range widely from +.047 (No. 1) to -1.683 (No. 12). This dispersion is not unanticipated. The user cost elasticities are partly determined by the underlying production technologies (cf. equation [5]), and it seems reasonable to expect that the degree of substitutability of labour and capital varies across sectors. Eight of the 11 user cost elasticities are negative and statistically significant.[36] In contrast to results with aggregate data (cf. Chirinko, 1993), most of these initial results are quite large and suggest the possibility of uncovering substantial elasticities with firm-level data.

Much recent work in investment has been concerned with the role played by financial conditions with cash flow as a proxy. Omitting cash flow from the regression may distort estimates, and this potential distortion is examined by including cash flow in the pooled regressions. In all regressions, the sums of cash flow coefficients are positive and statistically significant. This role for cash flow comes at the expense of the sales growth coefficients which are uniformly lower. Cash flow appears to be an important element in the investment equation.[37] Thus, in the remainder of this study, we focus on regressions with cash flow, though Table 2 also contains results without cash flow with which to draw comparisons.[38]

The pooled estimates considered so far are based on the potentially important homogeneity assumptions that the intercepts are the same across firms within a sector. The mean-difference and first-difference estimators allow for varying intercepts across firms. As reported in tables 2 and 3, estimates of the user cost elasticity based on the mean difference estimator are usually larger (in absolute value) than the pooled estimates. The information (No. 12) sector estimate is unchanged, while the user cost elasticities for chemicals (No. 4) and manufacturing (No. 9) are closer to zero. Thus, controlling for fixed effects is important in estimating user cost elasticities accurately.

First-differencing the data is an alternative way to eliminate fixed effects. If the model is specified properly, then the mean-difference and first-difference estimates will be close together. However, if measurement error is present in the user cost variable, the elasticities from the first-difference model would be closer to zero than the elasticities from the mean-difference model. For 10 of the 11 sectors, the first-differenced elasticities are either roughly equal to or greater than (in absolute value) the

TABLE 1

SUMMARY STATISTICS

Variable: $I_{i,t}/K_{i,t-1}$

Sector Name	Mean	Median	Standard Deviation (STD)	Within-Firm Standard Deviation (WFSTD)	No. of Firms	No. of Observ.
1. Plastics	0.153	0.118	0.152	0.121	193	1,369
2. Aerospace	0.213	0.168	0.230	0.193	205	1,351
3. Automotive	0.164	0.119	0.203	0.160	212	1,439
4. Chemicals	0.186	0.139	0.211	0.156	282	1,799
6. Fashion	0.179	0.139	0.179	0.141	513	3,264
7. Forest	0.153	0.115	0.166	0.137	150	1,072
8. Health	0.218	0.156	0.265	0.211	324	1,836
9. Manufacturing	0.167	0.118	0.208	0.171	1,393	9,451
10. Service	0.200	0.148	0.233	0.183	854	5,176
11. Transportation	0.166	0.122	0.181	0.144	313	1,910
12. Information	0.205	0.137	0.243	0.197	934	5,855
All Firms	0.178	0.128	0.209	0.165	3,296	21,516

Variable: $U_{i,t}$

Sector Name	Mean	Median	Standard Deviation (STD)	Within-Firm Standard Deviation (WFSTD)	No. of Firms	No. of Observ.
1. Plastics	0.210	0.213	0.024	0.012	193	1,369
2. Aerospace	0.218	0.215	0.019	0.014	205	1,351
3. Automotive	0.205	0.198	0.027	0.012	212	1,439
4. Chemicals	0.223	0.222	0.010	0.008	282	1,799
6. Fashion	0.224	0.223	0.023	0.012	513	3,264
7. Forest	0.229	0.226	0.014	0.013	150	1,072
8. Health	0.240	0.234	0.024	0.011	324	1,836
9. Manufacturing	0.213	0.211	0.018	0.012	1,393	9,451
10. Service	0.260	0.264	0.036	0.016	854	5,176
11. Transportation	0.221	0.217	0.052	0.017	313	1,910
12. Information	0.216	0.213	0.026	0.012	934	5,855
All Firms	0.226	0.220	0.033	0.013	3,296	21,516

(cont'd)

TABLE 1 (continued)
SUMMARY STATISTICS

Variable: $\Delta U_{i,t}/U_{i,t-1}$

	Sector Name	Mean	Median	Standard Deviation (STD)	Within-Firm Standard Deviation (WFSTD)	No. of Firms	No. of Observ.
1.	Plastics	-0.009	-0.014	0.048	0.045	193	1,369
2.	Aerospace	-0.029	-0.033	0.041	0.039	205	1,351
3.	Automotive	-0.014	-0.016	0.049	0.046	212	1,439
4.	Chemicals	-0.012	-0.018	0.045	0.044	282	1,799
6.	Fashion	-0.020	-0.023	0.043	0.040	513	3,264
7.	Forest	-0.024	-0.030	0.042	0.041	150	1,072
8.	Health	-0.018	-0.023	0.041	0.039	324	1,836
9.	Manufacturing	-0.019	-0.023	0.045	0.042	1,393	9,451
10.	Service	-0.020	-0.032	0.074	0.065	854	5,176
11.	Transportation	-0.004	-0.020	0.112	0.099	313	1,910
12.	Information	-0.024	-0.030	0.039	0.037	934	5,855
	All Firms	-0.019	-0.024	0.053	0.048	3,296	21,516

Variable: $S_{i,t}$

	Sector Name	Mean	Median	Standard Deviation (STD)	Within-Firm Standard Deviation (WFSTD)	No. of Firms	No. of Observ.
1.	Plastics	1,064.35	224.782	1,904.93	395.527	193	1,369
2.	Aerospace	1,439.90	97.249	3,351.23	902.301	205	1,351
3.	Automotive	2,913.14	104.918	12,075.80	2,534.490	212	1,439
4.	Chemicals	1,152.36	221.151	3,100.10	558.338	282	1,799
6.	Fashion	624.75	136.198	1,322.54	299.436	513	3,264
7.	Forest	1,227.87	177.682	2,559.60	620.107	150	1,072
8.	Health	806.98	114.249	1,855.38	466.271	324	1,836
9.	Manufacturing	1,613.01	107.632	7,432.74	1,491.650	1,393	9,451
10.	Service	1,236.21	196.489	5,463.41	1,155.910	854	5,176
11.	Transportation	883.02	202.733	1,717.22	490.606	313	1,910
12.	Information	772.78	71.194	3,386.74	717.665	934	5,855
	All Firms	1,425.34	153.385	5,996.73	1,217.360	3,296	21,516

(cont'd)

TABLE 1 (continued)

SUMMARY STATISTICS

Variable: $\Delta S_{i,t}/S_{i,t-1}$

	Sector Name	Mean	Median	Standard Deviation (STD)	Within-Firm Standard Deviation (WFSTD)	No. of Firms	No. of Observ.
1.	Plastics	0.037	0.019	0.241	0.213	193	1,369
2.	Aerospace	0.033	0.023	0.253	0.225	205	1,351
3.	Automotive	0.025	0.011	0.267	0.238	212	1,439
4.	Chemicals	0.054	0.039	0.261	0.225	282	1,799
6.	Fashion	0.032	0.022	0.241	0.213	513	3,264
7.	Forest	0.020	0.006	0.220	0.194	150	1,072
8.	Health	0.069	0.052	0.295	0.255	324	1,836
9.	Manufacturing	0.021	0.011	0.253	0.228	1,393	9,451
10.	Service	0.031	0.022	0.260	0.223	854	5,176
11.	Transportation	0.040	0.017	0.279	0.250	313	1,910
12.	Information	0.030	0.022	0.247	0.215	934	5,855
	All Firms	0.030	0.019	0.248	0.218	3,296	21,516

Variable: $CF_{i,t}/K_{i,t-1}$

	Sector Name	Mean	Median	Standard Deviation (STD)	Within-Firm Standard Deviation (WFSTD)	No. of Firms	No. of Observ.
1.	Plastics	0.198	0.169	0.280	0.192	193	1,369
2.	Aerospace	0.267	0.288	0.546	0.400	205	1,351
3.	Automotive	0.209	0.185	0.375	0.259	212	1,439
4.	Chemicals	0.309	0.256	0.661	0.291	282	1,799
6.	Fashion	0.267	0.231	0.485	0.285	513	3,264
7.	Forest	0.188	0.163	0.331	0.245	150	1,072
8.	Health	0.297	0.252	0.543	0.314	324	1,836
9.	Manufacturing	0.217	0.188	0.475	0.291	1,393	9,451
10.	Service	0.257	0.211	0.497	0.302	854	5,176
11.	Transportation	0.190	0.128	0.396	0.244	313	1,910
12.	Information	0.247	0.207	0.557	0.353	934	5,855
	All Firms	0.233	0.192	0.459	0.284	3,296	21,516

(cont'd)

TABLE 1 (continued)

SUMMARY STATISTICS

Variable: $K_{i,t-1}$

	Sector Name	Mean	Median	Standard Deviation (STD)	Within-Firm Standard Deviation (WFSTD)	No. of Firms	No. of Observ.
1.	Plastics	790.586	84.765	1,547.15	275.877	193	1,369
2.	Aerospace	394.649	24.302	949.63	266.056	205	1,351
3.	Automotive	943.181	31.484	3,976.47	538.661	212	1,439
4.	Chemicals	622.553	63.822	1,988.84	384.414	282	1,799
6.	Fashion	300.213	36.052	831.84	162.982	513	3,264
7.	Forest	852.120	54.470	1,756.04	352.370	150	1,072
8.	Health	344.705	26.669	837.80	215.231	324	1,836
9.	Manufacturing	969.291	34.294	4,565.90	604.364	1,393	9,451
10.	Service	227.212	34.938	588.58	151.496	854	5,176
11.	Transportation	1,048.560	104.335	2,418.63	580.730	313	1,910
12.	Information	886.490	22.166	7,135.74	2,728.760	934	5,855
	All Firms	884.997	44.697	4,903.31	1,495.610	3,296	21,516

Note: The within-firm standard deviation is computed by subtracting firm means from each variable before computing the standard deviation. This statistic measures variation in the time dimension only in the particular variable. Sector 5, Environmental Affairs, is missing because there are no corresponding firms in the Compustat data base. The statistics in the rows labelled "All Firms" are computed after all duplicate observations are removed.

mean-differenced elasticities. (The transportation sector [No. 11] is the exception.) Measurement error in the user cost variable does not appear to be a problem, and a prime suspect in prior low estimates of the user cost elasticity is found "not guilty."

The final econometric issue concerns simultaneity, and we employ the first difference estimator with instrumental variables.[39] The impacts are quite similar, as the user cost elasticity falls (in absolute value) in 10 sectors (health [No. 8] being the exception with a very modest increase).[40] The standard errors rise noticeably, and preclude firm inferences from being drawn. In all 11 sectors, the hypothesis that the user cost elasticity is zero cannot be rejected – but neither can the hypothesis that it is unity.

Two caveats should be kept in mind in interpreting these results. As noted in several places in sections two and three of this paper, the estimated elasticities represent an amalgam of technology, delivery lag and expectation parameters. The Lucas Critique is a reminder that these elasticities, regardless of how precisely they are estimated, may not be invariant to alternative policies and that policy evaluations must be tempered accordingly, especially when considering radical reforms.

A second caveat is that the sectoral elasticities presented here cannot be "weighted-up" (with capital or investment weights) to estimate an aggregate user cost elasticity. Given the definitions of the "Canadian sectors," some firms appear in more than one industry, and a weighted average would double-count the impact of these overlapping firms. Furthermore, the reported elasticities, which tend to be for established manufacturing and mining firms, are only a subset of the elasticities for all firms in the economy. The impact of these missing sectors may be sizable. For example, the manufacturing and mining sectors accounted for less than 25 percent of the capital stock in the United States in 1989, while transportation/public utilities and finance/insurance/real estate each accounted for approximately 20 percent.[41] While the estimates presented in this study are an accurate reflection of the sectors for which they are computed, they cannot form the basis for an aggregate user cost elasticity.

Summary, Conclusion and Future Research

THIS PAPER HAS PRESENTED A VARIETY OF ESTIMATES of the elasticity of investment spending to the user cost of capital. This elasticity is important for policy makers because it is one of two channels through which public policies can alter economic behaviour and enhance economic performance. At present, suitable data for Canadian firms do not exist, and elasticity estimates were computed for U.S. firms grouped to correspond to sectors in the Canadian economy. The data set contained substantial firm-level variation relative to prior studies, and the panel structure permitted an evaluation of several factors that might distort estimates of the user cost elasticity.

Summary estimates of the user cost elasticity for models with cash flow are presented in Table 3, which is ordered by the preferred estimates appearing in column 4. These first-difference/instrumental variable estimates range from -1.664 to -0.054. Unfortunately, the point estimates are accompanied by relatively large standard errors. In all 11 sectors, the hypothesis that the user cost elasticity is zero cannot be rejected, but the hypothesis that it is unity cannot be rejected either. Thus, the overall finding is that there is too much imprecision in these estimates to reach firm conclusions about the sensitivity of sectoral investment spending to variations in investment incentives.

A comparison of columns 3 and 4 of Table 3 reveals that much of this imprecision arises with the use of instrumental variables, which are necessary to control for simultaneity. This suggests searching for better instruments within the context of the first-difference estimator or using estimators that avoid simultaneity problems more efficiently. An alternative way to improve precision is to use more data. While expanding the data set would prove quite difficult, more data can be brought to bear for a given user cost estimate by defining the sectors more broadly. Estimation issues aside, while the sectoral groupings used here are valid, they can, nonetheless, only approximate the activities of firms in the Canadian sectors. The collection of suitable Canadian firm-level data must be a high priority for future research.

TABLE 2

SUMMARY REGRESSION RESULTS

Sector 1: Advanced Materials and Plastics

Regression Without Cash Flow:

$$I_{i,t}/K_{i,t-1}=\alpha_6(L)\Delta U_{i,t}/U_{i,t-1}+\beta_4(L)\Delta S_{i,t}/S_{i,t-1}+\phi_i+\epsilon_{i,t}$$

	Pooled Regression ($\phi_i=\phi$)	Fixed Effects Mean Difference	Fixed Effects First Difference	First-Difference Instrumental Variables
$SUM(\alpha)$	0.047 (0.243)	-1.034 (0.344)	-1.256 (0.584)	-1.178 (0.671)
$SUM(\beta)$	0.275 (0.033)	0.171 (0.040)	0.182 (0.080)	0.279 (0.148)
SSE	29.439	19.158	29.969	30.701
R-squared	0.066	0.037	0.029	0.015
Obs.	1,369	1,369	1,174	1,174

Regression Including Cash Flow:

$$I_{i,t}/K_{i,t-1}=\alpha_6(L)\Delta U_{i,t}/U_{i,t-1}+\beta_4(L)\Delta S_{i,t}/S_{i,t-1}+\gamma_4(L)CF_{i,t}/K_{i,t-1}+\phi_i+\epsilon_{i,t}$$

	Pooled Regression ($\phi_i=\phi$)	Fixed Effects Mean Difference	Fixed Effects First Difference	First-Difference Instrumental Variables
$SUM(\alpha)$	-0.203 (0.221)	-0.578 (0.341)	-1.080 (0.581)	-0.886 (0.730)
$SUM(\beta)$	0.109 (0.032)	0.050 (0.042)	0.105 (0.084)	0.200 (0.176)
$SUM(\gamma)$	0.326 (0.019)	0.286 (0.038)	0.178 (0.083)	0.174 (0.205)
SSE	24.087	18.216	29.337	32.708
R-squared	0.236	0.084	0.049	0.019
Obs.	1,369	1,369	1,174	1,174

(cont'd)

TABLE 2 (continued)

SUMMARY REGRESSION RESULTS

Sector 2: Aerospace and Defence

Regression Without Cash Flow:

$$I_{i,t}/K_{i,t-1}=\alpha_6(L)\Delta U_{i,t}/U_{i,t-1}+\beta_4(L)\Delta S_{i,t}/S_{i,t-1}+\phi_i+\epsilon_{i,t}$$

	Pooled Regression ($\phi_i=\phi$)	Fixed Effects Mean Difference	Fixed Effects First Difference	First-Difference Instrumental Variables
$SUM(\alpha)$	-0.802 (0.511)	-2.131 (0.649)	-1.837 (1.292)	-1.511 (1.894)
$SUM(\beta)$	0.626 (0.045)	0.419 (0.060)	0.228 (0.115)	0.459 (0.214)
SSE	60.740	46.855	68.628	77.660
R-squared	0.150	0.070	0.021	0.012
Obs.	1,351	1,351	1,144	1,144

Regression Including Cash Flow:

$$I_{i,t}/K_{i,t-1}=\alpha_6(L)\Delta U_{i,t}/U_{i,t-1}+\beta_4(L)\Delta S_{i,t}/S_{i,t-1}+\gamma_4(L)CF_{i,t}/K_{i,t-1}+\phi_i+\epsilon_{i,t}$$

	Pooled Regression ($\phi_i=\phi$)	Fixed Effects Mean Difference	Fixed Effects First Difference	First-Difference Instrumental Variables
$SUM(\alpha)$	-0.838 (0.488)	-1.515 (0.618)	-1.474 (1.266)	-0.054 (2.057)
$SUM(\beta)$	0.412 (0.047)	0.105 (0.063)	0.017 (0.123)	0.174 (0.274)
$SUM(\gamma)$	0.176 (0.016)	0.294 (0.026)	0.230 (0.056)	0.408 (0.142)
SSE	55.071	41.626	65.282	83.277
R-squared	0.230	0.174	0.069	0.021
Obs.	1,351	1,351	1,144	1,144

(cont'd)

TABLE 2 (continued)
SUMMARY REGRESSION RESULTS

Sector 3: Automotive

Regression Without Cash Flow:

$$I_{i,t}/K_{i,t-1}=\alpha_6(L)\Delta U_{i,t}/U_{i,t-1}+\beta_4(L)\Delta S_{i,t}/S_{i,t-1}+\phi_i+\epsilon_{i,t}$$

	Pooled Regression ($\phi_i=\phi$)	Fixed Effects Mean Difference	Fixed Effects First Difference	First-Difference Instrumental Variables
$SUM(\alpha)$	-0.642 (0.346)	-1.558 (0.471)	-1.916 (0.946)	-0.273 (1.280)
$SUM(\beta)$	0.498 (0.041)	0.271 (0.050)	0.197 (0.095)	-0.006 (0.185)
SSE	52.868	34.645	56.155	61.633
R-squared	0.107	0.054	0.019	0.015
Obs.	1,439	1,439	1,224	1,224

Regression Including Cash Flow:

$$I_{i,t}/K_{i,t-1}=\alpha_6(L)\Delta U_{i,t}/U_{i,t-1}+\beta_4(L)\Delta S_{i,t}/S_{i,t-1}+\gamma_4(L)CF_{i,t}/K_{i,t-1}+\phi_i+\epsilon_{i,t}$$

	Pooled Regression ($\phi_i=\phi$)	Fixed Effects Mean Difference	Fixed Effects First Difference	First-Difference Instrumental Variables
$SUM(\alpha)$	-0.470 (0.315)	-0.693 (0.452)	-1.376 (0.928)	-0.344 (1.318)
$SUM(\beta)$	0.192 (0.042)	0.019 (0.052)	0.018 (0.098)	0.065 (0.267)
$SUM(\gamma)$	0.307 (0.018)	0.361 (0.034)	0.328 (0.071)	-0.044 (0.189)
SSE	43.655	30.977	53.472	59.308
R-squared	0.263	0.154	0.066	0.018
Obs.	1,439	1,439	1,224	1,224

(cont'd)

TABLE 2 (continued)

SUMMARY REGRESSION RESULTS

Sector 4: Chemicals and Bio-technology

Regression Without Cash Flow:

$$I_{i,t}/K_{i,t-1}=\alpha_6(L)\Delta U_{i,t}/U_{i,t-1}+\beta_4(L)\Delta S_{i,t}/S_{i,t-1}+\phi_i+\epsilon_{i,t}$$

	Pooled Regression ($\phi_i=\phi$)	Fixed Effects Mean Difference	Fixed Effects First Difference	First-Difference Instrumental Variables
SUM(α)	-1.296 (0.402)	-0.512 (0.356)	-0.334 (0.699)	-0.426 (0.827)
SUM(β)	0.575 (0.036)	0.236 (0.053)	-0.137 (0.098)	-0.440 (0.225)
SSE	68.776	42.731	65.256	71.401
R-squared	0.137	0.029	0.018	0.017
Obs.	1,799	1,799	1,517	1,517

Regression Including Cash Flow:

$$I_{i,t}/K_{i,t-1}=\alpha_6(L)\Delta U_{i,t}/U_{i,t-1}+\beta_4(L)\Delta S_{i,t}/S_{i,t-1}+\gamma_4(L)CF_{i,t}/K_{i,t-1}+\phi_i+\epsilon_{i,t}$$

	Pooled Regression ($\phi_i=\phi$)	Fixed Effects Mean Difference	Fixed Effects First Difference	First-Difference Instrumental Variables
SUM(α)	-1.191 (0.397)	-0.533 (0.342)	-0.632 (0.684)	-0.615 (0.836)
SUM(β)	0.521 (0.037)	0.036 (0.054)	-0.315 (0.099)	-0.360 (0.271)
SUM(γ)	0.052 (0.008)	0.243 (0.024)	0.296 (0.051)	0.080 (0.235)
SSE	66.501	39.358	62.098	68.146
R-squared	0.166	0.106	0.066	0.022
Obs.	1,799	1,799	1,517	1,517

(cont'd)

TABLE 2 (continued)
SUMMARY REGRESSION RESULTS

Sector 6: Fashion, Leisure and Household Products

Regression Without Cash Flow:

$$I_{i,t}/K_{i,t-1}=\alpha_6(L)\Delta U_{i,t}/U_{i,t-1}+\beta_4(L)\Delta S_{i,t}/S_{i,t-1}+\phi_i+\epsilon_{i,t}$$

	Pooled Regression ($\phi_i=\phi$)	Fixed Effects Mean Difference	Fixed Effects First Difference	First-Difference Instrumental Variables
$SUM(\alpha)$	-0.529 (0.196)	-2.071 (0.330)	-1.720 (0.559)	-1.136 (0.794)
$SUM(\beta)$	0.446 (0.025)	0.268 (0.032)	0.207 (0.060)	0.216 (0.132)
SSE	93.482	61.862	98.783	98.841
R-squared	0.101	0.048	0.014	0.008
Obs.	3,264	3,264	2,749	2,749

Regression Including Cash Flow:

$$I_{i,t}/K_{i,t-1}=\alpha_6(L)\Delta U_{i,t}/U_{i,t-1}+\beta_4(L)\Delta S_{i,t}/S_{i,t-1}+\gamma_4(L)CF_{i,t}/K_{i,t-1}+\phi_i+\epsilon_{i,t}$$

	Pooled Regression ($\phi_i=\phi$)	Fixed Effects Mean Difference	Fixed Effects First Difference	First-Difference Instrumental Variables
$SUM(\alpha)$	-0.216 (0.189)	-1.695 (0.322)	-1.571 (0.552)	-0.798 (0.898)
$SUM(\beta)$	0.322 (0.025)	0.115 (0.034)	0.086 (0.063)	0.161 (0.375)
$SUM(\gamma)$	0.127 (0.008)	0.199 (0.017)	0.220 (0.038)	0.279 (0.208)
SSE	85.877	58.238	95.845	101.579
R-squared	0.174	0.103	0.043	0.011
Obs.	3,264	3,264	2,749	2,749

(cont'd)

TABLE 2 (continued)
SUMMARY REGRESSION RESULTS

Sector 7: Forest Industries and Building Products

Regression Without Cash Flow:

$$I_{i,t}/K_{i,t-1}=\alpha_6(L)\Delta U_{i,t}/U_{i,t-1}+\beta_4(L)\Delta S_{i,t}/S_{i,t-1}+\phi_i+\epsilon_{i,t}$$

	Pooled Regression ($\phi_i=\phi$)	Fixed Effects Mean Difference	Fixed Effects First Difference	First-Difference Instrumental Variables
SUM(α)	-0.381 (0.544)	-1.026 (0.530)	-1.750 (0.826)	-0.922 (1.081)
SUM(β)	0.570 (0.044)	0.383 (0.062)	0.349 (0.127)	0.262 (0.260)
SSE	24.874	18.955	31.849	33.097
R-squared	0.152	0.063	0.051	0.023
Obs.	1,072	1,072	918	918

Regression Including Cash Flow:

$$I_{i,t}/K_{i,t-1}=\alpha_6(L)\Delta U_{i,t}/U_{i,t-1}+\beta_4(L)\Delta S_{i,t}/S_{i,t-1}+\gamma_4(L)CF_{i,t}/K_{i,t-1}+\phi_i+\epsilon_{i,t}$$

	Pooled Regression ($\phi_i=\phi$)	Fixed Effects Mean Difference	Fixed Effects First Difference	First-Difference Instrumental Variables
SUM(α)	-0.028 (0.489)	-0.265 (0.487)	-1.604 (0.788)	-0.659 (1.112)
SUM(β)	0.233 (0.045)	0.103 (0.061)	0.080 (0.126)	0.184 (0.292)
SUM(γ)	0.269 (0.019)	0.393 (0.037)	0.545 (0.083)	0.400 (0.146)
SSE	19.900	15.654	28.716	29.577
R-squared	0.322	0.226	0.144	0.041
Obs.	1,072	1,072	918	918

(cont'd)

TABLE 2 (continued)
SUMMARY REGRESSION RESULTS

Sector 8: Health Care Industries

Regression Without Cash Flow:

$$I_{i,t}/K_{i,t-1}=\alpha_6(L)\Delta U_{i,t}/U_{i,t-1}+\beta_4(L)\Delta S_{i,t}/S_{i,t-1}+\phi_i+\epsilon_{i,t}$$

	Pooled Regression ($\phi_i=\phi$)	Fixed Effects Mean Difference	Fixed Effects First Difference	First-Difference Instrumental Variables
$SUM(\alpha)$	-1.710 (0.545)	-1.521 (0.550)	-1.079 (1.006)	-1.389 (1.243)
$SUM(\beta)$	0.489 (0.039)	0.005 (0.059)	-0.384 (0.115)	-0.221 (0.248)
SSE	115.269	78.830	120.894	124.295
R-squared	0.106	0.034	0.019	0.019
Obs.	1,836	1,836	1,510	1,510

Regression Including Cash Flow:

$$I_{i,t}/K_{i,t-1}=\alpha_6(L)\Delta U_{i,t}/U_{i,t-1}+\beta_4(L)\Delta S_{i,t}/S_{i,t-1}+\gamma_4(L)CF_{i,t}/K_{i,t-1}+\phi_i+\epsilon_{i,t}$$

	Pooled Regression ($\phi_i=\phi$)	Fixed Effects Mean Difference	Fixed Effects First Difference	First-Difference Instrumental Variables
$SUM(\alpha)$	-1.377 (0.533)	-1.474 (0.535)	-1.373 (0.990)	-1.426 (1.396)
$SUM(\beta)$	0.402 (0.039)	-0.196 (0.060)	-0.574 (0.117)	-0.047 (0.325)
$SUM(\gamma)$	0.138 (0.014)	0.315 (0.031)	0.414 (0.068)	-0.014 (0.315)
SSE	108.852	73.686	116.285	148.097
R-squared	0.156	0.097	0.057	0.021
Obs.	1,836	1,836	1,510	1,510

(cont'd)

TABLE 2 (continued)

SUMMARY REGRESSION RESULTS

Sector 9: Manufacturing and Processing Technologies

Regression Without Cash Flow:

$$I_{i,t}/K_{i,t-1}=\alpha_6(L)\Delta U_{i,t}/U_{i,t-1}+\beta_4(L)\Delta S_{i,t}/S_{i,t-1}+\phi_i+\epsilon_{i,t}$$

	Pooled Regression ($\phi_i=\phi$)	Fixed Effects Mean Difference	Fixed Effects First Difference	First-Difference Instrumental Variables
SUM(α)	-1.480 (0.133)	-1.821 (0.181)	-1.628 (0.358)	-1.667 (0.585)
SUM(β)	0.549 (0.016)	0.355 (0.021)	0.203 (0.044)	0.447 (0.106)
SSE	356.491	261.022	419.511	430.184
R-squared	0.126	0.052	0.013	0.012
Obs.	9,451	9,451	8,046	8,046

Regression Including Cash Flow:

$$I_{i,t}/K_{i,t-1}=\alpha_6(L)\Delta U_{i,t}/U_{i,t-1}+\beta_4(L)\Delta S_{i,t}/S_{i,t-1}+\gamma_4(L)CF_{i,t}/K_{i,t-1}+\phi_i+\epsilon_{i,t}$$

	Pooled Regression ($\phi_i=\phi$)	Fixed Effects Mean Difference	Fixed Effects First Difference	First-Difference Instrumental Variables
SUM(α)	-1.313 (0.130)	-1.102 (0.176)	-1.461 (0.350)	-0.968 (0.653)
SUM(β)	0.425 (0.017)	0.114 (0.022)	-0.002 (0.046)	0.261 (0.137)
SUM(γ)	0.126 (0.005)	0.299 (0.012)	0.309 (0.026)	0.399 (0.110)
SSE	334.966	238.010	402.004	478.648
R-squared	0.179	0.136	0.054	0.014
Obs.	9,451	9,451	8,046	8,046

(cont'd)

TABLE 2 (continued)
SUMMARY REGRESSION RESULTS

Sector 10: Service Industries and Capital Projects

Regression Without Cash Flow:

$$I_{i,t}/K_{i,t-1}=\alpha_6(L)\Delta U_{i,t}/U_{i,t-1}+\beta_4(L)\Delta S_{i,t}/S_{i,t-1}+\phi_i+\epsilon_{i,t}$$

	Pooled Regression ($\phi_i=\phi$)	Fixed Effects Mean Difference	Fixed Effects First Difference	First-Difference Instrumental Variables
$SUM(\alpha)$	-0.753 (0.118)	-0.917 (0.154)	-0.874 (0.332)	-1.308 (0.564)
$SUM(\beta)$	0.483 (0.021)	0.393 (0.029)	0.247 (0.061)	0.562 (0.117)
SSE	246.866	159.645	278.209	324.440
R-squared	0.121	0.077	0.020	0.012
Obs.	5,176	5,176	4,314	4,314

Regression Including Cash Flow:

$$I_{i,t}/K_{i,t-1}=\alpha_6(L)\Delta U_{i,t}/U_{i,t-1}+\beta_4(L)\Delta S_{i,t}/S_{i,t-1}+\gamma_4(L)CF_{i,t}/K_{i,t-1}+\phi_i+\epsilon_{i,t}$$

	Pooled Regression ($\phi_i=\phi$)	Fixed Effects Mean Difference	Fixed Effects First Difference	First-Difference Instrumental Variables
$SUM(\alpha)$	-0.481 (0.114)	-0.627 (0.148)	-0.612 (0.325)	-0.549 (0.577)
$SUM(\beta)$	0.330 (0.022)	0.226 (0.030)	0.153 (0.063)	0.459 (0.124)
$SUM(\gamma)$	0.168 (0.008)	0.261 (0.016)	0.267 (0.037)	0.298 (0.108)
SSE	225.445	145.026	265.659	301.138
R-squared	0.197	0.161	0.064	0.018
Obs.	5,176	5,176	4,314	4,314

(cont'd)

TABLE 2 (continued)
SUMMARY REGRESSION RESULTS

Sector 11: Transportation Industries

Regression Without Cash Flow:

$I_{i,t}/K_{i,t-1}=\alpha_6(L)\Delta U_{i,t}/U_{i,t-1}+\beta_4(L)\Delta S_{i,t}/S_{i,t-1}+\phi_i+\epsilon_{i,t}$

	Pooled Regression ($\phi_i=\phi$)	Fixed Effects Mean Difference	Fixed Effects First Difference	First-Difference Instrumental Variables
SUM(α)	-0.636 (0.103)	-0.897 (0.132)	-0.512 (0.271)	-0.647 (0.364)
SUM(β)	0.341 (0.028)	0.181 (0.036)	0.004 (0.069)	0.269 (0.119)
SSE	54.802	36.452	55.388	61.557
R-squared	0.119	0.085	0.008	0.015
Obs.	1,910	1,910	1,595	1,595

Regression Including Cash Flow:

$I_{i,t}/K_{i,t-1}=\alpha_6(L)\Delta U_{i,t}/U_{i,t-1}+\beta_4(L)\Delta S_{i,t}/S_{i,t-1}+\gamma_4(L)CF_{i,t}/K_{i,t-1}+\phi_i+\epsilon_{i,t}$

	Pooled Regression ($\phi_i=\phi$)	Fixed Effects Mean Difference	Fixed Effects First Difference	First-Difference Instrumental Variables
SUM(α)	-0.428 (0.100)	-0.723 (0.130)	-0.383 (0.270)	-0.373 (0.452)
SUM(β)	0.247 (0.028)	0.135 (0.035)	-0.059 (0.070)	0.346 (0.191)
SUM(γ)	0.165 (0.012)	0.187 (0.020)	0.279 (0.056)	0.404 (0.242)
SSE	49.804	34.122	53.609	85.063
R-squared	0.199	0.144	0.040	0.019
Obs.	1,910	1,910	1,595	1,595

(cont'd)

TABLE 2 (continued)

SUMMARY REGRESSION RESULTS

Sector 12: Information and Telecommunications Industries

Regression Without Cash Flow:

$$I_{i,t}/K_{i,t-1}=\alpha_6(L)\Delta U_{i,t}/U_{i,t-1}+\beta_4(L)\Delta S_{i,t}/S_{i,t-1}+\phi_i+\epsilon_{i,t}$$

	Pooled Regression ($\phi_i=\phi$)	Fixed Effects Mean Difference	Fixed Effects First Difference	First-Difference Instrumental Variables
$SUM(\alpha)$	-1.683 (0.279)	-2.597 (0.364)	-1.766 (0.706)	-2.998 (1.185)
$SUM(\beta)$	0.668 (0.022)	0.511 (0.031)	0.266 (0.066)	0.338 (0.184)
SSE	291.914	206.377	352.371	354.124
R-squared	0.158	0.091	0.020	0.009
Obs.	5,855	5,855	4,912	4,912

Regression Including Cash Flow:

$$I_{i,t}/K_{i,t-1}=\alpha_6(L)\Delta U_{i,t}/U_{i,t-1}+\beta_4(L)\Delta S_{i,t}/S_{i,t-1}+\gamma_4(L)CF_{i,t}/K_{i,t-1}+\phi_i+\epsilon_{i,t}$$

	Pooled Regression ($\phi_i=\phi$)	Fixed Effects Mean Difference	Fixed Effects First Difference	First-Difference Instrumental Variables
$SUM(\alpha)$	-1.747 (0.271)	-1.732 (0.349)	-1.777 (0.690)	-1.664 (1.407)
$SUM(\beta)$	0.479 (0.024)	0.170 (0.033)	0.012 (0.069)	0.571 (0.278)
$SUM(\gamma)$	0.135 (0.007)	0.309 (0.015)	0.299 (0.032)	0.134 (0.109)
SSE	273.754	185.799	335.989	458.880
R-squared	0.210	0.181	0.066	0.011
Obs.	5,855	5,855	4,912	4,912

Note: Estimates of equation (24) as described in the text. Standard errors are in parentheses. Individual coefficient estimates are available from the authors on request. The polynomials in the lag operators $\alpha_6(L)$, $\beta_4(L)$ and $\gamma_4(L)$ are of the order 6, 4 and 4 and contain contemporaneous values. $SUM(\alpha)$, $SUM(\beta)$ and $SUM(\gamma)$ are the sums of the estimated coefficients; ϕ_i is an estimated, firm-specific constant. For the fixed effect models, the R^2 statistic does not include the variance explained by the firm effects. These statistics are, therefore, not comparable across estimators. The instrumental variables are described in endnote 39.

Table 3

User Cost Elasticities

Equation (24) With Cash Flow

Sector	Least Squares			Instrumental Variable
	Pooled (1)	Mean Difference (2)	First Difference (3)	First Difference (4)
Information (No. 12)	-1.747 (.271)	-1.732 (.349)	-1.777 (.690)	-1.664 (1.407)
Health (No. 8)	-1.377 (.533)	-1.474 (.535)	-1.373 (.990)	-1.426 (1.396)
Manufacturing (No. 9)	-1.313 (.130)	-1.102 (.176)	-1.461 (.350)	-.968 (.653)
Plastics (No. 1)	-.203 (.221)	-.578 (.341)	-1.080 (.581)	-.886 (.730)
Fashion (No. 6)	-.216 (.189)	-1.695 (.322)	-1.571 (.552)	-.798 (.898)
Forest (No. 7)	-.028 (.489)	-.265 (.487)	-1.604 (.788)	-.659 (1.112)
Chemicals (No. 4)	-1.191 (.397)	-.533 (.342)	-.632 (.684)	-.615 (.836)
Service (No. 10)	-.481 (.114)	-.627 (.148)	-.612 (.325)	-.549 (.577)
Transportation (No. 11)	-.428 (.100)	-.723 (.130)	-.383 (.270)	-.373 (.452)
Automotive (No. 3)	-.470 (.315)	-.693 (.452)	-1.376 (.928)	-.344 (1.318)
Aerospace (No. 2)	-.838 (.488)	-1.515 (.618)	-1.474 (1.266)	-.054 (2.057)

Note: Elasticity estimates are from Table 2. Standard errors in parentheses. The rows are ordered from the largest to smallest elasticities (in absolute value) appearing in column 4.

Appendix A

Sector Definitions and Standard Industrial Classification

	Canada SIC	USA SIC[42]
1. Advanced Materials and Plastics (AMP)		
Plastics, Rubber Hose and Belting Industry	1520	305
Other Rubber Products	1590	267, 301, 305, 306
Plastic Products Industries	1600	26, 30
Plastic and Synthetic Resin Industry	3731	2821, 3087
2. Aerospace and Defence (AD)		
Aerospace and Defence		359, 372, 376
Aircraft and Aircraft Parts Industry	3210	3625, 3651, 3661, 3663
Other Communication and Electronic Equipment Industry	3359	3669, 3812, 7629
3. Automotive (AUTO)		
Motor Vehicle Industry	3230	371
Truck and Bus Body and Trailer Industries	3240	245, 371, 379
Motor Vehicle Engine and Engine Parts Industry	3251	3519, 3592, 3694, 3714
Motor Vehicle Wiring Assemblies Industry	3252	3647, 3694, 3714
Motor Vehicle Stampings Industry	3253	3465, 3714
Motor Vehicle Steering and Suspension Parts Industry	3254	3493, 3714
Motor Vehicle Wheel and Brake Industry	3255	3714
Plastic Parts and Accessories for Motor Vehicle Industry	3256	3089, 3714
Motor Vehicle Fabric Accessories Industry	3257	2396, 2399, 2531
Other Motor Vehicle Accessories, Parts and Assembly	3259	3429, 3599, 2531
Motor Vehicle Parts and Accessories, Wholesale	5520	3429, 3599, 3714
Automobile Dealers	6310	369, 371, 501, 753
Gasoline Service Stations	6330	551, 552
Automotive Parts and Accessories Stores	6340	554, 754
Motor Vehicle Repair Shops	6350	501, 553
Other Motor Vehicle Services	6390	753, 754
Tire and Tube Industry	1510	301

4. Chemicals and Biotechnology (CBI)		
Industrial Chemicals Industries N.E.C.	3710	281, 282, 286, 287
Agricultural Chemical Industries	3720	281, 287
Pharmaceutical and Medicine Industry	3740	283, 384
Paint and Varnish Industry	3750	285
Soap and Cleaning Compounds Industry	3760	284, 329
Toilet Preparations Industry	3770	284
Other Chemical Products Industries	3790	284, 286, 287, 289, 348
5. Environmental Affairs (EA)[43]		
Other Utility Industries N.E.C.	4990	495, 496
6. Fashion, Leisure and Household Products (FLHP)		
Leather Tanneries	1711	3111
Footwear Industry	1712	3021, 3142, 3143, 3144, 3149
Luggage, Purse and Handbag Industry	1730	3161, 3171, 3172
Other Leather and Allied Products Industry	1790	3131, 3172, 3199
Synthetic Fibre and Filament Yarn Industry	1811	2281, 2282, 2296, 2823, 2824, 3229 3229
Wool Yarn and Woven Cloth Industry	1821	2231, 2281, 2282
Other Spun Yarn and Woven Cloth Industry	1829	2211, 2221, 2261, 2262, 2269, 2281, 2282
Broad Knitted Fabric Industry	1831	2257, 2258
Natural Fibres Processing and Felt Products Industry	1911	2297, 2299
Carpet, Mat and Rug Industry	1921	2273
Canvas and Related Products Industry	1931	2394
Narrow Fabric Industry	1991	2241, 2258, 2397
Contract Textile Dyeing and Finishing Industry	1992	2231, 2253, 2254, 2257, 2258, 2261, 2262, 2269, 2295, 2396
Household Products Of Textile Materials Industry	1993	2211, 2221, 2258, 2391, 2392, 2591
Hygiene Products Of Textile Materials Industry	1994	3842
Tire Cord Fabric Industry	1995	2296

Other Textile Products Industries N.E.C.	1999	2259, 2284, 2298, 2299, 2392, 2393, 2395, 2396, 2399, 2672
Men's and Boys' Coat Industry	2431	2311, 2329, 2385, 2386
Men's and Boys' Suit and Jacket Industry	2432	2311, 2329
Men's and Boys' Pants Industry	2433	2325, 2329
Men's and Boys' Shirt and Underwear Industry	2434	2253, 2254, 2321, 2322, 2326
Men's and Boys' Clothing Contractors	2435	2311, 2321, 2322, 2323, 2325, 2326, 2329
Women's Coat and Jacket Industry	2441	2337, 2339, 2385, 2386
Women's Sportswear Industry	2442	2253, 2337, 2339
Women's Dress Industry	2443	2253, 2335
Women's Blouse and Shirt Industry	2444	2253, 2331
Women's Clothing Contractors	2445	2253, 2331, 2335, 2337, 2339, 2341, 2395
Children's Clothing Industry	2451	2253, 2254, 2341, 2361, 2369, 2385
Sweater Industry	2491	2253, 2329, 2339, 2369
Occupational Clothing Industry	2492	2311, 2326, 2337, 2339, 2389, 3842
Glove Industry	2493	2259, 2381, 3089, 3151, 384
Hosiery Industry	2494	2251, 2252
Fur Goods Industry	2495	2371
Foundation Garment Industry	2496	2342
Other Clothing and Apparel Industry, N.E.C.	2499	2253, 2254, 2322, 2323, 2329, 2339, 2341, 2353, 2384, 2385, 2387, 2389, 2396
Wooden Household Furniture Industry	2611	2511, 2517, 5712
Upholstered Household Furniture Industry	2612	2512, 2515
Other Household Furniture Industries	2619	2514, 2519
Metal Office Furniture Industry	2641	2522, 2531
Other Office Furniture Industries	2649	2529, 2522
Bed Spring and Mattress Industry	2691	2515

Hotel, Restaurant and Institutional Furniture	2692	2531, 2541, 2542, 2599, 3821
Other Furniture and Fixture Industry N.E.C.	2699	2426, 2499, 2591
Commercial Printing Industries	2810	273, 275, 276, 277, 278
Platemaking, Typesetting and Bindery Industry	2820	278, 279, 738
Publishing Industries	2830	271, 272, 273, 274
Combined Publishing and Printing Industry	2840	271, 272, 273, 274
Stationery Paper Products Industry	2792	2621, 2675, 2677, 2678, 2679
Small Electrical Appliance Industry	3310	363
Major Appliance Industry	3320	358, 363
Electric Lighting Industry	3330	322, 364, 399
Sporting Goods Industry	3931	3089, 3429, 3648, 3751, 3944, 3949
Floor Tile, Linoleum and Coated Fabric Industry	3993	2295, 3069, 3996
7. Forest Industries and Building Products (FLHP)		
Sawmill, Planing Mill and Shingle Mill Products Industries	2510	242, 244
Veneer and Plywood Industries	2520	243
Wooden Box and Pallet Industry	2561	2441, 2448, 2449
Coffin and Casket Industry	2581	3995
Pulp and Paper Industry	2710	249, 261, 262, 263
Paper Box and Bag Industries	2730	262, 263, 265, 267
Coated and Treated Paper Industry	2791	2671, 2672, 2679, 3861
Paper Consumer Products Industry	2793	2621, 2676
Other Converted Paper Products Industry	2799	2621, 2655, 2656, 2675, 2679, 3497
Sash, Door and Other Millwork Industries	2540	242, 243, 245, 249, 254
Other Wood Industries	2590	244, 249
8. Health Care Industries (HCI)		
Pharmaceutical and Medicine Industry	3740	283, 384
Toilet Preparations Industry	3770	284
Health and Social Service Industries	8600	41, 80, 83, 86, 87, 89, 96

9. Manufacturing and Processing Technologies (MPT)

Compressor, Pump and Industrial Fan Industry	3191	3561, 3563, 3564
Sawmill and Woodworking Machinery Industry	3193	3553
Other Machinery and Equipment Industries N.E.C.	3199	3519, 3524, 3537, 3541, 3542, 3545, 3546, 3547, 3549, 3552, 3554, 3555, 3556, 3559, 3562, 3564, 3565, 3567, 3569, 3582, 3586, 3589, 3999
Clock and Watch Industry	3913	3579, 3873
Ophthalmic Goods Industry	3914	3851
Sign and Display Industry	3970	399
Other Manufactured Products Industries	3990	209, 229, 239, 259, 274, 305, 306, 317, 329, 365, 369, 384, 393, 395, 396, 399, 807
Other Rolled, Cast and Extruded Non-Ferrous Metal Products Industry	2990	334, 335, 336, 339, 346, 349
Fabricated Structural Metal Products Industry	3020	344
Heating Equipment Industry	3070	343, 356, 358, 363
Machine Shop Industry	3080	351, 359, 371
Other Metal Fabricating Industries	3090	305, 329, 339, 342, 343, 344, 346, 348, 349, 359, 364, 382, 399
Agricultural Implement Industry	3110	352
Commercial Refrigeration and Air Conditioning Equipment	3120	358
Power Boiler and Heat Exchanger Industry	3010	344
Turbine and Mechanical Power Transmission Equipment	3194	3511, 3566, 3568, 3593, 3594
Electrical Industrial Equipment Industry	3370	351, 354, 361, 362, 367, 369, 769
Communications and Energy Wire and Cable Industry	3380	335
Other Electrical Industries (Batteries, etc.)	3390	362, 364, 366, 369
Electrical Power Systems Industry	4910	491, 493
Refined Petroleum Industries	3610	291, 299
Other Petroleum and Coal Products Industries	3690	295, 299
Gas Distribution Systems Industry	4920	492, 493

Construction and Mining Machinery and Materials Handling	3192	3531, 3532, 3533, 3534, 3535, 3536, 3537
Asphalt Roofing Industry	2720	262, 295
Primary Steel Industries	2910	331, 332, 339
Steel Pipe and Tube Industry	2920	331
Iron Foundries	2940	332
Non-Ferrous Metal Smelting and Refining Industry	2950	333
Aluminum Rolling, Casting and Extruding Industry	2960	335, 336, 339, 346
Copper and Alloy Rolling, Casting and Extruding	2970	335, 336, 339
Ornamental and Architect, Metal Products Industry	3030	254, 323, 344
Stamped, Pressed Coated Metal Products	3040	341, 344, 345, 346, 347, 349
Wire and Wire Products Industries	3050	331, 335, 339, 342, 345, 349, 354
Hardware, Tool and Cutlery Industries	3060	342, 352, 354, 399
Clay Products Industries	3510	145, 325, 326
Hydraulic Cement Industry	3520	324
Concrete Products Industry	3540	327
Ready-Mix Concrete Industry	3550	327
Glass and Glass Products Industries	3560	321, 322, 323
Abrasives Industry	3570	329
Lime Industry	3580	327
Other Non-Metallic Mineral Industries	3590	289, 305, 325, 327, 328, 329
Jewellery and Precious Metal Industries	3920	334, 335, 347, 349, 384, 391, 396
10. Service Industries and Capital Projects (SICP)		
Accounting and Bookkeeping Services	7730	729, 872
Advertising Services	7740	731, 733, 738, 873, 874
Architecture, Engineering and Other Scientific	7750	78, 138, 738, 871, 873, 874, 899
Offices of Lawyers and Notaries	7760	738, 811
Cons. and Business Finance Intermediary Industries	7100	60, 61, 67
Investment Intermediary Industries	7200	60, 61, 62, 63, 67
Insurance Industries	7300	63, 94
Other Financial Intermediary Industries	7400	60, 61, 62, 67
Real Estate Op. Industry (Except Developers)	7500	65
Insurance and Real Estate Agent Industries	7600	64, 65
Postal and Courier Service Industries	4840	421, 431, 738

Petroleum Products Industries, Wholesale	5100	51, 59
Food, Beverage, Drug and Tobacco Industries, Wholesale	5200	51
Apparel and Dry Goods Industries, Wholesale	5300	51
Household Goods Industries, Wholesale	5400	50, 51
Motor Vehicles, Wholesale	5510	501, 573
Metals, Hardware, Plumbing, Heating and Building	5600	50, 51, 52
Farm Machinery, Equipment and Supplies, Wholesale	5710	508, 769
Construction, Forestry and Mining Machinery Equipment	5720	508
Industrial Machinery, Equipment and Supplies, Wholesale	5730	508
Other Machinery, Equipment and Supplies, Wholesale	5790	502, 504, 506, 507, 508, 509, 762, 769
Other Products Industries, Wholesale	5900	50, 51
Shoe, Apparel, Fabric and Yarn Industries, Retail	6100	56, 59
Household Furniture, Appliances and Furnishings Industry	6200	57, 76
Recreational Vehicle Dealers	6320	555, 556, 557, 559, 769
General Retail Merchandising Industry	6400	53, 59
Other Retail Store Industries	6500	52, 53, 56, 59, 73, 76
Non-Store Retail Industries	6900	54, 59
Grain Elevator Industry	4710	422
Other Storage and Warehousing Industries	4790	422, 738
Pipeline Transport Industries	4610	461, 492
Service Industries Incidental to Crude Petroleum	0910	138
Service Industries Incidental to Mining	0920	108, 124, 148
Building Development and Construction	4000	15, 16
Industrial and Heavy (Engineering) Construction	4100	15, 16, 17
Trading Contracting Industry	4200	7, 16, 17, 73, 76
Service Industry Incidental to Construction	4400	17, 65, 73, 87
11. Transportation Industries (TRAN)		
Railroad Rolling Stock Industry	3260	346, 351, 374
Shipbuilding and Repair Industry	3270	373
Boatbuilding and Repair Industry	3281	3732
Other Transportation Equipment Industries	3290	375, 379
Other Service N.E.C.	9990	75, 609, 654, 738, 752, 769, 869, 899

Water Transport Industries	4540	441, 442, 443, 444, 448, 449
Public Passenger Transit Systems Industry	4570	411, 413, 414, 415, 417
Other Transportation Industries	4580	411, 412, 489
Air Transport Industries	4510	72, 138, 451, 452, 731, 733, 799, 829, 871
Service Industries Incidental to Air Transport	4520	458, 735
Railway Transport and Related Service Industries	4530	401, 448, 474, 478
Service Industries Incidental to Water Transport	4550	449, 473, 478
Truck Transport Industries	4560	421, 422, 423
Machinery and Equipment Rental and Leasing Services	9910	721, 735, 784, 799
Auto and Truck Rental and Leasing Services	9920	751
12. Information and Telecommunications Industries (ITI)		
Electronic Computing and Peripheral Equipment	3361	3571, 3572, 3575, 3577
Electronic Office, Store and Business Machine	3362	3578, 3579, 3596
Other Office, Store and Business Machine	3369	3578, 3579, 3581, 3596, 3861, 3999
Record Player, Radio and Television Receiver	3341	3651
Telecommunication Equipment Industry	3351	3661
Electronic Parts and Components Industry	3352	3661, 3663, 3671, 3672, 3674, 3675, 3676, 3677, 3678, 3679, 3699
Electrical Industrial Equipment Industries	3370	351, 354, 361, 362, 364, 367, 369, 769
Communications and Energy Wire and Cable Industries	3380	335
Indicating, Record and Controlling Instruments	3911	3491, 3492, 3822, 3823, 3824, 3825, 3829
Other Instruments and Related Products Industries	3912	3812, 3821, 3826, 3827, 3829, 3841, 3842, 3843, 3844, 3845, 3861
Cable Television Industry	4814	4841
Telecommunications Carriers Industry	4821	4812, 4813, 4822, 4899

Computer Machinery, Equipment and Software, Wholesale	5744	5045, 5734
Computer and Related Service	7720	737

ENDNOTES

1 This section draws on Chirinko (1993, sections II and III), which contains detailed references to the literature and a discussion of empirical results.

2 The only dynamic element remaining is the expected one-period capital gain affecting r_t in equation (2b).

3 The geometric adjustment process is employed in equation (4) because, since I_t and ΔY_t have pronounced trends, it is preferable to specify the investment equation so all variables enter as ratios or rates.

4 There may be additional interaction between these real decisions and financial decisions (Nadeau, 1988).

5 Since this alternative derivation depends on non-static expectations, it is plagued by an inconsistent treatment of delivery lags in the optimization problem.

6 A similar criticism applies to the importance of putty-putty vs. putty-clay capital. Even if putty-clay considerations contribute to relatively low price effects, the underlying expectation parameters can lead to an elimination or reversal of the estimated roles of output and user cost in econometric equations. (Abel [1981] offered an alternative reason why the estimated response of investment to changes in relative prices and output may not provide any evidence on putty-putty vs. putty-clay capital.) Since the length of the distributed lags need not be equal, the assumption of extrapolative expectations in equation (6) provides a justification for the differing lag lengths (H_U, H_Y) for user cost and output frequently found in empirical work.

7 The models analysed by Feldstein were examined critically by Chirinko (1987). See Feldstein (1987) for a response to Chirinko's study, and Feldstein and Jun (1987), Junge and Zarinnejadan (1986) and Sumner (1988) for further results.

8 Fullerton (1984) provided an excellent discussion of various definitions of and differences in average and marginal returns and tax rates.

9 With no loss in analytical insights but much saving in notation, it is assumed that production is affected by the end-of-period capital stock and, below, that the discount rate is constant.

10 Note that $p^{I'}_t$ is a relative price, and p^I_t, used in the implicit models elsewhere in the paper, is an absolute price.

11 An inconsistency (which is unlikely to be empirically important) enters many analyses because tax depreciation (z_t in equation [2b]), which accrues over time, is usually computed under the assumption of static expectations, but expectations of other variables are computed under non-static assumptions.

12 Under static expectations and an approximation about the steady-state capital stock, this adjustment cost model would also generate lags in an econometric equation. With these assumptions, we obtain the partial (or stock) adjustment model with I_t proportional to the spread between the actual and desired capital stocks.

13 Additionally, the user cost of capital (equation [2]) can be derived from equation (12b) or (12d) when adjustment costs are absent, expectations are static, and the optimization problem is stated in continuous time (cf. Jorgenson, 1967, pp. 140-144).

14 Key assumptions and empirical results are discussed in detail in Chirinko (1993, Section III).

15 Tax depreciation allowances accruing after period t on capital purchased prior to period t, i.e., past depreciation allowances, will enter as an additional positive term on the right side of equation (16). See Hayashi (1982, equations [5] and [14]). Interest and principal payments on debt existing prior to, but paid after, period t enter in a similar manner, though on the left side of equation (16). In applied work, net current financial assets, inventory stocks, and other capital assets are added to the right side of equation (16). Goodwill and firm-specific human capital should also be included, but are difficult to measure.

16 If adjustment costs are valued in terms of labour or new capital, then the term $p^{I'}_t$ in equation (17) would be replaced by p^I_t/w_t or 1.0 respectively.

17 Since u_t is correlated with the regressors, instrumental variables are needed to ensure consistency. The projection of an endogenous variable dated $t+1$ on the instruments dated t, $t-1$, etc. can be interpreted as a one-period ahead forecasting equation assumed stable over the sample period.

18 This section draws on Chirinko et al. (1996).

19 See Chirinko (1993, sections II and III) for a discussion of the empirical results and Oliner et al. (1995) for a comparison of the forecasting performance of several implicit and explicit models.

20 To see that the sum of the α's represent the elasticity of the long-run capital stock with respect to the user cost, consider the following abbreviated version of equation (24a): $I/K=\delta+I^n/K=\delta+\Delta K/K=\delta+SUM(\alpha)*(\Delta U/U)$. Cancelling δ's and dividing by $\Delta U/U$ yields an expression for the elasticity: $(\Delta K/K)/(\Delta U/U)=SUM(\alpha)$. Note that this derivation depends on the user cost elasticity being identical across firms.

21 Putty-clay considerations discussed in the second part of this paper also imply that the distributed lags on sales and user cost may differ.

22 See Eisner and Nadiri (1968, 1970), Eisner (1969, 1970), and Chirinko and Eisner (1982, 1983). Hall and Jorgenson (1969) comment on the first and third studies; Sinai and Eckstein (1983) on the fifth and sixth studies.

23 See Chirinko (1993) and Hubbard (1995) for recent surveys, Fazzari et al. (1988) for an important early contribution, and Chirinko and Schaller (1995) for a recent examination of Canadian firms.

24 If cash flow affected the long-run capital stock, then the *percentage change* in cash flow would enter the model. See Chirinko and Schaller (1995, Section 2.B).

25 To ensure reasonable long-run properties for equation (24), the cash flow term should be considered relative to its long-run value, $(CF/K)_{i,t} - (CF/K)^*_i$, where the effect of the latter firm-specific constant will be absorbed into ϕ_i.

26 Rather than being treated as fixed constants, the ϕ_i's are sometimes modelled as a random variable. The resulting random-effects estimator is more efficient than the mean-difference and first-difference estimators used in this study. However, the consistency of the random effects estimator depends on the effects being uncorrelated with the regressors, a condition that is usually rejected in panel data. See Chirinko et al. (1996) for the appropriate test.

27 See Hsiao (1986) for further discussion of panel data estimators.

28 See Auerbach (1983) and Chirinko (1993, Appendix) for details on the construction of the user cost variable.

29 These margins might include asset churning with insufficient recapture provisions, relations between the cost of leverage and the type of asset, alternative minimum taxes or endogenous capital depreciation and utilization.
30 See Griliches and Hausman (1986) or Hsiao (1986) for further discussion of this test for measurement error.
31 See Arellano and Bover (forthcoming) and Urga (1992) for further discussion.
32 These weights are from the Bureau of Economic Analysis capital flow tables and reflect asset usage by establishment. The Compustat data reflect ownership by company.
33 Since DRI user cost data are quarterly, we averaged them to obtain an annual user cost. The averages were computed at the firm level to account for different firm fiscal years. The user cost information is tailored to each firm's specific accounting period.
34 Data limitations prevent a separate analysis of plant and equipment spending.
35 Note that, given the use of lags and growth rates in the regression model, the dependent variable is defined for the period 1981 to 1991 for the pooled and mean-difference models, and for 1982 to 1991 for the first-difference models.
36 Statistical significance is only one means for assessing "relative importance." Other measures, such as economic significance, can also provide useful information, especially when evaluated with respect to specific policies.
37 Given the importance of cash flow and its effect on sales growth and user cost coefficients, future work should explore whether cash flow's significant role is related to finance constraints or represents a proxy for current and future demand.
38 Given this focus on models with cash flow, it may prove convenient to use Table 3 when examining only user cost elasticities.
39 The instruments are lags 2 to 8 for $\Delta S/S$ and CF/K, and lags 2 to 10 for $\Delta U/U$.
40 There is no discernible pattern as to which of the user cost lag coefficients have the greatest impact on investment spending. In several sectors (numbers 1, 4, 6, 8 and 9), the largest impact is at the fifth or sixth lag. In other sectors, the largest coefficient is on the contemporaneous variable (numbers 2 and 12). A hump-shaped pattern with the largest impact at the second lag is evident for sector numbers 10 and 11.
41 Even if data, which are representative of the economy as a whole, are available, an aggregate elasticity estimated as a weighted average of sectoral elasticities will not generally equal an aggregate elasticity estimated with data for all sectors. In the latter case, the weights are determined by each sector's contribution to the variance in the data, which need not correspond to capital-share or investment-share weights.
42 The SICs for the United States are on a 1992 basis.
43 No data available.

Acknowledgements

The authors would like to acknowledge the many helpful comments and suggestions received from Huntley Schaller and participants at the Industry Canada/Financial Research Foundation of Canada conference on "Capital Market Issues," especially from Albert Ando, Paul Halpern, Jack Mintz and our discussant, Serge Nadeau. Financial support from Industry Canada is gratefully acknowledged. This paper represents part of an ongoing project with Steven Fazzari, and the authors are particularly grateful for his advice and insights. All errors, omissions and conclusions remain the sole responsibility of the authors. The views expressed here do not necessarily reflect those of the Federal Reserve Bank of St. Louis nor the Federal Reserve System.

BIBLIOGRAPHY

Abel, Andrew B. "Dynamic Adjustment in a Putty-Putty Model: Implications for Testing the Putty-Clay Hypothesis." *International Economic Review*. 22, (February 1981): 19-36.

Arellano, Manuel and Olympia Bover. "Another Look at the Instrumental-Variable Estimation of Error-Components Models." *Journal of Econometrics*. (forthcoming).

Auerbach, Alan J. "Taxation, Corporate Financial Policy and the Cost of Capital." *Journal of Economic Literature*. 21, (September 1983): 905-940.

Ballentine, J. Gregory. "Three Failures in Economic Analysis of Tax Reforms." *National Tax Association – Tax Institute of America*. (1986): 3-6.

Chirinko, Robert S. "The Ineffectiveness of Effective Tax Rates: A Critique of Feldstein's Fisher-Schultz Lecture." *Journal of Public Economics*. 32, (April 1987): 369-387.

——. *Econometric Models and Empirical Findings for Business Investment*. New York: Basil Blackwell, 1993. (A monograph in the Salomon Brothers Center Series Financial Markets, Institutions & Instruments.)

Chirinko, Robert S. and Robert Eisner. "The Effect of Tax Parameters in the Investment Equations in Macroeconomic Econometric Models." In *Economic Activity and Finance*. Edited by Marshall E. Blume, Jean Crockett and Paul Taubman. Cambridge: Ballinger, 1982, pp. 25-84.

——. "Tax Policy and Investment in Major U.S. Macroeconometric Models." *Journal of Public Economics*. 20, (March 1983): 139-166.

Chirinko, Robert S., Steven M. Fazzari and Andrew P. Meyer. "What Do Micro Data Reveal About the User Cost Elasticity?: New Evidence on the Responsiveness of Business Capital Formation." Emory University, (November 1996).

Chirinko, Robert S. and Huntley Schaller. "Why Does Liquidity Matter in Investment Equations?" *Journal of Money, Credit and Banking*. 27, (May 1995): 527-548.

Coen, Robert M. "The Effect of Cash Flow on the Speed of Adjustment." In *Tax Incentives and Capital Spending*. Edited by Gary Fromm. Washington: Brookings Institution, 1971, pp. 131-196.

Eisner, Robert. "Tax Policy and Investment Behavior: Comment." *American Economic Review*. 59, (June 1969): 379-388.

——. "Tax Policy and Investment Behavior: Further Comment." *American Economic Review*. 60, (September 1970): 746-752.

Eisner, Robert and M. Nadiri Ishaq. "Investment Behavior and Neo-Classical Theory." *The Review of Economics and Statistics*. 50, (August 1968): 369-382.

——. "Neoclassical Theory of Investment Behavior: A Comment." *The Review of Economics and Statistics*. 52, (May 1970): 216-222.

Eisner, Robert and Robert H. Strotz. "Determinants of Business Investment." *Impacts of Monetary Policy*. By the Commission on Money and Credit. Englewood Cliffs, New Jersey: Prentice-Hall, 1963, pp. 60-337.

Fazzari, Steven M., R. Glenn Hubbard and Bruce C. Petersen. "Financing Constraints and Corporate Investment." *Brookings Papers on Economic Activity*. (1988:1): 141-195.

Feldstein, Martin S. "Inflation, Tax Rules, and Investment: Some Econometric Evidence." *Econometrica*. 50, (July 1982): 825-862.

——. "Tax Rates and Business Investment: Reply." *Journal of Public Economics*. 32, (April 1987): 389-396.

Feldstein, Martin S. and Joosung Jun. "The Effects of Tax Rules on Nonresidential Fixed Investment: Some Preliminary Evidence from the 1980s." In *The Effects of Taxation on Capital Accumulation*. Edited by Martin S. Feldstein, National Bureau of Economic Research. Chicago: University of Chicago Press, 1987, pp. 101-156.

Fullerton, Don. "Which Effective Tax Rate?" *National Tax Journal*. 37, (March 1984): 23-42.

Funke, Michael. "Asset Prices and Real Investment in West Germany: Evidence from Vector Autoregressive Models." *Empirical Economics*. 14, (1989): 307-328.

Gordon, Robert J. and John M. Veitch. "Fixed Investment in the American Business Cycle, 1919-83." In *The American Business Cycle: Continuity and Change*. Edited by Robert J. Gordon. National Bureau of Economic Research Chicago: University of Chicago Press, 1986: pp. 267-335.

Griliches, Zvi and Jerry A. Hausman. "Errors in Variables in Panel Data." *Journal of Econometrics*. 31, (1986): 93-118.

Hall, Robert E. and Dale W. Jorgenson. "Tax Policy and Investment Behavior: Reply and Further Results." *American Economic Review*. 59, (June 1969): 388-401.

Hayashi, F. "Tobin's Marginal q and Average q: A Neoclassical Interpretation." *Econometrica*. 50, (1982): 213-224.

Hsiao, Cheng. *Analysis of Panel Data*. Cambridge, England: Cambridge University Press, 1986.

Hubbard, R. Glenn. "Capital Market Imperfections and Investment." Columbia University, (1995).

Jorgenson, Dale W. "Capital Theory and Investment Behavior." *American Economic Review*. 53, (May 1963): 247-259.

——. "The Theory of Investment Behavior." In *Determinants of Investment Behavior*. Edited by R. Ferber. Universities-National Bureau Conference Series No. 18. New York: Columbia University Press, 1967, pp. 129-155.

——. "Econometric Studies of Investment Behavior: A Survey." *Journal of Economic Literature*. 9, (December 1971): 1111-1147.

——. "Investment Behavior and the Production Function." *Bell Journal of Economics and Management Science*. 3, (Spring 1972): 220-251.

Junge, Georg and Milad Zarinnejadan. "A Rate-of-Return Model of Investment Behavior for Switzerland." *Empirical Economics*. 11, (1986): 153-167.

Keynes, John Maynard. *The General Theory of Employment, Interest, and Money*. New York: Harcourt Brace, 1936. Reprinted in 1964, First Harbinger Edition.

Lucas, Robert E. Jr. "Econometric Policy Evaluation: A Critique." In *The Phillips Curve and Labor Markets*. Edited by Karl Brunner and Allan H. Meltzer. Amsterdam: North-Holland, 1976, pp. 19-46. Reprinted in Studies in Business Cycle Theory. Cambridge: Massachusetts Institute of Technology, 1981, pp. 104-130.

McCallum, Bennett T. "Topics Concerning the Formulation, Estimation, and the Use of Macroeconometric Models with Rational Expectations." *Proceedings of the American Statistical Association*. (1979): pp. 65-72.

McMillin, William D. "Money, Government Debt, q, and Investment." *Journal of Macroeconomics*. 7, (Winter 1985): 19-38.

Nadeau, Serge. "A Model To Measure the Effects of Taxes on the Real and Financial Decisions of the Firm." *National Tax Journal*. 41, (December 1988): 467-482.

Oliner, Stephen, Glenn Rudebusch and Daniel Sichel. "New and Old Models of Business Investment: A Comparison of Forecasting Performance." *Journal of Money, Credit and Banking*. 27, (August 1995): 806-826.

Sims, Christopher A. "Macroeconomics and Reality." *Econometrica*. 48, (January 1980): 1-48.

Sinai, Allen and Otto Eckstein. "Tax Policy and Business Fixed Investment Revisited." *Journal of Economic Behavior and Organization*. 4, (June 1983): 131-162.

Sumner, Michael T. "On Improving the Effectiveness of Effective Tax Rates on Business Investment." *Journal of Public Economics*. 35, (April 1988): 393-396.

Urga, Giovanni. "The Econometrics of Panel Data: A Selective Introduction." *Ricerche Economiche*. 44, (December 1992): 379-396.

Albert Ando
Department of Economics
University of Pennsylvania
and National Bureau of
Economic Research

& *John Hancock*
Department of Economics
University of Pennsylvania

& *Gary Sawchuk*
Industry Canada

3

Cost of Capital for the United States, Japan and Canada: An Attempt at Measurement Based on Individual Company Records and Aggregate National Accounts Data

ABSTRACT

A CONCEPTUAL BASIS IS LAID OUT FOR MEASURING THE COST OF CAPITAL for corporations from data typically available in countries such as the United States, Canada and Japan. Attempts are made to carry out the measurement based on both the accounting records of individual companies and the aggregate National Accounts data, supplemented by market information on the price of equity shares. For the United States, we find a consistent pattern from both sets of data, and the real cost of capital after depreciation and before taxes fluctuates around a point between 10 to 11 percent without a persistent trend. For Canada, the individual company data cover too few companies for a too short period, and it does not seem possible to obtain any reliable estimate from this set of data. The aggregate National Accounts data for Canada, supplemented by some unpublished data supplied by Statistics Canada, suggest that the cost of capital in Canada is equal to or somewhat lower than that in the United States. For Japan, the individual company accounts and National Accounts data yield results that are apparently inconsistent. Attempts have been made to identify the sources of inconsistency, with one of the conclusions being that Japan's Economic Planning Agency can clarify critical causes of the inconsistency by explaining more clearly a part of the procedure for deriving some of its National Accounts tables. Finally, we suggest that the extraordinarily high price of land and the persistent real capital gains enjoyed by companies on their ownership of land until 1990 were an important cause leading to an underestimation of the cost of capital when the standard procedure is applied to Japanese data. We believe this history is still affecting the expectations of market participants in Japan, and the current prices of land and equities are probably not sustainable unless a moderate but persistent rise in the real price of land is resumed. We believe this is an important question for the Japanese economy, and it makes the need for a better explanation of the National Accounts data by the Economic Planning Agency especially urgent.

INTRODUCTION

The cost of capital is an important component of the total cost of producing output for most firms and, therefore, its magnitude, both absolute and relative (especially in comparison with the cost of labour), is critical information affecting decisions by management on the choice of technology, the scale of operations and the location of plants. The magnitude and time pattern of the cost of capital faced by a group of firms, therefore, are an essential part of information needed by analysts wishing to understand the behaviour of these firms.

At the same time, the cost of capital is a notoriously difficult concept to measure in practice. First, it is in principle a forward-looking concept,[1] but we seldom have information on the subjective assessment of future values of variables used by managers. Consequently, most students of the subject measure the *ex post* cost of using capital from accounting records and hope such *ex post* measurements, if they are taken over many firms and cover a fairly long period of time, would converge to the similarly averaged value of the forward-looking concept used in managers' decisions.[2]

Second, the measurement of the cost of capital can be affected by a number of arbitrary accounting conventions and management decisions such as the choice of depreciation rules and inventory accounting methods. To establish some uniformity regarding these conventions among firms, especially among firms in different countries, can be an exceedingly difficult task.

During the 1980s, a perception developed among U.S. business executives, especially of corporations competing with Japanese firms, that the cost of capital was noticeably lower in Japan than in the United States, and this was one reason why Japanese corporations appeared to outperform their U.S. counterparts. Evidence for this proposition was not fully convincing and, relatively late in this debate, Ando and Auerbach (1988a,b, 1990) attempted to estimate the cost of capital for corporations in the United States and Japan using data for firms listed on the New York and Tokyo stock exchanges. The idea was that, by using more extensive data and making adjustments to them so data for Japanese and U.S. firms were as compatible as possible, we might come closer to settling the argument one way or another. More important, if the cost of capital was different in these two countries, we might gain some insight into the causes of such differences.

They concluded that, while in the United States, the accounting measure and the market measure of the cost of capital appeared reasonably close to each other when averaged over a fairly long period, in Japan the market measure appeared to be noticeably higher than the accounting measure. The market measure of the cost of capital appeared similar for the two countries and, therefore, the accounting measure of the cost of capital in the United States looked noticeably higher than in Japan. They explored a number of potential causes of this pattern and suggested, as a plausible hypothesis, a role played by the extraordinarily high price of land and the continual real capital gains which corporations in Japan enjoyed by their ownership of land. Since such real capital gains are not included in the measurement of earnings by firms, if these gains are in fact recognized by market participants and taken into account in valuing corporate shares, it may explain the discrepancy between the accounting and the market measures of the cost of capital and, hence, the difference between the cost of capital in the United States and Japan in terms of their accounting measures.

Since the price of land and the value of equity have both declined sharply in Japan since 1990, the most recent data seem to offer an opportunity to test this hypothesis. There is also an impression that the cost of capital in Canada is somewhat higher than in the United States. This seems surprising given the close integration of the capital markets of these two countries, at least for large companies with access to equity and bond markets in both countries.

In this paper, we take another look at the cost of capital in the United States, Japan and Canada. Since we rely heavily on the accounting measure of earnings by firms, and these earnings may include the contribution of physical capital to the total value added of the firm as well as oligopoly rent, in the next section, we attempt to clarify the relationship between the accounting measure of earnings and the user cost of capital as usually understood in the literature on investment. We then report on our empirical investigation using both aggregate data and individual firm data and conclude with a discussion of remaining puzzles and their potential explanations.

Some Conceptual Issues

Corporate Profit Tax, Oligopoly Rent and the Term Structure of Interest Rates

The user cost of capital is the amount of money a firm pays in order to use one dollar's worth of capital for a period of time (one year). In the absence of taxes and under the assumption of perfect markets, this cost must be equal to the real required rate of return in the market plus the economic rate of depreciation. We are, however, embarking on an empirical measurement of the cost of capital actually incurred by firms, so we must allow for corporate taxes, the presence of market imperfections and other issues. In order to arrive at an operational formulation in which a measurable quantity can be interpreted as an approximation to the cost of capital, we posit the following two equations:

$$T^c = \tau^c [P_x X - WE - \chi (\rho + \delta) P_k K] \quad (1)$$

$$(1 - \tau^c) P_x X = \mu [(1 - \tau^c) WE + (1 - \chi \tau^c)(\rho + \delta) P_k K] \quad (2)$$

where

T^c: corporate profit tax

τ^c: corporate profit tax rate

P_x: price of output (value added)

X: value added measure of output

W: gross compensation per man hour, including all fringe benefits

E: employment in manhours

ρ: real rate of interest per year prevailing in the capital market

δ: economic rate of depreciation per year

P_k: reproduction price of capital

K: net stock of capital used in production

z: rate of the depreciation allowed under the corporate profit tax law on K as a fraction of the total cost of capital, i.e., $Z=z(\rho+\delta)P_kK$ where Z is the depreciation allowed under the corporate profit tax

μ: markup factor, i.e., the pricing policy of the firm is assumed to require that the net of the tax value added is μ times the net of the tax cost of labour and the net of the tax cost of capital used.

Equation (1) is a grossly simplified description of the corporate profit tax system embedded in U.S. tax law. We assume that the tax rate is proportional and ignore many fine points of the law. We also assume that the corporate tax applies to profits net of other taxes such as real estate and sales taxes so, in our empirical work, we define the value added of the firm as net of these indirect taxes. Employment taxes are included in the rate of compensation W.

Equation (2) is the markup pricing rule applied to the net of tax prices. That is, it requires that the net of tax revenue (value added) should be μ times the net of tax cost.[3] For this equation to make sense, we must have a homogeneous production function of degree one underlying the whole process, and we assume that this is true in the range of production activities actually observed. We suppose that the markup factor, μ, may vary from one firm to another and over time but is not a function of the corporate tax rate τ^c or the rate of gross return $\rho+\delta$. It is instructive to rewrite equation (2) by dividing both sides of the equation by $\mu\ (1-\tau^c)$:

$$\frac{P_xX}{\mu} = WE + \frac{1-\tau^c z}{1-\tau^c}(\rho+\delta)\,P_kK \tag{2a}$$

In equation (2a), the left-hand side is the total value added before it is marked up. On the right-hand side, the first term is the gross wage bill, and the second term is the gross return on capital which the firm must earn in order to pay the corporate profit tax and the return required on funds obtained in the market, and to cover economic depreciation. It is perhaps helpful to note that this term can be split as follows:

$$\frac{1-\tau^c z}{1-\tau^c}(\rho+\delta)\,P_kK = (\rho+\delta)\,P_kK + \frac{\tau^c(1-z)}{1-\tau^c}(\rho+\delta)\,P_kK \tag{3}$$

The first term on the right-hand side is, of course, the market-required return and economic depreciation, and the second term is the tax payment. We may also note the identity:

$$P_xX = \frac{P_xX}{\mu} + \frac{\mu - 1}{\mu} P_xX \tag{4}$$

The first term on the right-hand side is gross value added, and the second term is the oligopoly rent earned by the firm. Substituting equation (2a) into equation (4) and then inserting the resulting expression into equation (1) and simplifying, we obtain:

$$T^c = \tau^c \frac{\mu - 1}{\mu} P_xX + \frac{(1 - z)\,\tau^c}{1 - \tau^c} (\rho + \delta)\, P_kK \tag{1a}$$

Equation (1a) says that the total corporate profit tax payment is the sum of the oligopoly rent times the full tax rate and the gross cost of capital net of tax times the factor $(1-z)\tau^c/(1-\tau^c)$. When z is unity, i.e., when the full cost of capital is deductible for corporate income tax purposes, the only corporate profit tax paid is on the oligopoly rent. The corporate profit tax, therefore, does not have any impact on input decisions by corporations and, in this sense, is neutral (Samuelson Theorem). When z is zero, i.e., when none of the cost of capital is deductible for corporate profit tax purposes, then corporations must earn $1/(1-\tau^c)$ times the cost of capital and pay $\tau^c/(1-\tau^c)$ times the cost of capital as well as τ^c times oligopoly rent as the corporate profit tax. We can now decompose total sales net of intermediate inputs and rearrange it so the decomposed parts can be interpreted as corresponding to familiar concepts appearing in the corporate sector of the national income and product accounts:

$$P_xX - WE - \delta P_kK = (1 - \tau^c) \frac{\mu - 1}{\mu} P_xX + \rho P_kK + \tau^c \frac{\mu - 1}{\mu} P_xX + \frac{\tau^c(1 - z)}{1 - \tau^c} (\rho + \delta)\, P_kK \tag{5}$$

The left-hand side of equation (5) represents, for the corporate sector, before tax corporate profits with inventory valuation adjustment and capital consumption adjustment plus interest payments.[4] On the right-hand side, the first term is the oligopoly rent after taxes, the second term is the market-required return on capital used, and the third and fourth terms are corporate profit taxes on oligopoly rent and the cost of capital, respectively. The important point here is that, on the basis of national income and product account data or on the basis of standard accounting data, such as those reported in the COMPUSTAT tape or its equivalent in other countries, we can, at best, compute only the left-hand side of equation (5) and not individual items on its right-hand side. In other words, we cannot directly measure separately the required return in the market $\rho P_k K$ and the oligopoly rent after the corporate profit tax

$$(1 - \tau^c) \frac{\mu - 1}{\mu} P_k K$$

although we can obtain data for the total profit tax paid, i.e., the sum of the last two terms on the right-hand side of equation (5)[5] and, therefore, the sum of $\rho P_k K$ and

$$(1 - \tau^c) \frac{\mu - 1}{\mu} P_k K$$

We have set out to estimate the rate of return on capital by computing the ratio of income accruing to capital to the market value of capital. We have argued above that, by relying on the standard accounting records for firms or on national income and product accounts, we can measure the sum of oligopoly rents and income accruing to capital, before or after corporate profit taxes, but not each of them separately. Let us now turn our attention to the measurement of the market value of capital.

Since there is no direct estimate of the market value of physical assets, the best we can do is to rely on the indirect estimate, namely, the total market value of the firm defined as the sum of the market value of equity outstanding and the market value of the debt of the firm.[6] There are two basic problems with this measure. First, it is very likely that the amount of debt reported in the accounting records of a firm is the face value of debt, not the market value. When the long-term rate of interest fluctuates significantly, the market value can deviate markedly from the face value of debt and, thus, our estimate of the total value of the firm may be subject to serious errors. The same observation applies to the aggregate value of the debt of corporations reported in the Flow of Funds accounts in the United States and in the National Accounts in Japan. Second, as we have discussed above, the total capital income of a firm includes oligopoly rent, and this means that the total market value of a firm must include the capitalized value of expected future oligopoly rent. In order to clarify the implications of the presence of oligopoly rent, consider a case in which the market value of physical capital is equal to its reproduction cost, and debt is also reported at its market value. Since economic depreciation is subtracted from the income accruing to capital, the existing capital can be perpetually replaced so current income may be viewed as a perpetuity. Under these assumptions and defining the ratio m by:

$$m = \frac{(1-\tau^c)\frac{\mu-1}{\mu}P_xX}{\rho P_kK}$$

the ratio of net of tax income from capital to the market value of the firm is given by:

$$\frac{(m+1)\,\rho P_kK}{(m\frac{\rho}{\rho+q}+1)\,P_kK} = \rho\,\frac{m+1}{m\frac{\rho}{\rho+q}+1} \qquad (6)$$

where q is the risk premium demanded by the market for capitalizing oligopoly rent. It is clear from the expression that, if q is zero, then the presence of oligopoly rent will not create any distortion when we measure the cost of capital by the ratio of total income accruing to capital as defined by the left-hand side of equation (5) to the total market value of the firm.

A parallel line of analysis applies to the effects of the ownership of natural resources by the firm. To see this, it is helpful to write down an alternative version of equation (5) in which it is assumed that there is no oligopoly rent, but that the firm can produce and sell (as a part of its product) N units of a natural resource, whose price is given to the firm as P_n. The government requires that a fraction d of P_nN be included in the corporate profit tax base. Equation (5) then becomes:

$$P_xX - WE - \delta P_kK = \rho P_kK + (1-\tau^c d)\,P_nN + \frac{\tau^c(1-z)}{1-\tau^c}(\rho+\delta)\,P_kK + \tau^c dP_nN \qquad (5a)$$

The value of the firm must now include the present value of the future stream of natural resources after tax, i.e., the future value of $(1-\tau^c d)P_nN$. In light of our discussion of oligopoly rent above, we know that the condition under which the cost of capital computed as the ratio of the left-hand side of equation (5a) to the total market value of the firm will be unbiased by the presence of the natural resources ownership, is that the value of natural resources included in the market value of the firm is $(1-\tau^c d)P_nN/\rho$.

We would venture a guess that this condition is more likely to be violated in the case of natural resources than with oligopoly rent. The reason for our conjecture is that natural resources may be exhausted fairly quickly at the current rate of exploitation or, alternatively, the stock of natural resources owned by the firm is much greater than the amount needed to enable its current rate of exploitation indefinitely. Since we have no information on the amount of natural resources owned by firms, we must proceed by ignoring its presence, having noted the nature of biases created due to our inability to deal with it explicitly.

We must now review another rather complex question. For a firm faced with a decision of whether or not to invest in capital equipment that may last for a fairly long time, where the nature of the equipment is basically putty-clay, the relevant rate of return is the real, long-term rate of return whose maturity is coincidental with the expected life of the equipment. On the other hand, for investors purchasing equities and the debt of the firm, presumably the most relevant measure of the profitability of such an investment is the one-period holding rate. The relationship between the one-period holding rate and the long-term real interest rate is a rather messy expression except in the limiting case of a perpetuity, whose rate of return we shall refer to as the capitalization rate. In that case, we have the relationship:

$$R_t^* = \rho_t^* - \left(\frac{\dot{\rho}_t^*}{\rho_t^*}\right)^e \tag{7}$$

where ρ^*_t is the capitalization rate for the perpetuity, $(\dot{\rho}^*/\rho^*)^e$ is the expected rate of change of ρ^*_t, and R^*_t is the one-period holding rate associated with the security whose capitalization rate is ρ^*_t. It is the one-period holding rate which would be equilibrated in the market and, since the expected rate of change of the capitalization rate is not necessarily uniform among market participants, the capitalization rate itself is not necessarily equilibrated in the market. Since the cost of capital, ρ, is closer to the capitalization rate than to the one-period holding rate, this is another reason why the cost of capital may not be fully equalized among markets in several countries.

Special Problems in Comparing the Cost of Capital across Countries

In addition to all the problems that we have raised above, the costs of capital in two or more countries have an additional reason for remaining differentiated, namely, the exchange risk. Let us recall the standard uncovered arbitrage equation involving the expected rate of change of the exchange rate and the differential of the short-term interest rate between two countries given by:

$$(R_t^d - R_t^f) - \left(\frac{\dot{e}_t}{e_t}\right)^e = \eta_t \tag{8}$$

where R^d and R^f are the real one-period interest rate in domestic and foreign countries, e_t is the real exchange rate, $(\dot{e}_t/e_t)^e$ is the expected rate of change of the real exchange rate and η_t is the risk premium plus random residual noise.[7]

Even assuming that the variation of η is relatively small, movements of the expected rate of change of the exchange rate are bound to be quite significant. Consider, for example, a case in which the exchange rate is expected to rise by 0.5 percent in a three-month period. This is equivalent to a 2 percent rise in the exchange rate at an annual rate, which creates a gap of 2 percentage points in the interest rates with a three-month maturity in the two countries in question measured at an annual rate. This is clearly a very significant difference between the two real interest rates. In Figure 1, we exhibit the three-month commercial paper rate for Japan and the United States. Between 1987 and 1994, we happen to have a direct measure of the expected rate of change of the exchange rates among several currencies including the exchange rate between U.S. dollars and the yen.[8] Taking advantage of this availability, we exhibit in Figure 2 what U.S. residents should have expected to receive in dollars by holding three-month commercial paper in Japan. In one case, it is assumed that the directly observed expectation data in fact represents the expectation of the person holding the commercial paper, and in the second case, perfect foresight is assumed. It is easy to see not only that the realized rate of return on such an operation is very different from holding a domestic commercial paper of similar quality, but the expectation and the realization can be very different from each other.

We have outlined the more important reasons why the cost of capital in two countries may not equalize even when the mobility of capital between the two countries in question is nearly complete. First, there may be a significant difference between the short-term real rate of interest in two countries due to the expected rate of change of the exchange rate, and this difference may be quite volatile over time. Second, even if the short-term interest rates in the two countries are the same, when this is translated into long-term rates through an expression such as equation (7), the expected rate of change of the capitalization rate must be taken into account, and there is no reason why the expected rate of change of the capitalization rate must be identical in two countries. Third, there are a number of measurement problems discussed above, and the order of magnitude of these measurement biases may not be the same between two countries.

There are reasons for the deviation in the cost of capital between two countries even before the more commonly cited reasons – different risk premiums and different fiscal systems – are introduced. These factors, moreover, are capable of creating quite large differences in the cost of capital among countries, and market forces would not necessarily eliminate these differences as long as the underlying causes persist. It would also be extremely difficult to attribute a specific magnitude for these differences to a particular cause, unless we have a direct measurement of such quantities as the expected rate of change of the capitalization rate and the expected rate of change of the exchange rate.

Under these circumstances, as it was done in the earlier papers of Ando and Auerbach, in this paper we concentrate on reporting the observed differences in the cost of capital in three countries, and leave our speculation as to their causes to a brief section at the end.

FIGURE 1

THREE-MONTH COMMERCIAL PAPER RATES IN THE UNITED STATES AND JAPAN

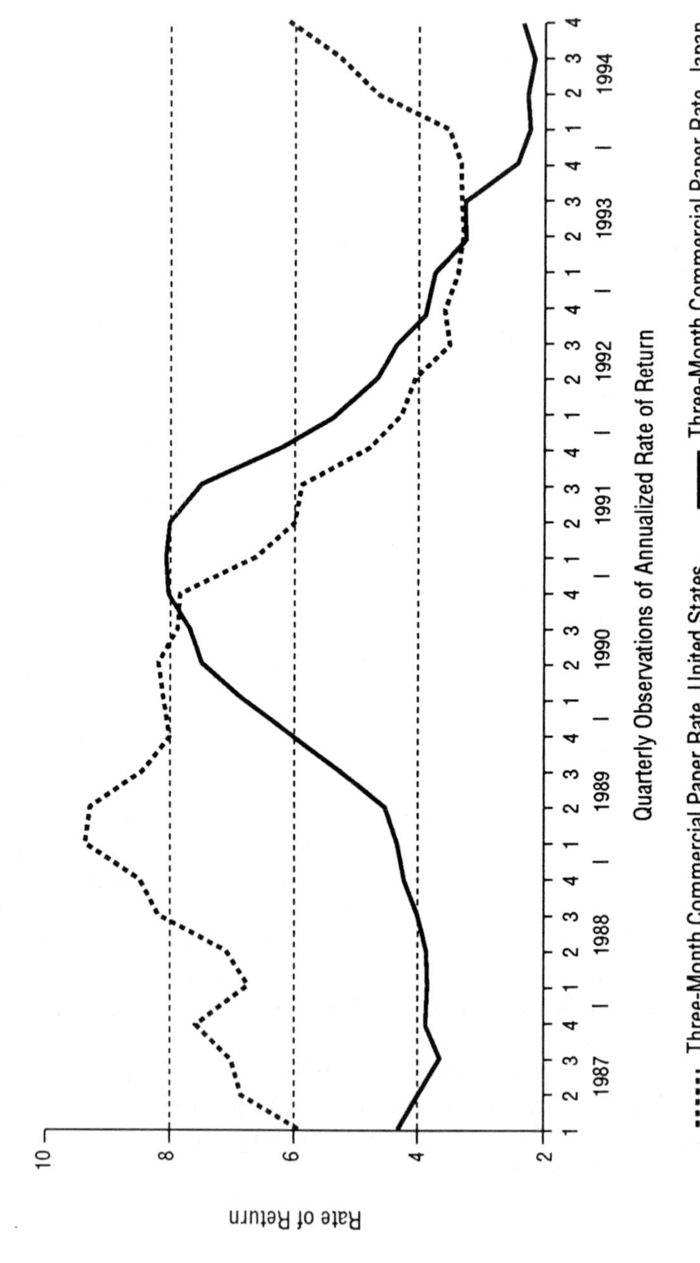

FIGURE 2

THREE-MONTH COMMERCIAL PAPER RATES IN JAPAN

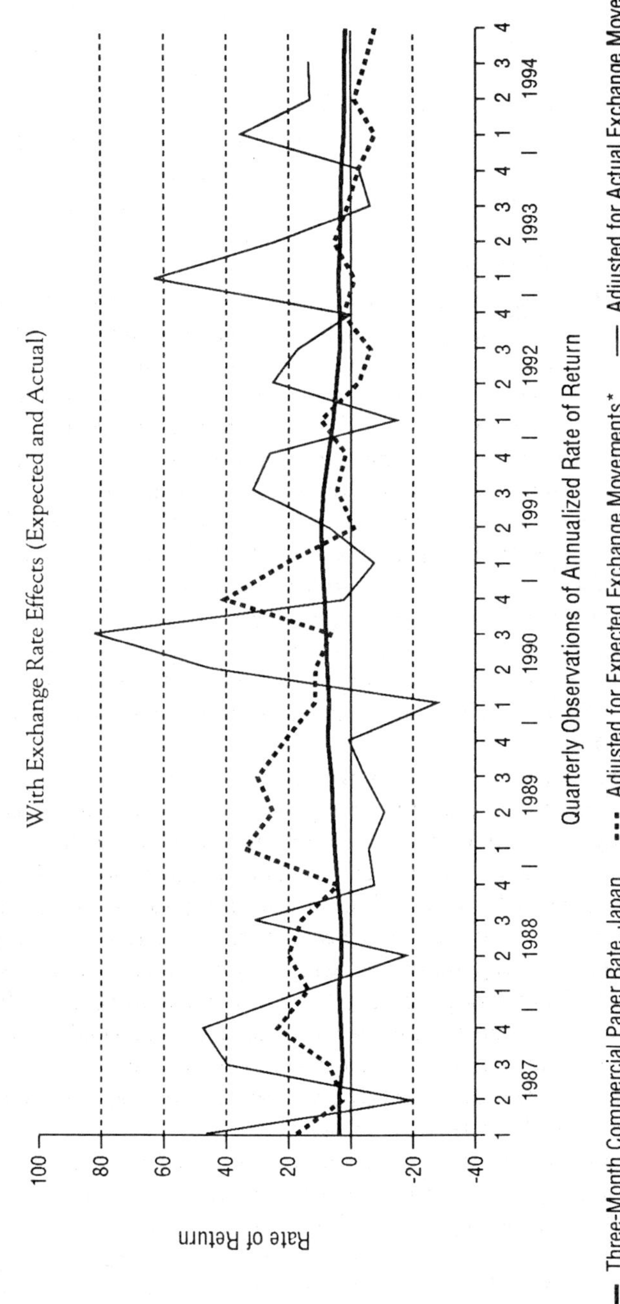

Notes: * The rate expected to be earned on three-month commercial paper in Tokyo from the point of view of an investor in New York.
** The rate actually earned on three-month commercial paper in Tokyo from the point of view of an investor in New York.

Marginal vs. Average Cost of Capital

It is often argued that the average rate of return on capital has little to do with the marginal rate, and it is the marginal rate that must be used in the construction of the gross rent for the use of capital which, in turn, must be equated to the marginal value product of capital. Professor Jack Mintz makes the point again in his written comment on an earlier version of this paper.

We have no quarrel with the observation that, in making a decision on whether or not to acquire a specific capital good, the manager must compare the present value of the future net income stream associated with the cost of acquiring it. The discount rate used to compute the present value here is closely related to the cost of capital we seek and, in principle, it may not be the same rate used to acquire capital goods in preceding periods. In this sense, the distinction between the marginal and average costs of capital appears to be well established.

For the purpose of measurement, however, we are prepared to make a case that errors introduced by approximating the marginal cost of capital by the average cost, computed using the market value of the firm as the denominator, are much smaller than potential errors of measurement involved in constructing the cost of capital directly from relevant interest rates, the depreciation rate, tax structure and even the markup factor to capture the oligopoly rent. Anyone who has attempted to estimate an investment equation can testify to the difficulty of carrying out the latter program. One of us, having struggled with the problem of constructing a direct estimate of the cost for many years, and having written on the cost of capital variable needed in the investment equation,[9] wanted to try an alternative approach. Accordingly, we present below an argument for why the average cost of capital may be a reasonable approximation of the marginal cost if the aim is simply to measure it.

The argument basically rests on the observation that, in period *t*, any capital goods acquired earlier by the firm must now have an economic value equal to the present value of the future stream of net revenues associated with the capital good in question by using the relative prices and price expectations held in period *t*, not those held in period *t-1* or earlier. One of the relative prices is the appropriate discount factor for converting expected future receipts to the present value in period *t*.

For example, suppose that the long-term interest rate increases significantly and unexpectedly in period *t*, other relative prices remaining stable. In such a case, it is clear that the market value of the equipment purchased in period *t-1* must decline to reflect the changes in the long-term interest rate, and the new long-term interest that must be used in period *t* is the same as the long-term rate used to make decisions on capital purchases in period *t*.

A perpetual inventory procedure for generating the depreciation of capital goods and the net stock of capital goods, however sophisticated it may be, would not be capable of reflecting many of these changes. In this sense, if we use the stock of capital generated by an accounting procedure involving a pre-fixed pattern of depreciation as the denominator of our estimate of the cost of capital, then the average cost of capital generated in this way may be significantly different from the marginal cost. The market value of equity, on the other hand, provided that the equity market functions well and all relevant information about the firm's operations and the relative prices it faces are made available to important market participants, must reflect all these changes, including changes in relative prices that may be caused by unexpected new technological improvements.[10]

This line of consideration leads us to expect that the average cost of capital estimated using the market value of equity as the denominator must approximate the marginal cost of capital as well as any measure can, and the objection that such a measure reflects the average rather than the marginal cost of capital is not strictly justified.

DATA

OUR ORIGINAL INTENTION WAS TO SUPPLEMENT EARLIER ESTIMATES by Ando and Auerbach (1988b, 1990) for the United States and Japan by adding data for the years 1988 to 1994, and to perform a parallel analysis for Canada. For the United States, the historical component of the COMPUSTAT file has become more easily accessible, and we have been able to revise our estimates using data for a longer period. For Japan, we have decided to use the Nikkei data set of consolidated accounts rather than the standard Nikkei-Needs data file, since the former appears to be more compatible with the U.S. accounts in the COMPUSTAT file.[11]

It turned out that, for Canada, COMPUSTAT started reporting individual company accounts only in 1976, and not until 1983 does the number of companies, with sufficient data for our calculations, exceed 100. Even after 1984, the number of companies hovered around 200, and we know from our experience with the U.S. and Japanese cases that this is not a large enough sample to generate reliable estimates.

These problems which we encountered in dealing with micro data led us to consider constructing an alternative estimate of the cost of capital for all three countries based on their aggregate national accounts data. Since the nature of the micro data and the number of adjustments we have undertaken to bring the accounting data as close as possible to the concepts needed to estimate the cost of capital have already been discussed in Ando and Auerbach (1988a,b, 1990), we comment here primarily on the nature of the aggregate data and the potential problems in using them.

For the United States, on the flow side, National Income and Product Accounts Table 1.16, Gross Domestic Product of Nonfinancial Corporate Business in Current and Constant Dollars, contains the records of corporate profits with an inventory valuation adjustment and a capital consumption adjustment. These two adjustments are, in principle, the same as those we have undertaken to correct the earnings of individual firms for their biases due to inflation in our dealing with the micro data. This table contains only net interest while we need gross interest paid, but the latter is separately reported in National Income and Product Accounts Table 8.17, Interest Paid and Received by Sector and Legal Form of Organization. Thus, all necessary data on the flow side are available in the National Income and Product Accounts subject to the normal measurement problems.

On the stock side, the most convenient source of data is the nonfinancial corporate sector of the Balance Sheets for the U.S. Economy, Flow of Funds Accounts, prepared by the Board of Governors of the Federal Reserve System. The basic problem with these balance sheets is that the basis of valuation varies for different groups of items and, hence, they contain a sizeable residual called "market valuation discrepancy." It is useful to be clear about these valuation problems and, for this purpose, we find it convenient to introduce a few simple notations:

ARR: Reproducible tangible assets valued at reproduction cost: equipment, structure and inventories.

ARN: Non-reproducible tangible assets, primarily land, valued, in principle, at market value.

AF: Financial assets, other than equities. Its components are, in principle, valued at their market value but, in practice, often reported at their face value.

LF: Financial liability. Components of this item too are, in principle, valued at their market value, but are often reported at their face value.

NWM: Equity outstanding at market value. Here it is netted against equity owned by these corporations.

NWR: Net worth at reproduction cost, to be defined below.

DMV: Market valuation discrepancy.

*LF**: LF less trade debts.

*AF**: AF less trade credit.

NWR is defined by the identity:

$$ARR + ARN + AF = LF + NWR \qquad (9)$$

and *DMV* is defined by another identity:

$$DMV = NWR - NWM \qquad (10)$$

As in our work with micro data, we propose to use the sum $NWM+LF^*$ as the denominator in our estimate of the cost of capital. This definition seems natural enough especially if *DMV* is relatively small. Unfortunately, *DMV* can be quite large and can fluctuate substantially over time, although its sign has remained positive until very recently.[12] The short-run fluctuation of *DMV* is largely due to cyclical fluctuations of the price of equity shares. The recognition of this problem implies that, to obtain a meaningful estimate of the cost of capital, we should confine ourselves to averages over a relatively long period so our estimate will not be affected by short-run fluctuations of the stock market.[13] The persistently large value of *DMV* indicates the presence of significant biases in estimates of some components of net worth reported in the balance sheet provided by the Flow of Funds accounts.

The market value of equity itself, *NWM*, is well known to be fairly accurate for large public corporations whose shares are listed on stock exchanges. Here, therefore, the source of error is the valuation of private unlisted companies, especially small ones. For the United States, the equity of large public corporations is a large enough fraction of the total value of equities of all corporations, so any bias in our estimates of the total value of equities of all corporations cannot be large enough to account for the average value of *DMV* over the last 40 years.[14]

Among financial assets and liabilities, we believe that the value of financial instruments with a relatively short maturity is reasonably accurately reported. The same cannot be said, however, for financial instruments with longer maturities, since the market value of these instruments depends not only on the relationship between the coupon rate and the market rate of interest given the length of the remaining period to maturity, but also on many complex provisions such as callability and convertibility. Because of these difficulties, the Flow of Funds Section often resorts to reporting the value of long-term financial instruments at their face value. The consequent bias in the estimate of the market value of a firm can be significant, and since corporations, on average, have much more long-term financial liabilities compared to long-term financial assets, one would expect that, by and large, when the long-term interest rate is high, we underestimate their net market value, while when the long-term interest is low, we overestimate their net market value. Thus, biases in the Flow of Funds estimate of financial assets and liabilities cannot explain the persistent positive value of *DMV*.[15]

These considerations leave the overvaluation of *ARR* as the most likely source of the persistent positive and large value of *DMV*. We believe that there are two possible mechanisms that can lead to the overvaluation of *ARR*. First, the depreciation rate used to carry out the perpetual inventory procedure may be simply too small. Second, in attributing the reproduction cost to existing capital stock, those responsible for the procedure may be underestimating the technical changes involved so they are imputing too high a level of productivity to older capital. This possibility would lead to two consequences. First, we may attribute to the older capital a market value that is too high. Second, we may underestimate the amount of capital which must be abandoned for economic reasons, because its productivity has become too low compared to that of new capital, so much so that the marginal cost of producing output using them has become larger than the total cost of producing the same output using new capital. Both of these situations could be mechanically described by saying that the rate of depreciation is too small. Let us, therefore, look at the consequence of using a depreciation rate smaller than the rate at which the value of capital declines in the market.

For the aggregate data, gross investment must be assumed to be accurately measured, so we will take gross investment I as given, and let us consider an economy in which output is increasing at a constant rate g, and the capital stock requirement is proportional to output and, therefore, also growing at the rate g. Let us designate the "true" depreciation rate and the "true" stock of capital by δ^* and K^* respectively. On the steady growth path, we must have the relationship:

$$I_t = gK^*_{t-1} + \delta^* K^*_{t-1}$$

implying:

$$K^*_{t-1} = \frac{I_t}{g + \delta^*} \tag{11}$$

for all t.

On the other hand, suppose an analyst adopted another depreciation rate δ, $\delta<\delta^*$, and kept the perpetual inventory according to:

$$K_t = I_{t-1} + (1 - \delta)\, K_{t-1}$$

starting from some K_0, presumably not too far from K_0^*, and using the same I_t as in equation (11). The analyst could find that his or her estimate of capital stock will eventually converge to:

$$K_{t-1} = \frac{I_t}{g + \delta} \tag{11a}$$

for all t.

To obtain a sense of the order of magnitude involved, suppose that g is 0.02 and δ^* is 0.15, while the analyst assumed that δ is 0.10. Then K^* is 5.88 times I, while K is 8.33 times I, making the analyst's estimate of the capital stock more than 40 percent too large relative to the true value. Somewhat surprisingly, however, the estimate of the amount of depreciation generated by the analyst is not very far from the true amount. We have:

$$\delta K_{t-1} = \delta \frac{I_t}{g + \delta} = \frac{0.1}{0.12} I_t = 0.83 I_t$$

$$\delta K^*_{t-1} = \delta^* \frac{I_t}{g + \delta^*} = \frac{0.15}{0.17} I_t = 0.88 I_t$$

Indeed, if g is zero, then the estimate of the depreciation amount prepared by the analyst is unbiased.

To summarize, in reviewing the aggregate balance sheet of nonfinancial corporations for the United States prepared by the Federal Reserve Board as a part of the Flow of Funds Accounts, we found the large and persistently positive value of the market valuation discrepancy to be the most disturbing feature of the data contained in the balance sheet. While it is possible that the discrepancy may be due to errors of measurement of the value of equity or of financial assets and liabilities, the most likely cause of the discrepancy is that the depreciation rate used in the perpetual inventory procedure by which capital stock was estimated from gross investment is too small as a measure of economic depreciation. However, even if this is so, the estimate of depreciation itself would not be seriously biased on the steady-state growth path as long as the accounting identities are consistently observed. In a sense, this is good news for working with the data for the United States because, for the ratio used to estimate the cost of capital, the numerator is affected by the amount of depreciation which is not badly biased, while for the denominator, we utilize $NWM+LF^*$, which appears to be estimated with less severe biases involved than *NWR*. Basically, the same comments apply to the micro data and, in the next section, we show that, for the United States, the estimates of the cost using micro data and aggregate data are almost identical (Figure 3).

We now come to a review of Canadian data. As mentioned earlier, micro data for Canada appear to be quite erratic, presumably because the sample size is too small, making it necessary for us to rely heavily on aggregate data to estimate the cost of capital in Canada. At the beginning, it looked as though the necessary aggregate data did not exist, but Statistics Canada was willing to make some unpublished data[16] available to us so we could carry out, for Canada, a computation very similar to the estimation procedure based on aggregate data for the United States.

There are, however, some problems. Financial data for Canada do not explicitly contain the value of equity outstanding for any group of corporations. However, Statistics Canada can generate dividends paid by nonfinancial corporations, while we can obtain the dividend-price ratios applicable to nonfinancial corporations listed on the Toronto Stock Exchange (TSE). Dividing dividends by the dividend-price ratio, we should be able to generate an estimate of the value of equity outstanding under the assumption that the dividend-price ratio for nonfinancial corporations not listed on the TSE is the same as the dividend-price ratio reported by the TSE. This is what we did, except that there is a large break in the time series on dividends from 1987 ($12,517 million) to 1988 ($26,274 million). Such a jump did not seem reasonable, and Statistics Canada informed us that this was partly due to a change in the method of the survey on which the dividend series is based. We have estimated an equation explaining dividends in terms of cash flow after taxes and previous years' dividends based on data up to 1987, and then used this equation to extrapolate the dividend series for the 1988 to 1994 period. We also had, from Statistics Canada, an alternative estimate of dividends for 1988 and 1989 based on the older survey method, and we eventually scaled our predictions up to match this additional information for 1988 and 1989. A detailed description of the procedure is given in Appendix A.

Liabilities of nonfinancial corporations were directly taken from the balance sheet of these corporations provided by Statistics Canada, except that we have excluded trade payable, corporate claims, shares and other liabilities. The sum of our

FIGURE 3

ADJUSTED ACCOUNTING R/K BEFORE TAX, UNITED STATES

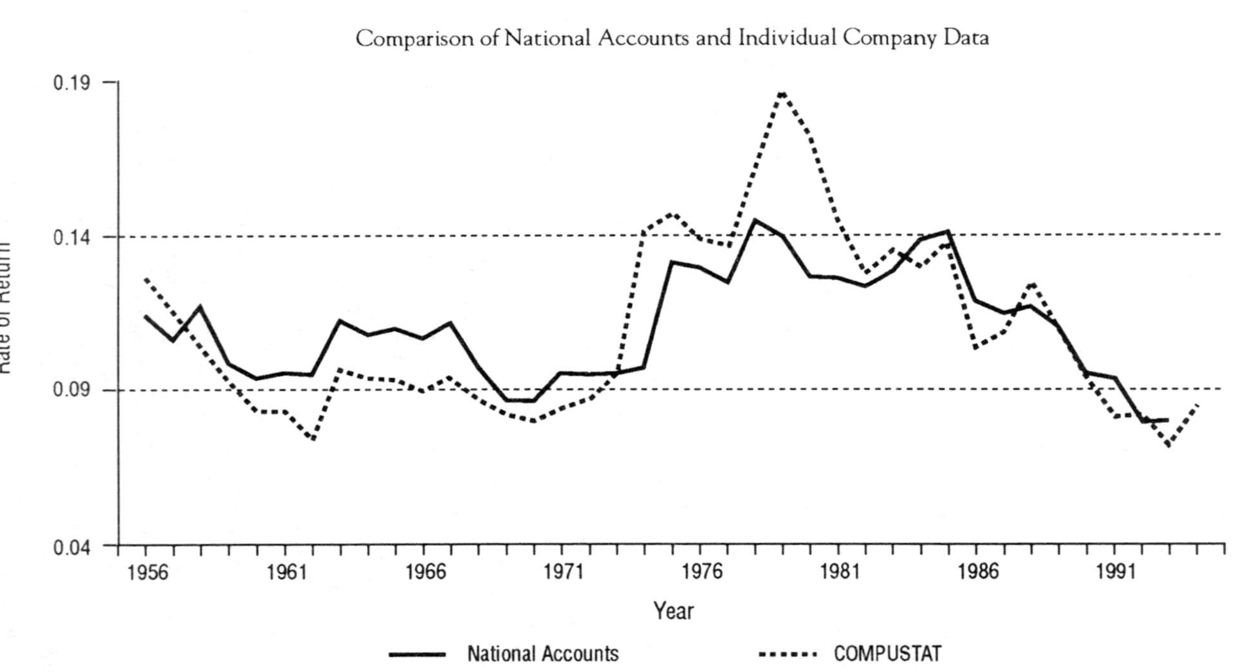

Note: R/K is the rate of return on capital.

estimated value of equity outstanding and total liabilities described above constitutes the denominator of our estimate for the cost of capital for Canada.

The numerator of the ratio is the profits of nonfinancial corporations before tax with capital consumption adjustments and inventory valuation adjustments as in the case of the United States, and these data are directly provided to us by Statistics Canada. As in the case of the United States, we make the final adjustment to the numerator by subtracting the real capital loss on the nominal financial assets of these corporations. The resulting ratio is reported in column (XIII), Table A6a (see Appendix A), and is discussed in the next section. Comparison of the results from the National Accounts data and from individual company data for Canada is provided in Figure 4.

We now have to make a few comments on the Japanese data, although the conclusion here is quite negative. The Japanese National Accounts data contain some critical defects for the purpose of estimating the cost of capital, making our estimates not meaningful. On the other hand, a comparison of the National Accounts data and corresponding estimates generated from individual company data provided by the Nikkei data files casts doubt on both sets of data, making our results for the Japanese case subject to serious concerns. We present below a brief description of the difficulties as we perceive them. A set of information which puts in focus differences between the National Accounts data and the individual company data provided by the Nikkei are shown in Table 1, supplemented by standard indicators compiled by the Tokyo Stock Exchange.

In the Japanese National Accounts, there are three basic tables for nonfinancial corporate enterprises. One shows income and outlays;[17] the second indicates investment in capital goods, inventory and land, and how these acquisitions are financed; the third is the balance sheet. With information provided in these three tables, it appears we could carry out the same procedure as we have described for computing the cost of capital in the U.S. case. Unfortunately, this is not the case.

First, it turns out that the depreciation of the capital stock reported in the first two tables of flow quantities is based on the original cost of investment, while the stock of capital reported in the balance sheet is based on their replacement costs. We have tried to reconcile the two, but we could not do so by using information reported in the National Accounts. In other words, in terms of the argument leading to equations (11) and (11a), not only is the depreciation rate used to compute depreciation in the flow tables an incorrect rate, and presumably too low, but the quantity of depreciation reported in the flow table is inconsistent with the stock of capital reported in the balance sheets and does not satisfy the accounting identity.

As we have shown in the discussion following equations (11) and (11a), this is a crucial issue because, if depreciation and the stock are consistently generated, the quantity of depreciation may be reasonably close to the true quantity even if the depreciation rate used is significantly different from the true rate. Since we do not know exactly how depreciation and the stock of capital are calculated in the Japanese National Accounts, we do not know what depreciation rate is used. If we simply compute the ratio of reported depreciation to depreciable real assets for nonfinancial corporations, we obtain a number a little below 0.1 for most years. On the

FIGURE 4

BEFORE TAX ACCOUNTING R/K, CANADA

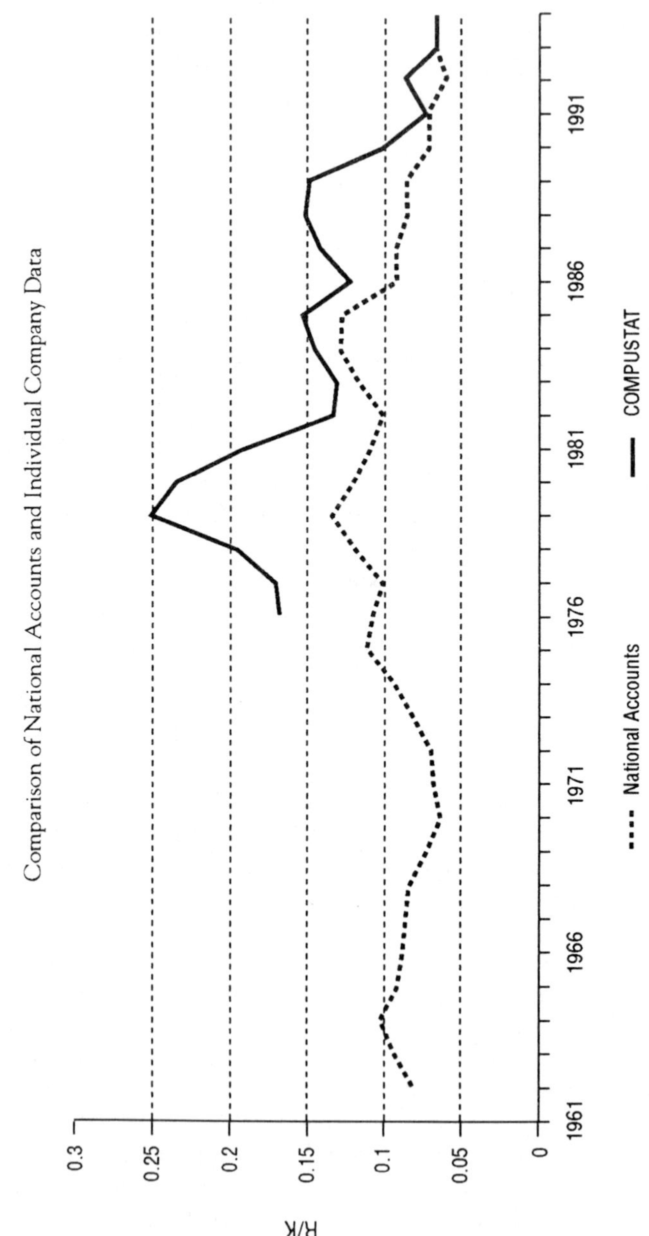

Note: R/K is the rate of return on capital.

TABLE 1

SOME CRITICAL RATIOS FOR JAPANESE DATA COMPUTED FROM NATIONAL ACCOUNTS AND INDIVIDUAL COMPANY DATA, NIKKEI, AVERAGED OVER 1985 TO 1993

	National Accounts	Nikkei	Tokyo Stock Exchange First Division
Depreciation rate[a]	0.092	0.206	
Debt-equity ratio[b]	1.541	0.918	
Dividend-price ratio	0.013	0.008	0.007
Earnings-price ratio[c]	0.043	0.023	0.021
$Land/ARR+AF^{*}$[d]	0.520	0.120	
$(NWR^{*}+LF^{*})/(NWM+LF^{*})$[e]	1.440	0.640	

Notes: [a] For the National Accounts, it is computed as a simple ratio of depreciation to the net stock. For the Nikkei, it is computed with adjustments to correct for inflation biases. Note that the inflation adjustments correct the net stock and depreciation of capital of the same vintage by the same proportion, so the depreciation *rate* is not much affected, although the amount of depreciation is.

[b] In both cases, debts exclude trade debts.

[c] For the National Accounts, earnings are computed as the sum of dividends and retained earning after tax ("saving"). For the Nikkei, it is adjusted for inflation biases.

[d] ARR and AF^{*} are defined just above equation (9) in the text. Note that this sum excludes the value of land.

[e] NWM is the market value of equity, LF^{*} is total financial liability excluding trade debts and NWR is net worth at reproduction cost defined by equation (9). NWR^{*} is equal to NWR for the National Accounts. For the Nikkei, NWR^{*} is equal to NWR except that the value of land is adjusted so the ratio of its value to ARR is equal to the ratio found in the National Accounts.

other hand, if we perform similar calculations using data from the Nikkei file of consolidated accounts, we obtain a number above 0.2 (see Table 1). For the United States, the corresponding number is between 0.06 and 0.08 computed both from individual company data supplied by COMPUSTAT and from the National Income and Product Accounts. For equipment, it may be between 0.1 and 0.2, but for structures, it must be below 0.1, so the figure of 0.2 for the average which emerges from the individual company data in Japan seems implausible.

Second, it is generally believed that the debt-equity ratio of Japanese corporations is much higher, on average, than the corresponding ratio in the United States. This ratio can move significantly even when the level of debt is fairly stable due to changes in the market value of equities. The average ratio for companies included in the Nikkei file of consolidated accounts was 1.22 in 1985. The ratio declined to 0.56 at the peak of the bubble in 1990 and increased again to 1.24 in 1993 as the bubble burst. Computing the same ratio from the nonfinancial corporation accounts in the National Accounts, gives us 2.07 in 1985, 0.81 in 1989 and

2.23 in 1993. Either smaller companies not listed on the Tokyo Stock Exchange have much higher debt-equity ratios, or we have some serious problems in the measurement of debt and/or equity. We find it hard to believe that the difference is due to a much larger debt-equity ratio of unlisted companies, since their debt-equity ratio would have to be extremely large in order to account for the difference.

Third, the standard measures of the rate of return on equity, the dividend-price ratio and the earnings-price ratio, as reported by the Tokyo Stock Exchange without any manipulation on our part, is, on average, only half the magnitude of the ratio computed from the National Accounts data.[18] Here again, we know that the National Accounts data cover, besides those corporations listed on the Tokyo Stock Exchange, many smaller firms that are not listed. Since the proportion of output generated by these smaller firms is quite large in Japan, if their behaviour is radically different from large corporations, then the larger difference between the earnings-price ratio for those firms listed on the Tokyo Stock Exchange and the ratio reported in the National Accounts is theoretically possible. Such a large difference, however, does not seem plausible and, since the measurement of dividend payments by corporations is unlikely to be badly biased, this observation raises the possibility that the value of equity reported in the National Accounts is underestimated.

The fourth and last observation on the Japanese data is related to the market valuation discrepancy.[19] In the National Accounts, this item is always positive as in the United States, but the ratio of this item to the total value of equity shares is extremely large in the case of Japan. The surprising finding is that, when the parallel concept is computed based on the Nikkei file of consolidated accounts, *DMV* is negative, and its ratio to the market value of equity is quite large. (See the sixth row of Table 1. Figures reported in this row are after the adjustment described in endnote 19.) There is an obvious bias in the estimate of this ratio from individual company accounts. In these accounts, it is most likely that the value of land is recorded at its original cost, and this in Japan is, of course, nonsense. Since we do not have any information on when the land was purchased nor where it is located in the consolidated version of the accounts in the Nikkei files, we have made a very gross adjustment to the value of land just to see if such an adjustment would make a material difference in our estimate of *DMV*.[20] This adjustment made a sizeable difference. Prior to this adjustment, the ratio of $DMV/(NWM+LF^*)$, averaged over all companies in the Nikkei file of consolidated accounts and over the years 1985 to 1993 was -0.53, while it became -0.36 after the adjustment. However, this contrasts with the corresponding figure computed from the National Accounts of 0.44.

We know that the market value of equity reported in the consolidated accounts of the Nikkei file is accurate, because we know precisely how many shares of these companies are outstanding, and we also know the precise market price of shares. Unfortunately, we do not know the value of the equities of the corporations which are not listed on the Tokyo Stock Exchange, and we cannot fully judge whether or not the market value of equity reported in the National Accounts is too small, although we suspect it is. On the other hand, we believe that the stock of reproducible tangible assets reported in individual company accounts in the Nikkei files is probably undervalued because of the unreasonably high rate of depreciation discussed earlier. Though we are not sure of either of these observations, we must keep them in mind as we proceed to review the results of our calculations to arrive at our estimate of the cost of capital.

RESULTS

WE REPORT TWO BASIC MEASURES OF THE COST OF CAPITAL:

(i) the total rate of return on capital before tax, designated as *R/K* (total income received by equity owners and bondholders before corporate profit tax and before personal taxes but after depreciation is subtracted); and

(ii) the total rate of return on capital after tax, taxed bonds (same as *R/K* except that the corporate profit tax paid is subtracted from the numerator: note that corporate profit tax paid is computed as though the interest on bonds is not deductible for tax purposes. See the discussion below.)

The denominator of the ratio is always the total market value of equity plus the market value of financial assets and liabilities. When the market values of some items in financial assets and liabilities are not available, we use the best available approximation for them.

Two alternative concepts are used as the numerator. The first is the accounting record of earnings accruing to equity owners plus interest paid to bondholders, adjusted for biases introduced into the standard accounting records when inflation is present. We will refer to this concept as the adjusted accounting measure. The second is the sum of the total gains accrued to equity owners in the market (dividends plus real capital gains from the ownership of shares) and interest earned by bondholders. We will refer to this second concept as the market measure. Note that the second measure is necessarily net of corporate profit tax, unless the tax liabilities are explicitly added back.

The net of tax measure of income is difficult to use in international comparisons, because interest payments on debt are usually deductible for tax purposes, making income net of tax dependent on the debt-equity ratio. The size of the debt-equity ratio, in turn, may be heavily affected by the tradition of a country, thus making income net of tax dependent on the institutional practices of a particular country. One way to get around this difficulty is to construct a hypothetical rate of return carrying out the computation under the assumption that interest payments to bondholders are not deductible and to use the resulting figure in estimating the rate of return after tax. We have prepared such estimates and report them from time to time. It is, however, subject to an objection that the concept is not commonly accepted, and any analysis in terms of such a concept is difficult to interpret. We therefore rely primarily on the total rate of return before tax in our discussion below.

The results of our calculations are summarized in Table 2, and the time pattern is given in various figures. One striking feature is that, for the United States, averaged over the longest possible period, 1956 to 1994, the adjusted accounting measure of the total return on capital before taxes (Table 2.B), based on individual company data, is identical to the market measure (Table 2.C), and they are, in turn, virtually the same as the parallel concept computed from the aggregate National Income and Product Accounts data (Table 2.B). They are all reported to be 0.109. They ought to be quite close to each other once they are averaged over a long period, but it is gratifying that they, in fact, become closer and closer as the period over which they are averaged becomes longer and longer. Thus, provided that we average over a long period and the quality of data is satisfactory, then any one of these three measures can provide a reasonable estimate of the order of magnitude of the average cost of capital for a country for the period covered.

Even when the period over which the averaging takes place is relatively short, the ratio computed for the United States from the National Income and Product Accounts and the average ratio computed from individual company accounts included in the COMPUSTAT file are quite close. This is evident from Figure 3, in which we graph each of these two ratios. The only periods in which the difference between them exceeds 2 percentage points are 1962, 1974 and 1979 to 1980.

For Canada, we originally produced estimates based on individual corporations but none based on the aggregate National Accounts data, because we understood from our colleagues at Industry Canada that it is not possible to locate the information necessary to adjust published data in order to match the concept laid out earlier in this paper. Somewhat to our surprise, our estimated cost of capital based on individual company data reported in the COMPUSTAT file turned out to be considerably higher than its counterpart for the United States. Furthermore, when we prepared the estimated cost of capital for broad classes of industries, we encountered a further surprise: the cost of capital is by far the highest in the industry in which it was expected to be relatively low, namely, the transportation and public utilities industry (Table 3).

We believe that these results are most likely due to the erratic variation of means of fairly small samples. We also observe, as a possible confirmation of this unreliability of the Canadian results based on individual company data, that the market rate of return for Canadian firms is dramatically lower than the adjusted accounting rate of return, 0.084 against 0.147. Confronted with these results, we appealed to Statistics Canada and, very fortunately, were supplied with a set of unpublished data on which we could base our estimate of the cost of capital for Canada. This set of data is not without problems, as discussed above and exhibited in detail in Appendix A.

The adjusted accounting rate of return before tax based on the aggregate National Accounts data for Canada for the years 1962 to 1993 turns out to be 0.094. This is only 1 percentage point over the market rate of return computed from individual company data, 0.084, for the period for which individual company data are available, 1976 to 1993. For comparison purposes, we computed the ratio based on the aggregate National Accounts for the period 1976 to 1993, and obtained the figure 0.100.

TABLE 2

AVERAGE RATE OF RETURN

A. ACCOUNTING RETURNS, UNADJUSTED

United States
Based on Individual Company Data

Period	Earnings-Price Ratio	R/K (Rate of Return on Capital) After Tax, Taxed Bonds	R/K (Rate of Return on Capital) Before Tax
(1) 1956-94	0.083	0.070	0.125
(2) 1967-94	0.091	0.076	0.135
(3) 1976-93	0.099	0.083	0.146

Japan
Based on Individual Company Data

Period	Earnings-Price Ratio	R/K (Rate of Return on Capital) After Tax, Taxed Bonds	R/K (Rate of Return on Capital) Before Tax
(2)* 1967-94	0.051	0.042	0.077
(2a) 1967-83	0.065	0.053	0.093
(2b) 1985-94	0.028	0.024	0.050
(4a) 1985-89	0.032	0.027	0.057
(4b) 1990-94	0.024	0.021	0.044

Canada
Based on Individual Company Data

Period	Earnings-Price Ratio	R/K (Rate of Return on Capital) After Tax, Taxed Bonds	R/K (Rate of Return on Capital) Before Tax
(3) 1976-93	0.167	0.124	0.179

Note: * 1984 is missing from averages reported in this row.

(cont'd)

TABLE 2 (cont'd)

B. ACCOUNTING RETURNS, ADJUSTED

United States
Based on Individual Company Data

Period	Earnings-Price Ratio	R/K (Rate of Return on Capital) After Tax, Taxed Bonds	R/K (Rate of Return on Capital) Before Tax
(1) 1956-94	0.085	0.054	0.109
(2) 1967-94	0.095	0.056	0.115
(3) 1976-93	0.104	0.061	0.124
Based on Aggregate National Accounts Data			
(1a) 1956-93			0.109
(3a) 1976-93			0.118
(4a) 1962-93			0.111

Japan
Based on Individual Company Data

Period	Earnings-Price Ratio	R/K (Rate of Return on Capital) After Tax, Taxed Bonds	R/K (Rate of Return on Capital) Before Tax
(2)* 1967-94	0.068	0.023	0.057
(2a) 1967-83	0.092	0.025	0.064
(2b) 1985-94	0.028	0.018	0.044
(4a) 1985-89	0.032	0.022	0.052
(4b) 1990-94	0.023	0.013	0.036

Canada
Based on Individual Company Data

Period	Earnings-Price Ratio	R/K (Rate of Return on Capital) After Tax, Taxed Bonds	R/K (Rate of Return on Capital) Before Tax
(3) 1976-93	0.163	0.093	0.147
Based on Aggregate National Accounts Data			
(3a) 1976-93			0.100
(4a) 1962-93			0.094

Note: * 1984 is missing from averages reported in this row.

(cont'd)

TABLE 2 (cont'd)

C. MARKET RETURN

United States
Based on Individual Company Data

Period	Earnings-Price Ratio	R/K (Rate of Return on Capital) After Tax, Taxed Bonds	R/K (Rate of Return on Capital) Before Tax
(1) 1956-94	0.080	0.053	0.109
(2) 1967-94	0.076	0.044	0.105
(3) 1976-93	0.102	0.061	0.126

Japan
Based on Individual Company Data

Period	Earnings-Price Ratio	R/K (Rate of Return on Capital) After Tax, Taxed Bonds	R/K (Rate of Return on Capital) Before Tax
(2)* 1967-94	0.072	0.018	0.053
(2a) 1967-83	0.075	0.016	0.057
(2b) 1985-94	0.066	0.020	0.045
(4a) 1985-89	0.249	0.113	0.141
(4b) 1990-94	-0.116	-0.072	-0.051

Canada
Based on Individual Company Data

Period	Earnings-Price Ratio	R/K (Rate of Return on Capital) After Tax, Taxed Bonds	R/K (Rate of Return on Capital) Before Tax
(3) 1976-93	0.065	0.025	0.084

Note: * 1984 is missing from averages reported in this row.

TABLE 3

ADJUSTED ACCOUNTING RATE OF RETURN ON CAPITAL BEFORE TAX

Industry Breakdown

Industry	United States 1955-1994	United States 1967-1993	Canada 1967-1993
Agriculture and primary industries	0.102	0.101	0.118
Manufacturing and construction	0.118	0.137	0.119
Transportation and public utilities	0.091	0.101	0.212
Trade	0.111	0.126	0.150
Services and public administration	0.108	0.122	0.042

This estimate of the cost of capital for Canada is somewhat lower than that for the United States. The corresponding figure for the United States computed from individual company data for 1976 to 1993 is 0.124 in terms of the adjusted accounting return, while it is 0.126 in terms of the market return. This contrasts with the Canadian figures of 0.147 and 0.084. As we noted earlier, the large difference between the two Canadian figures makes our Canadian estimates subject to some suspicion. Based on the aggregate National Accounts data, as we have noted above, the Canadian figure is 0.094 for the period 1962 to 1993, while the corresponding figure for the United States for the same period is 0.111.

Figure 5 exhibits the comparison of the total rate of return on capital before tax for the United States and for Canada, based on aggregate National Accounts data. The U.S. rate is almost uniformly higher than the Canadian rate by some 2 percentage points, so the average figures for the entire period are a good representative of the difference. We know that the U.S. pattern presented here is also very close to the U.S. pattern based on individual company data (Figure 3), while the Canadian figure is considerably lower than the pattern we would obtain using individual company data (Figure 4).

Given this somewhat mixed pattern that emerges in comparing the cost of capital between the United States and Canada, we are forced to speculate on which of these figures is more reliable, and how such considerations will affect our inference on whether or not the cost of capital in these two countries is the same and, if it is different, what is our best estimate of the difference.

We believe that the U.S figures are a little more reliable than the Canadian ones, for two reasons. First, the U.S. data cover a longer period. Second, for the United States, individual company data and the aggregate National Accounts data give roughly the same results. Of the Canadian data, we believe that the National Accounts data are somewhat more believable than individual company data, although we have no systematic and compelling evidence leading to such a conclusion. We simply find that the individual company data for Canada seem more erratic and cover relatively few

FIGURE 5

BEFORE TAX ACCOUNTING R/K

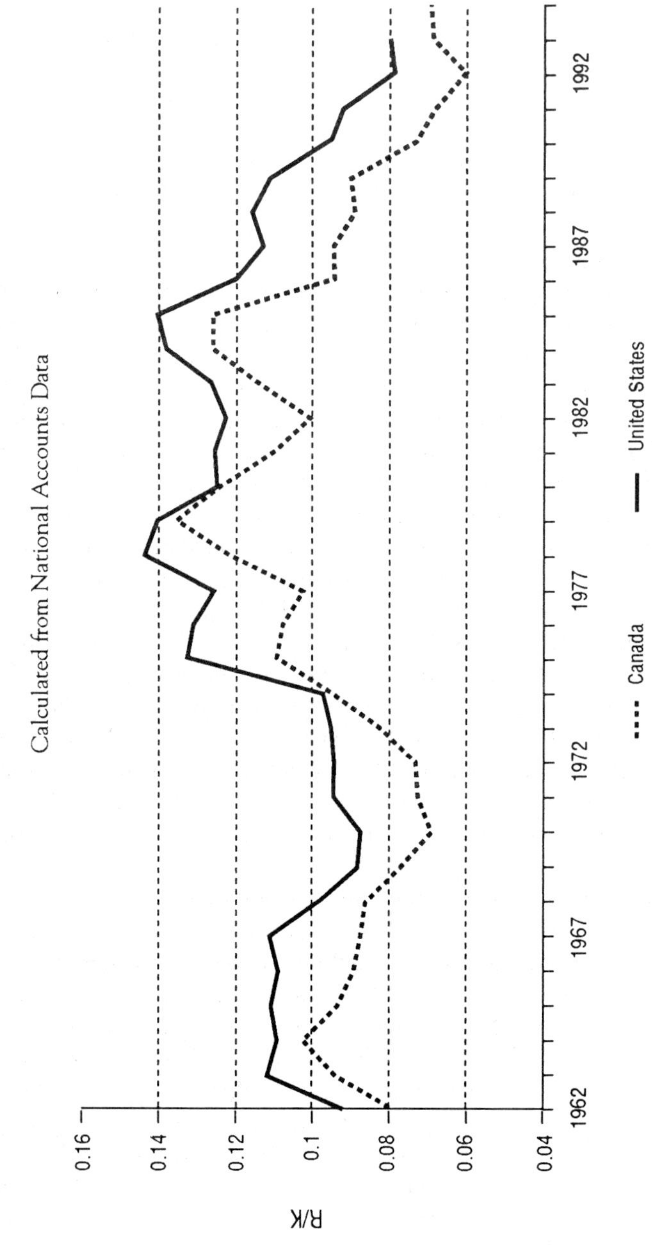

Note: R/K is the rate of return on capital.

firms over a very short period. The most suspicious feature of the National Accounts data is the very large break in the pattern for cash dividends series between 1987 and 1988. While this break is quite startling and makes the time series on cash dividends subject to serious doubt,[21] we believe it does not affect our estimate of the cost of capital very much. This is because, for Canada, we do not have direct estimates of the value of equity shares outstanding, and we estimate the value of equity by dividing the dividend series by the dividend-price ratio supplied by the TSE. In the end, we also add the same dividends to retained earnings, corporate profit tax and interest paid, and then divide them by the sum of the value of equity outstanding generated by the procedure just described and the value of financial liabilities less trade debt and a few other things. Thus, the dividend-price ratio is the critical variable, and the absolute size of dividends is used as a weight in this calculation. There is, of course, a possibility that retained earnings are underestimated, but we do not have any reason to suspect it.[22] We believe we were reasonably careful to select items among financial liabilities so the definition of financial liabilities should be very close to the one used for the United States.

There is one other indirect evidence that the cost of capital for Canada is quite close to that for the United States. Some Canadian companies are listed both on the TSE and on the New York Stock Exchange, and for these companies, the cost of capital must be very close to that for the U.S. corporations. If the cost of capital for Canada is higher than that for the United States, then the cost of capital for these cross-listed companies must be distinctly lower than the cost of capital for those Canadian firms which are not cross-listed. In Figure 6, we report the comparison between these two groups. There does not seem to be any systematic difference in the cost of capital between these two groups of companies.

Given the data at our disposal, we believe the only conclusion we can arrive at in comparing the cost of capital in Canada and that for the United States is that they are quite close and, if anything, the cost appears to be marginally lower for Canada than for the United States, but we cannot be sure. We can say that we have found no evidence supporting the proposition that the cost of capital is especially high in Canada.

For Japan, we must regrettably report that the current study confounds rather than resolves the difficulties of understanding Japanese data discussed in Ando and Auerbach (1988b, 1990). We have already outlined serious contradictions in the pattern of variables between the aggregate National Accounts data and individual company data included in the Nikkei data files. As a consequence of the differences noted earlier, if we proceed to calculate the rate of return based on the National Accounts data, we obtain a radically different result compared to individual company data.

In Figure 7, we exhibit the adjusted accounting measure of the total return on capital before tax based on individual company data, and the rate of return before tax that we calculated from the National Accounts data. We may note that the rate of return based on individual company data (represented by triangles) covering the period from 1970 to 1988 is taken from the earlier study of Ando and Auerbach (1990) and computed from the standard Nikkei file, while the figures for the later

FIGURE 6

ADJUSTED ACCOUNTING R/K BEFORE TAX, CANADA

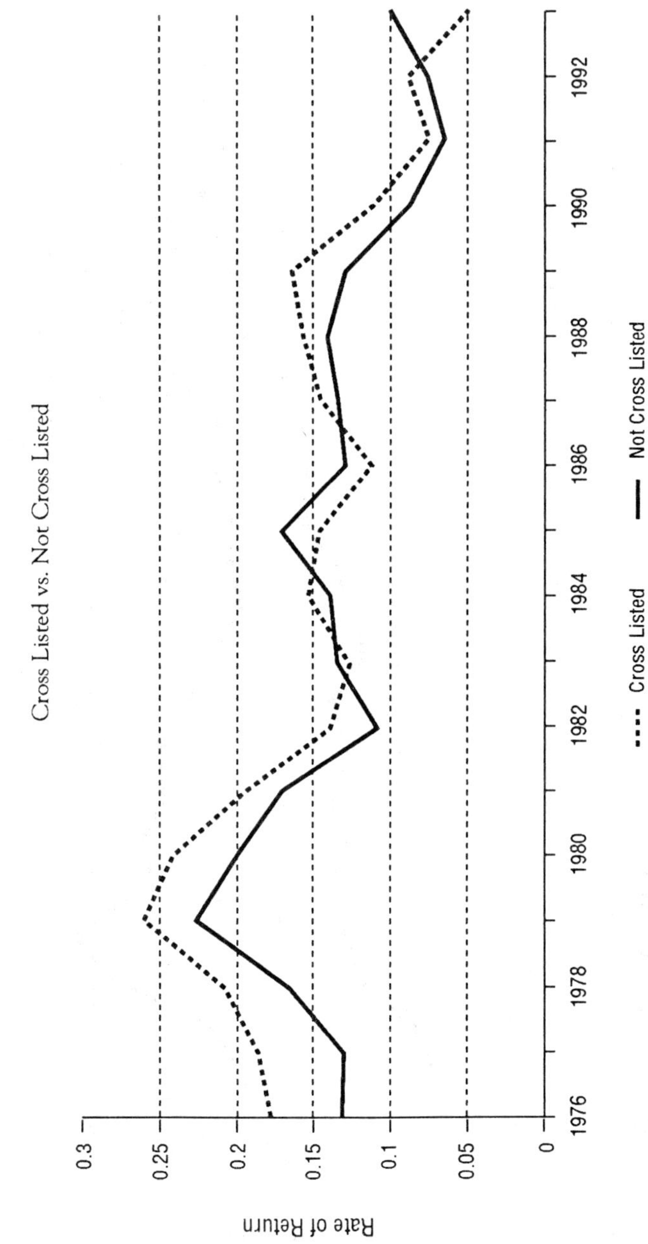

Note: R/K is the rate of return on capital.

FIGURE 7

ADJUSTED ACCOUNTING R/K BEFORE TAX, JAPAN

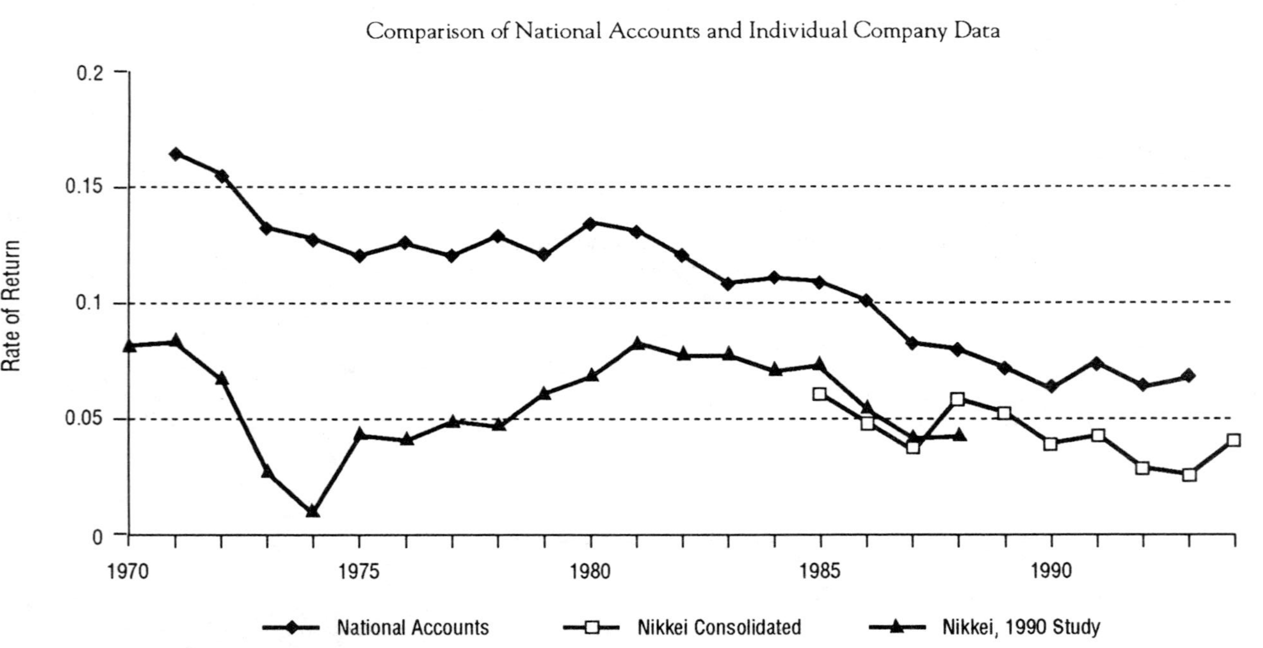

Note: R/K is the rate of return on capital.

period, 1985 to 1993, (represented by large squares) have been computed for this study using consolidated accounts from the Nikkei file. The latter covers a somewhat smaller number of companies, but the behaviour of these two series for 1985 to 1988, when they overlap, is close enough for us to suppose that there is no obvious selection bias. Results summarized by this graph line imply a very low level of return to capital before taxes. On the other hand, the graph line representing the result obtained using National Accounts data (represented by diamonds) indicates that the return to capital in Japan was exceptionally high until about 1982, and thereafter it becomes approximately the same as that for the United States.

For the rate of return based on the National Accounts data, we were unable to correct for inflation biases. Thus, the graph line of the rate of return based on the National Accounts data in Figure 7 is more like the unadjusted accounting measure rather than the adjusted accounting measure. Since the rate of inflation for Japan in the 1970s was quite high, this may make a significant difference. We have, based on individual company accounts data, a very rough indication of the quantitative effects of adjusting for inflation biases, since we have both unadjusted and adjusted accounting rates of return for Japan recorded in our tables. For example, in terms of the total return on capital, the unadjusted measure is 0.093 for the relatively high inflation period of 1967 to 1983 and 0.050 for the low inflation period of 1985 to 1994, while their adjusted counterparts are 0.064 and 0.044, respectively. Thus, the adjustment reduces the rate by 0.029 during the strong inflation period and only by 0.006 during the period of low inflation. This order of magnitude seems quite low to us, but since we have no other estimate, let us think through the consequences of the assumption that these adjustments are the right order of magnitude and that they can be transferred to estimates based on the National Accounts data.

Deducting 3 percentage points from the estimate based on the National Accounts data for the 1970s brings the average rate for this period down to a little over 10 percent, the number roughly comparable to the U.S. estimate based on the National Accounts data for the same period. For 1985 to 1993, our estimate for Japan based on the National Accounts data does not change much as the result of the adjustment and remains around 8 percent, which is noticeably lower than its counterpart for the United States. Compared with the corresponding estimates based on the individual company data for Japan, the difference has been narrowed, especially for the 1970 to 1983 period as we can see from Figure 7, but estimates based on the National Accounts data remain uniformly higher than those based on individual company data.

The fact that our estimate of the total rate of return on capital based on the National Accounts data for Japan turns out to be of the same order of magnitude as the estimate for their U.S. counterparts for a fairly long period, does not necessarily make the estimates believable. Earlier, we listed circumstantial evidence suggesting that the market value of net worth is substantially underestimated in the National Accounts, leading to a probable overestimation of the rate of return on capital. On the other hand, we also argue below that the unusually high price of land in Japan and the way it is handled in Japanese accounting practices would probably lead to a significant underestimation of the rate of return on capital. Before we come to these points, however, let us comment briefly on our estimates of the rate of return on capital based on individual company accounts.

The longest period for which we have an estimate of the rate of return on capital for Japan based on individual company data is from 1967 to 1994, and the adjusted accounting rate of return before tax for this period is reported to be 0.057. This contrasts with the rate of 0.115 for the same measure in the United States for the same period (see Table 2.B), making it appear that the Japanese rate is only half of its U.S. counterpart. In terms of the market measure, the pattern is basically the same. For 1967 to 1994, the Japanese figure is 0.053, while the figure for the United States is 0.105.

This pattern contradicts earlier findings of Ando and Auerbach (1990) who reported that the market measure of the rate of return for Japan was significantly higher than the adjusted accounting measure. The difference is due to the inclusion of the 1990 to 1994 period, when the market rate of return was strongly negative reflecting the burst of the bubble market in Japan of 1985 to 1989. Thus, on the surface, it seems difficult to deny that the cost of capital is lower in Japan than in the United States. We believe that several features of the data cast doubt on this conclusion.

Since nonfinancial corporations listed on the Tokyo Stock Exchange constitute a substantial fraction of all nonfinancial corporations in Japan, we should expect that the behaviour reported in the nonfinancial corporate sector of the National Accounts and that represented by nonfinancial firms in the Nikkei data file should exhibit similar patterns. The parallel expectation was largely fulfilled by the data for the United States, making our task of describing some aspects of the behaviour of U.S. nonfinancial corporations relatively straightforward. The difficulty we encountered in the case of Japan can be easily appreciated by referring back to Table 1, in which several critical ratios for these corporations are calculated according to both macro data from the National Accounts and the individual firm data reported by the Nikkei files. The difference between the two sets of ratios is quite striking, and yet we must attempt at least a partial reconciliation of these two sets of ratios if we are to say anything about the cost of capital faced by Japanese corporations.

Let us begin our review of potential biases by focusing on the question of land. Row (5) of Table 1 shows that the value of land is reported to be 0.52 of the reproduction cost of reproducible tangible assets and financial assets (excluding trade credits), while the parallel ratio computed from the Nikkei data is only 0.12. We believe that the figure from the National Accounts is clearly closer to the truth in this case, since the value of land reported in individual company records is almost surely based on its original purchase cost many years earlier, and the relative price of land has risen dramatically in Japan since the 1950s.[23]

Since individual company records in the Nikkei file do not report either the location or the physical size of land, there is no possibility of applying any reasonable correction to the value of land reported in these accounts. For our discussion here, we adjusted the value of land in individual records uniformly so that the ratio $Land/(ARR+AF^{*})$, on average, is equal to the ratio obtained from the National

Accounts data. We believe that this procedure is biased in the direction of underadjustment, since the value of $ARR{+}AF^{*}$ itself is probably underestimated in the Nikkei individual company records.

Second, row (1) of Table 1 indicates that the depreciation rate computed from the Nikkei file is more than twice as high compared with the one estimated from the National Accounts. We have never been able to understand the procedure followed by the National Accounts of Japan in handling depreciation. The description of National Accounts implies that the flow of depreciation is computed on an original cost basis, while the net stock reported in the balance sheet is on a reproduction cost basis. This statement has never made sense to us and we have not been able to duplicate the calculations generating the net stock of capital and its depreciation. Given this situation, the depreciation rate (0.092) for National Accounts reported in Table 1 is presumably not the rate used to construct the Accounts, because we are dividing the original cost flow by the reproduction cost stock to obtain this figure. Nevertheless, we believe that the true depreciation rate must be closer to 10 percent than to 20 percent, since we are dealing with both equipment and structures, and the weight of the structures appears to be more than one half.[24] Indeed, even the figure of 10 percent is considerably higher than the normal rate observed in most industrialized countries. Thus, the depreciation rate of 0.206 computed from the individual company records and reported in row (1) of Table 1 is clearly unreasonable, and it must lead to a serious underestimation of the net stock of capital. What happens to depreciation is not clear. If the net stock and depreciation are consistently generated from gross investment, then depreciation will be overestimated if the rate used is too high. The degree of overestimation will depend not only on the rate used and the true rate but also on the rate of growth of gross investment.[25] If depreciation and net stock are not generated consistently, as seems likely with such an exceptionally high rate, then anything is possible.

Pursuing the question of the underestimation of the net stock of capital, we observed that, according to figures reported in row (6) of Table 1, the total value of firms at their reproduction cost ($NWR^{*}{+}LF^{*}$) is only 64 percent of the total market value of these firms ($NWM{+}LF^{*}$) according to the Nikkei data. In this data set, we are reasonably sure that the market value of the firm is accurately measured, because we have the exact price and the number of equity shares outstanding. We can be reasonably sure, then, that in these accounting records of individual firms, the value of reproducible tangible assets is significantly undervalued even after its valuation is converted from an original cost basis to a reproduction cost basis.[26]

In terms of the National Accounts data, on the other hand, the total value of the firm at its reproduction cost is 1.44 times the market value of the firm. Unfortunately, in this case, we have no way of directly judging whether the market value is underestimated or the reproduction cost is overestimated. We suspect, however, that both the market value of firms is underestimated, and their value at the reproduction cost somewhat overestimated. To support this suspicion, we offer an observation reported in rows (3) and (4) of Table 1, that both the dividend-price ratio and the earnings-price ratio computed from the Nikkei individual company data are approximately the same as the ones recorded and published by the Tokyo Stock Exchange, while the corresponding ratios computed from the National Accounts data are almost twice as large. Since it is unlikely that dividends are badly overestimated in the National Accounts, we believe this observation strongly suggests that the market value of firms in the National Accounts is underestimated. The relative size of the debt-equity ratio, shown in row (2) of Table 1, also hints at the underestimation of the market value of the National Accounts, although this is by no means strong evidence.

To summarize implications of information given in Table 1 in evaluating our estimates of the rate of return for Japanese nonfinancial corporations from these sets of data, we believe that in the National Accounts, the market value of the firm is underestimated by as much as 20 percent or 30 percent, so the estimate of the total return on capital after the very rough inflation adjustment that we have cited at the beginning of this discussion, namely, 9 percent to 10 percent, is probably an overestimate and should be amended to around 8 percent. On the other hand, the estimate based on individual company records provided by Nikkei (reported in parts B and C of Table 2) of around 5 percent is significantly underestimated because of the overestimation of depreciation, and should be amended to 6.5 percent to 7 percent.

This is not, however, the final story in the case of the Japanese cost of capital. We must take account of the role played by the extraordinarily high price of land and steady rise of its price until 1990. This question was already discussed in Ando and Auerbach (1990), but to appreciate the issue, consider a firm whose market value is $1 million and is operating on a piece of land purchased at $100,000. The purchase cost of land is a part of the value of the firm and, therefore, if the firm earns the return of 10 percent or $100,000 per year, then it includes the rent on the land of $10,000. Suppose now that the price of land, for reasons that have little to do with the firm, suddenly goes up to $500,000. If the firm is unable to raise the price of output and earn the appropriate rent on the land of $500,000, it must move to a new location, realize the capital gain and distribute it to the firm's owners. Otherwise, the new market price of the firm, namely $1.5 million, is not sustainable, unless the price of land continues to rise at approximately 10 percent per year so the market value of the firm rises just enough to supplement the earnings of the firm and make the total return to shareholders 10 percent on average.

If this process goes on for a long enough period of time, then the conventional adjusted accounting measure of the rate of return will underestimate the full return earned by shareholders because real capital gains on land would not be included in such a measure, while the market for shares would recognize it and price the firm accordingly. It can be sustained only if the relative price of land is expected to rise continually, and actually does so. We believe that this is the process that operated in Japan from the 1960s to 1985, accelerated dramatically in the second half of the 1980s and then crashed at the beginning of the 1990s.[27]

Looking at the pattern of prices and rates of return in Japan immediately following the return of stability in asset prices in 1994 and 1995, the price of land and other associated prices do not seem to be low enough to be sustainable unless at least a moderate and steady real capital gain in land resumes, but we see no logical reasons why such steady capital gain should resume in Japan. We hasten to add that the period after the bubble and its subsequent burst has been quite short, and the market for land and equity does not seem to have recovered its equilibrium, so it is extremely difficult to interpret price patterns at this time.

We must conclude this long inquiry with less than a satisfactory assessment of the cost of capital in the United States, Japan and Canada. In the United States, the cost of capital measured as the total return on capital before tax and after depreciation has been a little more than 10 percent during most of the period since 1955. Though it does fluctuate substantially over time, it does not show any tendency to move up or down persistently. The order of magnitude cited above emerges whether we use individual company data collected in the COMPUSTAT tapes or macro data from the National Income and Product Accounts, and whether we use the adjusted accounting measure or the market measure.

For Canada, we are unable to use individual company data, since the number of companies for which data are available is too small and the period covered by the data is too short to generate reliable estimates. Based on National Accounts data supplemented by unpublished information supplied by Statistics Canada, we estimate that the cost of capital in Canada appears to be a little lower than that for the United States. Given that we had to make a number of approximations as discussed in Appendix A, it is probably best to conclude that there is no ground for believing that the cost of capital in Canada is significantly higher than in the United States.

The Japanese case is the most complicated, primarily because the patterns generated by individual company and National Accounts data are apparently inconsistent. After a lengthy review and reasoning which relied on a number of pieces of indirect evidence and on assumptions that are somewhat stronger than we would prefer to use, we have concluded that the cost of capital in Japan is somewhat lower than that in the United States, although not by a large margin. Furthermore, we have argued that this lower cost of capital was probably generated by a very high and continually rising price of land. If we are right in this hypothesis, only those firms which acquired land before the rapid rise in the real price of land began were able to take advantage of the lower cost of capital. Finally, again if we are right in this hypothesis, the current price of land and, hence, the current level of equity value, do not appear to be sustainable unless a moderate but persistently rising trend in the real price of land resumes in Japan.

To complete our presentation, in figures 8 through 11, we present a comparison of the rate of return in terms of various measures for each of the three countries, all based on individual company data. All reservations concerning the reliability of these estimates discussed above apply to these graphs. The adjusted accounting measures before and after tax show a similar pattern: the Canadian rate of return is slightly higher than that for the United States, while the Japanese rate of return is much lower than the other two countries. We should recall, however, that these measures, when computed from the aggregate National Accounts data, show the U.S. rate of return remains unchanged, while the Canadian rate becomes slightly less than the U.S. rate, and the Japanese rate becomes significantly higher than the U.S. rate.

The market rates of return are too volatile to allow us to make a detailed comparison even when they are smoothed by a moving average process. For the market rate, we believe that the only comparison possible is in terms of the averages over the entire period, as reported in Table 2.C.

We believe that these alternative measures of the rate of return do not change our main conclusion based on the adjusted accounting rate of return before tax, namely, that the Canadian rate of return has been about the same as that for the United States between 1962 and 1994, while not much can be concluded about the Japanese rate of return until its rate of return based on individual company data and the one based on its aggregate National Accounts data are reconciled.

FIGURE 8

ADJUSTED ACCOUNTING R/K BEFORE TAX

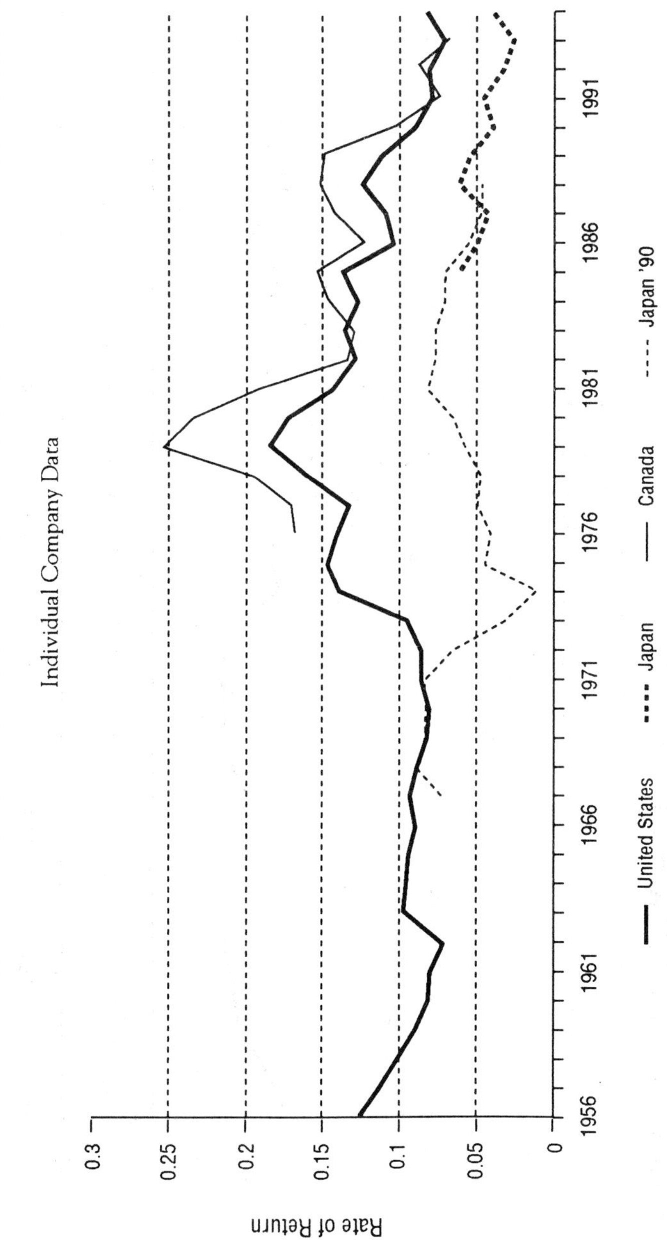

Note: R/K is the rate of return on capital.

FIGURE 9

ADJUSTED ACCOUNTING R/K AFTER TAX

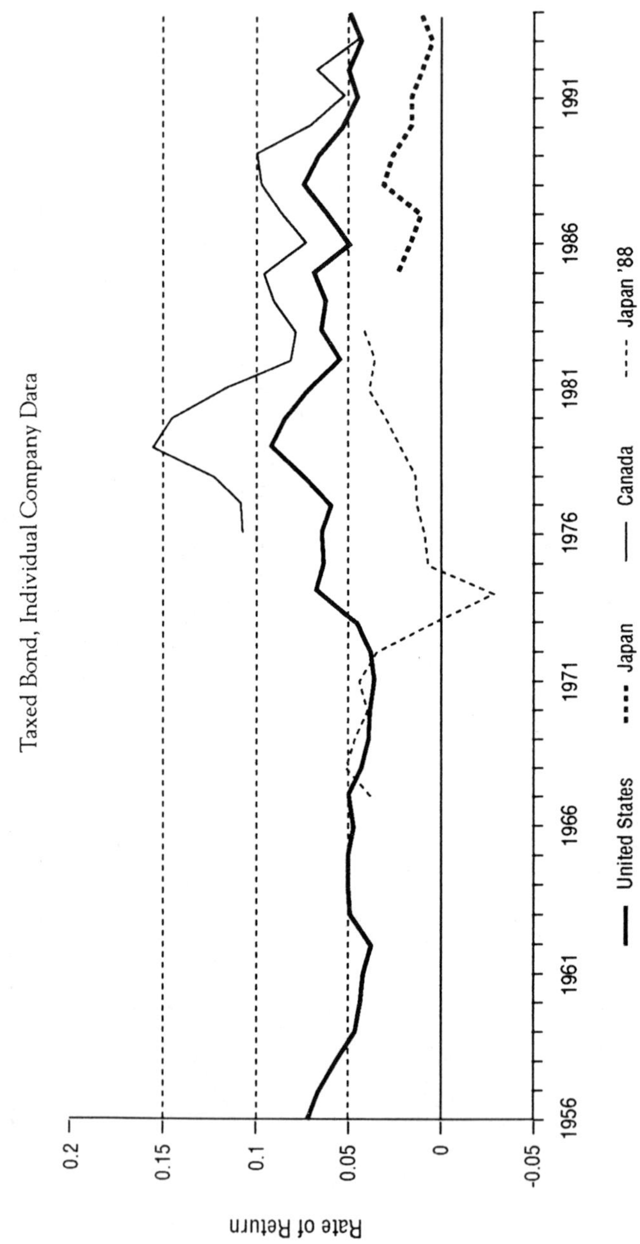

Note: R/K is the rate of return on capital.

FIGURE 10

MARKET R/K BEFORE TAX

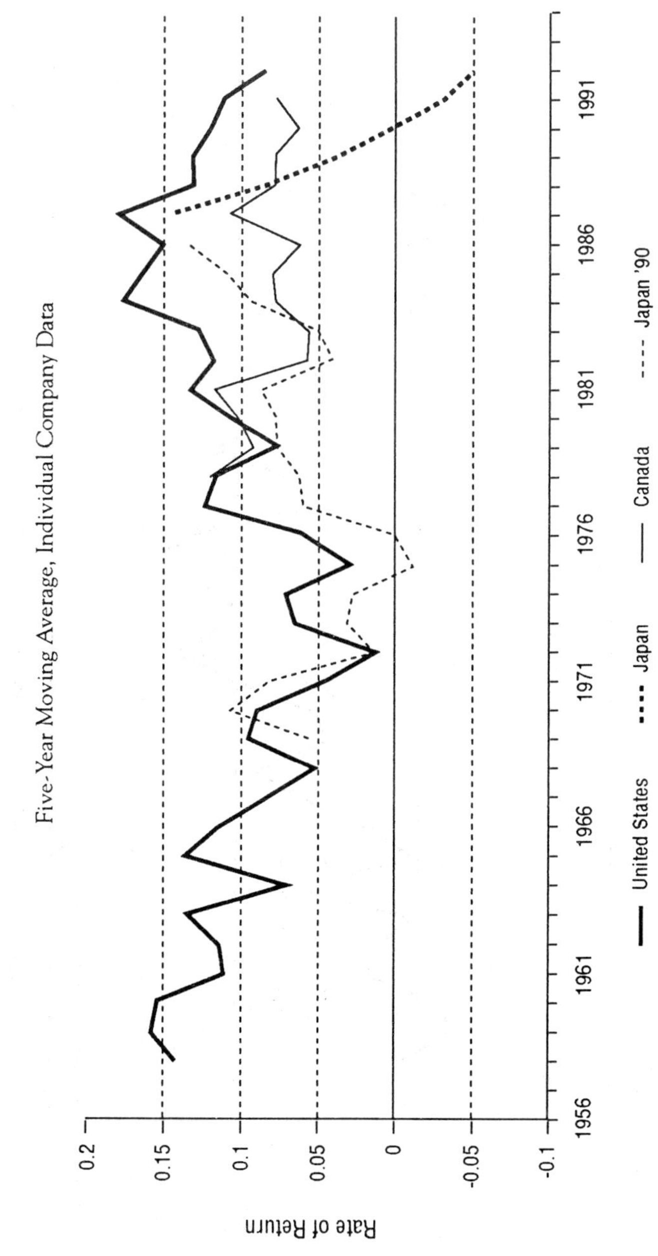

Note: R/K is the rate of return on capital.

FIGURE 11

MARKET R/K AFTER TAX

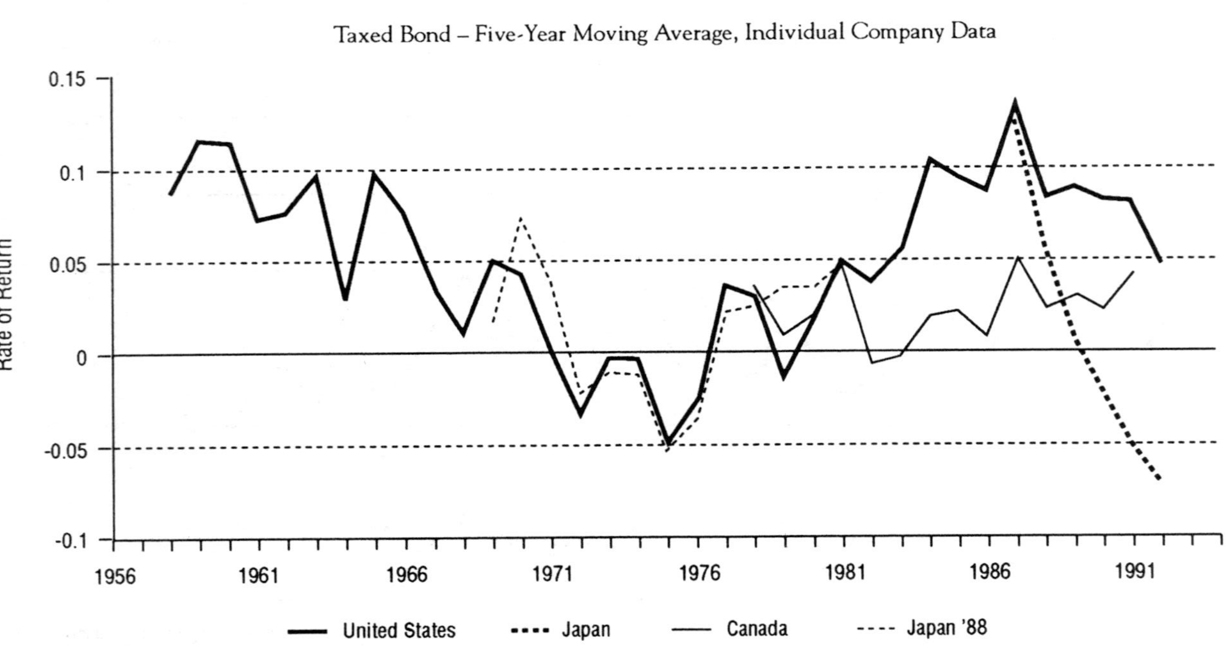

Note: R/K is the rate of return on capital.

APPENDIX A

DERIVATION OF THE COST OF CAPITAL FROM AGGREGATE NATIONAL ACCOUNTS DATA

TABLE A1

DIVIDENDS, DIVIDEND-PRICE RATIO, AND THE VALUE OF EQUITY FOR NONFINANCIAL CORPORATIONS, CANADA

Year	(I)[a] Dividends Reported ($M)	(II)[b] Predicted Value Based on Cash Flow ($M)	(III)[c] Adjusted Dividends ($M)	(IV)[d] Dividend-Price Estimated (%)	(V)[e] Estimated Value of Equity (III)/(IV) ($M)	(VI) Ratio to the Preceding Value of (V)	(VII)[f] Ratio to the Preceding TSE 300 Table 5, column (III)
1961	1,141	–	1,141	2.72	41,899	–	–
1962	1,171	–	1,171	3.25	36,066	0.861	–
1963	1,260	–	1,260	3.14	40,082	1.111	–
1964	1,345	–	1,345	2.90	46,290	1.155	–
1965	1,591	–	1,591	3.11	51,092	1.104	–
1966	1,798	–	1,798	3.70	48,545	0.950	–
1967	1,889	–	1,889	3.38	55,875	1.151	–
1968	1,990	–	1,990	2.90	68,519	1.226	–
1969	2,178	–	2,178	3.12	69,711	1.017	–
1970	2,289	–	2,289	3.33	68,657	0.985	–
1971	2,368	–	2,368	3.02	78,447	1.143	–
1972	2,293	–	2,293	2.49	92,247	1.176	–
1973	2,621	–	2,621	3.02	86,815	0.941	–
1974	3,199	–	3,199	5.29	60,522	0.697	–
1975	3,414	–	3,414	4.70	72,712	1.201	–
1976	3,523	–	3,523	4.46	79,042	1.087	–
1977	3,339	–	3,339	4.50	74,122	0.938	–
1978	4,417	–	4,417	4.22	104,668	1.412	–
1979	5,775	–	5,775	3.69	156,504	1.495	–
1980	6,595	–	6,595	3.43	192,274	1.229	–
1981	7,463	–	7,463	4.12	181,141	0.942	0.834
1982	6,923	–	6,932	3.66	189,399	1.046	1.013
1983	6,761	–	6,761	2.86	236,399	1.248	1.298

(cont'd)

TABLE A1 (cont'd)

Year	(I)[a] Dividends Reported ($M)	(II)[b] Predicted Value Based on Cash Flow ($M)	(III)[c] Adjusted Dividends ($M)	(IV)[d] Dividend-Price Estimated (%)	(V)[e] Estimated Value of Equity (III)/(IV) ($M)	(VI) Ratio to the Preceding Value of (V)	(VII)[f] Ratio to the Preceding TSE 300 Table 5, column (III)
1984	8,582	–	8,582	3.39	253,156	1.071	0.974
1985	10,459	–	10,459	2.89	361,903	1.430	1.168
1986	11,036	–	11,036	2.71	407,232	1.125	1.100
1987	12,517	–	12,517	2.43	515,103	1.265	0.972
1988	26,274	13,617	13,617	3.01	452,392	0.878	1.120
1989	25,755	13,644	13,644	2.94	464,082	1.026	1.128
1990	25,235	12,738	12,738	3.39	375,752	0.810	0.833
1991	22,157	11,614	11,614	2.83	410,389	1.092	1.091
1992	22,307	10,711	10,711	2.68	399,664	0.974	0.941
1993	20,336	11,120	11,120	1.98	561,616	1.405	1.314
1994	22,396	12,565	12,565	2.04	615,931	1.097	0.944
					Average (1981-1994):	**1.101**	**1.052**

Notes:
[a] Prepared by Statistics Canada.
[b] See the regression result, Table A3.
[c] 1961-1987 are the same as column (I). 1988 and 1989 are provisional estimates prepared by Statistics Canada using the old method. 1990-1994 values are scaled-up values of column (II) using the average of ratios of column (III) to column (II) for 1988 and 1989.
[d] Equal to Table A2, column (I) for 1988-1994. Equal 1.05*Table A2, column (II) for 1961-1977.
[e] Figures represent the value for the end of the year as closely as possible.
[f] A check on the pattern of column (VI). Since column (VI) reflects effects of new issues while column (VII) presumably does not, column (VI) should be on average slightly larger than column (VII), and they should be roughly parallel otherwise. We believe that column(VI) is a little too large, perhaps reflecting the jump of the series in column (III) in 1988.

TABLE A2

DIVIDEND-PRICE RATIO, CANADA

Year	(I)* Dividend-Price Nonfinancial Corporations (%)	(II)** Dividend-Price Total Corporations (%)	(III) TSE 300 Index (Average of Values for ends of Nov., Dec. and Jan.)
1961	–	2.86	–
1962	–	3.41	–
1963	–	3.30	–
1964	–	3.05	–
1965	–	3.27	–
1966	–	3.89	–
1967	–	3.55	–
1968	–	3.05	–
1969	–	3.28	–
1970	–	3.50	–
1971	–	3.17	–
1972	–	2.61	–
1973	–	3.17	–
1974	–	5.55	–
1975	–	4.93	–
1976	–	4.68	–
1977	–	4.73	–
1978	4.22	4.42	–
1979	3.69	3.99	–
1980	3.43	3.66	2,299
1981	4.12	4.49	1,918
1982	3.66	4.03	1,943
1983	2.86	3.22	2,521
1984	3.39	3.70	2,455
1985	2.89	3.13	2,867
1986	2.71	2.99	3,154
1987	2.43	3.08	3,065
1988	3.01	3.36	3,434
1989	2.94	3.25	3,872
1990	3.39	3.83	3,227
1991	2.83	3.18	3,519
1992	2.68	3.05	3,313
1993	1.98	2.26	4,352
1994	2.04	2.39	4,108

Notes: * Prepared by TSE at the request of Statistics Canada.
** TSE.

TABLE A3

REGRESSION OF DIVIDENDS ON CASH FLOW AND DIVIDENDS LAGGED, CANADA

Regression Statistics

Multiple R	0.99534
R-squared	0.99071
Adjusted R-squared	0.94866
Standard error	325.55176
Observations	26

Analysis of Variance

	df	*Sum of Squares*	*Mean Square*	*F*	*Significance F*
Regression	2.00000	271,259,767.17279	135,629,883.58639	1,279.72095	2.6E-24
Residual	24.00000	2,543,614.83835	105,983.95160		
Total	26.00000	273,803,382.01114			

	Coefficients	*Standard Error*	*t Statistic*	*P-value*	*Lower 95%*	*Upper 95%*
Intercept	0	NA	NA	NA	NA	NA
x1	0.10380	0.01572	6.60217	5.31E-07	0.07135	0.13625
x2	0.54201	0.08687	6.23932	1.33E-06	0.36272	0.72130

	Predicted Dividends ($ million)	**Cash Flow Used ($ million)**
1987	12,517	
1988	13,617	65,822
1989	13,644	60,337
1990	12,738	51,472
1991	11,614	45,371
1992	10,711	42,545
1993	11,120	51,194
1994	12,565	62,981

(cont'd)

TABLE A3 (cont'd)

DATA FOR REGRESSION (IN $M)

Year	X1(t)*	X2(t)=Y(t-1)	Y(t)**
1961	4,537		1,141
1962	4,979	1,141	1,171
1963	5,469	1,171	1,260
1964	6,283	1,260	1,345
1965	6,526	1,345	1,591
1966	7,192	1,591	1,798
1967	7,364	1,798	1,889
1968	7,939	1,889	1,990
1969	8,289	1,990	2,178
1970	8,604	2,178	2,289
1971	9,084	2,289	2,368
1972	10,558	2,368	2,293
1973	13,047	2,293	2,621
1974	15,353	2,621	3,199
1975	16,570	3,199	3,414
1976	18,701	3,414	3,523
1977	19,159	3,523	3,339
1978	23,286	3,339	4,417
1979	30,073	4,417	5,775
1980	34,382	5,775	6,595
1981	32,024	6,595	7,463
1982	29,978	7,463	6,932
1983	39,633	6,932	6,761
1984	47,304	6,761	8,582
1985	53,000	8,582	10,459
1986	52,178	10,459	11,036
1987	60,842	11,036	12,517

Notes: * Transferred from Table A5, column (V).
** Dividends of nonfinancial corporations; same as Table A1, column I. Prepared by Statistics Canada.

TABLE A4

CORPORATE TAX LIABILITIES, NONFINANCIAL AND TOTAL CORPORATIONS, CANADA

Year	(I)* Corporate Tax Liabilities, Total Corporations ($M)	(II)* Corporation Profits Before Tax, Total Corporations ($M)	(III) Effective Tax Rate (I)/(II)	(IV)** Corporate Tax Liabilities Reported, Nonfinancial Corporations ($M)	(V)** Profits of Nonfinancial Corporations GNP basis ($M)	(VI)*** Effective Tax Rate, Nonfinancial Corporations	(VII) Estimated Tax Liabilities, Nonfinancial Corporations (V)*(VI) ($M)
1961	1,629	4,120	0.395	–	3,454	0.314	1,086
1962	1,732	4,580	0.378	–	3,829	0.301	1,152
1963	1,874	5,115	0.366	–	4,355	0.291	1,269
1964	2,085	5,911	0.353	–	5,077	0.281	1,424
1965	2,188	6,466	0.338	–	5,367	0.269	1,445
1966	2,343	6,976	0.336	–	5,913	0.267	1,580
1967	2,382	7,158	0.333	–	5,858	0.265	1,551
1968	2,833	8,040	0.352	–	6,457	0.280	1,810
1969	3,199	8,504	0.376	–	6,849	0.299	2,049
1970	3,051	7,942	0.384	–	6,266	0.306	1,915
1971	3,332	8,955	0.372	–	7,048	0.296	2,086
1972	3,904	11,115	0.351	–	8,842	0.279	2,470
1973	5,064	15,697	0.323	–	12,934	0.257	3,319
1974	7,032	20,472	0.343	–	17,367	0.273	4,745
1975	7,464	20,003	0.373	–	16,226	0.297	4,816
1976	7,078	20,924	0.338	–	16,294	0.269	4,384
1977	7,202	22,045	0.327	–	17,154	0.260	4,458
1978	8,151	26,891	0.303	4,886	21,793	0.224	4,886
1979	9,966	35,984	0.277	6,302	30,679	0.205	6,302

(cont'd)

TABLE A4 (cont'd)

Year	(I)* Corporate Tax Liabilities, Total Corporations ($M)	(II)* Corporation Profits Before Tax, Total Corporations ($M)	(III) Effective Tax Rate (I)/(II)	(IV)** Corporate Tax Liabilities Reported, Nonfinancial Corporations ($M)	(V)** Profits of Nonfinancial Corporations GNP basis ($M)	(VI)*** Effective Tax Rate, Nonfinancial Corporations	(VII) Estimated Tax Liabilities, Nonfinancial Corporations (V)*(VI) ($M)
1980	11,943	39,795	0.300	7,615	33,663	0.226	7,615
1981	12,602	37,654	0.335	8,223	29,347	0.280	8,223
1982	11,514	26,848	0.429	8,012	21,984	0.364	8,012
1983	12,103	37,072	0.326	8,792	30,611	0.287	8,792
1984	14,749	45,855	0.322	10,317	38,501	0.268	10,317
1985	15,313	49,490	0.309	10,682	41,220	0.259	10,682
1986	14,373	45,355	0.317	8,693	36,187	0.240	8,693
1987	16,861	56,571	0.298	10,062	46,667	0.216	10,062
1988	17,506	64,667	0.271	12,489	51,763	0.241	12,489
1989	18,489	60,093	0.308	13,116	43,767	0.300	13,116
1990	16,651	44,814	0.372	11,363	28,726	0.396	11,363
1991	15,010	34,829	0.431	10,096	17,850	0.566	10,096
1992	14,423	35,060	0.411	9,868	17,156	0.575	9,868
1993	14,475	42,135	0.344	10,071	25,718	0.392	10,071
1994	16,890	57,357	0.294	11,918	38,274	0.311	11,918

Notes: * National Accounts of Canada.

** Estimated by Statistics Canada.

*** Equal to column (IV) divided by column (V), for 1978-1994. For 1961-1977, we first compute the average of the ratio of this column to column (III) for 1987-1994 and then apply the resulting average to figures in column (III).

Table A5

Estimated Cash Flow After Tax, Nonfinancial Corporations, Canada

Year	(I)* Corporate Profits ($M)	(II)** Corporate Tax Liabilities ($M)	(III)* CCA on an Historical Cost Basis ($M)	(IV)* IVA ($M)	(V) Estimated Cash Flow After Tax, (I)-(II)+(III)+(IV) ($M)
1961	3,454	1,086	2,199	(29)	4,537
1962	3,829	1,152	2,389	(87)	4,979
1963	4,355	1,269	2,534	(151)	5,469
1964	5,077	1,424	2,744	(114)	6,283
1965	5,367	1,445	2,896	(292)	6,526
1966	5,913	1,580	3,147	(288)	7,192
1967	5,858	1,551	3,398	(342)	7,364
1968	6,457	1,810	3,667	(375)	7,939
1969	6,849	2,049	4,010	(521)	8,289
1970	6,266	1,915	4,405	(152)	8,604
1971	7,048	2,086	4,758	(636)	9,084
1972	8,842	2,470	5,097	(910)	10,558
1973	12,934	3,319	5,795	(2,363)	13,047
1974	17,367	4,745	6,867	(4,136)	15,353
1975	16,226	4,816	7,758	(2,599)	16,570
1976	16,294	4,384	8,821	(2,030)	18,701
1977	17,154	4,458	9,943	(3,480)	19,159
1978	21,793	4,886	11,078	(4,699)	23,286
1979	30,679	6,302	12,960	(7,264)	30,073
1980	33,663	7,615	15,232	(6,898)	34,382
1981	29,347	8,223	17,647	(6,747)	32,024
1982	21,984	8,012	19,062	(3,056)	29,978
1983	30,611	8,792	20,296	(2,482)	39,633
1984	38,501	10,317	21,560	(2,440)	47,304
1985	41,220	10,682	24,084	(1,622)	53,000
1986	36,187	8,693	26,635	(1,951)	52,178
1987	46,667	10,062	27,294	(3,057)	60,842
1988	51,763	12,489	29,514	(2,966)	65,822
1989	43,767	13,116	31,130	(1,444)	60,337
1990	28,726	11,363	34,171	(62)	51,472
1991	17,850	10,096	35,851	1,766	45,371
1992	17,156	9,868	37,669	(2,412)	42,545
1993	25,718	10,071	38,459	(2,912)	51,194
1994	38,274	11,918	41,347	(4,722)	62,981

Notes: CCA: Capital Consumption Allowance.
IVA: Inventory Valuation Adjustment.
* Estimated by Statistics Canada.
** Table A4, column (VII).

TABLE A6

TOTAL RETURN ON CAPITAL BEFORE TAX, NONFINANCIAL CORPORATIONS, CANADA

Year	(I)* Estimated Value of Equity ($M)	(II)** Total Liabilities ($M)	(III)*** Interest Paid ($M)	(IV)**** Profit with CCAdj and IVA ($M)	(V) (III)+(IV) ($M)	(VI) (I)+(II) ($M)	(VII) Total Return on Capital Before Tax (V)/(VI)
1962	41,899	13,521	734	3,651	4,385	55,420	0.079
1963	36,066	14,683	782	4,104	4,886	50,749	0.096
1964	40,082	15,531	855	4,871	5,727	55,613	0.103
1965	46,290	16,953	980	4,935	5,914	63,243	0.094
1966	51,092	19,226	1,101	5,406	6,507	70,318	0.093
1967	48,545	22,119	1,201	5,241	6,443	70,664	0.091
1968	55,875	24,804	1,287	5,846	7,134	80,679	0.088
1969	68,519	26,568	1,423	6,032	7,455	95,087	0.078
1970	69,711	30,165	1,584	5,719	7,303	99,876	0.073
1971	68,657	33,374	1,790	5,845	7,635	102,031	0.075
1972	78,447	37,783	1,802	7,107	8,909	116,230	0.077
1973	92,247	40,832	2,182	9,628	11,810	133,079	0.089
1974	86,815	50,239	2,949	11,676	14,625	137,054	0.107
1975	60,522	59,696	3,336	11,459	14,795	120,218	0.123
1976	72,712	64,055	3,789	11,951	15,740	136,767	0.115
1977	79,042	74,847	5,234	11,098	16,332	153,889	0.106
1978	74,122	84,736	6,053	14,519	20,572	158,858	0.129
1979	104,668	95,257	8,267	20,865	29,132	199,925	0.146

(cont'd)

TABLE A6 (cont'd)

Year	(I)* Estimated Value of Equity ($M)	(II)** Total Liabilities ($M)	(III)*** Interest Paid ($M)	(IV)**** Profit with CCAdj and IVA ($M)	(V) (III)+(IV) ($M)	(VI) (I)+(II) ($M)	(VII) Total Return on Capital Before Tax (V)/(VI)
1980	156,504	113,949	12,005	24,375	36,380	270,453	0.135
1981	192,274	132,780	18,226	19,664	37,890	325,054	0.117
1982	181,141	176,124	24,664	14,185	38,849	357,265	0.109
1983	189,399	188,220	21,582	23,736	45,318	377,619	0.120
1984	236,399	183,618	22,992	31,285	54,277	420,017	0.129
1985	253,156	201,145	22,473	36,020	58,493	454,301	0.129
1986	361,903	212,980	23,559	31,240	54,799	574,883	0.095
1987	407,232	224,159	23,025	39,433	62,458	631,391	0.099
1988	515,103	243,105	26,240	43,899	70,139	758,208	0.093
1989	452,392	275,922	32,220	35,630	67,850	728,314	0.093
1990	464,082	312,233	37,072	22,474	59,546	776,315	0.077
1991	375,752	334,452	36,245	15,028	51,273	710,204	0.072
1992	410,389	342,939	33,399	12,225	45,624	753,328	0.061
1993	399,664	347,149	31,896	19,716	51,612	746,813	0.069
1994	561,616	358,762	33,663	30,469	64,132	920,378	0.070
					Average of column (VII):		**0.098**

Notes: CCA: Capital Consumption Allowance (in note below).
CCAdj: Capital Consumption Adjustment.
IVA: Inventory Valuation Adjustment.
* Table A1, column (V) shifted down to represent beginning of the year value.
** Total Liabilities (3100) – Trade Payable (3322) – Corporate Claims (3512) – Shares (3520) – Other Liabilities (3610).
*** Estimate by Statistics Canada.
**** Profits of Nonfinancial Corporations on a GNP basis + CCA of Nonfinancial Corporations on an historical cost basis – CCA of Nonfinancial Corporations on a replacement basis + IVA. Components are estimates provided by Statistics Canada.

TABLE A6a

TOTAL RETURN ON CAPITAL BEFORE TAX, ADJUSTED FOR CAPITAL LOSS IN FINANCIAL ASSETS NONFINANCIAL CORPORATIONS, CANADA

Year	(V) (from Table A6) (III)+(IV) ($M)	(VI) (from Table A6) (I)+(II) ($M)	(VIII) Nominal* Financial Assets ($M)	(IX) Deflator for GDP, Business Sector (P)**	(X) dP/P	(XI) (VIII)*(X) ($M)	(XII) (V)-(XI) ($M)	(XIII) Total Return on Capital Before Tax, Adjusted for Capital Loss in Financial Assets (XII)/(VI)
1962	4,385	55,420	4,711	25.8	0.0039	18	4,367	0.079
1963	4,886	50,749	5,022	26.2	0.0155	78	4,808	0.095
1964	5,727	55,613	5,383	26.5	0.0115	62	5,665	0.102
1965	5,914	63,243	5,582	27	0.0189	105	5,809	0.092
1966	6,507	70,318	5,847	28.1	0.0407	238	6,269	0.089
1967	6,443	70,664	5,856	29.1	0.0356	208	6,234	0.088
1968	7,134	80,679	6,333	29.9	0.0275	174	6,960	0.086
1969	7,455	95,087	6,976	30.8	0.0301	210	7,245	0.076
1970	7,303	99,876	7,047	32.6	0.0584	412	6,891	0.069
1971	7,635	102,031	7,120	33.4	0.0245	175	7,461	0.073
1972	8,909	116,230	8,007	34.9	0.0449	360	8,549	0.074
1973	11,810	133,079	8,281	38.2	0.0946	783	11,027	0.083
1974	14,625	137,054	9,796	44.2	0.1571	1,539	13,086	0.095
1975	14,795	120,218	11,551	50.1	0.1335	1,542	13,254	0.110
1976	15,740	136,767	12,484	53.4	0.0659	822	14,918	0.109
1977	16,332	153,889	13,172	56.7	0.0618	814	15,518	0.101
1978	20,572	158,858	16,512	61.2	0.0794	1,310	19,262	0.121
1979	29,132	199,925	19,469	67.8	0.1078	2,100	27,032	0.135
1980	36,380	270,453	26,561	75.5	0.1136	3,017	33,363	0.123

(cont'd)

TABLE A6a (cont'd)

Year	(V) (from Table A6) (III)+(IV) ($M)	(VI) (from Table A6) (I)+(II) ($M)	(VIII) Nominal* Financial Assets ($M)	(IX) Deflator for GDP, Business Sector (P)**	(X) dP/P	(XI) (VIII)*(X) ($M)	(XII) (V)-(XI) ($M)	(XIII) Total Return on Capital Before Tax, Adjusted for Capital Loss in Financial Assets (XII)/(VI)
1981	37,890	325,054	30,921	81.5	0.0795	2,457	35,433	0.109
1982	38,849	357,265	37,465	88.4	0.0847	3,172	35,677	0.100
1983	45,318	377,619	40,216	93.3	0.0554	2,229	43,089	0.114
1984	54,277	420,017	39,274	96.7	0.0364	1,431	52,846	0.126
1985	58,493	454,301	53,323	98.7	0.0207	1,103	57,390	0.126
1986	54,799	574,883	58,677	100	0.0132	773	54,026	0.094
1987	62,458	631,391	60,191	104.8	0.0480	2,889	59,569	0.094
1988	70,139	758,208	73,357	109.3	0.0429	3,150	66,989	0.088
1989	67,850	728,314	78,973	113.8	0.0412	3,251	64,599	0.089
1990	59,546	776,315	86,643	116.7	0.0255	2,208	57,338	0.074
1991	51,273	710,204	89,428	118.8	0.0180	1,609	49,664	0.070
1992	45,624	753,328	84,879	118.9	0.0008	71	45,553	0.060
1993	51,612	746,813	90,838	119.7	0.0067	611	51,001	0.068
1994	64,132	920,378	93,517	121	0.0109	1,016	63,116	0.069
						Average (1962-1994):		**0.093**
						Average (1976-1993):		**0.100**
						Average (1962-1987):		**0.099**
						Average (1962-1993):		**0.094**

Notes: * Financial assets on which capital loss due to inflation is assumed to accrue are: currency and bank deposits, deposits at other institutions, consumer credits, other loans, Canada and other short-term papers, mortgages and Canada, provincial, municipal and other bonds. Figures are reported for the beginning of the year.

** To estimate the inflation rate, we wish to use a price index as close as possible to the price index for value-added of nonfinancial corporations. We use the deflator for GDP originating in the business sector.

Table A7

Capital Loss on Financial Assets, U.S. Nonfinancial Corporations

Year	(I) Liquid Assets ($B)	(II) Foreign Deposits ($B)	(III) Consumer Credit ($B)	(IV) (I)-(II)+(III)* ($B)	(V) Deflator for Non-farm Business Less Housing**	(VI) Rate of Changes of (V)	(VII) (IV)*(VI) ($B)
1954	48.4	0.2	7.7		23.1		
1955	53.4	0.1	8.3	55.9	24.3	0.052	2.90
1956	48.9	0.1	8.6	61.6	25.1	0.033	2.03
1957	48.5	0.1	8.7	57.4	26	0.036	2.06
1958	51.0	0.1	8.8	57.1	26.2	0.008	0.44
1959	56.2	0.1	10.1	59.7	27.1	0.034	2.05
1960	51.4	0.1	9.6	66.2	27.5	0.015	0.98
1961	54.8	0.2	9.6	60.9	27.6	0.004	0.22
1962	57.9	0.8	10.4	64.2	28.2	0.022	1.40
1963	61.3	0.7	11.3	67.5	28.5	0.011	0.72
1964	61.7	1.1	12.3	71.9	28.9	0.014	1.01
1965	63.2	0.8	13.2	72.9	29.5	0.021	1.51
1966	61.3	0.9	13.4	75.6	30.5	0.034	2.56
1967	63.1	1.1	13.7	73.8	31.5	0.033	2.42
1968	68.6	1.6	13.8	75.7	32.9	0.044	3.36
1969	69.0	1.2	13.9	80.8	34.5	0.049	3.93
1970	69.5	0.8	14.5	81.7	36	0.043	3.55
1971	78.8	1.2	17.0	83.2	37.8	0.050	4.16
1972	88.0	2.2	17.7	94.6	39.1	0.034	3.25
1973	101.0	3.3	19.2	103.5	40.9	0.046	4.76
1974	105.4	4.9	20.3	116.9	45.2	0.105	12.29
1975	125.2	5.8	21.2	120.8	49.9	0.104	12.56
1976	139.8	7.4	23.5	140.6	53	0.062	8.73
1977	143.6	8.7	24.4	155.9	56.6	0.068	10.59

(cont'd)

TABLE A7 (cont'd)

Year	(I) Liquid Assets ($B)	(II) Foreign Deposits ($B)	(III) Consumer Credit ($B)	(IV) (I)-(II)+(III)* ($B)	(V) Deflator for Non-farm Business Less Housing**	(VI) Rate of Changes of (V)	(VII) (IV)*(VI) ($B)
1978	162.3	16.7	26.5	159.3	60.9	0.076	12.10
1979	170.8	21.8	28.3	172.1	66.4	0.090	15.54
1980	196.5	24.6	29.4	177.3	73.3	0.104	18.42
1981	220.4	23.0	30.3	201.3	80.7	0.101	20.32
1982	277.7	31.5	30.8	227.7	85.6	0.061	13.83
1983	415.7	125.4	35.4	277.0	88.9	0.039	10.68
1984	459.4	123.4	38.4	325.7	92	0.035	11.36
1985	508.1	134.1	42.5	374.4	95.3	0.036	13.43
1986	594.5	162.4	47.0	416.5	97.5	0.023	9.61
1987	643.0	174.4	54.0	479.1	100	0.026	12.28
1988	673.6	188.5	60.9	522.6	103.5	0.035	18.29
1989	740.5	236.6	63.8	546.0	107.9	0.043	23.21
1990	782.5	277.3	67.1	567.7	112.4	0.042	23.68
1991	801.2	268.0	63.0	572.3	116.6	0.037	21.38
1992	811.1	259.6	65.4	596.2	119.2	0.022	13.29
1993	812.8	258.3	80.4	616.9	121.5	0.019	11.90
						Average:	8.64

Notes: * Nominal Financial Assets. Defined as total liquid assets less foreign deposits plus consumer credits. (Balance Sheets for the U.S. Economy 1945-1994, Non-farm, Nonfinancial Corporate Business, pp. 32-37, row 9 - row 15 + row 21, shifted one year to give the initial rather than ending value for the year.

** Deflator for GDP for non-farm business less housing, National Income and Products Accounts, Table 7.14, row 4.

TABLE A8

TOTAL RATE OF RETURN ON CAPITAL BEFORE TAX, U.S. NONFINANCIAL CORPORATIONS

Year	(I)[a] Corporate Profit Before Tax with CCAdj and IVA ($B)	(II)[b] Monetary Interest Paid ($B)	(III) Capital Loss on Financial Assets Due to Inflation ($B)	(IV) (I)+(II)-(III) ($B)	(V)[c] Market Value of Corporations ($B)	(VI) Total Return on Capital Before Tax (IV)/(V)
1955	40.4	4.2	2.904	41.696	317	0.132
1956	38.5	4.8	2.028	41.272	381	0.108
1957	37.5	5.5	2.058	40.942	389	0.105
1958	38.2	6.0	0.439	43.761	376	0.116
1959	42.6	6.8	2.051	47.349	479	0.099
1960	40.0	7.6	0.977	46.623	509	0.092
1961	40.8	8.1	0.221	48.679	512	0.095
1962	48.2	9.1	1.396	55.904	596	0.094
1963	53.8	10.1	0.718	63.182	568	0.111
1964	60.0	11.0	1.009	69.991	646	0.108
1965	70.3	12.1	1.513	80.887	740	0.109
1966	74.9	14.4	2.563	86.737	814	0.107
1967	71.8	16.6	2.420	85.980	781	0.110
1968	76.0	19.5	3.364	92.136	948	0.097
1969	71.3	25.4	3.929	92.771	1,069	0.087
1970	57.1	31.2	3.552	84.748	982	0.086
1971	67.2	32.2	4.160	95.240	1,014	0.094
1972	77.0	34.8	3.253	108.547	1,158	0.094
1973	83.6	44.1	4.765	122.935	1,302	0.094
1974	70.6	56.2	12.290	114.510	1,194	0.096
1975	91.5	56.7	12.561	135.639	1,053	0.129
1976	111.5	57.7	8.735	160.465	1,251	0.128
1977	132.0	65.1	10.589	186.511	1,522	0.123

(cont'd)

TABLE A8 (cont'd)

Year	(I)[a] Corporate Profit Before Tax with CCAdj and IVA ($B)	(II)[b] Monetary Interest Paid ($B)	(III) Capital Loss on Financial Assets Due to Inflation ($B)	(IV) (I)+(II)-(III) ($B)	(V)[c] Market Value of Corporations ($B)	(VI) Total Return on Capital Before Tax (IV)/(V)
1978	146.1	79.8	12.102	213.798	1,505	0.142
1979	138.1	104.2	15.543	226.757	1,639	0.138
1980	120.7	134.4	18.424	236.676	1,894	0.125
1981	136.9	173.8	20.322	290.378	2,324	0.125
1982	111.5	188.3	13.826	285.974	2,345	0.122
1983	159.9	178.9	10.679	328.121	2,565	0.128
1984	214.3	207.6	11.357	410.543	2,942	0.140
1985	221.4	227.7	13.430	435.670	3,080	0.141
1986	203.8	240.4	9.615	434.585	3,624	0.120
1987	244.2	251.8	12.285	483.715	4,243	0.114
1988	274.4	286.1	18.291	542.209	4,613	0.118
1989	255.2	344.6	23.212	576.588	5,158	0.112
1990	256.4	354.5	23.676	587.224	6,081	0.097
1991	249.2	342.3	21.385	570.115	6,057	0.094
1992	276.6	307.2	13.294	570.506	7,179	0.079
1993	330.9	298.6	11.903	617.597	7,734	0.080
					Average (1955-1993):	**0.110**
					Average (1956-1993):	**0.109**
					Average (1976-1993):	**0.118**
					Average (1962-1993):	**0.111**

Notes: CCAdj: Capital Consumption Adjustment.
IVA: Inventory Valuation Adjustment
[a] National Income and Product Accounts, Table 1.16, line 27.
[b] National Income and Product Accounts, Table 8.17, line 7.
[c] Flow of Funds, Balance Sheet for the U.S. Economy, September 20, 1994, pp. 33-37, Total Liabilities (line 30) - Trade Debt (line 39) + Market Value of Equity (line 45).

ENDNOTES

1 It is forward looking in the sense that, since capital goods last for a number of periods, management must look forward to evaluate the cost of using them while they last, especially if the capital is not malleable once it is installed. If it is fully malleable, then it can be adjusted without cost to new relative prices in every period, so the managers need not look beyond the current period in designing the capital structure of the firm.

2 A little more than hope by analysts is involved here. Presumably, in assessing the future cost involved in maintaining a specific capital good, the manager summarizes his or her perception of various uncertain elements into a probability distribution and takes the expected value of the cost over this distribution. By averaging the *ex post* realization of the cost across firms and over time, analysts would be performing a similar operation though the information on which the expectations are conditioned may not be the same. If the *ex ante* estimates of the cost of capital used by managers in their decisions and the *ex post* measurement by analysts are substantially different from each other, even when they are averaged both across firms and over a fairly long period of time, then the presumption must be either that we are dealing with a very unstable system or there is something unusual about the process managers use to form their anticipations. To deal with such problems, we must have direct observations of managers' expectations in addition to *ex post* measurements of costs.

3 At the conference on which this volume is based, it was suggested that the markup factor should apply to the labour cost and capital cost net of depreciation. The markup rule is, in a sense, arbitrary and does not result from a rational optimization process, so what is reasonable is, in the final analysis, an empirical question. It may be pointed out, however, that a markup rule which excludes depreciation from the base is considerably more complex than equation (2). Furthermore, if the production function explains the value-added gross of depreciation and it is approximately Cobb-Douglas, then it is the markup on cost gross of depreciation that would be close to a constant fraction of the value-added measure of output.

4 This is so because we have interpreted the $\delta P_k K$ as the economic depreciation on all capital at replacement cost. This means that the depreciation of capital goods is based on their replacement costs, and the cost of inventory sold is also valued at its replacement cost.

5 This assertion is not quite true. Under our assumption, the total corporate profit tax collected by the authority is given by:

$$\tau^c \frac{\mu - 1}{\mu} P_x X + \frac{\tau^c (1 - z)}{1 - \tau^c} (\rho + \delta) P_k K = T^c \quad \text{(a)}$$

while the total profit after tax plus the depreciation allowance is given by:

$$(1 - \tau^c) \frac{\mu - 1}{\mu} P_x X + (\rho + \delta) P_x X = B + Dep \quad \text{(b)}$$

where B and *Dep* are profits after tax and the depreciation allowance reported to the tax authority. T^c, B and *Dep* are available from the tax data, and τ^c and z are computable from the tax codes. Hence, equations (a) and (b) above may be considered as two equations in two unknowns

$$\frac{\mu - 1}{\mu} P_x X \text{ and } (\rho + \delta) P_k K$$

and may be solved for these two quantities. In practice, however, this is an extraordinarily complex task because many detailed provisions of the corporate profit tax codes must be taken account of and data adjusted accordingly, and cyclical deviations of variables from their normal level must be reduced as much as possible. I may note that, whatever it may be worth, my attempt to carry out this program in the mid-1970s for the United States suggested that the value of μ was between 1.02 and 1.04. This does not mean, of course, that we can say anything about the value of μ for other countries. (This note by Ando.)

6 If all capital is malleable, we may rely on the reproduction cost of capital for its value since the putty content of capital is well defined, and it can be fully utilized as a component of a new capital good. Since, however, we believe that the nature of capital, especially of capital equipment, is putty-clay, the reproduction cost of capital is not well defined. We, therefore, believe that the only sensible measure of the value of capital to be used as the denominator of the rate of return must be the market value of capital. Note, however, that we have no alternative but to use a measure of depreciation on a reproduction cost basis (usually computed by adjusting the standard accounting records of depreciation for changes in capital goods prices) on the left-hand side of equation (5).

7 The relationship in equation (8) is often expressed in nominal terms rather than in real terms. Provided that the expectation of the inflation rate incorporated into interest rates and the one underlying the exchange rate expectation are the same, the formulations of equation (8), in real and nominal terms, are equivalent to each other.

8 *Currency Forecasters' Digest.*

9 Ando et al. (1974) and Ando (1976).

10 Most factors that may make estimation of the net income stream and discount factor complex are such that they can be introduced to affect either the income stream or the discount factor and, for most purposes, the results are equivalent. Here, however, we must make sure that we introduce them into our calculations in such a way that the discount factor applicable to the income generated by older capital is the same as the one applicable to the income generated by new capital.

11 Another reason for our choice was that, given the results reported in Ando and Auerbach (1988b, 1990), the fact that the Nikkei consolidated data file did not go back much earlier than 1980 did not seem important. Unfortunately, we found that the number of firms reported in the consolidated accounts file was quite small until 1984, and we had to start our analysis in 1985. Furthermore, some information was available in the standard Nikkei-Needs data file but not in the consolidated accounts file, forcing us to make some additional approximations. Ideally, we should have obtained both the standard data file and the consolidated accounts file, but the price charged by Nikkei for them and our budgets were not compatible with such an arrangement.

12 The unusual movement of *DMV* for the Flow of Funds accounts in the United States since 1989 is largely due to the reported movement of the value of land, which declined from $940 billion in 1989 to a mere $90 billion in 1993. This dramatic movement of the value of land has nothing to do with reality, but is simply due to the disappearance of the data source on which the Flow of Funds section at the Federal Reserve Board depended, and to the decision by the section to follow a specific procedure to deal with this problem which turned out to generate an unreasonable result after the fact. We believe that letting the value of land increase in proportion to, for example, the nominal value added measure of output of the nonfinancial corporate sector since 1989 would at least avoid the major distortion of the accounts and is preferable to the current procedure until an alternative source of the required information is found.

13 This is especially true when we work with the market measure of the rate of return rather than with the accounting measure. See the next section.

14 This may not be true in the Japanese case, as discussed below.

15 The size of *DMV*, which can be as large as 40 percent of *NWM* in some periods, cannot be accounted for by potential biases in the estimate of the value of financial instruments. Suppose that 50 percent of *NWM* is in long-term liabilities subject to the bias, and it is underestimated by as much as 50 percent due to the past movement of the long-term interest rate. This very extreme assumption would create *DMV* of some 25 percent of *NWM*.

16 Special tabulations and helpful information on the nature of the data were provided by Patrick O'Hagan of the National Accounts and Environmental Division at Statistics Canada.

17 These words are used in very specific senses. Total receipts here consist of operating surplus (not sales) plus income from properties not used in production and the benefits from casualty insurance policies. This is clearly different from the value added by enterprises. Outlays are the distribution of this concept of receipts among various items.

18 While the ratios calculated from the Nikkei file of consolidated accounts are quite similar to the ones reported by the Tokyo Stock Exchange, this cannot be considered independent information since companies in the Nikkei file are all listed on the Tokyo Stock Exchange.

19 In the balance sheets in the National Accounts of Japan, the market valuation discrepancy is designated as "Shomi Shisan," which can be literally translated as "True Net Assets." While definitions and names are arbitrary, in this instance, the designation used suggests that the original designers of these balance sheets had a serious misconception of what this item represented.

20 In the process of estimating the net earnings of companies in their individual accounts, we have estimated the value of the net stock of reproducible tangible capital at its reproduction cost as part of estimating depreciation at its reproduction cost. We then computed the ratio of the value of land to the value of reproducible tangible assets at reproduction cost for all companies in the Nikkei file of consolidated accounts and increased the value of land so this ratio matched the corresponding ratios in the National Accounts.

21 For most countries, dividends are a very stable quantity over time.

22 We wonder if very accurate estimates of these quantities, retained earnings, dividends, interest payments, corporate profit tax liabilities, etc. could not be directly available from tax records. For the United States, records at the Internal Revenue Service are the most important source of data for the income side of the corporate sector in the National Accounts.

23 One of us studied the value of land belonging to households and concluded that the aggregate estimate reported by the National Accounts seems reasonably accurate. See Hayashi et al. (1989). By way of contrast, for the United States, the balance sheet for nonfinancial corporations records the ratio of the market value of land to the reproduction cost of reproducible tangible assets plus financial assets less trade credits to be roughly 15 percent in 1989, the last year for which a reasonably reliable estimate of the value of land is available.

24 We do not seem to know the division of the total stock of reproducible tangible capital into equipment and structures for nonfinancial corporations. For the country as a whole and excluding residential structures, the division is roughly 70 percent structures and 30 percent

equipment. This is probably weighted too much toward structures when it is applied to the private sector, since we assume that most government capital is structures. Economic Planning Agency, (1994): p. 410.

25 See equations (11) and (11a) and the analysis following them.

26 Note that the value of land has also been adjusted up as described in note 5 of Table 1.

27 Ando and Auerbach (1990, Table XI) estimated that the adjusted accounting rate of return for Japanese firms may be biased down due to the implicit real appreciation of the land value by as much as 4 percent or more between 1976 and 1988. This is probably an exaggeration because the period covered had a very strong upward trend in the real price of land. As a working hypothesis, we suggest that the bias may be around 2 percentage points. Although the market measure of the rate of return should reflect the unrealized capital gains on land and, therefore, should not be biased due to this problem, it is hard to design a reasonable way to handle the dramatic large negative returns suffered by equity shareholders in the early 1990s, and we leave the analysis of this problem for a later occasion when we will have seen the final outcome for the pattern of the Japanese land price and of the equity value after the bubble and its subsequent burst.

ACKNOWLEDGMENTS

WE ARE GREATLY INDEBTED TO STATISTICS CANADA, especially to Mr. Patrick O'Hagan of the National Accounts and Environment Division for providing us with critical unpublished data and guiding us in their interpretation, and to Professor Jack M. Mintz of the University of Toronto for providing us with a useful set of written comments on the earlier version of this paper.

BIBLIOGRAPHY

Ando, Albert. "On the Definition of Cost of Capital for Investment Under Inflation When Corporate Profit Tax is Present." Unpublished note, Department of Economics, University of Pennsylvania, 1976.

Ando, Albert and Alan J. Auerbach. "The Corporate Cost of Capital in Japan and the United States: A Comparison." In *Government Policy Towards Industry in the United States and Japan*. Edited by John Shoven. London and New York: Cambridge University Press, 1988a.

——. "The Cost of Capital in the United States and Japan: A Comparison." *Journal of the Japanese and International Economies*. Vol. 2, (1988b): 135-158.

——. "The Cost of Capital in Japan: Recent Evidence and Further Results." *Journal of the Japanese and International Economies*. Vol. 4, (1990): 323-350.

Ando, Albert, Franco Modigliani, Robert Rasche and Stephen J. Turnovsky. "On the Role of Expectations of Price and Technological Change in an Investment Function." *International Economic Review*. Vol. 15, (1974): 384-414.

Collins, Julie H. and Douglas A. Shackelford. "Corporate Domicile and Average Effective Tax Rates: The Case of Canada, Japan, the United Kingdom and the United States." *International Tax and Public Finance*. 2, (1995): 55-84.

Currency Forecasters' Digest. Monthly publication, P.O. Box 139, Gedney Station, White Plains, NY 10605, Fax (914) 949-0303.

Economic Planning Agency. *Annual Report on National Accounts*. 1994.

Hayashi, Fumio, Albert Ando and Richard Ferris. "Life Cycle and Bequest Savings." In *Saving Behavior, Investment and Rate of Return on Capital in the United Sates and Japan: Comparative Analysis and Perspectives into 1990's*. Vol. 2, No. 1. Tokyo: National Institute for Research Advancement, 1989.

Duanjie Chen
International Centre For Tax Studies
University of Toronto

& *Kenneth J. McKenzie*
Department of Economics
University of Calgary

4

The Impact of Taxation on Capital Markets: An International Comparison of Effective Tax Rates on Capital

INTRODUCTION

THIS PAPER EXAMINES THE POTENTIAL IMPACT OF TAXATION on the accumulation of physical capital by calculating marginal effective tax rates (METRs) on capital for Canada and selected other countries. The METR on capital is a summary measure of the distortion in the return to capital caused by the imposition of personal and corporate taxes on capital. We also investigate the implications of risk and irreversibility for the impact of taxation on investment. Measuring the size of the distortion caused by the tax system reveals some insights into the potential impact of taxation on capital accumulation and, therefore, on economic growth.

The paper investigates just one aspect of the process linking taxation to growth. The underlying motivation is that the "transmission mechanism" by which the tax system may affect economic growth and productivity is its impact on investment in capital. Personal and corporate taxes on capital can drive a wedge between the gross and net-of-tax rates of return to capital. The size of this wedge is measured by the METR on capital. Neoclassical economic theory and its extensions suggest that this will, in turn, lead to a reduction in investment and capital accumulation, as well as to the introduction of intersectoral and interjurisdictional distortions to the extent that METRs vary by industry and location. These distortions can lead to an inefficient amount of capital employed in the economy and to an inefficient allocation of capital across assets and jurisdictions, potentially impeding economic growth and productivity.

Recently, much of the theoretical research on economic growth has focused on the role of externalities in technology development, and human and physical capital accumulation within the context of endogenous growth models.[1] In most of these models, taxes on capital are found to be growth reducing (see Milesi-Ferretti and Roubini, 1995). Despite this, empirical investigations have not been very successful in uncovering a statistically and economically significant relationship between tax rates and growth.

Yet there is some compelling "indirect" evidence that taxes affect growth, and many studies have found a relationship between capital accumulation and growth. For example, De Long and Summers (1991) used disaggregated investment data for several countries and found that, from 1960 to 1985, each extra percent of gross domestic product (GDP) investment in equipment was associated with an increase in GDP growth of one third of a percentage point per year. This is a very strong association which the authors suggest is causal.

Moreover, recent empirical evidence, such as Auerbach and Hassett (1992), Cummins and Hassett (1992) and Cummins et al. (1995), also based on disaggregated data, suggests that taxes on capital can have a significant impact on investment. Some of these results suggest that the elasticity of investment with respect to tax-driven changes in the user cost of capital may be as high as unity. While such a strong relationship is at odds with some previous work that investigated the relationship between the user cost of capital and investment (most of which used aggregate data), the fact that this recent work is based on firm-level data suggests that perhaps prices really do matter.[2]

Thus, although the statistical importance of capital taxes for growth has not been established, there is good theoretical reason that a relationship exists. Moreover, there is evidence linking capital accumulation to growth, and taxes to capital accumulation. This, we think, provides some important indirect empirical support for the view that taxes may affect growth through their impact on capital accumulation.

In this paper, we include an outline of the basic methodology used to calculate METRs followed by an international comparison of METRs among the G7 countries – Canada, United States, United Kingdom, Germany, Japan, France and Italy – as well as Mexico and Hong Kong. Then, we undertake an intersectoral and interprovincial comparison of METRs for Canada and consider the implications of risk and irreversibility for the measurement of METRs. The paper concludes with a summary of the key results and policy implications.

BASIC METHODOLOGY

THE METHODOLOGY EMPLOYED TO INVESTIGATE the potential impact of taxation on capital accumulation needs to be explained. While the basic approach is well established, various modifications are required to facilitate an international comparison and incorporate risk and irreversibility. Although a formal derivation based on neoclassical investment theory is possible, this paper follows a more intuitive approach to provide a basic understanding of the methodology to a broader audience.[3]

To consider how taxes may impinge on capital investment decisions, it is useful to begin by considering an economy without any taxes at all. Moreover, presume for the moment that all the funds for investment in capital are provided by domestic savers. In such an economy, firms invest in projects which generate a rate of return up to and in excess of a "hurdle" rate required by the financial market. This hurdle rate reflects the real (inflation adjusted), net-of-depreciation rate of return that investors (debt and equity holders) could earn in the next best alternative investment opportunity with similar characteristics.[4] If the proportion of investment financed by debt is β, the expected rate of inflation is π, the nominal interest rate on debt is I and the nominal required rate of return on equity is ρ, then the hurdle rate of return is a weighted average of the required rate of return on debt and equity, or $R=\beta I+(1-\beta)\rho - \pi$.[5]

If investment is continuously divisible and the marginal revenue product of capital (the increment to revenue arising from investing in one more unit of capital) eventually declines as the amount of capital employed increases, value-maximizing firms will invest in capital up to the point where the rate of return on the last unit of capital employed is equal to the real opportunity cost of the funds tied up in capital R, plus the loss in the value of the capital due to economic depreciation δ. If we denote the relative price of a unit of capital with respect to output by q, the expression $q(R+\delta)$ is referred to as the cost of capital. Denoting the marginal revenue product of capital by $MRP_K(K)$, the equilibrium condition is $MRP_K(K)=q(R+\delta)$, where capital is accumulated up to the point that the marginal unit breaks even in the sense that it earns just enough to cover the cost of capital.[6] This condition implicitly determines the demand for capital by domestic firms as a function of the rate of return on capital net of depreciation R.

We are now in a position to see how domestic taxes on capital, levied on either or both the suppliers and demanders of capital, can affect capital accumulation when funds are provided by domestic savers. Investors are concerned about the rate of return on their capital, net of both corporate and personal taxes. Consider first the imposition of personal taxes on interest income and on the return to equity. Denoting by m the personal tax rate imposed on nominal interest income, and by c the effective tax rate on equity, the weighted average net-of-personal tax real hurdle rate of return becomes $R^n=\beta I(1-m)+(1-\beta)\rho(1-c)-\pi$. In capital market equilibrium, in the absence of risk and capital market imperfections other than taxes, the after-tax rate of return on equity must equal the after-tax rate of return on debt. Thus, $I(1-m)=\rho(1-c)$ which implies that $\rho=I(1-m)/(1-c)$ in which case $R^n=I(1-m)-\pi$.

The imposition of corporate taxes affects investment by altering the cost of capital. There are several ways in which this can occur, depending on the details of the tax system. A somewhat stylized representation follows; details will vary by country.[7] As discussed above, firms accumulate capital up to the point where the rate of return generated by the last unit of capital is just equal to the cost of capital. To yield R^n after personal taxes, the marginal investment must earn $R=\beta I+(1-\beta)\rho - \pi$ after corporate taxes (and net of depreciation). R^g is the gross-of-corporate tax, net-of-depreciation rate of return required to yield R after corporate taxes. Treating capital as the numeraire, $R^g=MRP_K/q-\delta$. R^g will reflect various provisions of the corporate tax system. For example, the deductibility of nominal debt interest expenses for corporate income tax purposes lowers the nominal cost of debt finance to $I(1-u)$, where u is the statutory corporate income tax rate. Nominal interest deductibility lowers the cost of capital to the firm by reducing the weighted average opportunity cost of finance to $R^f=\beta I(1-u)+(1-\beta)\rho$.[8] The cost of capital is also lowered by the reduction in the effective purchase price of capital due to the presence of tax depreciation allowances and investment tax credits (ITCs). A company that is provided with an ITC at the rate ϕ and annual depreciation allowances that generate a reduction in taxes of uA in present value terms, A being the present value of the tax depreciation allowances on one dollar of capital,[9] faces an effective purchase price of capital that is lowered by the amount $\phi+uA$ per dollar. Recognizing that the incremental revenue generated by an additional unit of capital is taxed at the statutory tax rate, leaving $MRP_K(1-u)$ after taxes, the firm's value maximization condition becomes $MRP_K(1-u)=(R^f+\delta-\pi)(1-\phi-uA)$, where the after tax, marginal revenue product of capital is equal to its gross-of-depreciation after-tax user cost. Using this equilibrium condition, and recalling the definition of R^g above, the gross-of-corporate tax, net-of-depreciation rate of return on a marginal unit of capital is:

$$R^g = (R^f + \delta - \pi)\left[\frac{1 - \phi - uA}{1 - u}\right] - \delta \tag{1}$$

Equation (1) reflects the imposition of a corporate income tax. Other types of taxes may be levied on the capital as well. For example, capital may be subject to a sales or property transfer tax, special capital levies may apply, as may property taxes. Some jurisdictions also levy a gross receipts tax. Equation (1) may be modified to take all these types of taxes into account. For example, if the effective sales or property transfer tax rate is t_m the effective capital tax rate is t_c, the effective property tax rate is t_p and the gross receipts tax rate is t_g, then R^g becomes:[10]

$$R^g = (1 + t_m)(R^f + \delta - \pi)\left[\frac{1 - \phi - uA + t_c(1-u)/(\alpha + R^f + \pi)}{(1-u)(1-t_g)}\right] + \frac{t_p}{1 - t_g} - \delta \tag{2}$$

The imposition of both personal and corporate taxes affects the level of investment in the economy by driving a wedge between the after-tax rate of return required by savers (R^n) and the before-tax rate of return generated by firms (R^g). The METR on capital is a summary measure of the distortion to the return to capital caused by the imposition of the various taxes levied on capital. It is defined as the hypothetical rate of tax τ which, if applied to the gross-of-tax rate of return R^g, would yield the net-of-tax rate of return R^n. The METR thus solves $R^g(1-\tau)= R^n$ giving:

$$\tau = \frac{R^g - R^n}{R^g} \tag{3}$$

A METR may be computed using the above expressions for R^g and R^n for various types of capital in different countries, each imposing different tax systems and facing different interest rates, economic depreciation rates, inflation rates, etc. It is a convenient summary measure which allows users to evaluate and compare a diverse set of international corporate and personal tax systems in an economically meaningful way. Comparing the METRs across jurisdictions gives some insight into the potential impact of tax systems on the incentive to invest in capital. Specifically, the higher the METR, the greater the disincentive to invest in a particular type of capital in a particular jurisdiction. It should be noted that, if tax incentives are generous enough, METRs can also be negative, i.e., R^g can be less than R^n, in which case the tax system provides a subsidy to investment. If the METR is zero, the tax system is said to be neutral with respect to investment, i.e., taxes do not impinge on the investment decision.

The presentation to this point has assumed that capital for domestic investment is provided by domestic savers. If capital is provided by foreign investors, the analysis must be modified slightly. In terms of the above framework, the expressions defining the net-of-tax rate of return R^n and the after-tax opportunity cost of finance R^f must be altered to account for the presence of foreign investors. For example, if we presume that the investor is a multinational corporation from another country, the relevant cost of finance becomes:

$$R^{f'} = [\beta' I'(1 - u') + (1 - \beta')\rho'] \frac{1 - \gamma}{1 - x} + \gamma [I(1 - u) - \pi + \pi'] \qquad (4)$$

where β' is the debt-to-asset ratio in the home country of the multinational, I' is the cost of debt in the home country, u' is the statutory corporate income tax rate in the home country, ρ' is the cost of equity in the home country, γ is the proportion of funds borrowed within the host country, x is the weighted average withholding tax rate in the host country, I is the cost of debt in the host country, u is the statutory corporate income tax rate in the host country, π' is the inflation rate in the home country and π is the inflation rate in the host country. Equation (4) states that the cost of finance to a foreign multinational investor is the weighted average cost of funds raised in the home and host countries. The former is the weighted average cost of financing at home net of withholding taxes payable in the host country, and the latter is the after-tax cost of debt in the host country adjusted by the difference in inflation rates between the home and host countries.[11] In the case of investments undertaken by multinationals, R^f in equations (1) and (2) is replaced with the $R^{f'}$ in equation (4), and the inflation rate π used in equations (1) and (2) is replaced with π'.

Similarly, the net-of-tax rate of return required by a foreign multinational investor is:

$$R^{f'} = [\beta' I'(1 - u') + (1 - \beta I)\rho' - \pi'][(1 - \gamma) + \gamma(1 - \pi)] \qquad (5)$$

This is the net-of-tax rate of return on capital required by the suppliers of capital, including the multinational and its creditors in the host country.

Another important consideration which has been ignored in the above discussion is the implications of risk for the measurement of METRs. This has been the subject of numerous studies, many of which stress the importance of distinguishing between different sources of risk. For example, Gordon (1985), Bulow and Summers (1984) and Gordon and Wilson (1989) made the distinction between *capital risk* and *income risk*. Income risk refers to uncertainty regarding future net revenues, arising from the stochastic movement of output or current input prices. Capital risk refers to uncertainty regarding the economic rate of depreciation due to stochastic replacement prices for capital or physical rates of depreciation. Regardless of whether it is income or capital risk, risk has important implications for the size of the distortion caused by the tax system.

Consider income risk first. If the tax system grants full loss offsets, where companies effectively receive a full refund for taxable losses as they are incurred – an assumption maintained throughout the paper – the tax liability of the firm fluctuates perfectly with its income.[12] The government, therefore, shares equally in both the profits and losses of the company. In other words, the government shares in 100u percent of the profits and absorbs 100u percent of the income risk. The implication is that the cost of bearing income risk is, implicitly, fully deducted under a full loss offset tax system, and no additional distortions are introduced due to the presence of income risk, i.e., the METR on an income risky investment is the same as an otherwise identical riskless investment.

The implications of capital risk are very different. In most countries, including those considered in this paper, tax depreciation allowances are based on the *ex ante* or original purchase price of the asset with no adjustment for subsequent changes in the market value. This means that tax depreciation allowances do not fluctuate with unanticipated changes in the replacement value of capital, which is reflected in the economic rate of depreciation. The implication is that the tax system does not deduct the full opportunity cost of bearing capital risk. The presence of capital risk may be introduced into the above framework by adding a *systematic* capital risk premium h^c to the economic depreciation rate.[13] The sum $\delta+h^c$ is referred to as the risk-adjusted economic rate of depreciation. Rather than equation (2), the expression for R^g then becomes:

$$R^g = (1 + t_m)(R^f + \delta + h^c - \pi)\left[\frac{1 - \phi - uA + t_c(1 - u)/(\alpha + R^f + \pi)}{(1 - u)(1 - t_g)}\right] + \frac{t_p}{1 - t_g} - (\delta + h^c) \qquad (6)$$

As shown by Jog and Mintz (1989) and McKenzie and Mintz (1993), the presence of capital risk typically increases the METR on capital due to the failure of most tax systems to account for the capital risk premium in the tax depreciation rate. Thus, corporate tax systems tend to provide a disincentive to invest in capital risky assets. The implications of capital risk for the measurement of METRs are explored further below.

Another potentially important consideration which has been ignored in the above formulation is the implications of adjustment costs. The implicit assumption made above is that capital can be instantaneously adjusted to its optimal level. This is not likely to be the case in practice, as delivery lags, installation costs and imperfectly competitive capital markets give rise to costs associated with quickly adjusting the level of capital. Two types of adjustment costs have been considered in the effective tax rate literature. McKenzie (1993) explored the implications of the presence of continuous, convex adjustment costs for the neutrality of a corporate income tax system which relies on historic, or *ex ante*, depreciation allowances. Convex adjustment costs mean that the cost of installed capital increases at an increasing rate with the amount of capital employed. McKenzie (1993) showed that, in the simultaneous presence of risk and convex adjustment costs, the neutral tax depreciation rate – the tax depreciation rate that generates a METR of zero – will be stochastic.[14] The important implication is that, in the simultaneous presence of convex adjustment costs and risk, it is virtually impossible to design a neutral *ex ante* corporate tax system which relies on historic cost depreciation. Moreover, McKenzie (1993) showed that even when the tax system grants full loss offsets and, in contrast to the traditional case considered above, if convex adjustment costs exist, the presence of income risk does affect the METR. While a lack of data precludes METR calculations for investments which take place in this type of environment, it is nonetheless important to realize the implications of the presence of convex adjustment costs.

McKenzie (1994) considered a different type of adjustment costs. In this formulation adjustment costs are linear, as is implicitly assumed in the standard approach considered above, but investment is assumed to be irreversible in the sense that disinvestment can only occur slowly over time through depreciation, i.e., it is infinitely costly to adjust capital downward. The idea that many, if not most, types of investments are at least partly irreversible has become a focus of recent investment literature. If capital is valuable primarily in the use for which it was originally intended and/or it is very costly to reverse investment decisions or to convert capital to other uses, then the presence of different types of risk has important implications for how taxes may affect investment decisions. When capital is irreversible and there is capital and/or income risk, there are benefits to delaying capital investments which are not present when an investment is fully reversible. When this is the case, an investment can be thought of as a real option, where the decision to undertake the investment is analogous to exercising a financial call option. As discussed by McKenzie (1994), this idea can be incorporated into the framework established above by increasing the cost of capital to account for the opportunity cost of exercising the real investment option, i.e., the investment must earn an additional return to compensate for the fact that making the investment now precludes making it in the future when more will be known about the economic environment. Moreover, McKenzie (1994) illustrated that the distinction between capital and income risk discussed above plays an important role in the presence of irreversibility. Specifically, METRs are higher in the presence of both capital and income risk, even when there are full loss offsets. He also stressed another important distinction regarding the source of risk: distinguishing between *systematic* and *unsystematic* income and capital risk. The former reflects the correlation of the stochastic variable with the market while the latter reflects the idiosyncratic variance of the stochastic variable. Illustrative calculations showing the implications of risk and irreversibility for the measurement of METRs are presented below. To do this, R^g must be augmented as follows:

$$R^g = (1 + t_m)(R^f + \delta + h^c + H - \pi) \left[\frac{1 - \phi - uA + t_c(1 - u)/(\alpha + R^f + \pi)}{(1 - u)(1 - t_g)}\right] + \frac{t_p}{1 - t_g} - (\delta + h^c + H) \qquad (7)$$

where H is the opportunity cost of exercising the real investment option, which is a function of systematic capital and income risk (h^c, h^I) and unsystematic capital and income risk (σ^2_c and σ^2_I).[15]

Finally, the rate of return expressions presented above are for depreciable capital. Similar expressions can be developed for inventory capital and land. For inventories, the relevant expression for domestic investors is:

$$R^g = \frac{(1 + t_m)(R^f - \pi + u\pi\xi)}{(1 - u)(1 - t_g)} + t_c \qquad (8)$$

where t_m is the sales tax on inventory (if applicable), and $\xi = 1$ for first in, first out (FIFO) accounting method and 0 for last in, first out (LIFO).[16] For land, the relevant expression for domestic investors is:

$$R^g = \frac{(1 + t_m)(R^f - \pi)\,[1 + t_c(1 - u)/(R^f + \pi)]}{(1 - u)(1 - t_g)} + \frac{t_p}{1 - t_g} \qquad (9)$$

For international investors, the formulas are the same except that the real cost of finance should be the one relevant to the international investors, i.e., R^f should be replaced by $R^{f'}$.

International Comparison of METRs

In this section, the METRs for the G7 countries (Canada, United States, United Kingdom, Germany, Italy, France and Japan) as well as for Mexico and Hong Kong are discussed. Mexico is included due to its potentially close economic relationship with Canada under the North American Free Trade Agreement

(NAFTA). Hong Kong is included for comparative purposes. Only the manufacturing and services sectors are included in our broad international comparison as these are, by far, the largest targets of foreign direct investment. However, for Canada and the United States, we present calculations for eight industrial sectors. In each case, METRs are calculated for four broad asset categories – equipment, buildings, land and inventories – and then aggregated to form an overall, or aggregate, METR for each country.

The effective tax rates are calculated under what is called the open economy arbitrage assumption: capital is mobile in an open economy, and the required return to debt and equity is fixed by international financial markets. This implies that personal taxes levied on savings do not have a direct effect on domestic investment, but determine the proportion of that investment financed by foreigners. For all the countries, we present a set of calculations assuming that the marginal source of finance is the domestic investors. For Canada and the United States, we present an alternate set of calculations. For the United States, METRs are calculated under the assumption that the marginal investor is a Canadian multinational corporation.[17] Similarly, METRs are calculated for capital investment in Canada financed by a U.S. multinational. In this way, we can determine whether the tax systems in Canada and the United States provide an incentive for Canadian firms to invest at home rather than abroad. Similarly, by comparing the METRs of U.S. multinationals investing in Canada to the effective tax rate on domestic investment, we can determine whether U.S. investment in Canada is discouraged or encouraged relative to investment at home.

Before proceeding to a brief review of the statutory corporate tax treatment in the countries included in the study, a couple of caveats are in order. Although the basic methodology underlying the calculation of METRs is well accepted, as indicated above, different assumptions can be made regarding the country and tax status of the marginal investor. As such, different METR studies may have different results depending on the assumptions made in this regard. We employ an open economy arbitrage assumption, which seems the most appropriate given the open economy nature of most of the countries examined, particularly Canada.[18] Moreover, calculating METRs requires a great deal of aggregation. Differences in capital stock weights employed in different studies can also explain varying results. Many studies, for example, do not include inventories or land, both of which are included in this study. Finally, a related issue concerns the appropriate tax parameters used in the calculations. Effective tax rate calculations condense extremely complicated tax codes into a few key parameters. Studies may differ in the assumptions regarding the values of these parameters.

An Overview of the Statutory Tax Treatment

Table 1 presents a summary of some key aspects of the tax codes for the nine countries included in our study. Key elements are discussed below.

TABLE 1

CORPORATE TAX PROVISIONS, 1995

	Canada	United States	United Kingdom	Germany	France	Italy	Japan	Mexico	Hong Kong
General corporate income tax (CIT) rates									
National	29.12%	36%	33%	48.38%	33-1/3%	36%	37.5%	34%	16.5%
Local	8.9-17%	to 12%	No	5-25%	No	16.2%	see text	No	No
Investment allowance									
Structure	10% Atl	No	No	No	No	No	No	No	20%
Machinery	10% Atl	No	No	No	No	No	No	No	60%
Tax depreciation rate									
Manufacturing									
Structure	8% DB	32 year	4% SL	4% SL	5% SL	3% SL	4% SL	5% SL	4% SL
Machinery	36% DB	5-7 year	25% DB	15% SL	15% SL	13% SL	10% SL	10% SL	4% SL
Services									
Structure	11% DB	32 year	4% SL	4% SL	5% SL	3% SL	4% SL	5% SL	4% SL
Machinery	33% DB	5-7 year	25% DB	15% SL	15% SL	13% SL	10% SL	10% SL	4% SL
Dividend withholding tax									
To Canada		10%	10%	15%	15%	15%	10%	No	No
To United States	10%		10%	5%	15%	10%	10%	No	No

(cont'd)

Table 1 (cont'd)

	Canada	United States	United Kingdom	Germany	France	Italy	Japan	Mexico	Hong Kong
Property tax									
Structure	Yes	Yes	Yes	0.6%	Yes	0.4-0.6%	1.7%	Yes	Yes
Machinery	Yes/No	Yes/No	No	No	No	No	1.4%	No	No
Land	Yes	Yes	Yes	0.6%	Yes	0.4-0.6%	2.0%	Yes	Yes
Business tax	No	No	No	No	3.5-4%	No	No	No	No
Capital tax	0-0.6%	No	No	No	No	No	No	1.8% min. tax	No
Transfer tax	No	No	1%	No	6.4%	3-8%	3%	2%	No
Inventory accounting method	FIFO	F/LIFO	FIFO	LIFO	FIFO	LIFO	F/LIFO	LIFO	FIFO
Tax indexation	No	No	No	No	No	No	No	Yes	No

Notes: Atl: Atlantic Canada
DB: declining balance
SL: straight line
FIFO: first in, first out
LIFO: last in, first out

Corporate Income Taxes

Germany imposes the highest statutory tax rate at the federal level, followed by Japan and Italy. Five countries – Canada, United States, Germany, Italy and Japan – also impose income taxes at the sub-national (state/provincial) level. In all these countries, except Canada and Italy, provincial income tax is deductible for national income tax purposes. As a result, combined nation-wide income tax rates range from a high of 57 percent in Germany to a low of 16.5 percent in Hong Kong.

The corporate income tax systems in the United Kingdom, Mexico and Hong Kong are the simplest by virtue of their single national rate, with no sub-national tax. In contrast, Japan imposes three different types of local income taxes: a corporate enterprise tax (CET), a corporate inhabitants tax (CIBT) and an inhabitant per capita tax (IPCT). The IPCT is payable as a lump sum depending on the size of the corporation, regardless of net income or national tax liability. The CET is deductible for national income tax purposes, while the CIBT is levied like a surtax on national tax liabilities, with a rate that varies across locations.

In Germany, there are two income tax rates at the national level: one applied to retained earnings and another levied on distributed profits (at rates of 45 percent and 30 percent respectively). A solidarity surcharge of 7.5 percent is then levied on assessed corporate income taxes after the deduction of an imputed tax credit on dividends received from German companies. Local trade taxes are imposed at different rates by municipalities, based on capital employed and on business income. These local taxes are deductible for national income tax purposes.

In France, local business taxes, described below, are based on income, property, payroll and other criteria, and are deductible for national income tax purposes. In the United States, state income taxes are deductible for national income tax purposes. Canada and Italy are the only countries where federal and provincial governments share the same or similar income tax base.

Hong Kong has the most generous tax depreciation system. An initial write-off is allowed for both buildings and machinery, at the rates of 20 percent and 60 percent respectively. A regular annual deduction is then applied on the remaining balance at a rate of 4 percent per annum, using the straight line method.

The tax depreciation system is also relatively generous in both Canada and the United States in comparison to the other countries. In Canada, the average declining balance depreciation rate is about 8 percent to 10 percent for buildings and over 30 percent for machinery. Canada also grants a 10 percent investment tax credit for investments occurring in the maritime provinces.[19] In the United States, structures are written off over a 32-year period, and machinery is written off over from five to seven years, depending on the asset. The United States uses a mixture of straight line and declining balance depreciation over the relevant write-off period.

Dividend Withholding Taxes

The dividend withholding tax rates shown in Table 1 are bilateral treaty rates relevant to Canadian and U.S. investors. As the table shows, with the exception of Mexico and Hong Kong which do not impose such a tax, the rates in other countries range from 5 percent to 15 percent.

Other Taxes on Capital

Property Taxes

Property taxes are imposed mainly by local governments and are generally deductible for income tax purposes, the exceptions being Germany, Japan and Italy. In Germany, a 0.6 percent federal property tax is imposed on property owned by corporations. It is deductible for income tax purposes. In Japan, in addition to a national property tax imposed on both real estate and depreciable assets at 1.7 percent and 1.4 percent respectively, there is also a new land value tax at 0.3 percent imposed on large corporations. All these property taxes are deductible for income tax purposes. In Italy, the tax rate ranges from 0.4 percent to 0.6 percent of the registered value of real estate, according to the percentage established by each municipality, but it is not deductible for income tax purposes. In Canada, the property tax is imposed by municipal governments, with the base and rates varying according to location. Similarly, property taxes in the United States, United Kingdom, France and Mexico are decided by local governments. In Hong Kong, the property tax rate is 15 percent on the property's net rental value. However, corporations carrying on an active business are exempt from the property tax because income from property is aggregated with other income and subject to the profits tax.

Taxes on the Transfer of Immovable Property

In Italy there is a registration tax on the transfer price of land and buildings, with rates ranging from 3 percent to 8 percent. France levies a registration duty on the transfer of properties. The rate on the sale of buildings used by companies that set up or acquire plants is 6.4 percent. In Japan, an acquisition tax of 3 percent or 4 percent of the taxable value of real estate is imposed on land and other real property at the time of acquisition. In Mexico, the states impose a 2 percent tax on the acquisition value of property.

Although property transfer taxes do not exist in the United States or Canada, the presence of state and provincial sales taxes levied at the retail level does result in the imposition of sales taxes on some business inputs. In the United States, the effective sales tax rate on equipment is assumed to be about 4 percent; in Canada it is slightly higher.

Business Taxes

France imposes a business tax on all taxpayers carrying on business. The taxable base is the "annual rental" or "deemed rental" value of the company's tangible fixed assets plus 18 percent of gross salaries and benefits in kind. The rate varies according to location but minimum amounts apply and the base tax may also be limited to a percentage of turnover. In 1995, the maximum percentages ranged from 3.5 percent to 4 percent depending on the turnover.

In Japan, a business office tax is imposed at the rate of 600 yen per square metre and 0.25 percent of the annual payroll.

Capital Taxes

In Canada, half the provincial governments (British Columbia, Manitoba, Ontario, Quebec and Saskatchewan) impose a capital tax on non-financial firms, with rates ranging from 0.225 percent to 0.6 percent of paid-up capital.

In Mexico, there is a 1.8 percent tax on business assets. However, the corporate income tax is creditable against the asset tax and, as a result, the asset tax acts as a minimum corporate tax.

Comparative Analysis of METRs

Table 2 presents our estimates of the METRs for investments in capital employed in manufacturing and services undertaken by domestic investors in the G7 countries, Mexico and Hong Kong. Although, as discussed above, property taxes can play a significant role in some countries, the estimates presented in Table 2 exclude the impact of property taxes. This is because for many of the countries included in the study, property taxes are levied at the local level, and assessment procedures often vary widely within each country. As such, there are no reliable estimates of national averages. Therefore, rather than present calculations that could be misleading, property taxes were omitted from our calculations. It should be noted that, in some cases, the inclusion of property taxes can have a marked impact on METRs. For example, when property taxes are included, the METR for Japan increases by over 15 percentage points, while the METRs for some other countries go up by only about 2 percentage points. All the other taxes discussed above, including the taxes on capital, are included in the analysis.

Looking first at the manufacturing sector, our calculations indicate that Hong Kong faces the lowest METR of the countries in the study. This is a natural result of its very low corporate income tax rate, very generous investment allowances and the lack of any other taxes on income or capital. In contrast, Japan has the highest METR on manufacturing capital, due primarily to a relatively high corporate income tax rate and less generous depreciation deductions. Manufacturing in Germany faces a relatively high METR for similar reasons. Manufacturing capital in Canada faces the third highest effective tax rate, with lower METRs in the United States, United Kingdom France, Italy, Mexico and Hong Kong.

Table 2 shows that Canada imposes a slightly higher effective tax rate on manufacturing capital than most of the other countries in this study. Of particular interest is the fact that the Canadian manufacturing METR is 4 percentage points higher than for the United States. Although the combined federal-provincial statutory tax rate on manufacturing in Canada is about 4 percentage points lower than the combined rate in the United States (about 35 percent vs. 39 percent), there are four other mitigating factors. First, the tax depreciation regime is less generous in Canada, particularly with respect to structures. Second, there is a very high effective tax rate on inventories in Canada, primarily because of the mandatory use of FIFO accounting for tax purposes (U.S. companies may use LIFO). Third, Canada has capital taxes including a large corporation tax (LCT) at the federal level and various capital taxes levied by the provinces. Finally, the effective sales tax rate on manufacturing equipment is slightly higher in Canada, due to the presence of provincial sales taxes.

TABLE 2

INTERNATIONAL METRS, DOMESTIC INVESTORS, LARGE FIRMS

	Manufacturing	Services
Canada	25.5	32.2
United States	21.5	19.9
United Kingdom	20.2	19.0
Germany	27.5	33.1
France	21.9	25.5
Italy	22.1	34.1
Japan	32.0	33.9
Mexico	16.5	17.7
Hong Kong	11.9	3.7

Although the Canadian METR on manufacturing capital is only slightly higher than in the United States, the same cannot be said for services. Relative to the other countries studied, Canada has the fourth highest effective tax rate on capital investment in the service sector but, in contrast to the manufacturing case, the U.S. rate on services is substantially lower. Unlike in manufacturing, the combined statutory tax rate applied to the service sector in Canada is higher than in the United States, by about 4 percentage points. Coupled with the same factors that increased the Canadian rate on manufacturing above the U.S. rate – less generous depreciation allowances, FIFO accounting for inventories, a higher sales tax rate and the imposition of capital taxes – this substantially increases the Canadian effective tax rate on services. Indeed, with the exception of Italy, Canada is the only country that taxes capital in the service sector at a rate substantially higher than the rate imposed on manufacturing.

In sum, our calculations indicate that compared to domestic investors in some other countries in the study, particularly the United States, Canadian investors face a slightly higher METR on manufacturing capital. Canadian METRs on services are substantially higher than in the United States. As such, it appears that Canadian investors face larger tax-related disincentives to invest in capital relative to domestic investors in some other countries.

Consider Table 3, which illustrates METRs for a wider range of sectors facing Canadian and U.S. domestic and multinational investors. We focus on intercountry as opposed to intersectoral comparisons here. (A discussion of intersectoral differences in Canada is deferred to the following section.) Looking first at the sector METRs in the two countries for domestic investors, it is very clear that although the Canadian rate is only slightly higher than the U.S. rate in manufacturing, Canadian domestic investors face much higher METRs on investments in all the other sectors. As was the case with services, a higher statutory tax rate, less generous depreciation allowances, a high effective tax rate on inventories and the presence of capital taxes all contribute to the higher domestic Canadian rates. There is little question that relative to the United States, Canadian domestic investors face a greater tax disincentive to invest.

TABLE 3

INTERSECTORAL METRS, CANADA AND UNITED STATES, MULTINATIONAL AND DOMESTIC INVESTORS, LARGE FIRMS

	Canadian Domestic	U.S. Multinationals in Canada	U.S. Domestic	Canadian Multinationals in United States
Agriculture, fishing and forestry	31.3	27.6	17.9	14.6
Manufacturing	25.5	21.4	21.5	18.3
Construction	38.4	34.2	19.0	15.2
Transportation and storage	33.9	29.5	12.8	9.3
Communications	30.7	26.7	11.0	7.4
Utilities	34.0	29.8	13.1	9.7
Trade	36.7	32.4	23.4	20.5
Services	32.2	28.2	19.9	16.7

For both Canada and the United States, the METR for multinational investors is less that the METR of domestic investors. This is primarily due to two factors. First, foreign investors face a lower cost of financing (see equation [4]) because of the double deduction of interest costs in both the home and host countries (remember, we consider only "excess credit" cases for U.S. investors). Second, foreign investors require a slightly higher net-of-tax rate of return (see equation [5]).

Note also that the METRs for Canadian multinationals investing in the United States are lower than the METRs of Canadian firms investing domestically. The opposite is true for U.S. firms. This suggests that the tax systems in the two countries may act to attract capital from Canada to the United States. However, it should be stressed that this result is quite sensitive to the assumptions regarding the parameters. Also, the calculations ignore the interest allocation rules in the United States, assume that U.S. firms are in an excess credit position and ignore the role that other non-capital taxes may play in the location of production facilities.[20]

It is interesting to compare the data presented in tables 2 and 3 to the results of other international METR studies that have included some of the countries studied here. While the absolute level of our results differs from some of these previous studies, our general conclusions do not. Like these other studies, we conclude that capital in Canada is highly taxed relative to most of its major competitors, particularly the United States.[21]

INTERSECTORAL AND INTERPROVINCIAL METRs FOR CANADA

THE METRs PRESENTED FOR CANADA IN THE PREVIOUS SECTION are aggregated over the 10 provinces. METRs can vary substantially across provinces due to differences in tax systems as well as in industrial structure. In this section, we present METRs for various industrial sectors in each province.

Table 4 summarizes key provincial corporate tax rates for 1995. As the table shows, the general provincial corporate income tax rate ranges from a low of 8.9 percent in Quebec to a high of 17 percent in Saskatchewan, Manitoba and New Brunswick. All the provinces impose a lower CIT rate on small business, ranging from 5 percent to 10 percent. Alberta, Ontario, Prince Edward Island and Newfoundland also impose a lower CIT rate on manufacturing firms. Furthermore, five provinces including British Columbia, Saskatchewan, Manitoba, Ontario and Quebec impose a capital tax on non-financial firms which is deductible for income tax purposes. The rates range from 0.3 percent to 0.64 percent.

The provinces also impose special taxes on the oil and gas, and mining sectors. Due to the complexity of the mining tax systems, and the wide variation across the provinces, we present calculations for British Columbia, Ontario and Quebec, which together account for about 70 percent of investment in the mining sector. Similarly, with 85 percent of investment in oil and gas taking place in Alberta, we focus on that province for the oil and gas sector. It should be noted that neither mining taxes nor oil and gas royalties are deductible for federal corporate income tax purposes. Instead, companies are allowed to deduct a resource allowance equal to 25 percent of their net resource income. Historically, resource allowance deductions have tended to exceed provincial mining taxes and fall somewhat short of oil and gas royalties.

TABLE 4

PROVINCIAL CORPORATE TAX RATES (%) FOR NON-FINANCIAL INDUSTRIES, 1995

	Corporate Income Tax			Capital Tax	Mining	Oil & Gas
	General	Small	M&P	(Max. Rate)	Tax	Royalty*
British Columbia	16.5	10.0	16.5	0.30	13.0	n/a
Alberta	15.5	6.0	14.5	n/a	n/a	16.8
Saskatchewan	17.0	8.0	17.0	0.60	n/a	n/a
Manitoba	17.0	9.0	17.0	0.30	n/a	n/a
Ontario	15.5	9.5	13.5	0.30	20.0	n/a
Quebec	8.9	5.8	8.9	0.64	18.0	n/a
New Brunswick	17.0	7.0	17.0	n/a	n/a	n/a
Nova Scotia	16.0	5.0	16.0	n/a	n/a	n/a
Prince Edward Island	15.0	7.5	7.5	n/a	n/a	n/a
Newfoundland	14.0	5.0	5.0	n/a	15.0	n/a

Notes: * This is an effective royalty rate adopted from Chen, Mintz, Scharf and Traviza (1995).
M&P: manufacturing and processing
n/a: not applicable

Table 5 provides information on the industrial structure of each province. As the table shows, Ontario accounts for the largest share of all industries, except oil and gas which is highly concentrated in Alberta.

Table 6 presents METRs by industry and by province for 1995. METRs are calculated for both large and small firms in 10 industries in each of the 10 provinces. In addition to corporate income taxes and capital taxes, the METR calculations for the mining industry include mining taxes and those for oil and gas include royalties.

Focusing first on the intersectoral comparison, Table 6 shows that the mining, oil and gas, and manufacturing industries tend to be the most tax-favoured sectors, while construction and trade are the least favoured. This reflects not only differences in the tax treatment of the sectors, but also variations in capital structure and economic depreciation rates. In general, all else being equal, the higher the economic depreciation rate, the higher the cost of capital. This increases the effective tax rate for construction equipment in particular. Moreover, buildings and inventories tend to be taxed at a higher rate than machinery and land; the former as a result of low write-off rates and the latter due to the taxation of inflationary price changes as a result of the use of FIFO inventory accounting for tax purposes (except in agriculture, fishing and forestry). As such, sectors with a high share of buildings and inventories tend to face higher effective tax rates. This accounts, in part, for the relatively high METRs in trade, transportation and services.

TABLE 5

INDUSTRIAL DISTRIBUTION AMONG PROVINCES

	Agriculture, Fishing & Forestry	Mining	Oil and Gas	Manufacturing	Construction	Transportation	Communications	Utilities	Trades	Services
British Columbia	14.9	18.1	5.0	8.9	13.2	18.3	11.2	11.2	11.3	12.5
Alberta	18.2	7.1	85.4	5.5	12.0	15.8	14.9	14.9	9.7	11.3
Saskatchewan	16.2	8.2	8.6	1.2	4.3	6.0	2.8	2.8	2.8	3.2
Manitoba	6.9	6.3	0.5	2.3	3.8	5.5	4.4	4.4	3.6	3.5
Ontario	20.5	30.7	0.5	52.1	33.9	29.9	32.3	32.3	43.3	40.3
Quebec	15.0	17.9	0.0	25.6	24.5	19.0	26.5	26.5	23.3	22.9
New Brunswick	2.3	4.1	0.0	1.7	2.9	1.9	3.3	3.3	2.1	2.0
Nova Scotia	3.9	2.8	0.0	1.9	3.1	20.4	2.1	2.1	2.3	2.6
Prince Edward Island	0.9	0.0	0.0	0.1	0.4	0.3	0.3	0.3	0.3	0.3
Newfoundland	1.2	4.7	0.0	0.7	2.0	1.2	2.2	2.2	1.3	1.4
Aggregate	100.0	100.0	100.0	100.0	100.0	100.0	100.0	100.0	100.0	100.0

Source: Adopted from Chen, Mintz, Scharf and Traviza (1995).

TABLE 6

INTERSECTORAL AND INTERPROVINCIAL METRS, CANADA

		Agriculture, Fishing & Forestry	Mining	Oil and Gas	Manufacturing	Construction	Transportation	Communications	Utilities	Trades	Services
British Columbia	L	32.3	6.2	n/a	27.9	40.0	36.9	32.0	35.5	38.1	33.6
	S	10.5	n/a	n/a	14.5	18.8	18.3	22.3	17.4	19.0	15.5
Alberta	L	30.0	n/a	19.6	24.6	37.4	34.4	29.5	32.9	32.5	30.9
	S	8.8	n/a	n/a	12.2	16.0	16.1	20.7	15.0	16.1	13.0
Saskatchewan	L	34.8	n/a	n/a	30.8	42.7	39.7	34.8	38.2	41.0	36.3
	S	10.7	n/a	n/a	13.9	18.1	17.7	21.9	16.8	18.3	14.8
Manitoba	L	34.3	n/a	n/a	31.1	42.0	39.1	34.1	37.6	40.0	35.7
	S	10.5	n/a	n/a	14.5	18.8	18.3	22.3	17.4	19.0	15.5
Ontario	L	31.8	4.4	n/a	26.5	39.5	36.4	31.6	35.1	37.7	33.0
	S	10.1	n/a	n/a	13.9	18.1	17.7	21.9	16.8	18.3	14.8
Quebec	L	28.8	2.3	n/a	25.4	36.1	32.9	29.3	32.3	34.5	30.6
	S	8.7	n/a	n/a	12.1	15.9	16.0	20.7	14.9	16.0	12.9
New Brunswick	L	26.5	n/a	n/a	16.1	37.3	16.0	23.1	27.4	27.0	26.6
	S	0.0	n/a	n/a	0.1	11.6	-25.7	-11.9	2.6	10.5	9.5
Nova Scotia	L	26.1	n/a	n/a	15.6	36.8	15.2	22.7	26.9	30.0	26.1
	S	-2.1	n/a	n/a	-2.9	8.4	-30.3	-14.9	-0.6	7.1	6.7
Prince Edward	L	24.5	n/a	n/a	9.7	35.6	13.6	21.5	25.9	29.0	24.3
Island	S	-0.8	n/a	n/a	-1.0	10.4	-27.5	-13.1	1.4	8.0	8.5
Newfoundland	L	25.3	n/a	n/a	9.9	36.5	15.1	22.4	26.9	26.1	25.1
	S	-2.1	n/a	n/a	-2.9	8.4	-30.3	-14.9	-0.6	7.1	6.7
Aggregate	L	31.3	4.5	19.6	25.5	38.4	33.9	30.7	34.0	36.7	32.2
	S	9.0	n/a	n/a	12.3	17.2	16.2	21.4	16.0	17.5	14.1

Notes: L: large firms
S: small firms
n/a: not applicable

Of particular interest are the very low effective tax rates faced by the resource sector. This is due to generous write-offs for exploration and development expenditures as well as various resource-related allowances at both the federal and provincial level (particularly for mining). The low METRs in the manufacturing sector reflect its lower statutory income tax rate and high concentration of machinery and equipment, which are written off at a relatively fast rate.

Table 6 also provides an interprovincial comparison of METRs. For large firms in all industries, capital investments in Saskatchewan face the highest METRs. This is the combined effect of its high provincial CIT rate (17 percent) and high capital tax rate (0.6 percent). For a similar reason, in all industries except mining, companies in Manitoba, British Columbia and Ontario also face relatively high effective tax rates. Companies in Alberta face slightly lower METRs due to the absence of a capital tax and a slightly lower provincial tax rate. Of the provinces west of New Brunswick, Quebec imposes the lowest effective tax rates on capital because of the lowest provincial tax rate in the country, which more than offsets its high capital tax rate.

Table 6 highlights the fact that companies in the four Atlantic provinces face much lower effective tax rates than their western counterparts, despite imposing relatively high provincial tax rates. This is primarily due to the 10 percent regional investment tax credit offered by the federal government for investments in the Atlantic region. This significantly lowers the METR in all industries. The differences in METRs among the four Atlantic provinces reflect minor differences in the provincial CIT rates.

Also evident from Table 6 is the fact that small businesses face substantially lower METRs than large firms in all the provinces. This is due to the significantly lower federal and provincial tax rates imposed on small businesses. Indeed, in some cases in the Atlantic provinces, the effective tax rate on small firms is negative, indicating a subsidy offered by the tax system. Since there is no provincial capital tax imposed on small firms, the ranking of METRs across provinces for small firms primarily reflects differences in provincial CIT rates, as well as the presence of the federal investment tax credit in the Atlantic provinces.

On the basis of the intersectoral comparison of METRs, it would appear that Canada's tax system results in a very uneven set of tax incentives across industries. Some industries are highly taxed at the margin (construction and trade), while others face relatively low METRs (mining, oil and gas, and manufacturing). This intersectoral variation in METRs suggests potential efficiency costs which could impede economic growth. A similarly high degree of variation in METRs across the provinces, with particularly low effective rates in the Atlantic provinces, suggests more scope for efficiency losses due to interregional distortions.

The Impact of Risk and Irreversibility

THE CALCULATIONS PRESENTED ABOVE ignore the presence of risk and irreversibility in capital investments. These factors are considered here, as intersectoral METRs for Canada are calculated accounting for risk and irreversibility.

We begin by introducing capital risk, while ignoring irreversibility. As discussed in the second part of this paper, in the absence of irreversibilities, the presence of income risk has no impact on METRs, if full loss offsets are provided (or corporations are otherwise fully taxpaying). One of the problems in measuring METRs on risky capital is that it is difficult to measure the risk premium associated with capital risk. This section follows Bulow and Summers (1984), Jog and Mintz (1989) and McKenzie and Mintz (1993) who argued that the market value of a firm is equal to its asset value, so fluctuations in market value reflect changes in the value of the firm's underlying assets and, therefore, fluctuations in the economic rate of depreciation. This implies that we may use sectoral capital asset pricing model (CAPM) estimates for our capital risk premiums. Not everyone supports this approach. Gordon and Wilson (1989), for example, pointed out that it is the correlation between the economic cost of depreciation and consumption that is really relevant, and this correlation may well be negative. If this were the case, the use of CAPM estimates for the capital risk premiums would not be appropriate.

Calculations are presented for METRs in the presence of capital risk but only for Canada because of a lack of data.

Seven-year average capital risk premiums by industry estimated using the CAPM are presented in Table 7.[22] Since we lack access to market valuations for agriculture and fishing, the agriculture, fishing and forestry sector is excluded from our analysis. As Table 7 shows, the mining industry has the highest capital risk premium and construction and utilities the lowest.[23]

Note that, in some cases, the presence of capital risk can have a very significant impact on the METR. In other cases, the impact is more modest. For example, the METR for mining increases fourfold, the oil and gas METR increases by over 60 percent, while the utilities METR increases just over 10 percent. The differences in the impact of capital risk can be accounted for in large part by the differences in the capital risk premiums across sectors. For example, the risk premium in mining is the highest at 5.6 percent, while the utilities sector has the lowest risk premium at 1.5 percent. In general, the higher the capital risk premium, the higher the METR.

However, there are other reasons for the differental impact of capital risk across the sectors. In general, the higher the statutory income tax rate, the greater the impact of capital risk on the METR. The effective statutory rates in the resource sectors are relatively high because of the presence of mining taxes and royalties. This exacerbates the effects of the already high risk premiums. Capital risk also tends to increase METRs more for non-depreciable assets. Thus, sectors with high shares of land and inventories are affected more by capital risk. Hence, the relatively large increase in trade.

TABLE 7

METRS, CAPITAL RISK VS. NO CAPITAL RISK, LARGE FIRMS

	Risk Premium* (%)	No Capital Risk (%)	With Capital Risk (%)
Mining	5.6	4.5	19.3
Oil and gas	4.2	19.6	31.7
Manufacturing	3.8	25.5	37.1
Construction	1.6	38.4	45.0
Transportation and storage	2.6	33.9	39.9
Communications	3.2	30.7	40.2
Utilities	1.5	34.0	39.1
Trades	3.6	36.7	48.8
Services	3.7	32.2	44.7

Note: * Adopted from an ongoing study conducted by Prof. Vijay M. Jog; see endnote 22.

So what are the implications of capital risk for capital accumulation? First, METRs increase substantially in the presence of capital risk. This suggests that the distortionary impact of taxes may be much higher than indicated by METR calculations which ignore risk. As such, taxes may discourage capital accumulation more than previously suspected. Second, METRs generally increase as the amount of capital risk increases. This suggests that the tax system discriminates against risky investments vis-à-vis less risky investments, giving rise to yet another type of distortion in the economy. Third, due to variations in the capital risk premium across sectors, as well as differences in key tax parameters across industries, the presence of capital risk increases the variability in METRs across industrial sectors. This means that intersectoral tax distortions are even more pronounced than suggested by calculations which ignore capital risk.

Table 8 illustrates the implications of the irreversibility of capital in a risky environment for non-resource firms in Canada. The METRs are calculated under the assumption that systematic income risk is zero, systematic capital risk is measured by the CAPM estimates presented in Table 7 and total unsystematic risk, which incorporates the variance in both income and the replacement price of capital, is about $\sigma^2=10$. This adds approximately 7 percentage points to the risk premium for each sector, with slight differences across sectors due to different capital-labour ratios.[24] As can be seen from Table 8, irreversibility has significant implications for the distortionary effect of taxes. The METR on capital increases by a low of about 12 percentage points in transportation and storage, to a high of over 17 percentage points in construction. As such, the presence of irreversibility in a risky environment substantially increases the disincentive to invest caused by the tax system. Moreover, the variance in METRs across sectors is also increased. This implies that

TABLE 8

METRS, RISKY AND REVERSIBLE VS. IRREVERSIBLE INVESTMENTS,* LARGE FIRMS

	Riskless	Capital Risk Reversible	Capital Risk Irreversible
Manufacturing	25.5	37.1	51.2
Construction	38.4	45.0	62.5
Transportation and storage	33.9	39.9	51.8
Communications	30.7	40.2	54.0
Utilities	34.0	39.1	55.3
Trades	36.7	48.8	62.6
Services	32.2	44.7	59.0

Note: *See McKenzie (1994) for details on calculations.

the tax system may discourage risky, irreversible investment to a much greater extent than previously thought, and may also generate much larger intersectoral distortions.

SUMMARY AND CONCLUSIONS

THIS PAPER HAS EXAMINED THE POTENTIAL IMPACT OF TAXATION on capital accumulation by calculating marginal effective tax rates (METRs) on capital for Canada and selected other countries. The METR on capital is a summary measure of the distortion caused by the imposition of personal and corporate taxes on capital. We also investigated the implications of risk and irreversibility for the impact of taxation on investment. Measuring the size of the distortion caused by the tax system, provided some insights into the potential impact of taxation on capital accumulation and economic growth.

The international comparison of METRs included the G7 countries – Canada, United States, United Kingdom, Germany, Italy, Japan and France – as well as Mexico and Hong Kong. We included only the manufacturing and service sectors. In terms of the METR facing domestic savers investing in capital in their own country, Canadian investors face higher effective tax rates on both manufacturing and services than most of the other countries included in the study. The METRs facing domestic investors in Canada are the third highest of the nine countries studied in manufacturing and the fourth highest in services. Although third highest by rank, the METR on manufacturing investment in Canada is not out of line with the other countries, i.e., it is only 4 percentage points higher than the U.S. rate (25.5 percent vs. 21.5 percent). However, the effective tax rate on services is quite high, particularly vis-à-vis the United States (32.2 percent vs. 19.9 percent). In a closer comparison of METRs for eight sectors in Canada and the United States, we found similar results: Canadian rates are substantially higher than their

U.S. counterparts in other non-manufacturing sectors. This suggests that Canada's tax system may discourage capital investment in non-manufacturing sectors somewhat more than its key competitors on international markets.

In terms of the tax incentives provided for Canadian multinational firms to invest in the United States rather than at home, we found that there is a slight tax-induced incentive to invest in the United States. This suggests that the tax system in Canada may drive capital out of the country.

We also examined METRs across provinces and sectors within Canada and found that the variation in METRs across provinces is quite pronounced. This suggests that the tax system encourages an inefficient allocation of capital across the provinces. Moreover, there are substantial intersectoral distortions, as METRs vary significantly by industry.

When we incorporated risk into the analysis, we found that METRs increase substantially, as does the intersectoral variation. Thus, the tax system appears to not only discriminate against riskier investments, but the intersectoral distortions caused by taxation are more pronounced in the presence of risk.

Recent attention has focused on the implications of irreversibility for investment decisions. An investment is irreversible when the capital is sunk, and disinvestment cannot occur costlessly. When irreversibility is coupled with risk, METRs increase further still, as does the intersectoral variation. The very important implication is that, if capital is irreversible and risky, the tax system may impinge on investment decisions to a much greater extent than previously suspected.

We think the policy implications of these results are potentially quite important. In light of recent empirical evidence linking lower taxes to higher investment, and higher investment rates to higher productivity and growth, the scope for growth-enhancing changes to the capital tax system in Canada vis-à-vis the other countries included in the study, particularly the United States, becomes evident.[25] Moreover, Canada's tax system displays a great deal of intersectoral and interprovincial variation in effective tax rates, and discriminates against investments in risky and irreversible capital. In light of De Long and Summers' (1991) arguments that it is not so much the level of savings and investment that matters for economic growth, but rather whether that investment is allocated "appropriately," the presence of these distortions suggests scope for growth-enhancing changes to the business tax system in Canada.

Having said this, we close with the obligatory cautionary note that more research is required. The determinants of both growth and investment are not fully understood. While some suggestive evidence exists, there is no broad consensus in the literature regarding the role that taxes may play in promoting either investment or growth.

ENDNOTES

1 See, for example, Romer (1986).
2 Elasticities of this magnitude are somewhat unusual. Most empirical literature does not find such a strong relationship. However, there are substantial empirical and data difficulties involved with estimating investment functions, and the issue is still unresolved. See Chirinko (1993) for a discussion.
3 See Boadway (1987) for a formal derivation. Some of what follows is based on McKenzie and Mintz (1992).
4 The phrase "with similar characteristics" refers primarily to risk, although other factors, such as liquidity, could be important. The discussion which follows ignores risk and these other factors. Risk considerations are discussed later in this section.
5 In the absence of taxation, or other capital market imperfections, and risk, $I=p$.
6 Capital is implicitly treated as the numeraire.
7 These details are incorporated in the calculations performed later in this paper.
8 Note that the required rate of return to equity p is not deducted.
9 In the absence of various provisions such as the half-year rule (which is included in subsequent calculations but ignored here for simplicity), in Canada A is the infinite sum $A=(1-\phi)\sum_t \alpha(1-\alpha)^t/(1+R^f)^t=(1-\phi)\alpha/(R^f+\alpha)$, where α is the declining balance capital cost allowance (CCA) rate. This reflects the reduction in the tax depreciation base by the ITC. In other countries, slightly different approaches may be taken; these differences are reflected in the subsequent calculations.
10 See Chen and Mintz (1993).
11 See Mintz and Tsiopoulos (1994).
12 This presumes that the statutory corporate tax rate is flat and does not change with corporate profits.
13 The capital risk premium is systematic because it reflects the correlation of the economic rate of depreciation with the market.
14 McKenzie (1993) assumed that the tax system provides full cost of finance deductibility by allowing the opportunity cost of equity finance to be deducted at the corporate level along with the cost of debt.
15 See McKenzie (1994) for the specific form of the expression for H.
16 See Boadway et al. (1982).
17 METRs for U.S. multinationals are estimated under the assumption that the U.S. firm is in an "excess credit" position for U.S. tax purposes. This implies that the taxes paid to all foreign governments on dividends and other qualifying sources of income remitted to the home country are greater than the firm's U.S. tax liability on this income. In other words, the amount of U.S. tax owing on the remitted income is assumed to be zero. The estimates also ignore the interest allocation rules that result in U.S. interest being allocated for foreign subsidiaries based on the share of foreign net assets to worldwide assets. See Mintz and Altshuler (1995) for a formal theoretical analysis.
18 Not all studies make this assumption, as there seems to be a methodological debate in the literature regarding the appropriate financial arbitrage assumption to employ. Note in particular that the open economy arbitrage assumption differs from that advocated by King and Fullerton which is used in many METR studies. See Boadway (1987) and McKenzie and Mintz (1993) for a discussion.
19 Very little investment takes place in the Maritime provinces relative to the rest of the country.

20 On the latter, see McKenzie et al. (1996).
21 See, for example, McKenzie and Mintz (1993), Jorgenson and Landau (1993) and OECD (1991).
22 The risk premium estimates were provided by Prof. Vijay M. Jog, Carleton University. They are a part of his ongoing study of sectoral cost of capital in Canada.
23 This is despite the fact that precious metals are excluded from the CAPM estimates for mining.
24 See McKenzie (1994) for more details.
25 See Auerbach and Hassett (1992), Cummins and Hassett (1992), Cummins et al. (1995) and De Long and Summers (1991).

ACKNOWLEDGEMENTS

THE AUTHORS WOULD LIKE TO THANK JACK MINTZ for useful input. All conclusions are our own.

BIBLIOGRAPHY

Auerbach, A. and K. Hassett. "Tax Policy and Business Fixed Investment in the United States." *Journal of Public Economics*. 47, (1992):141-170.

Boadway, R. "The Theory and Measurement of Marginal Effective Tax Rates." In *The Impact of Taxation on Business Activity*. Edited by J. Mintz and D. Purvis. Kingston, Ontario: John Deutsch Institute for Economic Research, Queen's University, 1987.

Boadway, R.W., N. Bruce and J. Mintz. "Corporate Taxation and the Cost of Holding Inventories." *Canadian Journal of Economics*. 15, (1982): 279-293.

Boadway, R.W., N. Bruce, K.J. McKenzie and J.M. Mintz. "Marginal Effective Tax Rates for Capital in the Canadian Mining Industry." *Canadian Journal of Economics*. Vol. 20, (1987): 1-16.

Bulow, J. and L. Summers. "The Taxation of Risky Assets." *Journal of Political Economy*. 92, (1984): 20-39.

Chen, D. and J. Mintz. "Taxation of Capital in Canada: An Interindustry and Interprovincial Comparison." *Business Taxation in Ontario*. University of Toronto Press, 1993.

Chen, D., J. Mintz, K. Scharf and D. Traviza. "Taxation of Virgin and Recycled Materials." Prepared for the Canadian Council of Ministers of the Environment, mimeo, 1995.

Chen, D., J. Mintz, and D. Rolph. "The Effects of Ontario's Corporate Minimum Tax on New Investment." Prepared for the Ontario government, mimeo, 1995.

Chirinko, R. "Business Fixed Investment Spending: A Critical Survey of Modelling Strategies, Empirical Results, and Policy Implications." *Journal of Economic Literature*. 31 (December 1993): 1875-1911.

Cummins, G. and K. Hassett. "The Effects of Taxation on Investment: New Evidence from Firm Level Panel Data." *National Tax Journal*. 45, (1992): 243-251.

Cummins, J., K. Hassett and G. Hubbard. "Tax Reforms and Investment: A Cross-Country Comparison." Working Paper 5232, National Bureau of Economic Research, 1995.

De Long, J. and L. Summers. "Equipment Investment and Economic Growth." *Quarterly Journal of Economics*. (1991): 445-502.

Gordon, R. "Taxation of Corporate Income: Tax Revenues vs. Tax Distortions." *Quarterly Journal of Economics*. 100,(1985): 1-28.

Gordon, R. and J. Wilson. "Measuring the Efficiency Cost of Taxing Risky Capital Income." *American Economic Review*.79, (1989): 427-439.

Jog, V. and J. Mintz. "Corporate Tax Reform and Its Economic Impact: An Evaluation of the Phase I Proposals." In *Economic Impact of Tax Reform*. Edited by J. Mintz and J. Whalley. Canadian Tax Foundation, 1989.

Jorgenson, D. and R. Landau. *Tax Reform and the Cost of Capital: An International Comparison*. Washington, DC: Brookings Institution, 1993.

King, M. and D. Fullerton. *The Taxation of Income from Capital: A Comparative Study of the United States, United Kingdom, Sweden and West Germany*. University of Chicago Press, 1984.

McKenzie, K.J. "The Implications of Risk and Irreversibility for the Measurement of Marginal Effective Tax Rates on Capital." *Canadian Journal of Economics*. Vol. 27(3), (1994): 604-619.

—. "Neutral Ex Ante Income Taxation in the Presence of Adjustment Costs and Risk." *Public Finance*. Vol. 48(2), (1993): 111-128.

McKenzie, K.J. and J.M. Mintz. "Tax Effects on the Cost of Capital: A Canada-United States Comparison." In *Canada-U.S. Tax Comparisons*. Edited by J. Whalley and J. Shoven. National Bureau of Economic Research, Research Volume, University of Chicago Press, 1993, pp.189-216.

McKenzie, K.J., J.M. Mintz and K.A. Scharf. "The Measurement of Effective Tax Rates in the Presence of Multiple Inputs." Discussion paper, University of Chicago, 1996.

Milesi-Ferretti, G.M. and N. Roubini. "Growth Effects of Income and Consumption Taxes: Positive and Normative Analysis."Working Paper 5317, National Bureau of Economic Research, 1995.

Mintz, J. and R. Altshuler. "U.S. Interest Allocation Rules: Effects and Policy." *Journal of Public Economics*. (1995).

Mintz, J. and T. Tsiopoulos. "The Effectiveness of Corporate Tax Incentives for Foreign Investment in the Presence of Tax Crediting." *Journal of Public Economics*. 55(2), (October 1994).

OECD. *Taxing Profits in a Global Economy: Domestic and International Issues*. Paris, France, Organization for Economic Co-operation and Development, 1991.

Romer, P. "Increasing Returns and Long Run Growth." *Journal of Political Economy*. XCIV, (1986): 1002-1037.

Vijay M. Jog
School of Business
Carleton University

5

Investing in Canada: Estimation of the Sectoral Cost of Capital in Canada and Case Studies for International Comparisons

INTRODUCTION

THE PRIMARY OBJECTIVE OF THIS PAPER IS TO PROVIDE ESTIMATES of the cost of capital for Canadian industrial sectors. Three case studies are presented which deal with country and exchange risk, company and sector-specific risk, and the impact of using an alternative methodology for estimating the cost of capital for a specific sector. These case studies highlight some of the delicate and practical issues in cross-country estimation and comparisons of cost of capital, and the reasons for some of the observed differences. Two of the three case studies deal with Canada-United States comparisons in specific sectors; the third study highlights some of the issues in comparing cost of capital between Canada and one of its major European competitors (Finland) using the pulp and paper sector as an example. These case studies, together with the Canadian cost of capital estimates, address practical issues in estimating cost of capital and the impact of cost of capital differences on the competitiveness of Canadian firms and on Canada's ability to attract foreign capital for green-field investments in Canada. Due to the vast scope of the paper, the literature review has been kept to a minimum.

With these caveats in mind, the paper is organized as follows. The first section deals with the empirical estimates of Canadian sectoral cost of capital. These estimates are based on the standard notion of the weighted average cost of capital which reflects the rates of return demanded by shareholders and debtholders in order to earn appropriate risk-adjusted rates of return. The cost of equity estimates are based on the capital asset pricing model using data for companies listed on the Toronto Stock Exchange (TSE) from 1988 to 1994. The second section deals with a Canada-United States comparison of cost of capital with special emphasis on the country and exchange risk premiums. The results are used to highlight the impact of the cross-country differences in cost of capital on the competitiveness of a green-field investment in a lightweight coated (LWC) mill in each of the two countries. Next, the cost of capital differences are compared for the regulated telecommunications sector in the two countries. This section also highlights the practical difficulties of dealing with differential inflation rates and varying capital structures in a cross-country cost of capital comparison. The fourth section provides a practical example of difficulties faced in comparing cost of capital for the Canadian pulp and paper sector with its counterpart in Finland. In this sector, both countries compete in the North American capital and product markets and are each other's main competitors. This section also highlights the challenges in data collection and estimation. The paper ends with a summary and conclusion.[1]

Canadian Estimates of Sectoral Cost of Capital[2]

For various reasons, estimating the appropriate cost of capital continues to be a debatable subject. First, there is the selection of the appropriate model for estimating the risk-return trade-off. This debate is further complicated by the differences in opinion on the openness of the economy, the identification of the marginal investor in an increasingly global world, the ever-increasing importance of tax-exempt investors and the relevance of the user cost of capital used by economists in estimating the sectoral cost of capital. Since each of these areas can be (and has been) the subject of a series of papers, a solution which would be acceptable to all continues to present a challenge.

It is neither the intent nor the objective of this paper to cover the entire debate; the perspective here is much narrower. This section assumes one particular model of the return-generating process for estimating the cost of capital and providing empirical estimates based on its usage with the available data. Before looking at the methodology employed to estimate the cost of capital, a brief discussion of the two main schools of thought in the cost of capital estimation literature is in order. This is followed by a discussion of the basic tenets underlying the capital asset pricing model (CAPM), the dividend growth model (DGM) and capital structure theory. No attempt is made to justify the use of the CAPM; its application in this study is simply explained. The limitations of the model are well described in any standard finance textbook, and many papers exist which debate vigorously the use of the model and its empirical verification. Thus, there is little need for further elaboration here.[3] The types and sources of information used to estimate the costs of capital for individual sectors followed by the description of the estimation process of various components in the cost of capital are also described. The section ends with the aggregate results and conclusions.

The Cost of Capital Estimation Literature

At least two schools of thought are evident in the existing cost of capital estimation literature. The term "country averages" is used for those studies which attempt to estimate an overall country-specific cost of capital. The term "micro estimates" is used for those studies which utilize company-specific data to derive cost of capital estimates.

The Country Averages Approach

A typical recent study in this area is the one published by the National Advisory Board on Science and Technology (NABST) in 1990.[4] The study's main objective was to investigate whether or not the cost of capital in Canada is significantly different (higher) from that estimated for other countries. Based on an approach which relies on estimating an aggregate price-earnings ratio and adjusting it for depreciation and inflation, the report concluded that the overall cost of capital in Canada is higher than that of many of its trading partners except the United States. The report also provided possible reasons for this relatively high cost of capital and discussed policy prescriptions for overcoming this disadvantage. In the appendix of the report, there was a brief discussion on why an approach based on modern portfolio theory would be unreliable and, therefore, was not used by the study team. Also provided were some estimates of company-specific costs of capital using a variant of the well-known dividend growth model. These estimates were used to corroborate the macro results.

Although useful as an overall exercise, the NABST study approach is not without difficulties: its use of a country-level price-earnings ratio, the variety of adjustments made to it to arrive at a country-wide cost of capital, the lack of attention to country-wide differences in industrial structures, the dependence on price-earnings ratios of aggregate indices with radically different industrial composition and the inability to analyse the sectoral differences in the cost of capital within the country and across competing countries. These difficulties limit the usefulness of this approach for corporate decisions, particularly investment decisions.

This type of approach also does not lend itself to any conclusions about sectoral or company-specific differences. A better approach would be to compare sectors by matching companies across the various countries either at the level of sectoral indices or by choosing a subset of similar companies in each country. For competitiveness analysis, for instance, the relevant comparisons must be based on micro estimates and should account for, as a minimum, the sectoral level differences across competing countries.[5]

Another approach in determining country-level cost of capital is found in the literature on marginal effective tax rates (METRs). A recent paper by Bruce (1992) provides a good description of the approaches used in the METR studies and discusses some additional limitations of the NABST approach. As the main purpose of these studies is to evaluate how differences in country-specific tax systems affect investment decisions, the studies simply assume that the cost of capital for the Canadian corporate sector is determined at the international level by invoking the "open economy" notion of Canada. By keeping the cost of capital the same for all asset classes and sectors, these studies then concentrate on the determination of marginal effective tax rates across sectors and asset classes. Since many of these studies simply assume identical capital structures and identical costs of debt and equity for all sectors regardless of the fact that there are systematic differences in their underlying business risk, debt-to-equity ratios and costs of equity and debt, they are of no relevance to a corporate decision maker. There have been some recent METR studies which have attempted to account explicitly for the differences in the cost of capital in the estimation of METRs.[6] Their results indicate that the assumption of varying sectoral costs of capital has a significant impact on the METR estimates.

The Micro Approach

For simplicity, all studies under this category can be classified as belonging to the corporate finance, company-based approach. These studies explicitly account for differences in capital structure (amounts of debt vs. equity) and in costs of individual sources of capital (costs of debt and equity) at the company level. In many cases, the studies differ only in the way they estimate the costs of equity capital; the methodology used to estimate the cost of debt and the overall cost of capital is essentially the same.[7]

As many of these studies and their limitations are described in any standard corporate finance textbook, they are reviewed only briefly below. Under this approach, there is almost a consensus on the fact that there are three main models for estimating the company-specific cost of capital: the capital asset pricing model (CAPM), the dividend growth model (DGM) and the arbitrage pricing model (APM). A model which seems to be more popular in the investment dealer community is based on the price-earnings ratio.[8] This is sometimes used as a quick and dirty method of estimating the cost of equity capital as an inverse of the price-earnings ratio. This method has two major shortcomings: it relies on an accounting measure (earnings), and it completely ignores the differential growth rates in companies with the same current earnings. As a result, this method is considered the most unreliable and is almost never recommended for use in the decision-making framework.

As this section uses the CAPM approach to estimate the company-specific cost of equity, its underpinnings are explained in more detail below.[9] The dividend growth model (DGM), which is used in estimating the cost of capital in one of the case studies, is also described briefly.[10] As reported by Jog and Srivastava (1994), almost one third of Canadian firms indicate using a "risk premium" concept in estimating their cost of equity – a concept which underlies the development of CAPM. Fourteen percent of Canadian firms claim to use the DGM method to estimate their cost of equity capital.

Briefly, the CAPM relies on the simple concept that investors hold a diversified portfolio and require compensation, i.e., a higher expected return, for the risk that cannot be diversified away.[11] The CAPM provides a convenient way to quantify this non-diversifiable (or systematic) risk by measuring the beta of the firm. In other words, the return expected by the shareholders is made up of what they could earn in a riskless investment plus a risk premium proportional to the systematic risk coefficient of their stock. The higher the beta, the higher the expected return and, consequently, the higher the cost of equity for the firm. The actual risk premium would be determined by the beta coefficient times what is expected from holding a well-diversified portfolio, e.g., the TSE 300 index or the Standard & Poor's (S&P) 500 index. The latter, by definition, would have a beta of 1.0.

In the context of the CAPM, the risk-return relationship takes the following form:

$$R_S = R_F + Risk\ Premium \quad (1)$$

with the risk premium given by

$$beta \times (market\ return - risk\text{-}free\ return) \quad (2)$$

replacing equation (2) into equation (1)

$$R_S = R_F + Beta\ (R_M - R_F) \quad (3)$$

where R_S is the expected return on a security, R_F is the risk-free return and R_M is the expected return on the market portfolio.

This intuitively appealing formulation does not imply that this return would be realized each and every time but, on average, the relation must hold. Note that in equation (3), R_F and $(R_M - R_F)$ are economy-wide measures which should apply to any stock.

A straightforward application of the CAPM is the determination of a firm's cost of equity capital. Once the beta of the firm's stock is determined, the cost of equity can be calculated as:

$$cost\ of\ equity = risk\text{-}free\ rate + equity\ beta \times market\ risk\ premium \quad (4)$$

Three practical comments are in order here. First, a holding company would have to use as many costs of equity capital as it has main lines of business since the riskiness of the cash flows will generally be different from one line of business to the next. Second, each project can be seen as a mini-firm in itself for which a beta must be determined. And third, for a private firm or conglomerate, one must estimate the beta measures of independent similar firms operating in the same industry.

The Dividend Growth Model

The underlying rationale for the DGM for calculating the cost of equity is that the discount rate (or yield) makes the present value of the investment equal to its market value when it is used for discounting all future cash flows (ad infinitum). The DGM used for estimating the cost of equity was developed by Gordon and Shapiro (1956) and requires an estimate of future dividends that can be expected from holding shares of a company. Essentially, it implies that the current price equals the future dividend stream discounted at the required rate of return, i.e., cost of equity. By assuming a constant growth rate in dividends, the cost of equity under this model can be described as:

$$K_e = D_1/P_0 + g \quad (5)$$

where K_e is the cost of equity, D_1 is the next period dividends, P_0 is the current price and g is the estimated growth rate. Thus, the dividend growth model implies that if one can estimate growth rates for the company, one can estimate the company cost of equity.

A variety of approaches have been used to estimate the growth rates in empirical work. These include analysts' estimates, historical time series estimates and sustainable growth rates based on retention and book return on equity.

Capital Structure

In addition to equity capital, firms also resort to debt capital to finance their investments. On the one hand, debt capital provides a lower cost source since interest paid on debt is tax deductible. On the other hand, high reliance on debt also brings a higher possibility of bankruptcy or financial distress if the firm is unable to meet its interest obligations. Clearly then, the costs of equity and debt also depend on the capital structure, i.e., debt-to-equity ratio, of the firm. Intuitively, firms belonging to sectors which face higher variability in their business would resort to lower reliance on debt whereas firms in sectors facing lower levels of fluctuations in their earning streams would choose to rely on a higher level of debt.

In general, this trade-off between a lower after-tax cost of debt and a potentially higher probability of bankruptcy implies that the financing decisions of a firm must maximize the value of the firm. Therefore, the impact using various combinations of debt and equity to finance investments has on firm value and the costs of raising capital must be clearly understood before making capital structure decisions.

As taxes play a very important role in capital structure decisions, it is useful, as a starting point, to assume a case where no taxes or bankruptcy costs exist. It is in this case that Modigliani and Miller (1958) were able to show that the value of a firm would be independent of its capital structure; varying the degree of financial leverage would neither increase nor decrease the market value of the firm. However, the value of the firm is affected when corporate taxes are introduced since interest payments are deductible for tax purposes. This deductibility provides a tax-based incentive in the financing decision to rely on debt financing.

An important element in a decision about the appropriate level of debt is the notion of bankruptcy risk. A risk of bankruptcy means that the firm may be obliged to pay costs related to bankruptcy proceedings. Moreover, the possibility of bankruptcy may cause disruption in normal business relations: the potentially bankrupt firm may not be able to offer credible guarantees for its products or enter into long-term contracts with its customers and suppliers because of the threat of default.

Higher levels of leverage (debt) are associated with higher levels of bankruptcy risk. As such, both equity and debt investors will demand higher returns for the increasing levels of financial risk which, in turn, will reduce the value of the firm. The dilemma facing management when determining the optimal capital structure is the point where the costs associated with bankruptcy risk outweigh the benefits associated with the tax shield of the interest payments when increasing financial leverage. In practice, estimating the exact optimum level of debt at which firm value is maximized (or cost of capital is minimized) is difficult, if not impossible. It should also be noted that the systematic risk of the firm's equity not only reflects the underlying business risk faced by the firm but also the firm's financial risk. The latter is associated with the level of debt and the firm's ability to pay fixed interest obligations. The firm's cost of capital would thus depend on the level of debt and associated costs of equity and debt – the so-called weighted average cost of capital (WACC).

Cost of Capital – Empirical Estimation

The empirical estimates of the cost of capital presented in this paper are based on this basic framework of the CAPM and weighted average cost of capital. The individual components required for the estimation are outlined below.

Cost of Equity

The CAPM was used to compute the cost of equity. The use of the CAPM requires estimates of the risk-free rate, the equity beta and the market premium.

Risk-Free Rate

An approach by Myers (1993) was used to estimate the risk-free rate. The annual risk-free rate is estimated by subtracting a maturity premium of 1.2 percent from long-term government bond yields. Government of Canada long-term yields as of the end of each year studied were used.

Table 1 provides the inflation rate and the real and nominal risk-free rates used in estimating the cost of capital.

Equity Betas

Equity betas were computed by regressing each company's monthly return with the corresponding monthly returns of the TSE 300 index. The regressions were conducted on a rolling five-year basis for the 60 months immediately preceding the years for which the estimates were to be reported.[12] Due to the nature of the linear regression calculation, it is possible that the beta calculated for an individual firm may not have a great deal of explanatory power. This is due to the fact that the linear relationship represented by beta may only be useful over a specific range. If the returns used to calculate beta for a specific firm are highly volatile, the beta for that firm may not be indicative of the relationship between the stock returns and the TSE. To adjust for this problem, Vasicek (1973) suggested the following formula which compresses the betas of the sample, in this case the sector, toward the mean:

$$\beta_i^* = \beta_i^* \left(\sigma^2_{industry}/(\sigma^2_{industry} + \sigma(\beta_i)^2\right) + \beta^* \left(\sigma(\beta_i)^2/(\sigma^2_{industry} + \sigma(\beta_i)^2\right) \qquad (6)$$

TABLE 1
RISK-FREE RATES (%)

	1988	1989	1990	1991	1992	1993	1994
Nominal	9.16	8.49	9.31	7.77	7.34	5.92	7.96
Inflation	3.99	5.13	5.01	3.78	2.09	1.70	0.23
Real	4.97	3.20	4.09	3.84	5.14	4.15	7.71

where β_i^* is the Vasicek beta for stock i, β_i is the calculated beta for stock i, β is the average of the sector betas, $\sigma^2_{industry}$ is the variance of the sample betas in the corresponding industry sector and $\sigma(\beta_i)^2$ is the variance of the returns used to calculate beta for stock i.

Under this correction, the more uncertain the individual beta, the higher the weight given to the mean beta of that sector. The end result of this adjustment is a more robust series of beta values for the firms in the study.

Market-Risk Premium

There is no ideal method for estimating market-risk premium. In various rate studies and papers, any number from 4 percent to 8.5 percent has been used. All estimations in this paper use a 6 percent market-risk premium.[13] Clearly, any change in this premium may affect the cost of capital accordingly.

Cost of Debt

A simple method for obtaining a company's cost of debt is to use the current yield on the company's existing debt. However, the main obstacle with this approach is that, for many companies, their debt is not traded publicly and, therefore, current yields are not available. Even in cases where the debt is traded publicly, a current yield is only available if the debt is actively trading, otherwise, the yield will not reflect current market conditions.

Since, in most cases, the annual cost of company-specific debt was unavailable, the cost of debt had to be estimated in a more complex manner. First, the yield of all long-term corporate bonds was collected. This yield was used to represent the median of all corporate bond yields.[14] The median yields were then adjusted to reflect differences in the individual company's risk levels. To obtain the differences between companies, six different standardized criteria were used.[15]

Once the differences were computed, the individual companies were ranked (weighing each criteria equally) and assigned to one of 20 groups – the best ranked companies being assigned to group one, the second best companies to group two and so on. The groups were then assigned to one of seven bond ratings. Assigning

TABLE 2

COST OF DEBT ESTIMATES OBTAINED BY ADJUSTING THE MEDIAN YIELD OF ALL COMPANIES TO REFLECT DIFFERING CHARACTERISTICS OF EACH COMPANY

Groups of Companies Based on Rankings of Combined Six Criteria*	Assumed Bond Rating	Adjustment to Median Bond Yield (Basis Points)
1	AAA	-95
2,3,4	AA	-55
5,6,7,8	A+	-25
9,10,11,12	BBB	+75
13,14,15	BB	+125
16,17,18	B	+275
19,20	CCC	+600

Note: Group 1 represents the least risky (best) companies. Group 20 includes the most risky (worst) companies.

a bond rating made the yield calculations straightforward since spreads between bond ratings are available from many sources. Table 2 illustrates the groups, the corresponding bond ratings and the spreads that were used to compute the yields.

Cost of Preferred Equity

Since market data related to the current yields on preferred equity are very limited, measuring the cost of preferred equity can be complex. To simplify the estimation procedure, the spread between the yields on bonds and preferred equity was analysed over a nine-year period to determine if the cost of equity could be estimated in relation to the cost of debt. Government of Canada bond yields and preferred equity index yields were obtained from the preferred share quarterly report prepared by Burns Fry Limited (1994) and were compared, on a monthly basis, from 1985 to 1993. The average spread between the government bond yields and preferred equity yields over the period was 0.66 percentage points. As expected, the Government of Canada bond yield has been higher than the preferred equity yield.[16]

Since the above observations involved comparing low-risk government securities with higher-risk corporate securities, an adjustment was necessary to reflect the spread that has existed between corporate bond yields and corporate preferred yields. To adjust the Government of Canada bond yields to reflect the higher risk associated with corporate single-A rated bonds, the historical yields on Government of Canada bonds were compared with the historical yields on corporate single-A rated bonds provided in ScotiaMcLeod's *Handbook of Canadian Debt Market Securities*. The corporate single-A bond yields were approximately 1.3 percentage points to 1.5 percentage points higher than the government yields. Adding this adjustment to the

0.66 percent spread between Government of Canada bonds and preferred equity yields gives a spread of 1.96 percent to 2.16 percent between corporate single-A bond yields and preferred equity yields.

Having estimated the spread between corporate bond yields and preferred equity yields, the cost of preferred equity was then estimated by subtracting the spread (rounded to 2 percent) from the cost of debt estimated above.[17]

CAPITAL STRUCTURE

Market Value of Debt

Due to the unavailability of data regarding the market value of bonds, the market value of debt was assumed to equal the book value of debt. To ensure that a firm's use of permanent short-term debt as a substitute for long-term debt does not affect the estimates, one adjustment was made. Specifically, it was assumed that, in most cases, the value of a firm's current assets should at least be equal to the value of current liabilities. The first step was to calculate net working capital (current assets minus accounts payable) for each firm. If a firm had short-term debt greater than net working capital, it was assumed that the additional short-term debt was actually long-term debt and this difference was added to the long-term debt for the firm.

Market Value of Equity

The market value of common equity was computed by multiplying the year end market price by the number of shares outstanding at year end. The market value of preferred equity was computed under the assumption that the preferred dividend payment is a perpetuity. As such, the market value was computed by dividing the preferred dividend by the cost of preferred equity.

Market Value of Firm

The market value of the firm equals the sum of the market values of debt, common equity and preferred shares.

Effective Tax Rate

The effective tax rate was computed by dividing taxes paid by pre-tax income. In some cases, where this calculation produced meaningless values caused by various tax adjustments not reflected in the financial statements, the tax rate was assumed to equal 34.5 percent. Again, a different rate would change the estimation of the overall cost of capital.

Weighted Average Cost of Capital (WACC)

The following equation was used to compute the WACC:

$$WACC = k_d*(1 - T)*(D/V) + k_e*(E/V) + k_p*(P/V) \qquad (6)$$

where, k_d is the cost of debt before tax, k_e is the cost of common equity, k_p is the cost of preferred equity and D/V is the market value of long-term debt to the market value of the firm.

E/V is the market value of common equity to the market value of the firm, P/V is the market value of preferred equity to the market value of the firm, V is the market value of the firm (which equals $D + E + P$) and T is the effective tax rate.

Sectoral Estimates – Averaging of Company Results

To compute the sectoral cost of capital from the individual company estimates, some method of averaging was necessary. Two methods were used. The first computes a simple arithmetic average of all the companies' cost of capital within a given sector. The second computes a weighted average of all companies in a given sector. In the latter case, the weights used were the market values of the firm.

TABLE 3

SECTORAL GROUPINGS OF FIRMS

1	Metals and minerals
2	Gold and silver
3	Specialty stores
4	Paper and forest products
5	Technology
6	Industrial products
7	Real estate
8	Transportation and environmental services
9	Communications
10	Merchandising
11	Financial services
12	Conglomerates
13	Integrated oils
14	Oil and gas producers
15	Oil and gas, mining and forest services
16	Autos and parts
17	Beverages and tobacco
18	Food processing
19	Household goods
20	Biotechnology and pharmaceuticals
21	Utilities and pipelines
22	Services

Table 4

Average Beta for Canadian Sectors

Sector	1987	1988	1989	1990	1991	1992	1993	1994
Metals and minerals	1.46	1.43	1.36	1.28	1.31	1.18	1.08	1.11
Gold and silver	1.33	1.27	1.19	1.12	1.12	1.02	1.28	1.36
Specialty stores	0.86	0.83	0.84	0.82	0.86	0.86	0.86	0.80
Paper and forest products	1.20	1.26	1.36	1.26	1.30	1.21	1.16	1.10
Technology	1.02	1.03	1.04	1.00	1.04	1.18	1.16	1.13
Industrial products	0.98	1.01	1.02	0.97	0.99	1.10	1.04	1.03
Real estate	0.92	0.88	0.94	0.99	1.07	1.20	1.12	1.06
Transportation and environmental services	0.76	0.83	0.85	0.87	0.88	0.88	0.90	0.69
Communications	0.79	0.82	0.85	0.90	0.90	0.94	0.79	0.82
Merchandising	0.78	0.76	0.78	0.78	0.76	0.81	0.87	0.84
Financial services	0.98	0.95	0.96	0.94	0.95	0.84	0.98	0.90
Conglomerates	1.18	1.24	1.22	1.26	1.26	1.35	1.24	1.18
Integrated oils	1.09	1.04	1.05	0.94	0.87	0.58	0.75	0.73
Oil and gas producers	1.14	1.12	1.12	1.03	0.98	0.75	0.88	0.86
Oil and gas, mining and forest services	1.32	1.30	1.26	1.12	1.04	0.85	0.98	0.97
Autos and parts	0.83	0.83	0.91	0.79	0.83	0.78	0.79	0.75
Beverages and tobacco	0.79	0.81	0.85	0.80	0.80	0.83	0.76	0.75
Food processing	0.72	0.77	0.80	0.81	0.78	0.82	0.87	0.77
Household goods	0.86	0.86	0.87	0.82	0.85	0.96	1.00	0.92
Biotechnology and pharmaceuticals	0.87	0.89	0.96	0.96	1.02	0.91	0.95	0.97
Utilities and pipelines	0.47	0.48	0.54	0.56	0.58	0.61	0.57	0.63
Services	0.92	0.90	0.92	0.96	0.98	1.04	0.99	0.97

Results

The weighted average costs of capital were computed annually for all 714 companies in the study and were then grouped into 22 industrial sectors allowing the results to be presented in a reasonable manner. Table 3 shows the groupings of companies represented by the 22 sectors.

Main Results – Sectoral Costs of Capital

Table 4 shows the average beta for each of the 22 sectors listed above. Table 5 presents the corresponding cost of capital estimates, in real terms by sector, for each year of the study as well as the overall average cost of capital of the seven years considered.[18] These results show only the weighted average approach to computing the sectoral cost of capital. Simple averaging is not used because with this approach very small companies which represent a small portion of a sector will be given equal

TABLE 5

REAL WEIGHTED AVERAGE COST OF CAPITAL (WACC)

Sector	1988	1989	1990	1991	1992	1993	1994	Overall
Utilities and pipelines	6.41	5.25	6.18	6.35	7.37	6.44	9.30	6.76
Real estate	7.31	6.05	6.44	6.75	7.08	6.48	8.96	7.01
Transportation and environmental services	7.94	6.37	7.16	7.30	8.28	7.64	9.85	7.79
Communications	8.40	6.57	7.34	7.45	9.09	7.68	11.39	8.27
Autos and parts	8.59	7.56	7.22	7.66	8.80	8.14	10.70	8.38
Food processing	9.09	7.26	7.93	7.40	8.63	8.23	10.90	8.49
Merchandising	8.74	7.28	8.03	7.77	9.05	8.47	11.55	8.70
Beverages and tobacco	9.10	7.50	8.04	8.06	9.43	8.05	11.05	8.75
Household goods	9.13	7.27	7.37	7.64	9.47	8.93	11.64	8.78
Services	8.82	7.23	7.96	7.92	9.35	8.53	11.64	8.78
Integrated oils	10.20	7.97	8.65	7.99	8.11	7.88	11.26	8.87
Specialty stores	8.95	7.39	7.92	8.16	9.40	8.68	11.63	8.88
Conglomerates	9.60	8.05	8.44	8.29	8.61	8.98	11.80	9.11
Oil and gas producers	9.51	8.56	8.81	8.32	8.72	8.62	11.46	9.14
Financial services	9.55	7.89	8.45	8.48	9.13	9.00	11.90	9.20
Industrial products	9.30	7.78	8.08	8.12	9.67	9.13	12.33	9.20
Paper and forest products	10.20	8.73	8.74	8.83	9.74	9.21	11.88	9.62
Biotechnology and pharmaceuticals	9.46	8.21	9.12	9.68	10.03	9.29	12.57	9.77
Oil and gas, mining and forest services	11.00	9.24	9.59	8.99	9.17	9.72	13.19	10.13
Metals and minerals	11.79	9.69	9.57	9.45	10.55	9.57	12.95	10.51
Technology	10.45	8.56	9.04	9.35	11.45	10.71	14.02	10.51
Gold and silver	11.63	9.64	9.84	9.64	10.50	11.44	15.30	11.14
Average of sample	9.33%	7.73%	8.18%	8.16%	9.17%	8.67%	11.69%	8.99%

very small companies which represent a small portion of a sector will be given equal weight in computing the sectoral cost of capital resulting in potentially misleading results.

Tables 4 and 5 show that the utilities and pipelines sector has the lowest cost of capital averaging just under 7 percent which is consistent with its low beta, i.e., risk. At the other end of the spectrum, the gold and silver sector has the highest hurdle rate averaging just over 11 percent, which is consistent with its higher level of risk as measured by beta.

To test for the robustness of the cost of capital estimates over time, the WACCs of each sector were ranked in ascending order for each of the seven years in the study. The rankings, presented in Table 6, show that the results are quite robust over time with little change in the overall ranking of the sectors. At the bottom of Table 6, the value of Pearson year-to-year correlation coefficients are provided. This measure compares the correlations between the sectoral rankings of a given year with the rankings of the previous year. As the coefficients show, the correlations are high indicating that the rankings across time are fairly consistent.

Impact on the WACC of Changing the Market-Risk Premium

Table 7 presents the impact of changes of plus or minus 1 percentage point to the market premium (assumed to equal 6 percent) on the WACC. The results show that changes to the market premium assumption have a linear impact on the sectoral costs of capital. For instance, in the merchandising sector a 1 percentage point reduction in the market premium from 6 percent to 5 percent results in the WACC being reduced by -0.55 percentage point while a 1 percentage point increase in the market premium from 6 percent to 7 percent results in the WACC increasing by 0.55 percentage point. Thus, the sectoral WACCs can be adjusted according to the market-risk premium assumption used.

Sectoral Capital Structures

The overall capital structures of the sectors are illustrated in Table 8 which provides calculations based on both market values and book values. The figures present the sectoral equity-to-firm values computed by using the simple averages and the weighted averages of the companies in a sector. Overall, the capital structures do not differ significantly when market values are used as opposed to book values with the exception of utilities and pipelines, communications, beverages and tobacco, and technology where differences of greater than 10 percent exist.

In most sectors the amount of equity financing relative to total financing is in the range of 50 percent to 75 percent with the weighted average being 62 percent for book values and 72 percent for market values. In the real estate sector, however, the amount of equity financing used is considerably less than in all other sectors; the equity-to-firm ratio averages 37 percent (based on simple averages) for

TABLE 6

RANKINGS OF SECTORS BY WACC

Sector	1988	1989	1990	1991	1992	1993	1994	Overall
Utilities and pipelines	1	1	2	1	2	2	2	1
Real estate	2	2	1	2	1	1	1	2
Transportation and environmental services	3	3	3	3	4	3	3	3
Communications	4	4	5	4	10	4	8	4
Autos and parts	5	11	4	7	8	7	4	5
Food processing	12	8	10	5	6	8	5	6
Merchandising	6	6	9	8	9	9	10	7
Services	7	5	7	9	13	10	12	8
Household goods	9	7	6	6	15	14	13	9
Integrated oils	18	14	14	10	3	5	7	10
Beverages and tobacco	10	10	12	14	16	6	6	11
Specialty stores	8	9	8	13	14	12	11	12
Conglomerates	13	13	13	12	5	13	14	13
Industrial products	11	12	11	11	17	16	17	14
Oil and gas producers	14	18	17	15	7	11	9	15
Financial services	16	15	16	16	12	15	16	16
Paper and forest products	17	17	15	17	18	17	15	17
Biotechnology and pharmaceuticals	15	16	19	22	19	18	18	18
Oil and gas, mining and forest services	20	20	21	18	11	20	20	19
Metals and minerals	22	21	20	19	20	19	19	20
Technology	19	19	18	20	22	21	21	21
Gold and silver	21	22	22	21	21	22	22	22
Pearson year-to-year correlation coefficient	n/a	0.94	0.95	0.93	0.76	0.81	0.97	n/a

Note: n/a: not applicable.

TABLE 7

REAL WEIGHTED AVERAGE COST OF CAPITAL (OVERALL) IMPACT OF PLUS/MINUS 1 PERCENT CHANGE IN MARKET PREMIUM

Sector	5% MRP	6% MRP	Change in WACC	7% MRP	Change in WACC
Utilities and pipelines	6.43	6.76	-0.32	7.08	0.32
Real estate	6.63	7.01	-0.38	7.39	0.38
Transportation and environmental services	7.32	7.79	-0.47	8.26	0.47
Communications	7.70	8.27	-0.58	8.85	0.58
Autos and parts	7.79	8.38	-0.59	8.97	0.59
Food processing	7.89	8.49	-0.60	9.09	0.60
Merchandising	8.15	8.70	-0.55	9.25	0.55
Beverages and tobacco	8.13	8.75	-0.62	9.37	0.62
Services	8.12	8.78	-0.66	9.44	0.66
Household goods	8.13	8.78	-0.65	9.42	0.65
Integrated oils	8.26	8.87	-0.61	9.47	0.61
Specialty stores	8.24	8.88	-0.64	9.51	0.64
Conglomerates	8.48	9.11	-0.63	9.74	0.63
Oil and gas producers	8.40	9.14	-0.74	9.89	0.74
Financial services	8.47	9.20	-0.73	9.93	0.73
Industrial products	8.49	9.20	-0.71	9.91	0.71
Paper and forest products	8.85	9.62	-0.77	10.39	0.77
Biotechnology and pharmaceuticals	8.93	9.77	-0.84	10.61	0.84
Oil and gas, mining and forest services	9.24	10.13	-0.89	11.02	0.89
Metals and minerals	9.58	10.51	-0.93	11.44	0.93
Technology	9.56	10.51	-0.95	11.46	0.95
Gold and silver	10.07	11.14	-1.07	12.21	1.07

both book and market value based calculations. For this reason, the real estate sector has the second lowest WACC since the sector relies, to a much larger extent, on the much lower after-tax cost of debt as its major financing source.

Overall, the results of the study indicate that from 1988 to 1994 the real sectoral costs of capital ranged between 6.8 percent and 11.1 percent, averaging 8.99 percent with the assumption that the risk-free premium is 6 percent. The order of the sectors relative to one another has remained fairly constant during the period with utilities and pipelines having the lowest cost of capital and gold and silver having the highest cost of capital.

TABLE 8

CAPITAL STRUCTURE: EQUITY TO FIRM VALUE IN PERCENT BASED ON BOOK VALUE AND MARKET VALUE

Sector	Book Value		Market Value	
Averages	Simple	Weighted	Simple	Weighted
Utilities and pipelines	44	46	54	58
Real estate	37	25	36	27
Transportation and environmental services	52	49	51	56
Communications	50	47	62	66
Autos and parts	66	67	71	74
Food processing	72	81	74	84
Merchandising	65	57	68	65
Beverages and tobacco	65	64	77	75
Services	61	70	66	79
Household goods	65	61	69	66
Integrated oils	67	74	71	79
Specialty stores	71	71	75	79
Conglomerates	51	60	50	61
Oil and gas producers	65	66	74	76
Financial services	68	60	67	64
Industrial products	65	62	68	69
Paper and forest products	56	56	62	62
Biotechnology and pharmaceuticals	77	81	85	90
Oil and gas, mining and forest services	74	75	78	79
Metals and minerals	70	62	67	70
Technology	74	74	84	88
Gold and silver	76	78	84	90

CASE STUDY 1: CROSS-COUNTRY COMPARISON OF COST OF CAPITAL[19]

THIS SECTION EXAMINES THE ESTIMATION AND COMPARISON of the cost of capital between Canadian firms which may choose to raise funds in the United States and U.S. firms raising funds in the United States. There are a variety of reasons why a Canadian firm may choose to raise both debt and equity financing in the United States, e.g., export-oriented Canadian firms may want to reduce their exposure to exchange rate fluctuations or the size of domestic capital markets may not provide financing at attractive rates.

Since a main component of relative cost of capital is the risk-free rate, the differences between the risk-free rates in the two countries are examined first. These differences are analysed with respect to inflation, country and exchange rate risk. Next, the impacts of foreign exchange exposure and company-specific effects on the cost of capital are examined using the forest product sector as an example. Exchange rate exposure exists for companies which have their cash inflows and outflows denominated in more than one currency. Within this section, a numerical example is provided to illustrate the relative importance of the Canadian cost of capital disadvantage on a typical investment project. The example focuses on an investment decision to build a typical mill for producing LWC (magazine) paper, a product that is primarily sold to the U.S. market.

Differences in the Risk-Free Rate between Canada and the United States

As noted in the previous section, the cost of capital computation under the CAPM framework reveals that cross-country differences in the cost of equity and debt may arise, in part, from the fact that cross-country differences in the risk-free rates exist. Thus, to measure the differences in the cost of capital between Canada and the United States, a comparison of the risk-free rates between the two countries is in order.[20]

Nominal and Real Risk-Free Rates

To measure the difference in risk-free rates between Canada and the United States, the yields on three-month Canadian and U.S. treasury bills (t-bills) were compared. The historical yields on three-month Canadian and U.S. t-bills from 1983 to 1992 (inclusive) are shown in Figure 1. The figure illustrates that historically Canada has had a higher nominal risk-free rate (9.68 percent) than the United States (6.90 percent) with the historical spread between Canadian and U.S. treasury bills averaging 2.78 percent (Figure 2). This suggests that Canada has had, on average, a significantly higher nominal risk-free rate than the United States.

One reason for the higher Canadian risk-free rate could be the cross-country differential in inflation, since the above rates are given in nominal terms. During this 10-year period, Canada had an inflation rate which was approximately 0.9 percentage point higher than in the United States (which is lower than the 2.78 percentage point spread). As a result, the real spread between the Canadian and U.S. risk-free rates is reduced to 1.88 percent.

Components of Risk-Free Rate Differential

As Canada has traditionally been a net importer of capital relying largely on the United States, it may be interesting to evaluate this 1.88 percentage point spread from the viewpoint of a U.S. investor. A U.S. investor who is investing in Canadian government securities (denominated in Canadian dollars) faces two risks: an exchange rate risk and a country risk. The former arises from the changes in the exchange rate during the investment-holding period and the latter arises from a premium, if any, a U.S. investor would demand from investing in a Canadian government security.

FIGURE 1

CANADIAN AND U.S. THREE-MONTH TREASURY BILLS

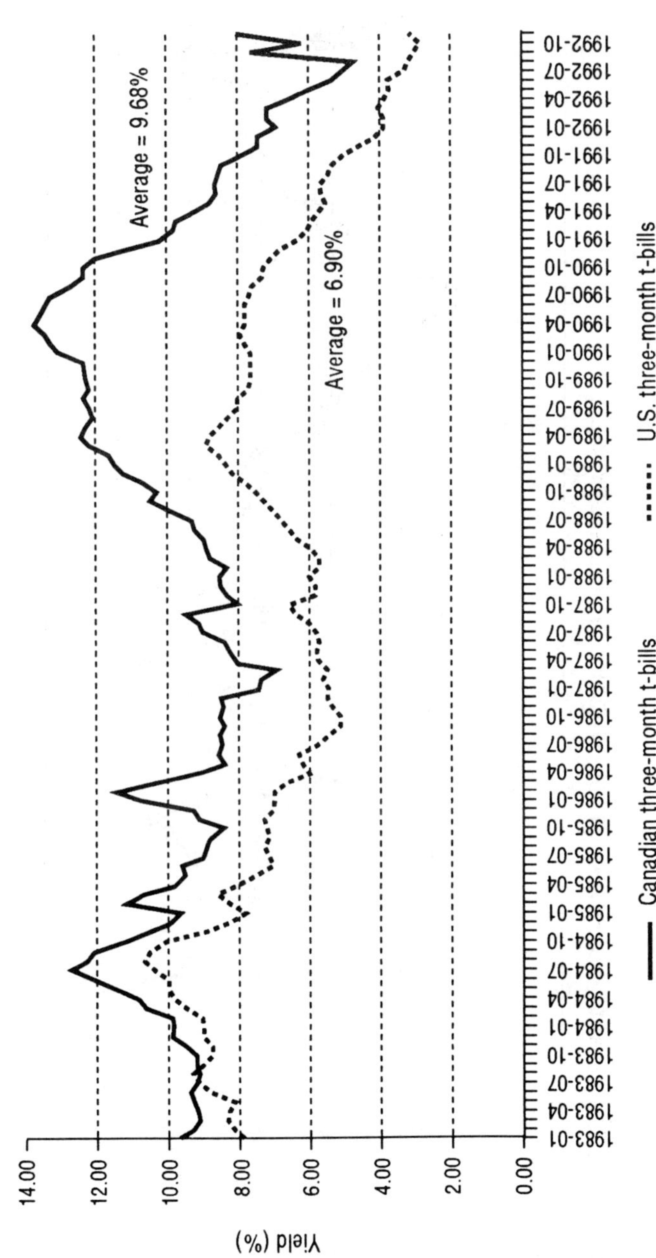

FIGURE 2

SPREAD BETWEEN THREE-MONTH CANADIAN AND U.S. TREASURY BILLS

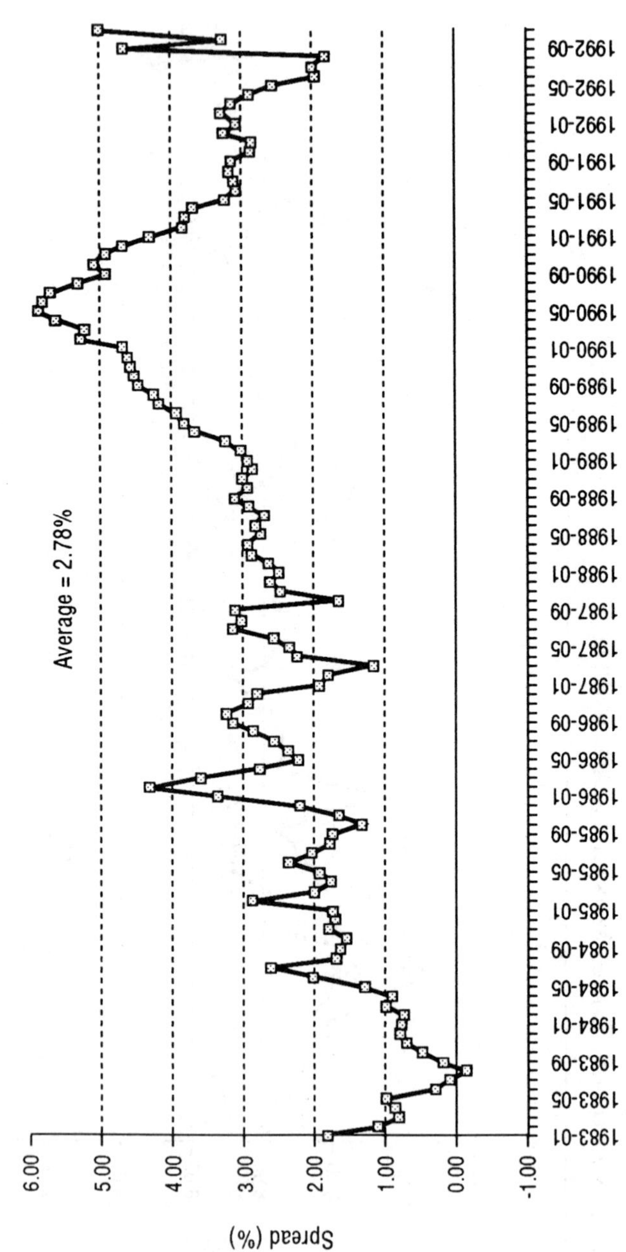

To isolate exchange rate risk from the Canadian-U.S. spread, the viewpoint of a U.S. investor is used to consider two investment options. The first option is to invest in a U.S. three-month t-bill. With the second option, the investment is in a Canadian three-month t-bill and the associated exchange rate exposure is hedged. Since the second option eliminates exchange rate risk associated with the Canadian denominated investment, any difference in the return between the second and first option must be due to country risk.

The following example illustrates how this can be accomplished using forward rates between Canadian and U.S. dollars.

In January 1991, Canadian three-month t-bills yielded 10.58 percent, U.S. three-month t-bills yielded 6.30 percent, the Canadian-U.S. spot exchange rate was $1.1629 and the three-month forward Canadian-U.S. exchange rate was $1.1730, i.e., a 101 basis point premium (1.1730 - 1.1629). The hedged yield for a U.S. investor investing in a three-month Canadian t-bill and converting the proceeds back to U.S. dollars at the end of the three months at the three-month forward exchange rate equals:

Beginning investment	US$1.0000
Convert to C$	C$1.1629
Ending Investment	
1.1629 + (1.1629 x .1058 x 3/12)	C$1.1937
Convert to US$ (@ 1.1730)	US$1.0176
Three-month return	1.76%
Annual return	**7.04%**

This illustrates that a U.S. investor could have earned, in U.S. currency, 7.04 percent on an annualized basis by investing in a three-month Canadian t-bill and hedging the currency exposure. In contrast, by investing in a U.S. three-month t-bill the yield was 6.30 percent, 74 basis points lower which reflects the Canadian country-risk premium.

Using this technique of accounting for the exchange risk faced by the U.S. investor in investing in Canadian t-bills, the historical absolute spreads shown in Figure 2 can be adjusted. These are shown graphically in Figure 3. For the 10-year period, the adjusted spread was 0.74 percentage points which represents the average additional yield investors demand for Canadian investments relative to U.S. investments in order to compensate themselves for the additional level of country risk they face when investing in Canada. Therefore, of the 1.88 percentage point real spread in the risk-free rates that exists between Canada and the United States, 0.74 percentage points is attributable to the country risk and 1.14 percentage points (1.88 - 0.74) is attributable to the exchange risk.

A second method of measuring the magnitude of sovereign country risk is to compare Canadian government securities with U.S. government securities, with both securities being issued in the same currency, thereby eliminating the exchange rate and inflation risk. For example, a study by Lessard et al. (1983) compared yields on

FIGURE 3

SPREAD OF HEDGED US$ INVESTMENT IN CANADIAN TREASURY BILLS VS. US$ INVESTMENT IN U.S. TREASURY BILLS

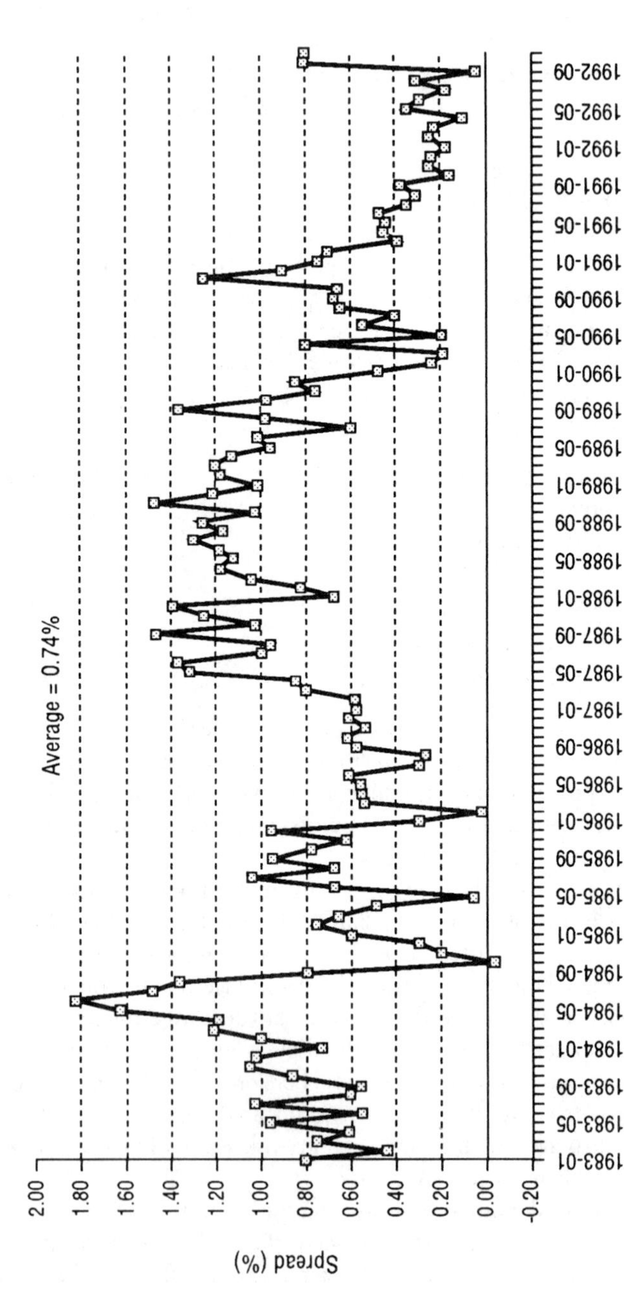

U.S. dollar denominated short and long-term bonds issued by both the Canadian and U.S. governments and government agencies in the Euromarkets and U.S. markets. Their study found that Canadian issuers averaged approximately 7.75 percent corresponding to an incremental yield differential that averaged approximately 0.80 percent. This finding is consistent with the 0.74 percent yield differential obtained above.[21]

Thus, even after adjusting for the exchange rate risk, U.S. investors received (or required) a 0.74 percent higher yield from investing in Canadian t-bills. The reasons for this differential can be many: the impact of variations in world economic activity on Canada, shifts in relative prices of natural resources and endogenous forces, such as monetary, fiscal, regulatory and labour market policies.

This estimation of 0.74 percent country-risk premium depends critically on the investment instruments used for comparison. Here the t-bill rate and the published forward rates have been used for separating the real rate differential. This estimation differs from Frankel (1991) who used the Eurodollar rates and forward rates from Barclays Bank for 1982 through to 1988. He concluded that, although there is a real rate differential between the United States and Canada during this period, there is no observed country-risk premium between the two countries; the entire difference in the real rate can be attributed to the foreign exchange premium.[22]

Foreign Exchange Exposure and Company-Specific Risk in the Forest Sector

Canadian corporations face, at a minimum, a real risk premium differential of 1.88 percent for the costs of both equity and debt from U.S. investors. However, there may be an additional risk premium demanded for those companies which have foreign exchange exposure due to their dependence on U.S. markets, i.e., a business risk premium. For example, any Canadian export-oriented firm is affected by the volatility of exchange rates since it has revenues denominated in U.S. dollars and costs denominated in Canadian dollars. Unfortunately, it is not possible to determine empirically this additional premium because it is impossible to find two firms, one in the United States and the other in Canada, which are identical in all respects except for their ownership and location. An indirect way of estimating (or detecting) whether any premium exists is to compare the yields on Canadian bond issues (by Canadian firms) denominated in U.S. dollars with bond issue yields received by their counterpart U.S. firms. This spread would represent the impact of foreign exchange exposure and the country-risk premium on the cost of debt.[23]

Because the Canadian forest products sector relies, to a large extent, on U.S. markets for its revenues, this sector is appropriate for making such a comparison. Accordingly, bond yields for a small sample of Canadian and U.S. pulp and paper companies have been obtained. In all cases, the bonds are issued in U.S. currency and the yields are those obtained by the U.S. investor. The average Canadian and U.S. debt costs, after being standardized for different maturities, are compared to determine the average spread between the two (the spread reflecting the difference in the cost of debt [before tax] between the two countries).

The average cost of debt for Canadian companies was found to be 10.72 percent and the average cost of debt for U.S. companies was 7.28 percent providing a spread of 3.44 percentage points. The spread is higher than the real rate differential as company and product-mix specific factors (illustrated by the debt ratings) are embedded in the individual costs of debt. It is also possible that this difference in the ratings may reflect the fact that the Canadian companies are located outside the United States and are automatically considered riskier. In any event, the debt ratings of Canadian companies are approximately two grades below that of U.S. companies. If it is assumed that each level of downgrading results in an average increase of 0.75 percentage points in the cost of debt, then the average Canadian cost of debt is approximately 1.50 percentage points higher than the average U.S. cost of debt because of the lower debt ratings. Thus, if the 1.50 percentage point company/industry-specific premium is removed from the total spread of 3.44 percentage points, then the spread without company/product-mix specific distortions becomes 1.94 percentage points.

Having estimated the spread between the Canadian and U.S. cost of debt for the forest product sector, it is also necessary to estimate the spread in the cost of equity. However, estimating the spread in the cost of equity using the same approach as that used for the cost of debt is more complex and beyond the scope of this paper.[24] As an approximation, it is reasonable to assume that the differential costs of equity will be at least equal to the 1.94 percentage points differential for debt securities.

An Example: Light Weight Coated Paper Mill

An example of an investment decision with respect to a representative and state-of-the-art LWC paper mill located in Canada relative to an identical mill located in the United States[25] is provided to illustrate the impact of the 1.94 percentage points higher debt and equity financing costs on the relative attractiveness of investing in Canada.

The estimation of the WACC for LWC mills located in the United States and Canada was carried out by estimating the cost of equity using the CAPM which requires estimates of the risk-free rate, the market premium and beta. Historically, the real risk-free rate (estimated from three-month U.S. t-bills less inflation) has averaged 2.97 percent. To convert the real risk-free rate to a nominal rate, an expected inflation rate of 2.25 percent was assumed giving an expected nominal risk-free rate of 5.28 percent.[26] The expected market premium was assumed to equal 6 percent. The equity beta of 1.21 was used as an estimate for the systematic risk of equity resulting in the cost of equity estimated to equal 12.54 percent.[27] The cost of debt (before-tax) was assumed to be 0.88 percentage points higher than the nominal risk-free rate and equal to 6.16 percent. Applying a tax rate of 34 percent gives an after-tax cost of debt of 4.07 percent. Using the typical capital structure of 40 percent debt and 60 percent equity in the forest sector, the U.S. WACC was computed to equal 9.15 percent nominal and 6.90 percent real.

To compute the Canadian WACC, the costs of equity and debt for the mill located in Canada were obtained by adding the 1.94 percentage point country and exchange premium to the U.S. costs of debt (before tax) and equity. Assuming the same capital structure for the Canadian mill, the real WACC is estimated as 8.57 percent. Comparing the real Canadian and U.S. WACCs reveals that the Canadian WACC is 1.67 percentage points higher than the U.S. WACC.

This difference in the Canadian and U.S. WACCs has a considerable impact on the attractiveness of an LWC mill investment. With the 1.67 percentage point higher Canadian WACC, the net present value of an LWC mill located in Quebec is reduced by a very significant $137 million (from $151 million to $14 million) compared to the net present value of an LWC mill located in the United States.

Conclusion

This case study illustrates some of the challenges in estimating cross-country differences in cost of capital using the micro approach. It is based on a specific sector and uses the data from a specific time period. The example from the forest products industry illustrates that, for export-oriented Canadian companies whose revenues are denominated in a foreign currency and costs in a domestic currency, a foreign exchange (business) risk premium exists. Canadian companies in the forest products sector, with exchange exposure, bear debt and equity costs that are 1.94 percentage points above their U.S. counterparts. The impact of this foreign exchange differential further decreases the competitive advantage for Canadian locations and companies. It has been shown that, for a typical Canadian LWC paper mill, the disadvantage reduces its net present value by $137 million. Thus, a small difference in cost of capital can have a major impact on location choices.

Case Study 2: A Case of Public Utilities[28]

The aim of this section is to uncover differences in the estimation of cost of capital between firms in Canada and the United States using a competing model for calculating cost of equity, the DGM. The telecommunications sector is chosen to illustrate this model for several reasons. First, this sector is regulated and faces similar risks in the two countries. Second, like other regulated utilities, the telecommunications sector has enjoyed stable cash flows and has maintained a relatively stable dividend stream. Several telecommunication companies (telcos) in both countries have been privatized with shares publicly traded on the open market. Further, the business environment and risks faced by telcos in the United States and Canada are sufficiently similar for case study purposes. Wherever relevant, the impact of the differences in the business environment between the United States and Canada on the estimation process is also discussed. The section begins with a discussion of the regulatory environment as it affects this study, followed by a description of the study sample and a brief comparison of the business risks faced by telcos in the two countries. A description of data, the empirical estimation procedure, results and the conclusion follow.

Telco Regulatory Environment

THE TELCO REGULATORY ENVIRONMENT, ON THE WHOLE, is very similar in Canada and the United States. In both countries, there has been a mix of national and state/provincial regulatory jurisdictions. Competition is permitted in both countries in most market segments; however, local service remains largely under the control of regulated monopolies. In both countries, telcos' regulated businesses must not cross-subsidize their non-regulated (competitive) businesses. A notable difference between the countries relates to long distance telecommunications services. Since the breakup of AT&T in 1984, the U.S. Baby Bells have been excluded from the right to deliver long distance services. However, they have retained "local long distance" toll services within their own areas and, for the most part, this business has been protected from competition. Canadian firms, in contrast, continue to participate significantly in both local and long distance services. Finally, both countries continue to distinguish between the carriage and content functions in the delivery of local network services. Accordingly, telephone industry investments in programming and in the provision of information services and other forms of "content" are not yet allowed among Baby Bells in the United States, and face regulatory restrictions in Canada.

Given this similarity in regulatory policy orientation, the proximity of the two countries and their participation in the same dramatic technological innovations, it is not surprising that the telecommunications regulatory climate has gone through similar changes in both countries in the recent past. However, although regulatory changes in Canada have tended to parallel actions taken in the United States, they have done so to a lesser degree and at a later date. The United States has tended to be quicker than Canada in relaxing the telco regulatory regime and in permitting greater competition. For example, U.S. telecom users were allowed to interconnect third-party terminal equipment in the mid-1970s, several years before similar changes in Canada. Also, long distance services were opened up to competition in the United States in the mid-1980s, whereas the Canadian long distance market remained a monopoly until June 1992. Finally, the Canadian industry has been slower to accept resale operators.

This leadership in the United States regarding the deregulation of telecommunication services continues. The United States is opening up "local" telecommunication services markets to competition more rapidly than Canada, permitting greater competition for business services. For example, as of 1992 in 43 U.S. states, new entrants in the industry (called "competitive access providers") can provide lower cost intra-state ("local long distance") telecommunications service and thereby undermine both Baby Bell toll revenues and local network access charges. In addition, long distance service providers will be able to by-pass Baby Bell local access charges by linking up with wireless systems. As a result, the local monopolies enjoyed by U.S. telcos have come under greater and increasing competitive pressure.

The difference between Canada and the United States regarding the regulatory environment does not relate merely to the extent and speed of the deregulation of telecommunication services. It also relates to the form of the telco regulations themselves. Traditionally, regulatory commissions have sought to control monopoly service rates through "rate of return" regulation. The aim is to constrain the monopoly firm's profits. However, under such a regime, there is less incentive to achieve lower costs (or avoid inefficient investment) since profit margins are capped. As a result, many of the U.S. regulatory agencies have switched to forms of "incentive" regulation. A popular kind of incentive regulation is called a "price cap." Here the agency controls prices rather than profits by limiting increases in regulated rates according to a formula that reflects the costs of providing regulated services, taking into account productivity gains. Another feature of some of these forms of incentive regulation is to permit the telco to make excess profits, but require that this excess be shared with ratepayers.

In Canada, by contrast, the Canadian Radio-television and Telecommunications Commission (CRTC) and provincial boards have continued to make use of the traditional rate base/rate of return regulation that is applied in most monopolistic utilities. While it is true that incentive-based schemes are not without their own problems, they would appear to be an advance on the traditional approach. Thus, here too, the Canadian regulatory environment lags behind the United States. It should be pointed out, however, that the CRTC has been investigating the possibility of moving toward an incentive-based system (Proceeding 78-92).

The Companies in the Sample

The U.S. sample consists of the seven regional telcos (or Baby Bells): Ameritech, Bell Atlantic, Bell South, NYNEX, Pacific Telesis, Southwestern Bell and US West. These companies are very large and of roughly equal size. In terms of the 1992 market value of invested capital (debt and equity), the value of these firms ranged from US$20.4 billion (US West) to US$32.8 billion (Bell South), with an average of US$25 billion. It should be noted that most of these firms have international businesses (including non-telecommunications activities, such as cable TV companies). Some also derive modest shares of their total revenues from other non-telecommunications businesses such as financial services and real estate. Thus, there is a mix of foreign ventures, cable TV, financial services and real estate that have an impact on their consolidated balance sheets.[29]

The Canadian sample consists of the following companies: BC Tel, Maritime Tel, Newtel, Quebec Telephone, Island Telephone and Bruncor. The largest, BC Tel, had a 1992 market value (debt and equity) of $3.7 billion. Maritime Tel is the second largest firm in the Canadian sample with a market value of $1.3 billion, including the $130 million value of its subsidiary, Island Telephone. The remaining three companies have market capitalizations ranging from $500 million to $900 million.

The market value of the entire Canadian sample is only $7.4 billion or roughly one quarter of the size of the average U.S. Baby Bell. The largest Canadian telco, Bell Canada, has a book value of debt and equity which is roughly equal to that of the smallest U.S. Baby Bell. If Bell Canada were added to the Canadian sample, it would increase the (1992) book value of that sample from $5.7 billion to $19.9 billion.

Unfortunately, Bell Canada's common shares are not publicly traded. Consequently, the market value of its common equity[30] cannot be estimated. Telus (largely made up of AGT), which is the third largest telecommunications company in Canada, was also excluded from the sample. It was not until the fall of 1990 that Telus became a private company and, as a result, available data for Telus for 1989 and 1990 were inadequate.

Among the Canadian firms, all but NewTel and Bruncor get all their revenues from telecommunication services. In the case of Bruncor, which has lines of business in real estate and financial services, 80 percent of assets and 95 percent of sales are derived from its telecommunications firm, NBTel. In the case of NewTel, 96 percent of both assets and sales are derived from its telecommunications firm, Newfoundland Telephone.

Comparison of Business Risk: United States vs. Canada

As a result of differences in the regulatory environment and the diverse operations of sample companies, it is necessary to discuss briefly the potential differences in their respective business risks, the most notable being in the degree of protection available to sample companies in the local and long distance markets.

Unfortunately, It is difficult to get a precise ratio of monopoly vs. competitive revenues for the U.S. and Canadian samples. With regard to the Canadian firms, and including Bell Canada, almost half of all 1992 revenues were derived from long distance services; another 36 percent (66 percent for U.S. telcos) came from local services, and 16 percent from "other services" such as directory advertising, equipment sales and cellular telecom revenues (24 percent for the United States). Within this mix, it is estimated that approximately 20 percent of Canadian telecommunication services were offered on a competitive basis.

In the United States, by contrast, only 10 percent of 1992 revenues came from long distance services, which, in the study period, continued to be largely a monopoly business for the Baby Bells. About two thirds of telecom revenues were derived from local services and access charges which are largely, but not entirely, a monopoly haven. Meanwhile, about 25 percent came from "other services" such as directory advertising, equipment sales and cellular services.

Although the exact percentage of U.S. revenues from competitive businesses is difficult to assess, it is safe to say that the U.S. firms in the sample have a higher business risk and face more competition than the Canadian firms. This is augmented by the fact that the Baby Bells would appear to be more involved in foreign ventures and non-telecom businesses which carry more risk.[31]

FIGURE 4

AS A PROPORTION OF TOTAL REVENUES, A LARGER SHARE OF BABY BELL REVENUE DERIVES FROM RISKIER BUSINESSES

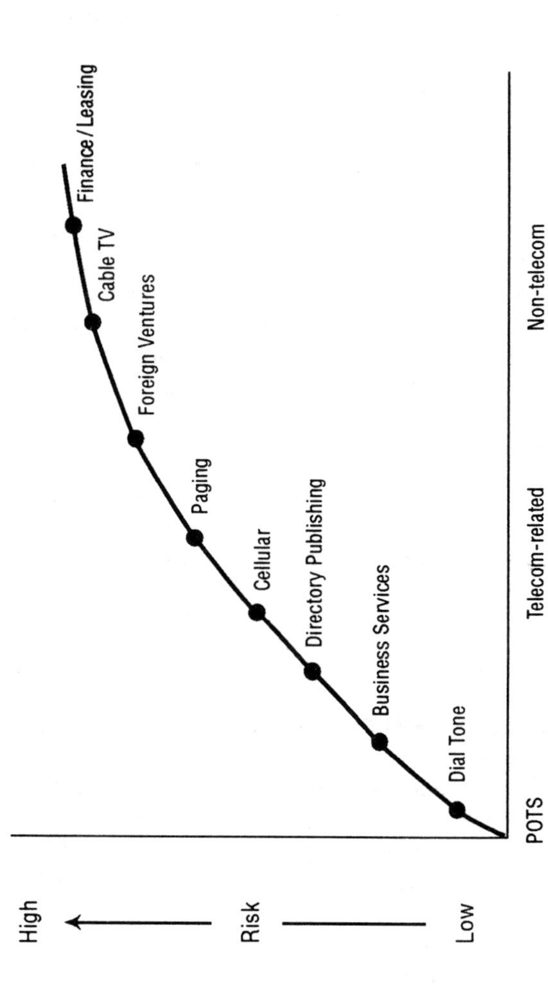

Note: POTS = Plain Ordinary Telephone Service.

DATA AND METHODOLOGY

RESULTS ARE BASED ON THE YEARS 1989 TO 1992. A simple average of the results is used in the final United States-Canada comparison. It is not surprising that a number of challenges were encountered in the empirical estimation of the cost of capital. These challenges can be grouped into five types: the unavailability of data on market values of debt and preferred shares due to non-trading, the ability to estimate future growth rates, the time of year at which the required market values are used for estimation purposes, the complexity of details including those associated with deferred taxes and minority interest, and some issues with respect to the part of the short-term debt that should be considered long-term debt.

TABLE 9

AVERAGE COST OF DEBT: 1989 TO 1992 U.S. TELCOS

Company	Nominal			Real	
	Pre-Tax Cost of Debt (%)	Effective Tax Rate (%)	After Tax Cost of Debt (%)	After Tax Cost of Debt (%)	Market Value of Debt: % of Firm Value
Ameritech	8.2	30.7	5.7	1.8	22
Bell Atlantic	8.2	32.2	5.6	1.7	29
Bell South	8.2	33.1	5.5	1.6	24
NYNEX	8.2	26.8	6.0	2.1	31
Pacific Telesis	8.2	37.0	5.2	1.9	26
Southwestern Bell	8.2	28.7	5.9	1.9	25
US West	8.2	30.5	5.7	1.8	32
INDUSTRY	8.2	31.3	5.7	1.7	27

AVERAGE COST OF DEBT: 1989 TO 1992 CANADIAN TELCOS

Company	Pre-Tax Cost of Debt (%)	Effective Tax Rate (%)	After Tax Cost of Debt (%)	After Tax Cost of Debt (%)	Market Value of Debt: % of Firm Value
BC Tel	10.1	43.6	5.7	2.7	36
Bruncor	10.1	44.7	5.6	2.6	52
Island Telephone	10.1	41.6	5.9	2.9	48
Maritime T&T	10.1	42.3	5.8	2.8	47
NewTel	10.1	47.4	5.3	2.3	52
Quebec Telephone	10.1	37.1	6.3	3.3	40
INDUSTRY	10.1	43.4	5.7	2.7	44

RESULTS

Cost of Debt

All telcos are assumed to have what amounts to AAA debt ratings, and have the same (pre-tax) cost of debt, namely, 25 basis points above the long-term government bond of the given country. A more refined methodology would have been to use provincial bonds, e.g., Quebec as the point of reference. If this had been done, the cost of debt differential between Canada and the United States would have been greater (Table 9).

Cost of Preferred Equity

The U.S. telcos did not have any preferred shares outstanding in the period under study. Meanwhile, 5 percent of the market value of firms in the Canadian sample was made up of preferred equity. To estimate the cost of preferred equity, historical yield data were used, when available. For BC Tel and Island Telephone the long-term government bond minus 75 basis points was used. One might consider using a wider spread over corporate bonds (up to 200 basis points) to estimate preferred share yields. However, given the small volume of preferred equity, such adjustments have a negligible impact.

Cost of Common Equity

Canadian firms had higher dividend yields than their U.S. counterparts. Also, despite a lower return on equity, the retention ratio was higher in Canada (35 percent vs. 24 percent), resulting in a higher value for the dividend growth rate. Thus, both in nominal and real terms, the cost of equity for firms in the Canadian sample was significantly higher than for firms in the U.S. sample[32] (Table 10).

Capital Structure

The final challenge arises as a result of the different capital structure found in the two countries, especially in market value terms. On a book value basis, U.S. companies had an average of 41 percent debt and 59 percent common equity. Meanwhile, Canadian firms had more leverage with 46 percent debt, 6 percent preferred shares and 48 percent common equity. However, on a market value basis, it was a different story. The market value based capital structure of U.S. firms was 27 percent debt and 73 percent common equity. Canadian firms, meanwhile, had market weights which were not too far removed from their book value weights: 44 percent debt, 4 percent preferred shares and 52 percent common equity (Figure 5). This difference between the relative market-to-book ratios of equity between the two countries has an impact on the estimates of cost of capital especially those based on the market value weights.[33] An explanation of the impact of this difference on the WACC estimates is attempted below.

TABLE 10

AVERAGE COST OF COMMON EQUITY: 1989 TO 1992 U.S. TELCOS

Company	Nominal Dividend Yield (%)	Return on Common Equity (%)	Growth Rate (%)	Nominal Cost of Common Equity (%)	Real Cost of Common Equity (%)	Market Value as % of Firm Value
Ameritech	5.8	16.5	4.9	10.7	6.6	78
Bell Atlantic	5.5	15.2	3.0	8.5	4.4	71
Bell South	5.6	12.3	2.5	8.2	4.1	76
NYNEX	–	–	–	–	–	69
Pacific Telesis	5.4	14.2	3.4	8.8	4.7	74
Southwestern Bell	5.7	13.0	3.5	9.2	5.1	75
US West	–	–	–	–	–	68
INDUSTRY	5.6	14.2	3.4	9.0	6.0	73

AVERAGE COST OF COMMON EQUITY: 1989 TO 1992 CANADIAN TELCOS

Company	Nominal Dividend Yield (%)	Return on Common Equity (%)	Growth Rate (%)	Nominal Cost of Common Equity (%)	Real Cost of Common Equity (%)	Market Value as % of Firm Value
BC Tel	6.2	12.6	4.9	11.1	7.9	60
Bruncor	7.1	11.5	2.7	9.8	6.7	45
Island Telephone	6.6	12.3	5.1	11.8	8.6	47
Maritime T&T	6.5	12.1	4.8	11.4	8.2	45
NewTel	7.6	10.4	2.3	9.9	6.7	41
Quebec Telephone	7.3	13.6	3.9	11.2	8.0	59
INDUSTRY	6.6	12.2	4.3	10.9	7.7	52

FIGURE 5

EVEN WITH THE HIGHEST MARKET-TO-BOOK PREMIUM IN THE CANADIAN SAMPLE, BC TEL IS STILL BELOW THE U.S. TELCOS

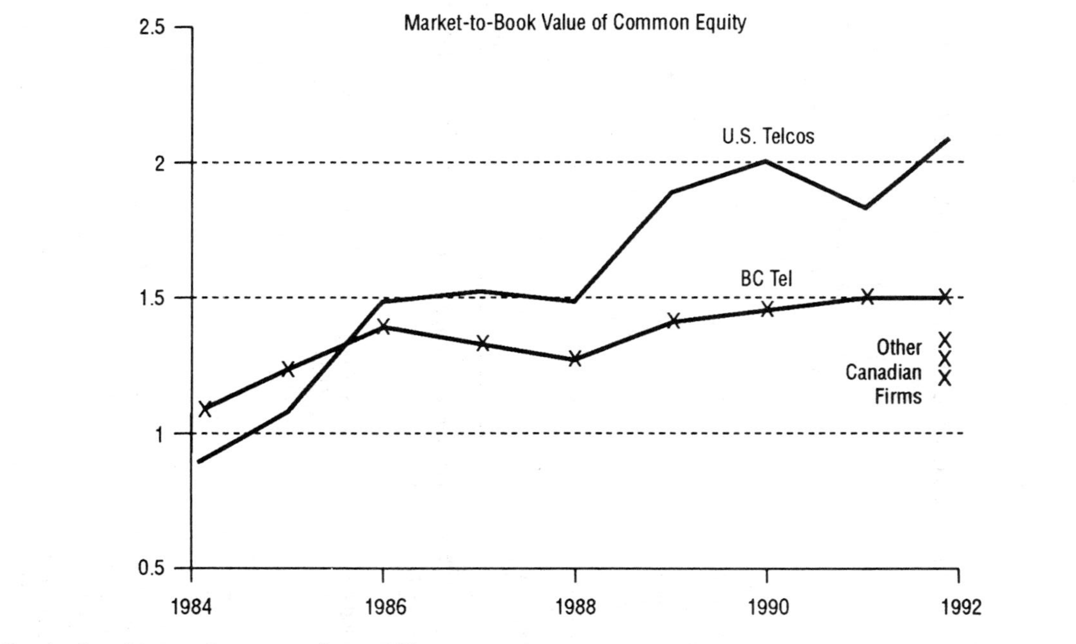

Note: U.S. value based on simple average of seven Telcos.

Weighted Average Cost of Capital

Based on these assumptions and analysis, Table 11 shows the results of a market value based cost of capital for the telcos in the two countries. The (real) cost of capital, when weighted by the market value of debt, preferred equity and common equity, was about 1.3 percent higher for telcos in Canada: 5.4 percent vs. 4.1 percent. Had book values been used to weight the cost of capital, then the gap between Canada and the United States would have been 1.6 percent (Table 12).

Table 11

Weighted Average Cost of Capital: 1989 to 1992 U.S. Telcos

Company	Real Cost of Debt (%)	Real Cost of Preferred Equity (%)	Real Cost of Common Equity (%)	Weighted Average Cost of Capital (%)
Ameritech	1.8	–	6.6	5.5
Bell Atlantic	1.7	–	4.4	3.6
Bell South	1.6	–	4.1	3.5
NYNEX	2.1	–	–	–
Pacific Telesis	1.3	–	4.7	3.9
Southwestern Bell	1.9	–	4.1	4.3
US West	1.8	–	–	–
INDUSTRY	1.7	–	5.0	4.1

Weighted Average Cost of Capital: 1989 to 1992 Canadian Telcos

Company	Real Cost of Debt (%)	Real Cost of Preferred Equity (%)	Real Cost of Common Equity (%)	Weighted Average Cost of Capital (%)
BC Tel	2.7	6.0	7.9	5.9
Bruncor	2.6	4.3	6.7	4.4
Island Telephone	2.9	6.0	8.6	5.7
Maritime T&T	2.8	4.7	8.2	5.4
NewTel	2.3	4.8	6.7	4.3
Quebec Telephone	3.3	6.1	8.0	6.1
INDUSTRY	2.7	5.3	7.7	5.4

TABLE 12

IMPACT OF MARKET AND BOOK VALUE WEIGHTS ON WEIGHTED AVERAGE COST OF CAPITAL

	Based on Book Values (%)	Based on Market Values (%)	Difference: (Market Minus Book) (%)
Canada	5.26	5.40	0.14
United States	3.64	4.11	0.47
Difference: (Canada minus United States)	1.62	1.29	

Impact of Capital Structure

Clearly, the estimates of cost of capital are affected by differences in the market-to-book ratio of equity across the two countries. To compare the cost of equity in the two countries on a similar basis, the impact of leverage needs to be removed. For example, if Canada's cost of capital is recalculated using U.S. market value proportions of debt and equity, it increases from 5.4 percent to 6.1 percent – almost 2 percentage points higher than for the United States.

The components of this 2 percent differential in the cost of capital can be broken down by progressively substituting Canadian values into the U.S. sample. First, use Canada's higher tax rates with respect to the tax savings firms enjoy from the tax deductibility of interest payments (and abstract from their impact on net income). The U.S. cost of capital would drop by 26 basis points. Then, subject the U.S. sample to the real cost of debt faced by the Canadian firms. The cost of capital would increase by 51 basis points, less the 26 basis points from Canada's larger tax shield, or a net increase of 25 basis points. Finally, insert into the U.S. sample the real cost of equity faced by Canadian firms (with the impact of leverage removed, i.e., 7.4 percent). The U.S. cost of capital increases by 177 basis points, reaching 6.1 percent. Thus approximately 1.75 percent of this 2 percent difference in the cost of capital originates from Canada's higher cost of equity (Figure 6).

SUMMARY AND CONCLUSIONS

WITHOUT ADJUSTING FOR THE DIFFERENCES IN LEVERAGE, the cost of capital premium paid by Canadian telcos compared with U.S. telcos was about 1.3 percent. Once normalized for leverage, the cost of capital differential increased to 2 percent. The higher Canadian cost of equity accounted for 1.75 percent of this 2 percent difference in the cost of capital. Meanwhile, the cost of debt, net of the tax shield, accounted for a modest 25 basis points.

FIGURE 6

MOST OF THE DIFFERENCE IN THE COST OF CAPITAL IS ACCOUNTED FOR BY CANADA'S HIGHER COST OF EQUITY

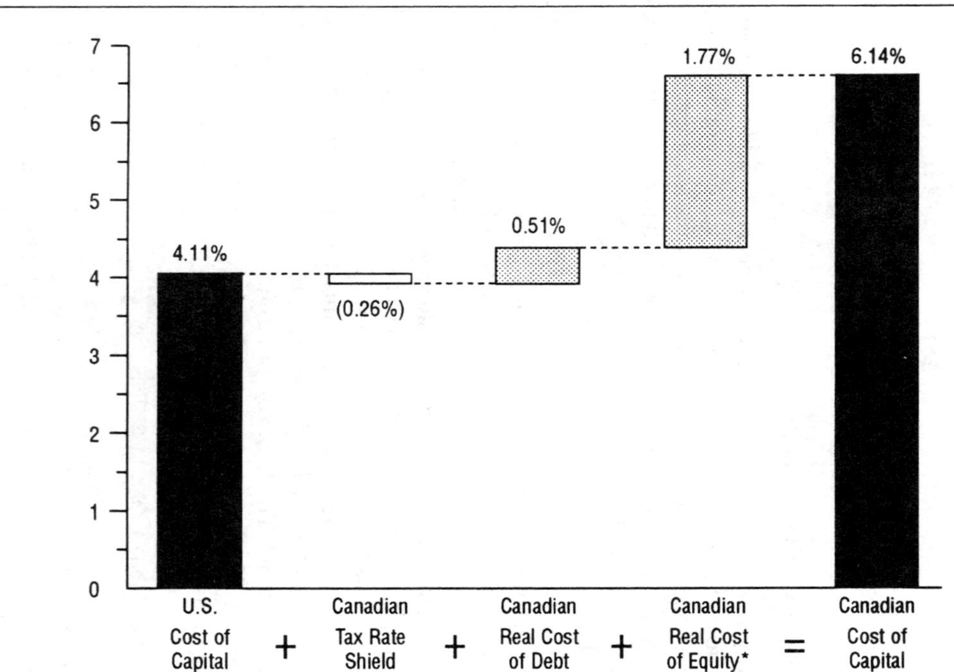

Note: Relevered to fit U.S. capital structure.

This is a surprising result, given that U.S. telcos would appear to have a higher level of business risk and a more competitive environment. If anything, they should face a higher cost of equity capital.

However, the cost of equity capital was higher for Canadian Telcos. The difference can be attributed to a variety of factors including the higher country risk faced by Canadian firms. It should be kept in mind that this analysis has been performed in "real" terms. However, U.S. inflation during the 1989-to-1992 period was approximately 1 percent higher than in Canada. This means that, in nominal terms, the cost of capital faced by Canadian telcos was only one percent above the United States cost.

CASE STUDY 3: COST OF CAPITAL – CANADA AND FINLAND[34]

THE OBJECTIVES OF THIS SECTION ARE TWOFOLD: to estimate the *ex ante* cost of capital for the Finnish pulp and paper industry and to compare the cost of capital for this sector in Finland to that in Canada. The Finnish pulp and paper sector was chosen for the comparison because many Finnish firms in this sector compete with Canadian firms in the North American product markets. If they are at an advantage due to a lower cost of capital, it would have a direct impact on the cost competitiveness of Canadian firms.

Not surprisingly, there is the inherent difficulty in obtaining the necessary data required for such comparisons. Moreover, analysis shows that there are significant differences between Canadian and Finnish firms in the areas of capital structure and those arising from the major restructuring of the Finnish economy in the late 1980s and early 1990s. These differences may increase even more over the next few years and require us to pay specific attention to the issue of using the actual *ex post* data to estimate the *ex ante* components.

In general, this section follows a format similar to the one used above. It estimates the marginal cost of capital in Finland with the United States as the benchmark. Having this common base allows for easy comparison of results between Finland and Canada.

After a brief overview of the Finnish economic situation, the risk-free rates in Finland and the United States are documented. The factors responsible for yield spreads between Finnish and U.S. corporate bonds are examined and the cost of debt in Finland is estimated. The cost of equity is looked at followed by the cost of debt and equity when combined to obtain the cost of capital.

FINNISH ECONOMIC SITUATION

IN MANY RESPECTS, FINLAND IS SIMILAR TO CANADA. It is a northern country, historically deriving its competitive advantage from its abundant natural resources. Over the last few decades, its economy has been moving away from the raw material based industries toward service sectors. In the 1960s, primary production industries were responsible for over a third of the Finnish economy. By 1990, primary production shrank to 10 percent, with the services sector swelling to 60 percent.

In the past, the Finnish government has followed an "interventionist" policy. Although only 5 percent of Finland's work force is directly employed by the government, it has played an active role in the economy at both the macro and micro levels. Throughout the 1980s, Finland experienced a healthy rate of economic growth. However, beginning in 1990, the situation changed dramatically. A combination of high real interest rates and a high Finnish markka (FIM), the disappearance of Finland's largest trading partner (the former Soviet Union), declining competitiveness due to high wages and taxes, and a general deterioration of the economic situation in Europe resulted in a negative gross domestic product (GDP) in Finland. In 1991, production in Finland dropped by 6.4 percent, and in 1992, it declined by another 3.6 percent. The rate of unemployment increased from approximately 3.4 percent in 1990 to the unprecedented high level of 18.5 percent by October 1993.

Similar changes can also be observed in Finnish financial markets. In 1987, Finland established a money market. In 1990, it reduced restrictions on foreign investment. In 1992, Finland discontinued the tax-exempt status of government bonds. The government has also started to phase out its subsidies and loan guarantees to the business sector.

In January 1993, the Finnish government implemented a major reform of corporate income taxation. The main aspect of the reform was to impose a uniform tax rate of 25 percent on all types of corporate income. (Corporations do not pay local or church tax, nor are they liable to any form of capital tax.) The new corporate tax rate is now the lowest among the Organization for Economic Co-operation and Development (OECD) countries.

Due to the structural changes taking place in Finland, using historical data may be inappropriate for extrapolation purposes. As a result, personal judgment has been used, at times, to choose the appropriate intervals of historical data for estimating the *ex ante* cost of capital.

Inflation Rates

Between September 1980 and July 1993, the inflation rate in Finland averaged 5.77 percent a year. Over the last decade, increases in consumer prices generally remained above those in the United States. On average, the difference in inflation rates was 1.42 percent a year.

Over time, the spread in monthly inflation rates between Finland and the United States narrowed. Between 1980 and 1985, it averaged 2.4 percent a year; since 1986, the average spread has dropped to 0.5 percent a year. However, the rate of inflation has also decreased. The ratio of spread to inflation declined by a smaller proportion than the spread itself. Between 1980 and 1985, the ratio was approximately 39 percent. Beginning in 1986, the ratio declined to approximately 20 percent and has more or less stabilized.

Therefore, it is assumed that, in the future, the inflation rate in Finland will continue to exceed that in the United States by a factor of 1.20. As such, based on the projected rate of inflation in the United States of 2.25 percent a year, the Finnish inflation rate is estimated to average 2.70 percent a year.

Risk-Free Rate

Since its introduction in 1987, the Helsinki Interbank Offered Rate (HELIBOR) has been calculated by the central bank of Finland as the average of offered rates for certificates of deposit (CD) quoted daily by the five largest banks. The central bank intervenes in the market one or two times a week by also bidding for government bills in an effort to guide the interest rates. Before HELIBOR, the central bank kept tight control over the system and adjusted money market rates in line with the monetary objectives at the time.

The risk-free rate in Finland has remained in double digits for a long time. However, in 1992, it declined significantly to below 7 percent. The nearly flat structure of the yield curve indicates the expectation that interest rates will remain low for the foreseeable future.[35]

Between September 1980 and July 1993, the 90-day Finnish HELIBOR rate was set, on average, 4.92% above the U.S. treasury bill rate (Figure 7). From the point of view of an American investor, Finnish CDs provide higher returns than U.S. t-bills, but also subject an investor to additional risks. Finnish investors, buying CDs in Finland, would have earned, on average, 3.28% a year more in real returns (in Finnish currency) than their American counterparts who invested in U.S. t-bills (Figure 8). This spread represents a premium for the sovereign exchange rate risk and country risk.

Differences in Yields on Corporate Debt: Finland and United States

Before examining the differences between yields of Finnish and U.S. corporate debt, it is assumed that the spread in the yields of two equally rated bonds, one issued by an American pulp and paper company and one by a Finnish company, is due to three factors: exchange rate risk premium, country-risk premium and corporate-risk premium. An implicit assumption is made that premiums for maturity and industrial risk in Finland and the United States are the same.

An examination of nominal yields on industrial bonds in Finland and the United States revealed that, over the last five years, the difference in nominal rates was approximately 2.96%. This spread is probably representative of the future, especially considering that the average value of the FIM over this period, in terms of U.S. dollars, was in line with its long-term historical average. Since Finnish financial markets have recently been undergoing substantial changes, it is not useful to examine spreads in yields over a longer period of time.

Table 13 compares real yields on Finnish industrial bonds to real yields earned on U.S. industrial bonds, with each security denominated in its respective domestic currency. Over the last five years, real rates in Finland have been, on average, 2.4 percent higher than the rates in the United States. Over the same period, the average difference in inflation rates between the two countries was just over 0.5 percent and the difference in nominal rates averaged a bit under 3.0 percent.

FIGURE 7

NOMINAL RISK-FREE RATES: UNITED STATES AND FINLAND

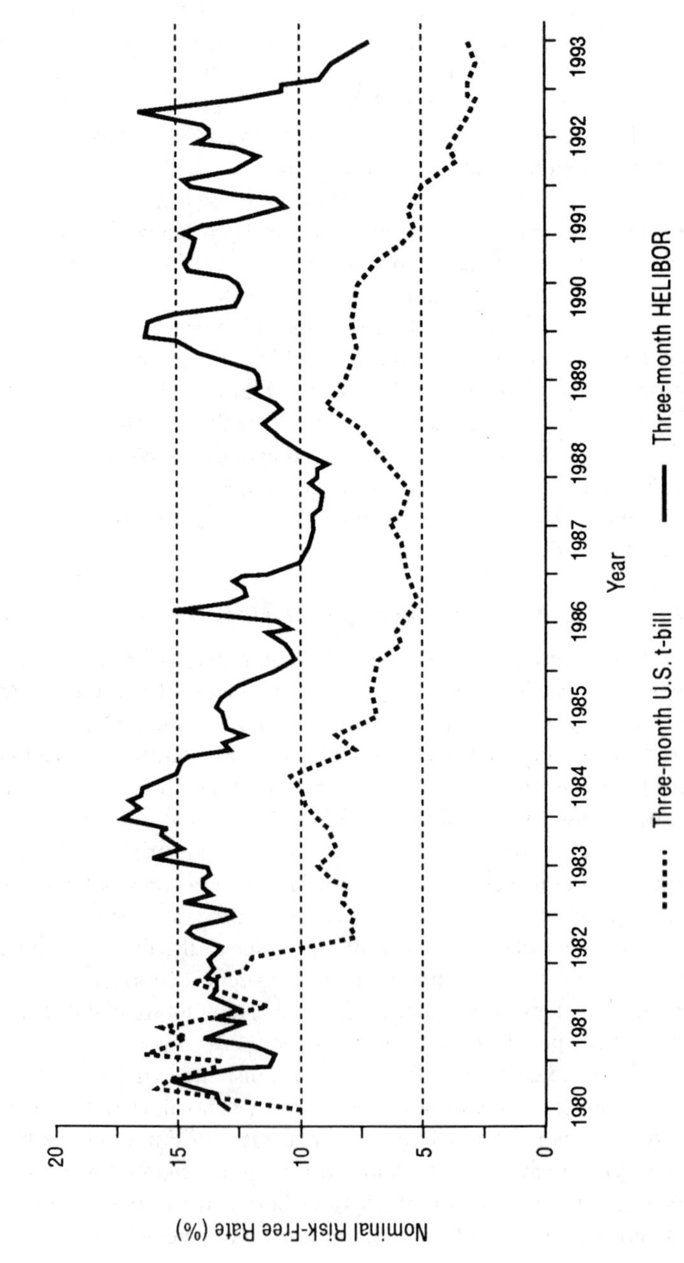

FIGURE 8

REAL RISK-FREE RATES: UNITED STATES AND FINLAND

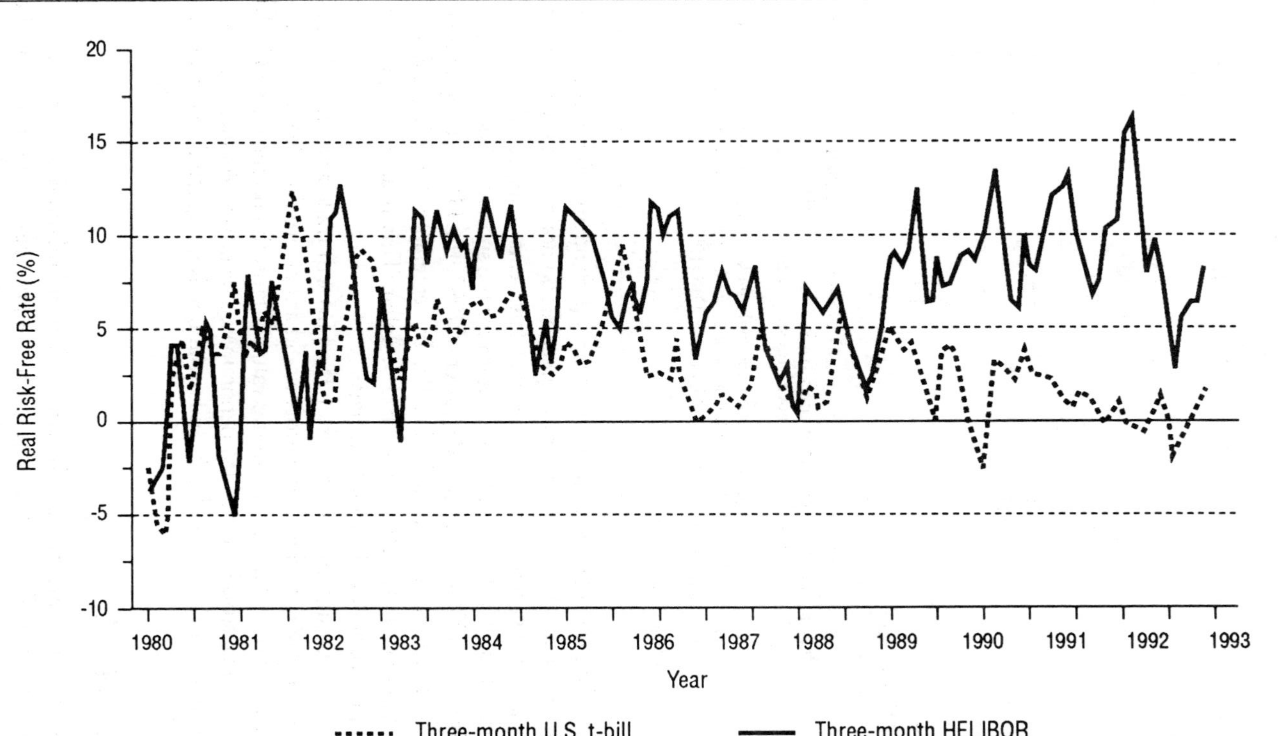

TABLE 13

REAL BOND YIELDS – FINLAND AND UNITED STATES

Year	Average Yields on Industrial Bonds		Difference Between Real Rates in the Two Countries (%)
	Finnish Issues in FIM[a] (%)	American Issues in US$[b] (%)	
1988	4.1	5.5	(1.4)
1989	5.5	5.1	0.4
1990	8.4	3.7	4.7
1991	8.7	6.2	2.5
1992	11.7	5.8	5.9
1993: Jan-April	9.8	n/a	n/a

Notes: [a] Nominal rates on issues with maturity of between three and six years were obtained from *Bulletin, Suomen Pankki*, Finlands Bank, June-July 1993. Inflation rates were calculated based on the monthly price index provided by Statistics Finland.

[b] Composite average of monthly nominal yields on industrial bonds provided by Moody's Industrial Manual, 1993. Inflation rates in the United States were calculated from the price index obtained from CANSIM data base, D139105.

n/a: not applicable.

Some readers may argue that an up trend in differences in yields can be detected over the last five years. I agree, but do not expect the pattern to continue. In fact, a reverse trend over the next few years is expected. The growth in the spread has been largely a compensation for the substantial devaluation of the FIM. Between 1990 and the second quarter of 1993, the FIM lost approximately 40 percent of its value against the U.S. dollar. In September 1993, the currency was trading at approximately FIM 5.78 to a U.S. dollar. This is about 20 percent below the Finnish currency's historical average.

Assuming that, in the future the FIM will trade at its historical average rate vis-à-vis the U.S. dollar, investors would anticipate the FIM to appreciate from its current levels. An increase in the value of Finnish currency would be beneficial to foreign investors holding FIM-denominated securities. As such, the spread between the yields of Finnish and U.S. industrial bonds is expected to narrow from its 1992 levels.

Cost of Debt

As previously mentioned, the cost of debt in Finland was estimated relative to the cost of debt in the United States. Table 14 provides the estimation methodology for estimating cost of corporate debt by using the United States as the base. Similar estimates are provided for Canada.

TABLE 14

COST OF DEBT – FINLAND, UNITED STATES AND CANADA

	Finland (%)	Canada (%)	Spread: Finland-Canada (%)
U.S. risk-free rate – real	2.97	2.97	
Plus: expected inflation	2.25	2.25	
U.S. risk-free rate – nominal	5.28	5.28	
Plus: debt premium	0.88	0.88	
Nominal cost of debt in the U.S.	6.16	6.16	
Premium due to country and corporate risk	2.96	1.94	1.02
Nominal cost of debt	9.12	8.10	1.02
Less: tax shield on debt	2.28	2.75	(0.47)
After-tax cost of debt	6.84	5.35	1.49
Less: expected inflation rate	2.70	2.25	0.45
Real cost of debt	**4.03**	**3.03**	**1.00**
% above the U.S. real cost of debt	2.25	1.25	1.00

Using the estimated nominal cost of debt in the United States at 6.16 percent and adding the corresponding premiums, the after-tax cost of debt in Finland is approximately 6.84 percent. This can be compared to the after-tax cost of debt in the United States of 4.07 percent, which is 2.77 percent lower than in Finland. In Canada, the nominal cost of debt is also lower than in Finland. In comparing the real cost of debt, Finland, again, has the highest real cost of debt of the three countries. (Finland, 4.03 percent; United States, 1.78 percent; Canada, 3.03 percent.)

It is important to point out that this estimated cost of debt would apply to corporations raising capital without the backing of government guarantees. In the past, the widely available government guarantees eliminated the need for a premium compensation for industrial risk, hence, *ceteris paribus*, the cost of corporate debt was lower.

Cost of Equity

The CAPM is used to estimate the cost of equity. This poses a variety of challenges. First, it is very difficult to obtain a historic estimate of market-risk premium in Finland over the three-month risk-free rate simply because Finnish money markets have only recently begun to develop. Tuutti (1992) estimated that the stock market premium was 6.8 percent above the long-term government bonds (average yield of 9.5 percent).[36] Malkamaki (1993) provided an estimate of the market-risk premium over the short-term interest rates as 9.3 percent. The short-term interest rates were computed from the Eurofutures market for the FIM based on U.S. treasury-bill rates.[37] Malkamaki's study also showed that the average rolling beta for a sample of pulp and paper companies over 17 years (1972 to 1989) was approximately 1.0.[38] A more recent study by Yli-Olli (1993) for the period 1988 to 1991 calculated betas of five Finnish pulp and paper companies as ranging from 1.14 to 1.26, with a weighted average beta of 1.2.[39]

Using a beta of 1.2 and a market premium of 9.3 percent, the nominal cost of equity for the Finnish pulp and paper industry can be estimated as 19.20 percent (Table 15). Because of the relatively high market-risk premium and the higher nominal risk-free rate, the cost of equity in Finland is significantly higher than in Canada and the United States.[40]

Capital Structure

The capital structure of the Finnish pulp and paper industry is highly leveraged, especially when compared to the capital structure of the North American industry. The debt-to-equity ratio of Finnish firms is in a range of 3:1 to 4:1.[41] Such an abnormal degree of leverage is possible because the Finnish government has traditionally guaranteed many corporate loans. On average, over US$1.5 billion is outstanding in such loan and bond guarantees.[42]

In Finland, the structure of debt is also different from North America. Long-term financing is primarily done through loans from financial and pension institutions. These private corporate loans make up at least 85 percent of Finnish companies' long-term debt, with some firms using 100 percent loans as the form of long-term debt financing. Capital markets are rarely used to raise long-term financing. Only two of the nine companies in the sample had bonds as a component of their long-term debt (4 percent in one case, and 30 percent in the other).

In the capital markets unguaranteed by government loan guarantees, such capital structure may not be possible. As Finnish markets continue to evolve, the capital composition of Finnish firms is expected to change. The transformation of capital structure is expected to be affected by two factors. First, Finnish financial markets are finding it increasingly difficult to finance large deals internally and, hence, domestic companies must often turn to Euromarkets. Second, in order to integrate the Finnish economy with that of other countries, the government reduced its guarantees of loans to business.

As a result, the capital structure of Finnish companies is expected to fall more in line with that observed in other developed countries. Consequently, aside from using the current capital structure in Finland to estimate cost of capital, the WACC in Finland is considered under three possible scenarios. The capital structure of Finnish firms remains as it is; the capital structure of Finnish firms resembles that in Sweden; and the capital structure of Finnish firms resembles that in the United States.

TABLE 15

COST OF EQUITY – FINLAND, UNITED STATES AND CANADA

	Finland	United States	Canada
Three-month risk-free rate – nominal	8.04%	5.28%	7.22%
Equity beta	1.20	1.33	1.33
Market premium	9.30%	6.00%	6.00%
Nominal cost of equity	19.20%	13.26%	15.20%
Less: expected inflation	2.70%	2.25%	2.25%
Real cost of equity	**16.07%**	**11.01%**	**12.95%**

WACC Using Current Finnish Capital Structure

If the capital structure in Finland was to remain the same as it has been, i.e., a debt-to-equity ratio of 3.5:1, the weighted cost of capital for the Finnish forest industry would be about 9.58 percent nominal and 6.70 percent real.

$$Nominal\ WACC_{Finnish\ Cap.\ Structure} = (6.84\%)(0.778) + (19.20\%)(0.222) = 9.58\%$$

$$Real\ WACC_{Finnish\ Cap.\ Structure} = [\ (1+9.58\%)\ /\ (1+2.70\%)\ ] - 1 = 6.70\%$$

As such, Finnish firms face a real cost of capital that is much lower than U.S. and especially Canadian companies.[43]

It is important to note that it is only during the last few years, as the government loan guarantees to business are being reduced, that the cost of funds in Finland is becoming more representative of the true forces of demand and supply. During the 1980s, Finnish companies had a significant advantage in the cost of capital due to their higher reliance on debt. In some years, the cost of debt for Finnish companies was even below the cost of debt in the United States. This, combined with the highly leveraged capital structure, gave Finnish pulp and paper firms an advantage over their North American competitors so they could easily cover their shipping costs and still compete on price in the North American product markets.

Impact of Using Alternate Capital Structures

Since the historical and current capital structure of Finnish firms is so different from their North American counterparts, it is interesting to evaluate the impact of potential changes to capital structure on the cost of capital estimates. There is, of course, no unambiguous method to determine what the equilibrium capital structure of

Finnish firms would be. Two potential scenarios are considered. First, the capital structure of Swedish firms is used as a benchmark. Then, the capital structure of U.S. firms is used as another benchmark.

The examination of the capital structures of eight Swedish pulp and paper companies between 1984 and 1991 revealed that the average debt-to-equity ratio remained relatively constant from year to year, as well as from company to company, at approximately 1:1. The highest debt-to-equity ratio was approximately 2:1, and the lowest was approximately 0.2:1.[44] In contrast, the capital of North American pulp and paper companies generally comprised 40 percent debt and 60 percent equity.

These capital structures can be applied to the corresponding costs of equity and debt. Note that equity betas are not re-leveraged to account for the reduction in the proportion of debt. I believe that investors view high-ratio government-backed corporate loans not as debt, but as a form of equity. Hence, they do not perceive the high amount of debt as a source of additional financial risk, usually associated with leverage.[45] The results are shown in Table 16.

Assuming that the capital structure of Finnish pulp and paper firms shifts toward a debt-to-equity ratio of 1:1, Finnish companies may face a cost of capital of approximately 13.02 percent nominal and 10.05 percent real. This is significantly higher than the estimate of the cost of capital of 9.58 percent nominal and 6.70 percent real, under the current highly leveraged capital structure. These figures clearly demonstrate that if pulp and paper companies in Finland were competing on an equal basis with U.S. firms, their financial costs, in real terms, would be higher than their counterpart firms in North America.

If the capital structure of the Finnish pulp and paper industry is assumed to be similar to that in North America, then Finnish companies would pay approximately 4.56 percent more for their capital because of the dramatic decline in leverage. In addition, they would pay another 0.5 percent to 0.75 percent due to the increase in the cost of debt. On balance, if the Finnish pulp and paper industry was facing a

TABLE 16

REAL COST OF CAPITAL UNDER ASSUMPTIONS OF VARIOUS DEBT-TO-EQUITY RATIOS

	Finland	United States	Canada
Finnish capital structure	6.70	n/a	n/a
Swedish capital structure	10.05	n/a	n/a
North American capital structure	11.26	6.90	8.57

Note: n/a: not applicable.

North American capital structure, its real cost of capital would be higher by over 4 percent compared to U.S. firms and approximately 3 percent over Canadian firms.

SUMMARY AND OVERVIEW

FOR YEARS, FINNISH COMPANIES ENJOYED RELATIVELY EASY ACCESS to inexpensive capital. This was the result of widely available government guarantees of business loans which, in turn, allowed Finnish companies to maintain highly leveraged structures and to borrow at rates almost the same as the Finnish government. Using historical capital structure, Finnish companies' real cost of capital was estimated as approximately 6.70 percent compared to the real cost of capital in the United States of 6.90 percent and in Canada of 8.57 percent. Thus, historically speaking, Finnish pulp and paper companies have held a significant cost of capital advantage over Canadian firms.

However, Finland has been undergoing significant changes to its financial and economic systems. As the restructuring proceeds, it is expected that the capital structure of Finnish companies will resemble, at the very least, that of Swedish firms, and possibly even that of North American firms. Further, the cost of debt is expected to rise as it begins to reflect the forces of demand and supply more accurately. It is estimated that Finnish firms will face a real cost of capital somewhere in the range of 10.05 percent to 11.26 percent, and will suffer a substantial decline in their competitive advantage.

OVERALL SUMMARY AND CONCLUSIONS

THIS PAPER HAS PROVIDED ESTIMATES OF THE COST OF CAPITAL for Canadian industrial sectors based on an analysis of publicly traded firms listed on the TSE. These estimates are based on a specific model of the return-generating process, namely, the CAPM. The paper provides estimates of systematic risk, the real cost of equity and capital, and capital structure. The estimates are provided on an average basis and can be used only if the firm or the project is expected to correspond to an average firm in that sector. If that is not the case, it would be inappropriate to use these estimates on an "as is" basis for undertaking an investment decision.

The three case studies are based on the work of many individuals. These studies are neither meant to be exhaustive nor definitive; they simply illustrate the methodological and empirical challenges in estimating the cost of capital of firms in a cross-country context. The studies clearly illustrate that the country-risk premium, as observed in differential real rates, provides an unambiguous cost of capital advantage to U.S. firms. If one adds the corporate-risk premium demanded by investors, then the cost of capital disadvantage for a typical Canadian firm is almost 2 percentage points. Since the analysis assumes that the market-risk premium and the systematic risk of Canadian firms is the same as for U.S. firms, I believe that the estimates are conservative at best. Knowing that Canadian firms in many sectors are thought of as swing suppliers to the U.S. markets and that Canada is a net importer of capital, I believe the cost of capital disadvantage is even higher in magnitude.

This 2 percent difference in the cost of capital, though small, has the potential to divert investment away from a Canadian location, all else being equal. This also indicates that, for Canada to compete, it must provide a higher degree of operational efficiency and cost advantage to counteract the 2 percent cost of capital advantage enjoyed by U.S. firms. One of the case studies also attempted to estimate cost of capital faced by a sector in a third country, Finland. Analysis indicated that the historical closeness of lenders and borrowers in Finland allowed Finnish firms to benefit from a much lower cost of capital. With the opening of capital markets and a continued withdrawal of the Finnish government from its involvement in the corporate sector, this advantage is expected to disappear in the coming years. However, the speed of this change is very hard to estimate given the continued close relationship between banks and the corporate sector in Finland as well as in many other countries around the world.

This study indicates that there is a significant cost of capital disadvantage to firms in a country where the real rates continue to be high, where the country-risk premium exists, where firms compete with foreign firms with a different capital market regime, and whose export markets treat them as swing suppliers. The use of Canadian data and Canadian estimates can be viewed as an attempt to determine empirically the magnitude and impact of these issues from a Canadian perspective.

ENDNOTES

1 All three case studies are based on data available as of June 1993, at the latest. Hence, the results presented here are illustrative rather than prescriptive.

2 This section is based on the work conducted by Vijay Jog and Jim Douglas in early 1994. It was updated by Vijay Jog and Colin Pattison in the fall of 1995.

3 For the most recent papers relevant to the applicability of this framework, see Fama and French (1992), Kim (1995), Kothari et al. (1995).

4 Also see Ando and Aurbach (1988), Department of Finance Canada (1992), Hatsopoulos (1983), Porter (1992) and Shoven and Topper (1992).

5 We ignore evidence based on survey results. For example, Jog and Srivastava (1993) reported that Canadian CEOs/CFOs perceive at least some significant disadvantage in terms of all three factors of competitiveness: the cost of capital, labour and material as well as the availability of equity capital.

6 See, for example, Jog and Mintz (1990), Chen and McKenzie (this volume) and McKenzie and Mintz (1992).

7 See, for example, Patterson (1993) and Booth (1993).

8 In a study on corporate financial decision making of Canadian firms, Jog and Srivastava (1994) reported that, in addition to the dividend growth model and risk premium type models, companies also use accounting rates of return, price-earnings ratios and subjective estimates for estimating their cost of capital. Similar conclusions are found in the U.S. survey results; see Gitman and Mercurio (1982) and Kim et al. (1986).

9 A recent critic of CAPM's validity in the United States can be found in Fama and French (1992). If one believes in their results, one could estimate cost of equity for companies using the following formulation: $K_e = R_f + B_s \times$ *firm size* $+ B_{bm} \times$ *book-to-market ratio* where firm size is the market capitalization of the firm's equity, B_s and B_{bm} are the sensitivities to these factors. The average risk premium can be estimated using cross-sectional regressions of the type used in testing the arbitrage pricing model by Chen et al. (1986). It is beyond the scope of this paper to test the validity of the Fama and French hypothesis for Canada.

10 This approach is quite useful in determining the cost of equity for regulated sectors where companies have a long history of dividend payments and follow stable and predictable capital structures. This method is used in many rate hearings.

11 Since this topic is covered quite extensively in any standard finance or investment textbook, no attempt is made here to provide further details.

12 For companies for which the monthly return data were not available or which had unsatisfactory R-squared (less than 0.1) or t-value (less than 1) statistics associated with the regressions, sector averages were used.

13 See Damodaran (1996) on this issue.

14 These yields (in percent) were 11.13, 10.75, 11.74, 10.74, 9.70, 8.02 and 9.95, respectively, from 1988 to 1994.

15 These were profitability, debt-to-service capacity, asset turnover, liquidity, equity-to-debt and assets.

16 Note that preferred equity is much less liquid than government bonds implying that a lag exists in the preferred equity market when adjusting to market conditions. Probably, the negative spread that existed in the 1990s was the result of government bond yields falling immediately in response to the changing market conditions while the preferred equity yields were much slower to respond to the changing market conditions.

17 Any changes to this assumption would have only a marginal impact on these estimates since preferred shares account for less than 5 percent of the aggregate capital.

18 Although not shown here, the WACC under the Myers approach in which inflation is removed at the end of the WACC calculation was also calculated for each sector. However, as the results were virtually identical, these are not shown here.

19 This section is based on a report written by Jim Douglas while he was a consultant to Industry Canada; the work was conducted jointly by Vijay Jog and Jim Douglas with assistance from Don Tate. The example uses updated estimates of cost of capital, capital structure and systematic risk to ensure consistency with the results in the previous section.

20 Note that while further differences may exist due to differences in the degrees of systematic risk (betas) between the two countries, it is assumed in this paper that the systematic risk does not vary between Canada and the United States.

21 Even after some research, it was difficult to find well-traded Canadian government bonds denominated in U.S. dollars that could be matched with their U.S. counterparts.

22 We thank A. Louis Calvet and John Crow for pointing out that the country risk premium results may be attributed to the choice of data, and we must explicitly address the Frankel (1991) results. Since the main intent is to show that there has been a real rate differential between the two countries and not to debate its exact source, we leave it to the reader to separate the difference in country risk and exchange risk premiums based on these two sets of results. To avoid the controversy we only refer to the overall difference in the rest of the paper.

23 Exchange risk is not relevant since the bonds are denominated in U.S. dollars and, therefore, the U.S. investor is not concerned with converting Canadian interest and principal payments received to U.S. dollars.

24 More specifically, it would require using a model such as the international CAPM and an adjustment for the capital structure to determine the cost of equity capital for the forest product sector companies in both countries. Due to time constraints, this is beyond the scope of this paper.

25 The choice of an LWC paper mill is for illustrative purposes since the author had access to some work in Industry Canada on the competitiveness of the forest product sector. All the operating and capital costs associated with the mill were provided by an internationally renowned engineering consulting firm.

26 Throughout this paper, the relationship between nominal and real rates is estimated as: *nominal rate = (1 + real rate)* X *(1+ inflation) - 1*.

27 The beta value of 1.21 and the average debt-to-equity ratio of 40:60 for 1992 are based on the results shown in the first part of this paper.

28 This section is based on work by Walter Sims of Industry Canada in May 1993.

29 Non-telecom businesses may have accounted for as much as 8 percent of Baby Bell revenue in 1992.

30 The degree of difficulty associated with the estimation of Bell's market value was illustrated by Halpern and Jog (1995).

31 Meanwhile, things are changing in Canada as well. With the recent Canadian Radio-television and Telecommunications Commission ruling regarding the opening up of long distance service to competition, a large chunk (virtually half) of Canadian telecom business revenue has lost its monopoly protection. As a result, the business risk faced by Canadian firms is also increasing.

32 Note that the data from US West and NYNEX have been excluded: their poor financial performance and low cost of equity in our time period were deemed to be unrepresentative.

33 We can speculate that this higher market-to-book ratio in the United States may have to do with expectations about more positive regulatory changes, and the positive impact of the incentive-based regulations which allow U.S. telcos to pass on the benefits of efficiency improvements to shareholders rather than to consumers.

34 This section is based on a study conducted by Igor Kotlyr while he was a consultant to Industry Canada. The example uses updated estimates of cost of capital, capital structure and systematic risk to ensure consistency with the results in the previous sections.

35 In October 1993, the yield on 11-year government bonds was approximately 7.60 percent; on eight-year, 7.45 percent; on five-year, 6.65 percent; on two-year, 6.3 percent; on one-year, 6.1 percent; and on three-month, 6.65 percent.

36 This is based on Petri Tuutti's unpublished graduate thesis at the Helsinki School of Economics. The thesis dealt with the *ex ante* cost of equity capital for Fiskars, a large Finnish metal company.

37 Average excess return from 1972 to 1989 is approximately 3.1 percent a year. This figure is similar to the projection of the *ex ante* market premium of 3.0 percent made by Professor Matti Viren of Turku School of Economics and Business Administration.

38 Three-year rolling beta mean (1972-1989): Enso-Gutzeit, 0.767; Kymmene, 1.088; Tampella, 0.935; United Paper Mills, 1.247. They are based on monthly observations.

39 Weighted average beta based on weekly data (1988-1991) is 1.21. Financial structure was used as the relative measure of weight. Individual betas are: Enso, 1.14; Kymmene, 1.26; Serla, 1.25; Yhtyneet (part of Repola), 1.10; Tempella, 1.21.

40 In estimating the Finnish cost of equity and comparing it to the United States and Canada, it is recognized that the use of different indices as the bases for regressions may have led to imprecise estimates of relative riskiness of pulp and paper industries in the three countries.

41 Based on the analysis of financial statements for a sample of nine Finnish pulp and paper companies (Enso-Gutzeit, Kymmene, Metsa-Serla, Kemi, Veitsiluoto, Metsa-Botnia, Sunila, Tampella, Ahlstrom) for 1989 through 1991.

42 Moody's Investment Services. *Moody's International Manual*, 1992, p. 1465.

43 This result is critically dependent on the expected market risk premium of 6 percent used in the estimation of cost of capital in North America. In the earlier work, a higher risk premium of 8.8 percent was envisioned: under that assumption, the Finnish firms enjoy an even higher advantage over their Canadian counterparts.

44 Our sample included: ASSI AB, Billerud AB, Kornas Aktiebolag, MODO, Munksjo AB, NCB, Stora, Svenksa Cellulosa.

45 Also note that the relatively high market risk premium in Finland may already reflect the overall higher reliance on debt by all Finnish companies.

Acknowledgements

THIS PAPER IS BASED ON THE WORK CONDUCTED at the Competitive Analysis Group of Industry Canada during 1993 and 1994 and updated by the author in 1995. The author acted as a consultant and supervised the various individual components. The author is indebted to Donald G. Tate who served as a special advisor at Industry Canada and provided extremely valuable direction, input and resources. Thus, the work presented here is a summary of the joint work of many individuals over a three-year period. Special thanks to Patty Dalcin, Jim Douglas, Igor Kotlyr, Brian Loveys, Colin Pattison and Walter Sims to bring this work to fruition. The paper has also benefited from comments by John Crow, Louis Calvet and Paul Halpern. All errors and omissions rest with the author.

Bibliography

Ando, A. and A. Aurbach. "The Cost of Capital in the United States and Japan: A Comparison." *Journal of Japanese and International Economies*. (1988): 134-158.

Booth, L. "Estimating the Cost of Equity Capital of a Non-traded Unique Entity: A Canadian Study." *Canadian Journal of Administrative Sciences*. Vol. 10, (June 1993):122-127.

Bruce, N. "The Cost of Capital and Competitive Advantage." *Bell Journal*. (1992): 77-117.

Burns Fry Limited. *Preferred Share Quarterly Report*. Toronto: Burns Fry Limited, 1994.

Chen, N., R. Roll and S.A. Ross. "Economic Forces and the Stock Market." *Journal of Business*. (1986): 383-403.

Damodaran A. *Damodaran on Valuation: Security Analysis for Investment and Corporate Finance*. New York: John Wiley and Sons, 1996.

Department of Finance Canada. "The Real Cost of Funds for Business Investment." *Quarterly Economic Review: Special Reports*. (1992): 55-67.

Fama, E. and K.R. French. "The Cross-Section of Expected Returns." *Journal of Finance*. Vol. 47, (1992): 427-465.

Finlands Bank. *Bulletin, Suomen Pankki*. June-July 1993.

Frankel, J.A. "Qualifying International Capital Mobility in the 1980's." In *National Savings and Economic Performance*. Edited by D. Bernheim and J. Shoven. Chicago: University of Chicago Press, 1991, pp. 227-260.

Gitman, L. J. and V.A. Mercurio. "Cost of Capital Techniques Used by Major U.S. Firms: Survey and Analysis of Fortune's 1000." *Financial Management*. (1982): 21-29.

Gordon, M.J. and E. Shapiro. "Capital Equipment Analysis: The Required Rate of Profit." *Management Science*. (1956): 102-110.

Halpern, P. and V. Jog. "Bell Canada Enterprises: Wealth Creation or Destruction." In *Corporate Decision Making in Canada*. Edited by R.J. Daniels and R. Morck. Calgary: University of Calgary Press, 1995, pp. 241-281.

Hatsopoulos, G. "High Cost of Capital: Handicap of American Sector, American Business Conference." Washington, 1983.

Hsia, C. "Estimating a Firm's Cost of Capital: An Option Pricing Approach." *Journal of Business Finance and Accounting*. (1991): 281-287.

Jog, V. and J. Mintz., "Corporate Tax Reform and its Economic Impact: An Evaluation of the June 18, 1987 Proposals." In *The Economic Impacts of Tax Reform*. Edited J. Mintz and J. Whalley. Canadian Tax Paper No. 84. Toronto: The Canadian Tax Foundation, 1990, pp. 83-124.

Jog, V. and A. Srivastava. "Capital Formation and the Cost of Capital in Canada." *The Canadian Investment Review*. Vol. 6, No. 3, (Summer 1993): 21-26.

——. "Corporate Financial Decision Making in Canada." *Canadian Journal of Administrative Sciences*. Vol. 11, No.2, (1994): 156-176.

Kim, D. "The Errors in the Variables Problem in the Cross-Section of Expected Returns." *Journal of Finance*. Vol. 50, (1995): 1605-1634.

Kim, S.S., T. Crick and S.H. Kim. "Do Executive Practice What Academics Preach." *Management Accounting*. (1986): 49-52.

Kothari, S.P., J. Shanken and R.G. Sloan. "Another Look at the Cross-Section of Expected Stock Returns." *Journal of Finance*. Vol. 50, (1995): 185-224.

Lessard, D., T. Bollier, R. Eckaus and R. Kahn. *Country Risk, Capital Market Integration, and Project Evaluation: A Canadian Perspective*. Massachusetts Institute of Technology, April 1983.

Malkamaki, O.M. *Essays on Conditional Pricing of Finnish Stocks*. Bank of Finland Publications, Helsinki: Oy Trio-Offset Ab, 1993.

McKenzie, K.J. and J.M. Mintz. "Tax Effects on the Cost of Capital: A Canada-United States Comparison." In *Canada-U.S. Tax Comparisons*. Edited by J. Whalley and J. Shoven. National Bureau of Economic Research, research volume, University of Chicago Press, 1992, pp. 189-216.

Miller M. "Debt and Taxes." *Journal of Finance*. Vol. 32, (1977): 261-275.

Modigliani F. and M. Miller. "The Cost of Capital, Corporation Finance, and the Theory of Investment." *American Economic Review*. (1958): 261-297.

Moody's Investment Services. *Moody's International Manual*. 1992, p. 1465.

Myers, S. "Estimating the Weighted Average Cost of Capital." Presented at the Financial Management Conference, Boston, 1993.

National Advisory Board on Science and Technology. "Under-Funding the Future: Canada's Cost of Capital Problem."1990.

Patterson, C. "The Cost of Equity Capital of a Non-traded Unique Entity: A Canadian Study." *Canadian Journal of Administrative Sciences*. Vol. 10, (June 1993): 115-121.

Porter, M. "Capital Disadvantage: America's Failing Capital Investment System." *Harvard Business Review*. (September/October 1992): 65-82.

J. Poterba. "Comparing the Cost of Capital in the United States and Japan: A Survey of Methods." *Quarterly Review of the Federal Reserve Bank of New York*. (Winter 1992): 20-32.

Roll, R. and S.A. Ross. "An Empirical Investigation of the Arbitrage Pricing Theory." *Journal of Finance*. (1980): 1073-1103.

Shoven, J. and M. Topper. "The Cost of Capital in Canada, the United States, and Japan." In *Canada-U.S. Tax Comparisons*. Edited by J. Whalley and J. Shoven. Chicago: University of Chicago Press, 1992.

Tuutti, Petri. Private conversation based on his graduate thesis at the Helsinki School of Economics, Helsinki, Finland, 1992.

Vasicek, O. "A Note on Using Cross-Sectional Information in Baysian Estimation of Security Betas." *Journal of Finance*. Vol. 8, (December 1973): 1233-1239.

Yli-Olli. Private conversation with Professor Yli-Olli, Helsinki School of Economics, Helsinki, Finland, 1993.

Comments on Session I: Cost of Capital

THE USER COST OF CAPITAL AND INVESTMENT SPENDING: IMPLICATIONS FOR CANADIAN FIRMS

Comment by Serge Nadeau
Industry Canada

THE PAPER BY ROBERT CHIRINKO AND ANDREW MEYER is an ambitious and welcome attempt at measuring the relationship between the user cost of capital and investment at the micro-economic level. However, as the authors are the first to admit, the results are too preliminary to be useful in policy design. These comments put the paper in a research context, discuss methodological issues and conclude by making specific suggestions for further research.

INVESTMENT AND THE USER COST OF CAPITAL

THE USER COST OF CAPITAL IS ONE OF THE CHANNELS through which government policies, e.g., tax and financial market policies, can influence business investment. Economists (Robert Chirinko in particular) have attempted for many years to quantify this influence, but with mixed results. Empirical evidence does not support the theory (and our intuition) that the user cost of capital should have a significant influence on investment. This is a classic example of the conundrum faced by scientists when empirical tests of a model fail: is it because of the model or the data? Improving the models has been the typical response in the past. Indeed, as reviewed by Chirinko and Meyer, several models (including refinements to existing models) have been proposed. To no avail, however. First-generation models, i.e., neoclassical Jorgenson models, still remain empirically superior to the more theoretically sophisticated models.

The paper by Chirinko and Meyer departs from the typical response of proposing "better" investment models to improve empirical results, by testing a narrow class of neoclassical models on a different data set. While investment models are usually estimated using data aggregated to some level, Chirinko and Meyer estimate their models using firm-level data. This is a welcome departure; estimating a neoclassical investment model using micro-economic data adds both methodological and policy points of view. From a methodological perspective, since the neoclassical model is fundamentally derived from micro-economic principles, it should be estimated using firm-level data. From a policy perspective, using estimates based on micro-economic data adds to the richness of the analysis by recognizing that the impact of policy changes may vary across sectors and firms.

METHODOLOGICAL ISSUES

UNFORTUNATELY, AS IS OFTEN THE CASE WHEN NEW GROUND IS BROKEN, the estimates obtained by Chirinko and Meyer are disappointing and suggest that the neoclassical model is incomplete in explaining investment behaviour at the firm level. Indeed, although the preferred model yields coefficients of the expected signs, they vary to an implausibly great extent across sectors and are very imprecise within sectors. For example, the estimated user cost elasticities vary from -0.272 to -4.345 across sectors and, statistically, are significantly different from zero in only one of the 11 sectors. As pointed out by the authors, "there is too much imprecision in these estimates to reach firm conclusions about the sensitivity of sectoral investment spending to variations in investment incentives."

My other methodology-related comments are more peripheral and relate to the modelling of cash flow; investment in structure, machinery and equipment; the availability of Canadian data; and the estimation and testing methodology.

Modelling of Cash Flow

Cash flow enters the investment equation in quite an ad hoc fashion. It would be preferable if it came as the result of a formal optimization process. As it is, the assumptions underlying the functional form are not clear.[1]

Another issue is the measurement of cash flow. It is not clear if cash flow is measured before or after dividends. It could be argued that it should be measured after dividends, unless it is assumed that the dividend decision and the investment decision are simultaneous.

Investment in Structure, Machinery and Equipment

The models in this paper do not distinguish between investment in structure and investment in machinery and equipment. It would be interesting to know if it is because of data limitation or some other reason.

The Availability of Canadian Data

As noted by the authors, sector-level information on the user cost of capital is not readily available in Canada. However, such series should not be too difficult to construct since the information required is similar to that necessary to compute marginal (sectoral) effective tax rates which have been done, e.g., Department of Finance in 1985, apparently without too much difficulty.

Firm-level information comparable to that for U.S. firms appears to be available for Canadian firms through Compustat. Although the sample is much smaller than that for the United States (about 900 firms compared to more than 4,000), it should be sufficient from a statistical point of view.

Estimation and Testing Methodology

The authors' favoured model assumes that regressors are endogenous and are estimated using instrumental variables. It would be useful if the authors specified which regressors they assume to be endogenous and/or perform exogeneity tests, such as Hausman tests.

I am also sceptical about their instruments, i.e., lagged regressors, being uncorrelated with the error term. As the authors point out, this necessitates an error term which is uncorrelated over time. However, at least at the aggregate level (and an almost universal feature of investment regression models) the error term is correlated over time.

Conclusion

In summary, the paper by Chirinko and Meyer is a worthwhile step are estimating investment functions using firm-level data. However, a lot remains to be done. In particular, technological changes will have to be modelled as well as expectations. Furthermore, specifically in the case of Canada, special consideration will have to be given to the small and open nature of the economy. For example, it may have to be assumed that Canada is a price taker on international capital markets, and the relationship between the cost of capital in Canada and the cost of capital in the rest of the world may have to be incorporated in the model.

Endnotes

1 For example, Coen (1971) assumed that cash flow affects the speed of adjustment.

Bibliography

Coen, Robert M. "The Effect of Cash Flows on the Speed of Adjustment." In *Tax Incentives and Capital Spending*. Edited by G. Fromm. Washington: Brookings Institute, 1971, pp. 131-196.

Department of Finance. *The Corporate Income Tax System: A Direction for Change*. Ottawa, May 1985.

Cost of Capital for United States, Japan and Canada

Comment by Jack M. Mintz
University of Toronto

THIS PAPER FOLLOWS THE CAREFUL APPROACH USED BY ANDO AND AUERBACH (1988a,b, 1990) to assess the cost of capital of major countries such as the United States and Japan. The value of this current work is that it includes Canada.

My main difficulty with this type of work is related to the information being sought. If we observe differences in rates of return on capital across countries, what should we conclude about this observation? I would suggest that there is little to conclude from a policy perspective. To clarify this point, I provide two general comments related to this paper.

- Why are we measuring the rate of return on capital as a cost of capital?
- What benchmark (financial arbitrage) should be used to determine equalized costs of capital?

Why Measure The Rate of Return on Capital?

ONE OF THE MOST IMPORTANT ISSUES THAT STRIKES THE READER of this paper is the rationale used for comparing the rate of return on capital by country as a proxy for the cost of capital. The motivation for this work is important because the measurements used can only be understood by relating them to objectives. For example, if I want to know what time it is, I need a clock to measure hours and minutes of the day. If I want to know the temperature of a room, I would have to have a thermometer to measure heat. I cannot use a thermometer for time and a clock for heat.

The very first question that should be asked is why measure the cost of capital at all? I suppose the argument is that it is important in determining the amount of capital stock held by firms. We may be particularly interested in knowing this amount since it is an important variable in determining the productivity and growth of an economy.

If this is the purpose of the cost of capital measurement, then the next question concerns how one would go about measuring it. Theory is useful here since economists would state that a firm will invest in capital until the marginal revenue product earned by holding capital is equal to its user cost of capital. The user cost of capital comprises three parts: the cost of depreciation, the cost of financing, including risk, and taxes.

Knowing the value of each component is important. The Ando-Hancock-Sawchuk paper concentrates on one part of the cost of capital: the cost of financing capital. We know that the cost of financing capital depends on the costs of issuing debt and new equity, and foregoing the distribution of profits (retained earnings).

Moreover, in today's global economy, firms can seek financing from different countries, not only from the host country where the investment takes place.

Generally, there are two approaches to measuring the cost of capital. The first is to take the *cost approach*: making calculations to capture the expected cost of financing capital. One, therefore, tries to measure interest rates for bond finance, the risk-inclusive cost of equity finance (using, for example, the capital asset pricing model) and other components that affect the cost of capital. The second is the *rate of return on capital approach*: measuring the competitive rate of return on capital earned by firms on their investments. With this approach, the rate of return on capital for competitive firms is presumed to equal the cost of holding capital. The Ando-Hancock-Sawchuk paper uses the latter approach.

Having this information, it would seem that there are several numbers we might be interested in:

- the cost of equity finance including risk;
- the cost of debt finance;
- the debt-to-equity ratio; and
- inflation.

To measure the cost of equity, the paper considers the earnings-to-price ratio. The cost of capital is measured by Ando-Hancock-Sawchuk in three ways:

1. the total return to capital before taxes: dividends, retained earnings, interest and taxes divided by the market value of debt and equity;
2. the total return to capital after taxes (bonds are untaxed): the same as method 1 except tax payments are omitted from the numerator; and
3. the total return after taxes (bonds are taxed): the same as method 2 except that interest, corrected for tax payments, is added to the numerator.

An important issue is how to treat the cost of debt finance, in particular, how to account for the deductibility of interest from corporate taxable income.

I have three problems with the methodology followed by the authors.

1. Does the Rate of Return on Capital Have Anything to Do with the Cost of Capital?

Taking profits and dividing the number by market value measures of capital provides an estimate of the average return on capital, not the marginal return which is expected to be equal to the cost of capital. One might argue that in competitive markets any economic rents should be dissipated so average and marginal returns on capital, on a risk-adjusted basis, are equal. However, in the presence of oligopoly (as discussed in the theory), fixed factors (such as natural resources which are important to Canada) and government regulations, there is no reason to expect that the average rate of return on capital would be equal to the marginal return on capital. Even in the absence of economic rents, average rates of return on capital, measured on a gross of risk basis as followed by the authors, will diverge across countries if there is country-specific risk or an industrial structure specific to countries.

Moreover, taxes paid on marginal investments are likely different than the average amount of tax paid for both infra-marginal and marginal investments. For example, governments might provide fast write-offs for capital that reduce substantially the cost of capital for marginal investments and result in a negative tax rate on marginal capital decisions yet still result in a positive tax rate for infra-marginal and marginal investments.

In addition, there is a difficulty in using the earnings-to-price ratio as a measure of the opportunity cost of equity. The authors carefully deal with problems related to the inflationary impacts on earnings. However, earnings also depend on accounting measures of profits and, as shown by Collins and Shackelford (1995), there is considerable divergence in accounting practices across countries. Moreover, even if there is an allowance for different accounting practices, one would like to have the expected rather than the actual earnings to measure the potential growth or decline in future income earned by the corporate sector.

As a minor point, I do not understand the theory in terms of the markup equation as discussed in the paper. If firms are marking up above costs, it would seem that costs should be corrected for depreciation that would be viewed as a charge against profits (otherwise an industry with a higher depreciation rate for capital would have greater markups). In other words, the markup should be based on costs net of depreciation, not gross of depreciation.

2. What Are the Components of Returns on Capital?

The return on capital is equal to the amounts of income received by shareholders and bondholders. Returns encompass business income plus financial income, including capital gains, held on assets. Should these returns be measured on a before-tax or after-tax basis? The paper uses various measures, but it would be useful to think of what question is being addressed first to know what type of measure is of interest.

If one were predicting that firms invest in capital so after-tax risk-adjusted rates of return are equalized across countries, then after-tax rates of return should be measured. The problem with this approach is that theory would predict that these after-tax rates of return on capital should be equal: any differences would have to be explained by theory.

On the other hand, if one wanted to know how high the rate of return on capital is needed to finance capital, then before-tax rates of return to capital, unadjusted for risk, should be measured. It would be interesting to measure the marginal rate of return on capital which is equal to the cost of capital rather than the average rate of return on capital. This is particularly important when considering the tax system.

Another approach is to measure the cost of finance for firms. This would be the weighted average of the opportunity cost of equity and the after-tax cost of bond finance. This is only one part of the total cost of capital of firms since it ignores depreciation and other parts of the tax system that influence the cost of capital. However, the information is helpful to analysts who estimate the user cost of capital.

3. What about Inflation?

The paper quite correctly adjusts returns for inflation. It is clear that profits are revised to correct the original cost of assets and nominal interest expense. However, are the rates of return measured on a real or nominal basis to compare across firms? Should they be or not – this gets into the issue of financial arbitrage.

WHAT IS THE BENCHMARK?

WHEN COMPARING THE COST OF CAPITAL ACROSS COUNTRIES, presumably, one would be interested in financial arbitrage. After all, what benchmark should we expect for measurements of after-tax-rates of return on capital that would be equalized across countries if capital flows across national boundaries? Financial arbitrage is a difficult issue for empirical estimation of the cost of capital since one cannot easily observe how taxes influence the determination of interest rates over time. The Ando-Hancock-Sawchuk paper assumes that differences in interest rates are solely due to expected appreciation of currencies. However, this ignores other institutional aspects of financial markets, particularly the presence of the tax system at the international level (see Boadway et al. [1984]).

Firms that finance capital can obtain it from three sources: individual investors, financial intermediaries and other corporations. The type of lender can operate from one of many countries. The taxes paid on income will depend on the existing tax regime of the country. For example, consider a marginal investor who pays taxes at the rate m on interest and at the rate c on the appreciation of a currency (foreign exchange earnings). Let I and I^* denote the nominal rates of interest on a bond issued in host and home countries. Let $\dot{e}$ be the appreciation of the host country's currency relative to the home country. In the presence of taxes, the investor will be indifferent between bonds held in home and host countries if the after-tax rates of return on assets are equal to each other:

$$I^*(1-m) = I(1-m) + \dot{e}(1-c) \Rightarrow I^* = I + \dot{e}(1-c)/(1-m) \qquad (1)$$

The above equilibrium suggests that the difference in nominal interest rates will not be equal to the expected change in the exchange rate. Instead, the difference will also be due to differential tax rates on foreign exchange earnings and asset returns. Some lenders, such as financial intermediaries, may face equal tax rates on all sources of earnings (so $c = m$ and possibly zero) while individuals or companies may face differential tax rates. Given that tax considerations will also influence the opportunity cost of equity, one is left with a quandry. If the objective of this type of work is to estimate the cost of capital, why would anyone want to ignore an important part of the tax system that influences the cost of financing?

It should be noted that real rates of return (nominal rates of return less inflation) will not be equalized across countries. For example, if the rate of increase in the value of foreign currency is equal to the difference between the anticipated inflation rates in the home and host countries, then $\dot{e} = \pi^* - \pi$, as under the assumption of purchasing power parity, then the following is implied:

$$I^* - \pi^*(l-c)/(l-m) = I - \pi(l-c)/(l-m) \qquad (2)$$

Real rates of return on assets will not be equalized due to differential taxes on different sources of income.

Financial costs are influenced by the possibility that firms may be in a non-taxpaying position for a particular time period. The Ando-Hancock-Sawchuk paper assumes that firms are fully taxpaying so the after-tax cost of debt finance is equal to the interest rate less the tax value of interest deductions from corporate taxable income: $I(l-t)$ (t being the corporate tax rate). However, for many countries including Canada, the United States and Japan, companies may be in a tax loss position. Thus, it is unclear what effective statutory corporate income tax rate should be used to measure the after-tax cost of debt finance.

Moreover, the appropriate measurement of the corporate income tax rate in Canada is especially complicated by differential manufacturing and non-manufacturing tax rates, provincial tax rates and special deductions given to resource companies that can influence the tax rate. Japanese and U.S. estimates are also complicated by the existence of state or local corporate income tax rates.

Given these tax considerations regarding financial arbitrage and the cost of finance, it is unclear what a researcher might conclude about differences in rates of return on capital across countries. If these differences are measured with the assumption that companies are paying taxes at a particular rate, are such differences important due to economic factors or are they a result of a mismeasurement of tax variables?

BIBLIOGRAPHY

Ando, Albert and Alan J. Auerbach. "The Corporate Cost of Capital in Japan and the United States: A Comparison." In *Government Policy Towards Industry in the United States and Japan*. Edited by John Shoven. London and New York: Cambridge University Press, 1988a.

—. "The Cost of Capital in the United States and Japan: A Comparison." *Journal of the Japanese and International Economies*. Vol. 2, (1988b): 135-158.

—. "The Cost of Capital in Japan: Recent Evidence and Further Results." *Journal of the Japanese and International Economies*. Vol. 4, (1990): 323-350.

Boadway, Robin, Neil Bruce and Jack Mintz. "Taxation, Inflation and the Effective Marginal Tax Rate in Canada." *Canadian Journal of Economics*. 17, (1984): 62-79.

Collins, Julie H. and Douglas A. Shackelford. "Corporate Domicile and Average Effective Tax Rates: The Cases of Canada, Japan, the United Kingdom and the United States." *International Tax and Public Finance*. 2, (1995): 55-84.

The Impact of Taxation on Capital Markets: An International Comparison of Effective Tax Rates on Capital

Comment by Michael Daly
Trade Policies Review Division
World Trade Organization

It is truly a pleasure to be invited to discuss this paper because it is clear, concise and extremely relevant to current Canadian and international tax policy. Moreover, while the paper contains much with which I agree, fortunately for me in my role as discussant, I can also find a few bones of contention, mainly regarding the international comparisons.

The paper contains a description of a well-known methodology used to derive marginal effective tax rates (METRs) applicable to income from domestic and cross-border investment. The methodology is broadly similar to that developed in a book edited by Mervyn King and Don Fullerton (1984), which focused on the manner in which taxation (in four countries, namely, the United States, Germany, the United Kingdom and Sweden) distorts the incentives to domestic savers to undertake different types of domestic investment financed in various ways. However, the paper by Chen and McKenzie is different from the seminal work by King and Fullerton in several notable respects.

First, the authors have adapted the methodology to incorporate capital risk and irreversibility. They show that both factors increase the level and intersectoral dispersion in METRs, thereby discouraging risk taking and exacerbating the potential distortions in investment caused by taxation.

Second, they compute METRs not just for various sectors in Canada as a whole, but also for various sectors in different provinces. The latter is particularly relevant given the existence of substantial interprovincial differences in taxation. Such differences further increase the dispersion in METRs.

Third, METRs are computed for domestic investments financed with domestic savings, as well as for foreign direct investment (FDI) undertaken by Canadian and U.S. multinational companies. On the basis of the estimates of METRs found in tables 2 and 3 of their paper, the authors draw the following conclusions.

a) Domestic savers investing at home are treated less favourably in Canada than in most of the other eight countries examined. Notable exceptions are Germany and Japan.

b) METRs faced by Canadian multinational firms investing in the United States are less than those applicable to similar investments in Canada.

c) Investments in Canadian manufacturing by U.S. multinationals are subject to slightly lower METRs than are investments in U.S. manufacturing undertaken by U.S. firms.

Conclusions b) and c) are especially noteworthy. They suggest that the interaction of the Canadian and U.S. tax systems tends to encourage Canadian and U.S. multinationals to undertake FDI in the United States and Canada, respectively, rather than invest domestically.

My critical remarks focus on the international aspects of the paper. The main point I would like to make is that international comparisons of tax systems using METRs or, indeed, any other tax indicators, tend to be much less robust and, therefore, potentially more misleading than purely domestic comparisons. Whereas METRs are very useful for highlighting intersectoral (and locational) differences in taxation within a country, as well as trends therein, international comparisons of METRs are more problematic. They require a common methodology together with very detailed knowledge of each country's tax system. While this paper satisfies the common methodology requirement, I am less sanguine that all the relevant features of all nine countries' tax laws are properly taken into account. The latter is, after all, an extremely daunting task, given the complexity of different countries' tax systems. As a compromise, studies such as King and Fullerton (1984) and, more recently, Jorgenson and Landau (1993), forego a strict common methodology, but rely on country experts to ensure that all the relevant provisions of each country's tax laws are taken into account. A more ambitious study conducted by the Organization for Economic Co-operation and Development (OECD, 1991) satisfies both requirements. The OECD study, like the Chen and McKenzie paper, entails an examination of cross-border as well as domestic investment, albeit in manufacturing only. As far as Canada's tax treatment of FDI is concerned, however, the OECD study provides a rather different picture from the one painted by Chen and McKenzie.

As shown in Table 1, other studies involving similar indicators (namely tax wedges and pre-tax hurdle rates of return) support the authors' conclusion a) that domestic savers investing at home are treated relatively less favourably in Canada than in the United States, the United Kingdom and Italy, at least in the case of a typical investment in manufacturing.[1] (Interestingly, the indicators of dispersion reported in the OECD study suggest that Canada's tax system treats domestic investments more uniformly than do the tax systems of several other countries, notably the United States, Japan and Italy.) A comparison of the rankings of countries in the different studies reveals some ambiguity regarding the characterization of the United States, Japan, Germany and France as high or low tax regimes.

Perhaps more importantly, the OECD (1991) study contradicts the authors' conclusions concerning the tax treatment of FDI. According to their conclusion b), Canada's tax system interacts with the U.S. tax system to encourage Canadian multinationals to invest in the United States. By contrast, the OECD study suggests that

TABLE 1

MARGINAL TAX INDICATORS APPLICABLE TO DOMESTIC INVESTORS IN MANUFACTURING

Country	Chen-McKenzie 1995 METR	Jorgenson-Landau 1990 METR	OECD 1990 Tax Wedge[a]	OECD 1990 Tax Wedge[b]	OECD 1990 Hurdle Rates[c]
United States	21.5	38.5	3.0 (1.7)[d]	2.6 (1.5)[d]	5.8 (2.5)[d]
Japan	32.0	27.7	2.8 (3.6)	–	6.4 (3.6)
Germany	27.5	31.9	0.9 (0.6)	0.9 (0.4)	5.6 (4.5)
France	21.9	53.8	2.3 (2.5)	1.4 (2.3)	5.4 (2.4)
United Kingdom	20.2	37.9	2.0 (0.8)	1.9 (1.0)	5.9 (2.3)
Italy	22.1	27.8	2.6 (2.2)	–	5.9 (3.6)
Canada	25.5	40.2	3.5 (1.1)	3.8 (1.2)	6.2 (2.4)
Mexico	16.5	–	–	–	–
Hong Kong	11.9	–	–	–	–

Notes: [a] The difference between the pre-corporate tax rate of return necessary when real interest rates are 5 percent post tax and the post-personal tax rate of return. Top marginal rate of personal taxes, average OECD inflation 4.5 percent, average weights.

[b] The difference between the pre-corporate tax rate of return necessary when real interest rates are 5 percent and the post-personal tax rate of return. Top marginal rate of personal taxes, country-specific inflation, country-specific weights. Only those countries with some information on weights are included.

[c] No personal taxes, average inflation at 4.5 percent, average weights.

[d] Figures in parentheses are standard deviations.

the pre-tax hurdle rate of 6.2 percent applicable to domestic investors in Canada is substantially lower than the corresponding rates (shown in column 2 of Table 2) for FDI undertaken abroad by a Canadian multinational. If this OECD finding is true, then this particular feature of Canada's tax system is undesirable as it reduces the overall returns Canadian investors can obtain on their savings and constitutes an impediment to the efficient global allocation of capital.

TABLE 2

HURDLE RATES FOR CANADIAN, U.S. AND OTHER FOREIGN MULTINATIONALS VS. DOMESTIC INVESTORS[a]

Country	(1) Domestic Investors	(2) Canadian Multinational	(3) U.S. Multinational	All Foreign Multinationals[b]
United States	5.8	7.2	–	7.5
Japan	6.4	7.9	7.7	8.1
Germany	5.6	6.6	6.3	6.4
France	5.4	8.1	7.3	7.9
United Kingdom	5.9	6.7	7.1	7.0
Italy	5.9	7.1	6.5	7.2
Canada	6.2	–	7.6	8.4
OECD Average	5.9	7.5	7.1	7.5

Notes: [a] Subsidiary financed by one-third loans from the parent, one-third new equity from the parent and one-third retentions by the subsidiary. Weighted average of three sources of finance by parent. Weighted average of three assets. Inflation of 4.5 percent everywhere. No personal taxes.

[b] Investment from all other OECD countries into named country.

Source: OECD (1991).

Nor is conclusion c) supported by the estimated pre-tax hurdle rates reported by the OECD (1991). As shown in column 3 of Table 2, the pre-tax hurdle rate of 7.6 percent faced by a U.S. multinational investing in Canadian manufacturing is not only substantially higher than the 5.8 percent rate applicable to domestic investors in the United States, thus tending to discourage U.S. multinationals from investing in Canada, it is also the highest among G7 countries.

The bias against FDI identified by the OECD study is not peculiar to Canada's tax system. In general, the study suggests that the interaction between countries' tax systems is such that together they tend to discourage both outward and inward FDI. It remains to be seen whether the discrimination against FDI (as reflected in the absence of both capital import and capital export neutrality) built into most countries' tax laws is addressed in the multilateral agreement on investment (MAI) currently being negotiated at the OECD.

By way of conclusion, it is important to bear in mind that the estimates of METRs reported by Chen and McKenzie as well as related indicators found in most other studies, including OECD (1991), ignore the fact that multinational companies have more scope for tax planning (often involving third countries) than do purely domestic firms. This enables the multinationals to avoid or evade taxes, thus reducing the METRs associated with FDI. Indeed, in many countries there is a widespread perception that foreign multinationals pay less rather than more taxes than do domestic firms as a consequence of creative accounting, financing and transfer pricing practices. The greater scope for tax planning arises as a consequence of wide differences in countries' tax systems and bilateral tax treaties. Multinational firms can reduce their global tax payments by shifting income to countries whose marginal tax rates are relatively low. The presence of real investment in a low-tax country facilitates the reporting of accounting profits there. Insofar as new investment in low-tax countries permits additional profit shifting, there is an implicit subsidy to FDI. Thus, real investment and profit shifting involve joint decisions.[2] This is especially true when intangibles are involved. It follows that METRs need to incorporate international tax planning/transfer pricing, etc. in order to provide a more accurate picture of the actual incentive to invest abroad.

ENDNOTES

1 A similar conclusion is found in a report by the Commission of the European Communities (1992), which used a methodology very similar to the one adopted by the OECD.

2 See Grubert and Slemrod (1994), for example.

BIBLIOGRAPHY

Commission of the European Communities. *Report of the Committee of Independent Experts on Company Taxation*. March 1992 .

Grubert, Harry and Joel Slemrod. "The Effect of Taxes on Investment and Income Shifting to Puerto Rico." Working Paper 4869, National Bureau of Economic Research, 1994.

Jorgenson D. and R. Landau. *Tax Reform and the Cost of Capital: An International Comparison*. Washington, DC: Brookings Institution, 1993.

King, M. and D. Fullerton. *The Taxation of Income from Capital*. Chicago: Chicago University Press, 1984.

OECD. *Taxing Profits in a Global Economy: Domestic and International Issues*. Paris: Organization for Economic Co-operation and Development, 1991.

INVESTING IN CANADA: ESTIMATION OF THE SECTORAL COST OF CAPITAL IN CANADA AND CASE STUDIES FOR INTERNATIONAL COMPARISONS

Comment by A. Louis Calvet
Faculty of Administration
University of Ottawa

IN HIS PAPER, PROFESSOR JOG ACCOMPLISHES THREE MAIN OBJECTIVES. First, he estimates the cost of capital for Canadian industrial sectors. He then extends the methodology used to account for country and exchange risks and, finally, he draws inferences about how international cost of capital differences affect the competitiveness of Canadian firms and the ability of Canada to attract foreign capital in an era of increased business globalization.

Professor Jog must be commended for his work and for being one of the first authors to apply modern finance theory in areas that have been the exclusive domain of economists working with aggregated data. The strength of this paper resides in the fact that its methodology is well suited for sectoral and company studies and, therefore, for performing a meaningful and pragmatic competitive analysis.

Besides providing numerous insights, the paper presents a number of strong conclusions that are very much dependent on its methodology. The validity of these conclusions is questionable. My comments mainly refer to the paper's theoretical framework and follow its outline.

In the first section, the author estimates sectoral costs of capital using the weighted average cost of capital (WACC) approach. For all its limitations (see Brealey and Myers, 1991, p. 465), the WACC can be implemented with relative ease, as compared to the more sophisticated approach which relies on asset betas and requires specifying the net tax advantage of corporate borrowing – a daunting and controversial task. In calculating the cost of equity based on the capital asset pricing model, Professor Jog uses, as the risk-free rate, the yield on long-term Government of Canada bonds minus a maturity premium. This gives a rough estimate of the expected yield on short-term treasury bills, as suggested by Brealey and Myers (1991). The choice of 6 percent as a market risk premium is arbitrary and some additional justification would have been welcome, particularly in light of the fact that 6 percent may appear low by many standards. Given the large sample of firms (714) studied, a wider index than the Toronto Stock Exchange (TSE) 300 would have been more appropriate.

A long series of ad hoc assumptions are subsequently made about how to compute the cost of debt, the cost of preferred equity, etc. There is no way to escape these assumptions when data are unreliable or unavailable. However, I would have liked to see a justification for the 22 sectors chosen and for the rules used to allocate firms to sectors (Standard Industrial Classification [SIC] codes, etc.). Furthermore,

I believe that Professor Jog's interpretation of Figure 4 as a relative risk-return relationship is incorrect: he is relating the sectoral costs of capital to equity betas, when the appropriate comparison, if any, would be to asset betas.

Table 5 gives the real WACC for each sector from 1988 to 1994. Two remarks come to mind when analysing this table. First, there is as much variability over time as across sectors: for instance, the real WACC of the utilities and pipelines sector in 1994 (the sector with the lowest overall real WACC) is very close to the real WACC of the gold and silver sector in 1991 (the sector with the highest overall real WACC). Second, there is a definite jump in the real WACC in 1994. Given that capital structures and tax effects are relatively constant over time and that the market risk premium is kept fixed, the increase in the real WACC is due solely to the increase in the real rate of interest, as can be appreciated from the data in Table 1. I wonder whether the estimate for 1994 can unduly influence the results when averaging over only seven years of data. I also find questionable allowing the real interest rate to change over time while keeping the market risk premium constant in the estimation of the cost of equity, and thus of the WACC.

The next section of the paper takes an international perspective by including foreign exchange risk and inflation differentials. The author's objective is to analyse how differences in risk-free rates between Canada and the United States can give rise to differences in the cost of capital between the two countries. Professor Jog shows that the 1.88 percent difference in real risk-free rates from 1983 to 1992 results from differences of 2.78 percent and 0.90 percent in the nominal and inflation rates, respectively. He then asserts that the 1.88 percent is made up of two components, a country premium and an exchange risk premium. The former is estimated at 0.74 percent from covered interest rate parity, whereas the latter equals 1.14 percent by difference. I believe this derivation is based on a definition of the exchange risk premium that differs from the usual one found in the literature. Let us first define the difference in real rates between Canada and the United States as:

$$r_c - r_{us} = (i_c - i_{us}) - (\pi_c - \pi_{us}) \tag{1}$$

where r is the real interest rate, i is the nominal interest rate and π is the expected inflation rate. The forward discount fd can be included in the above equation as follows:

$$r_c - r_{us} = (i_c - i_{us} - f_d) + (f_d - \pi_c + \pi_{us}) \tag{2}$$

Following Frankel (1991), the difference between the real interest rates is equal to the covered interest differential ($i_c - i_{us} - fd$), plus the real forward discount ($fd - \pi_c + \pi_{us}$). The first term can be called the political or country premium because it captures all barriers to the integration of financial markets across national boundaries: transaction costs, information costs, capital controls, tax laws, default risk and the risk of future capital controls. The second term may be called the currency premium because it pertains to differences in assets attributable to the currency in which they are denominated rather than in terms of the political jurisdiction in which they are issued. In fact, the currency premium can be broken down as follows:

$$(fd - \pi_c + \pi_{us}) = (fd - \delta e) + (\delta e - \pi_c + \pi_{us}) \tag{3}$$

where δe is the change in the spot rate. The first term $(fd - \delta e)$ is the exchange risk premium and the second $(\delta e - \pi_c + \pi_{us})$ is the expected real depreciation based on purchasing power parity (PPP). Equation (2) can be rewritten:

$$r_c - r_{us} = (i_c - i_{us} - fd) + (fd - \delta e) + (\delta e - \pi_c + \pi_{us}) \tag{4a}$$

or, in words,

$$r_c - r_{us} = \textit{country premium} + \textit{exchange premium} + \textit{expected depreciation based on PPP} \tag{4b}$$

We can contrast equation (4b) with the difference in real interest rates, as interpreted in Professor Jog's paper:

$$r_c - r_{us} = \textit{country premium} + \textit{exchange premium} \tag{5}$$

Clearly, the author's definition of exchange premium is at odds with the one used in the literature. His definition amalgamates two components: the exchange premium *per se*, i.e., the difference between the forward rate and the expected change in the spot rate, and the expected change in the spot rate based on PPP.

Another point deserves attention. It is well known that the covered interest differential $(i_c - i_{us} - fd)$ between Canada and the United states is effectively zero (see, for instance, Frankel, 1991). This is interpreted in the literature as proof of the integration of the two North American markets. The reason that Professor Jog finds a discrepancy of 0.74 percent is easily explained by his choice of yields on t-bills. Indeed, a currency's forward discount or premium is determined by arbitrage conditions in the offshore interbank market. When it is mentioned that there is no arbitrage possible between Canadian and U.S. funds, the literature refers to interest rates on Eurodollar deposits (or at least interest rates that reflect bank risk). If U.S. bank credit risk increases relative to Canadian bank credit risk, the Canadian dollar discount can decline (or its premium increase), which creates an arbitrage opportunity in Canadian t-bills hedged into U.S. dollars.[1] This surely cannot be taken as a measure of country risk as we are comparing instruments (t-bills and forward contracts) that are different in credit risk.[2] In fact, the existence of a difference between $(i_c - i_{us})$ and *fd* is more a measure of changes in the riskiness of the banking system than of the relative riskiness of Canada.[3]

In summary, the estimates of country and exchange premiums that are derived in the paper are rather controversial. This problem is compounded when the author adds a so-called business risk premium which is itself the result of foreign exposure risk detected in the bond yields of Canadian firms issuing bonds in U.S. dollars. As a result, both the costs of debt and equity capital of export-oriented Canadian companies are hit with an additional 1.20 percent differential (1.94 percent minus the already included 0.74 percent) which raises further their cost of capital. For example, according to the author, the WACC of the Canadian lightweight coated paper sector is 1.67 percent higher than its counterpart's WACC in the United States. Beyond the problems related to the methodology, I believe the rationale for increasing equity costs in Canada by 1.20 percent should be developed. Equally, Professor Jog should discuss the extent to which the above-mentioned business risk is systematic in nature, or can be influenced by diversification.

Jog then deals with the telecommunications sector and uses the dividend growth model to estimate the cost of equity. He leaves us with the puzzle that, although U.S. firms appear to have higher business risk than Canadian firms, the latter have substantially higher equity costs and, therefore, a higher WACC. I presume this suggests segmented equity markets in North America, a proposition that is hard to believe in view of recent results pointing toward increased integration.

Jog's final case study looks at the cost of capital for the Canadian and Finnish pulp and paper industries, using the United States as a benchmark. It appears to proceed along the same lines as section one, yet rather than taking the real rate spread between Canada and Finland as the result of the exchange risk and country risk premiums, this section uses nominal interest rates. Hence, we are told that the difference between Finnish certificates of deposits and U.S. t-bills is 4.92 percent, which can be broken down into a 1.29 percent country premium and a 3.63 percent exchange premium. Yet, if we were to use real rates, as in the first section, we would end up with a much smaller estimate of the exchange premium. More important, equation (3) unambiguously shows that the difference in nominal interest rates is not equal to a country premium plus an exchange premium.

To conclude, this paper is an interesting attempt at integrating currency and political risks in a sector's domestic cost of capital in order to proceed to international comparisons. Professor Jog's main finding is that Canadian firms are at a significant disadvantage in cost of capital, which he evaluates at 2 percent, vis-à-vis U.S. firms. I believe that this conclusion is open to debate. His work is, nevertheless, very useful and I encourage him to continue exploring these issues of great importance.

ENDNOTES

1 Note that the situation at the end of 1996 is the reverse since the Canadian dollar is at a premium to the U.S. dollar and U.S. t-bills have a higher yield.

2 Arbitrage between t-bills is a recurrent phenomenon, albeit of limited extent. There are different reasons for this: institutions cannot borrow at the t-bill rate, t-bills are held by institutions such as central banks that do not engage in arbitrage, the forward contract is risky and locking in a forward contract reduces liquidity since the investment can be unwound less easily and probably with higher transaction costs, etc.

3 In addition, the calculation of a possible differential should be done taking into account transaction costs (bid-ask spreads), taxes and the different ways of calculating yields between Canada and the United States. Indeed, U.S. t-bill yields are calculated following the commercial discount method and on the basis of 360 days in a year, whereas Canadian t-bill yields are true yields on a 365-day year.

BIBLIOGRAPHY

Brealey, R.A. and S.C. Myers. *Principles of Corporate Finance*. 4th edition. New York: McGraw-Hill, 1991.

Frankel, J.A. "Quantifying International Capital Mobility in the 1980's." In *National Saving and Economic Performance*. Edited by D. Bernheim and J. Shoven. Chicago: University of Chicago Press 1991, pp. 227-260.

Session II Financing Constraints and Small Firms

Raphael Amit, James Brander & Christoph Zott
Faculty of Commerce and Business Administration
University of British Columbia

6

Venture Capital Financing of Entrepreneurship in Canada

Executive Summary

THIS PAPER HAS THREE MAIN CONTRIBUTIONS. First, it provides overview information about venture capital investment in Canada using a data set generously made available to us by Macdonald & Associates Ltd. The second contribution is to infer four important empirical regularities (or stylized facts) from this information that require explanation. The third contribution is to set out a theoretical structure that is consistent with these stylized facts. Some preliminary econometric analysis is also presented. This combination of factual information and theoretical structure provides a foundation for further research on the venture capital industry and for relevant public policy analysis.

The data set used in this study has several important features. It is the most comprehensive and detailed data base about Canadian venture capital investments currently in existence, it is up-to-date, and it provides financial information about the investee firms, along with information about the decisions and practices of venture capitalists. From this data we make a number of interesting observations. First, to give some sense of the size of the industry, we estimate that there are approximately $300 million to $350 million of new venture capital investment annually by Canadian venture capitalists in Canadian companies, and there were at least $3 billion in Canadian venture capital funds under management in Canada in 1995.

Interestingly, the geographical pattern of venture capital activity does not match the geographical pattern of economic activity. Relative to overall economic activity, venture capital activity is high in Quebec and low in Ontario and Atlantic Canada. As expected, high-tech industries make up a relatively large share of venture capital investments. Investee firms are somewhat older than expected, as fully 10 percent of the post-1990 venture capital investments were made in firms founded before 1974, and one third of the investments were made in firms founded before 1984. The data also show that early-stage investments are smaller (by about 35 percent on average) and much less numerous than later-stage investments. Thus, we conclude that venture capital activity emphasizes expansion and growth stages rather than the start-up phase of a company's life cycle. Note, however, that much later-stage investment occurs in companies that did receive start-up financing.

Investees pay significant levels of tax (on average) and spend about 3 percent of revenues on research and development, which is about equal to the overall Canadian average and, therefore, somewhat lower than expected, given the high-tech nature of the investee population. The track record of financial returns to venture capital investments is particularly interesting. Many investments provide relatively low returns, but this is offset by a small number of "hits" that do very well. This general pattern is supported by information on employment growth, as aggregate growth exceeds median growth. Most investee firms grow slowly, but a few grow very rapidly.

The average venture capital equity (or ownership) share in investee firms is about 35 percent. The majority of Canadian venture capital investments are not syndicated as each round of investment is provided by a single venture capitalist in most cases, and about half the sample firms get only one round of venture capital. In comparison to the United States, we find that syndication is much less common in Canada, especially in the early stages. While venture capital investments can include both debt and equity, we observe that about two thirds of Canadian investments are pure equity.

Exit behaviour is particularly interesting. A substantial minority of investments (about 18 percent) are terminated by being written off – the venture capitalist loses the entire investment. A comparable share of investments (16 percent) are terminated following initial public offerings (IPOs) of stock (and these are generally successful investments). A substantial share of investments (13 percent) are terminated in third-party acquisitions, and these also tend to be successful investments. The largest category of exit (37 percent) is through management or company buyouts, as company insiders buy out the venture capitalist. Indeed, if we eliminate uncategorized exits (most of which are probably management buyouts) and write-offs, company buyouts account for 50 percent of remaining exits.

From this information, we distilled four empirical regularities that any successful theory of venture capital must accommodate. First, a theory must provide a reason for the existence of a specialized venture capital industry. Second, it must explain the emphasis on development rather than start-up. Third, it must explain the pattern of exit, where insider buyouts dominate, and it must be consistent with the skewed pattern of returns.

The theoretical framework we offer focuses on informational issues. Specifically, we view asymmetric information and limited liability (with low collateral) as the central features of venture capital investment. Both major forms of asymmetric information, hidden information (leading to adverse selection) and hidden action (leading to moral hazard) are included in our analysis. The model we present is complicated even though we abstract from several important features of the venture capital industry. We believe that this information-based approach is consistent with the major stylized facts characterizing the industry. For example, if inside information is important, it is not surprising that most exit is through company buyouts or acquisition by informed outsiders.

Our model implies that informational asymmetries lead to market failure, causing possible underfinancing. If adverse selection and moral hazard are important, it will be difficult for investors to earn a reasonable return in the industry, even if there are many potentially worthwhile projects, leading to underinvestment. Venture capitalists exist precisely because they can reduce information-based market failures through careful selection, monitoring and other means. The more skilled the venture capitalist is in reducing these sources of market failure, the more efficiently the venture capital sector will function. In a brief illustration of econometric analysis, we consider the implications of our theory for variations in the extent of venture capital ownership, then estimate the effect of venture capital ownership on several measures of success, including taxes paid, taxes per unit of assets and revenues per unit of assets. We also provide a review of the relevant literature in Appendix A.

INTRODUCTION

ENTREPRENEURIAL FIRMS IN CANADA HAVE BEEN GROWING in relative importance. For example, the rate of new business registrations approximately doubled between 1979 and 1989. Furthermore, the entrepreneurial sector is particularly interesting because of its close relationship to innovation and technological progress. However, despite the observed growth of this sector, it is often claimed that entrepreneurial activity in Canada is not as vigourous as it should be. More specifically, concerns have been raised about possible gaps or failures in financing the entrepreneurial sector.

One important source of financing for the entrepreneurial sector is the venture capital industry. Indeed, venture capital activity is normally defined as the provision of equity and mixed[1] financing to young privately held firms. Despite the significance of the entrepreneurial sector and the resulting importance of venture capital, relatively little is known about the Canadian venture capital industry. There is, by comparison, a much larger body of data and analysis related to other parts of the financial sector, such as banking, insurance, real estate finance and stock markets.[2] The primary objective of this paper is to address this lack of information by providing an empirical overview of venture capital financing in Canada.

Even the U.S. venture capital industry has not been subject to much rigorous empirical scrutiny, although recent work by Lerner (1994a, b) and Gompers (1995) provides a strong start in this direction. The venture capital industry has not been as closely studied as other elements of the financial sector, in part, because little of the relevant information is in the public domain, as almost all the firms that venture capitalists invest in (referred to as investees) are privately held and, therefore, not subject to the same reporting requirements as public companies. Public information is also more limited in the venture capital industry because there is no organized secondary exchange for venture capital investments that provides summary information. Furthermore, regulatory scrutiny of venture capital has been modest compared to the level of regulatory scrutiny of banks, insurance companies and stock exchanges, so the potential information that arises from regulatory proceedings and requirements is also relatively sparse. In addition to limited data availability, academic interest in the area seems to have been less than the level of interest in banking, stock markets and other parts of the financial sector.

The best available data on the Canadian venture capital industry is collected, using two surveys, by Macdonald & Associates Ltd. One of these surveys is supported financially by the Business Development Bank of Canada (BDC), and some of the information from this survey is reported in the annual (since 1993) BDC publication, *Economic Impact of Venture Capital*. Much of the information from the other survey is reported in *Venture Capital in Canada*, the annual statistical review and directory of the Association of Canadian Venture Capital Companies, prepared by Macdonald & Associates Ltd. We have, very fortunately, been allowed access, on an anonymous version (in which names of firms have been removed) of the Macdonald & Associates data base for this study.

In addition to reporting summary information, we infer a set of broad empirical regularities or stylized facts that we see as important aspects of the industry. We then provide a theoretically based explanation of these empirical regularities. In addition, we provide some preliminary econometric analysis of one central hypotheses that emerges from our theoretical analysis.

Thus, our paper provides useful new information about venture capital activity in Canada, along with a theoretical structure for interpreting this information and a brief econometric investigation of one key theoretical point. We emphasize that this paper is only a small step in a larger effort directed toward providing a better understanding of the venture capital industry. We believe that such an understanding is an important input to both public policy formulation and business practice in the area.

The next section describes the data base used in the paper followed by overview information drawn from the data base and a set of stylized facts from this information. A theoretical structure for interpreting the data is then presented along with some brief econometric results and concluding remarks. A literature review is provided as Appendix A.

THE DATA SET

AS INDICATED IN THE INTRODUCTION, the data used for this study were collected by Macdonald & Associates and made available on a confidential and anonymous basis. In addition, no individual firm-specific information is reported or discussed in our analysis.

The data are derived from two surveys. The first, referred to as the investment survey, began as an annual survey in 1991 and became quarterly in 1994. It asks approximately 66 Canadian venture capital providers (as of 1994) to identify the firms they invest in, i.e., their investees, and to give some financial information about each investee. Investees are recorded in the data base and follow-up information is requested in subsequent investment surveys. The investment survey asks about the amount and stage of each investment and seeks information about the venture capitalist's ultimate divestiture of its holdings in each investee.

The survey seeks to obtain comprehensive information from all Canadian venture capital providers. There is, however, no precise definition of venture capital provider, and some relevant firms may be missed from the survey. It is also possible that some surveyed venture capitalists do not report all their investments. Macdonald & Associates estimate that the investment survey identifies 90 percent to 95 percent of the underlying population of Canadian firms supported by Canadian venture capitalists. The survey is also sent to other investors, i.e., investors other than venture capitalists, who have investments in the venture-backed investees in an effort to get full information about the investee firms. The information from this survey covers the period from 1991 through the first quarter of 1995.

The second survey is an annual economic impact survey, that began in 1993. It seeks additional information about the investees identified in the investment survey. Economic impact information is sought about each investee that received an investment in or after 1991. Retrospective information was also requested. Suppose, for example, that an investee received an investment in 1991. The venture capitalist making the investment would have received a 1993 economic impact questionnaire asking for information about this investee going back as far as 1987. In many cases, not much retrospective information could be provided, but the data base contains economic information on a reasonable number of investees going back as far as 1987. The date of the investee's original start-up (which in some cases is well before 1987) is also reported.

The response rate for the economic impact survey over its three-year life has varied between 56 percent and 74 percent, i.e., information has been received on 56 percent to 74 percent of the targeted investee firms. If the investment survey identifies 90 percent to 95 percent of the relevant underlying population, then the effective sample coverage is between 50 percent (0.9 times 56 percent) and 70 percent (0.95 times 74 percent) of the underlying population. The economic impact survey collects balance sheet and income statement information on the investees (including revenues and taxes paid). It also collects information on the structure and amount of their employment, on the industry they are in and on the specific venture capital investments made in them.

A typical investee enters the data set when it receives its first investment from a venture capitalist. It may receive investments from additional venture capitalists as well. Subsequent rounds of investment may occur. Eventually, an investee leaves the sample. This occurs when all venture capitalists have either written off (in the case of failure) or "cashed in" their holdings in the investee. Thus, the data set contains a series of "life histories" for venture-capital-backed firms.

A record refers to information for one particular investee firm for one particular year. There are 372 investee firms in the data available from the economic impact survey, but information on about 20 is significantly incomplete. The remaining 352 firms provide 1,247 reasonably complete records and, therefore, have an average of just under four records each. Of these firms, 343 can be successfully matched[3] with firms in the investment survey data base, but the number of complete records falls to 424, primarily because there are no records in the investment survey before 1991. In addition, for each investee, matches occur only in years when investments occur. For example, an investee firm that received an investment in 1992 but in no other years would be matched only for 1992. Thus, as there are 343 firms and only 424 complete records, most firms have only one or two years of matched records. The investment survey data also include information on 476 additional Canadian investees.[4] For some purposes, complete matched records are necessary, but much interesting and relevant information is available from just the economic impact data (1,247 records on 372 companies) or just the investment data.

This data set targets Canadian investees supported by the Canadian venture capital industry. A Canadian entrepreneurial company that received support from venture capitalists based in the United States or Asia but no support from Canadian venture capitalists would not be in the data set. This set of firms is probably fairly small, but there is no hard data on its magnitude. It seems unlikely that this omission introduces much systematic bias over most subjects of interest in the data.

One possible source of systematic bias in the data arises from the fact that only 56 percent to 74 percent of the targeted investees are reported on in the economic impact survey for any one year. The informational requirements of this survey are fairly high, so it is not surprising that compliance is not perfect. Some venture capitalists do not provide any economic impact information in a given year, some provide information only on some of their investees and some provide only partial information on a given investee. We might reasonably suspect some selection bias from this source, as it seems likely that the absent investees or incomplete investee records would be smaller and/or less successful firms.

Despite some possible selection bias, this data set remains an important and unique data source. First, the coverage of the target population is good, partly due to the efforts and reputation of Macdonald & Associates and, for the economic impact survey, partly because of the sponsorship and influence of the Business Development Bank of Canada. Second, the data set has a significant time-series dimension, so firms can be tracked through time, allowing age effects, business cycle effects and other dynamic considerations to be investigated. Third, there is information on revenues, employees and taxes paid. Thus, the quality of information about measures of success is unusually high and unique for data sets dealing with entrepreneurial firms.

AN OVERVIEW OF VENTURE-CAPITAL-BACKED FIRMS AND INVESTMENTS

WE NOW TURN TO CONSIDERATION OF SUMMARY TABLES AND FIGURES that describe various aspects of the data. The summary statements apply to whatever subset of the 372 companies in the economic impact data base for which we have the

FIGURE 1

GEOGRAPHICAL DISTRIBUTION OF VENTURE ACTIVITY

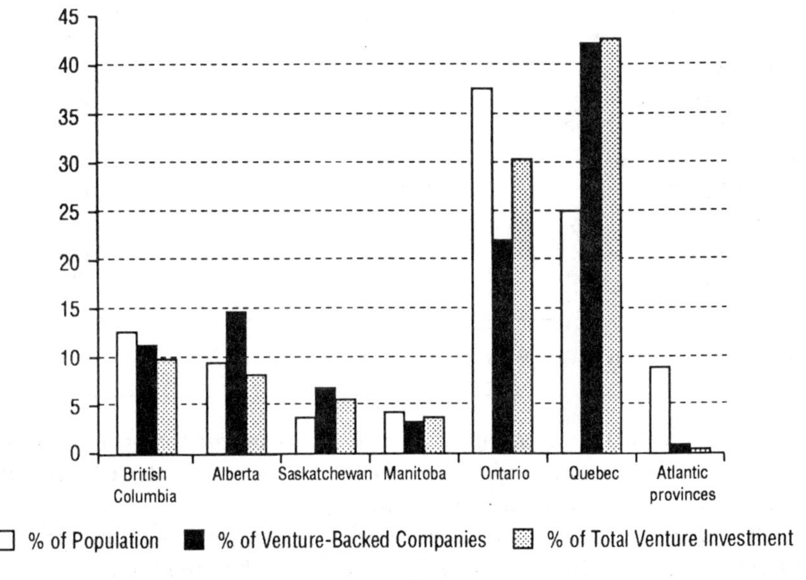

Source: Based on data provided by Macdonald & Associates Ltd.

relevant information. One noteworthy feature is that the geographical pattern of venture capital activity is not as closely matched to the geographical pattern of economic activity as one might expect. As shown in Figure 1, the proportion of venture-backed firms (shown by the solid bars) is high in Quebec (relative to population) and low in Ontario and in the Atlantic provinces. For example, Quebec has 25 percent of Canada's population (and produces 23 percent of Canada's national output), but is the home of 42 percent of the venture-backed firms in the data base. Ontario has almost exactly the reverse pattern. It has 38 percent of Canada's population, and produces 40 percent of Canada's output, but has only 22 percent of the venture-backed firms. Atlantic Canada has almost no venture-backed activity (less than 1 percent of the total) despite having 8 percent of Canada's population. The aggregate amount of venture investment (over the period 1991 to 1994), as shown by the lightly shaded bars, shows a similar, but less severe, pattern in that Ontario has a share of total venture investment more nearly commensurate with its relative size. The relatively high level of venture capital activity in Quebec may be partially due to the large and active labour-supported funds that operate in Quebec. These funds were created

TABLE 1
AGE OF VENTURE-BACKED COMPANIES

Year Founded	Number of Companies	Percentage of Total
1994	22	6
1993	21	6
1992	17	5
1991	25	7
1984-1990	163	44
1974-1983	81	22
Before 1974	38	10
Total	367	100

Source: Based on data provided by Macdonald & Associates Ltd.

by provincial legislation allowing favourable tax treatment for labour unions and other investors who participate. Other provinces have since followed suit, but the Quebec funds were the first and remain the largest.

If there is any bias in this data arising from the absence of firms supported by foreign venture capitalists, it is probably to understate the extent of venture-backed activity in British Columbia, as anecdotal evidence suggests that a disproportionate share of venture capital originating in Asia supports firms in British Columbia.

The companies in the data set are somewhat older than might be expected. As shown in Table 1, fully 10 percent of the 367 companies for which information on age is available were founded before 1974. As the data set is limited to firms that received at least one infusion of venture capital in 1991 or later, this means that some firms obtain venture capital financing long after being founded. In addition, this information appears to suggest that it takes longer than commonly perceived, and perhaps more venture capital than originally anticipated, to bring some investee firms to the stage at which exit is feasible. A company may be founded well before it obtains its first venture capital investment. These data seem to suggest that venture capital is focused on expansion of existing small companies rather than on the start-up phase.

Table 2 shows the industry breakdown (for 371 of the 372 companies). Venture capital financing is focused on the high-tech sector in that high-tech companies are much more strongly represented in this group of firms than they are in the economy as a whole.

The perception that venture-backed activity is closely related to the high-tech sector is supported by anecdotal comments from the venture capital industry itself.

TABLE 2

INDUSTRY CLASSIFICATION

	Number of Companies	Percent	High Tech?
Manufacturing	91	25	no
Miscellaneous	58	16	mostly no
Consumer related	50	13	no
Computer (hardware and software)	44	12	yes
Medical/health	28	7	yes
Electrical components and instruments	27	7	yes
Communications	26	7	yes
Energy/environmental technology	22	6	yes
Industrial equipment	13	3	yes
Biotechnology	12	3	yes
Total	371	100	

Source: Based on data provided by Macdonald & Associates Ltd.

Table 3 shows aggregate employment information for 352 of the 372 investees in the data set. While average employee numbers were very similar in 1987 and 1994, the 1987 and 1988 years were based on a small, and perhaps unrepresentative, group of firms reflecting the fact that only firms that received new venture capital infusions after 1990 are in the data set. It seems that 1993 and 1994 average employee levels were higher than earlier in the decade.

Of considerable interest are the indicators of growth provided in Table 3, e.g., the aggregate annual growth rate of continuing firms, shown in column 4. To see how this number is calculated, consider the 1994 year. There were 203 firms in the data that were present in both 1993 and 1994. Total employment in this group of 203 firms rose by 18 percent between 1993 and 1994. We might then say that the representative venture-backed firm grew by 18 percent over the year. To obtain column 5, we calculated a growth rate for each continuing firm, ordered the firms by growth rate and selected the median, i.e., the middle firm. Column 5 reports these median growth rates. Column 6 reports the growth rates for firms at the 60th percentile. We can see that the median growth rate is consistently, and significantly, less than the aggregate growth rate, and even the 60th percentile growth rate is less than the aggregate growth rate for several years. This reflects the fact that growth rates are skewed in the sense that most firms grow modestly if at all in any given year, but a few firms grow very substantially. This is similar to the "hit" phenomenon associated with the music business or the movie business, where a few "hits" account for most of the profits.

There are firms that leave the sample between any given pair of years. Column 7 shows the number of firms in the data and is used for calculating average and median employees, and the number of continuing firms available for calculating

TABLE 3

EMPLOYMENT IN VENTURE-BACKED FIRMS: LEVELS AND ANNUAL GROWTH

1900 (1)	Average Employees (2)	Median Employees (3)	Aggregate Growth of Continuing Firms (%) (4)	Median Growth per Firm (%) (5)	60th Percentile Growth per Firm (%) (6)	Number of Firms 2-3/4-6 (7)
1987	176	105	–	–	–	24/–/–
1988	118	47.5	8	1	4	52/22
1989	146	50	6	4	8	102/52
1990	150	42.5	13	3	12	136/102
1991	149	45	4	0	7	199/136
1992	151	45	7	0	6	236/194
1993	183	60	15	12	20	221/178
1994	178	52.5	18	10	20	270/203

Source: Based on data provided by Macdonald and Associates Ltd.

TABLE 4

SUMMARY FINANCIAL DATA: 1987 TO 1994 (IN REAL $1994)

(1)	Mean ($000s) (2)	Median ($000s) (3)	Standard Deviation (4)	Number of Records (5)
Total assets	22,074	5,423	67,758	1,228
Total equity	8,190	1,821	23,059	1,224
Venture capital-share of equity (%)	35	30	30	1,184
Retained earnings	720	143	10,076	1,081
Total fixed assets	9,615	1,967	40,749	1,208
Long-term debt	6,644	1,176	27,721	1,107
Revenue	23,210	5,902	54,692	1,237
Investments in plant, property and equipment	1,932	207	12,194	1,121
Research and development expenditures	812	74	2,073	1,035
Taxes paid	520	22	2,753	981
Number of Canadian employees	161	50	306	1,240

Source: Based on data provided by Macdonald & Associates Ltd.

aggregate growth and median growth rates for each year. The number of continuing firms is always less than the total number of firms as there are new venture-backed firms each year. For example, in 1994 there were 203 continuing firms of the 270 in the data set. This implies that 18 (=221-203) of the firms from 1993 exited before the 1994 survey, and 67 firms (=270-203) entered the data set in 1994. Note that omitting exiting firms from growth rate calculations is unlikely to bias the growth rates upward. Investees may leave the sample because they are unsuccessful (bankruptcy) but, more commonly, they leave because they are successful enough for the venture capitalist to sell out at a profit (following, for example, an initial public offering). Thus, if we could take all investee firms for a particular year and look at their employment growth, irrespective of whether they left the sample or not, this growth might well be higher than reported in Table 3.

Table 4 provides summary financial information for 352 firms (1,274 records). Some records fail to report the information for some variables, however. The number of records with the relevant information is indicated in column 5. All averages are in thousands of real 1994 Canadian dollars, i.e., nominal dollar amounts reported in the original data have been adjusted to account for inflation. This table shows that the data are skewed in the sense that there are a few large investees that make the averages much larger than the medians. Table 4 indicates that, on average, venture capitalists hold a (minority) share of 35 percent ownership in their investee firms. The data in Table 4 also imply that firms in the data set spend, on average, about

FIGURE 2

NUMBER OF VENTURE CAPITAL INVESTORS (SYNDICATION)

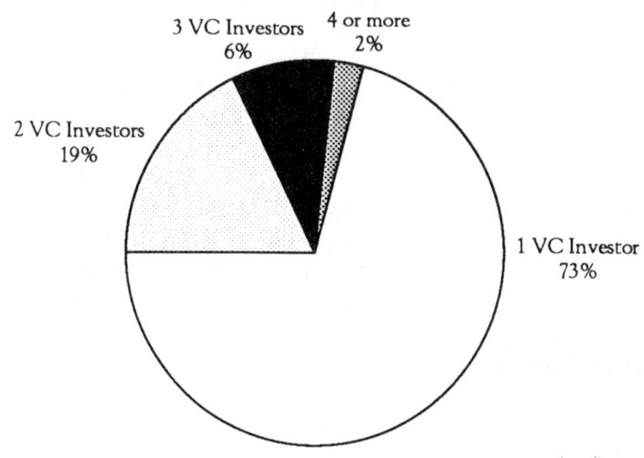

Source: Based on data provided by Macdonald & Associates Ltd.

3 percent of their revenues on research and development. This is about the same as the overall ratio of research and development spending to revenues for the Canadian economy as a whole. Revenues per Canadian employee are $144,000, and the average long-term debt-to-equity ratio is a conservative 0.81. The low debt-to-equity ratio may reflect the limited borrowing capacity of entrepreneurial firms. We note also that the average investee is profitable enough to pay non-trivial amounts of tax.

The next few tables and figures contain information about the structure of venture capital investment. This information is based on a subset of 343 investees for whom this information is available. In a given investment round, an investee may receive money from more than one venture capitalist. This is referred to as syndication. We refer to an infusion of capital (from one or more venture capitalists) in a given investment round as an investment package. The 343 investees received 532 investment packages in total. As shown in Figure 2, approximately 73 percent (387 of 532 investment packages) were stand-alone investments. About 19 percent of investment packages (102 out of 532) were syndicated across two venture capitalists, 6 percent (33 investment packages) had three venture capitalists involved and two percent (10) had four or more.

A given investee might go through several investment rounds, as implied by the fact that 343 investees received 532 packages. These 532 investment packages included 734 individual investments by venture capitalists. In our data, each investment

FIGURE 3

INVESTMENT ROUNDS

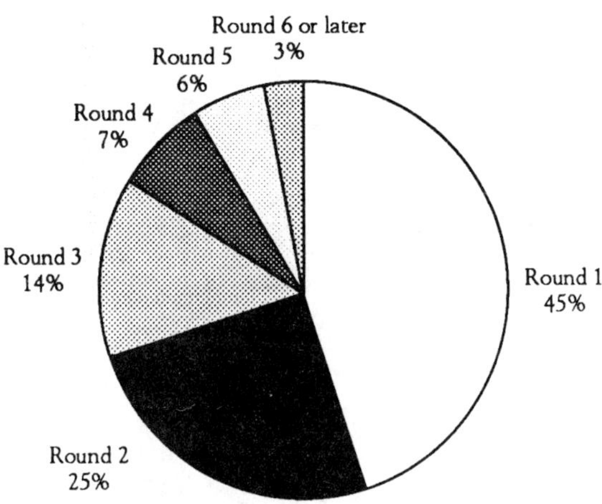

Source: Based on data provided by Macdonald & Associates Ltd.

package is identified by round. Thus, even if a given investee received only one round of investment in our sample period, the data indicate whether this investee had received earlier rounds of investment.

Figure 3 depicts the distribution of investment rounds for the 532 investment packages (covering 343 firms) in the data. Figure 3 shows that almost half (45 percent) of all investment packages were first-round investments. However, some investees have received multiple rounds of investment (up to a maximum of eight.)

Information about rounds and numbers of investors is provided in cross-tabulation form in Table 5. Syndication, in which an investment round is shared among two or more venture capitalists, is much less common than stand-alone investment, as 73 percent of investment packages are not syndicated.

Looking in particular at first-round investments, we see that 177 out of 242 were not syndicated. This contrasts with the United States where Lerner (1994b) reported that about two thirds of first-round investments in a sample of biotechnology firms were syndicated. Table 6 shows how many investments correspond to each stage in the entrepreneurial firm's life. It is based on 734 investments in the 343 firms in both the economic impact survey data and the investment survey data.

TABLE 5

NUMBER OF VENTURE CAPITAL INVESTORS AT EACH INVESTMENT ROUND

Number of Investors	Investment Round									Number of Investments
	1	2	3	4	5	6	≥ 7	Total	Percent	
1	177	95	57	27	19	9	3	387	73	387
2	43	26	13	8	7	3	2	102	19	204
3	16	10	2	2	2	1	–	33	6	99
4+	6	–	1	–	2	1	–	10	2	44
Totals	242	131	73	37	30	14	5	532	100	734
	45%	25%	14%	7%	6%	2%	1%		100	

Source: Based on data provided by Macdonald & Associates Ltd.

TABLE 6

NUMBER OF INVESTMENTS BY STAGE AND YEAR

Year	Early Stages			Later Stages					Count
	SE	ST	ES	EX	AC	TU	WC	OT	
1991	1	37	–	66	7	13	–	18	142
1992	9	43	–	57	16	30	2	34	191
1993	4	44	–	84	7	18	16	26	179
1994	3	54	4	99	10	13	–	6	189
1995(Q1)	1	4	4	20	–	2	–	2	33
Total	18	182	8	306	40	76	18	86	734

Note: SE: seed, ST: start-up, ES: other early-stage investments, EX: expansion, AC: acquisition, TU: turnaround, WC: working capital and OT: other.

Source: Based on data provided by Macdonald & Associates Ltd.

It includes investments made between 1991 and the first quarter of 1995. As already noted, a given investee may obtain financing from multiple venture capitalists, and may receive multiple rounds of investment from a given venture capitalist. Each investment is recorded separately. An investment may include debt, equity or both.

More than half of the "other" investments were management buyouts, in which an investee obtained investments from a venture capitalist to aid in buying out other investors in the company, including (quite possibly) other venture capitalists. As can be seen from this table, just about 27 percent of the investments are early-stage investments. This is consistent with the implication of Table 1 that most investees are fairly mature.

Table 7 shows investment size by stage. The early-stage average works out to be almost exactly $900 thousand per investment, while the late-stage average works out to $1.4 million. Combining the fact that early-stage investments are both smaller (from Table 7) and less numerous (Table 6) than late-stage investments, we can infer that the venture capital industry seems to focus more on growth and development of entrepreneurial firms, than on start-up activity.

Putting together information from tables 6 and 7 we can infer that in 1994 total new venture capital investment in the represented firms was about $237 million (189 investments at an average size of $1.25 million). Firms in this sample do not represent the entire population, but probably most large investments are included. A plausible rough estimate for total venture capital investment in 1994 would be in the range of $300 million to $350 million. By comparison, in 1994, U.S. venture capital firms invested roughly C$3.7 billion in 1,000 companies. Given the relative size of the two economies, venture capital investment is of similar importance in both countries.

TABLE 7

AVERAGE SIZE OF INVESTMENT BY STAGE AND YEAR (IN $000S)

Year	Early Stages			Later Stages					Total
	SE	ST	ES	EX	AC	TU	WC	OT	
1991	66	877	–	1,350	2,193	1,549	–	1,815	1,336
1992	494	1,032	–	1,192	1,414	645	480	1,800	1,156
1993	715	856	–	1,969	1,907	943	365	1,024	1,281
1994	983	945	1,102	1,297	2,155	1,239	–	1,000	1,254
1995	260	654	342	946	–	475	–	–	791
1991-95	589	924	722	1,406	1,822	967	378	538	1,230

Notes: 1995 values are based on only a few data points.
SE: seed, ST: start-up, ES: other early-stage investments, EX: expansion, AC: acquisition, TU: turnaround, WC: working capital and OT: other.

Source: Based on data provided by Macdonald & Associates Ltd.

Venture capital investments may include both debt and equity, although "pure" investments are much more common. About 66 percent (415 out of 734) investments in the 343 investees with full records were all equity, about 27 percent (198 out of 734 investments) were all debt, and the remaining 16 percent (121 investments) were mixed. A venture capitalist may provide equity at one stage and debt at a subsequent stage, so mixed debt and equity holdings are more common than mixed investments.

Figure 4 gives some idea of the relative importance of debt and equity. This figure shows an average or representative investment for each stage. There are, for example, 18 seed investments in total. The total debt in these 18 investments is $1.04 million, giving an average of only $57 thousand. This average is low because most seed investments have no debt whatsoever. Figure 4 shows that equity is relatively more important at the early stages, and debt becomes more significant later, although equity remains more important in absolute terms for every stage except working capital.

Because some investees receive investments from more than one venture capitalist, the average amount received per investee exceeds the average investment. Table 8 shows the average and median amounts received (including debt and equity) by an investee in a given round of investment.

Table 9 shows the average investment size by industry for early and late-stage investments. As expected, general manufacturing is a large category as measured by the number of investments. However, compared to their overall importance in the economy, communications and computer-based endeavours are heavily represented.

FIGURE 4

AVERAGE DEBT AND EQUITY BY INVESTMENT STAGE
1991 – Q1, 1995

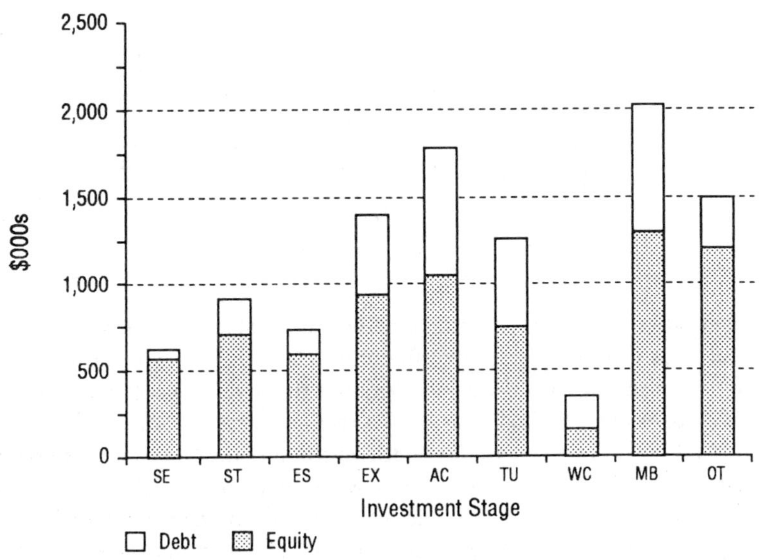

Notes: 1995 values are based on only a few data points.
SE: seed, ST: start-up, ES: other early-stage investments, EX: expansion, AC: acquisition, TU: turnaround, WC: working capital, MB: management buyout and OT: other.

Source: Based on data provided by Macdonald & Associates Ltd.

The comparison of early and late-stage investments varies by industry. In particular, biotechnology seems to require relatively heavy early-stage investments, and is the only industry category for which early-stage investments outnumber late-stage investments. This could, of course, reflect the relative youth of this industry, as few mature biotechnology companies exist.

Some of the most interesting information in the data set is related to exit by venture capitalists. Exit occurs when a venture capitalist either sells off or writes off its investment in an investee. Information is only available for 1992 to 1994 and the first quarter of 1995 (199 investee companies with 226 records).

Figure 5 shows the distribution of exit by type. As can be seen from this figure, IPOs make up only a modest portion of total exits.[5] The largest cause of exit is company buyouts, which occur when the officers or management of the investee buy out the venture capitalist.

TABLE 8

TOTAL AMOUNT RECEIVED BY INVESTEE IN AN INVESTMENT ROUND (DEBT + EQUITY)

Year	Mean		Median		Number	
	Early	Late	Early	Late	Early	Late
1991	1,204	2016	550	1,000	27	78
1992	1,526	1,703	535	700	32	101
1993	1,094	1,833	530	750	37	103
1994	1,328	1,700	400	1,000	44	105
1995	471	1,215	260	681	9	18
1991-1995	1,238	1,774	568	800	149	405

Source: Based on data provided by Macdonald & Associates Ltd.

From other information in the data set, we are able to make rough estimates of the real return to the overall investment for each class of exit. IPOs and acquisitions (which occur when a third party acquires the investee) both yield fairly high returns. Company buyouts show a large variance but, overall, provide slightly negative real returns. Generally, one can divide the entire group of investments into three broad categories: about one third do very well, about one third represent out-of-pocket losses or complete write-offs, and the middle third provide nominally positive but disappointing returns, i.e., returns below the rate of return on risk-free investments.

TABLE 9

SIZE OF INVESTMENT BY INDUSTRY

Industry	Mean		Median		Number	
	Early	Late	Early	Late	Early	Late
Communications	1,682	1,818	500	750	33	87
Computer	784	2,372	600	1,600	17	43
Electrical components and instruments	611	1,124	420	861	9	27
Energy and environmental technology	1,112	2,078	645	630	11	27
Health	1,197	2,360	525	1,200	14	27
Biotechnology	2,101	998	1,475	560	12	10
Industrial equipment	814	1,366	350	825	9	14
Consumer related	807	2,203	800	1,000	16	57
Manufacturing	1,301	1,382	400	600	27	109
Miscellaneous	814	1,485	375	640	24	74

Source: Based on data provided by Macdonald & Associates Ltd.

FIGURE 5

DISTRIBUTION OF VENTURE CAPITAL EXITS (PERCENTAGE OF EXITS)

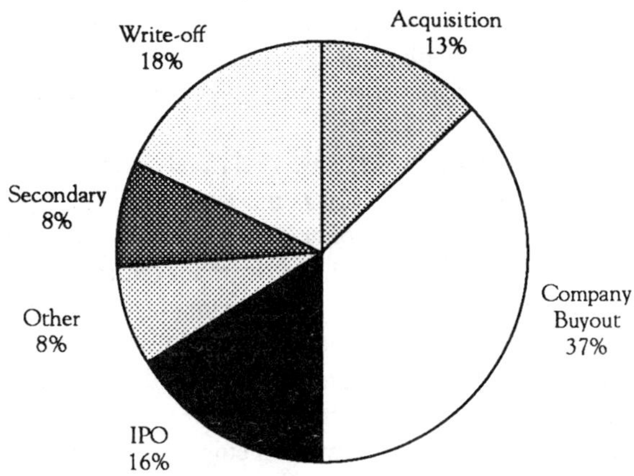

Source: Based on data provided by Macdonald & Associates Ltd.

In addition, there is a "star" or "hit" phenomenon in the data. Of the 226 exits, approximately 10 percent (22 investments) yielded annual real rates of return in excess of 50 percent per year.

MAJOR STYLIZED FACTS

BASED ON THE INFORMATION ALREADY PROVIDED, there are several major stylized facts that we wish to emphasize. Perhaps the primary observation is the simple fact that the venture capital sector exists at all. Venture capital firms constitute a specialized segment of the financial market that focuses on entrepreneurial companies. The research question arising from this observation is "Why does this specialized financial sector exist?" What makes the entrepreneurial sector sufficiently different from established firms to justify a dedicated set of financial intermediaries to serve it?

A second important stylized fact is that the venture capital sector focuses on later-stage financing. In our data, less than 3 percent of investments are "seed" investments and less than 30 percent are classified as early stage. Looking at the amount (rather than the number) of investments, early-stage investments account for roughly 20 percent of investment. Furthermore, even if this sample accounts for only 40 percent to 50 percent of the underlying population, the total number of seed and start-up investments is low relative to overall start-up activity. Thus, an appropriate characterization of venture capital is that it carries out development financing for firms, and is not the major factor in actual start-up activity. Any theory of venture capital must explain why start-ups would have relatively low representation in venture capital investment.

A third important stylized fact in the data is the nature of the exit. Typical textbook treatments of venture capital activity give the impression that the standard outcome of venture capital investments is an IPO. At some point, the firm becomes large enough and has strong enough prospects that it makes an initial share offering to the general public (an IPO) and becomes a publicly traded company. At or shortly after this point, the venture capitalist typically sells its shares in the company.[6]

However, as our data base shows, only a relatively small share (16 percent) of venture capital investments end in IPOs. Almost as many end in acquisitions, as a third party (often a competitor, a supplier or a customer) buys the firm outright. More than twice as many (37 percent) end in management buyouts. Thus, it is much more common for insiders (either company management or other firms that are close to the business) to buy out a venture capitalist than for a general public share offering to be made. Any theory of venture capital financing must explain or account for this dominance of insider activity at exit.

Finally, the other stylized fact we wish to emphasize relates to rates of return. The variance of returns is large, and most investments generate either disappointing or negative returns. We emphasize that this does not mean that there is anything "wrong" with the venture capital. Like several other industries (book publishing, music, movies) much of the profit in the industry comes from a relatively small number of "stars." High returns are associated with acquisitions and IPOs, although some management buyouts also provide very high returns. Management buyouts showed much higher variance in returns than the other forms of exit. One extremely valuable aspect of the data is that it contains enough information to estimate holding periods and rates of return, although this is a difficult estimation problem.

To recapitulate, any theory of venture capital activity must explain or accommodate the following empirical regularities:

- the existence of a specialized financial industry (the venture capital industry) that focuses on emerging privately held firms;
- emphasis, within the venture capital sector, on firms in the later stages of entrepreneurial development rather than on seed and start-up activity;
- the dominance of exit through insider buyouts rather than public share offerings; and
- high variance in returns with many disappointments and some "stars."

A Theory of Venture Capital Finance

Main Elements of the Theoretical Framework

THE KEY ELEMENT OF THE ENTREPRENEURIAL SECTOR that we believe might explain the existence of venture capitalists[7] is asymmetric information. There is a large volume of literature about asymmetric information, and some attempts have been made to apply this theory to the venture capital sector. A review of this literature is provided in Appendix A. We note here, however, that classic papers on asymmetric information include Akerlof (1970) and Jensen and Meckling (1976). Early attempts to apply these ideas to entrepreneurial finance include Amit et al. (1990, 1993) and Brander and Spencer (1989). MacIntosh (1994) provided a careful and detailed description of venture capital financing in Canada in which he emphasized the role of asymmetric information.

There are two types of asymmetric information: hidden information and hidden action. Hidden information refers to a situation in which the entrepreneur has better information about the firm's prospects than investors do. Thus, important information is hidden from the investor but known to the entrepreneur. As described more fully later, hidden information may give rise to *adverse selection*, in which low-quality entrepreneurial prospects dominate the venture capital market. The other form of asymmetric information is hidden action, (sometimes called *moral hazard*) which arises when the investor cannot observe the effort level of the entrepreneur. In its crudest form, moral hazard can lead to a situation in which the entrepreneurs can "take the money and run," while simply claiming bad luck as the reason for failure of the project. If adverse selection and moral hazard are more important in the entrepreneurial sector than among established firms, then we would expect the emergence of specialized investors (venture capitalist firms) which develop skills in selecting and monitoring investment targets. Thus, the existence of the venture capital industry is explained by the benefits from specializing in the selection and monitoring of investments.

Adverse selection and moral hazard might be particular problems in the entrepreneurial sector because of little collateral and limited liability. Firms in both the established sector and the entrepreneurial sector have limited liability. The key difference is that established firms normally have substantial amounts of collateral that can be used to secure debt finance and reduce the "down side" risk of equity investments. For such firms, hidden information and moral hazard may be present, but they are less important to the investor because the investor is partially protected by collateral. Entrepreneurial firms typically have very little collateral which implies that their limited liability is likely to be relevant to the investor in the sense that the investor may easily lose the entire investment if things do not work out well. (Recall that about one fifth of the exits in our data were write-offs.) In addition, the entrepreneur typically does not have much of a track record and, therefore, reputation is not as important in making assessments. For these reasons – the relative lack of collateral and track record – investors in the venture capital industry are more vulnerable to problems arising from informational asymmetries.

We assume that the entrepreneur has better information about the project than the venture capitalist. Perhaps, for example, the entrepreneur is an inventor who knows that some new product is really very close to being ready to sell, while the venture capitalist lacks the technical expertise to make such a determination. However, the opposite asymmetry may also arise. A venture capitalist may have a much more realistic appraisal of how well some new venture will do, because the venture capitalist might know the market better or entrepreneurs might be prone to "optimistic bias." In our analysis, we proceed on the supposition that entrepreneurs have better information about the project, but the alternative could also be investigated.

Very few (if any) theoretical studies exist that simultaneously consider the effect of moral hazard and adverse selection in the presence of limited liability. That is the task we undertake here. In order to focus on these aspects of venture capital finance, we abstract from other important considerations, in particular, from the risk-sharing aspect of venture capital finance, and assume that both the entrepreneur and the venture capitalist are risk neutral. We also abstract from bargaining between the venture capitalist and the entrepreneur. In our analysis, the venture capitalist offers a financing package to the entrepreneur, and this package is either accepted or rejected. In addition, we do not focus on any direct contribution by the venture capitalist to the management of the project. Its only contribution is equity finance. The other major abstraction we make is to focus only on a single interaction between the venture capitalist and the entrepreneur rather than considering a series of staged investments in a dynamic setting. All of these abstractions can be relaxed. Our first objective, however, is to focus as sharply as possible on the two informational asymmetries and on limited liability as we believe these issues are fundamental to venture capital financing.

We consider a one-period model with several stages. The entrepreneur wishes to launch a new venture that requires a certain amount of capital I, which we assume to be exogenous. The project has some underlying quality γ, which cannot be observed by the venture capitalist, but which is known to the entrepreneur.[8] γ is distributed according to probability density function $g(\gamma)$. Our analysis of the interaction between the entrepreneur and the venture capitalist starts after they have come into contact through some unspecified process.[9]

In this first contact, the venture capitalist obtains the available information about the entrepreneur and about the project. Based on this information, the venture capitalist forms an opinion about how likely particular levels of success might be. The first "move" in the game is made by the venture capitalist firm, which offers a contract to the entrepreneur. This offer might be nothing at all but, if the offer is positive, it includes a certain amount of equity capital E^v and an ownership share s. For example, the venture capitalist might say: I am willing to provide $1 million in return for 30 percent ownership in the firm.

FIGURE 6

STRUCTURE OF VENTURE CAPITAL FINANCING DECISION

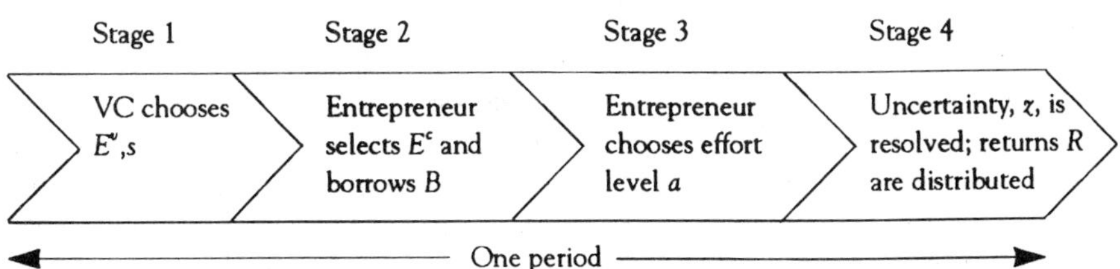

Stage 1
Stage 2
Stage 3
Stage 4
VC chooses E^v,s
Entrepreneur selects E^e and borrows B
Entrepreneur chooses effort level a
Uncertainty, z, is resolved; returns R are distributed
One period

The entrepreneur can accept or reject this offer. If the offer is accepted, the entrepreneur augments the equity capital in the firm by an amount $E^e > 0$ and borrows amount $B > 0$ from external lenders. Since the required investment is I, we have:

$$E^v + E^e + B = I \tag{1}$$

The face value of the debt (the amount that must be paid back) is denoted by D. It will exceed B. This face value D will be determined in a competitive debt market, ensuring that the debt offers the same expected return to lenders as alternative investments.

After financing is obtained, the entrepreneur provides an effort level (or action) a. This action causes disutility (or cost) $c(a)$ to the entrepreneur. The action a is unobservable to investors, creating a moral hazard problem. Finally, action a and the realization of some random variable z jointly determine the returns from the venture R. Figure 6 illustrates this sequence of events.

Figure 6 presents the model as a four-stage process. However, the last stage does not require any decisions to be made, and need not have been identified as a separate stage. It simply represents the final resolution of the payoffs, and might be thought of as occurring at the "end" of the third stage. The second and third stages are separated from each other only for expositional purposes. The model is exactly the same if these two stages are combined and the entrepreneur's equity input and effort are determined simultaneously. Therefore, the model is essentially a two-stage game. We assume that the players are sequentially rational. In particular, in the first stage, the venture capitalist correctly anticipates the effects of its investment E^v and of the sharing rule s on the entrepreneur's decisions in the second and third stages, especially on the optimal effort level a. We impose this requirement of sequential rationality by analysing the model with the method of backward induction. Consequently, we consider the third stage first.

Stage 3: The Entrepreneur's Effort Decision

Here the entrepreneur takes E^v as given from the first stage, and takes B, D and E^e as given from the second stage. We assume that the entrepreneur wishes to maximize utility, which is taken to depend on the action (or effort level) a and on the net income. The entrepreneur's expected net income y, depends on a, on γ (the underlying project quality), on the share of proceeds taken by the venture capitalist s, on the equity participation E^v and on debt D. The entrepreneur is taken to be risk neutral and, therefore, wishes to maximize expected income, net of any disutility associated with providing effort. Let the entrepreneur's expected utility be denoted U. The entrepreneur wishes to:

$$\underset{a}{\textit{Maximize}}\ U(a,y(a,s,\ldots)) = y(a,s,\ldots) - c(a) \qquad (2)$$

Market uncertainty is represented by random variable $z \in [0, 1]$. Variable z can be thought of as the "state of nature." It is distributed according to probability density function $f(z)$ with z ordered such that $z=0$ represents the worst possible state of nature, i.e., the worst possible realization, whereas $z=1$ describes the best possible outcome. Variable z influences the venture's terminal returns R, which are also taken to be increasing in project quality and in the entrepreneur's effort. Thus we can write:

$$R = R(a,\gamma,z) \qquad (3)$$

We can implicitly define a critical state z^* in which the new venture is just able to repay its debt.

$$R(a,\gamma,z^*) = D \qquad (4)$$

From equation (4), assuming a certain amount of mathematical regularity, we can use the implicit function theorem to write:

$$z^* = z^*(a,\gamma,D) \qquad (5)$$

The entrepreneur's income y, consists of what is left over from returns R after paying off any debts (represented by D), and turning over share sR to the venture capitalist. Provided $z > z^*$, then R exceeds D. If $z < z^*$, then $y=0$. The expected value of entrepreneurial income can be written as:

$$y = (1-s)\int_{z^*}^{1} (R(a,\gamma,z) - D)f(z)dz \qquad (6)$$

We can then substitute equation (5) into equation (6) which can be substituted into equation (2) and solve for the optimal effort level a as a function of γ and D. As D is predetermined in the second stage and γ is exogenous, this formally completes the specification of a and z^*:

$$a = a(\gamma,s,D);\ z^*=z^*(a(\gamma,s,D),\gamma,D) \tag{7}$$

Stage 2: The Determination of Entrepreneurial Financial Structure

At the second stage, sequential rationality implies that the entrepreneur anticipates how his or her effort will be determined as a function of D (the face value of debt) in the third stage and uses this knowledge in selecting the equity contribution in the second stage. This equity contribution will influence D and, therefore, will influence the final effort decision and the resulting payoffs. The central point in the analysis of the problem is the determination of D. Recall that investment I must be raised through a combination of E^v, E^e, and B, i.e., through equity and debt. However, in order to be willing to loan money to the entrepreneurial firm, outside lenders (assumed to be risk neutral) must expect to earn the same return from this risky loan as they would from a riskless alternative at the risk-free interest rate i.

To simplify this calculation, we assume that the entrepreneur's type is revealed at the beginning of the second stage. In practice, we might expect the lack of knowledge about the project's quality to persist and only gradually be eliminated, but this creates distracting algebraic complications that do not add to the main insight. The key point is that there is hidden information at the time the venture capitalist decides on what offer to make to the entrepreneur. The loan market constraint is then captured in the following equation:

$$B(1+ i) = D(1 - F(z^*)) + \int_0^{z^*} R(z,\ \gamma;\ a^*)\ f(z)dz \tag{8}$$

The left-hand side of equation (8) describes the lender's opportunity cost, which is the return that could be obtained if amount B were invested at riskless rate of return i. The right-hand side of equation (8) shows the lender's expected return from lending money to the entrepreneurial firm. If the face value of the debt is D, then the lender will receive D with probability $(1\text{-}F(z^*))$. This is the probability that $z \geq z^*$, which is the probability that the realization of uncertainty is sufficiently favourable that the entrepreneurial firm is solvent and able to pay its debts in full. Thus, the first term on the right-hand side of equation (8) is the expected value of being paid off in full. However, even if the lender is not paid off in full, i.e., if $z < z^*$, the lender still gets something. In particular, it receives the returns R, earned by the firm. The next term on the right-hand side of equation (8) is the expected value of these returns over states of nature where entrepreneurial default occurs.

If there were enough collateral, then contracts could be written on this collateral, eliminating concerns about incomplete payment of debt and, therefore, eliminating the relevance of limited liability. In such a case, lenders would receive the full amount D regardless of the state of nature. It would follow that $D=B(1+i)$, and neither venture capitalists nor entrepreneurs would have to worry about the effects of informational asymmetries on debt markets. Thus, it is the assumption that collateral is absent that makes equation (8) interesting, i.e., that prevents it from reducing to $D=B(1+i)$.

From equation (8), it is clear that D is a function of the amount borrowed B and, therefore, is also a function of underlying equity participation as:

$$B=I-E^v-E^e \tag{9}$$

where I is exogenous. Substituting this in equation (9) and equation (7) into equation (8) allows us to eliminate a, z^* and B and, in principle, solve for D as a (rather complicated) function of E^v, E^e, s and γ (and exogenous variables i and I). We write this expression as:

$$D=D(E^v, E^e, s, \gamma; I, i) \tag{10}$$

Equation (10) is just the debt market constraint, expressed as a function of predetermined variables and exogenous variables. Note that this incorporates the correct anticipation by lenders of third-stage incentives, as captured in equation (7).

The entrepreneur's objective in the second stage is to maximize overall utility, subject to equations (7) and (8) (or [10]). We assume that the entrepreneur's cost of providing equity capital is given by $C(E^e)$. Thus, by extending equation (2), the second stage utility of the entrepreneur is:

$$U=\gamma\{f[a(\gamma,s,D(E^v, E^e,s,\gamma)),s,\ldots] - c(a(\ldots))\} - C(E^e)$$

$$=U(\gamma,s,E^v, E^e) \tag{11}$$

The entrepreneur then maximizes equation (11) with respect to E^e, taking s and E^v as predetermined, with γ as exogenous. (Exogenous parameters i and I also affect utility through their effect on a and y, but they are suppressed for notational economy.) Assuming that such a solution exits, it can be written as:

$$E^e=E^e(\gamma,s,E^v;I,i) \tag{12}$$

The optimal amount of borrowed funds is then just I-E^v-$E^e(\ldots)$, and the optimal debt load follows from equation (10) with E^e at its optimal value.

First-Stage Selection of the Venture Capital Contract

So far, all solutions that have been derived (or, more precisely, are assumed to exist) are dependent on the exogenous parameters I and i, and on the venture capitalist's first-stage choice variables E^v and s. In the first stage, the venture capitalist anticipates subsequent incentives that will arise in subsequent stages and, therefore, incorporates the solution functions of the second and third stages into the first stage decision problem. This decision problem can then be written as follows:

$$\max_{E^v,s} \int_{\gamma_1}^{\gamma_2 1} \int_{z^*}^{1} s\,[R(z, \gamma; a) - D^*]\, f(z) g(\gamma)\, dz\, d\gamma - C^v(E^v) \tag{13}$$

As shown in equation (13) the venture capitalist seeks to maximize an expected value taken over the relevant states of nature, i.e., over states more favourable than z^* and over the relevant range of γ. Recall that γ reflects project quality. This quality is unknown to the venture capitalist in the first stage. When the venture capitalist makes an offer, only certain entrepreneurs will accept the offer. If an entrepreneur has a project that is very good, he or she may prefer not to sell a share of it to the venture capitalist. Conversely, if the project is very poor, then it may not be worthwhile for the entrepreneur to go ahead. In either case, the entrepreneur will decline the venture capitalist's offer. The highest-quality project that elicits an acceptance from the entrepreneur is denoted by $\gamma 2$, and the lowest quality project is $\gamma 1$. Only entrepreneurs with projects of quality between $\gamma 1$ and $\gamma 2$ will accept the venture capitalist's offer. Therefore, only this group of entrepreneurs are relevant for determining the expected return to the venture capitalist.

As incorporated in equation (13), the venture capital firm gets positive benefits from its share of net returns to the entrepreneurial venture, but incurs an opportunity cost of equity $C^v(E^v)$. Equation (13) is, therefore, an expected net value of the investment. This expected value is taken over all relevant states of nature and over all relevant project quality levels. Maximizing this expression over E^v and s allows the venture capitalist to select the optimal contract, consisting of an amount of equity investment and a proposed ownership share. Note that the "cut-off" values $\gamma 1$, $\gamma 2$ and z^* all depend on the values of s and E^v chosen by the venture capitalist, making the optimization indicated by equation (13) a significant computational exercise.

Solution and Interpretation of the Model

The model described in the preceding material captures the central features of venture capital investment. It is, however, a difficult model to solve. The greatest difficulty is created by the complicated self-selection by entrepreneurs that occurs at the first stage. The model can be solved using numerical methods for particular functional forms and parameter values. We do not report on the solution here, but we do summarize the main insights to be gained from the model.

The uncertainty about projects is contained in the perceived distribution of γ. The distribution of γ can be thought of as reflecting the uncertainty, from the investor's point of view, associated with any particular project's quality. If the venture capitalist has better information about γ than other investors, this is reflected in a tighter distribution for γ. A tighter distribution allows better decisions to be made and gives the venture capitalist an advantage in making investments.

Similarly, the "monitoring problem" arises because action is unobservable. If the venture capitalist can monitor the entrepreneur, we can think of this as changing the utility obtainable by the entrepreneur from a particular level of effort. More specifically, the venture capitalist would like to be able to punish low effort and reward high effort. It the venture capitalist can do this more effectively than other investors, this gives the venture capitalist an advantage. Thus, our primary explanation for the existence of the venture capital sector is its ability to specialize in selection and monitoring. (We note that MacIntosh, 1994 suggested the same rationale for the existence of the venture capital sector.)

Moral hazard and adverse selection create a market failure in venture capital financing, which might result in many worthwhile projects being unfunded or underfunded. The more skilled the venture capitalist is in reducing these sources of market failure, the more effectively this sector will function. Venture capitalists exist because they are better at this function than unspecialized investors. However, venture capitalists cannot eliminate adverse selection and moral hazard. Furthermore, these problems are more acute for younger firms, and most acute for start-ups. This explains why venture capitalists focus on the later-stage entrepreneurial firms. Later-stage firms have a track record that provides information to the venture capitalist, and they have enough assets to reduce the problem associated with limited collateral under limited liability. By virtue of their expertise, venture capitalists are better at dealing with informational problems than other investors (on average), but this advantage shows up most in later-stage entrepreneurial firms rather than at the start-up stage.

This theoretical structure can also explain the pattern of exit. If asymmetric information is important, and remains important even at the exit stage, then outside public investors will typically not be in the best position to evaluate the assets of the entrepreneurial firm. More commonly, it will be insiders who will be in the best position to buy out the venture capitalist's position. These insiders might be management or officers of the investee, or they might be other firms in a related business. Thus, if informational asymmetries are important, it is not surprising that IPOs account for only a modest fraction of exits.

Finally, the fourth empirical regularity we wish to explain is the pattern of returns. At this stage, our theory suggests only that the pattern of returns is a reflection of the underlying exogenous uncertainty associated with entrepreneurial projects. It is unclear whether the selection of financing process by the venture capitalist would magnify or reduce this underlying uncertainty. Magnification would arise if the best projects were the ones that received full financing, while lower-quality projects also received less financing. Thus, lower-quality projects would suffer two handicaps: lower basic quality *and* suboptimal financing given their quality. This effect would increase the variance of observed returns over and above the underlying variance in quality.

Econometric Analysis

So far, we have provided a descriptive overview of the venture capital industry in Canada and outlined a theoretical structure as a basis for interpreting this information. Ideally, we would like to test the important principles underlying the theory in some formal and rigorous way. Designing and carrying out such tests is a difficult task, but we report here on one preliminary step in this direction.

If moral hazard is important, then the higher the venture capitalist's share of equity becomes, the more important moral hazard becomes. If the venture capitalist has very little ownership in the firm, then the entrepreneur and other private investors bear the full consequences of the entrepreneur's actions, leading to a strong incentive to provide an appropriate effort level. As the venture capitalist's ownership increases, the entrepreneur's incentive to provide effort weakens. At the extreme, if the venture capitalist owned the entire firm, then the entrepreneur would have little incentive to provide effort and a strong incentive to convert the firm's assets to personal consumption. This effect suggests that the performance of an entrepreneurial firm might decline as venture capital ownership rose. On the other hand, it is possible that higher ownership levels by the venture capitalist would allow more effective monitoring, which suggests a positive effect of venture capital ownership on performance. In an effort to measure the relative strength of these effects, it seems reasonable to regress some measure of the entrepreneurial firm's success on the extent of venture capital ownership.

Ideally, we would like to use profits as a measure of success. We do not have a direct measure of profits, but we do have taxes paid which are a function of profits. Therefore, we can reasonably use taxes paid as a proxy for profits. This is far from ideal, but considerably better than nothing, and better than the performance indicators used in much analysis. Most of the firms in the data set paid some taxes, but many paid zero taxes. In effect, taxes paid are truncated from below by zero: a firm does not pay negative taxes, even if profits are negative. This truncation requires the use of a Tobit estimator (or some other appropriate estimator.) The results of a Tobit estimation for a regression of the venture capitalist's share of equity on taxes and on taxes per unit of assets are shown in Table 10. Table 10 also reports an ordinary least squares regression of the venture capital share on revenues per unit of assets. These regressions also contain age of the investee (in log form) as an explanatory variable.

As can be seen from this table, the venture capitalist share appears to be negatively associated with performance measures. However, the total amount of variation explained by the venture capital share is low. Thus, while the coefficient on the venture capital share is significant, variations in this share are, at most, a minor determinant of performance.

TABLE 10

EFFECT OF VENTURE CAPITAL SHARE ON PERFORMANCE

Dependent Variable	Explanatory Variable	Coefficient	Standard Error	t-Stat	P-value
Taxes paid	VCshare	-19.95	4.74	-4.21	.000
	log(Age)	706	146	4.85	.000
	Const.	-1,608	373	-4.31	.000
Taxes paid/assets (x10,000)	VCshare	-1.67	.71	-2.39	.019
	log(Age)	106	21	4.86	.000
	Const.	-146	56	-2.61	.009
Revenues/assets (x1,000)	VCshare	-4.73	1.66	-2.85	.004
	log(Age)	250	52	4.78	.000
	Const.	968	129	7.48	.000

We emphasize that the data are far from perfect. Taxes paid are not an ideal measure of performance and, in particular, do not provide much discrimination among the younger firms, most of which do not pay taxes. Using age as a regressor "corrects" for this, but it means that this group of firms contributes little to the venture capital share parameter estimate. The asset variable is also relatively "noisy."

At the interpretative level, it is very important to note that these results do not mean that venture capital investment should be viewed as a negative influence, nor do they mean that other sources of finance are better than venture capital. Venture capital investments could be an important positive influence on every firm in the data set, and could be the best source of financial capital available, and we could still observe a negative correlation between venture capital ownership and performance. What the negative correlation tells us is that the best-performing companies tend to be those in which the venture capital ownership share is not too high. This is consistent with the moral hazard idea that the entrepreneur will perform most effectively when he or she has a large stake in the company. However, if financial requirements are high and the owner's sources are meagre, then a high venture capital share might well be the best option, even if there is an associated moral hazard problem, as the alternative might be outright failure of the company. It is also possible that venture capitalists might, on average, require a higher ownership share in firms with less attractive prospects to compensate the venture capitalist for the anticipated weak performance. In any case, this table is intended only as an example of what can be done with this data set. More complete statistical analysis will be available in supporting documents from the authors.

CONCLUDING REMARKS

THIS PAPER PROVIDES PREVIOUSLY UNREPORTED DATA about venture capital investments in Canada. In addition, it sets out a series of four empirical regularities or stylized facts about the industry that emerge from the data. We also provide a theoretical structure that is consistent with these stylized facts, along with some preliminary econometric analysis. This material provides a basis for further rigorous examination of the Canadian venture capital industry and for addressing the role of public policy toward the industry.

The data set that has been used in this study has several important features. It is the most comprehensive and detailed data base about Canadian venture capital investments currently in existence, it is up-to-date and it provides financial information about the investee firms, along with information about the decisions and practices of venture capital firms. From this data we make a number of interesting observations. First, the geographical pattern of venture capital activity does not match the geographical pattern of economic activity. Relative to overall economic activity, venture capital activity is high in Quebec and low in Ontario and in Atlantic Canada. As expected, high-tech industries make up a relatively large share of venture capital investments.

Investee firms are somewhat older than expected, as fully 10 percent of the post-1990 venture capital investments were made in firms founded before 1975, and one third of the investments were made in firms founded before 1984. The data also show that early-stage investments are smaller (by about 35 percent on average) and much less numerous than later-stage investments. Thus, we conclude that venture capital activity emphasizes expansion and growth stages rather than the start-up phase of a company's life cycle.

Investees pay significant levels of tax (on average) and spend about 3 percent of revenues on research and development, which is about equal to the overall Canadian average. The track record of venture capital investments is particularly interesting. Most investments do not do particularly well, and provide lower returns than alternative risk-free investments, but this is offset by a small number of "hits" that do very well. This general pattern is supported by information on employment growth, as aggregate growth is higher than median growth. Most investee firms grow slowly, but a few grow very rapidly.

The average venture capital equity (or ownership) share in investee firms is about 35 percent. The majority of Canadian venture capital investments are not syndicated as each round of investment is provided by a single venture capitalist in most cases, and about half the sample firms get only one round of venture capital. While venture capital investments can include both debt and equity, about two thirds of Canadian investments are pure equity.

Exit behaviour is perhaps surprising. A substantial minority of investments (about 18 percent) are terminated by being written off, i.e., the venture capitalist loses the entire investment. Only a comparable share of investments (16 percent) are terminated in IPOs (and these are generally successful investments). A substantial share of investments (13 percent) are terminated in third-party acquisitions, and these also tend to be successful investments. The largest category of exit (37 percent) is through management or company buyouts, as company insiders buy out the venture capitalist. Indeed, if we eliminate uncategorized exits (most of which are probably management buyouts) and write-offs, company buyouts account for 50 percent of remaining exits.

From this information, we distilled four empirical regularities that any successful theory of venture capital must accommodate. First, a theory must provide a reason for the existence of a specialized venture capital industry. Second, it must explain the emphasis on development rather than start-up. Third, it must explain the pattern of exit, where insider buyouts dominate and, finally, it must be consistent with the skewed pattern of returns.

The theoretical framework we offer focuses on informational issues. Specifically, we view asymmetric information and limited liability (with low collateral) as the central features of venture capital investment. Both major forms of asymmetric information, hidden information (leading to adverse selection) and hidden action (leading to moral hazard) are included in our analysis. The model we present is complicated even though we abstract from several important features of the venture capital industry. In particular, our model does not deal with the risk-sharing motive for venture capital investment, nor does it deal with the dynamics or staged structure of venture capital investment. It also does not address the role of bargaining between the venture capitalist and the entrepreneur, or the role of gradual learning about project quality. While all these things are important aspects of venture capital and deserve scrutiny, we felt that the informational issues were the most central at this stage. We believe that this information-based approach is consistent with the major stylized facts characterizing the industry. For example, if inside information is important, it is not surprising that most exits are through company buyouts or acquisitions by informed outsiders.

We did not emphasize the implication that informational asymmetries lead to market failure, causing possible underfinancing. If adverse selection and moral hazard are important, it will be difficult for investors to earn a reasonable return in this industry, even if there are many potentially worthwhile projects. Venture capitalists exist precisely because they can reduce information-based market failures through careful selection, monitoring and other means. The more skilled the venture capitalist is in reducing these sources of market failure, the more efficiently the venture capital sector will function.

APPENDIX A: LITERATURE REVIEW

THE MODELLING FRAMEWORK IN THIS PAPER incorporates aspects of the theory of asymmetric information and the theory of finance and applies them to a financial contracting setting in which an entrepreneur may obtain funding from a venture capitalist. In particular, we suggest that moral hazard and adverse selection under conditions of limited liability create a link between the ownership structure of an entrepreneurial venture and its ultimate performance. By integrating these effects, we seek to capture the essence of the relationship between business founders and outside equity holders. This appendix provides a review of the relevant related literature.

Akerlof (1970) is normally regarded as the pioneering analyst of informational asymmetry. Akerlof described a situation in which sellers of used cars have hidden or private information about the specific quality of their vehicles, whereas buyers cannot discern quality differences before purchase. In this setting, there is reason to expect low-quality cars (or lemons) to dominate the market. This dominance is referred to as adverse selection as the market selects low-quality items. Akerlof showed that adverse selection is inefficient in the sense that potentially efficient, i.e., Pareto-improving trades will not take place. Thus, hidden information causes market failure.

It was quickly recognized that adverse selection problems can arise in many circumstances, especially in insurance markets, where buyers of insurance know their true risk better than insurance companies (as in Pauly, 1974), and in labour markets, where workers know their ability better than potential employers (as in Spence, 1973). Spence also pointed out that one natural market response to adverse selection is "signalling," where the informed party (usually the seller of the high-quality item) provides some signal of high quality to substitute for the inability of buyers to observe quality directly. Thus, for example, product warranties may be signals or indicators of high quality. Rothschild and Stiglitz (1976) emphasized the role of screening, under which the uninformed party offers a contract or set of contracts that cause informed parties to self-select. Thus, for example, insurance companies may offer contracts that low-risk types will buy but high-risk types will not. In general, the efficient response of the buyer may be to offer such "screening" or "separating" contracts, but sometimes the efficient response is to offer contracts that do not induce screening, resulting in "pooling" of different quality classes.

The other major informational asymmetry is referred to as hidden action (as opposed to hidden information). Hidden action occurs when one party to a transaction takes an action that is not observed by the other party, and this action affects the returns to both parties. This problem was first discussed in insurance markets, where insured parties can take actions that either decrease or increase the risk of hazard. For example, after purchasing auto insurance, the insured party can either drive safely or dangerously. This problem was originally referred to as moral hazard.

Early influential work on moral hazard includes Pauly (1974) and Arrow (1973) who showed that moral hazard causes market failure in the sense that it causes failures of Pareto efficiency.

Moral hazard problems are particularly important in situations where one party acts as an agent for another party (or principal), as when a client hires a lawyer or the seller of a house hires a sales agent. In these situations the principal cannot perfectly observe the effort (or other actions) of the agent. It was soon recognized that many situations of financial contracting are agency problems, and Jensen and Meckling (1976) argued that agency analysis was the key to understanding the modern firm. Thus, for example, the managers of the firm can be viewed as the agents of the owners, who might, in turn, be viewed as the agents of other investors in the firm. Classic papers on the agency problem include Holmstrom (1979) and Grossman and Hart (1983).

Agency theory also had an important influence on the debate over whether a firm's capital structure affects its value. In their influential article on the role of financing, Modigliani and Miller (1958) showed that, in the absence of any market frictions, the value of a firm's cash flow stream is independent of its capital structure. In other words, whether a firm is financed with debt or equity, or some combination, should not affect its performance. If we then consider the tax advantage of debt (as interest payments are deductible from corporate income), it follows that firms should be completely debt financed (see Modigliani and Miller, 1963). Given the indisputable fact that equity is an important financing tool, this cannot be the whole story. Most managers will say that the problem with relying excessively on debt is that the risk of bankruptcy becomes too high. Kraus and Litzenberger (1973) and Brennan and Schwartz (1978) solved for optimal capital structures based on the trade-off between tax savings and bankruptcy costs. It turns out that agency problems are central to the existence of bankruptcy costs. In addition, agency problems create a role for equity (and debt) even in the absence of bankruptcy costs.

Our analysis focuses in part on the capital structure of venture-backed firms. We observe that both equity and debt are important in venture capital finance. The fact that firms have limited liability adds an important feature of financial contracting as considered, for example, by Brander and Lewis (1986). Under limited liability, equity holders of firms will have an incentive to undertake riskier projects as debt increases in order to reap the fruits of the very good outcomes and have creditors bear the costs of the very bad outcomes. Thus, limited liability creates a link between the financial structure of a firm and its output market decisions (and its performance), enhancing the agency problems already present between owner-managers and providers of capital. This idea is one of the conceptual building blocks of our model.

The importance of limited liability has been investigated by Sappington (1983) who characterized an optimal contract between principal and agent in a setting where the agent receives a private signal after contracting but before taking action.[10] The optimal solution in this special case implies that, in the very bad states of nature, the agent does not exert any effort. In our model, however, uncertainty about the firm's profits is not resolved for either party until after the action choice of the entrepreneur, which we believe to be the empirically relevant case. In a related paper, Brander and Spencer (1989) showed that moral hazard under conditions of limited liability invalidates Modigliani and Miller's (1958) irrelevance result by creating a linkage between capital structure and output strategy (and firm value). The authors formally established consequences of changes in debt and/or investment on effort level and output decisions. However, Brander and Spencer did not distinguish between inside and outside equity holders, and they abstracted from the problem of adverse selection. Nevertheless, their two-stage model and the related solution method of backward induction are adopted in our modelling framework.[11]

Chan and Thakor (1987) examined the role of collateral under moral hazard and private information and concluded that collateral often efficiently resolves problems stemming from asymmetry of information. In other words, in such an informational setting (which is similar to the one that we explore in our model) insufficient collateral will lead to welfare losses. Despite the limitations of some of Chan and Thakor's assumptions for the characterization of the relationship between entrepreneur and venture capitalist,[12] we can learn several things from their analysis. First, collateral (or lack thereof) plays an important role under asymmetric information and must be considered. Second, results on market failures may depend heavily on assumptions about the notions of competition (between venture capitalists): the conceptualization of the equilibrium influences its characterization. Any results must, therefore, be interpreted very carefully.

The role of asymmetry of information in financial contracting in venture capital is widely recognized. Sahlman (1990), for example, postulated that contracting practices in the venture capital industry reflect uncertainty about payoffs and information asymmetries between venture capitalists and entrepreneurs. This distinction between market uncertainty on the one hand, and uncertainty resulting from an unequal distribution of information on the other, is also crucial for our analysis. In addition, Sahlman differentiated between problems related to private information about the skill level (adverse selection) and those related to the unobservable effort of the entrepreneur (moral hazard). He correctly argued that the lack of operational history aggravates the adverse selection dilemma, but does not mention the importance of collateral in that respect.

Amit et al. (1993) suggested that venture capitalists be regarded as financial intermediaries. The authors thoroughly characterized the relevant informational problems and identified a series of research questions, some of which are addressed in our model. In another review paper on new directions in venture capital research, Barry (1994) emphasized the relevance of private information of the entrepreneur with respect to the entrepreneur's abilities before contracting. Mitchell et al. (1995) explicitly used a principal-agent perspective to examine the (post-contracting) patterns of demand for accounting information by the venture capitalist. They found a greater intensity of scrutiny of investee performance by venture capitalists than by investors in established firms and concluded that the former demand more detailed information more frequently to combat the moral hazard problem. Bates (1990) empirically explored the linkage between financial structure (especially the effects of debt) and firm performance,[13] and hypothesized that information asymmetry may be a potentially severe cause of market failure. Furthermore, the problem of overly optimistic and confident entrepreneurs may create a bias, as pointed out by Kamien (1994).

In our model we attempt to highlight the implications of the moral hazard and adverse selection problems, in the presence of limited liability, on financing entrepreneurial ventures. Thus, we have made a series of simplifying assumptions, e.g., risk neutrality for both the entrepreneur and the venture capitalist, that allow us to focus the discussion. We do not consider any contracting practices that may mitigate adverse selection and/or moral hazard. However, as a number of authors have pointed out, there is empirical and anecdotal evidence of a variety of such practices which complicate the analysis of asymmetry of information.

Sahlman (1990) noted that staged investment which creates an option to abandon the venture is an important means for venture capitalists to minimize the present value of agency costs.[14] The active involvement of venture capitalists in the operation of their investee companies may mitigate the moral hazard problem as well.[15]

Other suggested solutions engineered by the venture capital industry to overcome problems arising from the asymmetry of information include the use of convertible preferred stock (see Barry, 1994) or syndication (see Lerner, 1994b). Lerner argued that syndicating first-round investments leads to better decisions about whether to invest. From the analysis of a sample of investment rounds in biotechnological firms he found that syndication in early stages often involves experienced and highly reputed venture capitalists, which seems to corroborate his hypothesis.

Chan (1983) highlighted the positive role of venture capitalists in mitigating the adverse selection problem in the market for entrepreneurial capital. He showed that an adverse selection result derives from the absence of any informed venture capitalists in the sense that only inferior projects are offered to investors. However, the introduction of informed investors may overcome this problem, leading to a Pareto-preferred solution. The key question raised by this analysis is the empirical issue of whether venture capitalists are as well informed about the project's prospects as the entrepreneur.

Chan et al. (1990) provided a proposed explanation for various "rules of thumb" contracting practices in venture capital, including absence of *de novo* financing, buyout options, performance requirements and earn-out arrangements. The central idea is that venture capitalists learn about the entrepreneur's ability as time proceeds, and then decide, in effect, whether to fire or retain the entrepreneur to manage the project. In a related paper, Hirao (1993) assumed that the agent's, i.e., the entrepreneur's, unobservable actions affect the learning process. As a result of the interaction of learning and moral hazard, she found that a long-term contract is not equivalent to a series of short-term contracts.

Amit et al. (1990) presented a principal agent model in which investors are uncertain about the entrepreneur's type when submitting bids for the company (this information asymmetry is resolved prior to actual contracting). The authors managed to relate the venture capital financing decision to the entrepreneur's skill level and predicted which entrepreneurs would decide to enter into an agreement with venture capitalists. They considered moral hazard problems, but had a limited treatment of moral hazard in which the entrepreneur's type becomes common knowledge between bidding and contracting. Also, entrepreneurs are assumed to be fully collateralized, which is an abstraction that eliminates the role of limited liability. Our current model can be viewed as an extension of this structure.

Amit et al. (1994) considered the role of different mechanisms for matching entrepreneurs and venture capitalists in mitigating adverse selection problems. They extended Rothschild and Stiglitz (1976) by incorporating some assumptions based on empirical regularities in the venture capital finance industry. Specifically, entrepreneurs have private information about their types; venture capitalists can get involved in the management of investees (at some cost) and thus contribute to the venture's success directly; entrepreneurs may shop around or venture capitalists may actively seek out attractive investment opportunities. With a three-stage game, the authors examined possible pooling and separating equilibria. Our model ignores the relevance of the matching regime for deriving such equilibria, but we regard this as an important potential extension of our model.

In a recent attempt to characterize the contract that allows optimal continuation decisions with staged finance, Admati and Pfleiderer (1994) found that venture capitalists should prefer a fixed-fraction contract. This contract stipulates that the venture capitalist owns a certain fraction of the final payoffs and also finances that same fraction of any future investment (if continuation of the project is desirable). This explains why later stages are not fully financed by the lead venture capitalist. It also attributes a positive role to the venture capitalist as a financial intermediary between the entrepreneur and outside investors. These analyses hinge, however, on some very restrictive assumptions.

Following Admati and Pfleiderer, Hellman (1994) built a multistage model involving staged investment. While it could be interesting to examine the extent to which the staging of capital input helps in mitigating the adverse selection problem, Hellman's focus was on explaining certain institutional features that he claimed would distinguish venture capital from more traditional methods of finance. For example, he explained that only a concentrated stake of the venture capitalist in investee companies would provide a sufficiently high incentive for active monitoring, which is necessary to avoid the problem of "short-termism" generated by staged finance.

The work that has been reviewed so far is model-based theory. In addition, there is a substantial descriptive literature on the venture capital industry. Two valuable papers of this type are Tyebjee and Bruno (1984) and Fried and Hisrich (1994) which depicted some activities undertaken by venture capitalists that may serve to diminish problems arising from asymmetry of information. For example,

Tyebjee and Bruno suggested that venture capital financing involves five sequential steps: deal origination, deal screening, deal evaluation, deal structuring and post-investment activities. Whereas the third to fifth steps have to do with the venture capitalist's actual choice problem and are explicitly dealt with in our model, the first two steps are more concerned with the construction of the choice set. While our model may capture some basic (informational) difficulties that arise in these early screening stages, we do not consider such mechanisms as referral processes or active screening by venture capitalists (or signalling by entrepreneurs, respectively). In other words, we do not model the matching process, although this issue was addressed analytically by Amit et al. (1994).

Some other useful overviews of the venture capital industry include MacMillan et al. (1985, 1987) and Low and MacMillan (1988). It is widely asserted that formal theory-driven research with clearly stated assumptions, different theoretical perspectives and formal decision models is relatively scarce in the literature on new venture financing. (See, for example, Low and MacMillan, 1988; Amit et al. 1993; Barry, 1994; and Hellman 1994.)

Endnotes

1 Venture capitalists may provide equity investments, debt investments or mixtures of debt and equity. In addition, they often provide managerial advice to their investee firms. Aside from venture capital, the other main sources of entrepreneurial finance include bank loans, equity provided personally by the entrepreneur and financing from other firms (including suppliers or customers), government grants and family and friends.

2 For example, in the standard (and very good) finance text, Brealy et al. (1992), only three pages out of over 1,000 are devoted to venture capital. Admittedly, much of the material in any finance text is general material that applies to all investments, but this is still very light coverage.

3 All 352 investee firms must have originated in the investment survey data base, but nine of them could not be matched with subsequent investment survey information.

4 These firms include investees for whom incomplete economic impact surveys exist, investees who received investments but who exited before an economic impact survey was completed, and firms that could not be matched, even though they are in both data bases. Most important, they include the investees for whom economic impact surveys were not returned. There are also investment records for 79 U.S. investees supported by Canadian venture capitalists. These firms are not tracked by the economic impact survey. In total, there are 898 firms in the investee data base, 819 of whom are Canadian.

5 An exit due to an IPO does not mean that the venture capital firm sold its shares on the date of the IPO. Regulation requires that venture capitalists keep most of their holdings for some period of time after the IPO. Furthermore, the underwriters of an IPO are normally even more restrictive in the limits they impose on the venture capitalist's ability to sell out. Typically, the venture capitalist sells a small part of its holding at the IPO, and sells its remaining holdings in several pieces beginning six months or more after the IPO.

6 Note that venture capitalists do not always cash out their entire investment when an IPO occurs. A few investees in the data are publicly traded companies in which venture capitalists have maintained investments. This may be due to regulatory escrow requirements or to expectation of future capital gains.

7 Very often the first explanation offered is the presence of "high risk" in the entrepreneurial sector. However, basic financial theory would suggest that investments made in high-risk ventures would be made by firms (or other investors) in the best position to diversify the associated risks and which were, in general, not risk averse. If anything, it is the large diversified financial intermediaries and investment firms which are in the best position to absorb or diversify such risks. The existence of relatively small specialized venture capital firms which are heavily invested in a few particular industries is, therefore, something of an anomaly if "higher risk" is the key factor that distinguishes entrepreneurial firms from established firms.

8 More commonly, the hidden information is assumed to be the ability or "type" of the entrepreneur. Both entrepreneur quality and project quality have the same implications.

9 We acknowledge that different assumptions about the underlying process that matches entrepreneurs and venture capitalists may have a substantial impact on the model. See Amit et al. (1994) for an analysis of the matching mechanism.

10 Another general treatment of moral hazard that deals with limited liability is provided by Innes (1990). Here the agent is an entrepreneur who owns a production technology but no capital. The implementation of the production technology requires an investment and the agent's effort. Innes shows that among monotonic contracts, debt contracts are optimal in that they will induce a higher action than any arbitrary contract, which makes both principal and agent better off. If the condition of monotonicity is relaxed, "live-or-die" contracts (according to which the principal gets all the profits below a cutoff value, and zero above) prove to be optimal. Important distinctions from our model are the absence of adverse selection and of any risk-sharing issues (Innes assumed risk neutrality for both parties).

11 For further developments in the theory of capital structure that focus on the link between financial decisions and product markets see Maksimovic (1986).

12 For example, they assume risk neutrality of both principal and agent and, therefore, ignore risk-sharing aspects. In addition, banks do not provide equity capital and do not get actively involved in their investee's management.

13 Bates (1990, p. 558) found that the amount of investment is "causally related to firm survival" – which is quite intuitive – and that "reliance upon debt capital is clearly not associated with business weakness or heightened market failure" which is a somewhat unexpected result, especially in light of our model.

14 Admati and Pfleiderer (1994) and Hellman (1994) provided models of staged finance in the venture capital context. They are discussed below.

15 This influence of the venture capitalist on probability distributions of a firm's success is explicitly modelled, for example, by Amit et al. (1994).

BIBLIOGRAPHY

Admati, Aviat R. and Paul Pfleiderer. "Robust Financial Contracting and the Role of Venture Capitalists." *Journal of Finance*. 49, (1994): 371-402.

Akerlof, G. "The Market for Lemons: Quality Uncertainty and the Market Mechanism." *Quarterly Journal of Economics*. 84, (1970): 488-500.

Amit, R., L. Glosten and E. Muller. "Entrepreneurial Ability, Venture Investments, and Risk Sharing." *Management Science*. 36, (1990): 1232-1245.

—. "Challenges to Theory Development in Entrepreneurship Research." *Journal of Management Studies*. 30, (1993): 815-834.

—. "Venture Capital Regimes and Entrepreneurial Ability." Working Paper University of British Columbia, 1994.

Arrow, K. *The Limits of Organization*. New York: Norton, 1973.

Barry, C. "New Directions in Research on Venture Capital Firms." *Financial Management*. 23, (1994): 3-15.

Bates, T. "Entrepreneur Human Capital Inputs and Small Business Longevity." *Review of Economics and Statistics*. 72, (1990): 551-559.

Brander, J. and T. Lewis. "Oligopoly and Financial Structure: The Limited Liability Effect." *American Economic Review*. 76, (1986): 956-970.

Brander, J. and B. Spencer. "Moral Hazard and Limited Liability: Implications for the Theory of the Firm." *International Economic Review*. 30, (1989): 833-849.

Brealey, R., S. Myers, G. Sick and R. Giammarino. *Principles of Corporate Finance*. 2nd Canadian Edition, Toronto: McGraw Hill Ryerson, 1992.

Brennan, M. and E. Schwartz. "Corporate Income Taxes, Valuation, and the Problem of Optimal Capital Structure." *Journal of Business*. 51, (1978): 103-114.

Business Development Bank of Canada. *Economic Impact of Venture Capital*. Montreal, 1993, 1994, 1995.

Chan, Y. "On the Positive Role of Financial Intermediation in Allocations of Venture Capital in a Market with Imperfect Information." *Journal of Finance*. 38, (1983): 1543-1561.

Chan, Y. and A. Thakor. "Collateral and Competitive Equilibria with Moral Hazard and Private Information." *Journal of Finance*. 42, (1987): 345-363.

Chan, Y., D. Siegel, and A. Thakor. "Learning, Corporate Control and Performance Requirements in Venture Capital Contracts." *International Economic Review*. 31, (1990): 365-381.

Fried, V. and R. Hisrich. "Toward a Model of Venture Capital Investment Decision Making." *Financial Management*. 23, (1994): 28-37.

Gompers, Paul A. "Optimal Investment, Monitoring, and the Staging of Venture Capital." Harvard University working paper, 1995.

Grossman, S. and O. Hart. "An Analysis of the Principal-Agent Problem." *Econometrica*. 51, (1983): 7-45.

Hellman, T. "Financial Structure and Control in Venture Capital." Stanford University working paper, 1994.

Hirao, Y. "Learning and Incentive Problems in Repeated Partnerships." *International Economic Review*. 34, (1993): 101-119.

Holmstrom, B. "Moral Hazard and Observability." *Bell Journal of Economics*. 10, (1979): 74-91.

Innes. R. "Limited Liability and Incentive Contracting with Ex-ante Choices." *Journal of Economic Theory*. 52, (1990): 45-67.

Jensen, M. and W. Meckling. "Theory of the Firm: Managerial Behavior, Agency Costs, and Ownership Structure." *Journal of Financial Economics*. 3, (1976): 305-360.

Kamien, M. "Entrepreneurship: What Is It?" *Business Week: Executive Briefing Service*. 7, (1994).

Kraus, A. and R. Litzenberger. "A State-Preference Model of Optimal Financial Leverage." *Journal of Finance*. 33, (1973): 911-922.

Lerner, J. "Venture Capitalists and the Decision to Go Public." *Journal of Financial Economics*. 35, (1994a): 293-316.

—. "The Syndication of Venture Capital Investment." *Financial Management*. 23, (1994b): 16-27.

Low, M. and I. MacMillan. "Entrepreneurship: Past Research and Future Challenges." *Journal of Management*. 14, (1988): 139-161.

Macdonald & Associates Ltd. Venture Capital in Canada: *Annual Statistical Review and Directory*. Toronto: Association of Canadian Venture Capital Companies, published annually.

MacIntosh, Jeffrey G. "Legal and Institutional Barriers to Financing Innovative Enterprise in Canada." Discussion Paper 94-10, School of Policy Studies, Queen's University, Kingston, 1994.

MacMillan, I., R. Siegel, and P. Narashima. "Criteria Used by Venture Capitalists to Evaluate New Venture Proposals." *Journal of Business Venturing*. 1, (1985): 119-128.

MacMillan, I., L. Zemann and P. Narashima. "Criteria Distinguishing Successful from Unsuccessful Ventures in the Venture Screening Process." *Journal of Business Venturing*. 2, (1987): 123-137.

Maksimovic, V. "Optimal Capital Structure in Oligopolies." Ph.D. Dissertation Harvard University (1986).

Mitchell, F., G. Reid and N. Terry. "Post Investment Demands for Accounting Information by Venture Capitalists." *Accounting and Business Research*. 25, (1995): 186-196.

Modigliani, F. and M. Miller. "The Cost of Capital, Corporation Finance, and the Theory of Investment," *American Economic Review*. 48 (1958), 261-297.

—. "Taxes and the Cost of Capital: a Correction." *American Economic Review*. 53, (1963): 261-297.

Pauly, M. "Overinsurance and Public Provision of Insurance: the Roles of Moral Hazard and Adverse Selection." *Quarterly Journal of Economics*. 88, (1974): 44-54.

Rothschild, M. and J. Stiglitz. "Equilibrium in Competitive Insurance Markets: an Essay on the Economics of Imperfect Information." *Quarterly Journal of Economics*. 90, (1976): 629-649.

Sahlman, W. "The Structure and Governance of Venture-Capital Organizations." *Journal of Financial Economics*. 27, (1990): 473-521.

Sappington, D. "Limited Liability Contracts between Principal and Agent." *Journal of Economic Theory*. 29, (1983): 1-21.

Spence, M. "Job Market Signalling." *Quarterly Journal of Economics*. 87, (1973): 355-374.

Tyebjee, T. and A. Bruno. "A Model of Venture Capital Investment Activity." *Management Science*. 30, (1984): 1051-1066.

Williamson, O. "Markets and Hierarchies: Analysis and Anti-trust Implications." New York: Free Press, 1975.

Wilson, C. "Adverse Selection." In: *The New Palgrave*. 1, London: MacMillan, 1987, pp. 32-34.

Jeffrey G. MacIntosh
Faculty of Law
University of Toronto

7

Venture Capital Exits in Canada and the United States

THE IMPORTANCE OF EXIT FOR VENTURE CAPITALISTS

THIS PAPER DEALS WITH VENTURE CAPITAL EXITS – the means by which venture capitalists (VCs) dispose of their investments. How important is exit? This question is perhaps best answered by pointing out that venture capital investing is primarily equity investing. Moreover, many investee firms are young and lack the cash flow (and profitability) that would enable them to pay dividends. Thus, most of the VC's return is in the form of capital gains. Because of this, there are two prices that dominate the investment decision: the entry (purchase) price and the exit price. The VC's initial decision to make an investment, the cost of the investment and the structuring of the investment will depend on the prospective profitability of available exit mechanisms. Entry and exit are inextricably linked. Effective exit mechanisms tend to lower the early stage cost of capital. For this reason, knowing how VCs exit their investments is vital to understanding the venture capital investment process.

It is not surprising that evidence suggests that the prospect of a profitable exit is a factor VCs consider when deciding whether to invest and on what terms. For example, MacMillan et al. (1985, p. 119) sent questionnaires to U.S. VCs to determine investment selection criteria. Preliminary questioning resulted in the identification of 24 major criteria. Survey respondents were asked to rank the importance of these factors on a scale from 1 to 4 (where 1 meant the criterion was irrelevant, and 4 meant it was essential). One of these criteria was "I require an investment that can be easily made liquid, e.g., taken public or acquired." This criterion received an average score of 3.17, with a standard deviation of 0.89, and ranked eighth of the 24 factors.

Moreover, of the five financial criteria on the questionnaire, liquidity scored the second highest (after "I require a return equal to at least 10 times my investment within 5-10 years"). Of the 10 requirements most frequently ranked as essential, liquidity ranked sixth. Forty-four percent of VCs surveyed indicated that they would refuse to invest absent liquidity, regardless of the potential of the project or the market (MacMillan et al., 1985, p. 123).

Further analysis isolated six factors which seemed to be particularly important in the VC's decision-making process. One of these, "bail out risk," included both the timing and availability of exit mechanisms.[1]

A study by Carter and Van Auken (1994) offered further evidence regarding the importance of exit. Carter and Van Auken also asked capitalists to rate the importance of different factors in their decision-making process.[2] Unlike MacMillan et al., Carter and Van Auken attempted to determine whether investors with a preference for investing at the early or later stages of a firm's development had different evaluative criteria.

The results are striking. On a scale of 5, the mean rating given to "exit potential" by early stage investors was 2.46 (with a standard deviation of 1.17), which was the single most important factor of 21 evaluative criteria. While the mean rating given to exit potential by later stage investors was only 1.94 (with a standard deviation of 0.83), this was, nonetheless, the fourth most important factor of 21. It is understandable that exit would be a less important factor for later stage investors, given that the likelihood of finding a suitable exit is probably higher from the outset.

In addition, Carter and Van Auken found evidence that early stage investors were more interested in exiting via an initial public offering (IPO) than were later stage investors. They concluded that this was consistent with the heightened risk of early stage investing, and the commensurately enhanced required rate of return (1994, p. 72).

In short, the evidence suggests that the availability of a liquid and profitable exit is a primary concern for venture capital investors.

A Decade and a Half of Venture Capital in Canada

In a longer version of this paper (MacIntosh, 1996), I presented historical data on the venture capital industry in Canada between 1978 and 1994. These data paint a portrait of venture capital investing in Canada and highlight some differences between the Canadian and U.S. venture capital industries. The data suggest the following points.

1. VCs Invest in Private Companies

Between 1978 and 1994, Canadian VCs invested about 90 percent of their capital in private companies.

2. VCs Invest in Small Companies

It has become common to categorize the financing provided by VCs into different stages, which are commonly characterized as early stage financing, expansion stage financing and acquisition/buyout financing.[3]

Early Stage Financing

Seed financing normally helps prove a concept. While there may be some product development there is rarely any initial marketing.

Start-up financing is used in product development and initial marketing. Perhaps the company is being organized or has only been in business for a few months, but has not yet sold its product commercially. Generally, a firm looking for start-up financing would have assembled its key management and prepared a business plan.

Expansion Stage Financing

First stage financing helps companies that have started to sell their product but expended their initial capital. They may require additional funds to begin full production and sales.

Second stage financing provides additional support for companies that are making progress but may not yet be profitable.

Mezzanine financing (or third stage expansion financing) provides the capital for major growth expansion when a company's sales are increasing and the company is either breaking even or profitable. The funds may be used for plant expansion, marketing, working capital or new product development. Often, this type of financing involves subordinated debt instruments (unsecured loans) with equity kickers or provisions which entitle the investor to some common shares if the company succeeds.

Acquisition/Buyout Financing

Leveraged buy out financing provides capital for operating management or outside investors to acquire a product line, a division or a company. Companies involved in these transactions normally have highly leveraged assets to minimize the equity required.

The fourth type of investment – turnaround financing – involves investment in a company in financial distress so it can overcome current obstacles and achieve profitability. Acquisition and turnaround investments are generally made at a later stage in a company's life cycle.

The historical data indicate that VCs concentrate their investments in small companies, in particular, those in the early and expansion stages of development. While the proportion of turnaround investing has almost never exceeded 10 percent of all investments, it appears to have increased in the last four years. As discussed in MacIntosh (1996), this trend is likely due to the growth of the labour-sponsored venture capital corporations (LSVCCs), which often pursue job creation rather than pure profit maximization.

As indicated above, early stage investing consists of seed and start-up capital (and, in some classifications, "development" capital). The historical data show that while VCs invest heavily in early stage financing, little of this money (generally less than 4 percent per annum) is directed to seed capital investing.[4]

The historical data also show that, in Canada, the proportion of acquisition financing has fluctuated substantially over the last decade. Such financing peaked in the last half of the 1980s and the first part of the 1990s. In recent years, the proportion of venture capital finding its way to acquisition financing has dropped sharply.

3. Canada vs. the United States: Acquisition, Early and Expansion Stage Financing

The historical data show that Canadian VCs have historically invested more heavily in acquisition investments than U.S. VCs, who invest more heavily in early and expansion stage investments. Acquisition financing is generally low risk compared to investments made at earlier stages in a company's existence. This suggests that investments made by Canadian VCs have a somewhat lower risk profile than those made by U.S. VCs. This, in turn, suggests that Canadian VCs should be expected to earn somewhat lower returns.

4. VCs are High-Risk Equity Investors

Historical data indicate that more than three quarters of all investments made in Canada between 1978 and 1994 involved some equity component – common shares (the most common form of equity investment), convertible debt, convertible preferred shares or some combination of the foregoing. The data also indicate a trend in Canada toward structuring venture capital investments with common shares alone.

5. Canadian and U.S. Differences in Industry Focus and Degree of Specialization

Data presented in MacIntosh (1996) indicate that U.S. VCs have historically invested more heavily in the high-technology sectors than Canadian VCs. U.S. VCs have invested less in manufacturing and consumer-related firms than their Canadian counterparts.

There is anecdotal evidence that U.S. VCs have specialized to a much greater degree than their Canadian counterparts (Macdonald & Associates, 1992; Sahlman, 1990, p. 489). While most Canadian funds have historically been willing to entertain investments in virtually any industry, many U.S. funds have limited themselves to investments in particular areas of the high-technology spectrum, e.g., biotechnology or computers (Bygrave and Timmons, 1992).

Both industry focus and specialization are likely to enhance VC profits (MacIntosh, 1996, pp. 12-14). The comparative lack of focus and specialization in Canada are two more factors that would lead us to expect Canadian VCs to earn lower profits than U.S. VCs.

6. PRIVATE FUNDS, PUBLIC FUNDS AND HYBRID FUNDS

MACDONALD & ASSOCIATES (1992) HAS CLASSIFIED THE CANADIAN INDUSTRY into five different types of funds. Each type of fund employs expert venture capital managers to invest the money of others: the difference arises in the source of funds. "Private independent" funds are funded mainly by public and private pension funds and wealthy individuals. "Corporate industrial" funds are wholly owned venture capital subsidiaries of corporations, while "corporate financial" funds are wholly owned subsidiaries of financial institutions. These three types of funds are referred to below as "private" funds. "Government" or "public" funds are venture capital corporations owned and run by the federal or provincial governments. Finally, hybrid funds are "funds which are formed in response to a government incentive or an investment by government alongside private investors, or which have secured more than 50 percent of their capital from another hybrid fund" (Macdonald & Associates, 1994, p. 4, note 3). The most important type of hybrid fund is the LSVCC which must be incorporated by a labour union. The labour union must also control the board of directors (although in the typical case, the union's only financial interest in the fund will be the sponsorship fee it receives for creating the fund). Despite the labour union affiliation, anyone can invest in an LSVCC. Management of LSVCCs is invariably contracted out to expert venture capital managers.

The following stylized facts, garnered from MacIntosh (1996) characterize the last five years of venture capital investing in Canada.

1. There has been a rapid increase in new capital commitments compared to historical experience.
2. Much of this new capital has flowed into the LSVCCs.[5]
3. LSVCC investors are individuals. Since institutional investors (with some admixture of wealthy individuals) have historically driven venture capital investing, the shift toward individual contributors marks a significant shift in the source of venture capital funds in Canada.
4. The rapid influx of capital has resulted in many LSVCCs being unable to find qualified managers to invest their committed capital. This, in turn, has led to the hiring of many inexperienced VC managers.
5. LSVCC funds must invest certain percentages of their committed funds by statutorily mandated deadlines. This (coupled with fund manager inexperience) has led many of the LSVCC funds to focus on comparatively large, non-technology investments.
6. Private, public and hybrid funds have differing investment objectives. Private funds invest purely for profit. Public and hybrid funds are constrained profit maximizers. They maximize profits within the peculiar constraints thrust on them by their statutory and/or sponsorship mandates. Public funds target small, early stage technology investments that often cannot secure funding through other channels. They invest almost entirely in firms with their

principal facility in Canada. Hybrid funds mix the goal of profit maximization with that of job creation (and/or investing in enterprises with a union affiliation), although some (such as Working Ventures Canadian Fund) have publicly stated that they will pursue pure profit maximization. Provincially incorporated hybrid funds are also constrained by a requirement to invest in firms with their principal business in the province in which the fund is incorporated.

The differing investment strategies of public, private and hybrid funds will likely have an impact on the manner in which investments are exited. For example, one would expect public funds, which invest more heavily in small (and risky), high-technology firms, to have higher write-off rates than private or hybrid funds. Hybrid funds, which tend to invest in larger more mature companies, would be expected to exit fewer investments via IPOs. The determinants of exit strategy are discussed below.

The mixing of public, private and hybrid funds in the Canadian data is also likely to affect comparisons of the profitability of venture capital investing in Canada and the United States. The U.S. data examined below consist of a sample of private venture capital funds only. Because private funds tend to pursue profits more vigorously than other types of funds, this is another factor that would lead us to expect higher profits in the U.S. venture capital industry than in the Canadian industry.

Explaining the Choice of Exit

Types of Exits

In general, VCs will exit their investments by one of five methods: an IPO, acquisition, buy back, secondary sale or write-off.

Initial Public Offering

In an IPO, the firm sells shares to members of the public for the first time. Typically, the VC will not sell his or her shares into the public market at the date of the public offering, for reasons discussed below. Rather, securities will be sold into the market over a period of months or even years following the public offering. Alternatively, after the offering the VC may dispose of the investment by making a dividend of investee firm shares to the fund's owners.

Despite the fact that the VC will usually not sell more than a small fraction of shares at the time of the IPO (if any at all), in the data below (and by common useage), exits effected by sales *subsequent* to the IPO are classified as IPO exits.

Acquisition

Sometimes, a VC will exit when the entire firm is purchased by a third party. One way in which this is accomplished is to sell all the shares of the company, in return for cash, shares of the acquiring company or other assets. Alternatively, the transaction may be a sale of the firm's assets. As discussed below, the buyer will often be a larger established company seeking a foothold on the technology possessed by the selling firm. In some instances, the buyer will be another VC.

Buy Back

In a buy back, the entrepreneur and/or other firm managers (referred to as "the entrepreneur" below) or the company will repurchase the shares held by the VC.

Secondary Sale

The VC may also exit by means of a sale of shares to a third party. This type of exit differs from an acquisition in that only the shares of the VC are sold to the third party. As in an acquisition, the third party will often be a larger corporation seeking a foothold on the company's technology.

Write-Off

A write-off occurs when the VC walks away from his or her investment. While a write-off often involves the failure of the company, the VC may continue to hold shares in an essentially non-viable enterprise.

Factors that Affect the Method and Timing of Exit

The following discussion identifies factors that are important in the VC's choice of exit. The list of factors is based on informal interviews with VCs, financial theory and empirical evidence.[6] Later, hypotheses developed in this section are tested against the survey data.

Economic Factors

A variety of economic factors will affect the VC's choice of exit strategy.

Exhaustion of the VC's Skill Set

Aside from their ability to evaluate prospective investments and separate the wheat from the chaff, VCs are specialized monitors who offer investee firms valuable guidance once the investment has been made. VCs monitor and sometimes replace management, participate in strategic decisions and offer informal advice on decisions of lesser importance. The ability to monitor is closely connected with the ability to resolve information asymmetries. It is only by virtue of a keen understanding of the enterprise and what is needed to achieve success that the VC can monitor effectively. In turn, monitoring not only addresses problems of moral hazard, but reduces information asymmetry by resulting in enhanced information flow between the entrepreneur and the VC.

VCs bring other benefits to the enterprise. Experienced VCs will have webs of contacts that assist the firm in sourcing materials and finding other sources of funding. VCs can also use their experience to help the firm find skilled lawyers, accountants, investment bankers, marketers and other professional advisors.

When the VC exits the investment, all these potential benefits are lost. By the time exit occurs, however, the enterprise may be sufficiently mature that the VC is no longer in a position to create significant additional value. Once the firm has an established product and has demonstrated profit potential, other sources of funding may become available. Management may have matured sufficiently that the marginal value of the VC's monitoring, advice and participation in strategic decisions has greatly declined. Contacts between the firm and suppliers, marketing experts, lawyers and investment bankers may be in place and need little further massaging by the VC. At this point (aside from choosing the timing and means of exit), the VC's unique skill set is no longer particularly useful to the enterprise, and it is time for the VC to turn his or her investment into cash and move on to other ventures.

In some cases the investment has proven to be a failure; again, it is time to move on. Exhaustion of the VC's skill set is the common thread that binds the various means of exit.

Ability of the New Owners to Resolve Information Asymmetry, Value the Firm and Monitor the Investment

When the time comes for the VC to exit, the degree of information asymmetry between firm insiders and outsiders will be less severe than when the VC initially invested in the firm. Older firms that have benefited from VC guidance tend to have a proven product, an established market, relatively experienced management, and more elaborate internal control and information systems than when the VC's first investment was made. This attenuates many of the risks that confront investors in the earlier stages of a firm's existence.[7]

Nonetheless, the degree of information asymmetry will be high compared with that of a typical public company. A public company will have a lengthier operating history. Moreover, much more information about a public firm will be on the public record, both as a consequence of the operation of private information gathering networks and mandatory disclosure requirements.

The severity of the information asymmetry confronting the firm will be a factor in the choice of exit. Investors who do not understand the firm's product and/or market will rationally discount the value of the firm to reflect this lack of understanding. Those who are best able to overcome the asymmetry will tend to put the highest value on the enterprise.

The ability to resolve information asymmetry is closely connected with monitoring capability. Knowledgeable buyers who can critically evaluate the information they receive from management can better determine when the managers are not performing adequately, i.e., they can more readily recognize moral hazard problems.

The ability of the buyer(s) to monitor managers will depend on the identity of post-exit shareholders (and their ability to resolve information asymmetries) and on the post-exit concentration in shareholdings. In general, managers will be disciplined more effectively by a controlling (and non-managerial) shareholder than by an unrelated group of small shareholders.

Different forms of exit result in sales to buyers with differing abilities to resolve information asymmetries and to monitor managers, as discussed below.

IPOs: When information asymmetries between insiders and outsiders are particularly large, public buyers may not possess the ability to gauge the worth of the company accurately. In such cases, a sale in the public market may result in a price that represents a lower multiple of earnings than in the case of a strategic acquisition. Indeed, public buyers will often be less well positioned to resolve information asymmetries than a strategic buyer.

An IPO generally involves the sale of a minority interest to public investors, leaving a controlling shareholder or coalition of shareholders in place. While the existence of a controlling shareholder may bring some discipline to the managers, the managers themselves will often form a significant part of the controlling coalition. Moreover, after an IPO, control will often be split among a variety of shareholders. As a result, the control coalition may be subject to collective action and defection problems. By contrast, with a strategic acquisition, a single shareholder will usually hold all the firm's equity. Thus, one could conjecture that a strategic acquisition by a knowledgeable buyer will result in better post-exit monitoring of managers than with an IPO.

Acquisitions: In a sale of the entire firm to a third party, the buyer will often be a "strategic buyer" – usually a large company in the same or similar business as the purchased firm, either as competitor, supplier or customer (see, for example, Venture Economics, 1995), which will integrate the company's technology with its own following the acquisition. That strategic buyers are usually in the same or a closely related business to the acquired firm is not accidental. Just as VCs are specialists at resolving information asymmetries in the earlier stages of investing, so strategic buyers are particularly well positioned to evaluate the firm's product, technology and management. Knowledge of the particular business enables the buyer to evaluate the firm's potential and, following the acquisition, provide useful monitoring and strategic advice. Indeed, because of its bargaining power, a strategic buyer will tend to have better access to inside information about the firm than many other types of buyers (such as purchasers in secondary sales). Finally, following the acquisition, the strategic buyer will own 100 percent of the firm. It will be optimally positioned to discipline wayward managers.

Secondary Sales: In a secondary sale, the buyer often possesses the same ability as a strategic acquirer to overcome information asymmetries. (Indeed, strategic and secondary buyers are often the same parties.) However, a secondary sale results in a very different configuration of post-exit shareholdings than an acquisition. Because VCs most often purchase minority interests, the buyer of the VC's shares will also acquire a minority interest. The buyer's ability to acquire information and monitor and discipline management will be far less than if the buyer purchases the entire firm.

The lessened ability to monitor and discipline is not merely a consequence of the fact that the buyer will be a minority shareholder. Before the sale, the VC will have carefully nurtured a relationship with the entrepreneur and other shareholders. In a successful venture capital investment, the VC will seldom, if ever, have to resort to the formal powers of a shareholder or director; informal powers of persuasion will be exercised through an amicable relationship with the entrepreneur. The purchaser of the VC's shares, however, will have no pre-existing relationship with the non-selling shareholders in the firm. As a result, the purchaser will not (at least immediately) be able to use a position as a minority shareholder as effectively as the VC. For this reason, a buyer will normally prefer to make a strategic acquisition rather than a secondary purchase of the VC's shares.

Buy Backs: Two factors suggest that buy backs should be a preferred means of exit. First, whether the corporation or insider group actually purchases the VC's shares, the insiders are the true buyers. For obvious reasons, the problem of information asymmetry disappears, since the insiders know more about the enterprise and its prospects (and their own activities) than anyone else. Second, because the entrepreneur and/or firm will usually have to borrow money to purchase the VC's shares, the buy back will often substantially enhance the entrepreneur's or the firm's debt load. The higher level of fixed interest payments will act as a discipline on management (see, for example, Jensen, 1986, p. 323).

The buy back also has significant disadvantages. One concern is that the buy back will jettison a specialized monitor (the VC) without bringing any replacement monitor on board. Indeed, an objective of the buy back may be to eliminate external monitors, so the entrepreneur may indulge a taste for leisure in a way that he or she was unable to do when the company had minority investors. The entrepreneur may be interested in doing so when he or she is less concerned about becoming fabulously wealthy than about running a "lifestyle" company, i.e., one that furnishes profits that are adequate to pay the interest on the firm's new debt and provide a reasonable return without the extraordinary commitment generally demanded by a VC. Indeed, a buy back may be evidence that the VC initially failed to appreciate the entrepreneur's work/leisure preferences.

Summary: While the buy back best addresses problems of information asymmetry, it eliminates an effective external monitor without substitution of a new one. A buyer in a strategic acquisition or secondary sale will usually be well placed to resolve information asymmetries but, in an acquisition transaction, the buyer will be better able to monitor managers than following a secondary sale. Public shareholders will often be both comparatively incapable of resolving information asymmetries and less effective monitors than strategic acquirers or secondary purchasers.

Managerial Incentives

Empirically, managerial share ownership is an important determinant of the degree of alignment between managerial and shareholder interests (see, for example, Jensen and Murphy, 1990, p. 225). However, there is conflicting evidence on the nature of this relationship. There is evidence, for example, that as managerial ownership increases, the value of the firm first rises, falls and then rises again (see, for example, Wruck, 1988, p. 3; Morck et al., 1988, p. 293). There is also evidence that the value of the firm rises and then falls as management ownership increases (McConnell and Servaes, 1990, p. 595). In either case, the explanation for the non-linear relationship between management ownership and firm value appears to be that as managers acquire more shares, their ability to resist a hostile takeover (the entrenchment effect) increases. As ownership increases, the incentive to act in the best interests of all shareholders (the alignment effect) also increases. By itself, the former tends to diminish the value of the firm, while the latter increases it. Over some ranges of share ownership, the entrenchment effect apparently dominates the alignment effect. Unfortunately, without consistent evidence concerning the nature of the relationship between management ownership and share value, it is difficult to predict how ownership changes associated with the VC's exit will affect firm value.

Different forms of VC exit tend to be associated with different post-exit managerial shareholdings.

IPOs: IPOs generally leave the existing management in place; raising new capital will significantly dilute their shareholdings and will result in a diminished alignment effect. However, it will also result in a diminished entrenchment effect. Thus, the effect of this change in ownership on the value of the firm cannot be predicted *a priori*.

Strategic Acquisition: Because a strategic acquisition involves the purchase of the entire firm, managers (whether part of the old management team or not) will have no ownership interest in the enterprise. While compensation schemes can be used to enhance managerial incentives, these do not appear to be as effective as share ownership in aligning manager and shareholder interests (MacIntosh, forthcoming). A strategic acquisition will tend to result in inferior post-exit management incentives when compared to forms of exit in which the managers retain a non-trivial shareholding interest.

Secondary Sales: A secondary sale of just the VC's interest will generally not affect managements' shareholdings. Thus, the degree of alignment between management and shareholder interests will not change.

Buy Backs: A buy back will also leave management in place. However, it will almost always result in the insider/managers owning a large portion (perhaps all) of the firm. At very high levels of ownership, the alignment effect is likely to dominate the entrenchment effect (although the empirical evidence is mixed). Thus, buy backs are the only form of exit that might be hypothesized to enhance managerial incentives.

Transaction Synergies

Some venture capital exits result in the realization of transaction synergies, while others do not.

IPOs: In an IPO, the firm is not combined with any other entity. Thus, an IPO will not generally result in the realization of any transaction synergies. It may, however, result in an indirect synergy premium. An IPO increases the likelihood of a hostile takeover. In a market characterized by rational expectations, any anticipation of a hostile acquisition for synergistic (or other) motives will be incorporated into the price at which the firm's shares trade in the public market. This premium should be reflected in the price at which the shares are initially sold to the public. In this way, some expectation of the realization of future synergies may be captured by those exiting the firm at the time of, or following, the IPO.

Strategic Acquisition: The purchase of the firm by a strategic buyer will often result in the realization of synergies. The decision to purchase the firm will frequently be the outcome of a so-called "make or buy" decision. Such a decision arises when the buyer reaches a critical juncture at which it would be advantageous to develop a specific product or technology to complete or complement an existing product line. Rather than developing the product or technology itself, the buyer will identify a firm that possesses what it needs and will purchase the firm.

Especially in the technology industries, strategic buyers often place idiosyncratically high values on the target firm, often because the buyer has already spent considerable money developing similar or complementary products or technologies. Because of these expenditures, the buyer will be uniquely positioned to bring the product or technology to market without substantial additional investment. The buyer may also possess distribution networks that are well adapted to marketing the seller's product or technology. In some cases, a strategic buyer may be a high-valuing purchaser wishing to keep the firm's technology out of the hands of competitors.

Secondary Sales: Transaction synergies are less likely to be realized with secondary sales than with acquisitions, primarily because the buying firm will have less ability to combine the target's assets with its own. Legally effecting a combination of assets will generally require both directors' and shareholders' resolutions, whether the combination is through amalgamation, a sale of the target's assets to the purchaser or by other means. If the buyer possesses only a minority interest in the target enterprise, securing such resolutions will be difficult or impossible.

Even when the buyer purchases a controlling interest from the departing VC, the buyer is taking on as many partners as there are other shareholders. Attempts to transfer assets from the target to the buyer may result in a suit by one or more of these shareholders for breach of fiduciary duty or oppression. Moreover, in some jurisdictions, cumbersome and potentially insurmountable procedural requirements must be satisfied before substantial assets may be transferred from one company to another. In Ontario, for example, securities laws compel a buyer wishing to transfer significant assets to a related firm to secure a valuation of the firm and obtain approval of the transaction by minority shareholders.[8]

Buy Backs: There are no transaction synergies with buy backs.

Summary: Strategic acquisitions routinely result in the realization of transaction synergies; no other exit method will have a similar result.

Capital Raised

Exit techniques differ in the extent to which they are associated with the raising of new capital for the firm.

IPOs: An IPO is associated with a large infusion of fresh capital. It is the only exit technique that invariably has this result.[9]

Acquisition: On the face of it, an acquisition raises no fresh capital; it merely rearranges ownership interests, i.e., transfers the company to new owners. However, an acquisition transaction will often be the prelude to fresh investment of new capital by the strategic buyer, with a view to further development of the product or technology.

Secondary Sales: A secondary market sale of shares will result in no new investment. It is also less likely than an acquisition to presage the investment of new capital by the buyer. As indicated above, strategic buyers often want to obtain 100 percent of the company before investing new capital. However, even if the buyer will not be immediately investing fresh capital in the business, it will sometimes purchase the VC's shares with a view ultimately to making an acquisition and investing new capital.

Buy Backs: To effect a buy back, either the company or the entrepreneur will usually borrow money, replacing the VC's shares with debt. In either case, servicing the loan will put additional strain on the firm's cash resources.

Summary: IPOs invariably raise new cash for the firm. Other forms of exit may presage new investment by the buyer, but often do not. The buy back will typically result in a cash drain, which may make it more difficult to raise external capital.

Scale of Acquisition and Ability to Meet Future Capital Requirements

An acquirer will obviously have to possess sufficient capital to effect the acquisition, whether of the VC's shares alone or the entire company. Indeed, companies that are suitable for an acquisition by a strategic buyer or by public investors (in an IPO) will often be high-growth companies. Thus, the acquiring firm must be able to anticipate that it will have sufficient capital (or the ability to bring further investors on board) to meet the acquired firm's further capital needs as it continues to grow. Because the public market is the deepest capital well from which the firm may drink, large capital requirements will tend to favour a sale into the public market.

Aside from the firm's present and future capital requirements, its present financial status and future promise will affect its current valuation. An extraordinarily successful firm (or one with tremendous prospects of future success) will command a high price. The buyer must have sufficient resources to pay this price.

This has an important implication for buy backs. In cases where the VC's investment is very successful, the entrepreneur or the company will lack the resources to repurchase the VC's interest. Because high-growth companies are almost always cash-starved, entrepreneurs who anticipate rapid growth may be unwilling to effect a buy back if the resulting cash drain or diminution in borrowing capacity means that the firm will have insufficient cash resources to effect that growth. In this sense, the buy back may be evidence that the entrepreneur and VC are in agreement that the firm lacks significant upside potential.

Risk-Bearing Considerations

Purchase of the entire firm by a single person or entity may result in underdiversification for the purchaser – at least if the purchaser is an individual or private company. In theory, underdiversification should not be of concern to an acquirer that is a public company (or other tradeable entity); the shareholders of a public company may themselves diversify the unsystematic component of the firm's risk by purchasing portfolios of securities. An individual or private company, however, may not have sufficient capital to diversify fully the unsystematic risk, even if it has sufficient capital to effect the acquisition. Indeed, even managers of public companies may have incentives to avoid high net present value but high risk investments to the extent that such investments result in managerial underdiversification (Coffee, 1986, p. 1). Because the ability to bear risk will be priced, risk-spreading considerations will, at the margin, bias the exit decision toward a sale to a (large) public firm or to public shareholders.

The Value of a Common Exit Strategy in Promoting Teamwork and Enhancing the VC's Reputation

A venture capital investment is, by definition, a relational investment, and a strong and amicable working relationship between the VC and the entrepreneur is the hallmark of a successful investment. When the parties agree, explicitly or implicitly, to work toward a common exit strategy, this increases the perception that the parties are "on the same team." Thus, aiming for a co-operative exit strategy can assist in fulfilling the VC's expectations of profit. For this reason, working toward a secondary sale that results in the disposition of the VC's interest alone is inferior to a common exit strategy. A secondary sale may, in fact, be evidence of a breakdown in the VC-entrepreneur relationship – and reason to believe that secondary sales should be associated with poorer profitability than co-operative exit strategies.

Evidence of the value of a common exit strategy arises in the frequency with which "go along" or "piggyback" rights are observed in agreements between VCs and entrepreneurs. Such rights may be held by the VC, the entrepreneur or both. They enable the holder of the right to sell at the same time and price as the other (or veto the sale) in the event of a third-party offer.

Even without such express stipulation, an experienced VC will often take management's preferences into account when choosing an exit option, even when this results in a less profitable exit than might otherwise be the case. Cultivating the entrepreneur's interests protects and enhances the VC's reputation in the entrepreneurial community, leading to a higher probability of capturing future venture capital business.

The VC's Cash Preference: VCs often say that "cash is king." This homily expresses the VC's preference for a cash exit, as opposed to one in which he or she acquires shares in another company or can only dispose of an interest in the investee firm over an extended period of time (such as an IPO).

A cash exit is preferable for a number of reasons. VCs bring value to their investments by engaging in active, hands-on management. They have no particular advantage in administering purely passive investments. Thus, once the VC's skill set has been exhausted, it makes sense to cash out and move on.

When VCs dispose of some or all of their shares at the time of a public offering, outside investors may view this as a signal of a lack of confidence in the firm which could result in an inferior price (see Bygrave and Timmons, 1992, p. 175; Leland and Pyle, 1977, p. 371). Thus, even when regulatory hold and escrow requirements do not apply, underwriters will typically negotiate a lock-in arrangement with key shareholders which forbids those shareholders (including the VC) from selling their shares into the secondary market for a stipulated period following the IPO. The lock-in generally ranges to six months. Even when a secondary sale of VC stock occurs contemporaneously with a prospectus offering of the firm's shares, the VC will almost never dispose of more than 10 percent of his or her stock.

The VC's cash preference tends to favour acquisitions, secondary sales or buy backs, which all tend to result in a cash disposition of the VC's interest.

Psychological Factors

IPOs: There is evidence that IPO pricing is subject to psychological factors, and not merely investment fundamentals. The operation of these psychological factors may result in periodic market overvaluations of IPO firms. IPOs will be a particularly attractive means of exit during these periods of overvaluation.

The best evidence that psychological factors operate in IPO markets is evidence of long-term overpricing. A number of studies have found that in the three to six years following an IPO, when IPOs are overpriced compared either to a relevant market benchmark or a matched sample of public firms (see Ritter, 1991, p. 3; Levis, 1993, p. 28; Loughran and Ritter, 1993; Loughran, 1993, p. 241; Jog, "Climate," this volume). Ritter's pioneering study, for example, found that "a strategy of investing in IPOs at the end of the first day of public trading and holding them for three years would have left the investor with only 83 cents relative to each dollar from investing in a group of matching firms listed on the American and New York stock exchanges (Ritter, 1991, p. 23). Ritter also found that "younger companies and companies going public in heavy volume years did even worse than average."[10] Ritter concluded that purchasers of IPOs were overoptimistic about the prospects of IPO firms. He concluded that the "evidence presented here is broadly consistent with the notion that many firms go public near the peak of industry-specific fads." (Ritter, 1991, p. 23).

Numerous other studies have confirmed and extended Ritter's findings.[11] For example, Levis (1993) looked at a sample of U.K. IPOs and found that IPOs exhibiting the best first-day performance, i.e., the greatest short-term underpricing, were the worst underperformers in the three years after going to market. Like Ritter (1991), Levis suggested that the initial underpricing may be due to market "over-reaction" at the time of the issue. Vijay Jog's study in this volume offers evidence that Canadian IPOs are also overpriced in the longer term.

Loughran et al. (1994, p. 165) found further evidence supporting the view that investors cyclically overprice IPOs and that firms time their offerings to coincide with "hot issue" markets. In 14 of 15 countries, they found a positive correlation between inflation-adjusted stock market prices and the annual volume of IPO activity. At first blush, this is not necessarily inconsistent with economic theory. In a strong economy, stock prices will rise and better investment opportunities will exist for small firms. This, in turn, will create a demand for capital to fund these opportunities. Thus, the correlation between rising stock prices and a strong IPO market may be nothing more than a case of common causation; each is a product of a strong economy.

Nonetheless, Loughran et al. found that the frequency of IPO offerings is more closely correlated with the stock market than with real economic factors. They concluded that the "evidence from around the world is consistent with the view that private companies have some success in timing their IPOs to take advantage of misvaluations."[12]

Venture capitalists may play some role in timing market cycles. For a sample of biotechnology IPOs, Lerner (1994) found that more experienced VCs were better able to time market cycles than were less experienced VCs.

There is also evidence that long-term overpricing is concentrated among small risky young non-venture capital backed firms. As noted above, Ritter found that younger companies had the worst long-term performance. In their multi-country review of IPO studies, Loughran et al. (1994) concluded that the worst after-market performance was in markets with an abundance of IPOs of risky firms. Most recently, Brav and Gompers (1995) found that "underperformance is almost entirely concentrated in the smallest deciles of nonventure capital-backed issuers." They noted that purchasers of non-venture capital backed IPOs tend to be retail rather than institutional investors and speculated that such investors are more likely to be influenced by emotional, rather than purely fundamental factors.[13]

In sum, there is some (albeit not unambiguous) evidence that markets periodically overvalue IPO firms and that venture capitalists play a role in timing IPOs at the peaks of these market cycles. Clearly, during a market peak, IPOs will be the favoured means of exit.

Buy Backs: The other context in which psychological factors may operate is the buy back. An entrepreneur may have an emotional attachment to the firm, having played a key role in creating and nurturing the enterprise. If so, the entrepreneur may be willing to buy out the VC even if, from a financial point of view, it would be better for the entrepreneur to exit the investment.

Selection Bias

As the data below and other studies make clear, the IPO occupies a place of central importance in venture capital investing. Success has historically been driven by one or more home runs (spectacularly successful investments) in the VC's investment portfolio (Bygrave and Timmons, 1992; Huntsman and Hoban, 1980). Moreover, the evidence presented below is consistent with the view that a much larger share of home runs are realized through IPOs than by any other exit method. Indeed, Bygrave and Timmons (1992, p. 169) suggested that a "healthy IPO market gives the venture capital industry its vitality. Without IPOs the venture-capital investment process would not be viable." Bygrave and Timmons noted that IPOs can result in huge returns on the initial investment. They cite Apple Computer which yielded a return of 235 times the initial investment, Lotus 63 times and Compaq 38 times.

What makes the IPO such an important means of exit? A number of economic factors have already been suggested. In particular, the public markets are the deepest source of capital, and an IPO spreads risk efficiently among a variety of buyers. The psychology of the marketplace may also result in artificially high valuations in some periods, tempting venture capitalists to exit via IPOs.

The high returns associated with IPOs may also result, in part, from selection bias. The IPO differs from other exit techniques in that it alone always results in a large infusion of cash. A firm that goes public must be a high-growth company with prospects for using the proceeds of the offering profitably. And, while firms that are exited via IPOs must invariably jump this hurdle (high growth, good prospects), firms exited by other means need not.

This selection bias results in high average returns for IPOs. Because IPOs are available only to firms that are either very profitable or show great promise of profitability, we should expect firms that are exited via IPOs to yield superior returns for the departing VC. These superior returns need not result from some innate characteristic of the IPO; they may simply reflect this bias. The use of the IPO as a means of exit may, therefore, be the symptom of profitability, rather than its cause.

Legal Factors

As identified by MacIntosh (1994), Robinson (this volume) and Andrews (1995), a number of legal factors may affect the VC's choice of exit. This section briefly touches on those legal factors affecting exit choices not discussed in the aforementioned sources.

Public and hybrid funds operate under legal constraints that sometimes influence their choice of exit. Innovation Ontario, for example (a public fund), is required to give the entrepreneur a call option to repurchase the VC's interest (although it appears to be the only government fund that is required to do so). If the business starts to become profitable, the entrepreneur will typically exercise the option and cash out its public investor.

By affecting the initial choice of investments, the legal constraints under which the LSVCCs operate will tend to colour a fund's exit strategy.

- Under federal and provincial legislation for LSVCCs, a fund will be penalized if it fails to invest a stated percentage of its committed capital within a certain period following receipt of that capital.
- LSVCCs are essentially open-ended mutual funds from which investors may withdraw at any time. While investors may withdraw only after five years without being subject to recapture of the investment tax credit (now eight years in the federal legislation), investors in private funds are often locked in for 10 years (although investors in the Fond de solidarité des travailleurs du Québec must normally wait until retirement to withdraw from the fund). This creates a need to maintain a greater percentage of the investment portfolio in comparatively liquid form, as compared to a private or government fund.

For both these reasons, LSVCCs have tended (at least until recently), to make larger and less risky mezzanine investments in older more traditional industrial sectors. This, in turn, is likely to influence the type of exits used by LSVCCs; such investments may lack the upside potential of earlier stage technology investments. If so, they are more likely to be exited via buy backs than via IPOs or acquisitions.

Tax Factors

The differential taxation of various exit techniques may constitute a reason for cross-sectional variations in patterns of exit use, both within Canada and between Canada and the United States. Taxation factors may also account for changes in exit strategies over time. While no attempt was made to determine systematically the tax consequences of all means of exit both in Canada and the United States discussions with VCs suggested that tax factors were relatively unimportant in the choice of exit strategy. Whether shares are sold by the VC in an IPO, a secondary market sale, an acquisition or a buy back, the VC will generally pay capital gains tax on the appreciation in the value of its holdings.

Summary

Clearly, a variety of factors touch on the VC's choice and timing of exit. As a result, there is no clear hierarchical ranking of exit techniques that applies to all types of investments in all states of nature. However, it is important to bear in mind that VCs make the lion's share of their returns via home runs. Investee firms that are home runs will be extremely high-growth firms with high-market valuations and significant present and future capital requirements. Theory and empirical and anecdotal evidence all suggest that the most profitable means of exiting such investments will be the IPO. While, to some extent, the high returns that accompany IPOs result from selection bias, public markets are frequently the deepest and best source of capital for high-growth firms.

Acquisitions will also be an attractive means of exiting profitable growth firms, particularly those that can benefit from a strategic union with an established industry player. For some investee firms and in some economic environments, acquisitions will dominate IPOs.

Secondary sales will be inferior to strategic acquisitions, mainly because they do not afford the buyer the same ability as an acquisition to merge the acquirer's and target's assets and exploit transaction synergies. There will be cases in which a strategic buyer would prefer to purchase the entire firm, but cannot convince the entrepreneur to exit at the same time as the VC. The strategic buyer may be sufficiently anxious to "get a foot in the door" to purchase a minority interest. By so doing, the buyer may be able to place a representative on the board and secure a strategic window on the firm's technology. A purchase of the VC's interest may also be a prelude to further attempts to buy the entire company. Because the strategic buyer's willingness to purchase a minority interest will usually reflect a high valuation of the target firm, such an exit will sometimes result in a very good price for the exiting VC.

Despite some apparent advantages over other forms of exit, the buy back transaction is often the exit of last resort, short of a write-off. Venture capitalists often classify their investments into three varieties: home runs, living dead and write-offs. Living dead investments are those that generate enough cash flow to keep the company afloat, but lack significant upside (home run) potential. A VC's comparative advantage (and source of profits) lies in nurturing potential star performers – not living dead. For this reason, VCs will unload living dead at the first opportunity. In many cases, the only available opportunity will be a buy back. Because of the firm's mediocre prospects, an IPO will generally be out of the question. Nor will the firm tend to attract a strategic buyer.

VCs often include a put option in their initial contract with the entrepreneur. This put option (which can generally only be exercised after five years from the date of the contract) functions as an escape hatch that enables the VC to escape a living dead investment via a buy back if the firm's prospects turn sour.

In some cases, the VC will grant the entrepreneur a call option on the VC's shares (which can generally be exercised after seven years). A typical scenario for a call option involves less risky investments lacking significant upside potential. While the investment will appear to offer some promise, the VC's initial assessment will be that an IPO or acquisition exit will be relatively unlikely. The buy back will, therefore, result in reasonably good, but not spectacular profits for the VC. In other words, the investment will be at the upper end of the living dead part of the returns spectrum.

Buy backs may also be negotiated in the absence of contractual arrangements. Either the entrepreneur or the VC may approach the other and request a buy back. This is likely to happen when the investment is doing badly, and/or the relationship between the entrepreneur and the VC is poor. In either case, a negotiated buy back will result in a mediocre exit price.

One caveat is in order. For the entrepreneur or company to be able to effect a buy back, the firm must be sufficiently profitable to enable the entrepreneur or company to borrow funds to repurchase the VC's shares. This emphasizes the point that living dead investments are *moderately*, but not spectacularly successful companies.

A Comparison of Two Early Studies of Venture Capital Exits in Canada and the United States

Two early surveys, one in Canada (VEC, 1986), and the other in the United States (VE, 1988) tracked venture capital exits. These surveys are compared below, and reviewed in light of the aggregate industry data found in MacIntosh (1996) and the above discussion of the pros and cons of various forms of exit. While the broader data presented in MacIntosh (1996) allow some opportunity to check the survey results for selection bias, the comparison is imperfect, given that the periods covered by the aggregate data and the survey data differ.

The most probable survey bias is likely to be the underreporting of unprofitable exits, simply because VCs who have profited handsomely from their investments are more likely to be willing to take the time and effort to respond to the survey. This may artificially inflate average profitability figures for the different exit techniques.

Exit Techniques

Generally, the exit techniques examined in the two surveys are those explored above. However, among the two early studies, only the U.S. survey deals with secondary sales as a distinct method of exiting an investment. In the Canadian survey, secondary sales were not accounted for separately. This is reflected in the comparatively large number of "other" types of exits in Table 1.

The U.S. survey also breaks acquisitions into two categories: acquisitions and liquidations. The latter includes asset sales, as opposed to a sale of all the shares of the company (VE, 1988, p. 6).

Periods Covered by the Studies

The Canadian survey, conducted by Venture Economics Canada Limited (VEC, 1986), examined 167 exits between 1975 and 1985 by 22 venture capital firms. The U.S. survey, by Venture Economics (VE, 1988), examined 544 exits between 1970 and mid-1988 by 26 venture capital firms. Thus, the two studies cover somewhat different periods. This diminishes their comparability as discussed below.

Size of Investments

Table 1 indicates that, on average, survey investments made by U.S. VCs were somewhat larger than those made by Canadian VCs. It should be kept in mind that the Canadian figures are in Canadian dollars, while the U.S. figures are in U.S. dollars.

TABLE 1

DISTRIBUTION OF EXITS IN CANADA (1975 TO 1985) AND THE UNITED STATES (1975 TO 1988)

	Canada			United States		
Exit Method	Number of Portfolio Companies	Percent	Average Investment (C$000s)	Number of Portfolio Companies	Percent	Average Investment (US$000s)
IPO[a]	27	16	999	193	35	814
Acquisition	29	17	700	118	22	988
Company buy back	37	22	453	33	6	595
Secondary sale[b]	n/a	n/a	n/a	46	8	715
Liquidation[c]	n/a	n/a	n/a	32	6	1,030
Write-off	53	32	6,13[d]	114	21	961
Unknown	4	2	n/a	–	–	–
Other	7	10	421	8	2	n/a
Total	167	99	647	544	100	851

Notes: [a] In Canada, IPO includes one reverse takeover.

[b] In Canada, secondary sales were not recorded separately. They are likely reflected in the "other" category.

[c] In Canada, liquidations were not recorded separately. They may be reflected in either the "acquisition" or "other" categories.

[d] Excludes one extraordinary transaction which, if included, increases the average investment to $741,000.

n/a: not available.

Source: VEC (1986, p. 6); VE (1988, pp. 7, 10).

Industry of Portfolio Firms

Table 2 indicates the distribution of exits by portfolio company industry for both the Canadian and U.S. studies. It accords well with the broader data presented in MacIntosh (1996) and reflects the higher concentration of U.S. venture capital investments in technology-related areas, and a lower concentration in consumer-related and manufacturing concerns.

Distribution of Exits by Portfolio Company Stage at Date of Investment

Table 3 shows the distribution of exits by portfolio company stage at the time of the investment, for investments by both Canadian and U.S. VCs. The survey results agree with the broader industry data presented in MacIntosh (1996) insofar as they show that U.S. VCs invested more heavily than Canadian VCs in early and expansion stage financings. However, there are fewer acquisition transactions, and more early stage investments in the Canadian survey data than in the broader data.

Comparison of Different Exit Techniques

Table 1 reveals some interesting divergences in exit methods between Canada and the United States. In the United States, the most common exit method was an IPO (35 percent), followed by an acquisition of the entire firm (22 percent) and a write-off (21 percent). These three exit methods accounted for 78 percent of the total sample. By contrast, in Canada the most common exit method was a write-off

Table 2

Distribution of Exits by Portfolio Company Industry

	Canada (%)	United States (%)
Communications	10	14
Computer related	12	41
Other electronic	5	1
Biotechnology	1	2
Medical/health related	5	9
Energy related	10	4
Consumer related	16	6
Industrial products	15	5
Other	23	0
Unknown	4	–
Total	101	100

Source: VEC (1986, p. 15); VE (1988, p. 18).

TABLE 3

DISTRIBUTION OF EXITS BY PORTFOLIO COMPANY STAGE

Portfolio Company Stage	Percent of Exits	
	Canada (%)	United States (%)
Early stage	36	48
Expansion stage	27	45
Acquisition/leveraged buyout	8	7
Turnaround	7	0
Other/unknown	23	0

Source: VEC (1986, p. 13); VE (1988, p. 15).

(32 percent), followed by a share buy back (22 percent), IPO (16 percent[14]) and acquisition (17 percent). These four methods (with rounding of fractions) accounted for 88 percent of the Canadian exits.

Frequency of IPOs

The data from these two studies add support to the view that the IPO has been used more frequently as an exit mechanism in the United States than in Canada. Many Canadian VCs attribute this difference to the greater receptivity of U.S. institutional investors to IPOs. Some support for this belief is found in the fact that Canadian VCs exited their U.S. holdings via IPOs at the same rate (about one third of the time) as did U.S. VCs (VEC, 1986, p. 11). Indeed, this suggests that U.S. markets are receptive only to IPOs involving U.S.-based firms. Otherwise, one would expect Canadian VCs to use the U.S. IPO exit route as often for their Canadian investments as their U.S. investments.[15]

This interpretation of the evidence is based on the assumption that Canadian and U.S. investments are drawn from similar underlying populations and should thus show similar IPO rates of exit. Both the survey data and the aggregate data explored in MacIntosh (1996) suggested that Canadian and U.S. portfolio investments are not drawn from the same underlying population. In particular, there is a higher concentration of technology-related firms in the United States, and a lower concentration of firms in more traditional sectors such as consumer products and manufacturing. Thus, it is difficult to draw more than very tentative conclusions about the comparative receptivity of Canadian and U.S. markets to IPOs.

The Canadian study suggests that the tax incentives associated with the Quebec Stock Savings Plan (QSSP) increased the number of Canadian IPOs in the 1975 to 1985 period.[16] One quarter of the exits from Quebec companies were IPOs (all occurring in 1984 and 1985), compared to only 8 percent for Ontario companies (VEC, 1986, p. 11). Indeed, of the 26 IPOs in the Canadian sample, seven occurred in Quebec, compared to eight in the rest of the country (and 11 in the United States) (VEC, 1986, p. 11). This is consistent with other evidence suggesting that the QSSP resulted in a large number of IPOs in Quebec that would not have occurred but for the tax incentives (Jog and Riding, 1990).

Frequency of Acquisitions

U.S. VCs exited their investments through acquisitions somewhat more frequently (22 percent) than did Canadian VCs (17 percent).[17]

Frequency of Company Buy Backs

A significant difference relates to the relative use of company buy backs in the two countries. In Canada, buy backs constituted 22 percent of the sample; in the United States, only 6 percent. Canadian VCs exited only 11 percent of their U.S. investments via a company buy back.[18] This suggests that some feature of the economic or regulatory environment in the United States makes buy backs less attractive (or other exit options comparatively more attractive).

Frequency of Write-Offs

The number of write-offs also appears to differ substantially between the two countries. In the United States, 21 percent of investments were written off, vs. 32 percent in Canada. Canadian VCs, however, wrote off their Canadian and U.S. investments at an identical rate (32 percent) (VEC, 1986, pp. 6, 10).

CHANGES IN THE USE OF EXIT METHODS OVER TIME

TABLES 4 AND 5 INDICATE THAT THE USE OF DIFFERENT EXIT METHODS has varied considerably over time. It is difficult to discern many patterns in these variations. It does appear, however, that there was increasing reliance in Canada on IPO exits over the 1975 to 1985 period. Out of 40 exits between 1975 and 1980, only 10 percent were IPOs. By contrast, 19 percent of the 117 exits between 1981 and 1985 were IPOs. The data also appear to show a decreasing reliance on company buy backs. While 43 percent of all exits in the 1975 to 1977 period were through buy backs, only 22 percent of all exits from 1984 to 1985 were buy backs.

There was also an increase in the percentage of write-offs by Canadian VCs over the sample period. Between 1975 and 1980, 23 percent of exits were write-offs. Between 1981 and 1985, 33 percent were write-offs. As discussed in MacIntosh (1996), this may reflect the rapid increase in funding for venture capital in the early 1980s which resulted in the hiring of many inexperienced venture capital managers (Gompers, 1994, p. 1; Bygrave and Timmons, 1992).

TABLE 4

USE OF EXITS OVER TIME IN CANADA

	1975-1977		1978-1980		1981-1983		1984		1985		Date Unknown		Total	
Exit vehicle	Number	%	Number	%	Number	%	Number	%	Number	%	Number	%	Number	%
IPO	0	0	3	9	6	19	5	19	11	19	1	10	26	16
Acquisition	0	0	5	15	8	25	5	19	9	16	2	20	29	17
Buy back	3	43	10	30	4	13	4	15	15	26	1	10	37	22
Reverse	0	0	1	3	0	0	0	0	0	0	0	0	1	1
Write-off	1	14	8	24	9	28	11	41	19	33	5	50	53	32
Other	3	43	6	18	5	16	2	7	4	7	1	10	21	13
Totals	7	100	33	100	32	100	27	100	58	100	10	100	167	100

Source: VEC (1986, p. 8).

TABLE 5

USE OF EXITS OVER TIME IN THE UNITED STATES

Exit Vehicle	1/70-12/79 (%)	1/80-12/81 (%)	1/82-12/82 (%)	1/83-6/84 (%)	7/84-9/85 (%)	10/85-9/87 (%)	10/87-6/88 (%)
IPO	32	62	33	54	16	34	5
Acquisition	19	16	33	17	30	21	26
Buy back	7	2	8	8	4	7	3
Secondary sale	23	11	8	6	11	5	13
Liquidation	–	2	–	6	7	8	10
Write-off	19	7	17	9	32	25	43
Totals	100	100	99	100	100	100	100
Total number of portfolio companies	31	45	24	125	88	182	39

Source: VE (1988, p. 23).

These apparent trends may be no more than an artifact of cyclical variations in business conditions that affect the relative availability and/or profitability of various forms of exit. For example, from 1991 to 1994, write-offs by Canadian VCs were only 22 percent of all exits, while buy backs were 39 percent of all exits. These figures make it difficult to conclude that there is any particular trend in the use of exit techniques by Canadian VCs.

The U.S. data show a similar pattern of changes in the use of exit techniques over time. The use of IPO exits, for example, fluctuated substantially over the sample period. This should be no surprise. As discussed earlier, there is very strong evidence that VCs time IPO exits to correspond to variations in stock market cycles. It would be surprising if there was no variation in the use of IPOs over time.

The earlier discussion of exit preferences also suggests that there is likely to be an inverse relationship between the use of IPO and acquisition exits. When stock markets are doing poorly and the IPO market is on the downswing, acquisition exits should become relatively more attractive. Casual inspection of the U.S. data suggests that this is the case.

While one should be cautious in discerning trends in the data, the level of exits effected by secondary sales in the United States appears to have been lower in the 1980s than in the 1970s. This may reflect the growing experience of strategic buyers with the adverse consequences of purchasing minority interests and a commensurately enhanced preference for purchasing the entire firm. Indeed, while the number of secondary sales was lower in the 1980s, the number of acquisitions was higher.

The number of write-offs in the United States increased dramatically from mid-1984 to mid-1988. Once again, this probably reflects the influx of inexperienced VCs into the venture capital industry in the early to mid-1980s.

Relative Profitability of Exit Methods

TABLE 6 INDICATES THE RELATIVE PROFITABILITY OF VARIOUS EXIT TECHNIQUES. For Canada, profitability is calculated as an internal rate of return (IRR) (per annum). For the United States, profitability is calculated as a "gain multiple" per annum, i.e., the total proceeds of the disposition less the total purchase cost, divided by the holding period. While differences in computing profitability interfere with cardinal intercountry comparisons, they do not interfere with ordinal comparisons.

In the United States, the IPO was the most profitable way of exiting a venture capital investment in the survey period, by a wide margin. Acquisitions, buy backs and secondary sales appear to have been equally profitable, despite the fact that 22 percent of investments were exited via acquisition and only 6 percent and 8 percent respectively through a company buy back or a sale in the secondary market (see Table 1).

In Canada, IPOs were also the most profitable means of exiting venture capital investments, with an average IRR of 197 percent. Share repurchase was the second most profitable way of exiting investments in the 1975 to 1985 period, yielding an

TABLE 6

PROFITABILITY AND HOLDING PERIODS FOR DIFFERENT EXIT TECHNIQUES

	Canada		United States	
Exit Method	Average Holding Period (Years)	Average Internal Rate of Return (%)	Average Holding Period (Years)	Average Gain (or Loss) per Year as a Multiple of Cost
IPO	2.3	197	4.2	1.95
Acquisition	4.1	21	3.7	0.40
Company buy back	5.7	44	4.7	0.37
Secondary sale	n/a	n/a	3.6	0.41
Liquidation	n/a	n/a	4.1	(0.34)
Write-off	3.4	n/a	3.7	(0.37)

Note: n/a: not available

Sources: VEC (1986, p. 6); VE (1988, p. 10).

internal rate of return of 44 percent – although removing one outlier results in an average return of 31 percent (VEC, 1986, p. 7). Acquisition was the third most profitable, yielding an IRR of 21 percent. Sales in the secondary market were not accounted for separately and may make up a sizeable portion of the "other" category in the survey, which constituted 10 percent of all exits (VEC, 1986, p. 5).

There is some indication that a number of highly profitable acquisition investments may have skewed the Canadian sample results for IPO returns. Out of 26 IPO exits, only four had an IRR in excess of 125 percent (VEC, 1986, p. 17), and these four investments accounted for 50 percent of the $16 million invested in companies that eventually were taken public (VEC, 1986, p. 6). All four investments were held for less than 24 months and may have been acquisition investments. Given that the IRR calculation in the report is effectively value-weighted,[19] these transactions clearly had a major impact on the average IRR. Indeed, acquisitions as a group were the most profitable form of investment, yielding an average IRR of 55 percent.[20] Of the 26 IPOs in the sample, seven were acquisitions (VEC, 1986, p. 15).

Unfortunately, the original data no longer exist. There is no way of checking to see if these four transactions involved investments in acquisition financings. VEC has indicated a belief that not all the four transactions involved acquisition financing. Moreover, even if these four transactions are removed from the sample, the distribution of returns reported in Table 7 suggests that IPOs were still the most profitable means of exiting investments.

TABLE 7

DISTRIBUTION OF RATES OF RETURN BY EXIT VEHICLE USED, CANADA

IRR Range (%)	IPO Number	IPO %	Buy Back Number	Buy Back %	Acquisition Number	Acquisition %
> 200	2	8	–	–	–	–
126-200	2	8	–	–	–	–
76-125	4	15	1	3	–	–
51-76	1	4	–	–	4	14
26-50	2	8	6	16	2	7
16-25	4	15	6	16	2	7
0-15	3	12	11	30	10	35
< 0	–	–	3	8	2	7
Incomplete data	8	30	10	27	9	30
Total	26	100	37	100	29	100

Note: IRR: internal rate of return

Source: VEC (1988, p. 17).

Acquisition investments do not appear to have exerted a strong influence on the healthy returns realized in U.S. IPOs. Out of 544 exits, only 10 were IPO exits from acquisition investments (VEC, 1986, p. 15). While the "gain multiple" calculated by Venture Economics is a value-weighted statistic (treating all investments and exits as if they were a single investment) (VE, 1988, p. 10), most of the investments in the sample were early or expansion stage financings (VE, 1988, p. 3). Thus, it seems clear that the handsome returns from IPO exits do not result from acquisition outliers.

Figure 1 (reproduced from the U.S. survey) is a vivid illustration of the fact that most of the profit from venture capital investing has historically been derived from home runs or spectacularly successful investments with returns greatly in excess of those experienced on other investments.[21] Figure 1 highlights a surprising discontinuity in venture capital returns. The distribution of gains and losses on investments suggests the existence of two underlying populations of investments. One is reflected in the left-skewed distribution reflecting gains and losses of less than $5.5 million. The second is reflected in the startling spike at the upper tail of the distribution. While a spike will normally be produced by aggregating all occurrences above a cut-off point (as the Figure 1 has done), the spike appears to be much larger than would be expected on aggregating the right tail of the distribution.

FIGURE 1

DISTRIBUTION OF PORTFOLIO COMPANY GAINS AND LOSSES BY EXIT METHOD (EARLY SURVEY RESULTS)

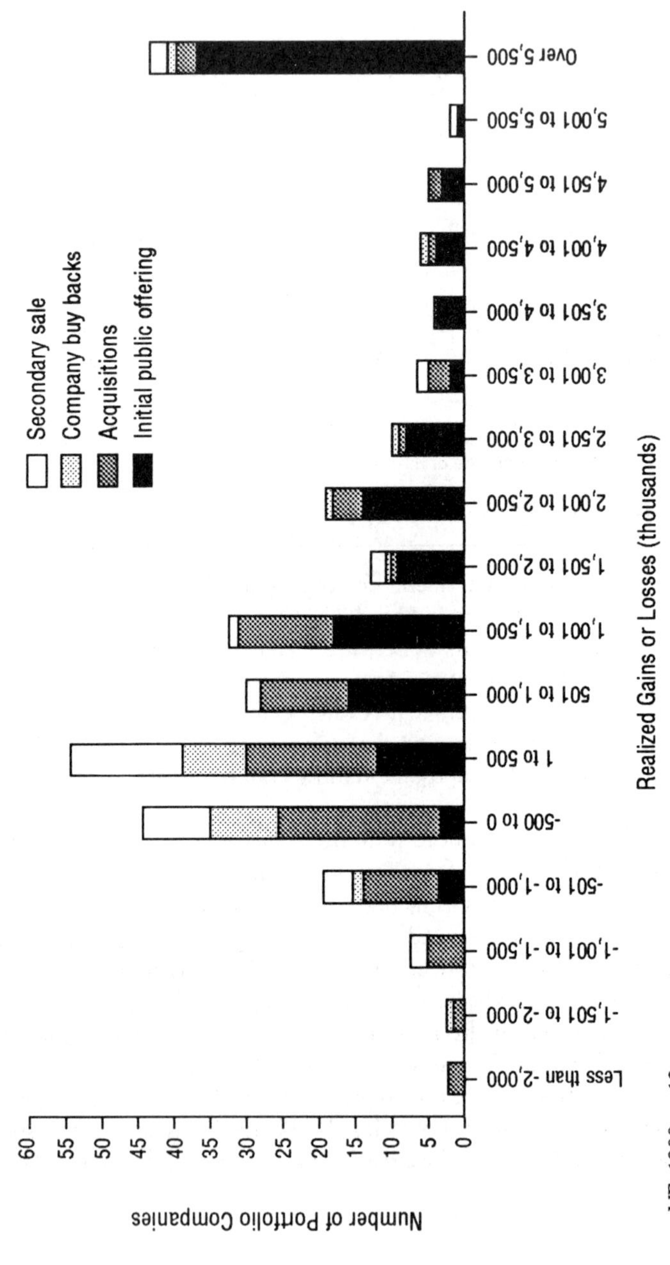

Source: VE, 1988, p. 13.

The distribution to the left is composed of two kinds of investments – living dead and write-offs. The latter are represented by all investments yielding a negative return. Living dead are investments that yield a positive return, but unspectacular profitability. The spike at the right tail of Figure 1 represents home runs. (Unfortunately, because all the cases making up the spike are lumped together, we do not know whether the home run returns are normally distributed.)

The Canadian survey results also show that more home runs were realized via IPOs than by any other exit technique. Table 7 indicates that 35 percent of all IPO exits resulted in IRRs of 51 percent or better. The comparable percentages for acquisitions and buy backs were 14 percent and 3 percent, respectively.

While the division of investments into write-offs, living dead and home runs fits with the VC's traditional description of venture capital investments, it also suggests a puzzle. Why are some investments so much more profitable than others? It seems counterintuitive to believe that there are two underlying populations of investments – home runs and everything else.

One explanation for the right-tailed spike is that it is not an artifact of the underlying distribution of firms, but of the manner in which newly public firms are valued in the public market. As presented earlier, evidence suggests that IPOs, on average, are overvalued by public investors. Therefore, the spike in Figure 1 may be an artifact, not of the underlying population of firms, but of the manner in which firms are valued in the public market.

This explanation does not seem persuasive. As Figure 1 discloses, it is only a subset of the firms brought to the public market that are home runs. Ignoring the spike, the distribution of IPO returns approximates a normal distribution, although it is somewhat skewed to the right. Why would the public market vastly overvalue a subset of IPOs and not all IPOs? In order for this to be the case, firms with certain arbitrary characteristics must be "hot issues" that are greatly overpriced compared with other public offerings.

This seems unsatisfactory. It suggests that IPO home runs constitute a subset of the population of IPOs that possess some arbitrary characteristic unrelated to investment fundamentals, and this arbitrary characteristic results in extreme overpricing. While there is some evidence that there are fads in IPO offerings, Brav and Gompers' (1995) evidence suggests that it is non-venture-backed IPOs sold to retail investors that are overpriced. If venture-backed IPOs are, on average correctly priced, the hypothesis that home runs are a result of market mispricing appears to collapse.

Many VCs, nonetheless, believe there are fads in public markets, and these fads tend to focus on particular industrial sectors, e.g., biotechnology in one cycle and computer-related investments in another. Clearly, more investigation is in order. In particular, there has been virtually no empirical investigation of the efficiency of Canada's speculative junior markets in British Columbia and Alberta. Many of the IPOs sold in these markets are sold mainly to retail investors. If retail investors are routinely subject to emotional flights of fancy that induce them systematically to overpay for new issues, then we would expect a high degree of overpricing in these markets. It would be useful to know if this is the case.

Earlier, it was suggested that the profitability of VC exits will be greatest for IPOs, followed by acquisitions, secondary sales, buy backs and write-offs. The Canadian survey data on profitability offers only partial support for this view. IPOs were clearly the most profitable exits. Buy backs, however, were the second most profitable, easily topping the returns received from acquisitions. Moreover, buy backs occurred with a slightly higher frequency than acquisitions. The low number of acquisitions may reflect a lack of mature firms in Canada either willing or able to act as strategic acquirers, when compared to the depth of the pool of strategic acquirers in the United States. The relative profitability of secondary sales, unfortunately, is unknown.

The U.S. data offer greater support to the hypothesized exit preferences of VCs. Again, IPOs were easily the most profitable, and such exits were used more than one third of the time. While acquisitions, buy backs and secondary sales were approximately equal with regards to profitability, acquisition exits were used with greater frequency (22 percent of all exits) than were buy backs (6 percent) or secondary sales (8 percent). This suggests that there are fewer opportunities for profitable exits via buy backs or secondary sales than via acquisitions.

Stage of Investment, Exit Method and Returns

The Canadian survey indicates the relative profitability of exits for firms at various stages of development at the time of investing. In the time period under examination, leveraged buyouts were the most profitable investments, with an IRR of 55 percent. Leveraged buyouts were followed by turnaround financing (23 percent), expansion financing (22 percent) and seed/start-up financing (16 percent) (VEC, 1986, p. 13).

These data are counterintuitive. *A priori*, one would expect early stage financing to be the riskiest and, therefore, to result in the highest average returns. Early stage firms are young and unproven, usually without a product that is ready to sell, much less an established market. Their future is highly uncertain. Firms in later stages of development will have had to survive various developmental hurdles in order to proceed to these later stages. Thus, it seems natural to assume that the earlier the stage at which financing occurs, the higher the risk, and the higher the required and realized rates of return. In other words, the most profitable investments should be early stage financing, followed by expansion and acquisition financing.

There is evidence that risk and required rates of return are higher for early stage investments. Ruhnka and Young (1991) found that rates of return required by venture capitalists were 73 percent for seed capital investments, 55 percent for start-up investments and 35 percent for later stage investments.[22] Sahlman (1990, p. 511) suggested that U.S. VCs' required rates of return are higher for early stage as opposed to expansion stage financing, and higher for expansion stage financing than acquisition financing. Bygrave and Timmons (1992, p. 168) also adduced evidence suggesting that early stage investments are riskier than other forms of investing. Table 8 indicates that there are substantial differences in the type of exit a Canadian VC can expect to use for investments made at different stages. Leveraged buyout (acquisition) investments, for example, are more likely to result in an IPO exit than

TABLE 8

EXITS USED FOR INVESTMENTS MADE AT DIFFERENT STAGES, CANADA

Type of Exit	Seed/Start-Up		Expansion		Leveraged Buyout		Turnaround		Unknown		Totals	
	Number	%	Number	%	Number	%	Number	%	Number	%	Number	%
IPO	4	7	10	22	7	50	1	9	4	11	26	16
Acquisition	8	13	6	13	3	21	4	36	8	22	29	17
Buy back	12	20	11	24	1	7	3	27	10	27	37	22
Reverse	1	2	0	0	0	0	0	0	0	0	1	1
Write-off	30	50	11	24	1	7	3	27	8	22	53	32
Other	4	7	6	13	2	14	0	0	5	14	17	10
Unknown	1	2	1	2	0	0	0	0	2	5	4	2
Totals	60	100	45	100	14	100	11	100	37	100	167	100

Note: IPO: initial public offering

Source: VEC (1986, p. 14).

TABLE 9

DISTRIBUTION OF EXITS BY PORTFOLIO COMPANY STAGE, UNITED STATES

Portfolio Company Stage	Total Number of Exits	IPO (%)	Acquisition (%)	Company Buy Back (%)	Secondary Sale (%)	Liquidation (%)	Write-Off (%)	Total[a] (%)
		Percent of Exits						
Early stage	261	30	22	3	7	5	31	98
Expansion stage	244	43	23	5	9	7	12	100
Leveraged buyouts	36	28	17	30	19	–	6	99
All stages	544	35	22	6	8	6	21	98

Note: [a] May not total 100 percent due to "other" exit types.

Source: VE (1988, p. 15).

an investment at the early (seed/start-up/development) stage. Generally, excluding turnaround investments, the later the stage at which the investment is made, the more likely it is to be exited via an IPO (the most profitable form of exit). Again excluding turnaround investments, early stage financings have the largest write-off rate (fully 50 percent were written off), followed by expansion stage financings and acquisitions. Given that IPOs are the most profitable exits, and write-offs the least profitable, this evidence supports the view that the earlier the financing stage, the greater the investment risk.

The U.S. evidence presented in Table 9 is similar. The write-off rate is easily the highest for early stage investments, followed by expansion stage and leveraged buyout investments. The proportion of IPO exits is also higher for expansion financings than for early financings. However, the proportion of IPO exits for leveraged buyout financings is no higher than that of early stage investing.

Turnaround investments appear to present a somewhat unique case. Table 8 indicates that, in Canada, turnaround investments were more likely to be exited via an acquisition or a company buy back than were any other type of investment. The write-off rate is second only to that experienced with early stage investing. This is not surprising. Turnaround investments are made, by definition, in firms experiencing financial difficulties. *A priori*, one would, therefore, expect a low number of home runs and a high number of write-offs (although it is easy to overstate the case; most small firms in the early or expansion stages will also be cash-strapped). The risk of turnaround investments appears to be reflected in the average return to such investments (VEC, 1986, p. 13).

Investment Size, Exit Method and Profitability

The Canadian survey indicated that, on average, larger investments were more profitable (VEC, 1986, p. 18). Initially, this appears counterintuitive. One might expect that larger investments would generally be made in larger and more mature firms with established products and track records. Such investments should be less risky and, hence, less profitable.

The explanation likely lies in the fact that VCs often provide funds more than once to their investee firms. Successful investments will succeed in attracting additional investment at subsequent stages of development, while unsuccessful investments will be abandoned. Thus, in many cases, the size of the investment will be a function of the success of the firm, rather than the other way around.

If it is true that the total size of the investment is closely correlated with the success of the investment, then, in keeping with the earlier hypotheses about the relative profitability of different exit methods, the largest investments should be in firms exited via IPOs, followed by acquisitions, secondary sales and buy backs. The Canadian evidence offers some support to the joint hypothesis about relative profitability and the correlation between size and profitability. The average investment in a firm that is eventually taken public is larger than the average investment in a firm that is exited via some other route.[23] Investments that are later repurchased by the firm are about half the size of investments in firms exited through IPOs.[24] Investments in firms exited via acquisitions were midway in size between those exited via buy backs and IPOs.[25] However, investments that were eventually written off were larger than those that were the subject of a buy back.[26] It is not clear if this high average resulted from large initial investments or multiple-staged investments.

U.S. survey data (not reproduced) offer little support for the view that larger investments will be exited via an IPO more frequently than smaller investments. Indeed, all investments in excess of $100,000 had a similar likelihood of being exited via an IPO. The U.S. survey also indicated that only investments under $100,000 were more likely to be exited via a company buy back or a write-off than investments above this threshold (VE, 1988, p. 19).

Venture Capital Manager Skill in Canada and the United States

As noted above, the write-off rate was higher (32 percent) for Canadian VCs than for U.S. VCs (21 percent). There are a number of plausible explanations for this difference.

Less Experienced Venture Fund Managers in Canada

The higher write-off rate experienced by Canadian VCs may reflect the influx of inexperienced managers into the venture capital industry over the survey period. This view is supported by the fact that the Canadian write-off rate shows a rising trend in the 1975 to 1985 period (see Table 4). Further, the average IRR realized on exits occurring in 1984 and 1985 is somewhat lower than the average IRR in the 1975 to 1983 period.[27]

The rapid growth theory, however, fails to consider the rapid growth that occurred in the U.S. venture capital industry in the early 1980s. This growth started in approximately 1980 and culminated in banner years in 1983, 1984 and 1985 (VE, 1986, p. 14). Indeed, 39 percent of the venture capital funds in the U.S. survey made their first investments in 1981 and 1982.[28] Further, 75 percent of all investments from which exits were taken in the 1970 to 1988 period were made in 1980, 1981, 1982 or 1983 (VE, 1988, p. 5). Perhaps most telling, the write-off rate was sharply higher during the last four years of the survey – mid-1984 to mid-1988 (see Table 5), the period in which many of these new managers would have begun to harvest their investments. These data strongly suggest that the U.S. funds surveyed were also populated by a large number of inexperienced VCs in the survey period.

This view is given further credence by a number of histories of the U.S. venture capital industry. Historical accounts by Bygrave and Timmons (1992) and by Gompers (1994) suggested that the massive influx of funds into the U.S. venture capital industry in the early and mid-1980s resulted in a large number of novice venture capital managers entering the industry. Both accounts attributed the significant reduction in venture capital returns in the mid to late-1980s to investments made by these inexperienced managers.

While it is difficult to obtain figures comparing the growth of the venture capital industry in Canada with that in the United States in the early 1980s, there is evidence that rapid growth in the Canadian industry lagged that in the United States by approximately two years. While there was an increase in venture capital investing as early as 1980,[29] the most rapid growth appears to have occurred in 1985.[30] Given that the Canadian survey terminates in 1985, the lemons taken on by inexperienced Canadian venture capital managers would not show up in the survey results – but they clearly show up in the U.S. results. This suggests that the timing difference between the U.S. and Canadian surveys may make the U.S. write-off results look comparatively worse, and the Canadian results look comparatively better than they would if the survey periods were exactly matched. In short, it seems implausible that a rapid inflow of inexperienced managers into the Canadian venture capital industry is responsible for the higher write-off rate in Canada.

Lower Skill, Holding Experience Constant

An alternative view is that, with experience held constant, Canadian venture capital managers are less skilled at venture investing. This hypothesis is plausible given that, historically, Canadian VCs have been generalists, while U.S. VCs have tended to specialize in particular industrial sectors, with a greater focus on early and expansion stage investments in the high-tech sector. Given the manner in which VCs bring value to the firms in their portfolios, specialization is likely to result in higher returns. Specialized VCs can bring a higher degree of expertise to their craft at all stages of the investment, including choosing and structuring the investment, raising funds from other parties at critical junctures, monitoring the investment, offering expert advice and formulating exit strategies.[31]

A comparison of tables 8 and 9 supports this view. Not only were write-off rates substantially lower for early and expansion stage investments by U.S. VCs but, in addition, these investments were more likely to result in an IPO. While the difference in IPO rates may also reflect the greater receptivity of U.S. investors to IPOs, this factor would not account for the difference in write-off rates.

Survey Timing

The Canadian sample ended in 1985, while the U.S. sample ended in 1988. As noted earlier, many of the investments in both the Canadian and U.S. surveys took place in the early 1980s. In venture capital investing, "the lemons ripen within two and a half years while the plums take seven or eight" (Bygrave and Timmons, 1992, p. 13). Had the Canadian study terminated in 1988, then perhaps more of the plums would have ripened and been harvested, lowering the percentage of exits taken as write-offs.[32]

As described above, there was a large influx of inexperienced managers into the Canadian venture capital industry at about the time that the Canadian survey ended. If the Canadian experience was like the U.S. experience, this would have resulted in higher, rather than lower write-off rates in the late 1980s.

Summary

Because of the timing difference in the surveys, the higher write-off rate in Canada is not unambiguous evidence that Canadian venture capital managers were either less experienced than their U.S. counterparts or less skilled, (holding experience constant). Nonetheless, the higher write-off rate in Canada is most consistent with the view that Canadian VCs were less skilled than their U.S. counterparts over the survey periods.

Comparison of Current Canadian and U.S. Survey Results

To update the early survey results just discussed, new surveys were sent to both Canadian and U.S. VCs. The survey was formulated in consultation with, and administered by, Macdonald & Associates in Toronto and Venture Economics in Boston.

In Canada, the questionnaire was mailed to members of the Association of Canadian Venture Capital Companies (ACVCC) and to non-ACVCC VCs identified by Macdonald & Associates. In total, 37 questionnaires were mailed out and 22 VCs responded. The responses covered 134 exits between 1992 and 1995 (inclusive). Given that the questionnaire was mailed in early November 1995, and most of the questionnaires returned in November and December, the results for 1995 are not complete in relation to exits taken in the last two months of 1995. The 134 exits constituted 59 percent of the total universe of exits identified by Macdonald & Associates as having taken place in this period.

The questionnaire data have been supplemented with data covering venture capital exits by members of the ACVCC between 1991 and 1994 (inclusive). (Data for 1995 are not yet available.) These data cover 199 exits by 44 VCs. Unless otherwise indicated, the data discussed below derive from the survey results.

The U.S. questionnaire was sent to members of the American Venture Capital Association. Twenty venture capitalists responded, providing data for 112 exits. The U.S. data were matched in time with the Canadian data, i.e., exits not occurring in the same period of time were discarded.

Geographic Distribution of Exits

Tables 10 and 11 indicate the geographic distribution of exits in Canada and the United States. When compared to the aggregate table presented in MacIntosh (1996), it is apparent that, in the survey data, exits in Ontario and foreign countries are overrepresented, and exits in Quebec underrepresented. The geographic distribution of investments in the United States is broadly similar to the geographic distribution in aggregate industry data compiled by Venture Economics, save for the absence of any exits in New York (VE, 1995, pp. 24-25).

TABLE 10

GEOGRAPHIC DISTRIBUTION OF EXITS IN CANADA

Location	Number	Percentage
British Columbia	13	10
Prairies	17	13
Ontario	49	37
Quebec	30	22
Atlantic	1	1
United States	21	16
Other countries	3	2
Total	134	100

Source: Macdonald & Associates.

SIZE OF INVESTMENTS

TABLES 12 AND 13 INDICATE THE SIZE OF THE AVERAGE INVESTMENT. Note that the Canadian figures are in Canadian dollars, while the U.S. figures are in U.S. dollars. As in the earlier survey, the average investment made by U.S. VCs was somewhat larger than the average investment by Canadian VCs.

INDUSTRY OF PORTFOLIO FIRMS

THE PROPORTION OF INVESTMENTS IN TECHNOLOGY INDUSTRIES (biotechnology, communications, computers, electronics, energy/environmental, industrial automation and medical/health) was 62 percent in the United States and 54 percent in Canada (data not reproduced). The difference between the two countries was mainly due to

TABLE 11

GEOGRAPHIC DISTRIBUTION OF EXITS IN THE UNITED STATES

Location	Number	Percentage
California	26	23
Connecticut	7	6
Illinois	12	11
Massachusetts	28	25
Minnesota	8	7
New Hampshire	6	5
Pennsylvania	6	5
Other states	19	17
Total	112	100

Sources: Venture Economics; Macdonald & Associates.

TABLE 12

FREQUENCY AND PROFITABILITY OF EXITS IN CANADA

Vehicle	Exits		Average Holding Period (Years)	Average Investment (C$000s)	Average IRR (%)
	Number	Percentage			
IPO	36	27	4.73	2,006	21
Acquisition	16	12	5.89	2,643	12
Company buy back	41	31	5.28	997	8
Write-off	27	20	3.08	512	–
Secondary sales	12	9	1.98	662	38
Other	2	1	5.00	3,350	9
Total	134	100	4.53	1,372	16

Notes: IRR: internal rate of return

IPO: initial public offering

Source: Macdonald & Associates.

TABLE 13

FREQUENCY AND PROFITABILITY OF EXITS IN THE UNITED STATES

Vehicle	Exits		Average Holding Period	Average Investment	Average IRR
	Number	Percentage	(Years)	(US$000s)	(%)
IPO	30	27	4.27	1,964	45
Acquisition	29	26	4.34	1,625	23
Company buy back	6	5	3.50	759	49
Write-off	33	29	4.28	1,966	–
Secondary sales	9	8	6.00	462	12
Other[a]	5	4	3.40	1,119	3
Total	112	100	4.35	1,651	25

Notes: [a] One merger and four unknown.

IRR: internal rate of return

IPO: initial public offering

Sources: Venture Economics; Macdonald & Associates.

TABLE 14

PROFITABILITY OF EXITS BY TYPE OF INVESTMENT IN CANADA

Stage	Number	Percentage	Average Holding Period (Years)	Average Cost (C$000s)	Average IRR (%)
Early stage	64	48	5.07	932	17
Expansion	61	46	3.76	1,830	11
Acquisition/buyout	3	2	7.61	426	30
Turnaround	6	4	3.81	1,875	28
All stage	134	100	4.53	1,372	16

Note: IRR: internal rate of return

Source: Macdonald & Associates.

TABLE 15

PROFITABILITY OF EXITS BY TYPE OF INVESTMENT IN THE UNITED STATES

Stage	Number	Percentage	Average Holding Period (Years)	Average Cost (US$000s)	Average IRR (%)
Early stage	72	64	4.28	1,570	27
Expansion	34	30	4.54	1,969	25
Acquisition/buyout	2	2	3.00	1,725	27
Turnaround	4	4	4.25	543	21
All stage	112	100	4.35	1,651	25

Note: IRR: internal rate of return

Sources: Venture Economics; Macdonald & Associates.

higher U.S. investment in the communication and computer industries. The relative proportions of technology and non-technology investments were reasonably close to those in aggregate industry data for Canada and the United States presented in MacIntosh (1996).[33] The aggregate data show that Canadian VCs invested more in technology-related investments from 1991 to 1994 than between 1987 and 1991, and somewhat more than in the 1978 to 1986 period.

In the survey results, the proportion of manufacturing investments was higher in Canada (16 percent) than in the United States (5 percent), but the proportion of consumer-related investments was higher in the United States (28 percent) than in Canada (13 percent).

Nature of Investments

A comparison of aggregate industry data presented in MacIntosh (1996) and tables 14 and 15 indicate that early stage investments are overrepresented in the survey data in both Canada and the United States. This overrepresentation is particularly pronounced in the U.S. data.

Frequency of Exits

General

IPOs

The current survey results show some differences in the relative use of exit methods by Canadian and U.S. VCs. While in the earlier survey, IPO exits were used with greater frequency by U.S. VCs than by Canadian VCs, this is not the case in the current survey. Tables 12 and 13 indicate that both U.S. and Canadian VCs exited 27 percent of their investments via IPOs.

The aggregate Canadian industry data reported in Table 16 indicate that there is a much higher percentage of IPO exits in the survey data (27 percent) than in the aggregate data (16 percent). This may be because VCs with more profitable exits were more likely to respond to the survey, and IPO exits tend to be more profitable exits. If this is the case, the U.S. results should be similarly biased. As a result, the Canadian and U.S. results should still yield useful comparative information about the relative frequency and profitability of exit techniques.

Acquisitions and Buy Backs

While IPOs were used with equal frequency in Canada and the United States, there were substantial differences in the frequency with which other exit techniques were used. Tables 12 and 13 indicate that exit by acquisition was much more common in the United States (26 percent) than in Canada (12 percent). Conversely, company buy backs were used far more often in Canada (31 percent) than in the United States (5 percent).

In Canada, the greater frequency of buy backs, and the lower frequency of acquisitions were common to the earlier and later surveys. Both differences, however, were more pronounced in the current survey.

TABLE 16

FREQUENCY OF CANADIAN EXITS, 1991 TO 1994 (AGGREGATE INDUSTRY DATA)

Vehicle	Number	Percentage
IPO	44	16
Acquisition	31	11
Merger	6	2
Company buy back	107	39
Write-off	59	22
Other	24	9
Total	271	100

Note: IPO: initial public offering

Source: Macdonald & Associates.

Write-Offs

In the earlier surveys, the write-off rate was higher in Canada than in the United States (32 percent vs. 21 percent). This reversed in the current survey. Tables 12 and 13 indicate a higher write-off rate in the United States (29 percent) than in Canada (20 percent). This may be an artifact of the high degree of overrepresentation in the U.S. survey data of early stage investments, which are expected to have a high write-off rate.

Frequency of Exits by Type of Investment

Table 14 indicates that in the survey results, the vast majority of Canadian exits were taken from investments in early and expansion stage financings. While the bulk of venture capital investing in Canada is concentrated in early and expansion stage financings, the aggregate industry data presented in MacIntosh (1996) indicate that acquisition and turnaround investments were underrepresented in the survey data.

The same bias exists in the U.S. survey results; comparing aggregate data in MacIntosh (1996) with Table 15, clearly indicates that acquisition and turnaround (included in "other") transactions were underrepresented in the survey results.

Tables 17 and 18 indicate that the pattern of exits was broadly similar for early and expansion stage investing in Canada and the United States although, in both countries, the write-off rate was higher for early stage investments. This lends further support to the view that early stage investing is riskier than expansion stage investing (the sample of acquisition and turnaround investments is too small in

TABLE 17

FREQUENCY OF EXITS BY STAGE OF INVESTMENT IN CANADA

Vehicle	Early Stage		Expansion		Acquisition Buyout		Turnaround		Total	
	Number	%	Number	%	Number	%	Number	%	Number	%
IPO	19	30	15	25	0	0	2	33	36	27
Acquisition	5	8	10	16	1	33	0	0	16	12
Company buy back	21	33	18	30	2	67	0	0	41	31
Write-off	14	22	9	15	0	0	4	67	27	20
Secondary sales	5	8	7	11	0	0	0	0	12	9
Other	0	0	2	3	0	0	0	0	2	1
Total	64	100	61	100	3	100	6	100	134	100

Note: IPO: initial public offering

Source: Macdonald & Associates.

TABLE 18

FREQUENCY OF EXITS BY STAGE OF INVESTMENT IN THE UNITED STATES

Vehicle	Early Stage		Expansion		Acquisition Buyout		Other		Total	
	Number	%	Number	%	Number	%	Number	%	Number	%
IPO	20	28	9	26	1	50	0	0	30	27
Acquisition	20	28	7	21	0	0	2	50	29	26
Company buy back	1	1	4	12	0	0	1	25	6	5
Write-off	23	32	8	24	1	50	1	25	33	29
Secondary sales	5	7	4	12	0	0	0	0	9	8
Other	3	4	2	6	0	0	0	0	5	4
Total	72	100	34	100	2	100	4	100	112	100

Note: IPO: initial public offering

Sources: Venture Economics; Macdonald & Associates.

either country for meaningful comparisons). However, contrary to the earlier survey, in both countries early stage investments resulted in a slightly higher proportion of IPOs than did expansion stage financings. The difference is not large in either country.

Investment Size and Exit Method

As tables 12 and 13 show, in both Canada and the United States, investments that were exited via IPOs or acquisitions were larger than investments exited by other means. The only exception was write-offs taken by U.S. VCs. The average investment that was written-off was of comparable size to investments exited by IPOs. This contrasts sharply with the experience in Canada, in which investments exited via write-offs were the smallest investments, on average, in the sample.[34]

The data in tables 12 and 13 offer some support to the hypothesized VC exit preferences. It was suggested earlier that investments exited via IPOs and acquisitions are, on average, more successful than investments exited by other means. More successful investments will receive more rounds of financing. On this basis, we would expect IPO and acquisition investments to be the largest investments. However, we would also expect write-offs to receive the least investment. As noted, the latter is the case in the Canadian, but not the U.S., survey data. It is unknown if outliers are responsible for the U.S. result.

In both Canada and the United States, there is a substantial difference in size between exits taken as acquisitions and exits taken as secondary sales. This suggests that exits taken as secondary sales tend to be made after fewer rounds of venture capital financing than acquisition exits. Note, however, that while the average holding period for investments exited via secondary sales in Canada was much shorter than the average holding period for investments exited via acquisitions, that was not the case in the United States.

In both countries, the size of investments repurchased in a buy back was much smaller than the size of investments exited via an IPO or an acquisition. This is consistent with the buy back being an inferior form of exit from living dead investments.

Investor Type and Exit Mechanism

Table 19 indicates the frequency with which Canadian public, private and hybrid funds used different exit methods. Government funds have very high write-off rates. This is not unexpected. Government funds invest in early stage, high-risk technology investments; in many cases, these are firms that have found difficulty securing funding from private venture capital investors. It would be surprising if the write-off rate was not high.

What *is* surprising is the high rate at which government investments were exited via IPOs. The early survey results suggested that early stage investments were less likely than later stage investments to be exited by IPOs. The high IPO rate may reflect the concentration in technology investing; survey results not reproduced here suggest that technology investments are more likely than other forms of investment to result in IPOs.

TABLE 19

FREQUENCY OF EXITS BY INVESTOR TYPE

Investor Type	Mechanism/Vehicle	Number of Exits	%
Corporate	Acquisition	3	30
	Company buy back	4	40
	IPO and subsequent sales	2	20
	Other	1	10
Corporate total		10	100
Government	Acquisition	2	8
	Company buy back	7	27
	IPO and subsequent sales	9	35
	Write-off	8	31
Government total		26	100
Hybrid	Acquisition	4	20
	Company buy back	4	20
	IPO and subsequent sales	4	20
	Secondary sales	5	25
	Write-off	3	15
Hybrid total		20	100
Private independent	Acquisition	7	9
	Company buy back	26	33
	IPO and subsequent sales	21	27
	Other	1	1
	Secondary sales	7	9
	Write-off	16	21
Private independent total		78	100
Total		134	100

Note: IPO: initial public offering

Source: Macdonald & Associates.

Hybrid funds demonstrated no particular exit preferences, while buy backs, IPOs and write-offs dominated the exit sample for private independent funds.

Yearly Variations in Distribution of Exit Types

Tables 20 and 21 disclose that, as in the earlier survey, there were significant variations over time in the relative use of different exit techniques. As discussed earlier, much of this variation is likely attributable to changes in the economic environment.

TABLE 20

FREQUENCY OF EXITS BY YEAR IN CANADA

Vehicle	1992		1993		1994		1995		Total	
	Number	%	Number	%	Number	%	Number	%	Number	%
IPO	5	25	6	19	9	26	16	33	36	27
Acquisition	4	20	5	16	2	6	5	10	16	12
Company buyout	8	40	10	32	9	26	14	29	41	31
Write-off	3	15	7	23	12	35	5	10	27	20
Secondary sales	0	0	1	3	2	6	9	18	12	9
Other	0	0	2	6	0	0	0	0	2	1
Total	20	100	31	100	34	100	49	100	134	100

Note: IPO: initial public offering

Source: Macdonald & Associates.

TABLE 21

FREQUENCY OF EXITS BY YEAR IN THE UNITED STATES

Vehicle	1992		1993		1994		1995		Total	
	Number	%	Number	%	Number	%	Number	%	Number	%
IPO	5	19	10	29	8	28	7	32	30	27
Acquisition	8	30	8	24	9	31	4	18	29	26
Company buyout	2	7	1	3	3	10	0	0	6	5
Write-off	6	22	11	32	1	3	10	45	28	25
Secondary sales	4	15	3	9	6	21	1	5	14	13
Other	2	7	1	3	2	7	0	0	5	4
Total	27	100	34	100	29	100	22	100	112	100

Note: IPO: initial public offering

Sources: Venture Economics; Macdonald & Associates.

PROFITABILITY OF EXITS

Overall

Tables 12 and 13 indicate that, on average, exits by U.S. VCs resulted in an IRR of 25 percent vs. only 16 percent for Canadian VCs. The lower profitability in Canada is consistent with a number of factors identified earlier, including a lower degree of VC specialization, the admixture of public and hybrid funds in the survey data, the comparative absence of strategic acquisition partners, lower risk profile (due to substantially fewer early stage Canadian investments), fewer technology investments and less receptive public markets.

Profitability by Exit Method

Table 12 indicates that secondary sales in Canada were the most profitable form of exit (with an IRR of 38 percent), although comparatively few exits were taken by this method. IPOs were the second most profitable exit method (21 percent), followed by acquisitions (12 percent) and write-offs.

These results can be compared to the aggregate industry data collected in Table 14.[35] While Table 22 indicates only cost and exit value (hold periods were unavailable for calculating IRRs or gain multiples), it nonetheless supplies useful additional information. The data suggest that exits taken as IPOs and acquisitions were very profitable, while buy backs were largely unprofitable. Table 22 offers support to the hypothesized ranking of exit methods by profitability.

In the United States, company buy backs were the most profitable (49 percent). The profitability of IPO exits (45 percent) was approximately the same as that of buy backs, but many more exits (30 of 112) were taken this way. Aside from write-offs, secondary sales were the least profitable exits (12 percent), with acquisitions occupying the middle ground (23 percent).

These results lend strong support to the predicted relationship between exit method and profitability. The only anomaly is the high average profitability of buy backs. It is important to note, however, that the number of exits taken by this method was small (six of 112) and the high average profitability was driven by just two of the six exits taken as buy backs. Thus, it would appear that this anomalous result is driven by outliers.

Tables 23 and 24 shed some additional light on the relative profitability of different types of exits both in Canada and the United States. As in the earlier survey, the U.S. IPO distribution is significantly more skewed to the right than any other exit technique; 41 percent resulted in home runs (exits with IRRs of 51 percent or greater) compared to only 17 percent of buy backs, 17 percent of acquisitions and none of the exits taken as secondary sales or by other methods. As in the earlier sample, IPOs accounted for a disproportionate share of home runs.

In Canada, the distribution of IPOs was also significantly skewed to the right, with 28 percent of IPOs yielding IRRs of 51 percent or better, compared to only 19 percent of acquisitions and 2 percent of buy backs. In sharp contrast to the United States, however, the distribution of secondary sales was even more skewed to the right

TABLE 22

FREQUENCY AND PROFITABILITY OF CANADIAN EXITS BY INVESTMENT STAGE, 1991 TO 1994 (AGGREGATE INDUSTRY DATA)

Vehicle	1991			1992			1993			1994		
	Number	Cost ($M)	Exit Value ($M)	Number	Cost ($M)	Exit Value ($M)	Number	Cost ($M)	Exit Value ($M)	Number	Cost ($M)	Exit Value ($M)
Acquisition	7	14	70	6	15	40	10	30	59	8	26	50
Company buy back	9	21	36	22	26	27	38	30	29	38	32	37
IPO	9	16	36	4	4	19	13	49	71	18	18	78
Merger	0	9	0	1	3	3	0	0	0	5	14	14
Write-off	15	18	0	7	7	0	16	21	0	21	19	0
Other[a]	n/a	n/a	n/a	n/a	n/a	n/a	17	61	116	7	8	9

Notes: [a] Primarily secondary sales, but before 1994, includes sales following an IPO in addition to secondary sales.

n/a: not available

IPO: initial public offering

Source: Macdonald & Associates.

TABLE 23

DISTRIBUTION OF PROFITABILITY BY TYPE OF EXIT IN CANADA

IRR Range	IPO		Buy Back		Acquisition		Secondary	
(%)	Number	%	Number	%	Number	%	Number	%
> 200	1	3	0	0	1	6	1	8
126-200	1	3	0	0	0	0	2	17
76-125	4	11	1	2	0	0	0	0
51-76	4	11	0	0	2	13	2	17
26-50	10	28	2	5	2	13	2	17
16-25	3	8	8	20	1	6	0	0
0-15	10	28	20	49	9	56	3	25
< 0	3	8	10	24	1	6	2	17
Total	36	100	41	100	16	100	12	100

Notes: IPO: initial public offering

IRR: internal rate of return

Source: Macdonald & Associates.

TABLE 24

DISTRIBUTION OF PROFITABILITY BY TYPE OF EXIT IN THE UNITED STATES

IRR Range	IPO		Buy Back		Acquisition		Secondary		Other	
(%)	Number	%	Number	%	Number	%	Number	%	Number	%
> 200	2	7	0	0	0	0	0	0	0	0
126-200	3	10	0	0	2	7	0	0	0	0
76-125	2	7	0	0	0	0	0	0	0	0
51-76	5	17	1	17	3	10	0	0	0	0
26-50	9	30	1	17	2	7	1	11	0	0
16-25	6	20	0	0	6	21	0	0	1	20
0-15	2	7	4	67	11	38	3	33	3	60
< 0	1	3	0	0	5	17	5	56	1	20
Total	30	100	6	100	29	100	9	100	5	100

Notes: IPO: initial public offering

IRR: internal rate of return

Sources: Venture Economics; Macdonald & Associates.

than that of IPOs, with 42 percent of secondary sales resulting in returns of 51 percent or better. It should be noted, that there were twice as many home runs through IPOs (10) than through secondary sales (five). Moreover, the number of secondary sales (12) was small, and the large number of secondary sale home runs may be an artifact of the survey data rather than a result with general implications. Nonetheless, this is an unexpected result.

Profitability by Stage of Investment

Tables 14 and 15 indicate the profitability of investments by stage of investment. The results are meaningful only for early and expansion stage investments, given the small number of acquisition and turnaround investments in both Canada and the United States. If early stage investments are more risky than expansion investments, as hypothesized, they should yield a higher return on average. In the United States, returns on early stage investments were only marginally greater than returns on expansion stage investments. In Canada, the difference was more pronounced.

Table 25 indicates that in Canada, more expansion stage investments (20 percent) resulted in home runs than did early stage investments (11 percent). In the United States, (Table 26) early and expansion stage investments accounted for an identical share of home runs (15 percent).

Overall, these results offer weak support to the view that early stage investments are riskier than expansion stage investments.

Profitability of Exits Taken by Different Types of Canadian Venture Capital Funds

Table 27 presents the profitability of Canadian exits by investor type, using aggregate industry data. It was not possible to calculate IRRs for these data, given that hold periods were unavailable for some investments. Nonetheless, the data strongly suggest that hybrid and government funds were not nearly as profitable as private funds (corporate financial, corporate industrial and private independent funds). While private funds generated substantial profits on their investments, public and hybrid funds appeared to do little better than break even.

Table 27 offers support to the hypothesis that government and hybrid funds will exhibit a lower degree of profitability than private funds. This, in turn, lends support to the view that the Canadian venture capital data (with an admixture of government and hybrid funds) can be expected to show a lower degree of profitability than the U.S. data, which includes only private funds.

Profitability by Year of Exit

Tables 28 and 29 indicate some divergence in the profitability of exits by year in Canada and the United States. In Canada, exits taken in 1995 were the most profitable, and those taken in 1992, 1993 and 1994 were of about equal profitability. In the United States, exits taken in 1995 were the least profitable, with some variation in the profitability of exits taken in 1992, 1993 and 1994.

TABLE 25

DISTRIBUTION OF PROFITABILITY BY STAGE OF INVESTMENT IN CANADA

IRR Range	Early Stage		Expansion		Acquisition/Buyout		Turnaround	
(%)	Number	%	Number	%	Number	%	Number	%
> 200	1	2	2	3	0	0	0	0
126-200	0	0	3	5	0	0	0	0
76-125	2	3	3	5	0	0	0	0
51-76	4	6	4	7	0	0	0	0
26-50	5	8	7	11	2	67	2	33
16-25	6	9	6	10	1	33	0	0
0-15	22	34	21	34	0	0	0	0
< 0	24	38	15	25	0	0	4	67
Total	64	100	61	100	3	100	6	100

Note: IRR: internal rate of return

Source: Macdonald & Associates.

TABLE 26

DISTRIBUTION OF PROFITABILITY BY STAGE OF INVESTMENT IN THE UNITED STATES

IRR Range	Early Stage		Expansion		Acquisition/Buyout		Other	
(%)	Number	%	Number	%	Number	%	Number	%
> 200	1	1	1	3	0	0	0	0
126-200	4	6	1	3	0	0	0	0
76-125	1	1	1	3	0	0	0	0
51-76	5	7	2	6	1	50	1	25
26-50	9	13	5	15	0	0	0	0
16-25	8	11	4	12	0	0	0	0
0-15	13	18	8	24	0	0	2	50
< 0	31	43	12	35	1	50	1	25
Total	72	100	34	100	2	100	4	100

Note: IRR: internal rate of return

Sources: Venture Economics; Macdonald & Associates.

TABLE 27

FREQUENCY AND PROFITABILITY OF CANADIAN EXITS BY INVESTOR TYPE, 1991 TO 1994 (AGGREGATE INDUSTRY DATA)

	1991			1992			1993			1994		
	Number	Cost ($M)	Exit Value ($M)	Number	Cost ($M)	Exit Value ($M)	Number	Cost ($M)	Exit Value ($M)	Number	Cost ($M)	Exit Value ($M)
Corporate[a]	9	14	27	7	13	10	15	74	135	2	1	3
Government	6	17	19	10	10	16	24	9	9	22	14	16
Hybrid	4	6	4	1	4	10	5	7	5	30	44	42
Private independent	21	33	93	24	28	53	50	102	125	43	61	128
Total	40	70	143	42	55	89	94	192	274	97	119	168

Note: [a] Includes corporate financial and corporate industrial

Source: Macdonald & Associates.

TABLE 28

PROFITABILITY OF EXITS BY YEAR IN CANADA

	Number of Exits	Average Holding Period (Years)	Average Investment (C$000s)	Average IRR (%)
1992	20	4.60	1,423	10
1993	31	4.10	1,340	11
1994	34	3.97	1,279	12
1995	49	5.17	1,435	20
All years	134	4.53	1,372	16

Note: IRR: internal rate of return

Source: Macdonald & Associates.

Profitability by Extent of Disposition

There is reason to believe that partial exits should be more profitable than full exits. In general, once the VC's skill set is exhausted, it is time to "cash out" and move on. However, when the firm has good future prospects, the VC may be unable to cash out at a price which fairly reflects the true prospects of the firm. This is a consequence of the VC's informational advantage over potential purchasers. In the face of this information asymmetry, a purchaser will rationally conclude that there is some probability that the VC is selling his or her interest only because the investment lacks promise. The price will be discounted accordingly. When the VC

TABLE 29

PROFITABILITY OF EXITS BY YEAR IN THE UNITED STATES

	Number of Exits	Average Holding Period (Years)	Average Investment (US$000s)	Average IRR (%)
1992	27	3.81	1,518	23
1993	34	4.15	1,237	32
1994	29	4.34	2,246	27
1995	22	5.32	1,702	5
All years	112	4.35	1,651	25

Note: IRR: internal rate of return

Sources: Macdonald & Associates.

TABLE 30

PROFITABILITY BY EXTENT OF DISPOSITION IN CANADA

	Number of Exits	Average Holding Period (Years)	Average Investment (C$000s)	Average IRR (%)
Partial	35	5.41	1,219[a]	21
Full	99	4.13	1,353	13
Total	134	4.53	1,372	16

Notes: [a] Excludes one large transaction.

IRR: internal rate of return

Source: Macdonald & Associates.

retains an ownership interest in the firm, it signals the VC's confidence in the future of the firm and results in a more favourable exit price (Leland and Pyle, 1977).

The VC might also make a partial exit when the firm does not have good prospects. However, even if this results in a better price for the shares sold in the partial exit, making only a partial exit condemns the VC to remain involved in a losing investment. In short, ownership retention is more costly when the firm has poor prospects. This is what makes the ownership retention signal credible. Hence, partial exits should result in higher average profitability than full exits.

Tables 30 and 31 offer some support to this hypothesis. In Canada, partial dispositions of investments resulted in greater profits (21 percent) than full dispositions (13 percent). While this was also true in the United States, the difference was small (29 percent vs. 25 percent).

TABLE 31

PROFITABILITY BY EXTENT OF DISPOSITION IN THE UNITED STATES

	Number of Exits	Average Holding Period (Years)	Average Investment (US$000s)	Average IRR (%)
Partial	25	4.96	1,347	29
Full	87	4.17	1,747	25
Total	112	4.35	1,651	25

Note: IRR: internal rate of return

Sources: Venture Economics; Macdonald & Associates.

TABLE 32

REASONS FOR EXIT IN CANADA

	Number of Exits	Average Holding Period (Years)	Average Investment (C$000s)	Average IRR (%)
Pre-planned	35	6.2	2,262	16
Market conditions	35	3.41	1,321	23
Unsolicited offer	27	5.57	1,405	13
Others	37	3.78	555	–
Total	134	4.53	1,372	16

Note: IRR: internal rate of return

Source: Macdonald & Associates.

Reasons for Exit and Profitability of Investments

The survey asked VCs to identify their reasons for making exits. The Canadian and U.S. survey results showed some differences in this respect. Table 32 indicates that in the Canadian survey, 26 percent of exits were designated as "pre-planned." The profitability of pre-planned exits was the same as the mean return of the sample.

In the United States, (Table 33) the percentage of exits that were pre-planned was similar (30 percent), but their profitability was greater than the mean of the sample (34 percent vs. 25 percent).

TABLE 33

REASONS FOR EXIT IN THE UNITED STATES

	Number of Exits	Average Holding Period (Years)	Average Investment (US$000s)	Average IRR (%)
Pre-planned	34	4.76	1,675	34
Market conditions	39	3.82	1,688	8
Unsolicited offer	10	4.00	1,675	38
Others	24	4.92	1,160	17
Unknown	5	3.60	3,860	49
Total	112	4.35	1,651	25

Note: IRR: internal rate of return

Sources: Venture Economics; Macdonald & Associates.

In the United States, more exits were taken in response to market conditions than in Canada (35 percent vs. 26 percent). However, in the United States, those exits were much less profitable than the mean (8 percent vs. 25 percent), while in Canada such exits were more profitable than the mean (23 percent vs. 16 percent).

Exits in response to unsolicited offers were more frequent in Canada than in the United States (20 percent vs. 9 percent). But in Canada, they were slightly less profitable than the mean (13 percent vs. 16 percent), while in the United States they were substantially more profitable than the mean (38 percent vs. 25 percent).

SUMMARY AND CONCLUSIONS

What Explains Venture Capital Exits?

Earlier, it was suggested that IPOs should be the most attractive form of exit for venture capitalists, followed by acquisitions, secondary sales, buy backs, and write-offs. The data support the view that IPOs are the most profitable form of exit. Both in Canada and the United States, more home runs resulted from IPOs than from any other form of exit, although in Canada (contrary to expectations), secondary sales also accounted for a significant number of home runs. In the current survey data, IPO exits were used with equal frequency in Canada and the United States. This is a marked change from the earlier survey, in which IPOs were used by Canadian VCs with only about half the frequency of that in the United States.

The evidence suggests an interesting puzzle relating primarily to IPOs. As noted, IPOs accounted for a disproportionate share of venture capital home runs. It was not clear, however, if the aggregate distribution of returns was extremely skewed to the right, or if there were two distinct distributions of returns: write-offs plus living dead, and home runs. This intriguing puzzle deserves further investigation.

The evidence offers mixed support to the above predictions about the comparable profitability of other forms of exit. In the earlier Canadian survey, buy backs were the second most profitable form of exit, followed by acquisitions. No separate data were available concerning secondary sales. In the earlier U.S. survey, acquisitions, buy backs and secondary sales were about equally profitable, although acquisitions were used with greater frequency than secondary sales or buy backs. In the later Canadian survey as well as in the aggregate industry data, buy backs were frequently used but were the least profitable form of exit. In the later U.S. survey, buy backs were the most profitable form of exit, but were almost never used, and the high average profitability was driven by just two very profitable buy backs. The low frequency with which this exit technique is used in the United States supports the view that it is regarded as an inferior form of exit.

Both the earlier and later surveys suggest that buy backs were used with greater frequency in Canada than in the United States. Preliminary inquiries suggested that tax factors are not responsible for this difference, although further investigation is in order. It may be that the high Canadian buy back rate reflects the comparative lack of strategic acquirers in Canada. This would make acquisition exits less likely, and increase the relative frequency of buy backs. The fact that in both surveys acquisitions were used with greater frequency in the United States than in Canada adds some credence to this view.

The U.S. evidence is fairly supportive of the hypothesis that acquisitions are a more profitable form of exit than secondary sales. In the earlier U.S. survey, acquisitions and secondary sales were equally profitable, but acquisitions were used more frequently. In the later U.S. survey, acquisitions were significantly more profitable than secondary sales and were used with a much higher frequency.

The Canadian evidence, however, is not supportive. While data on secondary sales were not available from the earlier survey, in the later Canadian survey secondary sales were the most profitable means of exit. Moreover, the number of exits taken as secondary sales (12) was not very different from the number of exits taken as acquisitions (16). Further, after IPOs, there were more home runs via secondary sales than by any other exit technique. This result is puzzling.

The evidence did not offer great support to the view that acquisitions are more profitable than buy backs. Acquisitions were only slightly more profitable than buy backs in the earlier U.S. survey, and substantially less profitable than buy backs in the earlier Canadian survey. In the later U.S. survey, acquisitions were also less profitable than buy backs, but were used with a higher frequency. In the later Canadian survey, acquisitions were somewhat more profitable than buy backs, but were used less often.

The percentage of exits taken as write-offs also showed some differences between the two countries. In the earlier period, the frequency of write-offs was about 50 percent higher in Canada than in the United States. In the later period, this result was almost exactly reversed, with the U.S. write-off rate about 50 percent higher than the Canadian rate. The later result may be an artifact of the greater frequency of early stage investing in the U.S. data.

There appears to be little consistency in the data, either cross-sectionally or over time. A larger data sample stretching over a longer period might be more useful in testing the hypotheses advanced above. The need for a larger data sample is also suggested by the high degree of variation over time in both the chosen means of exit and the profitability of VC investments.

Have Canadian VCs Become More Skilled Over Time?

Earlier, it was argued that aggregate industry data and early survey results support the view that Canadian VCs are less skilled than their U.S. counterparts. However, write-off rates declined substantially from the earlier to the later survey. Further, in the later survey, more portfolio firms and, in particular, firms that first received funds in their early stages, were brought to the public market.

Venture capital investing is a young industry in Canada. As in the United States, substantial funds were not committed to the venture capital industry until the early 1980s. It is natural to expect that as venture capital managers gain experience in picking portfolio companies, shepherding them through the growth process, securing other sources of funding and choosing appropriate exit techniques, they will become better at what they do. Experience is a vital ingredient in venture capital investing, and experienced managers are likely to be more capable managers.

One difficulty in disentangling evidence relating to profitability is that a large number of factors affect the profitability of venture capital funds. Some of these factors are purely cyclical in nature, while others reflect long-term trends. This section briefly looks at some of these factors.

The aggregate industry data presented in MacIntosh (1996) showed that the proportion of technology-related investing in Canada has climbed quite rapidly in recent years. Moreover, like their U.S. counterparts, Canadian VCs are starting to specialize in technology investing, and even in particular areas of the technology spectrum. Specialization and skill go hand in hand.

A comparison of early and latter survey results initially suggests that the average profitability of venture capital investments declined from the early to the later period. However, as Poitevin pointed out in his comment on an early draft of this paper, returns in both surveys are based on nominal dollar amounts. Poitevin suggested that, accounting for inflation, real profitability was approximately the same in both survey periods. Because the environment for venture capital investing was less welcoming over the later than the earlier survey period, this suggests that Canadian venture capitalists have become more skilled. In general, the profitability of Canadian firms was poor in the 1992 to 1995 period. Canadian firms have struggled to overcome the effects of the recession that plagued both Canada and the United States in the early 1990s. Indeed, in the early 1990s, investing in the stock market lagged investment in t-bills. Viewed against this background, the returns to venture capital investing in the later survey period are cast in a more favourable light.

There is, however, reason to believe that the average skill level of venture capital managers has varied cyclically (and not merely increased linearly) over time. As indicated above, the mid-1980s was a period of rapid growth in the Canadian venture capital industry, and it seems likely that (as in the United States) many inexperienced managers were hired by venture capital funds. If the Canadian experience was like that in the United States, many of these managers made poor investments. To the extent that these investments resulted in exits in the survey period, they would have an adverse impact on overall profitability.

The late 1980s and early 1990s, however, witnessed a substantial shake out in the venture capital industry in Canada. New capital in 1989 dropped to $200 million from $600 million the year before and stayed at that level in 1990. Indeed, netting out profits returned to investors and new funds raised, there was a net outflow of funds in 1990 and 1991.[36] Anecdotal evidence suggests that declining fund profitability was the cause of reduced financial commitments from institutional investors. This shake out is likely to have eliminated the weaker venture capital managers and left only the more capable ones. To the extent that investments by these more capable managers are reflected in the survey data, this should result in enhanced profits over the survey period. Indeed, because fewer managers were chasing attractive deals, i.e., the demand for investments diminished relative to their supply, the average deal price should have declined, enhancing profitability.

Superimposed on these cyclical factors are a number of long-term trends including the supply of quality investments. It may be that the supply of these investments was greater from 1975 to 1985 than from 1992 to 1995. During the earlier period, the venture capital industry was still young. Given that VCs supply funds typically not available from other suppliers of capital, it is not unreasonable to suppose that there was a backlog of quality projects awaiting funding. The large inflow of funds in the early and mid-1980s would have reduced or eliminated this backlog, resulting in greater competition among funds for deals in the later 1980s and early 1990s.[37] Increasing competition would increase the average deal price, resulting in reduced profitability. This factor is long term, rather than cyclical in nature.

Gompers (1994, pp. 13-15) suggested that increasing institutional investment in venture capital funds in the early to mid-1980s resulted in pressure for venture capital managers to achieve short-term results. As a consequence, many venture capital managers made unwise investment decisions. Institutional pressure may also have affected the profitability of the venture fund industry in Canada. In the upsurge of venture capital investing in the mid-1980s, much of the new capital originated with pension funds.

The argument that institutional investors are responsible for inducing a short-term focus in their investees, however, remains speculative. There is evidence that institutional investors do not inappropriately discount the long-term prospects of the firms in which they invest.[38] Thus, Gompers' argument may be overstated.

Other factors may have played a role in putting downward pressure on venture capital profits over the later survey period. In particular, in the last three decades Canadian product markets have become significantly more competitive. The high-technology business (the focus of much venture capital investing) has matured, and the number of competitors in areas such as computer hardware and software and biotechnology has increased substantially. The free trade agreements, as well as the General Agreement on Tariffs and Trade, have played a role in rendering Canadian markets more competitive. These agreements have opened up many Canadian markets to U.S. and Mexican competitors.

The balance between private and hybrid funds started to change dramatically at the start of the 1990s. The first such fund (Fond de solidarité des travailleurs du Québec) was created only in 1983. Hybrid funds grew from 17 percent of the industry in 1989 to 48 percent in 1994 (MacIntosh, 1996, Table 5). If such funds are less profitable than private funds (as preliminary evidence suggests), this would clearly diminish the profitability of the Canadian venture capital industry in the later survey period. The increasing dominance of the LSVCCs in Canadian venture capital investing suggests that the overall profitability of the industry may be depressed for many years to come.

In short, there is no easy answer to the question "Have Canadian VCs become more skilled over time?" The answer is partly yes and partly no. There are many more experienced venture capital managers in the industry now than in the 1970s or 1980s. Among the experienced managers, skill levels are likely to have increased. However, the growth of the venture capital industry in Canada has resulted in many inexperienced managers being hired in recent years. Among these new and inexperienced managers, skill levels are likely to be low.

The divergence in the objectives and profitability of the different types of funds in Canada strongly suggests that future examinations of the Canadian venture capital industry should differentiate, as much as possible, between different types of funds.[39]

POLICY IMPLICATIONS

GENERAL

THE EVIDENCE PRESENTED IN THIS PAPER ADDS SUPPORT TO THE VIEW that IPOs are central to the venture capital process. On average, IPOs are more profitable than other means of exit. Moreover, venture capital returns are largely driven by home runs, and more home runs take place through IPOs than through any other means of exit. Clearly, a healthy IPO market is important for the venture capital industry. This emphasizes the importance of ensuring that regulatory hurdles to accessing public markets are cost-effective and not unduly onerous. It also emphasizes the importance of healthy secondary trading markets (i.e., the stock exchanges and over-the-counter markets). There is an inextricable link between primary and secondary markets. Typically, securities can be sold into the public markets only if investors can anticipate some degree of secondary market liquidity.[40] Moreover, once the firm goes public, secondary markets provide valuable information about how subsequent equity offerings should be priced. Thus, it is just as important to ensure that regulatory requirements in secondary markets are as cost-effective as those in primary markets.

There is, however, evidence that in the longer term (three to six years) IPOs are (on average) overpriced. This is disturbing, since overpricing is evidence of allocative inefficiency. If IPOs are overpriced, the IPO market may be privately remunerative for VCs and other early stage investors, but costly from a broader social perspective. At first blush, this suggests that additional regulation should be aimed at curtailing IPO overpricing, whether through additional mandatory disclosure, merit regulation or other means. The most recent U.S. evidence suggests that the overpricing observed in IPO markets is primarily associated with small non-venture-backed IPOs sold to retail investors. If so, then any additions to the regulatory apparatus should be directed solely at that sector of the IPO market.

Even in relation to very small IPOs sold to retail investors, it is questionable whether additional regulation can cure the problem. If emotion and excitement drive the retail market, rather than investment fundamentals, then it is not obvious that additional disclosure of investment fundamentals will make any difference. Moreover, because regulators are not well positioned to evaluate new issues, merit regulation is likely to be a clumsy and ineffective tool in preventing only overpriced issues from going to market. The only truly effective means of preventing overpricing would be a ban on sales of IPOs in very small firms. Such a ban would likely do more harm than good.

There is much to support Loughran and Ritter's (1993) view that many investors purchase new issues in primary markets because they dream of purchasing the next Microsoft. This view is given a good deal of credence by recent events in Canada's junior resource markets. The enormous success of two junior mining companies – Bre-X Minerals and Diamond Fields Resources – has given a boost to the entire junior mining sector (Northfield, 1996). Diamond Fields is reported to have discovered a "mammoth nickel deposit" in Voisey Bay in Labrador, while Bre-X made an equally impressive gold discovery in Indonesia. Writing in *The Globe and Mail*, Northfield (1996, p. B1) quoted one mining promoter as stating that: "The hype at the moment is unbelievable.... The comment I keep getting is that we don't want to miss another Voisey Bay."

In the same article, Northfield further reported that:

> Fuelled by dreams of riding the next stock rocket to untold riches, investors have developed an insatiable appetite for junior exploration plays. Each day, it seems, a different junior stock blips up on Bay Street's radar screens and gets propelled to nosebleed levels. Some investor are getting fabulously wealthy, others, inevitably, will lose their shirts.

While citing several changes in underlying fundamentals that might make junior mining plays more attractive, *The Globe and Mail* article opined that "none of that really matters. The only things that really matter are Diamond Fields Resources Ltd., and Bre-X Minerals Ltd." (Northfield, 1996, p. B1). The power of regulation to contain such speculative binges appears to be limited.

Indeed, markets for junior issues are far from unregulated at present. A great deal of mandatory disclosure is required in primary markets, and Canadian securities regulators have a very broad mandate to intervene on merit grounds to prevent an issue from going forward if they object to particular features of the offering.[41]

It should be noted that Simon (1989) found evidence supporting the view that the mandatory disclosure introduced by the *Securities Act of 1933* in the United States significantly improved the returns realized by investors in small IPOs (but not subsequent equity offerings) floated over regional stock exchanges. Simon's evidence demonstrates that the introduction of mandatory disclosure was useful in 1933 – not that additional mandatory disclosure (or other regulation) would be useful in 1996. It may be that any gains from mandatory disclosure have already been exploited, and that additional disclosure would accomplish little or nothing. Moreover, securities markets are significantly more institutionalized than in 1933. Sophisticated institutional buyers are more likely to play a key role in pricing small IPOs floated over regional exchanges. If Simon's evidence is to be taken as confirmation that mandatory disclosure assists retail buyers in evaluating new offerings, then such disclosure is likely to be of assistance only in relation to the smallest (i.e., less than $10 million) IPOs in which there is no substantial institutional component.

Whatever the policy implications for securities markets, one thing is clear. More research should be undertaken into the long-term overpricing of IPOs. While

Jog's research ("Climate" this volume) strongly suggests that it is not just retail investors who tend to overvalue IPO offerings, more direct evidence would be helpful.

The evidence also indicates that buy backs are used with a greater frequency in Canada, and acquisitions with a lower frequency compared to the United States. The comparative dearth of acquisition exits is troubling, given that this form of exit can generate handsome gains for VCs. It may be that there is little that government policy can do to correct the situation – at least in the short term. The lack of strategic partners in Canada is likely a product of the fact that Canadian markets are smaller and less developed than those in the Untied States. Nonetheless, policy makers should be aware that factors which create a more vibrant, competitive large firm sector will also indirectly affect small firms, by furnishing more possible strategic partners and more potentially profitable opportunities for venture capital exits.

Differences between the Canadian and U.S. Venture Capital Industries and an Agenda for Further Research

One primary purpose of this paper was to compare the Canadian and U.S. venture capital industries, especially in relation to exit strategies. There is both utility and peril in making intercountry comparisons. The utility arises from the identification of differences in exit techniques between Canadian and U.S. VCs. For example, Canadian VCs use buy backs with much greater frequency, and acquisitions with much lower frequency than U.S. VCs. This is a cause of some concern, since the buy back appears to be a less preferred form of exit.

The identification of differences is only the first step in addressing the policy issue, however. Differences in exit methods may arise from market, regulatory or taxation factors, or from some combination of all three. It is unlikely that univariate explanations tell the whole story. Some of the more important differences, and some possible policy implications, are briefly summarized below.

VC Specialization

Canadian VCs have funded both traditional and high-technology businesses. They have also tended to be generalists, rather than specializing in any particular industrial sector. By contrast, U.S. VCs have concentrated more heavily on the funding of high-technology businesses. They have also tended, more than their Canadian counterparts, to be specialists, focusing their efforts on one particular industrial sector (such as computers, biotechnology, etc.). I have argued that this specialization is likely to result in higher value added returns to the investee enterprise.

Does this have policy implications? Can the government affect the degree of venture capital specialization and hence increase the returns to venture capital investing? In my view, the answer in each case is no. The degree of venture capital specialization is most probably a product of economies of scale. A VC situated in Silicon Valley, for example, can afford to specialize in computer hardware or software because of the abundance of computer-related entrepreneurial activity in that region. A VC in Toronto, by comparison, must consider a wider range of industrial sectors because of the comparative absence of concerted entrepreneurial effort in any one sector. As the Canadian market grows, Canadian VCs will be increasingly able to exploit economies of scale, and VC specialization will become more common. This process is already under way, and government efforts to promote specialization do not seem to be indicated.

Underwriter Specialization

There is little systematic evidence on the comparative nature of Canadian and U.S. underwriting industries. However, anecdotal evidence suggests that in the United States, there are proportionately more underwriters willing to bring small and medium-sized firms to the public market than in Canada. While Canada does not entirely lack for underwriters willing to service the small end of the market (*Profit*, 1994), the Economic Council of Canada (1982, p. 29) reported that:

> while there are about four times as many national brokers in the United States as in Canada, there are about 34 times as many regional brokers (2,887 compared with 86 in Canada). Regional broker-dealers are crucial to the secondary and the initial-public-offering markets because they manage the majority of small offerings. In the 1972-80 period, regional broker-dealers managed 79 per cent of all initial public offerings in the United States and 92 per cent of the offerings of issues of less than $10 million in annual sales. In Canada, about three-quarters of the initial public offerings of industrial shares under $2 million in the 1970-72 period were managed by regional broker-dealers.

This research from the early 1980s has not been updated. However, anecdotal evidence suggests that in the last decade many regional dealers have been bought up by the national dealers and integrated into the latter's national operations. The large national dealers are typically not interested in public offerings of less than $15 million or $25 million.

Anecdotal evidence also suggests that U.S. underwriters play a more active role than their Canadian counterparts *after* a small firm goes public, functioning either as market makers, i.e., standing ready to buy or sell the firm's shares for their own account, or price quoters. Because the anticipation of secondary market liquidity is an important inducement in effecting primary market sales, the willingness of underwriters to play this dual role tends to ensure greater access to the primary market for small firms. The U.S. market is also characterized by the existence of niche underwriters that service the high-technology market; there are no such players in Canada (MacIntosh, 1994).

While it is possible that regulatory factors have played a role, these differences may again simply reflect the comparative size of the two economies. The greater concentration of small firm underwritings in particular regions of the United States allows underwriters to exploit economies of scale. Given the importance of the

IPO to the venture capital process, further research should be undertaken on the comparative structures of the underwriting industries in Canada and the United States.

Economies of Scale in the Product Market

Canada's product market is small compared to the United States (the "one-tenth" rule of thumb applies). This has important implications for the development of small firms. As the Premier's Council (Ontario, 1988, Vol. 1, p. 171) stated, the smallness of the Canadian market can frequently mean that Canadian companies "must begin exporting their product without the benefit of a solid domestic sales base." The U.S. market is sufficiently large that American firms do not suffer this disadvantage. This is yet another reason for believing that U.S. VCs should generate more profits than their Canadian counterparts. From a policy perspective, it stresses the need for openness in Canada's trade policy. Many small, technology-based companies must tap into foreign markets to survive and grow. The door must be kept open for them.

Tax Incentives

A number of U.S. commentators have detailed various changes to the tax structure in the United States which gave an enormous impetus to the development of the venture capital industry in the late 1970s and early 1980s (Bygrave and Timmons, 1992, pp. 23-25; Gompers, 1994, pp. 10-13). The tax structure in the United States has also affected the VC's choice of organizational form; 80 percent of venture capital firms are organized as limited partnerships.[42]

Aside from research into the effects of Quebec's QSSP, little or no research has been done in Canada on the effect of the tax structure on venture capital financing. Research is clearly warranted.

The Supply of New Technologies

VCs must necessarily rely on others to produce the ideas they fund. There is good reason to believe that the supply of new technologies has been greater in the United States than in Canada. Gompers (1994, p. 22) noted that "[m]any technologies and companies have been spawned from large corporations as a by-product of government-funded research.... Spending on space and defense research created the electronics, modern communication, and computer industries."

Lacking major space or defence-related initiatives, spending on research and development (R & D) by the Canadian government has been much more modest (Ontario, 1988, Vol. 1, pp. 145-147) (although the government has provided generous tax incentives for R & D) (Kastner, 1995, p. 289).

Moreover, even aside from space and defence-related expenditures, U.S. firms have historically done more R & D than Canadian firms (Ontario, 1988, Vol. 3, pp. 186-187, 191-193). Canada has a resource-based economy. While resource-based firms may innovate in various ways to reduce their costs of production, a resource-driven economy is likely to produce fewer innovations than an economy built on an industrial base. Further, Canada's economy has historically been a "branch plant" economy. R & D work has often been done by foreign parent corporations, rather than in Canada. The less abundant supply of new technologies has been a factor in the tendency of Canadian VCs to be generalists and not specialists.

Government spending and tax incentives for R & D are not the only way in which the government can influence the supply of new technologies. Experience suggests that there is an interaction between the entrepreneurial and venture capital communities in which each contributes to the growth of the other. Where there is an active venture capital community, entrepreneurs are encouraged to develop innovations, knowing that sources of funding are likely to be available. And VCs are likely to situate where there is a good supply of innovations. Innovators and VCs flourish together in symbiotic communities such as the Route 128 area in Boston, Silicon Valley in California and, in Canada, in the Ottawa-Carleton and Waterloo-Guelph areas. Such communities almost always centre around universities, which have proved a fertile source for many innovative ideas. The government should give further attention to the issue of how it can foster and promote the growth of symbiotic university-venture capitalist relationships, in order to foster the growth of more symbiotic high-technology communities in Canada.

Regulatory Environment

VCs are subject to a variety of regulations that affect the cost of carrying on business. Securities regulatory requirements, for example, have a significant impact on the cost of taking a firm public (MacIntosh, 1994). Securities regulatory requirements also affect other types of investors, such as angel and love capital investors (MacIntosh, 1994). This has an indirect impact on VCs. If fledgling firms cannot surmount the seed and start-up stages because of an inability to tap love capital or angel investors, they may never get to the stage when a VC can provide further funding.

There is some evidence that the regulatory environment in the United States is more accommodating to small firms than that in Canada (MacIntosh, 1994). Further study should be undertaken of the impact of securities regulatory requirements on small firms and on the venture capital community, in order to ensure that the regulatory burden is not excessive.

Governance Structures of Venture Capital Funds

Governance structures of U.S. venture capital organizations have been extensively studied (Sahlman, 1990; Bygrave and Timmons, 1992). In general, there are three agency problems. The first arises from the relationship between fund investors and fund managers. The last two arise from the relationship between fund managers and entrepreneurs. As Sahlman pointed out, in some contexts the entrepreneur can be regarded as the agent and the VC as the principal. In others, the VC assumes the role of agent, and the entrepreneur that of principal.

There is little research into the governance structures of Canadian venture capital organizations, at any of these three levels. However, anecdotal evidence suggests that there may be differences between Canadian and U.S. funds in organizational structures and compensation schedules for the venture capital managers. Both LSVCCs and government funds have unique governance structures. More research is clearly warranted.

Secondary Market Liquidity and Institutional Investor Appetite for Small Firms

The liquidity of secondary market trading is an important determinant of the ability of small firms to sell securities in the primary market. While the empirical record is slender, there is some reason to believe that secondary market trading mechanisms offer investors in small firms greater liquidity in the United States than in Canada. This may result from differing appetites of institutional investors for small firms. Canadian institutions are often said to be more risk averse than U.S. institutions, and less predisposed either to buying small firm IPOs or to trading small firms in the secondary markets.

Institutional trading creates a public good, in the sense that an institutional decision to buy or sell creates an opportunity for a trader on the other side of the market. By creating liquidity, institutional activity in secondary markets also facilitates public offerings by small firms. This emphasizes the importance of regulating institutional purchases in a manner which does not restrict the purchase of small firms.[43]

It also suggests further avenues for research. Is it true that Canadian institutions have been more reluctant purchasers of small firm securities? To date, no analysis has been undertaken of the nature of institutional portfolios in Canada and the comparative willingness of institutions in Canada and the United States to purchase shares in smaller firms. Nor has any analysis been undertaken of the comparable efficiency and liquidity of the regional stock exchanges in the United States and Canada, and their ability to contribute to a low cost of capital for new issuers. Again, further research is warranted.

Endnotes

1 MacMillan et al. (1985, p. 126). Also divided the universe of VCs into three groups: "purposeful risk managers," "determined eclectics" and "parachutists." For the latter, the availability of a reliable exit mechanism was controlling. In the absence of liquidity, such investors would decline to invest in a particular project, p. 128.

2 Carter and Van Auken, (1994, p. 60). See also Kahn (1987, p. 193); Bruno and Tyebjee, (1985, p. 61).

3 The definitions that follow are reproduced verbatim from Macdonald & Associates (1992, pp. 8-9). These definitions are used both in Canada and the United States. See VE (1988, Appendix A). The use of the term "stage" may be somewhat misleading, in that acquisition or turnaround financing may be supplied at a variety of different stages in a company's development.

4 Amit et al. (this volume) make a similar finding. Between 1991 and 1995, seed capital investments constituted only about 2.5 percent of all venture capital investments.

5 This growth is purely tax driven. Before the most recent federal budget, investors in LSVCCs received a 20 percent provincial plus a 20 percent federal tax credit on an investment of up to $5,000. Under the March 1996 federal budget, the government's tax credit is now 15 percent on a maximum investment of $3,500.

6 I have also benefited greatly from Michel Poitevin's perceptive suggestions on the determinants of venture capital exit strategies.

7 These risks are described in Sahlman (1990); MacIntosh (1994).

8 Ontario Securities Commission Policy 9.1. These rules will apply to most venture-backed private companies. See MacIntosh (1994, pp. 131-133). In this respect, the rules in the United States are typically less demanding.

9 By contrast, the reverse takeover, a close cousin of the IPO, does not automatically result in the raising of new capital (although in practice a fresh infusion of capital will usually occur in connection with this type of transaction).

10 Ritter (1991, p. 23). Loughran (1993) also found similar results for a sample of NASDAQ IPOs, in the six years following the offering.

11 Ritter (1991); Levis (1993); Loughran and Ritter (1993); Loughran (1993); Jog, "Climate" (this volume). The study by Loughran and Ritter, for example, found that between 1968 and 1987 IPOs consistently underperformed the market, providing an average annual return of just 2 percent for investors in the five years following issuance. Loughran and Ritter suggested that firms going public are able to time their market offerings near market peaks to maximize offering proceeds. Loughran et al. (1994) pooled the results of studies done in different countries and found that long-term (three-year) overpricing holds in Brazil, Finland, Germany, Singapore, United Kingdom and United States. There does not appear to be long-term overpricing in Japan, Korea or Sweden. The authors, however, cautioned that, except for studies in the United States and United Kingdom, sample sizes for these studies are generally small.

12 Loughran et al. (1994, p. 191). See also Lerner (1994, p. 293) who found that the number of IPOs, but not private financings, peak when equity values are at their maximum.

13 See also MacIntosh (1993, p. 371) who makes a similar speculation.

14 This figure includes reverse takeovers (1 percent), which appear to be included in the IPO total from the U.S. example.

15 There is other evidence suggesting that Canadian and American markets for smaller firms are segmented. See Mittoo (1992, p. 2035), Jorion and Schwartz (1986, p. 603).

16 The QSSP was introduced by the Quebec government in 1979. See Jog and Riding (1990).

17 In fact, as noted above, the U.S. study catalogues "liquidations" separately from acquisitions. If all those exits classified as liquidations were "acquisitions" within the meaning of the Canadian study, then 28 percent (rather than 22 percent) of all exits would have been effected via "acquisitions," resulting in a more pronounced difference in the use of acquisition exits between Canada and the United States. However, the data on profitability presented in Table 12 suggests that "liquidations" are more akin to write-offs than to acquisitions by a strategic buyer.

18 VEC (1986, p. 10). Given that U.S. portfolio investments constituted one quarter of the sample, this means repurchase exits were used at more than twice the rate for Canadian than for U.S. investments.

19 The IRR was calculated by treating the total amount invested by all VCs as if it were a single investment, and calculating the IRR based on total exit price.

20 This was followed by turnaround financing (23 percent), expansion financing (22 percent), and seed/start-up financing (16 percent). VEC (1986, p. 13.)

21 VEC (1986, p. 17) makes a similar observation in respect of the Canadian data: "The distribution of rates of return by exit mechanism ... confirm one of the basic expectations of venture capital investing... a small number of highly profitable investments can produce a superior rate of return overall. Only 15% of the exits generated annual returns of more than 50%. These investments clearly played a critical role in producing an average annual return of 23% across the total sample." With respect to U.S. data, see the VE (1988) study and Bygrave and Timmons (1992, p. 167).

22 See also Wetzel (1983) Rev. 23 finding that rates of return required by angel investors decline with advancing stages of investment.

23 VEC (1986, p. 6). The average investment was $999,000.

24 Ibid. The average investment was $453,000.

25 Ibid. The average investment was $700,000.

26 Ibid. The average investment was $613,000. Note, however, that the large size of investments in firms that were eventually taken public almost certainly reflects the influence of acquisition investments. Acquisition investments tend to be larger on average than early stage, expansion stage or turnaround investments (VEC, 1986, p. 13). Such investments accounted for seven of the 26 Canadian investments that resulted in IPOs. The average acquisition investment was $1,098,000, vs. $545,000 for early stage investments, $707,000 for expansion stage investments and $879,000 for turnaround investments.

27 The average IRR from 1975 to 1980 was 25.8 percent. From 1981 to 1983, it was 22.8 percent. In 1984, it was 14.1 percent, and in 1985, it was 23.9 percent. While the IRR in 1985 alone is no lower than that for 1975 to 1983, combining 1984 and 1985 yields a lower IRR. Given that the average holding period for exits in 1984 and 1985 was 3.1 years and 4.1 years respectively, many of the exits made in 1984 and 1985 were from investments made in 1981 and 1982 (VEC, 1986, p. 18).

28 VEC (1988, p. 1). A new fund need not have inexperienced managers; it may be operated by an experienced venture capital company or it may hire experienced managers. However, the flow of new funds into the venture capital industry in the early 1980s was so great that, inevitably, many of the newly formed funds employed managers lacking in experience. See Bygrave and Timmons (1992); Gompers (1994).

29 The rapid influx of capital into the Canadian venture capital industry in the early 1980s is indicated by the ratio of new deals to exits in each year covered by the survey. This ratio jumped from 3:3 in 1980 to 25:8 in 1981. It fell to 8:9 in 1982 and to 3:7 in 1983. The only years (aside from 1981 and 1982) in which the ratio was above six were 1975 (7:0) and 1976 (6:7). VEC (1986) at 4.

30 VEC (1987, Table 1; 1986, Table 1). Between 1984 and 1992, growth patterns in the two countries were broadly similar, with the Canadian industry growing somewhat more rapidly than the U.S. industry. See Macdonald & Associates (1994, p. 2).

31 On the benefits of specialization, see Bygrave and Timmons, (1992).

32 VEC (1986, p. 7) commented: "It is important to note that writeoffs were expected to account for a high proportion of the exits at the outset, given the nature of the sample. Many of the reporting funds have been formed in the past three to five years, and these funds can legitimately be expected to have taken writeoffs by now without having realized

the gains on their more successful investments (which are still in their portfolio). If the sample included only those funds which have completed a full investment cycle, the proportion of writeoffs would, in all likelihood, have been significantly lower."

33 There is a slight timing mismatch between the aggregate data (which includes 1992 to 1994, but not 1995) and the survey data (which extends from 1992 to 1995).

34 Note that in the earlier Canadian sample, a number of large acquisition investments may have accounted for the large size of investments exited by IPOs. This is clearly not the case with the current survey results. In the later Canadian survey, no acquisition investments were exited via IPOs, and only two of 36 turnaround investments were exited via IPOs. The balance were all investments in early and expansion stage financings. In the current U.S. survey, 29 of 30 IPO exits involved investments in the early or expansion stages.

35 Unfortunately, in the aggregate industry data, figures on secondary sales are available only for 1993, and are pooled with secondary sales following IPOs (which, in the survey data, were simply classified as IPOs). Thus, the aggregate data are not entirely comparable to the survey data.

36 Macdonald & Associates, (1994, p. 3). See also Figure 1 on p. 2 (showing that the total capital under management was essentially unchanged between 1988 and 1992).

37 Gompers (1994) made a similar argument.

38 With respect to U.S. data, see e.g., Office of the Chief Economist, 1985. With respect to Canadian data, see Johnston and Pazderka (1993, p. 15); Giammarino (1995, p. 575).

39 Macdonald & Associates declined to break the survey data into fund types to determine profitability, indicating that in their view there were too few observations to lead to meaningful results.

40 On the value of liquidity to investors, see, e.g., Amihud and Mendelson (1986, p. 223; 1989, p. 479).

41 See e.g., Ontario *Securities Act*, R.S.O. 1990, c. S.5 ("OSA"), s. 61.

42 Gompers (1994). Non-tax reasons also exist for structuring venture capital funds as limited partnerships. See Sahlman (1990).

43 Legal restraints on institutional investors have played an uncertain role in institutional purchases of small firm stocks. Even restrictive "legal for life" statutes have "basket clauses" allowing purchases of risky small firm shares, although recent federal adoption of "prudent person" investing standards may encourage more small firm investment. See generally Gelfand (1993); MacIntosh (1994, p. 19).

BIBLIOGRAPHY

Amihud, Yakov and Haim Mendelson. "Asset Pricing and the Bid-Ask Spread." *Journal of Financial Economics*. 15, (1986).

——. "The Effects of Beta, Bid-Ask Spread, Residual Risk, and Size on Stock Returns." *Journal of Finance*. 44, (1989).

Andrews, Michael. *Initial Public Offerings by Canadian Growth Companies*. Ottawa: The Conference Board of Canada, 1995.

Brav, Alon and Paul A. Gompers. "Myth or Reality? The Long-Run Underperformance of Initial Public Offerings: Evidence from Venture and Nonventure Capital-Backed Companies." Unpublished working paper, Harvard Business School, July 1995.

Bruno, A. and T. Tyebjee. "The Entrepreneur's Search for Capital." *Journal of Business Venturing*. 1, (1985).

Bygrave, William D. and J.A. Timmons. *Venture Capital and the Crossroads*. Boston: Harvard Business School Press, 1992.

Carter, Richard B. and Howard E. Van Auken. "Venture Capital Firms' Preferences for Projects in Particular Stages of Development." *Journal of Small Business Management*. 32:1, (1994).

Coffee, John C. "Shareholders Versus Managers: The Strain in the Corporate Web." *Michigan Law Review*. 85, (1986).

Economic Council of Canada. *Intervention and Efficiency*. Ottawa: Economic Council of Canada, 1982.

Gelfand, Brian Z. *Regulation of Financial Institutions*. Toronto: Carswell, 1993.

Giammarino, Ronald M. "Patient Capital? R & D Investment in Canada." In *Corporate Decision-Making in Canada*. Edited by Ronald J. Daniels and Randall Morck. Calgary: University of Calgary Press, 1995.

Gompers, Paul A. "The Rise and Fall of Venture Capital." *Business and Economic History*. 23:2, (1994).

Huntsman, B. and J. Hoban. "Investment in New Enterprise: Some Empirical Observations on Risk, Return, and Market Structure." *Financial Management*. (Summer 1980).

Jensen, Michael C. "Agency Costs of Free Cash Flow, Corporate Finance and Takeovers." *American Economic Review*. 76, (1986).

Jensen, Michael C. and Kevin J. Murphy. "Performance Pay and Top Management Incentives." *Journal of Policy Economics*. 98, (1990).

Jog, V.M. and A.L. Riding. "Tax Assistance and the Performance of IPOs in Canada: The Case of the Quebec Stock Savings Plan (QSSP)." Paper presented at 1990 ENDEC World Conference, Singapore.

Johnston, Lewis D. and Bokumir Pazderka. "Firm Value and Investment in R & D." *Managerial and Decision Economics*. 14, (1993).

Jorion. P. and E. Schwartz. "Integration versus segmentation in the Canadian stock market." *Journal of Finance*. 41, (1986).

Kahn, A.M. "Assessing Venture Capital Investments with Non-Compensatory Behavioral Decision Models." *Journal of Business Venturing*. 2, (1987).

Kastner, Peter. "Tax Credit Aspects: Tax Climate for R & D: A Canadian Perspective." *Canada-United States Law Journal*. 21, (1995).

Leland, H. and Pyle, D. "Information Asymmetries, Financial Structure and Financial Intermediation." *Journal of Finance*. 32, (1977).

Lerner, Joshua. "VCs and the Decision to Go Public." *Journal of Financial Economics*. 35, (1994).

Levis, Mario. "The Long-Run Performance of Initial Public Offerings: The UK Experience 1980-1988." *Financial Management*. 22, (1993).

Loughran, T. "NYSE vs NASDAQ returns." *Journal of Financial Economics*. 33, (1993).

Loughran, Tim and Jay Ritter. "The Timing and Subsequent Performance of IPOs: Implications for the Cost of Equity Capital." University of Illinois, April 27, 1993.

Loughran, Tim, Jay R. Ritter and Kristian Rydqvist. "Initial Public Offerings: International Insights." *Pacific-Basin Finance Journal*. 2, (1994).

Macdonald & Associates. *Venture Capital in Canada: A Guide and Sources*. Toronto: Macdonald & Associates, 1992.

—. *The Venture Capital Market in Canada: An Analysis of 1993 Venture Capital Activity*. Toronto: Macdonald & Associates, 1994.

MacIntosh, Jeffrey G. "The Role of Institutional and Retail Shareholders in Canadian Capital Markets." *Osgoode Hall Law Journal*. 31, (1993).

—. "Legal and Institutional Barriers to Financing Innovative Enterprise in Canada." Discussion Paper 94-10, Government and Competitiveness Project, School of Policy Studies, Queen's University, Summer 1994.

—. "Venture Capital Exits in Canada and the U.S." Corporate Governance Project, WPS#1-96, 1996.

—. "Executive Compensation: The Importance of Context." Toronto: C.D. Howe Institute, forthcoming.

MacMillan, Ian C., Robin Siegel and P.N. Subba Narashimha. "Criteria Used by VCs to Evaluate New Venture Proposals." *Journal of Business Venturing*. 1, (1985).

McConnell, J.J. and H. Servaes. "Additional Evidence on Equity Ownership and Corporate Value." *Journal of Financial Economics*. 27, (1990).

Mittoo, Usha R. "Additional Evidence on Integration in the Canadian Stock Market." *Journal of Finance*. 47, (1992).

Morck, Randall, Andrei Shliefer and Robert W. Vishney. "Management Ownership and Market Valuation." *Journal of Financial Economics*. 20, (1988).

Northfield, Stephen. "Juniors gone wild." *The Globe and Mail*. March 16, 1996, p. B1.

Office of the Chief Economist, Securities and Exchange Commission. "Institutional Ownership, Tender Offers, and Long-Term Investments." April 19, 1985.

Ontario. *Competing in the New Global Economy*. Report of the Premier's Council, Province of Ontario, 1988.

Profit. "Top Brokers in Small-Cap IPO Market First-Half 1994." (Fall 1994).

Ritter, J. "The Long-Run Performance of Initial Public Offerings." *Journal of Finance*. 46, (1991).

Ruhnka, J.C. and J.E. Young. "Risk in Venture Capital Investing." *Journal of Business Venturing*. 6, (1991).

Sahlman, William A. "The structure and governance of venture-capital organizations." *Journal of Financial Economics*. 27 (1990).

Simon, Carol J. "The Effect of the 1933 Securities Act on Investor Information and the Performance of New Issues." *American Economic Review*. 79, (1989).

VE (Venture Economics). *Venture Capital Yearbook 1986*. Wellesley: Venture Economics, 1986.

—. *Exiting Venture Capital Investments*. Wellesley: Venture Economics, 1988.

—. *Venture Capital: 1995 Annual Review*. Wellesley: Venture Economics, 1995.

VEC (Venture Economics Canada). *Exiting from Venture Capital Investments: The Canadian Experience*. Venture Economics Canada Limited, 1986.

—. *Unaudited Information Regarding the Investment Activities of the Association Members, Association of Canadian Venture Capital Companies (For the year ended December 31, 1986)*. Toronto: Venture Economics Canada Limited, 1987.

—. *Unaudited Information Regarding the Investment Activities of the Association Members, Association of Canadian Venture Capital Companies (For the year ended December 31, 1985)*. Toronto: Venture Economics Canada Limited, 1986.

Wetzel, W.E. "Angels and Informal Risk Capital." *Sloan Management Review*. 24, (1983).

Wruck, Karen Hopper. "Equity Ownership Concentration and Firm Value." *Journal of Financial Economics*. 23, (1988).

Vijay M. Jog
School of Business
Carleton University

8

The Climate for Canadian Initial Public Offerings

INTRODUCTION

FOR AN ENTREPRENEURIAL FIRM, a public listing of its shares on a stock exchange is often considered a major event. Going public through an initial public offering (IPO) can be considered as the coming of age for a firm.

This paper provides empirical evidence on four issues related to the process of going public based on Canadian IPOs from 1971 to 1994. More specifically, the paper provides evidence on: underpricing of IPOs, the long-term stock market performance of IPOs, the financial performance of firms in the post-IPO period compared to their pre-IPO period and the actual process of going public as seen from the viewpoint of individual firms. The evidence for the first three issues is based on secondary data available in the public domain; the evidence on the last issue comes from responses to questionnaires received from firms which went public during the late 1980s and early 1990s.[1]

The next section provides an overall perspective on the importance of increasing knowledge of the IPO environment in Canada. This perspective reflects that of the government as well as the entrepreneur. The terms "entrepreneur" and "firm" are used interchangeably throughout the paper. The following section provides a very brief overview of the Canadian IPO market and institutional environment. Subsequent sections provide empirical evidence on the four main issues noted above. The paper ends with summary and conclusions.

IMPORTANCE OF THE IPO ENVIRONMENT

ACCESS TO EQUITY CAPITAL BY CANADIAN ENTREPRENEURIAL FIRMS has generated considerable interest and debate, beginning with the Economic Council study in 1982, and continuing up to the report produced by the Small Business Working Committee (Industry Canada, 1994). The basic notion behind all the analysis and concern with respect to the IPO environment is that, for a country like Canada to compete effectively, Canadian capital markets must be efficient and effective in providing equity capital to entrepreneurial firms.

If this access to equity capital is cost effective, both from a transaction and a pricing and valuation viewpoint, then Canadian firms will be able to create and sustain new innovations, create jobs, generate corporate and personal tax revenues, and compete internationally. Thus, from an economic perspective, it is clear that Canada must have a vibrant IPO market.

There are important additional reasons for having a vibrant IPO environment. First, entrepreneurs are provided with an additional impetus to start a business and nurture it if they have a reasonable expectation that, if and when necessary, capital markets will provide them with monetary rewards by purchasing their equity in the firm at an attractive price. Second, a vibrant IPO market provides exit possibilities for investors who provide private capital to a firm before it is ready for an IPO. These informal investors and venture capitalists can, therefore, provide seed capital without being overly concerned about locking in their investment for long periods.

A third and even more important reason for having a vibrant IPO market is the contemporary structural change in the global business environment. It is undeniable that, to compete globally, Canada must change its focus from a bricks and mortar industrial base to a knowledge-based economy, where efficient access to external equity capital is even more important. Traditional sources of debt financing can effectively finance the purchase of assets that have high collateral value. These lenders are comfortable with the knowledge that, in a worst case scenario, they can find buyers for the underlying assets of the firm. In a knowledge economy, no such collateral exists. Assets walk out at 5 p.m.; they are not collateral if they don't come back the next day. Traditional sources of debt financing are not attracted to financing this sort of entrepreneurial firm. Worse still, even if lenders wanted to lend against these "soft" assets, the incentives necessary for a proper valuation may be absent in a lending environment where the up side returns are fixed, but the down side risk is not. Although there is no empirical evidence of the potential difficulty of raising funds for these knowledge-based firms, it is fair to say that a strong IPO environment may be another necessity for a country attempting a shift to a knowledge-based economy.

The benefits a strong IPO environment presents to entrepreneurs and firms are easy to identify. Not only does the company receive equity financing when it goes public, but it also has easier access to equity capital in the post-IPO period. Because it is evaluated more regularly by capital market participants, it can also be argued that going public potentially reduces the cost of equity capital for the firm since these investors hold diversified portfolios and require a risk premium for only the non-diversifiable portion of the firm risk. Some studies have indicated that a typical venture capital firm expects to earn at least 25 percent (in inflation-adjusted terms) on its investment, whereas typical required rates of return demanded by a capital market participant may be in the range of 15 percent to 19 percent.[2] Raising equity capital also implies less reliance on bank debt financing. Additional intangible benefits may include increased credibility vis-à-vis lenders, suppliers and domestic and international buyers, an increased ability to attract key personnel, the ability to provide stock options as a part of the compensation for key employees and a potential for improvement in a firm's operational and organizational structure due to increased scrutiny.[3]

Of course, along with the publicly traded status come some impediments and costs. These costs include the legal and underwriting expenses associated with the IPO and the subsequent ongoing expenses associated with filing requirements, information demands by investors and analysts, more stringent and formal legal and corporate governance requirements, exchange listing requirements and filing needs, disclosure rules, etc. Clearly, a strong and vibrant IPO market can exist only if the benefits far outweigh the costs of going (and staying) public.

Historical Overview and Institutional Characteristics

Given the importance of the IPO environment, it is scarcely surprising that federal and provincial governments have taken a variety of initiatives to foster an easier and more cost-effective environment for accessing external equity capital. While it is not possible to provide a complete review of these initiatives here, the following brief summary highlights some major initiatives and notes similarities and dissimilarities. While these initiatives do not directly affect the IPO environment, they need to be considered in the context of the life cycle of a firm's quest for growth. This begins with raising capital from love money,[4] then moving on to informal capital, then to venture capital, and finally culminating in an IPO. Each of these three early stages is important to a firm's growth and will influence the timing and decision of an IPO.

In Canada, the interest of various levels of governments in the issue of access to capital by entrepreneurial Canadian firms began mainly after the recession in the early 1980s. This interest resulted from the decreasing importance of traditional large firms in creating jobs and growth, and the emergence of a large number of small and medium-sized businesses. Access to various financing sources was extremely important if these firms were to grow and achieve some stability. Although they could rely on banks for traditional working capital and short-term financing, there was a need for access to other sources for both debt and equity capital. Consequently, many new initiatives were introduced by both the public and private sectors to fulfil these financing needs.[5] The result was the emergence of provincially backed venture capital firms, less-stringent requirements for stock exchange listing and increased access to various tax-based initiatives implemented by the provinces, such as investment tax credits and higher depreciation rates for calculating provincial taxes. Although most of these initiatives were not directly targeted to IPOs, they did influence the growth of these firms, resulting in a larger number of firms with the potential to go public.

The most direct incentive affecting a firm's decision to go public was introduced in Quebec. The Quebec Stock Savings Plan (QSSP), introduced in 1979, became more targeted to small and medium-sized businesses in the early 1980s. It provided investors with tax assistance for their investment in newly issued common equity by Quebec-based firms. At inception, this tax credit was available to all Quebec-based firms irrespective of size; later the program was (and is) primarily targeted to smaller firms. This plan had two objectives: to furnish the equity capital required by Quebec-based small and medium-sized firms and to encourage individuals to invest in the shares of these firms. By all standards, the QSSP has been a success in achieving its objectives.[6]

In a parallel development, the country's leading stock exchange, the Toronto Stock Exchange (TSE), introduced new initiatives to reduce the listing requirements and facilitate the going public process for small firms.[7] These measures, coupled with the robust equity markets of the mid-1980s, encouraged many firms to go public.

Although not exhaustive, the above discussion indicates that access to equity financing for small firms has been a focus of continued interest in Canada. This focus has resulted in initiatives by both the public and private sector, to facilitate access to equity capital from a variety of sources. Many Canadian firms have taken advantage of these initiatives by raising equity capital through an IPO.

It is in this context that empirical evidence on issues that arise in the IPO environment is provided here, beginning with the issue of underpricing of IPOs in Canada.

Underpricing of Canadian IPOs

One important aspect of a firm's decision to go public is that of receiving a "proper" price for its common shares. Since the firm, by definition, is a private firm before going public, it must rely on investment bankers and underwriters to provide recommendations on the reasonable price at which it can sell its shares to investors. It cannot judge the validity of these recommendations until the shares are priced, sold to investors and begin to be traded on the stock exchange. Ideally, the firm would like the price at which shares begin trading to be very close to the price at which the shares were sold to investors – the issuing price.[8] If the initial trading price is much higher than the issuing price, i.e., the shares are significantly underpriced, then the firm will have received less financing than it could have for the same number of shares issued. This would also imply that the initial owners of the firm suffered a higher dilution of their holdings and the underpricing resulted in a much lower level of wealth for them. Thus, if on average, IPOs are significantly underpriced, many eligible firms would become reluctant to choose an IPO as a means of raising equity capital. On the other hand, if overpricing is seen as a norm, investors will be unwilling to buy IPOs at issuance, preferring to wait a day or two after the issue and buy the same share at a lower price. Thus, the degree of under (or over) pricing may have a significant influence on the overall IPO environment.[9]

In this section, the evidence on the underpricing of Canadian IPOs during the last 20 years is reviewed. These results are from Jog and Srivastava (1994), who updated the underpricing results provided by Jog and Riding (1987). According to their results, based on the 1984 to 1992 period, the percentage of underpricing for Canadian IPOs is decreasing almost continuously, and is now significantly better than every other country except France.[10]

Earlier Results

In the earlier paper, Jog and Riding (1987) provided the first comprehensive evidence on underpricing in Canadian IPOs. Their results, based on a sample of 100 IPOs between 1971 and 1983, indicated that the average degree of underpricing ranged from 9.5 percent to 11.0 percent. The degree of underpricing varied significantly across issues, and approximately 40 percent were overpriced.[11]

In recent years, there has been a growing interest about the underpricing of IPOs in other countries. Table 1 summarizes the data for the G7 countries given by Loughran et al. (1994) who summarized international evidence on underpricing. According to their summary table, the average underpricing for U.S. IPOs is 15.3 percent. Underpricing ranges from a low of 4.2 percent in France to highs of 78.5 percent in Brazil and 166.6 percent in Malaysia.[12] The average underpricing in Europe is 47.4 percent (11 countries, a total of 972 issues), 54.2 percent in South America (three countries, 118 issues) and 66.6 percent in Asia, including Australia and New Zealand (nine countries, 1,372 issues). Most of these results are based on evidence gathered during the 1970s and 1980s.

Table 1

Evidence on Underpricing in G7 Countries

Country	Sample Size	Time Period	Underpricing (%)
Canada	100	1971-1983	9.3
France	187	1983-1992	4.2
Germany	172	1978-1992	11.1
Italy	75	1985-1991	27.1
Japan	472	1970-1991	32.5
United Kingdom	2,133	1959-1990	12.0
United States	10,626	1960-1992	15.3

Source: Loughran et al. (1994).

The Updated Results

The results below are based on the extension of the 1987 Jog and Riding study to IPOs from 1984 to 1992 as reported by Jog and Srivastava (1994) and to 1993 and 1994 for this paper. The main source of data is the IPO listing provided by the

(TSE).[13] A total of 383 common equity IPOs were identified over this period, 100 of which were from the Jog and Riding sample.[14] Data on stock returns were obtained from the TSE-Western Database.

The IPOs covered in these listings include only those firms which raised equity financing through the TSE. As the TSE is the largest stock exchange in Canada, the firms in the sample are also generally larger than those which have gone public on other exchanges. Consistent with the tradition in Canada, all these IPOs were issued on a best-efforts basis. To ensure consistency with previous results, comparisons are also provided between the updated results and those of Jog and Riding (1987).[15]

Table 2 shows summary statistics for the entire sample, from 1971 to 1994. Two major conclusions can be drawn from this table. First, the degree of underpricing is markedly lower from 1984 to 1994 than that reported for the earlier period. The average underpricing in the 1984 to 1994 period is 7.89 percent compared to 9.96 percent for the earlier period. Due to the very high dispersion in underpricing in the years 1971 to 1983, this difference of 2.07 percent in underpricing is not statistically significant. However, the annual underpricing from 1984 to 1994 has stayed below 7 percent in most of the years, and has been exceeded only marginally in two of the 11 years. The average annual standard deviation is also significantly lower in the latter period, the difference being statistically significant at the 1 percent level. These results clearly indicate that the degree of underpricing in Canada was much lower in the 1980s and the early 1990s than had been reported for previous periods.[16] Table 2 also indicates the nature of the overall market by showing the annual returns on the TSE 300 Composite Index. Although not shown in the table, there is a positive relationship between the degree of underpricing and the state of the market.[17] Thus, there is some evidence that IPOs issued in bull markets are, on average, more underpriced than those issued in bear markets.

Figure 1 graphically shows the decline in the degree of underpricing as well as its extent during the last 20 years in Canada. Figure 2 shows the annual variation in the percentage of underpriced IPOs. Consistent with the results of Figure 1, the percentage of underpriced IPOs is also decreasing each year in Canada. From 1971 to 1983, the percentage of all underpriced IPOs was 62.0 percent. The corresponding number for the 1984 to 1994 period was less than 50 percent.[18]

Summary

This 23-year perspective updates the evidence on underpricing in Canada, its cross-sectional variation and the percentage of IPOs which are underpriced each year. Based on the average degree of underpricing from 1984 to 1992, Canada now ranks as the second best (after France) among the 25 countries surveyed by Loughran et al. (1994). These results indicate that Canadian capital markets are doing a good job in allocating risk capital to entrepreneurs, and that Canadian

TABLE 2

UNDERPRICING BY YEAR (1971 TO 1994)

	Year	Average Underpricing (%)	Standard Deviation of Underpricing (%)	High (%)	Low (%)	Number	TSE Total Returns (%)
Jog and Riding (1971-1983)	1971	5.31	19.62	34.88	-16.67	8	8.01
	1972	12.36	19.78	80.00	-11.82	22	27.38
	1973	3.87	33.70	80.00	-35.42	17	0.27
	1974	28.54	85.35	88.89	-31.82	2	-25.93
	1976	25.00	0.00	25.00	25.00	1	18.48
	1978	18.48	0.00	18.48	18.48	1	29.72
	1979	9.05	21.65	27.78	-20.97	4	44.77
	1980	26.80	39.87	82.50	-13.89	8	30.13
	1981	4.25	20.77	62.50	-17.65	17	-10.25
	1982	19.82	32.12	65.79	-10.71	5	5.54
	1983	6.21	17.01	43.85	-21.05	15	35.49
	1971-1983	9.96	26.48	88.89	-35.42	100	
Jog and Srivastava (1984-1992)	1984	3.80	9.46	32.00	-3.75	14	-2.39
	1985	5.87	6.02	17.65	0.00	6	25.07
	1986	7.11	16.53	74.24	-15.67	70	8.95
	1987	7.13	18.58	87.50	-15.85	30	5.88
	1988	1.33	4.07	8.11	-2.78	4	11.08
	1989	1.21	7.02	12.57	-13.64	10	21.37
	1990	-3.80	5.70	0.00	-14.74	5	-14.80
	1991	3.73	7.84	20.69	-2.63	5	12.02
	1992	5.26	8.02	20.63	-3.03	10	-1.43
	1993	14.03	33.32	200.00	-11.36	77	32.55
	1994	5.44	15.38	80.00	-16.13	52	0.18
This paper Jog (1993-1994)	1984-1994	7.89	23.37	200.00	-16.13	283	
	1971-1994	8.43	24.07	200.00	-35.42	383	

entrepreneurs and policy makers need not be too concerned about IPO underpricing in Canada and its impact on the motivation to go public. The reasons for this declining average underpricing are unclear and require further research.

FIGURE 1

CANADIAN IPO UNDERPRICING (1971 TO 1994)

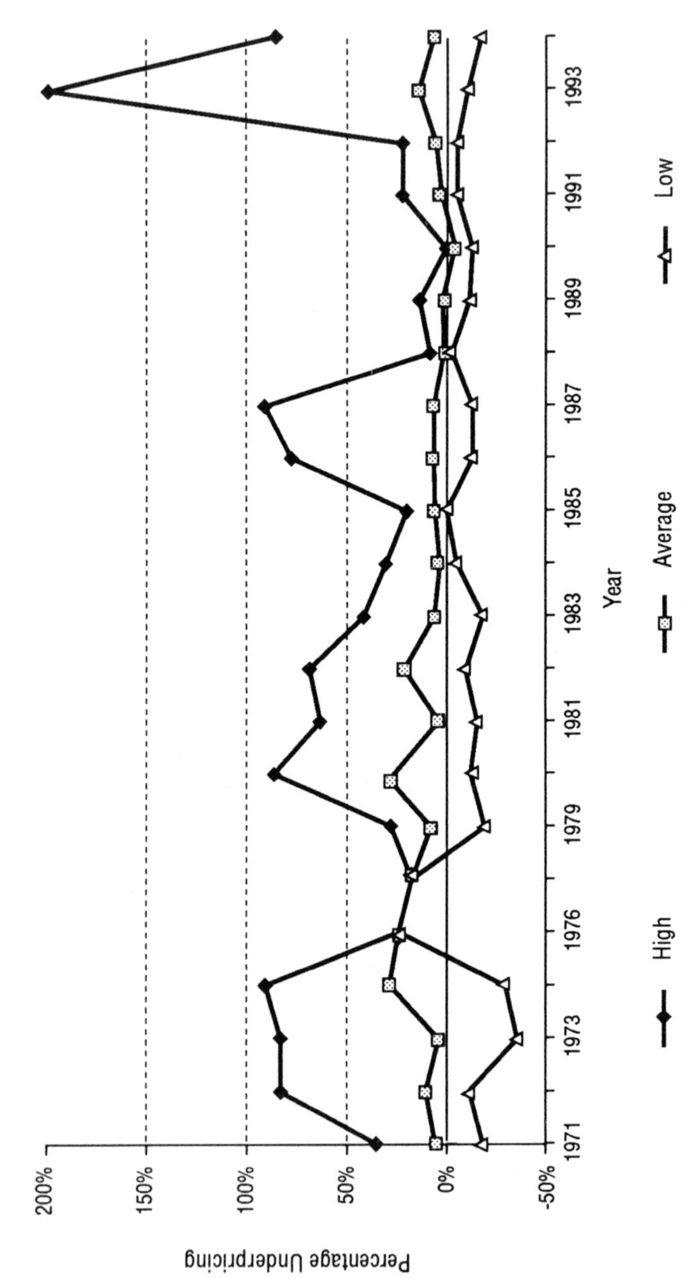

FIGURE 2

PERCENTAGE OF ALL IPOS UNDERPRICED BETWEEN 1971 AND 1994

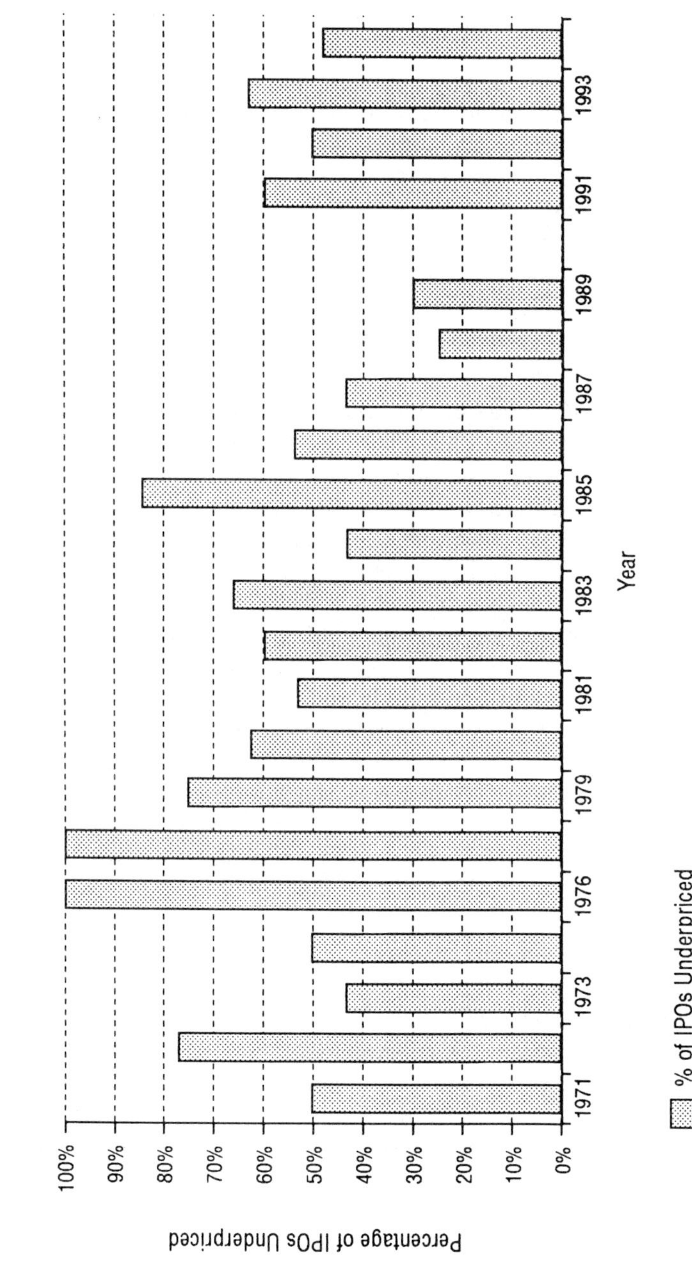

Long-Term Performance of Canadian IPOs

In addition to evaluating the underpricing of IPOs, recent studies have examined the performance of IPOs in other countries including the United States.[19] These studies document the existence of positive average initial returns followed by strongly negative returns over an extended period following the IPO. In this section, Canadian evidence on long-term IPO performance is reviewed based on the returns that an investor would earn from an IPO stock. The evidence is derived from a subset of 254 equity IPOs, between 1971 and 1992, used by Jog and Srivastava (1995).

Methodology

Typically, the long-term performance of a group of stocks is analysed by investigating the returns earned by an investor whose investment strategy is to invest in each IPO as it lists on the stock exchange. However, since this performance may be affected by the overall performance of the stock market, it is also necessary to analyse it on a relative basis by comparison with widely based stock market indices. Appendix A provides the details of the two methodologies used to conduct this relative performance analysis. The first methodology provides an estimation of relative abnormal returns earned by IPOs over and above the benchmark portfolio.[20] The second methodology measures the wealth creation or depletion (called residual cumulative wealth from now on, and explained in the appendix) which would have resulted from investing in a portfolio of sample IPOs, relative to an investment in a benchmark portfolio. This residual cumulative wealth represents an investor's returns from an arbitrage strategy of investing in the sample IPO stocks who simultaneously holds a short position in the benchmark portfolio. A negative return on such a strategy implies that the investor would have done better by investing in the benchmark portfolio.

Since the measurement of long-term performance may be sensitive to the choice of benchmark, as suggested by Ritter (1991), Jog and Srivastava (1995) used two benchmarks to evaluate abnormal performance for the sample stocks: the TSE 300 Composite Index and the value-weighted index of TSE-Western Database. The analysis was conducted over a 72-month period in the post-IPO period. (The first month begins on the 21st trading day following the IPO listing.) To be included in a particular year, the stock must have had return data in the data base for at least 10 of the 12 months. Since the analysis was based on 72 months of post-IPO returns, the number in the sample decreases as the length of the period increases. For example, since return data ends in 1994, the 1992 IPOs are included only in the results for the first 24 months. This explains the declining number of stocks in Table 3.

FIGURE 3

CUMULATIVE RAW RETURNS

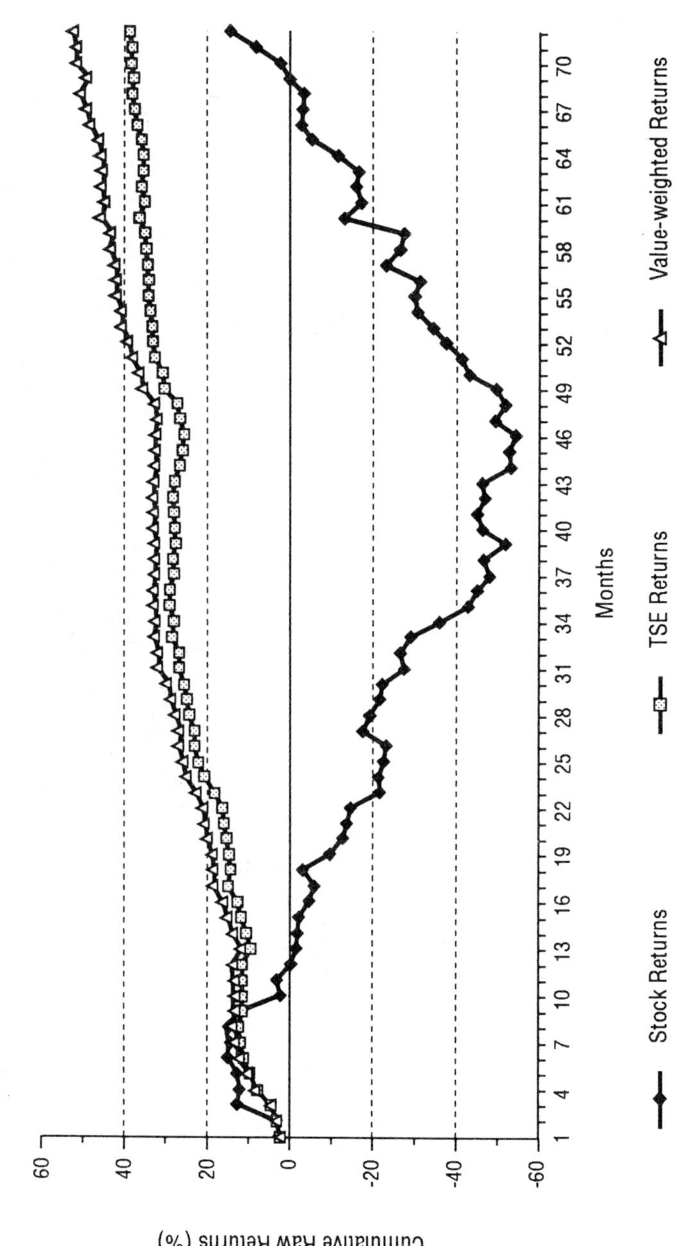

FIGURE 4

RESIDUAL CUMULATIVE WEALTH

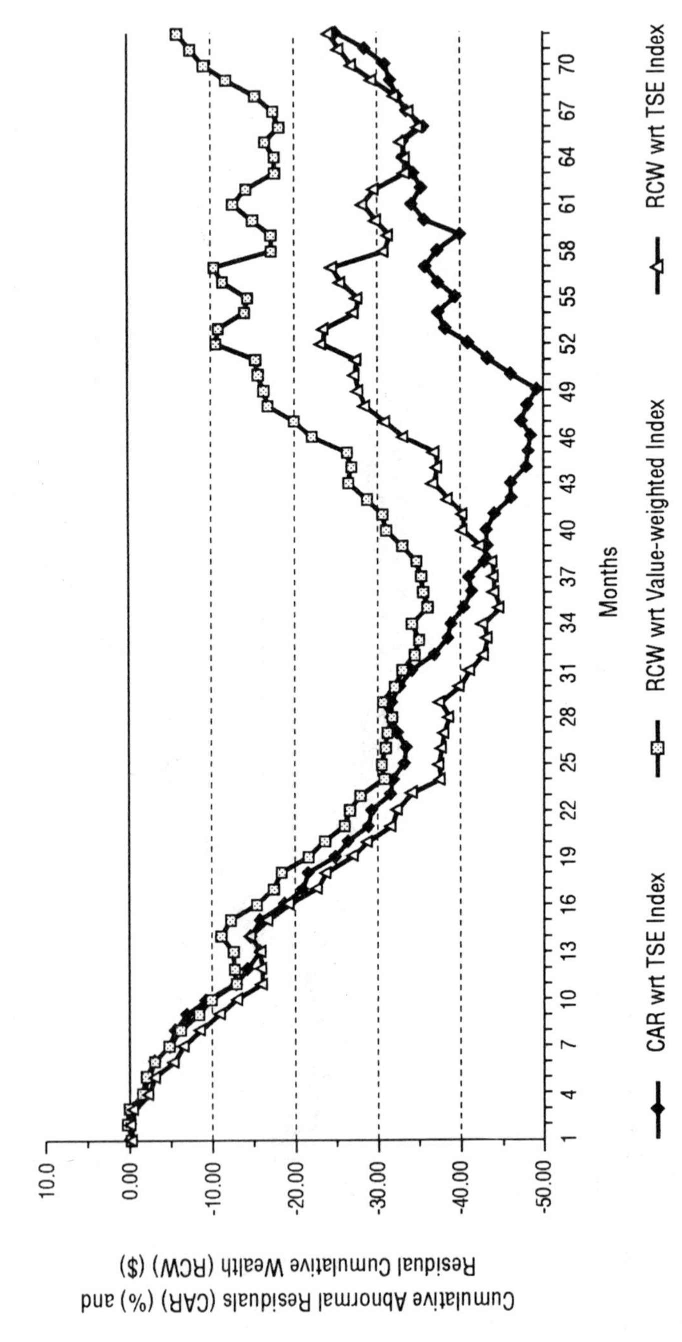

Note: wrt: with respect to.

TABLE 3

CUMULATIVE ABNORMAL RESIDUALS (CAR), RESIDUAL CUMULATIVE WEALTH (RCW)

Month	Number of Firms	CAR wrt TSE 300 (%)	t-Statistic	RCW wrt TSE 300 ($)	RCW wrt VW Index ($)
1	149	-0.19	-0.13	-0.23	-0.54
12	148	-14.36	-2.22	-12.92	-15.76
24	150	-31.99	-3.49	-30.83	-37.28
36	130	-41.02	-3.39	-35.15	-43.66
48	117	-48.37	-3.28	-17.17	-28.32
60	98	-35.28	-1.96	-15.26	-29.82
72	96	-24.72	-1.24	-6.19	-23.92

Note: wrt: with respect to.

LONG-TERM PERFORMANCE RESULTS

FIGURE 3 SHOWS MATCHED CUMULATIVE (UNADJUSTED) RETURNS for an average stock in the portfolio relative to cumulative returns on the two benchmarks used in the study, namely, the TSE 300 Composite Index, and the value-weighted TSE-Western Database index. The latter two represent the investor's accrued returns from investing in benchmark portfolios instead of IPOs. As can be seen, over the 72-month period, returns on an average stock fell significantly below the cumulative return provided by either of the two benchmarks, the difference being in the order of 80 percent in month 47. From this point on, IPO returns seemed to exhibit an upward trend. However, for the overall period, it is evident that the portfolio of IPOs significantly underperformed the market for at least 72 months following the IPO listing.

Figure 4 provides evidence on relative performance with respect to the TSE 300 index while Table 3 provides a summary of results with respect to both the benchmarks. It is clear from these results that an average IPO, as measured by cumulative abnormal residuals (CARs), underperformed the TSE 300 by close to 50 percent over the first 49 months of trading, and this underperformance was highly significant. From this point on, the underperformance, as well as its significance, dropped and by the end of 60 months, the underperformance was not statistically significant in relation to the benchmark. For the sake of brevity, the results with respect to the value-weighted benchmark are not reported since they are very similar to the reported results relative to the TSE 300 index.

This arbitrage strategy of going long in the portfolio of IPO stocks and short in the benchmark also seems to have resulted in substantially negative residual cumulative wealth. Based on Table 3 results, a zero initial investment in the arbitrage portfolio would have resulted in a loss to the investor of $35.15 by the end of 35 months in the post-IPO period with the benchmark being the TSE 300 index, or $43.66 if the benchmark used is the value-weighted index. While the arbitrage portfolio strategy shows a loss of only $6.19 by the end of 72 months, the value-weighted index shows a much larger loss of $23.92. The upward trend in the CARs, as well as residual cumulative wealth with respect to either benchmark, may be the result of a survivorship bias. Clearly, those IPOs which continue to be listed for a long period provide returns similar to other companies on the stock market.

Distribution of CARs and Sample Characteristics

Table 4 presents the distribution of CARs and residual cumulative wealth for the full sample of IPOs at 12-month intervals using the TSE 300 Index as the benchmark. All CARs and proportions are statistically significant at the 5 percent level unless marked with an asterisk. Not only the overall performance is statistically significant. The proportion of firms showing negative CARs in each of these intervals is significantly greater statistically (at the 5 percent level) than the number of IPOs with positive CARs. Clearly, an average IPO stock exhibits statistically and economically significant negative abnormal returns over as long a period as 48 months. Similarly, the arbitrage strategy of taking a long position in the sample IPOs and a short one in the TSE 300 benchmark returns a significant loss over the 72 months. However, the relationship exhibits a U-shaped character perhaps indicating a survivorship bias.[21]

Table 4 also presents the distribution of CARs for various subsamples. While all sample partitions exhibit statistically significant underperformance in the post-IPO period of 72 months after the issue, there is evidence of a statistically significant differential performance across individual subsample partitions. Using 1992 dollars, an average IPO priced below $10 produced a CAR by month 36 which was lower by almost 13 percent than the average IPO priced at or above $10, the difference being statistically significant at the 5 percent level. This trend seems to reverse itself beyond month 36, although the CARs for low-priced IPOs are all statistically insignificant beyond month 36. The difference in CARs between the two subsample partitions continues to be statistically significant to month 60 at the 5 percent level.

While both overpriced and underpriced stocks underperform significantly in the after-market, overpriced stocks perform significantly worse than underpriced stocks over the first 48 months. This is contrary to existing non-Canadian evidence, which indicates that underpriced stocks show a more negative long-term performance. Instead, in the sample of IPOs, stocks which are undervalued i.e, overpriced, by the market in relation to the underwriter's assessment at the time of issue underperform even more in the after-market.

Issues with gross proceeds of $10 million or more (using 1992 dollars) perform significantly better than those under $10 million. The difference by month 48 is close to 30 percent and is statistically significant at the 5 percent level. From there on, neither the CARs nor the differences in CARs across the two sample partitions are statistically significant.

TABLE 4

SUBSAMPLE CHARACTERISTICS AND CARS

Sample	Month 12	Month 24	Month 36	Month 48	Month 60	Month 72
Full sample CAR	-14.36% 148 (54:94)	-31.99% 150 (49:101)	-41.02% 130 (37:93)	-48.37% 117 (37:80)	-35.28% 98 (36:62)	-24.72%* 96 (45:51)&
Full sample cumulative wealth	-12.92 148	-30.83 150	-35.15 130	-17.17 117	-15.26 98	-6.19 96
Price < $10.00	-13.61* 64 (24:40)	-36.92 66 (18:48)	-48.70 54 (12:42)	-43.49* 48 (14:34)	-22.49* 40 (14:26)	4.45* 38 (17:21)&
Price ≥ $10.00	-15.37 83 (29:54)	-28.92 83 (30:53)	-35.78 76 (25:51)	-51.48 69 (23:46)	-44.42 58 (22:36)	-44.97 58 (28:30)&
Overpriced	-19.97* 50 (13:37)	-43.13 51 (14:37)	-56.33 44 (13:31)	-64.32 37 (9:28)	-39.40* 29 (9:20)	-41.20* 28 (10:18)&
Underpriced	-11.62* 97 (40:57)	-26.81 98 (34:64)	-33.60 86 (24:62)	-40.38 80 (28:52)	-32.89 69 (27:42)	-17.26* 68 (35:33)&
Proceeds > $10 M	-18.41 72 (22:50)	-33.37 71 (22:49)	-35.13 61 (21:40)	-49.74 55 (16:39)	-33.24* 45 (15:30)	-15.10* 45 (22:23)&
Proceeds ≤ $10 M	-7.50 38 (15:23)&	-41.16 38 (9:29)	-75.12 32 (3:29)	-80.29 26 (3:23)	-50.67* 22 (6:16)	-26.53* 22 (8:14)&
Bull market	-8.95* 79 (35:44)&	-31.49* 79 (31:48)	-41.88* 71 (21:50)	-51.92* 63 (21:42)	-35.01* 50 (21:29)&	-20.41* 48 (26:22)&
Bear market	-20.42 69 (19:50)	-32.50 71 (18:53)	-39.94 59 (16:43)	-44.33 54 (16:38)	-35.74* 48 (15:33)	-29.38* 48 (19:29)&
Industrials	-17.21$ 122 (42:80)	-34.95$ 122 (36:86)	-43.39● 107 (29:78)	-46.73$ 97 (28:69)	-30.70*$ 85 (34:51)	-21.50*● 83 (40:43)&
Mines	14.31* 10 (5:5)&	0.39* 11 (7:4)&	-38.69* 9 (4:5)&	-71.05* 7 (3:4)&	-100.17* 5 (1:4)&	-3.41* 5 (3:2)&
Oil and gas	-13.56* 15 (6:9)&	-32.82 16 (5:11)&	-26.21* 13 (4:9)&	-56.58 12 (5:7)&	-44.14* 7 (0:7)	-79.52* 7 (1:6)

Notes: Each cell (other than the ones with residual cumulative wealth) contains CAR percentage, number of sample (or subsample) firms and the number of positive CARs vs. negative CARs.

* Not significant at 5 percent level of significance.

● Not significantly different from the CAR of mining IPOs at 5 percent level of significance.

$ Not significantly different from the CAR of oil and gas IPOs at 5 percent level of significance.

& The proportion of negative CARs is not significantly greater statistically than that of positive CARs at 5 percent level of significance.

In the sample segmented by whether the market was in the bull or bear market phase, the CARs for IPOs made during both phases are significantly different statistically from zero through to month 48.[22] From that point on, the underperformance is statistically insignificant.

When the sample is segmented by sector, industrial IPOs exhibit statistically significant underperformance through to month 48. Mining IPOs exhibit CARs which are not significantly different statistically from zero. Oil and gas IPOs do exhibit statistically significant underperformance at months 24 and 48. For these two sample partitions, the sample size is too small to make any reasonable parametric statistical inferences. If the relative performance of these sample partitions is analysed, industrial issues perform poorly relative to mining issues over the first 24 months of market seasoning; but the trend reverses beyond that, with industrial issues performing better over the long haul. No such inference can be made with respect to oil and gas IPOs.

Overall, these results clearly indicate that the long-term performance of the sample IPOs has not been stellar. Although, on an absolute basis, these IPOs generated positive returns to the investor in the first year, after holding them for over five years (see Figure 4), their relative performance was much worse. The decline in performance seems to start approximately 10 months after the IPO and continues through to the end of the fourth year. The improvement in performance after the first four years may have more to do with survivorship bias and a reduced sample size than with any fundamental changes to the underlying characteristics of the sample firms. The various subsample results show that sample characteristics may have some influence on long-term performance; however, no firm conclusions can be reached using this univariate analysis.

Relationship between Under-Performance and Issue-Specific Factors

To assess the relationship between CARs and issue-specific factors in a multivariate context, six ordinary least squares regressions were performed over the 72 months at 12-month intervals. The regression equation has the following form:

$$CAR^{i}_{1,s} = \alpha_0+\alpha_1 UP_i+\alpha_2 PROC_i+\alpha_3 PRICE_i+\alpha_4 MARKET_i+\alpha_5 INDUS_i+\epsilon_{is} \quad (1)$$

where s takes on a value of 12, 24, 36, 48, 60 or 72. UP_i is the underpricing in stock i and $PROC_i$ is the inflation-adjusted gross proceeds in 1992 dollars. $PRICE_i$ is the issue price for stock i, and $MARKET_i$ is a dummy variable taking on a value of 1 if the market is in a bull phase and 0 otherwise at the time the IPO was issued. $INDUS_i$ captures the industrial classification of the IPO and takes on a value of 1 for mining issues, 2 for oil and gas and 3 for industrial issuers.

Table 5 presents results from these six regressions. First, no obvious statistically significant relationship emerges which is stable over time. The cross-sectional regressions using CARs for up to 48 months show no statistically significant positive relationships between any of the variables and the respective CARs. The conclusion is that although the proportions of firms with negative and positive CARs are different, the variations in performance are too large to be statistically significant. A somewhat stronger pattern can be observed for long-term performance (post 48 months) between CARs and some of the variables. For example, in cross-sectional regressions at months 60 and 72, the degree of underpricing is shown to have a statistically significant positive relationship with cross-sectional CARs, suggesting that larger underpricing implies better performance over the long haul. However, the overall strength of the specification is not very strong.

SUMMARY

THE MAGNITUDE OF UNDERPERFORMANCE in the Canadian IPO market is found to be similar to the results reported for other countries. In particular, the cumulative abnormal residual for the Canadian sample by month 36 is -41.02 percent compared to -29.13 percent for Ritter's (1991) IPOs in the United States. The sample IPOs in the Canadian study continue to show statistically significant underperformance for four years after the issue date.

An examination of the sample partitions of IPOs reveals some regularities. For example, irrespective of the type of sample segmentation, all subsamples show high underperformance over 72 months of market seasoning. Other regularities include the fact that low-priced stocks perform better than high-priced stocks over the long run, but the relative performance is period-dependent; overpriced stocks perform significantly worse than underpriced stocks; larger issues perform significantly better than smaller issues through 48 months; and industrial issues seem to perform better than either the mining issues or oil and gas issues. However, the longitudinal analysis of CARs fails to uncover any systematic relationships with some firm-specific factors that are stable over time.

The evidence presented by Jog and Srivastava (1995) on long-term underperformance provides limited support for the hypothesis of Allen and Faulhaber (1989) and Welch (1989) who contended that issuers use underpricing to signal the quality of issue. As such, high-quality issuers who can afford to offer higher underpricing than low-quality issuers, will do so. This hypothesis predicts better performance in the after-market by issues that have been more underpriced. While both the underpriced and overpriced issues underperform the market over 72 months of market seasoning, the underpriced IPOs perform significantly better statistically than the overpriced IPOs by as much as 23 percent through 48 months of market seasoning.

TABLE 5

RELATIONSHIP OF CUMULATIVE ABNORMAL RESIDUAL WITH FIRM-SPECIFIC FACTORS

Dependent Variable	Independent Variables						f-Statistics
	Constant	Underpricing	Proceeds	Price	Bull/Bear	Industry	
CAR (1,12)	69.672 (0.47)	-0.024 (0.81)	-0.116 (0.47)	0.044 (0.78)	0.066 (0.51)	-0.135 (0.18)	0.773 (0.57)
CAR (1,24)	-151.126 (0.21)	0.004 (0.97)	0.165 (0.31)	-0.027 (0.87)	-0.037 (0.71)	-0.092 (0.37)	0.572 (0.72)
CAR (1,36)	-329.898 (0.03)	-0.016 (0.88)	0.320 (0.08)	-0.021 (0.91)	0.024 (0.82)	-0.099 (0.35)	1.798 (0.12)
CAR (1,48)	-375.032 (0.09)	0.026 (0.83)	0.288 (0.15)	-0.025 (0.90)	0.080 (0.48)	-0.168 (0.15)	1.398 (0.24)
CAR (1,60)	-260.704 (0.21)	0.315 (0.02)	0.162 (0.44)	0.124 (0.55)	0.121 (0.33)	0.001 (0.99)	1.666 (0.16)
CAR (1,72)	-124.218 (0.61)	0.322 (0.01)	0.079 (0.70)	0.112 (0.56)	0.108 (0.38)	-0.204 (0.11)	2.142 (0.07)

Note: The values in the bracket are the levels of significance, e.g., the value of (0.01) for the underpricing coefficient in the last row indicates that the coefficient is significant at the 1 percent level.

Post-IPO Financial Performance

As noted above, the empirical evidence on the long-term performance of IPOs, from the viewpoint of shareholders, is not very attractive. It is possible that this disappointing performance is due to the high initial price paid by investors for the IPO and their subsequent disillusionment, leading to poor market performance. However, this need not imply a disappointing economic performance by firms which raise equity financing from external investors.

To shed further light on financial performance, accounting information was collected on a sample of firms which raised financing through an IPO on the TSE during the 1985 to 1992 period. The emphasis was on non-resource firms, since the purpose of this part of the study was to analyse the financial performance of predominantly industrial and service sector companies. This required information on some relevant accounting variables from the prospectuses filed by these firms. The main objective was to compare their performance in the pre-IPO years with the immediate post-IPO years.

Data

Since there is no readily available data base in Canada on IPOs, the required data were collected by searching the prospectuses of IPOs available in the Toronto Public Library, the main public source of such hard copy, inexpensive data in Canada. A total of 83 prospectuses were collected, and the relevant data identified for the two years preceding the IPO year and two years following the IPO year for 54 of the firms. Of these, four firms were extremely large (Petro-Canada, Repap, Co-Steel and Quebecor) and were eliminated from further analysis because of the focus on the performance of smaller firms, which raised equity financing from the stock market as a logical consequence of their growth. Thus, the remainder of the analysis in this section concentrates on a 50-firm sample.[23] It should be mentioned that this cannot be considered a random sample – it is a "convenience" sample. The ability to increase the sample size is constrained by two forces. First, not all firms report the pre-IPO performance; second, the available resources do not allow for contacting each firm and then coding the data manually. The hope is that others will provide comparable results using a much larger data set.

The 50 sample firms came from a variety of industries. Table 6 shows their sectoral distribution. It should be noted that this sample does not necessarily represent the overall distribution of IPOs in that period; it is under-represented in the natural resource sector by design. The sample firms span 28 industry groupings with some concentration in the technology sectors. There are 12 firms which represent the hardware, software and biotechnology sectors.

TABLE 6

INDUSTRY DISTRIBUTION OF THE SAMPLE FIRMS

Industry	Number
Mining	1
Oil and gas, mining and forest services	1
Paper and forest products	3
Building materials	2
Autos and parts	1
Breweries and beverages	2
Food processing	1
Household goods	5
Biotechnology/pharmaceutical	3
Hospitality	3
Specialty stores	2
Business services	2
Chemicals and fertilizers	1
Electrical and electronic products	1
Fabricating and engineering	1
Speciality industries	1
Steel distributing and servicing	1
Technology – hardware	6
Technology – software	3
Transportation and environmental services	2
Telephone utilities	1
Broadcasting	1
Publishing and printing	1
Real estate and construction	1
Leasing, financing, mortgages	1
Insurance	2
Conglomerates	1

RESULTS

TABLES 7 AND 8 PROVIDE THE MEAN AND MEDIAN VALUES for the 50 sample firms for all the accounting variables collected from their prospectuses and their annual reports following the IPO year. These variables include the standard accounting variables used in a typical corporate financial analysis, as well as some of the financial ratios that can provide indications of financial and operating performance. While more variables and details might be desirable, the necessary information is often unavailable in the prospectuses which provide only the most aggregate information. These two tables provide aggregate information on eight income statement variables, five

TABLE 7
MEAN VALUE OF EACH VARIABLE OR RATIO FOR ANY GIVEN YEAR BETWEEN -2 AND +2

	Year				
	-2	-1	0	1	2
Revenues	$44,411.29	$85,877.78	$100,598.12	$125,263.04	$127,828.70
Depreciation	$2,639.10	$3,976.19	$4,259.47	$5,770.82	$4,658.08
Earnings before interest and taxes	$5,761.57	$16,783.80	$16,863.86	$14,108.47	$15,329.06
Interest	$2,186.68	$5,328.72	$4,130.39	$4,560.90	$4,450.28
Taxes	$963.31	$2,625.96	$2,937.04	$4,552.29	$4,697.56
Net income	$1,314.27	$7,552.50	$9,337.18	$4,852.47	$7,493.72
Dividends – preferred	$22.94	$26.81	$119.00	$274.27	$469.76
Dividends – common	$294.39	$624.49	$2,969.92	$2,482.02	$3,798.46
Short-term debt	$2,319.16	$8,807.51	$9,303.92	$8,943.63	$8,374.90
Long-term debt	$19,566.69	$31,802.59	$42,411.02	$37,933.20	$51,666.80
Preferred equity	$747.71	$1,442.67	$4,135.69	$4,943.10	$6,806.40
Net fixed assets	$43,119.57	$61,184.58	$73,395.57	$75,015.59	$93,368.72
Total assets	$97,108.78	$152,954.74	$204,303.78	$203,164.29	$227,102.28
Return on assets	0.057	0.083	0.063	0.006	-0.040
Profit margin	-0.006	0.052	0.073	-0.256	-0.131
Payout	0.264	0.114	0.160	0.355	0.104
Debt-to-asset ratio	0.282	0.262	0.196	0.188	0.230
Sales-to-asset ratio	1.527	1.356	1.081	0.991	0.886

TABLE 8

MEDIAN VALUE OF EACH VARIABLE OR RATIO FOR ANY GIVEN YEAR BETWEEN -2 AND +2

	Year				
	-2	-1	0	1	2
Revenues	$22,685.00	$23,348.00	$39,408.00	$48,009.00	$47,864.00
Depreciation	$752.00	$936.00	$1,287.00	$1,512.00	$1,095.00
Earnings before interest and taxes	$2,575.00	$3,761.00	$6,497.00	$4,770.00	$2,190.50
Interest	$501.00	$532.50	$470.00	$446.00	$410.50
Taxes	$550.00	$1,083.00	$1,942.00	$1,824.00	$630.00
Net income	$881.00	$1,491.00	$2,921.00	$2,217.00	$1,134.00
Dividends – preferred	$0.00	$0.00	$0.00	$0.00	$0.00
Dividends – common	$0.00	$0.00	$0.00	$0.00	$0.00
Short-term debt	$899.50	$898.00	$629.00	$807.00	$1,520.00
Long-term debt	$3,806.00	$3,083.00	$3,113.00	$3,312.00	$2,089.00
Preferred equity	$0.00	$0.00	$0.00	$0.00	$0.00
Net fixed assets	$3,779.00	$5,112.50	$9,062.00	$12,779.00	$8,851.00
Total assets	$16,433.50	$19,664.00	$34,117.00	$45,285.00	$48,711.00
Return on assets	0.055	0.057	0.058	0.040	0.033
Profit margin	0.045	0.056	0.063	0.046	0.026
Payout	0.000	0.000	0.000	0.000	0.000
Debt-to-asset ratio	0.274	0.276	0.158	0.146	0.206
Sales-to-asset ratio	1.402	1.210	0.954	1.038	0.882

balance sheet variables and five ratios constructed from 13 accounting variables. It should also be noted that no attempt was made to express these in inflation-adjusted dollars. The analysis that follows provides a more detailed picture of performance.

Although these two tables do not provide a firm by firm perspective, some general conclusions can still be made. First, it is clear that the asset base of the firm increases after the IPO since it now has a much higher level of equity capital. The results indicate that the primary result of an IPO is to increase the firm's working capital, since the net fixed assets seem to increase more slowly than the total assets. This is not surprising since many IPO firms raise equity financing to build inventories or finance accounts receivable. This increase in asset base also implies the ability of the firm to increase sales in cases where assets had been the constraining factor. As can be seen, there is a corresponding increase in sales. For example, the mean and median value of sales show an increase of 25 percent in the year following the IPO (year 1). Thus, it is clear that the IPO allows the firm to increase assets and have the necessary capital base to support higher levels of sales. As a consequence of the IPO, this increase in sales and assets can now be financed without increasing the firm's debt load. As can be seen, there is no discernable trend in interest expense or the levels of short and long-term debt. The debt-to-asset ratio (second last row) actually declines. Thus, the IPO has achieved one of its main functions, a reduction in the reliance on debt by the firm.

Unfortunately, the mean and median values of performance indicators show that the growth in sales and assets comes at the expense of profitability and turnover. The sales-to-assets ratio (last row) declines significantly, indicating an inability to increase sales in proportion to the increase in assets. Also seen is a decline in the return on assets and profit margin in the years following the IPO. These aggregate numbers imply that a typical IPO firm may actually display a deteriorating performance once it raises external equity capital.

These conclusions must be viewed with caution, because they are based on aggregate values and may be caused by a specific subset of the sample firms. To investigate this possibility, tables 9 through 19 provide the distribution among firms of the various performance measures shown in tables 7 and 8. This distribution-based analysis also allows us to make more precise conclusions about the sample firms.

Table 9 provides the distribution in terms of the percentage change in total assets. The columns show the comparisons for the various post and pre-IPO years for total assets. For example, row one compares the total assets in year 0 (the year of the IPO) with year -2 (two years before the IPO). It shows that in 5.1 percent of the sample firms, the total assets in year 0 declined by over 10 percent as compared to year -2. Similarly, in 87.2 percent of the cases (the last column value in the first row), the total assets grew by at least 10 percent. The second row compares assets in year 0 with assets in year -1 and so forth, with the last row comparing assets in year 2 with assets in year 1. Thus, all years are expressed in relation to the year of the IPO which is designated as year 0. A similar format is followed in the rest of the tables, and a variety of conclusions emerge.

TABLE 9

DISTRIBUTION OF IPO FIRMS IN TERMS OF PERCENTAGE CHANGE IN TOTAL ASSETS

Year	x < -10% (%)	-10% ≤ x < -5% (%)	-5% ≤ x < 5% (%)	5% ≤ x <10% (%)	x ≥10% (%)
0 – -2	5.1	0.0	5.1	2.6	87.2
0 – -1	5.8	1.9	5.8	3.8	82.7
1 – -2	2.6	0.0	2.6	0.0	94.9
1 – -1	5.8	0.0	1.9	0.0	92.3
1 – 0	11.5	0.0	15.4	11.5	61.5
2 – -2	17.5	0.0	2.5	0.0	80.0
2 – -1	18.9	1.9	0.0	0.0	79.2
2 – 0	24.5	5.7	1.9	3.8	64.2
2 – 1	24.5	5.7	17.0	11.3	41.5

There is an overall increase in assets (Table 9) and a corresponding increase in the number of firms reporting increases in depreciation expenses (Table 10). This is not surprising since there is a large infusion of additional capital into the firm, some of which is used to increase the firm's net fixed assets.

TABLE 10

DISTRIBUTION OF IPO FIRMS IN TERMS OF PERCENTAGE CHANGE IN DEPRECIATION

Year	x < -10% (%)	-10% ≤ x < -5% (%)	-5% ≤ x < 5% (%)	5% ≤ x <10% (%)	x ≥10% (%)
0 – -2	12.8	0.0	7.7	2.6	76.9
0 – -1	14.0	4.0	10.0	6.0	66.0
1 – -2	7.7	0.0	5.1	0.0	87.2
1 – -1	8.0	0.0	6.0	4.0	82.0
1 – 0	2.0	6.0	8.0	0.0	84.0
2 – -2	27.5	2.5	5.0	0.0	65.0
2 – -1	21.6	5.9	2.0	0.0	70.6
2 – 0	21.6	2.0	5.9	3.9	66.7
2 – 1	22.0	2.0	14.0	2.0	60.0

Table 11 shows the changes in the revenues of sample firms. Given that the external equity financing was likely being raised to sustain growth, it is not surprising that a majority of the firms experienced high growth rates in the pre-IPO years. Similar high growth rates seem to continue in the post-IPO years, but at a declining rate.

TABLE 11

DISTRIBUTION OF IPO FIRMS IN TERMS OF PERCENTAGE CHANGE IN REVENUE

Year	x < -10% (%)	-10% ≤ x < -5% (%)	-5% ≤ x < 5% (%)	5% ≤ x <10% (%)	x ≥10% (%)
0 – -2	4.4	0.0	2.2	0.0	93.3
0 – -1	13.2	0.0	7.5	3.8	75.5
1 – -2	2.2	2.2	2.2	2.2	91.1
1 – -1	7.5	1.9	1.9	3.8	84.9
1 – 0	9.6	3.8	11.5	1.9	73.1
2 – -2	15.2	2.2	2.2	0.0	80.4
2 – -1	27.8	1.9	0.0	1.9	68.5
2 – 0	24.5	5.7	3.8	1.9	64.2
2 – 1	26.4	1.9	15.1	11.3	45.3

TABLE 12

DISTRIBUTION OF IPO FIRMS IN TERMS OF PERCENTAGE CHANGE IN DEBT-TO-ASSET RATIO

Year	x < -10% (%)	-10% ≤ x < -5% (%)	-5% ≤ x < 5% (%)	5% ≤ x <10% (%)	x ≥10% (%)
0 – -2	62.8	2.3	7.0	27.9	0.0
0 – -1	62.7	3.9	2.0	0.0	31.4
1 – -2	71.4	4.8	4.8	2.4	16.7
1 – -1	66.7	2.0	2.0	5.9	23.5
1 – 0	47.9	4.2	8.3	2.1	37.5
2 – -2	53.5	7.0	2.3	2.3	34.9
2 – -1	48.1	3.8	5.8	1.9	40.4
2 – 0	38.8	2.0	8.2	2.0	49.0
2 – 1	31.9	4.3	14.9	2.1	46.8

Although sample firms raise equity financing, their reliance on debt does not necessarily decrease: roughly as many firms showed an increase in the debt-to-assets ratio as those showing a decrease (Table 12). This indicates that, in over one-third of the sample firms, asset growth forced them to continue to rely on higher levels of debt. This may be more feasible due to their public status.

TABLE 13

DISTRIBUTION OF IPO FIRMS IN TERMS OF PERCENTAGE CHANGE IN COMMON DIVIDEND

Year	x < -10% (%)	-10% ≤ x < -5% (%)	-5% ≤ x < 5% (%)	5% ≤ x <10% (%)	x ≥10% (%)
0 – -2	18.2	0.0	70.5	0.0	11.4
0 – -1	16.0	0.0	66.0	0.0	18.0
1 – -2	11.4	0.0	68.2	0.0	20.5
1 – -1	17.6	3.9	60.8	0.0	17.6
1 – 0	17.6	0.0	58.8	0.0	23.5
2 – -2	13.3	0.0	68.9	0.0	17.8
2 – -1	21.6	2.0	58.8	0.0	17.6
2 – 0	25.0	0.0	57.7	0.0	17.3
2 – 1	12.2	0.0	73.5	2.0	12.2

TABLE 14

DISTRIBUTION OF IPO FIRMS IN TERMS OF PERCENTAGE CHANGE IN PAYOUT RATIO

Year	x < -10% (%)	-10% ≤ x < -5% (%)	-5% ≤ x < 5% (%)	5% ≤ x <10% (%)	x ≥10% (%)
0 – -2	25.0	0.0	68.2	0.0	6.8
0 – -1	24.0	0.0	64.0	0.0	12.0
1 – -2	22.7	2.3	68.2	0.0	6.8
1 – -1	25.5	0.0	60.8	0.0	13.7
1 – 0	21.6	0.0	60.8	2.0	15.7
2 – -2	24.4	0.0	66.7	0.0	8.9
2 – -1	29.4	0.0	60.8	0.0	9.8
2 – 0	28.8	0.0	59.6	0.0	11.5
2 – 1	15.2	0.0	69.6	0.0	15.2

In contrast to the aggregate results shown in tables 7 and 8, Table 13 shows that there was no increase in common dividends in the post-IPO years; only one fifth of the firms showed an increase in dividends, and a majority of the firms showed no increase. Similar conclusions can be drawn from Table 14, which shows most firms maintaining their payout ratios, but with almost one fourth showing a decline.

Next, attention focuses on performance measures. Tables 15 and 16 show the changes in the earnings before interest and taxes (EBIT) levels and the EBIT-to-sales ratio for the sample firms. Table 7 indicates that the level of EBIT had increased for all the firms in the years before the IPO (year -1 and year 0 compared to the preceding year). But as Table 15 shows, the actual number of firms with an increase in the level of EBIT in the post-IPO years was almost the same as the number of firms where the EBIT level decreased. Moreover, the comparison of the EBIT-to-sales ratio in Table 16 indicates a more disappointing picture. In all post-IPO years, almost two thirds of the sample firms showed a decline in this ratio, thereby indicating worsening operating margins. These results provide partial support to some recent work which contends that there may be a degree of earnings management by firms immediately before the IPO. This earnings management implies that one would expect to find a relative decline in reported earnings in the post-IPO years.[24]

Table 17 confirms this deterioration in performance, although the difference here is not as substantial as for the operating margins. Again, almost two thirds of the sample firms show a decline in the profit margin. Table 18 analyses the profitability performance using the return on assets measure, which shows the productivity of the asset base. Here again, performance is disappointing: over two thirds of the sample firms showed a decline in their performance.

TABLE 15

DISTRIBUTION OF IPO FIRMS IN TERMS OF PERCENTAGE CHANGE IN EARNINGS BEFORE INTEREST AND TAXES

Year	x < -10% (%)	-10% ≤ x < -5% (%)	-5% ≤ x < 5% (%)	5% ≤ x <10% (%)	x ≥10% (%)
0 – -2	24.4	0.0	4.4	2.2	68.9
0 – -1	22.6	1.9	7.5	1.9	66.0
1 – -2	28.9	0.0	4.4	2.2	64.4
1 – -1	39.6	0.0	5.7	0.0	54.7
1 – 0	48.1	0.0	5.8	3.8	42.3
2 – -2	43.5	0.0	4.3	0.0	52.2
2 – -1	53.7	0.0	1.9	3.7	40.7
2 – 0	56.6	0.0	0.0	1.9	43.4
2 – 1	46.0	2.0	4.0	2.0	46.0

TABLE 16

DISTRIBUTION OF IPO FIRMS IN TERMS OF PERCENTAGE CHANGE IN EARNINGS BEFORE INTEREST AND TAXES-TO-SALES RATIO

Year	x < -10% (%)	-10% ≤ x < -5% (%)	-5% ≤ x < 5% (%)	5% ≤ x <10% (%)	x ≥10% (%)
0 – -2	42.2	0.0	6.7	2.2	48.9
0 – -1	28.3	3.8	15.1	5.7	47.2
1 – -2	51.1	6.7	15.6	0.0	26.7
1 – -1	56.6	5.7	11.3	1.9	24.5
1 – 0	61.5	3.8	17.3	1.9	15.4
2 – -2	60.0	0.0	5.0	0.0	35.0
2 – -1	63.8	4.3	4.3	2.1	25.5
2 – 0	63.0	4.3	10.9	0.0	21.7
2 – 1	54.5	4.5	20.5	0.0	20.5

TABLE 17

DISTRIBUTION OF IPO FIRMS IN TERMS OF PERCENTAGE CHANGE IN PROFIT MARGIN

Year	x < -10% (%)	-10% ≤ x < -5% (%)	-5% ≤ x < 5% (%)	5% ≤ x <10% (%)	x ≥10% (%)
0 – -2	44.4	0.0	4.4	2.2	48.9
0 – -1	37.7	1.9	7.5	3.8	49.1
1 – -2	57.8	4.4	4.4	0.0	33.3
1 – -1	60.4	1.9	3.8	0.0	34.0
1 – 0	61.5	1.9	3.8	1.9	30.8
2 – -2	60.9	4.3	0.0	2.2	32.6
2 – -1	63.0	0.0	1.9	1.9	33.3
2 – 0	73.6	0.0	1.9	3.8	20.8
2 – 1	61.5	3.8	5.8	1.9	26.9

Table 19 uses the changes in turnover ratio as another indicator of performance. As this table shows, the sample firms were unable to generate an increasing level of sales per dollar of invested assets. More firms showed a decline in this performance ratio than showed an improvement.

TABLE 18

DISTRIBUTION OF IPO FIRMS IN TERMS OF PERCENTAGE CHANGE IN RETURN ON ASSETS

Year	x < -10% (%)	-10% ≤ x < -5% (%)	-5% ≤ x < 5% (%)	5% ≤ x <10% (%)	x ≥10% (%)
0 – -2	55.6	0.0	6.7	2.2	35.6
0 – -1	52.8	0.0	13.2	3.8	30.2
1 – -2	62.2	2.2	6.7	2.2	26.7
1 – -1	67.9	0.0	5.7	0.0	26.4
1 – 0	57.7	1.9	5.8	5.8	28.8
2 – -2	71.7	0.0	0.0	2.2	26.1
2 – -1	70.4	1.9	1.9	0.0	25.9
2 – 0	69.8	3.8	3.8	0.0	22.6
2 – 1	63.5	1.9	7.7	1.9	25.0

TABLE 19

DISTRIBUTION OF IPO FIRMS IN TERMS OF PERCENTAGE CHANGE IN SALES-TO-ASSETS RATIO

Year	x < -10% (%)	-10% ≤ x < -5% (%)	-5% ≤ x < 5% (%)	5% ≤ x <10% (%)	x ≥10% (%)
0 – -2	43.6	5.1	17.9	5.1	28.2
0 – -1	46.2	7.7	23.1	1.9	21.2
1 – -2	46.2	15.4	10.3	7.7	20.5
1 – -1	50.0	1.9	15.4	11.5	21.2
1 – 0	30.8	7.7	15.4	7.7	38.5
2 – -2	65.0	5.0	5.0	0.0	25.0
2 – -1	58.5	13.2	7.5	1.9	18.9
2 – 0	45.3	7.5	7.5	3.8	35.8
2 – 1	39.2	11.8	13.7	7.8	27.5

SUMMARY

OVERALL, THESE RESULTS INDICATE THAT THE SAMPLE FIRMS managed to increase their sales and assets and improve their working capital in the post-IPO years. They also managed to reduce their reliance on debt due to the infusion of the external equity capital. No major changes were observed in their dividend payments or payout ratio, indicating that there was no additional withdrawal of funds by shareholders.

However, the performance of these firms actually worsened. Almost two thirds showed a deterioration in the standard performance measures traditionally used in the corporate finance framework. Since the sample size was small and the distribution properties of the ratios not known, there is little possibility that sophisticated statistical analysis can be conducted on this data. However, the distribution of firms is such that the overall deterioration in performance in the post-IPO years cannot be explained away as a statistical artifact. It should also be noted that even if the analysis is extended to more firms, there is little chance that these results will change significantly. Since these 50 firms were chosen simply on the basis of data availability, there is no reason to believe that another set of 50 firms would display radically different performance characteristics. These results also confirm the overall negative long-term performance of the IPO firms in the stock market. Similar results are presented by Jain and Kini (1994), who found a noticeable deterioration in operating performance in the post-IPO period for a much larger sample of U.S. firms.

Entrepreneurs' Views

In the sections above, the emphasis was placed on issues related to pricing, valuation and performance of IPOs in Canada. The analysis was based on data available in the public domain. This section, however, assesses the issues that arise during the IPO process. The analysis is based on the results of a survey questionnaire sent to entrepreneurs who were instrumental in taking their firms public.[25] The reason for this work was to obtain some direct evidence on the IPO process in Canada, rather than relying on secondary research on underpricing and stock market or accounting-based performance.

Five aspects of the IPO process were considered important: the decision to go public, contractual details of the IPO, IPO-specific aspects, the post-issuance process and the entrepreneurs' views on the reasons for underpricing IPOs. The individual questions were intended to solicit the detailed responses which are unavailable from secondary data sources.

Data

The questionnaires were sent to 140 potential respondents whose IPOs covered the years 1982 through 1993. Each questionnaire had a total of 105 questions. The 54 responses came predominantly from recent IPOs, with 29 from 1993, 10 from 1988 to 1992 and 15 from the pre-1988 years. In terms of dollars raised by the sample firms, the smallest amount was $2 million (in 1993 dollars) and the largest was $565 million.[26] Of the 47 respondents who indicated the amount raised, five can be considered IPOs of very large established companies, which raised over $200 million each from the stock market.[27] Since the sample is small, no attempt was made to distinguish individual respondents representing large IPOs from that of small IPOs. In most cases, little difference was found between the responses of the large and small IPO firms.

RESULTS

THE FIRST SET OF QUESTIONS REFERRED TO THE ISSUES surrounding the entrepreneur's (firm's) decision to go public. The questions were about the best time to go public, the reasons for going public, the intended use of the capital being raised, the importance of underwriters and the influence of venture capital financiers on the timing to go public. As can be seen from Table 20, the timing of IPOs seems to be related to the need for external equity financing coupled with an inability to raise capital from other sources, e.g., private equity or debt, the state of the stock market, i.e., the bullishness sentiment, and the owners' need for liquidity. Although not shown here, capital raised though the IPO was used for financial restructuring (40 percent of the respondents), paying off the founding owners (25 percent), financing business acquisition (24 percent) and purchasing equipment (22 percent).[28] Other uses mentioned include investing in research and development, retiring debt and general expansion of the business.

Table 21 shows that the choice of underwriter was dependent mainly on reputation, quality of service, previous success in raising capital and institutional experience, rather than the location or size of the retail staff or even the history of under/over-pricing. Not a single respondent mentioned the cost of service as the most important consideration. Thus, it seems that handholding experience and the ability to raise capital through institutional investors seem to be key factors that can be emphasized by underwriters in marketing their services to potential IPO clients.

On the issue of venture capital influence on the IPO decision, only 11 IPOs had received financing from such firms. In four cases, these venture capitalists were instrumental in the firm's decision to go public. In half the cases, venture capitalists continued to maintain the same level of ownership even one year after the IPO. Thus, the exit requirements of venture capital financing were not a major aspect of the IPO decision, at least for these sample firms. These results are not surprising given the much lower levels of involvement of venture capital in Canada than in the United States.

The next section of the questionnaire focused on the costs of IPO issuance and the contractual obligations of the firm with its underwriter. Many of these agreements had either an over-allotment option or a compensation option.[29] Thirty-three firms had granted their underwriters either an overallotment option (20), or a compensation option (five) or both (eight). The overallotment option was in the range of an additional 10 percent to 15 percent of the initial issue, whereas the compensation option was generally less than 10 percent of the initial issue. In both cases, the share price at which either of these options could be exercised was the IPO price. Since compensation options allow an underwriter to buy shares during the subsequent 24 months, underwriters stand to benefit in addition to the normal underwriting fees.

In most cases, underwriters who were granted either or both of these options exercised them. The existence of these options was not restricted to small issuers only, but were equally present among all issuers. In at least 50 percent of the cases, another 15 percent to 20 percent in additional shares were issued to the under-writing syndicate under these options. It is also interesting to note that of the 34 issuers whose shares were oversubscribed, only 10 had neither of these options. Of the remaining firms, 14 had one of the two options, and 10 had both options. These observations indicate that oversubscription may be a norm rather than an exception and that underwriters benefit further from these options if the oversubscription leads to higher prices in the immediate post-issuance period or if the stock price remains above the IPO price in the near term.[30]

These observations indicate that, in addition to fixed underwriting commissions, an underwriting syndicate can also benefit from the receipt and the subsequent exercise of the overallotment and compensation options. If the stock price increases over the IPO price in subsequent periods, the underwriting syndicate can exercise either of the options and receive up to 20 percent in additional shares at the IPO

TABLE 20

DECISION THAT IT WAS BEST TIME TO GO PUBLIC

	Best Reason	Second Best	Third Best	Total
You felt ready	5	6	4	15
The business had an exceptionally good year	1	1	3	5
The business had a well-defined business plan to expand	11	11	4	26
The current sources of financing were starting to dry out	7	5	7	19
The business wished to enter new markets	2	8	2	12
The business was looking at diversifying	3	0	1	4
The stock market was favourable to high-priced issues	10	7	6	23
The owners wanted liquidity for their shares	1	8	11	20
The owners wanted to sell a part of their ownership	6	0	3	9
The owners wanted the respect a public firm enjoys	2	0	2	4
Others	5	2	5	12

price. The evidence in the previous sections indicates that IPO stock prices, on average, increase by 10 percent to 15 percent in absolute terms in the two years after the IPO issuance. This implies that the underwriters can earn an additional 1.5 percent to 2.5 percent of the IPO amount by exercising these options.[31]

Another issue investigated in this questionnaire concerns the out-of-pocket costs associated with an IPO issuance process. It is well known that there are minimum fixed costs associated with the IPO process. These include the underwriting commission, and issuing and legal costs. Forty respondents provided information on these two categories of costs. Since the sample spans 10 years, these costs are reported in 1993 dollars as well as in relation to the amount of financing raised through the IPO. In addition, due to the presence of a few large IPOs, the median results are reported wherever appropriate and exclude the large IPOs when drawing general conclusions. Expressed in 1993 dollars, the median (mean) levels of issuing expenses were $525,000 ($1 million) and $1.6 million ($2.8 million) for the underwriting commission for a

TABLE 21

CHOOSING AN UNDERWRITER FOR IPO

Reason for Choosing an Underwriter	Very High	High	Average	Low	Very Low	Most Important
A good reputation	27	23	3	0	0	11
The quality of service	21	26	4	1	0	10
The cost of service	2	13	29	7	1	0
Proximity of underwriter's office	0	3	14	16	19	1
Underwriter's success with previous issues	19	25	8	1	0	20
History of under/overpricing of issues	1	14	21	13	3	2
The size of the retail sales staff	5	11	17	13	6	1
Experience with large institutional clients	14	21	15	2	1	4
Market share	4	14	23	9	2	1

median (mean) IPO financing of $26 million ($69.5 million). Table 22 expresses these expenses as a percentage of the total financing raised through the corresponding IPO.

The issuing costs (legal, printing, travel, etc.) represent 2.3 percent, and the underwriting commission represents 6 percent of the IPO amount raised, bringing the total expense of a typical IPO to 8.3 percent of the amount raised. Obviously, these figures vary from issue to issue, and are partially dependent on the size of the IPO since there is a component of fixed and variable costs associated with an issue.[32] The following regression equations show the nature of the relationship between expenses and IPO value, both expressed in 1993 dollars for IPO issues of under $60 million.[33]

Issuing expense = 167,806 + 0.02 x IPO value (R-squared = 0.31)
Underwriting commission = 171,048 + 0.05 x IPO Value (R-squared = 0.81)
Total expenses = 338,854 + 0.069 x IPO Value (R-squared = 0.80)

These results confirm the observations based on simple analysis: in a typical IPO issue, the fixed costs are about $300,000 to $400,000 in addition to the variable costs of 6 percent to 8 percent of the IPO value. A further 1.5 percent to 2.5 percent of the IPO value is also received by the underwriter through the exercise of the overallotment and compensation options.

The next section of the questionnaire dealt with the process immediately surrounding the actual IPO issuance. In over 70 percent of the respondents, the finalization of the IPO price seemed to take place two weeks before the offering date,

Table 22

Issuing and Underwriting Expenses as a Percentage of Equity Capital Raised (Number of Firms)

Percent Range	Issuing Expenses	Underwriting Expenses	Total Expenses
0-1	8	2	1
1-2	8	2	1
2-3	7		
3-4	8	1	
4-5	3	4	1
5-6		7	3
6-7	1	15	6
7-8	1	2	6
8-9			4
9-10			6
10 and above		1	7

with another 16 percent fixing the offering price in the four weeks before the date. The influence of institutional investors was also quite apparent from the responses. On average, 60 percent of the shares were bought by institutional investors; in 20 IPOs, institutional investors purchased over 75 percent of the shares offered. Moreover, the respondents also stated that, not only were the institutional investors important in the initial purchase, they continued to hold what they purchased. In over 50 percent of the cases, they bought more shares in the month following the IPO. Investors sold their shares soon after purchase; additional buying by these retail investors occurred in only 13 percent of the cases. These findings reinforce the importance IPO firms attach to the influence underwriters have with institutional investors.

Given that one of the main functions of the underwriter is to provide service and support to the firm, it is interesting to note the respondents' opinions about the post-issuance support they received. Table 23 shows the responses to four key questions about post-issuance support. As can be seen, the degree of underwriter support is said in most cases to be "above average" or "excellent." The perception is that underwriters do a better job in providing the support required by institutions than by retail investors. When asked specifically about support provided by the underwriter in assigning an analyst and in providing the coverage and analysis required after the IPO, over 90 percent of the respondents indicated that the lead underwriter had assigned an analyst, and 60 percent were satisfied with the subsequent coverage and analysis provided to the firm. It is also interesting to note that, of the 18 respondents who issued additional common shares, 14 of them used the services of the same underwriter. This observation indicates that, despite the less than excellent ratings they give their underwriters, firms continue to deal with their original underwriters for subsequent issues. This finding is also important given the fact that only 40 percent of the respondents showed "above average" satisfaction with the price of their IPO and the current price of their common stock.

Another important purpose of the questionnaire was to elicit response to the underpricing issue. As noted earlier, much of the literature provides theoretical justification for the existence of underpricing. However, there is little or no direct

TABLE 23

OPINIONS ABOUT UNDERWRITER SUPPORT IMMEDIATELY FOLLOWING IPO ISSUANCE

	Poor	Below Average	Average	Above Average	Excellent
Overall support		3	19	17	11
Quality of service		1	15	21	14
Retail market support	2	8	23	15	3
Institutional support	2	4	13	24	7

TABLE 24

UNDERPRICING EXISTS BECAUSE

	Agree Strongly	Agree Moderately	Indifferent	Disagree Moderately	Disagree Strongly
Investors require a discount for future uncertainty	3	33	7	5	1
It reduces the possibility of underwriters' losses due to undersubscription	7	22	12	5	2
IPOs are generally oversubscribed and demand exceeds supply	4	19	15	9	1
Underwriters do not want a legal suit	1	13	16	13	5
Underwriters can benefit their preferred customers	4	20	6	14	4
Underwriters must leave something on the table	6	20	12	8	2

corroborative evidence on these competing theoretical hypotheses from the firms which actually raise the capital. Table 24 shows the responses to these competing hypotheses. The results partially corroborate all the theoretical hypotheses, with stronger corroboration for the discount based on future uncertainty as a major reason for underpricing. Given the generally low levels of litigation in Canada, it is not surprising to find only weak support for the legal argument for underpricing; a similar question may result in stronger agreement in the United States. Moreover, although not reported here, none of these responses depend on the size of the issue; there is virtually no difference between responses by small issuers and those of large issuers to these and other questions in this section.

SUMMARY

THE MAIN REASON FOR FIRMS GOING PUBLIC is that other sources of financing can no longer satisfy their financing needs. This, coupled with the state of the stock market and the owner's need to seek liquidity, may result in a firm's decision to go public. The underwriters who can get the IPO business will be those who have a good overall reputation, are known for their quality of service, can demonstrate their success in raising capital and can show their knowledge of institutional investors. The costs of raising external financing via an IPO are in the range of $300,000 to $400,000 plus another 6 percent to 7 percent in underwriting costs. In addition, underwriters are often allocated an overallotment or a compensation option, bringing the total compensation of the underwriters to about 8 percent to 10 percent of the amount raised. There is a general recognition of the fact that underpricing of an IPO can be justified in the context of uncertainty about the future price of the IPO and in order to ensure that the required financing is raised. These results also indicate that there are competing hypotheses for the underpricing, and no one hypothesis can provide a complete explanation for the existence of underpricing in IPOs.

CONCLUSIONS

THIS PAPER EVALUATED THE ENVIRONMENT for Canadian initial public offerings based on historical evidence. The empirical evidence was in four areas: underpricing, long-term stock market performance, accounting-based performance in the post-IPO period and the IPO process as viewed by firms which went public in the mid to late 1980s and early 1990s. All results in this paper are based on IPOs for firms that qualified for listing on the TSE. As a result, generalizations from this study may apply to IPOs on other Canadian exchanges which cater to IPOs of smaller firms.

The following major conclusions arise from this paper. First, the evidence reviewed here reveals that the degree of underpricing of Canadian IPOs is much less than that reported in most other developed countries. Moreover, the degree of underpricing decreased in the 1980s compared to the 1970s. Thus, there is no reason to be concerned about the pricing mechanism for Canadian IPOs. As noted above, the evidence is restricted to firms which qualified for listing on the TSE and may not be applicable to other stock exchanges where listing requirements are less restrictive.

The results associated with the long-term performance of Canadian IPOs are disappointing and are similar to those reported for the United States. Although an investment in an average IPO provides positive absolute returns, the returns that are adjusted for the underlying stock market performance reveal a high degree of negative returns. On a market-adjusted basis, an average IPO shows a relative loss of 40 percent in four years. The performance is mostly negative beginning within a year of the IPO, continuing through to the end of the fourth year and turning somewhat positive in the fifth and sixth years. This apparent improvement must be viewed with caution due to the small sample size and the obvious implication of the survivorship bias. IPOs which were overpriced perform even more negatively than those which were underpriced, an observation at odds with some U.S. results.

A smaller and more recent sample of IPOs reveals that the post-IPO performance as revealed by standard accounting-based measures can be considered mediocre or worse. A majority of IPO firms show decreased turnover and profitability. These results are consistent with the long-term performance results and further reinforce the view that IPOs, from an investor viewpoint, may show disappointing performance. There is no reason to believe that these results are specific to the sample studied. They are consistent with some U.S. studies which show evidence of active earnings management in the pre-IPO period.

In terms of some primary evidence about the IPO process as seen from the viewpoint of the firms, there is an overall degree of satisfaction about the support received from underwriters and about the pricing of the IPOs. The costs of a typical IPO seem to be in the range of $300,000 to $400,000 plus 6 percent to 7 percent of the IPO value. Underwriters also receive further compensation (2 percent to 3 percent) due to compensation and overallotment options. The sample firms seem to be perfectly willing to live with some underpricing as a compensation to investors for the underlying uncertainty involved. No expression of dissatisfaction about the process was reported.

From the viewpoint of an entrepreneur, the Canadian IPO environment is an attractive one. The degree of underpricing is low; investors seem to buy all the IPOs offered despite below-average returns and performance; there is no evidence of underallotment; and the support by underwriters seems to be satisfactory.

From an investor's viewpoint, the results are quite disappointing. Although, on an absolute basis, there is no great loss from an initial investment, a typical IPO provides large negative returns when adjusted for the underlying market movement. This less than attractive performance is also confirmed by the accounting-based analysis conducted for a small sample of recent IPO firms.

The overall evidence presented here indicates that the Canadian capital markets are doing a good job in allocating risk capital to entrepreneurs. It should also be noted that this evidence is based on sample firms from the TSE and may reflect the experience of somewhat larger firms. Also, by definition, the evidence reflects those firms which have gone public; little is known about firms which tried to raise equity capital via an IPO but failed to get the necessary support. More research is certainly needed to explore these issues for other exchanges.

Clearly, an improvement in underlying performance by IPO firms in post-IPO years would be welcome news if Canadian investors were expected to channel their savings into IPOs. However, the managers of these newly public firms seem to be unable to perform according to initial expectations. The post-IPO performance is poor both on the basis of stock market performance and accounting-based performance measures although the latter is based on a non-random small sample. No empirical evidence exists on the post-IPO governance characteristics of these IPO firms. Neither is there any evidence on the adequacy and ability of the management skills of these firms to manage in the new environment. The evidence presented here indicates that, if anything, these firms in their post-IPO period performed less than satisfactorily for their shareholders.

APPENDIX A
METHODOLOGY FOR LONG-TERM PERFORMANCE ANALYSIS

RITTER'S (1991) METHODOLOGY IS USED to evaluate how an average IPO stock performs over the 72 months following the IPO.[34] A second methodology is used to measure the wealth creation or depletion (referred to as residual cumulative wealth and explained below) which would have resulted from investing in a portfolio of sample IPOs, relative to an investment in a benchmark portfolio. This residual cumulative wealth represents returns from an arbitrage strategy to an investor who invests in the sample IPO stocks and simultaneously holds a short position in the benchmark portfolio. A negative return on such a strategy implies that the investor would have done better by investing in the benchmark portfolio.

To ensure consistency with the Ritter results, monthly returns are defined as the 21-trading-day returns starting with the closing price on day 21 of trading in the post-IPO period. Month 1, therefore, consists of days 22 to 43, followed by month 2 including days 44 to 65, etc. Similarly, monthly residual returns are calculated as the monthly raw return on a stock less that on the benchmark for the corresponding 21-day period.

More specifically, the monthly abnormal return for stock i in month t with respect to the benchmark is defined as:

$$AR_{it} = R_{it} - R_{mt} \tag{1}$$

where R_{it} and R_{mt} are the return on stock i in month t and the return on the benchmark in month t. The average benchmark-adjusted abnormal return for month t is the equally weighted arithmetic average of the abnormal returns for individual stocks.

$$AR_t = \frac{1}{n_t} \Sigma_{i=1}^{n_t} AR_{it} \tag{2}$$

where n_t is the number of stocks in the portfolio in month t and the summation is over 1 to n_t.

The cumulative benchmark adjusted abnormal return in the after-market from month q to month s is the summation of the average benchmark adjusted abnormal returns for individual stocks over this period where the summation is done from month q to month s.

$$CAR_{q,s} = \Sigma_{t=q}^{s} AR_t \tag{3}$$

When a firm is delisted from the TSE-Western Database, the portfolio return for the next month is computed as an equally weighted average return of the surviving firms in the portfolio. The computation of CAR, therefore, requires monthly rebalancing, with the proceeds of a delisted firm equally allocated among the surviving members of the portfolio for each of the subsequent months.

For the second methodology, the residual cumulative wealth is computed as follows. Cumulative wealth from investing in stock i until month t, CW_{it}, is given as:

$$CW_{it} = \Pi_t(1+R_{it}) \qquad (4)$$

The residual cumulative wealth, RCW_{it}, for stock i until month t is given by:

$$RCW_{it} = CW_{it} - CW_{mt} \qquad (5)$$

where CW_{mt} is the cumulative wealth accumulated by investing in the benchmark until month t. Then, the average cumulative residual wealth, $ARCW_t$, until month t is computed as an equally weighted average of the residual cumulative wealth for all stocks which form part of the portfolio in month t.[35]

$$ARCW_t = \frac{1}{n_t}\Sigma_{i=1}^{n_t} RCW_{it} \qquad (6)$$

Since the measurement of long-term performance may be sensitive to the choice of benchmark, as suggested by Ritter (1991), two benchmarks to evaluate abnormal performance for the sample stocks – the TSE 300 Composite Index and the value-weighted index of the TSE-Western Database stocks – are used.[36]

ENDNOTES

1 These four issues are, of course, not the only ones that are associated with the IPO environment. Various papers have covered other aspects of the IPO environment which are neither reviewed nor discussed here. See, for example, Drake and Vetsuypens (1993), Garfinkel (1993) and Krinsky and Rotenberg (1989).

2 See Jog et al. (1991) for the expected returns required by venture capitalists. The 15 percent to 19 percent range of required real returns for IPOs is an estimate based on the fact that historical average rates on a broad market index have been around 6 percent to 8 percent above the risk-free rate. Since one can conjecture that IPOs may be viewed as relatively risky, investors may demand an additional risk premium of 4 percent to 6 percent. If the real risk-free rate is assumed to be 5 percent, then the cost of equity capital for an IPO can be estimated at between 17 percent and 22 percent.

3 See Desroches and Jog (1991).

4 Love money refers to the initial injection of capital from parents, relatives and friends of the entrepreneur. Informal investors include business associations or wealthy individuals who provide the next round of financing, followed by the more formal venture capital firms.

5 It is beyond the scope of this report to review all these developments and specific legislative changes. The purpose of this section is to provide an overall perspective on the environmental factors that have affected the financing of small and medium-sized businesses. For more details, see Jog (forthcoming).

6 This is not to say that investors received an above normal return or that the entrepreneurs received a higher than equilibrium price for their shares due to the tax incentive. For an analysis of the valuation and pricing of QSSP stock, see Jog and Riding (1990). Also see Suret and Cormier (this volume) for a more complete and up-to-date evidence.

7 These initiatives include the Exchange Offering Prospectus and the Canadian over-the-counter system. Also see Robinson (this volume) for an in-depth review of various provincial initiatives.

8 It should be noted that the pricing of share issues does not necessarily relate to the proper valuation of an IPO. More specifically, one could argue that, in a risk-averse society, IPOs would be valued at a level lower than in a less risk-averse society. Thus, even though one may find a lower degree of underpricing, it need not mean that IPOs are valued correctly. Whether this argument holds in the context of Canada relative to the United States is anybody's guess.

9 A variety of explanations are available about the existence of underpricing; none is reviewed here. Interested readers can see Logue (1973), Smith (1986), Beatty and Ritter (1986) and Rock (1986), among others. For a more complete up-to-date review of this literature, see Robinson (this volume).

10 Underpricing is measured as the difference between the closing price on the first day of trading and the initial offering price expressed as a percentage of the initial offering price.

11 Another paper, Clarkson and Merkley (1993), using IPOs from 1984 to 1987 showed a similar degree of underpricing.

12 The Malaysian results are based on a relatively small sample of 21 issues. The most exhaustive sample is from the United States – 10,626 issues. A casual glance at Table 1 from Loughran et al. (1994) indicates that underpricing of over 20 percent can be found in 15 of the 25 countries reported.

13 Details of the Canadian capital markets in relation to IPOs and the history of IPO underpricing is available in Jog and Riding (1987), and is not repeated here. There has been relatively little change in the institutional framework since their discussion.

14 Closed-end funds, unit issues and issues involving both debt and equity were excluded from the sample. Some other Canadian studies seem to have included these IPOs in their sample, however.

15 The IPOs in the 1984 to 1994 period had a higher representation of consumer and industrial product IPOs compared to the sample of Jog and Riding (1987). In that sample, resource sector industries were the dominant source of IPOs, representing well over 40 percent of the sample in value and numbers. This shift in the industrial composition of the sample corresponds to the shift in Canada from reliance on the resource sector to reliance on non-resource sectors of the economy. In the 1984 to 1994 period, the $10 to $20 price range dominated. This is also quite different from the finding of Jog and Riding (1987) where the $5 to $10 price range dominated. This difference could simply be the result of inflation, or it could also represent the resource sector dominance in the earlier sample which typically favours low price IPO offerings.

16 The average underpricing is actually lower than these results indicate since one IPO in 1993 had a 200 percent underpricing, thereby affecting the overall results considerably for that year.

17 A regression analysis between the average degree of underpricing and the TSE 300 total returns (excluding the years 1974, 1975 and 1978, which had less than two IPOs each) shows that the slope coefficient is positive and the R-squared is 26 percent. No statistically meaningful relationship is found between the standard deviation and the TSE 300 returns.

18 This percentage implies that the degree of underpricing (or overpricing) is almost random and not systematic.

19 See, for example, Ritter (1991), Levis (1993) and Aggarwal et al. (1993).

20 Ideally, an equally weighted index or a control portfolio of matching firms needs to be used. The former, although available in Canada, is suspect due to some abnormally high returns exhibited by the series; the latter is not feasible given existing resources.

21 Friedlan et al. (1994) studied the long-term underperformance of Canadian IPOs in the mid-1980s and concluded that the poor performance of their sample was not due to the poor performance of stocks that left the exchange. They concluded that stocks that were no longer traded included those that had done well as well as those that had done poorly.

22 The market is defined as a bull (bear) market if the returns on the TSE 300 index are higher (lower) than the annual t-bill rate for that year.

23 Over 50 percent of the IPO firms (26) raised funding in 1986, following the strong performance of the stock market in 1985, followed by 1987 (eight), where before the October crash, the mood of the equity markets was buoyant. Since the post-IPO data were needed for comparison purposes, the firms which went public after 1992 were not selected.

24 See, for example, Teoh et al. (1994).

25 The questionnaires were sent to IPO firms in late 1993 and early 1994.

26 Unless otherwise stated, all dollar figures in this section are in 1993 dollars, using the consumer price index for adjustments.

27 These five companies are: Quebcor, Petro-Canada, West Fraser Timber, Potash Corporation and Telemedia Inc.

28 The percentages add to more than 100 since multiple responses were allowed.

29 In an overallotment option, the firm agrees to issue additional shares to the underwriter at a fixed price in case of oversubscription within 60 days of the IPO. Under a compensation option, the firm grants the underwriters a long-term (up to 24 months) option to buy additional shares of the company at a predetermined exercise price.

30 Unfortunately, no data are available in the public domain on the actual number of oversubscribed shares. Neither the Ontario Securities Commission nor the TSE keeps such data. Attempts to get this type of data through this questionnaire also failed, since of the 34 issuers reporting oversubscriptions, only 11 reported the actual number of oversubscribed shares.

31 More specifically, this amount is estimated by multiplying the average increase in share price by the average percentage of shares received under either of the two options.

32 The lowest (highest) issue expenses were reported as $30,000 ($14.5 million) and the lowest (highest) underwriting expenses were reported as $40,000 ($26.6 million).

33 All coefficients are statistically significant.

34 This 72-month period was chosen for convenience. It preserves the sample size and includes IPOs in the sample that were listed in the post-1986 period.

35 The two methods provide a complementary perspective on the long-term performance of the sample IPOs. The first methodology is similar to an arithmetic average of abnormal returns whereas the second methodology corresponds to a geometric return.

36 See endnote 20.

ACKNOWLEDGEMENTS

THIS PAPER COULD NOT HAVE BEEN WRITTEN without the co-operation of my colleague, Ashwani Srivastava, in my ongoing joint work with him in this area. The research assistance of Bo Li, Jim Douglas, Marni Halpern and Samuel Asiedu for the new work conducted specifically for this paper is much appreciated. I am also thankful to Bill Horsman of Industry Canada for many stimulating discussions. Research funding from Industry Canada and the Social Sciences and Humanities Research Council is greatly appreciated. The paper has also benefited from the comments of Elizabeth Maynes, Robert Chirinko, Paul Halpern, two anonymous referees appointed by Industry Canada, the participants at the Northern Finance Association conference and the finance workshop at the University of Toronto. All errors and opinions expressed in this paper are the sole responsibility of the author.

BIBLIOGRAPHY

Aggarwal R., R. Leal and L. Hernandez. "The Aftermarket Performance of Initial Public Offerings in Latin America." *Financial Management.* (1993): 42-53.

Allen, F. and G. Faulhaber. "Signalling by Underpricing in the IPO Market." *Journal of Financial Economics.* (1989): 303-323.

Beatty, R.P. and J.R. Ritter. "Investment Banking, Reputation and the Underpricing of Initial Public Offerings." *Journal of Financial Economics.* (1986): 312-332.

Clarkson, P. M. and J. Merkley. "Ex Ante Uncertainty and the Underpricing of Initial Public Offerings: Further Empirical Evidence." *Canadian Journal of Administrative Sciences.* Vol. 11, No. 1, (1993): 54-67.

Dalcin, P.E. "Canadian Informal Investors: Towards a Framework for Policy Initiatives." Unpublished master's thesis, School of Business, Carleton University, Ottawa, 1993.

Desroches, J. and V. M. Jog. *Entrepreneurs and Initial Public Offerings.* Quebec City: The Institute for Research on Public Policy, 1991.

Drake, P.D. and M.R. Vetsuypens. "IPO Underpricing and Insurance against Legal Liability." *Financial Management.* (1993): 64-73.

Economic Council of Canada. *Intervention and Efficiency.* Ottawa, 1982.

Friedlan, J., E. Maynes and S. Verma. "The Long Run Performance of Canadian Initial Public Offerings," Working paper, Schulich School of Business, York University, 1994.

Garfinkel, J.A. "IPO Underpricing, Insider Selling and Subsequent Equity Offerings: Is Underpricing a Signal of Quality?" *Financial Management.* (1993): 74-83.

Industry Canada. *Breaking Through the Barriers: Forging Our Future.* Small Business Working Committee, Report to Ministers. 1994.

Jain, B.A. and O. Kini. "The Post-Issue Operating Performance of IPO Firms." *Journal of Finance.* Vol. 49, (1994): 1699-1726.

Jog, V.M. "Canadian Economy, Financial System, and Environment for Business Financing." In *Government and Business Finance: Global Perspectives on Economic Development.* Edited by Richard D. Bingham and Edward W. Hill. CURR Press, Rutgers University, forthcoming.

Jog, V.M. and A. L. Riding. "Underpricing of Canadian IPOs." *Financial Analysts Journal.* (November-December 1987): 48-55.

—. "Technology Firms and Canadian Capital Markets: A Survey and Overview." Proceedings of the International Council for Small Business – Canada, VIth Annual Conference, Windsor, Ontario, 1989.

—. "Tax Assistance and Performance of IPOs in Canada: The Case of the Quebec Stock Savings Plan." Proceedings of ENDEC International Entrepreneurship Conference, Singapore, 1990, pp. 49-54.

Jog, V.M., A.L. Riding and W. Lawson. "The Venture Capitalists-Entrepreneur Interface: Expectations, Conflicts and Contracts." *Journal of Small Business and Entrepreneurship.* Vol. 8, (Jan-March 1991): 5-20.

Jog, V.M. and H. Schaller. "Sources of Financing for Small- and Medium-sized Businesses in Canada." In *Tax Effects on the Financing of Medium and Small Public Corporations*. Edited by Roy D. Hogg and Jack M. Mintz. John Deutsch Institute for the Study of Economic Policy, Queen's University, Kingston, Canada, 1991, pp. 7-23.

Jog, V.M. and A.S. Srivastava. "Underpricing of Canadian IPOs 1971-1992 – an Update." *Fineco*. Vol. 4, No. 1, (1994): 81-89.

—. "Long term performance of Canadian IPOs 1971-1992." School of Business, Carleton University, mimeo, March 1995.

Krinsky, I. and W. Rotenberg. "The Valuation of Initial Public Offerings." *Contemporary Accounting Research.* Vol. 5, No. 2, (1989): 501-515.

Levis, M. "The Long-Run Performance of Initial Public Offerings: the UK Experience 1980-1988." *Financial Management.* (1993): 28-41.

Logue, D. "On the Pricing of Unseasoned Equity Issues, 1965-1969." *Journal of Financial and Quantitative Analysis.* (1973): 91-103.

T. Loughran, J.R. Ritter and K. Rydqvist. "Initial Public Offerings: International Insights." *Pacific-Basin Finance Journal.* (May 1994):165-199.

Ritter J.R. "The Long-Run Performance of Initial Public Offering." *Journal of Finance.* (1991): 3-27.

Rock, K. "Why New Issues Are Underpriced?" *Journal of Financial Economics.* (1986): 187-212.

Smith, C. "Investment Banking and the Capital Acquisition Process." *Journal of Financial Economics.* (1986): 3-30.

Teoh, S.H., T.J. Wong and G.R. Rao. "Earnings Management and the Long Term Performance of Initial Public Offerings." Unpublished manuscript, University of Michigan, 1994.

Welch, I. "Seasoned Offerings, Imitation Costs and the Underwriting of IPOs." *Journal of Finance.* (1989): 695-732.

Comments on Session II: Financing Constraints and Small Firms

Venture Capital Financing of Entrepreneurship in Canada

Comment by Ralph A. Winter
Department of Economics
University of Toronto

AMIT, BRANDER AND ZOTT OFFER A CAREFUL AND INSIGHTFUL description of an extraordinary data set on venture capital financing in Canada. The Macdonald data allow the authors to lay out basic facts of the market that were previously unavailable to academic researchers; and they do this in a very clear and interesting way. Not all of these facts are what we had expected. The authors offer an overview as well of the most prominent approach that economists have taken to understanding the venture capital market, the theory of imperfect information. They sketch a model of asymmetric information with the aim of explaining particular features of the market.

The Factual Questions

LAYING OUT THE BASIC FACTS OF THE VENTURE CAPITAL market is overdue. This paper will save academic researchers from spending years offering explanations of stylized "facts" that are false. The first general question that one might want to ask about the paper is, how do the industry facts compare with the U.S. venture capital market? In Canada, the size of the venture capital market, relative to the Canadian economy, is of the same magnitude as in the United States where between $3 billion and $4 billion are invested annually. The rates of high success and of write-offs are very similar between the two countries.[1] The distribution of returns to ventures is skewed in the United States as well, according to the paper by Jeffrey MacIntosh in this volume, i.e., there are a small number of big "hits." A striking difference between the two venture capital markets is that more ventures end in insider buy-outs in Canada than in the United States, again by comparison of this paper with the MacIntosh results.

The second factual question that one might ask about the paper concerns the additional stylized facts about the market that one might want to investigate, as the authors pursue their project. One is more detail on the specific nature of the financing instruments and contracts between venture capitalists and entrepreneurs. The authors note that, in Canada, three quarters of venture capital financing is through equity. It would be interesting to know if convertible preferred equity is the dominant form of financing, as in the United States.[2] How explicit are the obligations of entrepreneurs and venture capitalists in the contracts? This is a natural question because the focus of economic theory (contract theory) for problems like this has been on the form of the contracts.

On another theme, the authors mention the difference in regional concentration of venture capital activity relative to general economic activity. It would be interesting to know the extent to which this is due to different industrial patterns across regions and especially to the different government subsidies of small businesses, especially in the high-tech sector. Casual observations suggest that the latter is responsible for a large part of the relatively high venture capital activity in Quebec. The Quebec government has established a $300 million fund for high-tech firms, financing that could be complementary to private venture capital. As well, the first Canadian labour-sponsored venture capital corporation, Solidarité, was established in Quebec in 1983; these corporations receive large government subsidies through tax exemptions for investors.

But analysis of this regional issue must first deal with a measurement problem: Figure 1 of the Amit et al. paper is interpreted as describing venture capital activity. Actually, it describes the number of venture-backed firms, not the total investment. My guess is that the average venture-backed company in Quebec is smaller than it is in Ontario.

The Academic Question

The authors state that a theory of the venture capital market must account for four empirical regularities. To what extent does the *general* theory that they offer – informational asymmetries between entrepreneurs and venture capitalists – explain these regularities? And to what extent does the specific structure they offer predict or account for these regularities? We consider the authors' stylized facts in sequence.

The Existence of a Specialized Venture Capital Market

This reflects more basic facts about the financing life cycle of a firm. When the firm is small, it receives capital (through debt and equity) from only a small number of investors. It is efficient for the market to channel investment through a small number of investors (say, one) because this saves any duplication of expenditure on information by the capital market participants. Incentives for information acquisition among capital providers are efficient because the benefits from this acquisition are internalized in the single provider of capital. As a firm gets larger, this effect is offset by the advantages to the firm of casting a wider net in raising financial capital, and the firm goes public. So at a general level, the venture capital market exists because of differences in information within the economy and efficient incentives to acquire information. (Another aspect of the existence of the venture capital market is the specialization by commercial banks in less-risky lending than venture capitalists; regulatory restrictions on bank financing play some role in this specialization.)

The existence of a specialized venture capital market can be explained, therefore, by the lack of perfect information on the part of the providers of capital. Is an asymmetry necessary for the explanation? The role of superiority of the entrepreneur's information is unclear. If entrepreneurs were simply individuals who came up with ideas, then got them funded by investors who are just as well informed, then a specialized venture capital market would still exist.

The Emphasis on Development rather than Start-up

It seems to me that if we *did* observe relatively high investment by venture capitalists at start-up, we would not reject the information asymmetry model. Information asymmetries are at least as strong at start-up. The greater involvement by venture capitalists at the development stage may reflect the fact that this is the point of greatest investment from *all* sources rather than an indication of information asymmetries. On the other hand, the emphasis on informational asymmetries is consistent with the typical provision of initial capital by the entrepreneur herself or himself, or through so-called love capital, which is provided by relatives, friends and business associates who have inside information on the integrity of the borrower.

Insider Buyouts Dominate

This is a very interesting observation – one that has not been fully appreciated by the literature on venture capital, perhaps because the rate of insider buyouts is lower in the United States than in Canada. It supports the hypothesis of superior information on the part of insiders – whether the insider buyout is negotiated *ex post* or whether the option to buy back equity is included *ex ante* in the original contract.

When buy backs are negotiated *ex post*, then the venture is being allocated to the entrepreneurs. It is well-established that capital markets will allocate assets to the individuals who are best informed about the value of the assets. So this is consistent with hidden information on the part of entrepreneurs. Buy backs, like leveraged buyouts, can be an efficient response to hidden action or moral hazard problems for a corporation that has enough internal capital or debt capacity to fund the buyout.

The *ex ante* inclusion of an option for an agent to purchase more equity in a venture in the future is, I would conjecture, an optimal response to the type of agency problem that the authors analyse in the paper: limited liability with hidden action and information. The challenge facing the principal in this kind of agency problem is to design a contract that balances the goals of attracting good projects and offering good incentives for the agent (through the offer of a high residual claim to the agent) with the extraction of a high proportion of the profits from the venture. (In agency problems with hidden information and limited liability, high-quality agents will be left with profits, termed "informational rents.") With straight equity, options are a means of increasing the agent's share of residual claim (the marginal profit) under better states of the world; options come into the money at higher levels of profit. Why is this efficient? Let's consider the moral hazard aspect of the agency problem and identify the costs and benefits of raising the agent's residual claim over some small range of profit. The benefit is that this increases the agent's incentives, since a larger share of the marginal return to effort is captured by the agent. But the cost to the principal is the *level* of the share of profits to the agent for all higher realizations of profit; this increases the agent's share of profits. But this cost is smaller for higher realizations of profit than it is for poorer realizations; so it is optimal to offer the agent a share of marginal profits that is higher for higher levels of profits. (For some classes of agency problems, the agent gets the entire margin at the highest level of profits, and there is "no distortion at the top.") The role of options is to implement this pattern of residual claim. In short, the frequent insider buy backs as a pattern of exit are consistent with the asymmetric information view of the venture capital market.

One can also identify an adverse selection (or more precisely, a *screening*) explanation for options of this type, i.e., the marginal rate of substitution of options for equity increases with the quality of an asset; so the essential condition for a screening equilibrium (a condition referred to as the "single crossing property"[3]) is satisfied. By offering contracts with buy back options, not just retention of equity to entrepreneurs, the venture capitalist will select higher-quality projects.

This discussion is an example of looking to the form of the contracts to see whether they reflect the informational problems alleged. In discussing the adverse selection or, more precisely, the screening aspect of the problem, we should keep in mind that venture capitalists reject more than 95 percent of the projects proposed to them; the asymmetries in information that we analyse are among those projects that are accepted.

The Skewed Pattern of Returns

My reaction is that this observation is not a point in favour of the asymmetric information model, at least not for the adverse selection hypothesis. In general, before considering informational asymmetries, we might expect investment returns to have approximately a lognormal distribution, like a lot of random variables in nature or in economics – the returns on securities or the size distribution of firms, for example. The lognormal is a skewed distribution. But the adverse selection perspective on the venture capital market (that Professor Amit has developed elsewhere as well) would suggest that a greater proportion of those projects that are going to be "hits" are financed outside the venture capital market, with the entrepreneur's own capital or with debt. So the upper tail of the distribution of returns should be *thinner*, and the thinner it is, the more important is adverse selection. In other words, asymmetric information, of the type the authors consider, should decrease the skewedness of distribution of returns, not increase it.

The Econometric Evidence

Amit et al. present evidence of a negative correlation between performance of ventures and the share of equity owned by the venture capitalist. The authors note that this is consistent with a moral hazard hypothesis, since a higher share owned by outsiders diminishes the incentives for insiders. The negative correlation is also consistent with the hidden information or adverse selection aspect of their problem, since the higher share required by venture capitalists (in return for more investment or more managerial input) will deter the higher-quality ventures. The opposite correlation would be predicted by a model with hidden action or information on the part of the venture capitalists. The finding can, therefore, be interpreted as supporting the view that the entrepreneurs are the better-informed side of the market, or the agents whose incentives are most prone to moral hazard.

As a final remark, I note that the authors do not analyse the normative economic issue of whether the equilibrium in a venture capital market under imperfect information can be improved by government intervention – by an ideal, government agency motivated solely by aggregate economic efficiency. The authors do use the term "market failure," but they use it to mean that the market does not achieve the same performance as it would if agents had perfect information. Specifically, there is underfinancing in the sense that inherently viable projects do not attract financial capital. The modern use of the term, in the economic literature on markets under imperfect information, refers to the issue of whether a mechanism is available to a planner or perfectly motivated government that out performs the market when the planner has no more information than the market participants. More practically, we would not want to assume, in assessing the need for intervention, that governments are better at picking winners than venture capitalists. Whether asymmetric information can justify or explain intervention in the form of government agencies that subsidize or guarantee financing to entrepreneurs, is a topic that the authors have wisely left for further research.

Endnotes

1 This is based on a comparison of the figures reported in this paper with those reported in Perez (1986).

2 Marx (1993) offers a number of references for this empirical regularity.

3 See Andreu Mas-Colell et al. (1995), Chapter 13.

Bibliography

Marx, Leslie M. "Negotiation and Renegotiation of Venture Capital Contracts." Working paper, University of Rochester, 1993.

Mas-Colell, Andreu, Michael Whinston and Jerry Green. *Microeconomic Theory*. Oxford University Press, 1995.

Perez, Robert. *Inside Venture Capital*. New York: Praeger Publishers, 1986.

VENTURE CAPITAL EXITS IN CANADA AND THE UNITED STATES

Comment by Michel Poitevin
Department of Economics
Université de Montréal

THIS PAPER SEEKS TO COMPARE VARIOUS EXIT TECHNIQUES USED by venture capitalists in the United States and Canada over two distinct periods. Ample data are provided and analysed. Venture capitalists (VCs) have used mainly six different means of exiting their investments.

1. Initial public offerings (IPO) are a public sale of the assets owned by the VCs (and possibly some of the original owners) through a share offering.
2. Exit by acquisition refers to the private sale of all the assets of the company, those of the VC as well as those of the original owner, to a private party.
3. A company buy back occurs when the financed firm reacquires the VC's share of the firm.
4. A secondary sale involves the sale of only the VC's share of the firm to a private party.
5. Liquidation refers to the sale of the dismantled assets of the firm.
6. A write-off occurs when the financed firm goes bankrupt and no asset is worth liquidating.

In this comment, I try to provide a theoretical framework for the analysis of exit which should help to identify the data that should be looked at and interpreted.

The issue of exit is important because it influences initial financing terms, the governance of the relationship between the firm and the VC, and the VC's returns. The first issue is whether exit should be made easy or difficult for the VC. The more liquid the investment, the easier it will be to exit when desired. Liquidity, therefore, seems to be a desirable property of these types of financial investments. There is, however, a caveat. The relationship between a VC and a firm is not exactly the same as the one between a shareholder and a large corporation. It is better characterized as an agency relationship in which the VC must provide the firm with incentives to perform and, in doing so, must monitor the firm's actions. The difference lies in the incentives to monitor: a VC has more incentives to monitor the firm and get involved in management than an ordinary shareholder of a large corporation.

In a typical agency relationship, lengthening the horizon over which the relationship takes place often has benefits for both parties as incentives are more efficiently provided when rewards and penalties can be spread out over time. It may then be argued that an easy exit by the VC may not provide the necessary commitment to exploit these long-term benefits. Furthermore, an easy exit may encourage the VC to consider only the short term in the choice of investment and technology by the firm. There is, then, a trade-off between liquidity of investment and the commitment necessary to reduce agency costs.[1] This issue has important policy implications when considering the relative efficiency of different means of exit.

A second issue to consider before analysing means of exit is to determine why VCs exit at all. It is not sufficient to argue that they do so to focus on their core business of monitoring and managing small and risky projects, because they could still do so without exiting past projects by raising external capital to finance their risky ventures. Exiting allows the VC to earn returns from a relatively small set of projects. This imposes large risks on the VC, but these risks may be necessary to provide the incentive to monitor and manage new projects. Without such risks, diversification would turn VCs into "institutional investors" without much incentive to invest in monitoring activities. The necessity for such risks can explain why large financial institutions are not present in the venture capital industry.

A VC's action of exiting from a firm can be analysed in the same way as an entrepreneur selling shares in his or her own firm. What does economic and financial theory have to say about such action? There are two important elements that should be considered when analysing the sale of financial assets by a VC. First, these assets are relatively risky despite the human capital investment already made by the VC. Second, the VC, as well as the owner (insiders) of the firm, generally have superior information about the quality of these assets than do third parties. These elements can help in understanding the patterns of exit by VCs.

When considering a risky asset, any buyer will take into account the size of the asset and its perceived underlying risk and how this fits his or her existing portfolio. For risk purposes, the important distinction is whether the sale is public or private. A private sale of a risky asset imposes a large risk on the buyer while a public sale spreads the risk across many buyers. Among the various means of exit, only IPOs involve the sale of the assets to more than one buyer and, hence, can be considered as a public sale. When the proceeds of the sale are large enough that acquisition by a single buyer is too risky and many buyers would be necessary, IPOs should be used. The data reported by the author seem to indicate that this intuition is right. IPOs have been used mainly to exit from large initial investments and investments in high-technology industries. Although the proper criterion would be to relate the occurrence of IPOs with the proceeds of the sale (rather than the initial investment), one may conjecture that these two measures are positively correlated. IPOs, therefore, diversify the risk associated with a single firm when no single buyer is large enough to be willing to support it all. It is not surprising that IPOs are positively correlated with returns on initial investments. According to this theory, IPOs are used because the initial investment has been profitable, instead of that investment being profitable because the VC divested through an IPO. Furthermore, this may also explain why, in the early period, more IPOs were used in the United States. Investments in the United States were larger and more likely to be in high-technology industries which have a large upside potential. This is also consistent with the fact that Canadian VCs exited their American investments in much the same manner as their American counterparts.

The second element of the sale of financial assets by VCs focuses on informational asymmetries between insiders (the owner and the VC) and external financial markets. Economic theories based on informational assumptions do not say much with respect to means of exit per se. They do say something, however, about how much to divest when one has privileged information. Theory predicts that a credible signal of asset value is the share of the firm withheld by the insider. This share should be increasing in the value of the firm. For example, if asymmetric information is important, one would expect both the owner and the VC to divest fully from a non-profitable firm. This divestiture is rationally interpreted by the buyer who then puts a low value on the assets. Acquisitions should then be correlated with low returns following the sale of the assets.[2] Secondary sale may not be such an adverse signal as the owner is retaining his or her share of the firm. IPOs could be an intermediate case depending on the amount withheld by the VC and that required by law. For example, if the VC retains a larger share of the assets than what is prescribed by the law, then buyers rationally interpret that the assets have high value and price them accordingly. Company buy backs only involve the two informed agents, and theory does not say much about them. It may be argued that these are low-value assets the entrepreneur buys back because he or she attributes a personal value to the firm being kept alive. This theory implies that the retained share of the firm is the relevant variable to study not the type of exit *per se*. It also suggests an interesting research avenue if data are available. One could look for a correlation between the withheld share of the firm by the VC (and the owner) and the profitability of the firm following the sale of its financial assets.

Finally, I have more specific comments. The author argues that the profitability of Canadian VCs has decreased over time, from 23 percent in 1975 to 1985 to 16 percent in 1992 to 1995. If these rates of return are in nominal terms, then this direct comparison is not appropriate. It should consider inflation, which was significantly different between the two periods. During the 1975 to 1985 period, average inflation was 8.3 percent, while it was 1.4 percent from 1992 to 1995. Converting the nominal rates of returns to real rates of return yields 14.7 percent (23-8.3) for the earlier period and 14.6 percent (16-1.4) for the later period. This implies that profitability seems to have remained fairly constant over time. This argues for converting, when possible, nominal rates of return to real rates of return.

The paper includes many comparisons of averages across different samples. Given that the samples are often small for some sub-categories, it would be helpful to refine the statistical analysis to take into account standard deviations in each sample. Simple statistical tests exist to compare means of different samples. Otherwise, it is hard to see whether the stated differences are significant or not.

ENDNOTES

1 On a more general note, this trade-off is central to the current debate as to whether the German and Japanese financial systems, based on long-term relationships between financiers and firms, are better performers than the U.S., Canadian and British systems which are based on more liquid and short-term relationships.

2 Note that this theory implies that what is relevant are the expected returns of the sold assets, not those that the VC realized on the initial investment.

THE CLIMATE FOR CANADIAN INITIAL PUBLIC OFFERINGS

Comment by Elizabeth Maynes
Schulich School of Business
York University

THIS PAPER PRESENTS EMPIRICAL EVIDENCE ON FOUR ASPECTS of taking a company public through an initial public offering (IPO): pricing the issue, long-run stock market performance of the issue, performance of the issuing firm, pre- and post-IPO measured with accounting data and the process of going public from the perspective of the issuer/entrepreneur. On the basis of the evidence reported, the study concludes that for the entrepreneur, the Canadian IPO environment is attractive. However, from the investor's perspective, the poor long-run performance of IPOs suggests that the investors do not do well by investing in IPOs.

Before turning to the details of the paper, a few general comments are warranted. First, the focus of the report is on successfully completed IPOs listed on the Toronto Stock Exchange (TSE). Although the TSE is Canada's largest exchange, it is dangerous to assume that results drawn from it necessarily apply to the other public equity markets. To assess the Canadian climate for IPOs, information on the Montreal Exchange, the Vancouver Stock Exchange, the Alberta Stock Exchange and the Canadian Dealer Network (the over-the-counter market) is needed. What percentage of IPOs are completed in the various exchanges? Differences in both the firms seeking to list on various exchanges, and the listing requirements and other regulatory aspects of the various exchanges may affect the IPO process. For example, firm size may be smaller for some exchanges. So too may be the involvement of institutional investors in some markets. It would be interesting to know whether underpricing and long-run performance results are similar for these other exchanges.

A second feature of this report is its focus on successful IPOs. Little is known about companies that sought access to the public equity market but failed. Granted, it is likely more difficult to get access to information about such firms. However, the analysis of the Canadian IPO market is incomplete without it.

For these reasons, I believe the report's very strong conclusion that the IPO environment is an attractive one for Canadian entrepreneurs may be premature.

Further research on the rest of the Canadian IPO market is needed. I should add that the author is not responsible for the fact that insufficient research has been conducted on Canadian IPO markets. The works of Michael Robinson and Jean-Marc Suret and Elise Cormier in this volume are encouraging beginnings to the study of the other Canadian new public equity markets.

Now I would like to make some comments on specific aspects of the report.

Possible Linkages between the Studies

The paper consists of four different studies of the IPO process. Each raises interesting questions about aspects of IPOs and provides useful information about the IPO process for firms seeking a listing on the TSE. However, I think the opportunity to link the studies has not been fully exploited. Some suggestions for further work are outlined below.

The Role of Market Timing

Table 2 of Jog's study clearly demonstrates that IPOs come in waves. Boom years were 1972 to 1973, 1981, 1983 to 1984 and 1986 to 1987. What drives these waves? The survey of entrepreneurs revealed that the second most important factor leading to a public offering was that "the stock market was favourable to high-priced issues." Do the IPO waves bear this out? Are the boom years associated with bull markets?

The evidence on the relationship between market conditions and IPOs reported by Jog is scattered and needs clarification. For example, in Table 4, which reports various long-run stock market performance data, the difference in long-run performance of issues made in bull and bear markets is examined. The difference in the long-run performance is reported to be statistically significant in all but month 60, with issues made in bull markets experiencing less underperformance than those issued in bear markets. What is unusual is that only 19 issues are identified as bull market issues and 129 are bear market issues. This is in stark contrast to the entrepreneurs' high weight given to favourable market conditions. Furthermore, endnote 23 refers to 26 issues in 1986 when the market rose significantly, suggesting to me that this might be considered a hot IPO market. Clarification of the definition of market conditions is needed. It would seem reasonable to measure market conditions just before the decision to go public. Such a measure would imply that companies that decided to issue in July 1987 faced very different market conditions than those which decided to issue in November 1987, after the market crash of October 1987.

The impact of market conditions is also considered in the underpricing study where market condition is measured as the average annual return on the TSE 300 total return index, reported in endnote 17. At a minimum, the impact of inflation should be considered. Furthermore, as with the long-run performance analysis, prevailing market conditions at the time of the issue are a more relevant measure than an average annual return.

The study of long-run performance based on accounting data offers an opportunity to examine the relationship between market conditions, the financial health of a firm and the decision to go public. For example, are firms that go public in hot markets less in need of external financing than those which elect to go public in a cold market?

What Causes the Negative Long-Run Performance of Stocks and Firms?

Two of the studies deal with long run performance and both suggest that IPO firms, on average, perform badly. It seems unfortunate that no link is made between the analysis of the accounting performance and the market performance. Do the firms with the most negative accounting performance also experience the most negative stock performance?

The Role of Venture Capitalists

Only limited information about venture capitalists was found through the survey of entrepreneurs. Surely, the 83 prospectuses contain information about the shareholders, including any venture capitalists. It would be interesting to use this information to see if the presence of a venture capitalist has any effect on the underpricing and long-run performance, measured both with market and accounting data. This might shed light on the interesting observation made in the paper that the evidence draws into question the adequacy of management skills of the firm after the IPO. Do firms with a relationship with a venture capitalist perform differently?

STUDY-SPECIFIC ISSUES

Underpricing

The underpricing of IPOs is a well-established phenomenon. However, the evidence of a decline in underpricing during the 1984 to 1992 period relative to the 1972 to 1983 period is an interesting twist. Has the IPO boom of 1993 and 1994 changed the result?

What are the reasons for the decline in underpricing? For example, is this a reflection of a change in the underwriters' ability to assess the market's reaction to IPOs? Could it be due to a shift in the type of firms coming to market on the TSE? Is it a reflection of the increasing importance of institutional investors? Are these results true for other stock exchanges in Canada? It would seem important to explore the reasons for the change before drawing conclusions about the ability of Canadian capital markets in allocating risks.

Long-Run Performance

The results of the poor long-run performance of IPOs are rather sobering, in light of all the media hype about the initial stock run of companies such as Open Text and iStar. In a related study by John Friedlan et al. (1994) poor long-run performance was not due to the poor performance of stocks that subsequently left the exchange. Stocks that were no longer traded included both those that had done well and were purchased by another company and those that had failed.

Table 4 of the Jog paper presents a number of different categorizations of the long-run performance data. It would be interesting to know the correlation between the categories. For example, drawing from the underpricing study, there would appear to be a correlation between degree of underpricing and whether the issue was made during a bull market. How correlated are the factors? If the independent variables are correlated, the statistical significance of the individual variables, reported in Table 5, will be lowered.

Post-IPO Financial Performance

Much more work can be done to relate the accounting performance data with both the degree of underpricing and the long-run stock market performance. For example, do firms that use the funds to increase assets rather than to reduce debt have different underpricing or long-run performance? As it stands, it is difficult to draw a conclusion on the basis of the information presented.

Entrepreneurs' Views

Surveying entrepreneurs' views on the process of going public is an interesting way to collect information. Unfortunately, the survey leaves me with questions. For example, when choosing an underwriter, entrepreneurs were asked to assess the importance of reputation, quality of service, cost of service and previous success. Unfortunately, reputation would seem to me to depend on quality and cost of service and previous success. Are these independent measures? How are entrepreneurs measuring quality? How did entrepreneurs gather information about underwriters? Did they approach several before selecting one?

As far as motives for going public, I am curious to know the basis on which the conclusion is drawn that the "main reason for firms going public is that other sources of financing can no longer satisfy their financing needs." Table 20 of the Jog paper reports that the primary reason was the "business had a well-defined business plan to expand." It would seem to me that this does not necessarily imply that firms need new financing. Furthermore, the specific choice of "current sources of financing were starting to dry out" was only the fourth choice overall. Again, I'm not sure how to interpret the data provided.

SUMMARY AND CONCLUSION

OVERALL, I FOUND THIS TO BE AN INTERESTING PAPER that raises many important issues. It seems clear that underpricing exists and has changed over time. Also, over the first four years, IPOs underperform various benchmark portfolio. Some evidence indicates that the accounting performance of these firms deteriorates from the pre-IPO period to the post-IPO period. The survey of entrepreneurs provides insight into the decision to go public but offers little information on either underpricing or long-run underperformance. Many questions remain, including explanations of the underpricing and the underperformance. The issue of market timing needs to be explored more fully. Can firms raise equity financing when they need it or are they forced to wait until market conditions are right? What can a firm needing equity financing do when the IPO market is not receptive to new issues? Furthermore, these results relate to companies which successfully list on the TSE. We still have much to learn about the other public equity markets and the firms which fail in their attempts to go public before we can conclude that Canada has a vibrant market for initial public offerings.

BIBLIOGRAPHY

Friedlan, John, Elizabeth Maynes and Savita Verma. "The Long Run Performance of Canadian Initial Public Offerings." Working paper, Schulich School of Business, York University, Toronto, 1994.

Session III Dinner Speech

Edward P. Neufeld
Centre for International Studies
University of Toronto

9

Reshaping Canada's Financial System: Who Wins, Who Loses?

IT IS A VERY REAL PLEASURE FOR ME TO PARTICIPATE IN THIS CONFERENCE – a pleasure professionally and personally. My interest in Canada's financial system, its evolution and its functioning, goes back a number of years to the days when I was an academic at the University of Toronto. At that time, there were not many academic researchers interested in the financial services sector, and it is most encouraging to see the increased interest today. I am greatly indebted to Harry Hassanwalia, Deputy Chief Economist, Royal Bank of Canada, for his assistance in the preparation of this paper.

That sector, after all, is enormously important for the functioning of the Canadian economy. It is one that has been undergoing basic restructuring, both because of market developments and because of legislative changes. There is much that should be analysed and appraised, particularly now that government is again contemplating important changes to the legislative framework of the financial services sector. I would like to comment on the restructuring of the financial system, past, present and future.

In 1992 we saw the introduction of major amendments to virtually all our federal financial legislation and, around about that time, to much provincial financial services legislation as well. The process of review had been an extraordinary long and detailed one, beginning with the federal government green paper in 1986. There followed the Wyman report (deposit insurance), the Blenkarn report (House of Commons Finance Committee), several Senate reports, the Estey report (failed banks) and a federal government white paper in December 1986 that recommended substantial services integration across the "four pillars" of the financial system – banking, insurance, trust and investment. A series of legislation drafts relating to the *Bank Act*, and trust and loan, insurance and co-operative credit acts followed. I have not even mentioned the provincial studies and reports such as the Ontario Dey report of the Ontario Securities Commission relating to the opening up of the industry and the Dupré report on financial services generally in Ontario.

Now you might think that such an intensive review and such a blizzard of amendments would have sufficed for some time. Wrong. There was an undertaking in the new legislation to conduct a further review within five years, i.e., by 1997, instead of following the historical pattern of the decennial revision of the *Bank Act*. So there are now two broad legislative initiatives under way. One initiative deals with the supervisory and regulatory system for federal financial institutions, including the powers of the Office of the Superintendent of Financial Institutions (OSFI), and the Canada Deposit Insurance Corporation (CDIC). The other deals with the powers and operations of the federal financial institutions themselves. I will come back to these two initiatives in a moment.

Why all this frantic legislative activity over the last decade? There is really only one fundamental reason: legislators and regulators were and are trying desperately to keep up with the restructuring going on in the marketplace in Canada and abroad. Historically, Canadian financial legislation was based on the separation of banking, insurance, trust and investment. In reality that separation was being eroded in the marketplace.

Years ago, for example, trust companies began to go beyond their trust powers to engage in deposit banking; banks offered credit insurance and traded in a range of debt securities; life companies offered a variety of non-life products; investment dealers, in their commercial paper activities, were in the business of short-term corporate lending in direct competition with the banks. New players, such as the consumer loan and sales finance companies, and credit unions and caisses populaires emerged to provide various kinds of banking services, and leasing companies had, in a substantive way, become finance companies. In some respects, these newcomers had greater flexibility than the older institutions.

In light of all this, what was the logic of trying to maintain walls between the players, old or new? What was the logic of trying to maintain a structure based essentially on legislative rigidities and not market efficiencies that frustrated the emerging preferences of borrowers, lenders and investors? There really was very little left of the logic that had existed in the circumstances of earlier times.

But to introduce legislative change is complicated by the fact that institutions whose current operations rest even partially on existing legislative barriers to entry will, naturally, strongly oppose it. We witnessed this in events leading to the 1992 amendments, and it is very much in evidence in the current review process.

As an aside, let me say that this conference, because of the detachment of many of its program participants and because of the technically difficult and important subjects examined, can make a fine contribution to the development of policy that is in the best interests of the country as a whole and not just individual players.

The focus of the conference on the various aspects of the cost of capital and its implications was particularly welcome. I have read with great interest most of the draft papers presented in this volume. I recall some years ago studying historical differences between long-term interest rates in Canada and the United States and puzzling over exactly why the cost of long-term capital, in real terms, appeared always to have been higher in Canada than in the United States. Theoretical possibilities are easy to identify but empirical testing is another matter – as the current papers amply illustrate. What is clear is that the Canadian economy has always had a higher cost of capital than the United States and has developed in spite of it.

In the absence of solid analysis of the kind that is emerging, there is a danger that facile conclusions will be drawn and used to introduce further legislative rigidities into the financial system. I am thinking, for example, of new controls on lending and schemes for the subsidization of some borrowers and issuers of equity capital through guarantees or tax preferences. Several papers in this volume are quite interesting on this point. One day I would dearly wish to know if the capital, in the aggregate, attracted by government subsidies, guarantees and tax preferences, subsequently achieved a competitive rate of return. There is also a danger that very exaggerated notions of Canada's actual ability to influence fundamentally the cost of capital in the short run will prevail and will influence policy.

But I must resist going down the cost-of-capital path and return to the restructuring of the financial system.

It would be a mistake to think that further restructuring of the Canadian financial system is needed because it, somehow, is lagging behind that of other industrial countries. In fact, one of the most remarkable aspects of our financial system is how highly developed it has become. One way of measuring this is to trace the growth of financial intermediaries, e.g., banks, insurance companies, trust companies, mutual funds, etc., in relation to the growth of the Canadian economy. In 1870, financial intermediary assets amounted to only about 30 percent of gross domestic product (GDP). This rose steadily reaching 100 percent by 1930, 150 percent by 1980 and in 1994 it stood at 218 percent – high by international standards. Generally, in terms of day-to-day servicing of clients and the cost of financial services, few countries are better served by their financial services industry than is Canada.

So when we speak of restructuring our system, this refers to a system that, for many historical reasons, is already highly developed. In some areas, such as banking, it is a more mature system than in the United States. By the way, the rapid increase of the intermediation ratio over the last two decades shows how misplaced has been the fear of some intermediaries of a trend toward, what they call, "disintermediation" – a phenomenon confined essentially to short-term corporate bank lending.

What lay behind this rapid development of the financial system in Canada? The heritage of English and Scottish financial legislation gave the various sectors a remarkably good legislative framework from the beginning, and the decennial revision of the *Bank Act* ensured timely amendments in that sector. Several royal commissions that examined "skulduggery" in banking and insurance speeded the process. Also, the major types of financial institutions appeared early on in Canada, and so the system has had many decades of evolution.

Fire and casualty insurance first appeared in 1809, chartered banks 1817, savings banks 1819, building societies 1844, life insurance companies 1847, post office savings bank 1867, government pension account 1870, trusteed pension plans 1874, trust companies 1882, caisses populaires and credit unions 1900, closed-end investment trusts 1901, finance companies 1916, consumer loan companies 1928 and mutual funds 1932 – not to mention the federal crown corporations that were formed along the way.

But one of the most significant reasons for the highly developed nature of the Canadian financial system, even in comparison with that of the United States, is the absence, over the whole of its almost two centuries of development, of obstacles to the development of national institutions. Whereas, for example, the U.S. banking system has been shaped, even contorted, by the existence of strong state legislation and limitations on branch banking, the Canadian system developed all across the country as fast as the banks could throw up branches in new communities. Economies of scale were never frustrated by legislative restrictions.

Underneath the aggregate numbers, to which I have referred, lies another significant reason why the Canadian financial system is well developed. The reality is that the system has been remarkably flexible and change over time has inevitably involved the disappearance of losers, the diminution of dominant players and the emergence of new winners. I will give you a few examples.

In 1870, the chartered banks accounted for about 75 percent of financial intermediary assets. By 1940, this was down to 40 percent and it reached a post World War II low of 28 percent in about 1966. Banks had seen their intermediary business invaded by the trust companies, credit unions and caisses populaires, sales finance and consumer loan companies, and they were missing out on the long-term investment market to the life companies, trusteed pension funds and closed-end and mutual investment funds.

The winners by far in long-term investments up to the 1930s were the life insurance companies. They had only about 2 percent of financial intermediary assets in 1870 but, by 1934, this had grown to a peak of 34 percent. They then entered a period of relative decline as Canadians began to shift away from whole life insurance into other forms of long-term investments. By 1980, life insurance companies accounted for less than 9 percent of financial intermediary assets.

Mutual funds, which first emerged in Canada in 1932, only had assets of $4.6 billion even by 1980. Then they exploded. By 1990, their assets had grown to $35.2 billion and, by 1994, to $131.8 billion, of which $28.6 billion were in funds sponsored by the chartered banks. This represented about 8 percent of total financial intermediary assets, up from 1 percent in 1980. Such growth is spectacular. But again, historical perspective is instructive. Life insurance companies moved from 13 percent of total financial intermediary assets in 1920 to 26 percent in 1930, an even faster pace than mutual funds in the 1980s. They then began a very steep relative decline.

How did the banks and the life insurance companies respond to their decades-long relative decline? The short answer is, "not quickly."

Round about the mid-1960s the banks realized they had a problem. In fact, their problem was a lack of innovation in savings and lending instruments – partly because of legislative restraints but also because of rather rigid views as to what constituted banking. Recall that they had never asked for residential mortgage lending powers. These powers were handed to them by a government that wanted more house financing. Also, only the Canadian Bank of Commerce, as it then was known, took advantage of a *Bank Act* loophole that enabled it to make small consumer loans at rates above the interest ceiling.

Things began to change in banking in the late 1960s. Legislative obstacles to banks engaging in consumer and residential mortgage financing were removed in the 1967 revision of the *Bank Act*, including abolition of the interest rate ceiling, and the banks soon showed they could provide financing at lower cost to consumers than their competitors.

The dominance of the consumer loan and sales finance companies soon faded and, by 1994, they accounted for only 1.5 percent of financial intermediary assets compared with almost 6 percent in the 1970s. Similar aggressiveness developed in mortgage financing, as the banks increased their role and provided competition for the traditional players in this area – the life insurance, trust and mortgage loan companies. Greater convenience and lower mortgage costs appear to have been the outcome of that invasion.

Very significant was the removal of the barriers separating commercial and investment banking in 1987 and the rapid takeover by the banks of a major part of the investment dealer industry. This was followed in the early 1990s by bank acquisition of the major trust companies and by a sharply accelerating bank role in the mutual fund business.

The life insurance companies too became much more aggressive in the long-term savings business, particularly in annuities and, by 1994, held 10 percent to 11 percent of financial intermediary assets, up from less than 9 percent. So, after several decades of relative decline, they were holding their own and a bit more. Indeed, in the last few years their assets have grown a bit faster than those of the banks.

So what system restructuring remains to be accomplished in the period ahead, beginning with the upcoming legislation, and what principles should guide that restructuring? While policy changes must pay attention to achieving a smooth transition from the existing regime to an altered one, they should not be impeded by the notion that change will hurt some and help others. The history of the evolution of the Canadian financial system is replete with examples of the rise and fall of groups of financial institutions and of individual ones – an essential reason, as I have already noted, why the Canadian system is so highly developed. We have seen the rise and fall of building societies, private bankers, mortgage loan companies, sales finance and consumer loan companies, and the relative declines in the chartered banks, life insurance companies and trust companies. We have also seen a major restructuring of the investment dealer industry and the trust companies, while the recent rising stars have been the mutual funds and trusteed pension funds. At the same time, and significantly, in almost all areas, a number of niche players exist that are nicely surviving the changes and operating profitably.

Indeed, apart from the need for further substantial changes in the insurance industry and some in the leasing industry, institutional restructuring across the "pillars" is largely complete. Since World War II, we have seen the joining of consumer and commercial bank lending and mortgage lending in the same institutions – contrary to what had existed in preceding decades. We have seen the combining of investment and commercial banking, still absent in the United States and, after 1992, the banks, trust, investment and insurance companies have had the power to engage in each other's businesses, albeit only through separate subsidiaries. However, the two exceptions I noted – insurance and leasing – are not unimportant. In both, there would appear to be room for reduced distribution costs to consumers through additional restructuring.

Even taking into account several recent failures and the merging of a few large companies, the insurance industry faces adjustment for two reasons. First, there has been relatively little consolidation within the industry. Contrary to what has happened over the years in banking and the investment business, there are almost 150 companies in the life and health insurance business, and none has more than 10 percent of the market. This is not the outcome of market forces but rather the outcome of decades of apparent bias against mergers on the part of former superintendents of insurance, and legislative restrictions in a complex industry with both mutual and stock companies. Emerging legislation should remove such restrictions for the sake of the future efficiency of the industry.

The second reason for the likelihood of significant restructuring of the insurance industry is the inevitability, sooner or later, of life insurance distribution through branches of all deposit-taking institutions as is currently the case in many other advanced industrial countries.

Current legislation also prohibits financial institutions from engaging in car and household property leasing even though leasing, in many instances, has become a substitute form of financing. Since considerable international practice argues in favour of financial institutions engaging in such activity, this is likely to emerge as an important issue in the upcoming debate on new financial services legislation.

While many of the major legislative barriers to integrating the pillars have been removed, some obstacles remain. Banks and federal trust companies cannot directly underwrite insurance risks in Canada or distribute insurance or annuities through their branches; insurance companies cannot directly take deposits or participate in the payments system; banks and insurance companies cannot directly act as trustees; and financial institutions cannot engage in car leasing or even have car leasing subsidiaries. You see here the results of a nice *political* balance struck by the government in enacting the 1992 legislation, a balance that did not seem *economically* logical in 1992 and seems even less so today.

As in the past, the real world of the marketplace moves on in spite of legislation. On January 23, 1996, the National Bank of Canada and the Metropolitan Life Insurance Co. announced that they were forming a joint venture whereby a new company, called National Bank Financial Services Inc., would begin selling each other's products through agents reporting to regional offices in all parts of Canada. From an economic efficiency point of view, this is probably a second-best solution, with the first-best solution probably being the one present in Europe, some states in the United States and some credit unions, and all the caisses populaires in Quebec, i.e., direct distribution of insurance through branches of deposit-taking financial institutions. Similar critical appraisal, of the other obstacles to integration to which I have referred, is also justified such as in house trust powers for insurance companies and banks, and deposit taking by insurance companies. So where is government policy now? I mentioned earlier that there were two broad legislative initiatives in play at present – deposit insurance and regulatory and supervisory powers and procedures of the OSFI and CDIC, and amendments to the legislation outlining the powers and operations of the financial institutions.

In late 1992, there began a long parliamentary review of the first. The federal Department of Finance undertook a review of the deposit insurance system and related supervisory powers of the OSFI and the CDIC with the help of an advisory committee drawn from the public and private sectors. Work was completed in mid-1994. House of Commons and Senate committees held hearings. The House of Commons Standing Committee on Finance examined and reported on deposit insurance following the failure of some trust companies. The Standing Senate Committee on Banking, Trade and Commerce, in April 1994, began to conduct a review of regulatory issues including deposit insurance and, by the end of the year, had come up with an influential report containing 42 recommendations.

This laid the groundwork for a federal government policy paper issued by the Secretary of State for Finance, the Hon. Doug Peters, on February 9, 1995. It was entitled *Enhancing the Safety and Soundness of the Canadian Financial System*. Ignoring widespread advice, it argued against co-insurance to strengthen the deposit insurance system through making depositors more sensitive to where they put their money and confined itself to reducing "stacking" of the $60,000 deposit limit. The paper favoured some form of risk premiums. So it appears that basic restructuring of deposit insurance remains for another day. The hands of the OSFI and the CDIC were to be strengthened through permitting earlier and strong intervention in the affairs of troubled institutions, and a new entity was to be formed for insuring policy and annuity holders of insurance companies.

In June 1995, the government introduced Bill C-109, later changed to Bill C-15, reflecting the Peters report, and sent it to the House of Commons Finance Committee, which reported on it in December 1995. The bill became law in June 1996.

As for the second initiative, in 1995, the Senate Banking Committee began to review issues relating to legislation governing federal financial institutions, and interested parties submitted briefs. The Department of Finance submitted a background paper entitled *Developments in the Financial Services Industry Since Financial Sector Legislative Reform*. The Committee reported on the issues but did not make specific recommendations. The Department of Finance had preliminary discussions with the industry and invited briefs. It released a white paper on June 19, 1996. Unfortunately, the white paper did not deal with the major controversial issues, leaving them for consideration by a task force and advisory committee. The task force has not yet been formed. In short, as of today we do not know what the government will propose in terms of further restructuring of the financial institutions. What *should* they propose?

Quite apart from having to deal with the exceedingly important questions of opening up insurance distribution, and car and household property leasing to all regulated financial institutions, there are other issues lurking around the review process which could affect the further restructuring of the system. These include the issues of concentration, real/financial mixing, wide ownership and the 10 percent rule, international reciprocity, access to the payments system, federal-provincial harmonization, corporate governance, unaffiliated directors' minority interest investments, related party rules, privacy, consumer protection and holding companies.

Let me reassure you immediately that I do not propose to comment on each of these matters – only on several of them.

Concentration

In the current process of legislative revisions, a prominent issue is that of concentration. It is referred to, for example, by the life insurance industry as a major reason for opposing the entry of banks into the retail distribution of insurance through bank branches. There is need to take a very objective view on this matter.

It is interesting and significant that while banks have branched out in their intermediary business in a remarkable way, their share of intermediary business today, at about 40 percent, is no higher than it was in 1980 or even 1940. And if you take the foreign banks out of that figure, it is 4 percentage points lower. Furthermore, after comparing such things as interest rate spreads and the share of market in individual product areas, such as deposits, mortgages, mutual funds and rates of return on equity, with those of other countries, it is difficult to make the case either for excessive concentration or lack of competition.

Furthermore, the constant pressure of foreign competition in most areas of the financial system casts grave doubt on the usefulness of concepts of domestic concentration, not to mention the apparent reality coming out of research that competition is intense even when there are relatively few companies in individual industry sectors. I suspect that, before the decade is out, we will be discussing the need to *increase* the size of even the largest Canadian financial institutions, through mergers among them, in order for them to have a sufficiently large domestic base for surviving in the global financial system. This may well go to the point of questioning the continued usefulness of the 10 percent individual shareholder ownership limitation for Schedule I chartered banks, even though I do not expect that it will be an issue in the current revision.

Mixing of Industrial and Financial Activity

An important principle that has guided past banking legislation is the separation of real and financial activities. (Banks cannot own industrial companies, and industrial companies cannot own banks either directly or indirectly.) However, the principle has not held in the case of other financial institutions, such as trust companies, and it is not observed in Europe. My own view is that the principle is a good one and, where it has been applied, has served the system well. While Europe has permitted such mixing, even in the case of the most prominent example of it, the Deutsche Bank, there have been questions concerning its desirability. A number of examples now exist internationally where trouble in the industrial company has impaired the position of the financial institution in the group. It seems that when push comes to shove, the financial institution in such a mixed group will not be shielded from trouble in the industrial affiliates. Certainly, regulating financial institutions is simplified if mixing of real and financial activity is prohibited.

Access to the Payments System

One area where the Canadian financial system is lagging other industrialized countries is its payments clearing and settlement system. Alternative clearing mechanisms made possible by electronic transfer mechanisms, such as debt cards, underscore the need to restructure the system. One element of reform, the Large Value Transfer System, is being developed and may be introduced by the Canadian Payments Association next year. There is also increasing pressure from non-bank institutions, both financial and non-financial, to gain access to the payments system. The recent consent order filed by the director of the federal Bureau of Competition Policy with the Competition Tribunal requiring the opening up of the Interac system to other regulated financial institutions, is a straw in the wind. Not nearly enough work has been done on reforming the payments system to move forward on it. My own feeling is that, with the rapidly changing character of many financial institutions, there is a need to examine the system in detail and codify preconditions, including regulatory and supervisory requirements, for ensuring the safety and soundness of the payments system. This could pave the way for entry into the system of any institutions that meet those requirements. The essential challenge is to have a system that leads to each player being prepared to accept the other's credit risk.

One researcher who has studied the matter with some care, Professor Neil C. Quigley, has even concluded that the basic character of the payments system should be changed. He feels that the monopoly position of the Canadian Payments Association should be broken, and there should be no requirement that the chartered banks must be members of it. It will be very interesting to see how this part of the financial system evolves.

Federal-Provincial Harmonization of Regulation

I noted earlier that one major reason why the Canadian financial system is highly efficient is because there were no major obstacles to the development of national institutions. We see this in all areas – banking, insurance, trust, investment and leasing. However, while the system permitted the realization of economies of scale, the existence of joint federal-provincial jurisdictions in areas other than banking has meant a proliferation of regulatory regimes. It is the existence of this unnecessary regulatory burden that has stood in the way of achieving maximum economic efficiency in the national financial system.

This has become increasingly recognized in recent years, and some attention has been paid to possible improvements. However, the results so far have been quite disappointing. Provinces began as early as 1988 to try to harmonize trust legislation but have still not succeeded. Nor is national harmonization much advanced in areas of insurance and securities legislation. The European Community is more advanced than the Canadian provinces with its principle that institutions regulated in their home jurisdiction have access to the whole of the Community. The federal government has made a proposal for a national securities regulator but no one should hold his or her breath on that possibility.

You can guess from what I have already said that we are in for another interesting period of legislative restructuring with some important and controversial issues to be resolved. History makes it quite clear that the system can absorb substantial change without significant disruption, so we should not be phased by it. We must all hope that emerging government policy will lead to Canadian consumers being the winners, not the self-interested players.

Session IV Financing Constraints and Large Firms

Usha R. Mittoo
Faculty of Management
University of Manitoba

Seasoned Equity Offerings and the Cost of Equity in the Canadian Market

ABSTRACT

THIS STUDY EXAMINES THE STOCK PRICE EFFECTS of the seasoned equity offerings by the Toronto Stock Exchange (TSE) 300 firms to identify the determinants of the cost of equity for Canadian firms. The results reveal that the issuing firms experience a significant drop in their share price around the announcement date. The cross-sectional analysis shows that large firms experience a more pronounced negative reaction while issuers interlisted on both Canadian and U.S. stock exchanges have a less negative market reaction. The results suggest that the main determinants of the equity capital are related to the smaller size of the Canadian equity market. The findings of this study also confirm the previous evidence that the Canadian market is segmented from the U.S. equity market, and segmentation is more severe for the non-interlisted Canadian stocks.

INTRODUCTION

THE GLOBALIZATION OF CAPITAL MARKETS IN RECENT YEARS has created a worldwide surge in cross-border security offerings and investments. Cross-border equity flows have increased rapidly in the last decade: one in five share trades featured a foreign investor or a foreign equity in 1992. Gross sales and purchases of bonds and equities by domestic and foreign residents in the United States rose from 9 percent of the American gross domestic product (GDP) in 1980 to 135 percent in 1993. The total cross-border ownership of securities that could be traded in 1992 was estimated to be $2.5 trillion.[1]

Two recent trends in capital markets have accelerated the pace of cross-border trading and the globalization of markets. First, institutional investors have become major players in the market place buoyed by the phenomenal growth in mutual and pension funds. Institutional investors now manage almost two fifths of American households' financial assets, up from one fifth in 1980.[2] In Canada, institutions, such as mutual and pension funds, and insurance companies, held 70 percent of the market value by 1990 and about two thirds of the traded value on the TSE in 1991.[3]

Second, the number of firms listing on foreign exchanges has increased dramatically, making it easier for investors to buy the foreign stocks at home. For example, 372 foreign firms were listed on the London Stock Exchange between 1987 and 1992. The cross-exchange trading, buying and selling of foreign shares at home was $875 billion in 1990, nearly 40 percent of all international equity trades.[4] In 1994, the purchase and sale of foreign equities on the New York Stock Exchange (NYSE), the American Stock Exchange (AMEX) and the National Association of Security Dealers Automated Quotation (NASDAQ) reached $715 billion, and the volume of trading in foreign stocks accounted for about 10 percent of total trading.[5] Availability of foreign stocks for trading on domestic exchanges has reduced the cost of acquiring and trading foreign securities.

What implications do these trends have for Canadian investors and corporate managers? Cross-border investments serve to eliminate barriers to international investments across countries and to increase the integration of capital markets. In segmented capital markets, securities with the same risk earn differential rates of return. Thus, firms with similar risk characteristics may have different costs of capital, depending on the degree of segmentation and the special characteristics of the home country economy. Barriers to international capital flows can cause segmentation in financial markets along national boundaries. These barriers can be legal ones that pertain to government restrictions on the flow of capital across countries. They can also be indirect barriers arising from investors' reluctance to invest in foreign securities because of difficulties in collecting information about, or transacting in, foreign stocks. While most legal barriers have been either eliminated or considerably reduced, the indirect barriers still remain strong. Cross-border listing allows firms to reduce indirect barriers to investment since foreign stocks listed on domestic exchanges are as easy to trade as domestic stocks.

Many recent studies have investigated the integration of the Canadian and U.S. equity markets. These studies concluded that while Canadian markets had been segmented from U.S. equity markets, in recent years there has been a move toward integration. Also, Canadian stocks interlisted on U.S. stock markets are priced in a relatively integrated market compared to their domestic counterparts.[6]

Segmentation of the Canadian and U.S. equity markets implies that the cost of equity capital for the Canadian firms depends largely on the demand and supply of equity capital within Canada. Since the Canadian economy is small and resource based, many risk factors may be priced in the Canadian market that are diversified away in the larger U.S. economy. Consequently, Canadian firms are likely to face a higher cost of capital relative to their U.S. counterparts. In a survey of Canadian managers, Jog and Srivastava (1993) reported that all respondents believed that they had at least some cost of capital disadvantage over a comparable U.S. firm. Since a lower cost of capital is a major competitive advantage for firms in a globalized market economy, understanding the factors that determine the cost of capital for Canadian firms is important to reduce the negative effects of these factors.

The purpose of this paper is twofold: to identify factors that are likely to influence the cost of equity capital in Canada and to study the effect of interlisting on a firm's cost of capital. These issues are investigated by studying seasoned equity offerings in Canada – a relatively unexplored area of research. In efficient markets, market reaction at the time of the equity issuance provides information on the significance of the factors that are relevant in determining the cost of equity.

The next section discusses the potential determinants of the cost of equity for Canadian firms, followed by a description of the sample and methodology. The final sections include empirical results, a summary of the findings and a discussion of the policy implications.

DETERMINANTS OF THE CANADIAN COST OF EQUITY

THE CAPITAL ASSET PRICING MODEL (CAPM) SPECIFIES that systematic risk or beta is the only determinant of risk that is relevant for pricing securities. This model is, however, based on the strong assumptions of perfect and frictionless capital markets that may be inadequate to capture the complexities of the marketplace. In particular, Merton (1987) observed that the models developed in a perfect market setting rarely provide explicit and important roles for either financial institutions, complicated financial instruments and contracts, or regulatory constraints, despite their observed abundance in the real financial world. Merton developed a model of capital market equilibrium under the more realistic assumptions that investors generally know about or are "aware" of only a subset of available securities and these subsets vary across investors depending on individual investors' degree of recognition of different securities. Under these assumptions, many risk factors are priced in addition to the market factor. The model predicts that expected returns increase with systematic risk, firm-specific risk and relative market value, and decrease with the relative size of the firm's investor base.

The risk factors relevant for asset pricing may vary greatly across countries depending on the special characteristics and the institutional and capital market structure prevalent in different economies. Canadian markets have several unique features that may be relevant for security pricing. First, the Canadian market is small and dominated by resource-based, and infrequently traded, stocks. As a result, risk factors, such as industry and stock liquidity, may be priced in the Canadian market that are likely to be diversified away in the larger U.S. economy. Second, Canada has a large number of securities that are interlisted on U.S. stock exchanges. The effects of interlisting on the cost of equity need to be explored fully. Third, institutional and regulatory differences between Canada and the United States may play a role in the demand and supply of Canadian stocks. These factors are discussed below to identify the potential determinants of the demand or supply of equity capital in the Canadian market.

INDUSTRIAL STRUCTURE

AS MANY RECENT STUDIES HAVE DOCUMENTED, industry is an important factor in asset pricing. King (1966) first identified the presence of an industry factor in addition to the market factor as a determinant of U.S. stock returns. Lessard (1974, 1976) documented the importance of an industry factor for international stock returns. Roll (1992) showed that an industry factor is an important determinant of the differences in the correlations and of the volatility among country index returns. Griffin and Karolyi (1995) concluded that an industrial mix of the portfolios affects the portfolio diversification benefits in an economically significant way, and Mittoo (1995) found that sensitivity to risk factors varies across industries in a matched sample of Australian, Canadian and U.S. stocks.

The Canadian stock market is dominated by resource firms which are more volatile than non-resource firms. Although the percentage of resource firms has been decreasing over time, their concentration in Canada is still significant relative to their proportion in the United States.[7] Rao and Lee-Sing (1995) compared a sample distribution of Canadian and American firms by industry grouping and found that the U.S. sample had only 13 percent of the firms in mining and resource-intensive manufacturing compared to 30.7 percent in Canada. Thus, industry is likely to be a significant factor in the Canadian market, and Canadian investors may demand a higher risk premium for holding the resource stocks relative to the non-resource stocks.

STOCK LIQUIDITY

STOCK LIQUIDITY IS AN IMPORTANT ATTRIBUTE since highly liquid stocks can be bought and sold with minimal impact on the stock price. In contrast, an illiquid stock increases the overall cost of trading for investors because of the difficulty in trading in stock. Liquidity is also a determinant of the bid-ask spread, and less-liquid stocks have generally larger spreads. Investors are likely to require a higher expected return for holding an infrequently traded stock to compensate for its higher trading costs. Amihud and Mendelson (1986) developed a theoretical model in which expected returns are an increasing and concave function of liquidity. They provided evidence that, after controlling for differences in beta and firm size, differences in expected returns reflect differences in liquidity.

Infrequent trading is a major problem in the Canadian stock market. Fowler et al. (1980) reported that out of the 1,800 securities listed on the TSE for at least 12 months during the period January 1970 to December 1979, only 4.3 percent of the stocks traded on the last day of each month, only 37.5 percent exhibited at least one trade every month and the remaining 58 percent had at least one month in which no trade was recorded. In contrast, Foerster and Keim (1987) reported that in the 1972 to 1987 period, the percentage of stocks that did not trade on an average day was 1.6 percent for all NYSE stocks and 15.9 percent for all AMEX stocks. Highly liquid stocks are particularly preferred by large institutional investors who have become the dominant investors in the Canadian stock market in the 1990s.

Thus, the demand for highly liquid Canadian stocks is likely to be greater than the supply of such stocks, and investors may demand a higher risk premium for holding thinly traded stocks.

FIRM SIZE

BANZ (1981) FIRST DOCUMENTED THE SIZE ANOMALY, i.e., the existence of a negative association between abnormal returns and firm size after controlling for the risk measured by beta. Banz reported that small firms, on average, earned risk-adjusted returns of about 12 percent per annum in the 1926 to 1975 period. Many other studies have confirmed these findings, and the estimates of the size premium vary from 10 percent to 20 percent per annum. Moreover, empirical support for the association between size and average returns is about as strong as the association between beta and average returns. Thus, an alternative model based on size and expected return would seem to have as much empirical validity as the one based on beta and expected return (Schwert, 1983). Berk (1993) provided a theoretical framework in which the firm size is actually a measure of risk.

Canadian firms are much smaller, on average, compared to U.S. firms. For example, only nine Canadian companies were included in the *Fortune* (1992) list of 500 largest industrial companies compared to 157 U.S. firms. Rao and Lee-Sing (1995) confirmed that Canadian firms were much smaller than their U.S. counterparts in their comparative sample of Canadian and U.S. firms. Small-firm stocks are also generally less liquid and trade infrequently – attributes that make these stocks unattractive for large institutional investors. Consequently, Canadian investors are likely to demand a higher risk premium for holding small Canadian stocks relative to the large-firm stocks.

OWNERSHIP STRUCTURE

OWNERSHIP STRUCTURE IS THE MOST STRIKING DIFFERENCE between Canadian and U.S. firms. Canadian firms, in general, are closely held, and many domestically owned corporations have a control block of shareholders. Rao and Lee-Sing (1995) reported that, in more than three quarters of the Canadian corporations in their sample, at least one large blockholder controlled 20 percent or more of the voting shares and, in over half the firms, a single blockholder controlled more than 50 percent of the voting shares. Differences in the ownership structure are more pronounced for the largest size category. Morck and Stangeland (1994) found that only 16 percent of the 550 largest Canadian corporations are widely held in Canada. Thain and Leighton (1991) found that 73 percent of the top 100 corporations in the United States are widely held compared to only 15 percent in Canada.

In widely held firms, each shareholder owns a small portion of the firm with no effective control. In such firms, agency problems arise because managers may work in their own interest rather than in the interest of the shareholders. While conflict of interest between managers and shareholders is reduced when a single shareholder has effective control of a firm, conflict of interest between majority and minority shareholders may also emerge. Thus, two opposite effects can be attributed to the differences in the ownership structure of Canadian firms relative to their U.S. counterparts. First, in contrast to widely held firms, the agency costs that arise from the divergence between the interests of managers and shareholders are reduced in closely held firms. On the other hand, agency costs that stem from the conflict of interest between the dominant and other shareholders are likely to be higher in the closely held firms. Thus, the net effect of ownership structure on the cost of equity and on investors' demands for the stocks of closely held firms depends on which of the two effects dominates.

DIVIDEND YIELD

THE IMPACT OF DIFFERENTIAL TAXATION ON DIVIDENDS and capital gains on equity value has been the subject of considerable debate in Canada. In particular, non-residents do not receive the dividend tax credit, and Canadians do not receive the dividend tax credit on dividend income from foreign investments. Booth (1987) argued that the dividend tax credit induces segmentation in the Canadian market by encouraging Canadians to invest in Canadian securities and provided evidence consistent with this hypothesis. McKenzie and Thompson (1995) found that taxes affect stock prices and that changes in the domestic taxation of dividends have a differential impact on high and low-dividend-yield securities. The effect of stock dividend yield, however, is likely to be minimal in recent years because of tax reforms during the last two decades that have reduced the tax differential between dividends and capital gains considerably.

CANADIAN INTERLISTED STOCKS

THE CANADIAN SECURITY MARKET HAS TWO DISTINCT SEGMENTS: interlisted securities that are listed on both U.S. and Canadian stock exchanges and purely domestic stocks that are listed only on their domestic stock exchanges. Until the early 1980s, very few Canadian firms listed on U.S. exchanges. For example, only 110 TSE firms were interlisted on U.S. exchanges in December 1986. Since then, the pace of U.S. listings has increased rapidly, spurred by the globalization of financial and product markets: 75 TSE firms were interlisted on U.S. exchanges between January 1987 and December 1995. The interlisted securities form a significant portion of the Canadian market value, and their traded value comprises more than 50 percent of the total dollar traded value on the TSE. About half of the TSE 35 firms and about one third of the TSE 100 firms are interlisted on U.S. stock exchanges.

BENEFITS AND COSTS OF INTERLISTING

WHY DO CANADIAN FIRMS SEEK U.S. LISTINGS? In a survey of Canadian firms, managers cited various reasons (Mittoo, 1992b): to access larger U.S. capital markets, to broaden the shareholder base, to increase liquidity, to appeal to institutional investors and to enhance visibility. Other reasons related to increasing the marketing efforts and the prestige and image of the company.

The major cost associated with the listing was the U.S. Securities and Exchange Commission's (SEC's) reporting and compliance requirements. Further, the costs of legal and accounting fees, and of staff involvement – factors related to the stringency of the reporting requirements – were considered more important than the listing fees. The survey also found that the perceptions of managers about the net benefits of interlisting were highly positively correlated with the trading volume of their firm's stock on U.S. exchanges. Also, firms that conducted a higher percentage of business abroad and had issued securities in foreign markets had higher trading volumes on U.S. markets. Foerster and Karolyi (1993) and Mittoo (1996) also found that U.S. listings by TSE firms were accompanied by an increase in total trading volume and trading volume on domestic stock exchanges. The average trading volume in the interlisted stocks more than doubled in the months following interlisting.

Canada-United States Multijurisdictional Disclosure System and Interlisting

For years, Canadian companies issuing securities in the United States have been required to meet that country's tougher requirements for disclosure and financial reporting. Canadian companies interlisted on U.S. exchanges had to produce lengthy filings such as 10-K and 10-Q reports and U.S. style proxy statements. Although the U.S. and Canadian securities regulations are similar, SEC regulations require extensive disclosure of proxy requests, executive compensation, the relationship between management and directors, and broader liability provisions than those required under Canadian regulations. These disclosure requirements are onerous and costly for many firms and deter Canadian companies from accessing U.S. capital markets.

On July 1, 1991 Canada and United States implemented the Multijurisdictional Disclosure System (MJDS) that eliminates the need for interlisted public companies to file two sets of documents and meet two sets of regulations. Under MJDS, Canadian companies are deemed to have met the U.S. requirements simply by filing Canadian documents with the SEC. The System has reduced the costs of interlisting considerably and represents a major step in the integration of Canadian and U.S. markets. The number of U.S. interlistings has grown rapidly since the implementation of the MJDS. Between July 1991 and December 1995, 54 TSE firms interlisted their securities on U.S. exchanges, up from 23 between January 1987 and June 1991.[8]

Overall, interlisted Canadian firms may be preferred by Canadian investors for their higher trading volumes, broader shareholder base and their easy access to U.S. markets, and investors may pay a premium for these stocks relative to their domestically listed counterparts.

DATA AND METHODOLOGY

SAMPLE AND DATA DESCRIPTION

THE SAMPLE ANALYSED IN THIS STUDY consists of seasoned equity issuances by the TSE 300 firms during the 1982 to 1993 period. The initial sample of equity offerings was identified from Compact Disclosure, and the search for announcement dates of the offerings was done in Canadian Business and Current Affairs (CBCA) data base. To qualify for inclusion in the study, an equity issuance had to satisfy the following criteria.

1. The firm issuing the equity was included in the TSE 300 index as of December 1993.
2. The issue was a public seasoned offering made by a non-financial firm. Initial public offerings (IPOs) were excluded.
3. The equity issue did not have any warrants or other sweeteners attached.
4. The announcement date of the equity issue was available in *The Globe and Mail* or *The Financial Post*, and there was no other major firm-specific event on the announcement date.
5. The daily stock returns for the security were available on the Canadian Financial Markets Research Centre (CFMRC) data base, and sufficient stock returns data were available around the offering announcement for empirical analysis.
6. The information on firm-specific variables was available for the cross-sectional analysis. The data on firm-specific variables were collected from Compustat, Compact Disclosure, *Toronto Stock Exchange Review* and *The Financial Post* data base.

These selection criteria resulted in a sample of 106 equity offerings.

METHODOLOGY

THE STANDARD EVENT STUDY FRAMEWORK WAS USED with a two-step estimation procedure to test the significance of the specified factors. In the first step, the abnormal returns to the announcements of the equity issuance by each firm were estimated. In an efficient market, the stock market reaction at the time of the announcement will capture the effects of the equity offering on the firm value. The second step involved a cross-sectional analysis of the relationship between stock price effects and determinants of the cost of equity.

Research has shown that stock markets react negatively to announcements of seasoned equity issuances. According to these studies, seasoned equity offerings are accompanied by a drop in the issuer firm's price, and larger equity issues have a more pronounced negative reaction.[9] A negative stock price reaction for larger issues is consistent with the theoretical model developed by Myers and Majluf (1984) under the assumption that managers and investors have asymmetric information about a firm's prospects. In their model, managers issue equity when the share price is too high relative to the managers' assessment of the share price based on the future cash flows to the firm. As a result, the equity issue signals bad news to the market. Jog and Schaller (1993) provided evidence in support of the asymmetric information hypothesis in the Canadian market. Another explanation for the negative stock price reaction is the price pressure hypothesis which states that firms face a downward-sloping demand curve for their stock. The announcement of a new equity issue results in an increase in the supply of a firm's stock and a decrease in the price of their equity. Based on these theories, the effect of larger issues needs to be controlled in the cross-sectional analysis.

Estimation of Abnormal Stock Returns

THE DAILY ABNORMAL RETURNS FOR ANY STOCK ARE DEFINED as the difference between the observed returns and the expected returns predicted by a single factor market model of expected returns. The market model is specified as:

$$R_{jt} = \alpha_j + \beta_j R_{Mt} + \epsilon_{jt} \quad (1)$$

where R_{jt} is the rate of return on security j on day t, R_{Mt} is the rate of return on the value-weighted market portfolio provided by CFMRC on day t and ϵ_{jt} is the error term of security j on day t.

Abnormal return for the common stock of firm j on day t is defined as $AR_{jt}=R_{jt}-(\hat{\alpha}_j+\hat{\beta}_j R_{Mt})$, where $\hat{\alpha}_j$, $\hat{\beta}_j$ are ordinary least squares estimates of firm j's market model parameters. Event day 0 is defined as the day of the first announcement of the equity issue in a Canadian business newspaper. The parameters of the model are estimated from trading days -200 to -50 prior to the announcement day. For a sample of N firms, daily average abnormal return AR for each day t is obtained:

$$AR_t = (1/N)\Sigma_{j=1}^{N} AR_{jt} \quad (2)$$

The expected value of AR_t in the absence of any abnormal returns is zero, and the difference from zero captures the abnormal returns due to the market reaction to the announcement. To examine whether the average daily abnormal return is different from zero, the average standardized abnormal return SAR_t is calculated as:

$$SAR_t = \frac{1}{N} \Sigma_{j=1}^{N} \frac{AR_{jt}}{S_{jt}} \quad (3)$$

where S_{jt} is the estimated residual standard deviation of firm j from the market model regression.

For calculating the significance of the abnormal returns, the following z-statistic is calculated for a portfolio of N securities for each day t:

$$Z_t = \sqrt{N}\, SAR_t \tag{4}$$

Assuming that the individual abnormal returns are normal and independent across securities, the z-statistic follows a unit-normal distribution and is used to test the hypothesis that the average standardized abnormal return equals zero.

Since there may be a leakage of information before the publication date, the cumulative abnormal returns (CARs) are calculated for a two-day period (-1, 0) which includes the event day and the trading day before the publication date.

CROSS-SECTIONAL REGRESSION

THE FOLLOWING MULTIPLE REGRESSION MODEL IS ESTIMATED to examine the significance of the hypothesized factors:

$$SCAR_j = \alpha_0 + \beta_1 RESOURCE + \beta_2 TURNOVER + \beta_3 SIZE + \beta_4 OWNER$$

$$+ \beta_5 DIVYLD + \beta_6 ISSUESIZE + \beta_7 INTERLST + \epsilon_j$$

where $SCAR_j$ is the two-day (-1, 0) standardized cumulative abnormal return, and the independent variables are the hypothesized determinants of the equity capital.

RESOURCE is the proxy for the industry factor and is a dummy variable which takes the value one if the equity issuance is by a resource firm and zero otherwise. TURNOVER is the proxy for the stock liquidity and is the ratio of the number of a firm's shares traded to the average number of shares outstanding in the year prior to the equity issue. The data on number of shares traded on Canadian and U.S. stock markets were collected from various issues of the *Toronto Stock Exchange Review*. Stock liquidity is expected to be positively related to stock market reaction. The SIZE variable represents the firm size and is expected to be negatively related to the market reaction. SIZE is measured by the natural logarithm of the book value of the total assets of the firms in the year prior to the equity issue. (These data were collected from Compustat.) OWNER is the proxy for the ownership structure of a firm and is a dummy variable that takes the value one for firms that are closely held and zero otherwise. A firm in which a single shareholder owns more than 20 percent of the voting shares outstanding is defined as a closely held firm.[10] The data on stock ownership are collected from various issues of *The Financial Post*. DIVYLD is the stock dividend yield in the year prior to the issue, and the data are collected from Compustat. INTERLST is a dummy variable which takes the value one if the firm issuing equity was interlisted on Canadian and U.S. stock exchanges and zero otherwise. ISSUESIZE is a proxy for the size of offerings and is included to test the predictions of the price pressure and asymmetric information hypotheses. ISSUESIZE is measured as the ratio of the number of new shares offered to the number of shares outstanding at the end of the year prior to the issue.

The method of underwriting the equity issues also varies across offerings. In recent years, a majority of Canadian issues have been done on a bought deal basis. In a bought deal, investment dealers buy an entire issue of shares with their own money and then resell it, usually in large blocks, to institutional investors. In the fully marketed method, the underwriter brings the deal to the market and all investors participate in the deal. In a bought deal, the underwriter negotiates directly with large investors. As a result, the industry perception is that institutional investors have a better price that comes at a cost to the current shareholders. This results in a price decline and a loss by current shareholders.[11] Schwartz (1994) examined these claims by studying the stock market reaction to two samples of equity offerings issued under different methods of underwriting: bought deals and fully marketed deals. He found that, contrary to industry perceptions, the bought deal sample of equity issues had a less negative market reaction compared to the fully marketed sample. To control for the method of underwriting, a dummy variable BOUGHT has been used. It takes the value one if the offering was made using the bought deal method and zero otherwise.

EMPIRICAL RESULTS

SAMPLE CHARACTERISTICS

TABLE 1 PRESENTS THE FREQUENCY DISTRIBUTION of the sample offerings by the year of offering and the interlisting status. Most of the sample is concentrated in the 1991 to 1993 period where about 60 percent of the sample offerings occur. Equity offerings by the interlisted firms comprise 40.5 percent of the sample offerings. The sample equity issues by the interlisted and non-interlisted firms follow a similar distribution over time. The number of offerings by NASDAQ-listed firms is approximately the same as for NYSE-listed firms, and most of these offerings are in the 1991 to 1993 period. In contrast, the number of offerings by AMEX-listed Canadian firms is much smaller, and most of these offerings occur before 1991. It may be relevant to note that most Canadian interlistings since 1991 were on the NYSE and NASDAQ.

Table 1 also provides a breakdown of the sample offerings by the bought deal transactions. Forty-three of the 106 offerings were issued using the bought deal method of underwriting. A preponderance of bought deals also occurred in the 1991 to 1993 period, a pattern that is consistent with the drastic increase in bought deal issues observed in this period. The concentration of the sample (1991 to 1993) coincides with a period when there were many security offerings in the Canadian markets. A record number of equity issues worth $20.85 billion occurred in 1993, up from $12.04 billion in 1992. Loughran and Ritter (1995) found that seasoned equity issues in the U.S. stock markets are associated with business cycles. The recent wave of seasoned equity issues in the Canadian market coincided with a buoyant stock market. Since there were many significant trends in the Canadian market in the 1991 to 1993 period (including a surge in institutional investors and an increase in Canadian interlisted securities), this period needs closer examination to draw implications about the determinants of the cost of equity.

TABLE 1

FREQUENCY DISTRIBUTION BY YEAR, BY BOUGHT DEAL TRANSACTIONS AND BY U.S. EXCHANGE OF LISTING OF THE SAMPLE OF SEASONED EQUITY OFFERINGS BY THE TSE 300 FIRMS (1982-1993)

Year	Total	Bought	Non-Interlisted	Interlisted	U.S. Exchange of Listing		
					NYSE	AMEX	NASDAQ
1982	3	0	1	2	2	0	0
1983	5	0	3	2	1	1	0
1984	3	0	2	1	0	1	0
1985	7	0	5	2	0	2	0
1986	6	0	5	1	1	0	0
1987	7	3	3	4	0	2	2
1988	1	0	0	1	0	1	0
1989	5	5	3	2	1	0	1
1990	4	2	2	2	1	1	0
1991	17	10	11	6	3	1	2
1992	22	8	15	7	3	1	3
1993	26	15	13	13	5	0	8
Total	106	43	63	43	17	10	16
Percentage	100.0	40.5	59.5	40.5	16.0	9.4	15.1

Table 2 provides summary statistics of issuers and characteristics of offerings with a breakdown between interlisted and non-interlisted firms. The average book value of the assets of the sample firms is $1,582.19 million. Interlisted firms are larger in size compared to non-interlisted firms, but they also have higher standard deviations that may reflect the existence of a large number of NASDAQ-listed firms in the sample. On average, 7.3 million shares with an average dollar amount of $106.25 million per issue were offered. Although interlisted firms have larger security offerings in terms of the number of shares and the dollar amount offered, sample firms that are domestically listed have significantly larger issue sizes measured as a percentage of the number of shares outstanding.

Table 2 reveals no significant differences between the interlisted and domestic samples in the ownership structure, dividend yield or percentage of bought deals. The major differences are in stock turnover and industry of the firms. The stock turnover for the interlisted sample firms is almost four times that of their domestic counterparts based on both U.S. and Canadian trading volumes. Using only the trading volume on Canadian stock exchanges, the interlisted firms still have almost two times the turnover relative to that of the domestically listed firms. The interlisted sample is also dominated by resource firms. Given a preponderance of resource stocks among the interlisted securities, this is not surprising.

TABLE 2

DESCRIPTIVE STATISTICS OF ISSUER AND OFFERING CHARACTERISTICS BY INTERLISTING STATUS

	Mean			Standard Deviation		
	All	Non-interlisted	Interlisted	All	Non-interlisted	Interlisted
Total assets (book value)[a] (in millions)	$1,582.19	1,403.36	1,844.21	2,012.83	1,697.67	2,399.16
Number of shares offered (in millions)	7.30	6.04	9.15	10.20	7.24	13.29
Issue size[b]	0.15	0.163	0.137	0.11	0.105	0.113
Estimated amount offered[c] (in millions)	106.25	87.70	133.38	103.66	73.03	133.13
Dividend yield (percentage)	1.98	2.07	1.84	2.11	2.16	2.05
Stock turnover[d]						
Canadian markets[e]	0.30	0.24	0.40	0.27	0.21	0.35
U.S. and Canadian markets[f]	0.47	0.24	0.82	0.54	0.25	0.65
Percentage of sample offerings						
By closely held firms[g]	0.56	0.63	0.44	0.50	0.49	0.50
By resource firms	0.38	0.27	0.53	0.49	0.45	0.50
Bought deals	0.41	0.40	0.42	0.49	0.49	0.50

Notes: [a] Average book value in the year prior to the year of offerings.
[b] Calculated as the number of shares issued divided by the number of shares outstanding in the year prior to the offering.
[c] Based on the number of shares issued multiplied by the share price immediately prior to the issue.
[d] Calculated as the ratio of the number of shares traded in the year prior to the issue to the average number of shares outstanding in the year prior to the issue.
[e] Stock turnover based on the number of shares traded only on Canadian stock exchanges.
[f] Stock turnover based on the number of shares traded on U.S. and Canadian stock exchanges.
[g] A firm is defined as closely held if a single shareholder owns more than 20 percent of the voting shares.

ABNORMAL RETURNS

TABLE 3 PRESENTS THE AVERAGE DAILY ABNORMAL RETURNS (AR) in the period -10 to +10 days relative to the announcement day of the offerings. The first column presents the event day. Column 2 contains the average abnormal returns on each

TABLE 3

DAILY AVERAGE ABNORMAL RETURNS (AR), T-STATISTICS, Z-STATISTICS AND PROPORTION OF POSITIVE AND NEGATIVE ABNORMAL RETURNS AROUND THE ANNOUNCEMENTS OF THE SEASONED EQUITY ISSUES BY THE TSE 300 FIRMS (1982-1993)

Event Day (1)	AR (2)	t-Statistic (3)	z-Statistic (4)	Proportion Positive: Negative (5)
-10	0.003	1.48	1.50	60:40
-9	0.004	1.40	1.49	59:41
-8	-0.004	-1.76	-1.11	41:59
-7	0.0014	0.37	1.10	53:47
-6	0.0002	0.08	0.35	45:55
-5	0.004	1.51	2.12*	51:49
-4	0.0010	0.36	1.22	46:54
-3	0.0007	0.31	0.67	49:51
-2	-0.0002	-0.11	0.00	46:54
-1	-0.0150	-5.75**	-8.69**	28:72
0	-0.0029	-1.05	-2.55*	39:61
+1	0.0032	2.18*	1.71	58:42
+2	0.0002	0.086	-0.38	44:56
+3	0.0003	0.177	-0.36	43:57
+4	-0.005	-2.60*	-1.92	36:64
+5	-0.004	-2.14*	-2.13*	36:64
+6	0.0015	0.82	0.13	54:46
+7	-0.003	-1.46	-1.79	35:65
+8	-0.003	-1.20	-1.50	37:63
+9	-0.0002	-0.08	0.052	48:52
+10	0.0017	0.90	0.52	47:53

Notes: The average two-day (-1,0) cumulative abnormal return is -0.018 with t-statistic=-4.99, z-statistic=-7.97.

The z-value for the binomial sign test for the negative abnormal returns is -5.05 for day -1 and -1.95 for day 0.

The average two-day (-1,0) cumulative abnormal return for the interlisted equity issues is -0.00865 with z-statistic=-2.07. For the non-interlisted issues, it is -0.0238 with z-statistic= -8.63. The z-statistic for the difference between the average two-day (-1,0) cumulative abnormal returns for the interlisted and non-interlisted firms is 3.90 and is significant at the 0.01 level.

* Significant at the 0.05 level.
** Significant at the 0.01 level.

event day. The t-statistics for testing the significance of the average abnormal returns and z-statistics for testing the significance of the standardized average abnormal returns are given in the next two columns. The last column depicts the proportion of positive and negative average abnormal returns.

The evidence reveals that the stock market reaction is significantly negative to the announcement of the seasoned equity offerings, a finding that is consistent with most of the previous evidence in the United States and Canada. The abnormal return on day -1 is -1.5 percent of the issuer firm's equity value with a z-statistic of -8.69 which is significant at less than the 0.001 level. The abnormal return on the announcement day is -0.29 percent and the z-statistic is significant at the 0.05 level. The average two-day CAR for days -1 and 0 is -1.80 percent and is statistically significant at less than the 0.001 level. For most days before and after the event, there are no significant abnormal returns. This is consistent with market efficiency.

Table 3 also reveals that the proportion of negative abnormal returns is much higher on the event days. The proportion of positive and negative abnormal returns is approximately the same on most non-event days. However, 72 percent of the abnormal returns on day -1 and 61 percent of the returns on day 0 are negative. A binomial sign test is used to determine the significance of the negative abnormal returns. The z-value for the number of negative abnormal returns is -5.05 for day -1 and -1.95 for day 0. According to the evidence, the negative market reaction is not a result of a few extreme observations.

There appears to be significant cross-sectional variation in the market reaction across firms. For example, the average two-day CAR for the interlisted issues is -0.87 percent compared to -2.38 percent for the non-interlisted issues. The z-statistic to test the difference between the two is 3.85 which is significant at the 0.01 level. The average two-day CAR for the bought deal issues is -2.1 percent compared to -1.5 percent for the non-bought deal issues. However, the difference between the two samples is not significant. The next section examines the potential determinants of the cross-sectional variation in market reaction.

Cross-Sectional Regression Analysis

TABLE 4 PROVIDES THE SUMMARY STATISTICS OF THE HYPOTHESIZED VARIABLES. Panel A presents the mean and standard deviation of the variables. Fifty-six percent of the sample issues are by closely held firms and 38 percent are by resource firms. Bought deals comprise about 40.5 percent of the sample. Panel B presents the correlation coefficients among the variables. These are small with few exceptions. The low correlation between SIZE and INTERLST reflects the large number of NASDAQ-listed firms in the sample that are much smaller in size than the NYSE-listed firms.

A few large correlation coefficients can also be observed among some of the variables, and these may present potential multicollinearity problems in the cross-sectional regressions. In particular, the correlation between DIVYLD and SIZE is

TABLE 4
SUMMARY STATISTICS OF THE HYPOTHESIZED DETERMINANTS OF THE COST OF EQUITY FOR CANADIAN FIRMS

Panel A: Mean and Standard Deviation

	DIVYLD	SIZE	CDTURNOVER	ISSUESIZE	RESOURCE	INTERLST	OWNER	BOUGHT	USCDTURNOVER
Mean	1.98	20.38	0.30	0.15	0.38	0.406	0.56	0.406	0.47
Standard deviation	2.11	1.42	0.27	0.11	0.49	0.49	0.50	0.49	0.54

Panel B: Correlation Coefficients

	DIVYLD	SIZE	CDTURNOVER	ISSUESIZE	RESOURCE	INTERLST	OWNER	BOUGHT	USCDTURNOVER
DIVYLD	1.0	0.47	-0.19	-0.172	-0.144	-0.054	-0.153	-0.12	-0.206
SIZE		1.00	-0.103	-0.165	0.093	0.018	-0.065	-0.09	-0.078
CDTURNOVER			1.00	0.002	0.066	0.29	-0.31	0.19	0.78
ISSUESIZE				1.00	-0.064	-0.116	0.087	0.0128	-0.14
RESOURCE					1.00	0.268	-0.245	-0.088	0.05
INTERLST						1.00	-0.191	0.022	0.53
OWNER							1.00	-0.11	-0.16
BOUGHT								1.0	0.027

Notes: RESOURCE is a dummy variable which takes the value one for the resource firms and zero otherwise.
CDTURNOVER is the ratio of the number of firms' shares traded on Canadian stock exchanges to the average number of shares outstanding in the year prior to the equity issue.
USCDTURNOVER is the ratio of the number of firms' shares traded on Canadian and U.S. stock exchanges to the average number of shares outstanding in the year prior to the equity issue.
SIZE is the natural logarithm of the book value of the total assets of the firms in the year prior to the equity issue.
OWNER is a dummy variable that takes the value one for firms in which a single shareholder owns more than 20 percent of the voting shares outstanding.
DIVYLD is the dividend yield in the year prior to the issue.
ISSUESIZE is the ratio of the number of new shares offered to the number of shares outstanding at the end of the year prior to the issue.
INTERLST is a dummy variable which takes the value one if the firm issuing equity was interlisted on the Canadian and U.S. stock exchanges and zero otherwise.
BOUGHT is a dummy variable which takes the value one if the seasoned equity was a bought deal and zero otherwise.

0.47 which indicates that large firms in the sample have higher dividend yields. The correlation between USCDTURNOVER and INTERLST is 0.53, which is not surprising because interlisted firms have much higher trading volumes than their domestic counterparts. To reduce the multicollinearity problem, an alternative measure of the stock turnover CDTURNOVER has been constructed using the trading volume only on the Canadian stock exchanges. This variable has a correlation of 0.78 with the USCDTURNOVER but has a much lower correlation with INTERLST. The analysis has been conducted using both these variables to examine the robustness of the estimates.

Table 5 presents the results for the cross-sectional regressions of the standardized two-day cumulative abnormal returns (SCAR) on the potential determinants of the cost of equity for Canadian firms. Regressions (1) to (3) are estimated using CDTURNOVER while regressions (4) to (6) are estimated using USCD-TURNOVER. Regressions (1) and (4) are estimated with all independent variables, regressions (2) and (5) exclude the BOUGHT variable, and regressions (3) and (6) exclude both the BOUGHT and DIVYLD variables to deal with the potential multicollinearity problem.

The results strongly support that SIZE and INTERLST are the most significant determinants of stock market reaction to seasoned equity offerings. The coefficients of SIZE and INTERLST are significant at either the 0.05 or the 0.01 levels in all regressions. The coefficient of SIZE has a negative sign which implies that larger firms have a more pronounced negative reaction at the announcements of the equity issue. The coefficient of INTERLST is positive which suggests that investors prefer equity issues of the interlisted firms relative to those of the non-interlisted firms. None of the other variables, RESOURCE, OWNER, DIVYLD or TURNOVER, has significant coefficients at any conventional levels. The coefficient of BOUGHT is negative but not significant. Thus, the results in this study do not support the hypothesis that bought deals result in larger losses to shareholders than their fully marketed counterparts. The results are similar whether the stock turnover is calculated using the trading volume on the Canadian markets or on both the U.S. and Canadian markets. The coefficients of INTERLST are, however, less significant in regressions (4) to (6) that use USCDNTURNOVER because of the multicollinearity problem.

As noted earlier, the period 1991 to 1993 was characterized by many significant events and trends in Canadian markets that included the implementation of the MJDS, a significant increase in the market power of institutional investors, an increased incidence of interlistings on U.S. stock markets and a large number of bought deal issues. Also, Canadian markets were more segmented in the early 1980s. Thus, it is reasonable to expect that the factors affecting the cost of equity may have changed over time. To gain useful insights, samples of equity issues from 1982 to 1987, 1988 to 1993 and 1991 to 1993 were examined.

TABLE 5

ESTIMATES OF THE CROSS-SECTIONAL REGRESSIONS OF THE TWO-DAY STANDARDIZED CUMULATIVE ABNORMAL RETURNS SCAR (-1, 0) ON THE HYPOTHESIZED DETERMINANTS OF THE COST OF EQUITY FOR CANADIAN FIRMS (T-STATISTICS ARE IN PARENTHESES)

Regression	(1)	(2)	(3)	(4)	(5)	(6)
INTERCEPT	3.59	3.53	3.81	3.61	3.54	3.80
	(1.72)	(2.07)*	(1.96)	(1.74)	(2.06)*	(1.97)
SIZE	-0.21	-0.21	-0.23	-0.21	-0.21	-0.23
	(-2.06)*	(-2.07)*	(-2.51)*	(-2.07)*	(-2.08)*	(-2.55)*
CDTURNOVER	0.19	0.15	0.19			
	(0.34)	(0.27)	(0.37)			
USCDTURNOVER				0.11	0.11	0.141
				(0.30)	(0.39)	(0.50)
ISSUESIZE	-0.78	-0.87	-0.81	-0.72	-0.80	-0.73
	(-0.64)	(-0.72)	(-0.68)	(-0.59)	(-0.66)	(-0.61)
RESOURCE	-0.125	-0.101	-0.070	-0.12	-0.09	-0.06
	(-0.43)	(-0.35)	(-0.26)	(-0.39)	(-0.31)	(-0.22)
INTERLST	0.74	0.74	0.74	0.70	0.69	0.68
	(2.64)**	(2.64)**	(2.65)**	(2.19)*	(2.18)*	(2.16)*
OWNER	-0.11	-0.09	-0.06	-0.13	-0.10	-0.078
	(0.29)	(-0.31)	(-0.22)	(-0.46)	(-0.37)	(-0.30)
DIVYLD	-0.034	-0.031		-0.32	-0.027	
	(-0.61)	(-0.40)		(-0.14)	(-0.36)	
BOUGHT	-0.165			-0.15		
	(-0.65)			(-0.56)		
R-SQUARED	0.147	0.144	0.142	0.147	0.144	0.143

Notes: RESOURCE is a dummy variable which takes the value one for the resource firms and zero otherwise.
CDTURNOVER is the ratio of the number of firms' shares traded on Canadian stock exchanges to the average number of shares outstanding in the year prior to the equity issue.
USCDTURNOVER is the ratio of the number of firms' shares traded on Canadian and U.S. stock exchanges to the average number of shares outstanding in the year prior to the equity issue.
SIZE is the natural logarithm of the book value of the total assets of the firms in the year prior to the equity issue.
OWNER is a dummy variable that takes the value one for firms in which a single shareholder owns more than 20 percent of the voting shares outstanding.
DIVYLD is the dividend yield in the year prior to the issue.
ISSUESIZE is the ratio of the number of new shares offered to the number of shares outstanding at the end of the year prior to the issue.
INTERLST is a dummy variable which takes the value one if the firm issuing equity was interlisted on the Canadian and U.S. stock exchanges and zero otherwise.
BOUGHT is a dummy variable which takes the value one if the seasoned equity was a bought deal and zero otherwise.
* Significant at the 0.05 level.
** Significant at the 0.01 level.

TABLE 6

ESTIMATES OF THE CROSS-SECTIONAL REGRESSIONS OF THE TWO-DAY STANDARDIZED CUMULATIVE ABNORMAL RETURNS SCAR (-1, 0) ON THE HYPOTHESIZED DETERMINANTS OF THE COST OF EQUITY FOR CANADIAN FIRMS (T-STATISTICS ARE IN PARENTHESES)

Regression Period	(1) 1982-1987	(2) 1988-1993	(3) 1991-1993	(4) 1982-1987	(5) 1988-1993	(6) 1991-1993
INTERCEPT	3.17	6.45	4.90	3.37	6.38	4.81
	(1.19)	(2.51)*	(1.88)	(1.40)	(2.51)*	(1.88)
SIZE	-0.15	-0.40	-0.31	-0.16	-0.39	-0.31
	(-1.13)	(-3.19)**	(-2.44)*	(-1.54)	(-3.15)**	(-2.42)*
CDTURNOVER	-1.23	0.83	0.66			
	(-1.86)	(1.33)	(1.02)			
USCDTURNOVER				-1.07	0.55	0.53
				(-2.43)*	(1.69)	(1.63)
ISSUESIZE	-6.430	0.95	- 0.05	-6.85	1.26	0.23
	(-2.63)**	(0.70)	(-0.04)	(-3.08)**	(0.92)	(0.15)
RESOURCE	0.55	-0.108	-0.23	0.46	-0.081	-0.20
	(1.44)	(-0.31)	(-0.62)	(1.32)	(-0.23)	(-0.54)
INTERLST	0.33	0.87	1.02	0.78	0.66	0.79
	(0.71)	(2.67)**	(2.99)**	(1.65)	(1.80)	(2.11)*
OWNER	0.05	0.06	-0.101	0.12	-0.045	-0.045
	(0.13)	(0.17)	(-0.27)	(0.36)	(-0.14)	(-0.14)
R-SQUARED	0.37	0.25	0.26	0.46	0.27	0.27

(cont'd)

TABLE 6 (cont'd)

Notes: RESOURCE is a dummy variable which takes the value one for the resource firms and zero otherwise.

CDTURNOVER is the ratio of the number of firms' shares traded on Canadian stock exchanges to the average number of shares outstanding in the year prior to the equity issue.

USCDTURNOVER is the ratio of the number of firms' shares traded on Canadian and U.S. stock exchanges to the average number of shares outstanding in the year prior to the equity issue.

SIZE is the natural logarithm of the book value of the total assets of the firms in the year prior to the equity issue.

OWNER is a dummy variable that takes the value one for firms in which a single shareholder owns more than 20 percent of the voting shares outstanding.

ISSUESIZE is the ratio of the number of new shares offered to the number of shares outstanding at the end of the year prior to the issue.

INTERLST is a dummy variable which takes the value one if the firm issuing equity was interlisted on Canadian and U.S. stock exchanges and zero otherwise.

BOUGHT is a dummy variable which takes the value one if the seasoned equity was a bought deal and zero otherwise.

* Significant at the 0.05 level.

** Significant at the 0.01 level.

Table 6 presents the results of this analysis using two different measures of stock turnover for each period. The explanatory powers of regressions are much higher in each period compared to overall which suggests that there are significant differences across periods.

From 1982 to 1987, ISSUESIZE is the most significant variable, and it has the predicted negative coefficient. The significance of ISSUESIZE is consistent with the price pressure and the asymmetric information hypotheses. Larger issues that could not be easily absorbed in the smaller Canadian market experienced more negative market reaction. The coefficient of the INTERLST variable is not significant in this period. This can be interpreted as consistent with segmentation of the Canadian equity market in the earlier period. However, since interlisted firms in this period had higher disclosure levels consistent with the SEC's requirements, the support for the asymmetric information hypothesis is weak. Also, the negative coefficient of stock turnover in this period is puzzling. Overall, the evidence appears consistent with the price pressure hypothesis.

The results from 1988 to 1993 and 1991 to 1993 are similar to those in the overall period. Both SIZE and INTERLST are significant at either the 0.05 or the 0.01 level. According to these results, the higher trading volumes and broader shareholder base of the interlisted stocks make these stocks particularly attractive to Canadian institutional investors who comprised about 75 percent of the Canadian market in 1993.

Conclusions and Policy Implications

This study provides evidence on the determinants of the cost of equity for Canadian firms by conducting a cross-sectional analysis of the market reaction to the announcements of the seasoned equity issues by the TSE 300 firms from 1982 to 1993. Overall, the market reacts negatively to announcements of equity issuances. The larger firms experience a more pronounced negative reaction while interlisted firms have a more favourable market reaction.

The findings confirm previous evidence that the Canadian market is segmented from the U.S. equity market and that the segmentation is more severe for the non-interlisted stocks. These results suggest that the main determinants of equity capital are related to the smaller size of the Canadian equity market. Larger non-interlisted firms appear to face a downward-sloping demand curve resulting in a larger drop in their share price at the time of new equity issues. Overall, the results suggest that large Canadian non-interlisted firms are likely to face a higher cost of capital relative to their U.S. counterparts.

Since most of the sample is from the 1988 to 1993 period, these findings should be interpreted in the context of recent trends in the Canadian and global equity markets. The number of cross-border offerings has been increasing at a rapid pace in recent years, and this trend is likely to continue. Security offerings across different markets are likely to reduce a firm's cost of equity relative to offerings in the domestic market. Since a firm's ability to raise capital at a lower cost is a major competitive advantage in the increasingly globalized capital markets, government policy should be aimed at reducing the impediments to cross-border offerings.

One major impediment is that issuers have to comply with the requirements of multiple jurisdictions. The costs of meeting accounting and regulatory requirements of two jurisdictions can be very onerous, time consuming and costly for most firms. Until the early 1990s, the SEC's stringent reporting and compliance requirements were a major deterrent for many Canadian issuers in gaining access to the larger U.S. stock market. The recent Canada-United States MJDS is a first step toward establishing a North American capital market. However, the MJDS was initially available only to "substantial" issuers of securities with a public float of US$150 million for investment grade bonds and preferred shares, and of US$300 million for other securities. In November 1993, the SEC adopted a new set of measures and proposals to simplify the issue of securities by foreigners. These rules are designed to simplify the registration and reporting process for foreign issuers seeking access to U.S. capital markets, and to accommodate foreign market making and trading practices concerned with offerings in the United States.[12] These rules expand the availability of the MJDS to more Canadian firms by eliminating the market capitalization requirement and establishing a minimum public float of US$75 million, reducing the reporting history requirement to 12 months and accepting ratings organizations recognized by the Canadian regulators.

Since the accounting and auditing practices of Canada are similar to those in the United States, the MJDS should be made available to more Canadian firms, and government policy should be aimed at persuading the SEC to move in that direction. Such a move would also make Canadian stocks accessible to foreign institutional investors who trade in the U.S. markets since the institutional portfolio managers prefer to invest in foreign stocks with high liquidity and information availability. As Kang and Stulz (1995) documented, foreign investors invest heavily in those Japanese firms that disclose more information.

This study has provided evidence that the factors determining the cost of equity capital in Canada are closely linked to the growth in institutional investors and interlistings observed in Canadian and worldwide markets during the 1990s. Future research should explore the relationship between these trends and the cost of capital more fully.

ENDNOTES

1 *The Economist*. October 7, 1995 and January 11, 1992.
2 *The Economist*. October 7, 1995.
3 *The Financial Post*. November 17, 1992.
4 *The Economist*. January 11, 1992.
5 Cochrane et al. (1995).

6 Jorion and Schwartz (1986) found strong evidence, using the capital asset pricing model (CAPM) that Canadian stocks were priced in a segmented Canadian market rather than in an integrated market (the Canadian and U.S. stock markets) in the 1968 to 1982 period. Mittoo (1992a) confirmed their findings in the 1977 to 1981 period using both the CAPM and the arbitrage pricing theory (APT) but found that there was a move toward integration in the 1982 to 1986 period. Foerster and Karolyi (1993) and Mittoo (1992a) concluded that the pricing of Canadian stocks interlisted on U.S. stock markets is done in a relatively integrated market. Evidence by Booth and Johnston (1984) on ex-dividend day behaviour of stock prices also supports these findings.

7 For example, in 1982, 122 firms in the TSE 300 index belonged to the resource sectors of metals and minerals, gold and silver, oil and gas, and paper and forest products with a relative weight of 33.2 percent. In contrast, the number of resource firms in the TSE 300 index in 1992 declined to 98 with a relative weight of 25.3 percent.

8 The U.S. stock exchanges also increased their marketing to attract Canadian listings, see for example, *The Globe and Mail*, August 12,1991, p. B5.

9 See Jog and Schaller (1993) and Eckbo and Verma (1992) for Canadian evidence and Loderer et al. (1991), Lucas and McDonald (1990), Kalay and Shirmat (1987), Masulis and Korwar (1986), Asquith and Mullins (1986), Mikkelson and Partch (1986) and Smith (1986) for the U.S. evidence.

10 A threshold of 20 percent is commonly used in Canadian studies to define closely held companies. See for example, Morck and Stangeland (1994). The Ontario Securities Commission also allows cumulative share acquisition up to 20 percent of votes before a takeover offer must be extended to all shareholders.

11 See for example, *The Globe and Mail*, February 24, 1992, p. B1. The Investment Dealers Association of Canada (IDA) wants to change the way bought deals are done and argues that the current practice favours large institutional investors.

12 *Euromoney*, December 1993, p. 20.

Acknowledgements

The author would like to thank Paul Halpern and Andrew Karolyi for many valuable comments and suggestions and Vijay Jog for providing data on the bought deal transactions. The financial support from Industry Canada and the Social Sciences and Humanities Research Council of Canada is gratefully acknowledged.

Bibliography

Amihud, Y. and H. Mendelson. "Asset Pricing and the Bid-Ask." *Journal of Financial Economics*. 17, (1986): 223-249.

Asquith, P. and D.W. Mullins. "Equity Issues and Offering Dilution." *Journal of Financial Economics*. 15, (1986): 61-91.

Banz, R.W. "The Relationship between Return and Market Value of Common Stock." *Journal of Financial Economics*. 9, (1981): 3-18.

Berk, J. "A Critique of the Size Related Anomalies." Working paper, University of British Columbia, Vancouver, 1993.

Booth, L. "The Dividend Tax Credit and Canadian Ownership Objectives." *Canadian Journal of Economics*. 20, (1987): 321-339.

Booth, L. and D. Johnston. "The Ex-dividend Day Behaviour of Canadian Stock Prices: Tax Changes and Clientele Effects." *Journal of Finance*. 39, (1984): 457-476.

Cochrane, J., J. Shapiro and J. Tobin. "Foreign Equities and U.S. Investors: Breaking Down Barriers Separating Supply and Demand." Working Paper 95-04, New York Stock Exchange, 1995.

Eckbo, E. and S. Verma. "Ownership Structure and Valuation Effects of Security Offerings." Working paper, York University, Toronto, 1992.

The Economist. "The World Economy." (October 7, 1995).

—. International Equities: Trading Places." (January 11, 1992).

Euromoney. "SEC announces new initiatives for foreign issuers." (December 1993): 20.

The Financial Post. "Brokers chase small players again." November 17, 1992.

Foerster, S. and A. Karolyi. "International Listings of Stocks: the Case of Canada and the U.S." *Journal of International Business Studies*. Vol 24, (1993): 763-784.

Foerster, S. and D. B. Keim. "Direct Evidence of Non-trading of NYSE and AMEX Securities." Working paper, University of Pennsylvania, 1987.

Fortune. "The Global 500: The World's Largest Industrial Corporations."(July 27, 1992): 175-232.

Fowler, D.J., H. Rorkie and V. Jog. "Thin Trading and Beta Estimation Problems on the Toronto Stock Exchange." *Journal of Business Administration*. 12, (1980): 77-90.

The Globe and Mail. "Bought deals changing the way Bay Street works: Little guy being shut out of market." February 24, 1992, p. B1.

— "Amex Out to Convert Canadians: U.S. market begins drive to attract listing under new cross-border rules." August 12, 1991, p. B5.

Griffin, J.M. and G. Karolyi. "Another Look At the Role of the Industrial Structure of Markets for International Diversification Strategies." Working paper, Ohio State University, 1995.

Jog, V. and H. Schaller. "Share Prices and New Equity Issues: New Cross-Sectional Evidence on Asymmetric Information." Working paper, Carleton University, Ottawa, 1993.

Jog, V. and A. Srivastava. "How Capital Formation Hinders Canada's Competitiveness Against Foreign Firms." *Canadian Investment Review*. (1993): 21-26.

Jorion, P. and E. Schwartz. "Integration vs. Segmentation in the Canadian Stock Market." *Journal of Finance*. 41, (1986): 603-614.

Kalay, A. and A. Shimrat. "Firm Value and Seasoned Equity Issues: Price Pressure, Wealth Redistribution, or Negative Information." *Journal of Financial Economics*. 19, (1987): 109-126.

Kang, J. and Stulz, R. "Why Is there a Home Bias? An Analysis of Foreign Ownership Portfolio Equity Ownership in Japan." National Bureau of Economic Research Working Paper No. 5166, 1995.

King, B.F. "Market and Industry Factors in Stock Price Behaviour." *Journal of Business*. 39, (1966): 139-190.

Lessard, D.R. "World, National and Industry Factors in Equity Returns." *Journal of Finance*. 29, (1974): 379-391.

——. "World, Country and Industry Relationships in Equity Returns: Implications for Risk Reduction through International Diversification." *Financial Analyst Journal*. 32, (1976): 32-38.

Loderer, C., D. Sheehan and G.B. Kadlec. "The Pricing of Equity Offerings." *Journal of Financial Economics*. 29, (1991): 35-57.

Loughran, T. and J.R. Ritter. "The New Issues Puzzle." *Journal of Finance*. 50, (1995): 23-51.

Lucas, D.J. and R.L. McDonald. "Equity Issues and Stock Price Dynamics." *Journal of Finance*. 45, (1990): 1019-1043.

Masulis, R.W. and A. Korwar. "Seasoned Equity Offerings: An Empirical Investigation." *Journal of Financial Economics*. 15, (1986): 91-118.

McKenzie, K. and A. Thompson. "Dividend Taxation and Equity Value: The Canadian Tax Changes of 1986." *Canadian Journal of Economics*. 28, (1995): 463-472.

Merton, R.C. "A Simple Model of Capital Market Equilibrium with Incomplete Information." *Journal of Finance*. 42, (1987): 483-510.

Mikkelson, W.H and M. Partch. "Valuation Effects of Security Offerings and the Issuance Process." *Journal of Financial Economics*. 15, (1986): 31-60.

Mittoo, U.R. "Additional Evidence on Integration in the Canadian Stock Market." *Journal of Finance*. 47, (1992a): 2035-2056.

——. "Managerial Perceptions of the Net Benefits of Foreign Listing: Canadian Evidence." *Journal of International Financial Management and Accounting*. Vol. 4, No. 1, (1992b): 40-62.

——. "Industrial Structure and Cross-Country Stock Returns: Evidence from the Australian and Canadian Stock Markets." Working paper, University of Manitoba, Winnipeg, 1995.

——. "Market Regulation, Cross-Country Listing and Trading Volume: Canadian Evidence." Working paper, University of Manitoba, Winnipeg, 1996.

Morck, R. and D. Stangeland. "Shareholder Type and the Competitiveness of Firms: An Examination of Large Canadian Corporations." Working Paper No. 9-91, University of Alberta, 1994.

Myers, S.C. and N.S. Majluf. "Corporate Financing and Investment Decisions when Firms Have Information that Investors Do Not Have." *Journal of Financial Economics*. 13, (1984): 187-221.

Rao, P.S. and C.R. Lee-Sing. "Governance Structure, Corporate Decision Making and Firm Performance in North America." *Corporate Decision-Making in Canada*. University of Calgary Press, 1995.

Roll, R. "Industrial Structure and the Comparative Behaviour of International Stock Market Indices." *Journal of Finance*. 47, (1992): 3-41.

Schwartz, L. "Bought Deals: the Devil that You Know." *Canadian Investment Review*. (1994): 61-66.

Schwert, G.W. "Size and Stock Returns and Other Empirical Regularities." *Journal of Financial Economics*.12, (1983): 81-88.

Smith, C.W. Jr. "Investment Banking and the Capital Acquisition Process." *Journal of Financial Economics*. 15, (1986): 3-29.

Tripathy, N. and R.P. Rao. "Adverse Selection, Spread Behavior, and Over-the-Counter Seasoned Equity Offerings." *Journal of Financial Research*. 15, (1992): 39-56.

Thain, D. and D. Leighton. "Ownership Structure and the Board." *Canadian Investment Review*. (1991): 61-66.

Jean-Marc Suret & *Jean-François L'Her*
CIRANO[1] CIRANO[1]

11

The Evolving Capital Structure of Large Canadian Firms

SUMMARY

THIS STUDY EXAMINES THE EVOLVING CAPITAL STRUCTURE of large Canadian firms from 1960 to 1994. It is divided into three parts: the first is devoted to trends in indebtedness, the second offers an aggregate analysis of financing choices, and the third examines econometric models used to explain corporate financing decisions.

The first part of the study shows that a significant increase in the level of total corporate debt, as occurred in the United States, was not observed in Canada. The book value of total debt did rise from 1960 to 1982, but it then started to decline, reaching in 1994 a level 500 basis points above its 1960 level. If allowance is made for the market value of equity, however, total debt was actually lower in 1994 than in 1960. The relative stability of total debt hides an increase in long-term debt and a decline in corporate short-term liabilities. This means that the concerns expressed by U.S. authors about the rapid rise in corporate indebtedness are not applicable to Canada. Only long-term debt has increased in this country, a phenomenon unconnected to developments in the United States.

The second part of the study investigates the relationship between financing decisions and prevailing economic and market conditions. Financing decisions are measured by the proportion of total financial requirements (including depreciation and dividends) that are financed through the various sources of funds. Over the period, cash flow was used to meet 61.2 percent of the financial requirements of growing firms, on average, while long-term debt covered 20 percent of needs. Equity issues accounted for only 9.8 percent of financial requirements, and dividend payments far exceeded the amounts raised through equity. The relatively limited use of equity issues is common to other industrialized countries, but again the phenomenon is less pronounced in this country than in the United States, where net issues became negative (because of stock repurchases) according to some recent studies. In Canada, there has been an increase recently in the proportion of financing raised through equity issues (22.1 percent of financial requirements in 1993). The relative importance of the various methods of financing appears to be strongly influenced by economic conditions. Inflation and stock market levels are positively related to debt financing and equity issues, respectively. On the other hand, there appears to be no link between tax changes and the behaviour of firms in the aggregate. For example, tax changes that made debt financing more attractive did not translate into an increase in indebtedness. Real interest rates are negatively related to long-term debt but do not appear to have any significant influence over total debt. Lastly, periods of recession generally coincide with debt financing, likely because of lower cash flows. The financing decisions of Canadian firms thus largely depend on prevailing economic and financial conditions but do not seem to be affected by tax changes. There is significant variation at the firm level, however, a subject examined in the final part of this study.

Four models help explain the relative use of the various financing methods at the firm level, and several estimation methods are applied to a sample of 7,833 annual observations from 1963 to 1994. The results for profitability and growth are consistent with the behaviour predicted by the "pecking order" theory. The main determinants of financing decisions are profitability and growth. Internal financing is positively related to higher profitability and negatively related to growth. Dividend policy is perceived as a constraint. In our explanatory models, the variable for the relative size of non-debt tax shields has a positive sign – the opposite of what theory predicts. The most heavily indebted firms are also those eligible for non-debt tax shields. This appears to confirm the key role of profitability and collateral in explaining indebtedness. Finally, size is positively related to debt financing. The introduction of macro-economic variables into the models generally confirms the relationships observed at the aggregate level. However, the amount of tax gain associated with debt is significantly and negatively related to debt financing, which runs counter to expectations. One possible explanation for this result is that some of the tax changes coincided with an economic slowdown and with changes in the ownership structures of firms.

In conclusion, we did not find significant long-run change in the debt levels of Canadian companies. Their financing decisions are influenced mainly by economic and market conditions. At the firm level, the two major factors explaining financing decisions are growth and profitability, and the tax system does not appear to affect these choices to any significant extent.

INTRODUCTION

IN THE UNITED STATES, SEVERAL AUTHORS (Bernanke and Campbell, 1988; Friedman, 1986; Taggart, 1986) became concerned about the rapid rise in corporate debt levels during the 1980s, and the chairman of the Federal Reserve Board cited this trend among the factors explaining the slow economic recovery following the 1990-1991 recession (Gertler and Hubbard, 1993). But other researchers have regarded these high debt levels as a positive factor that may help reduce the extent and frequency of suboptimal behaviour among managers (Jensen, 1986). The analysis and explanation of the changing structure of medium and long-term financing have thus become a major focus of research. In Canada, however, virtually no work has been done in this area. The comparative data available tend to show that the indebtedness of Canadian companies was higher than that of U.S. firms in 1991, but that debt levels grew very little from 1982 to 1992 (Rajan and Zingales, 1995, tables II and III). According to Grant et al. (1990), indebtedness declined during the 1980s, contrary to what was observed in the United States. Finally, Fillion (1992, p. 5) reports that total debt followed an irregular and volatile pattern from 1964 to 1990, based on the market value of equity. What is needed, therefore, is an in-depth study of firm indebtedness in Canada. That is our objective in the first part of the study, which seeks to describe how the capital structure of Canadian firms has evolved between 1960 and 1994.

Trends in indebtedness identified in this section refute the hypothesis that changes in corporate debt in Canada have mirrored those in the United States, as well as the hypothesis that the capital structure of Canadian firms remained unchanged. The growth and subsequent fall in debt levels show that the relative importance of various sources used to finance growth fluctuated over the study period and vary from the estimates yielded by average debt levels. The obvious question is: What broad factors may explain the financing decisions of Canadian firms? In the second part of the study, we tackle this question by studying the linkages between financing decisions and economic and financial conditions. Flow models are then estimated using such dependent variables as the proportion of funds coming from various sources for the purpose of financing growth. This work differs from conventional research on corporate financing in Canada and the United States, which has relied on cross-sectional models using debt *levels* at a particular point in time as the dependent variable.[2]

Moreover, under a given set of economic circumstances, the choices of firms appear to be tied to factors that are firm-specific. In the final section of the study, the financing choices of each firm are explained by combining factors unique to the firm with factors related to market conditions. We then attempt to answer the following question: Can individual financing decisions made by Canadian firms be explained by their particular characteristics within the larger economic picture?

LONG-TERM TRENDS IN INDEBTEDNESS

PREVIOUS RESEARCH

TRENDS IN INDEBTEDNESS HAVE BEEN STUDIED IN THE UNITED STATES since 1926 (Taggart, 1985, 1986). The ratio of total debt to assets rose from 30 percent in 1945-1946 to 55 percent in 1979 (Taggart, 1986, Table 1.1). After adjustment for the market value of capital stock and capital replacement costs, the increase in indebtedness is much smaller and appears to be concentrated in the 1970s. It accelerated during the 1980s, however, as has been pointed out by several authors reporting generally similar results (Bernanke and Campbell, 1988; Friedman, 1986; Taggart, 1986; Rajan and Zingales, 1995). From 1982 to 1992, the average debt-to-equity ratio in a constant sample of firms rose from 0.32 to 0.46 in the United States (Rajan and Zingales, 1995, Table III). Such a rapid rise in indebtedness was not common to all industrialized countries, however.

To our knowledge, there are no recent Canadian studies dealing with the capital structure of firms over long periods. Only Fillion (1992), in his analysis of financing costs, reported aggregate data for the period 1963 to 1990 (p. 58). The debt ratio measured at quasi-market value (market value of equity plus book value of total debt) increased from 0.37 in 1963 to a peak of 0.56 in 1982, then declined to 0.44 by 1990. Rajan and Zingales (1995)[3] provided data comparing trends in financing methods in Canada and in other G7 countries. There appears to be no significant difference among Canadian, U.S., French and Japanese firms in terms of debt levels, adjusted for accounting-system differences. Only Germany and the United Kingdom show lower debt levels. The average debt-to-equity ratio of Canadian firms would have fallen from 0.42 in 1982 to 0.40 in 1991. Grant et al. (1990) reported a significant decline in the indebtedness of Canadian companies between 1983 and 1989 but noted an increase in the United States over the same period. Ross et al. (1995, p. 469) suggested that tax differences were the likely cause. However, the period studied by Grant et al. is too short to draw definite conclusions, while the data from Statistics Canada, used in the Gagnon and Papillon study (1984), are for the period before 1980.

A few cross-sectional studies have been done for Canada. Davis (1994) tested the tax substitution hypothesis of DeAngelo-Masulis (1980). Gagnon et al. (1987) found a significant inverse relationship between debt and profitability, but no significant tax effect. On the other hand, Bartholdy et al. (1989) showed that corporate tax rates have a significant (and large) impact on the debt levels of Canadian firms. None of these studies covers a long period, except that of Mandron (1993). The author used data from 1967 to 1987, but relied on observational averages for each firm and for each period or subperiod. It should be noted that all these studies analyse debt levels rather than flows and none uses data later than 1987. The present study is therefore justified by our limited knowledge of the financial behaviour of Canadian firms, and the lack of research on trends in corporate indebtedness and on how these trends are related to the broader economic and financial conditions.

Trends in Indebtedness in Canada

The data used in the study are derived from the 1991 version of *The Financial Post* data base, which covers 30 years (1960 to 1990). They are supplemented by data from Compustat to compensate for the major changes made by *The Financial Post* to the structure of the data base and to individual items.[4] The latter contains information on almost 1,000 stocks. Because of the length of the study period, however, complete data for every year are available only for a subgroup of about 400 companies. Excluding financial firms, the sample falls to about 350 stocks. Thus, it is not possible to construct a sample from that data base comprising the same firms year after year, and the results reported here are for all non-financial firms.

Using all the observations available for each year from 1963 to 1990, we calculated the level of total book indebtedness (measured from balance sheet data only), for both short and long-term debt. Short-term debt is that normally reported on the balance sheet, while long-term debt excludes both deferred taxes and minority interests.[5] The portion of long-term debt maturing during the year was assigned to long-term debt. Each measure of debt was compared to total firm assets in order to calculate three ratios: the total debt ratio (short-term liabilities plus long-term debt divided by total assets), the short-term debt ratio (short-term liabilities divided by total assets), and the long-term debt ratio (long-term debt divided by total assets). Total debt at market value was also estimated by dividing the book value of debt by the quasi-market value of assets, the latter obtained by summing the book value of debt and the market value of equity. The market value of equity was calculated by multiplying the number of common shares issued by their closing price at fiscal year end. The value of preferred shares, if any, was measured in the same way. This measure does not take into account possible fluctuations in the market value of debt, which cannot be estimated in the absence of transactions.

Figure 1 shows the various measurements of indebtedness for major Canadian firms from 1960 to 1994. The average numerical values are reported in Table 1. Long-term debt, which rose only very slightly from 1960 to 1979, increased rapidly from 1980 to 1982, hitting a peak of 25.1 percent before declining slightly. Total debt, measured by the book value of assets, rose from 1960 to 1981, reaching a peak of 47.8 percent. It then contracted slowly, reaching 43 percent by 1994.[6] The relative proportions of short and long-term debt changed during the study period. The use of short-term debt (measured as the difference between the total debt ratio and the long-term debt ratio) grew substantially from 1960 (18.24 percent) to 1979 (25.6 percent), but fell back to 19 percent by 1994. During the period 1960 to 1980, the increase in total debt primarily reflected an increase in short-term debt. The trend reversed afterward. When equity is measured by the market value of shares, the measure of total debt becomes more volatile, reflecting fluctuations in stock prices. On average, debt measured at book value remained roughly comparable to debt measured by the market value of equity until 1980, as shown by the six-period moving average for the series. After 1980, debt measured by the market value of shares is lower. This phenomenon may be linked to the inflation of the 1980s and the fairly steady rise in stock prices since 1982. Figure 1 also shows a measure of debt corrected for cash flow. Total adjusted debt is measured as the ratio of debt net of cash flow (cash plus short-term investments) to the book value of assets. This measure of debt follows a trend similar to that noted above, but the decline in indebtedness since 1982 is sharper because of rising cash flows. In 1994, total adjusted debt was 31.8 percent, compared with 29.7 percent in 1960.

FIGURE 1

INDEBTEDNESS OF LARGE CANADIAN FIRMS, 1960 TO 1994[a]

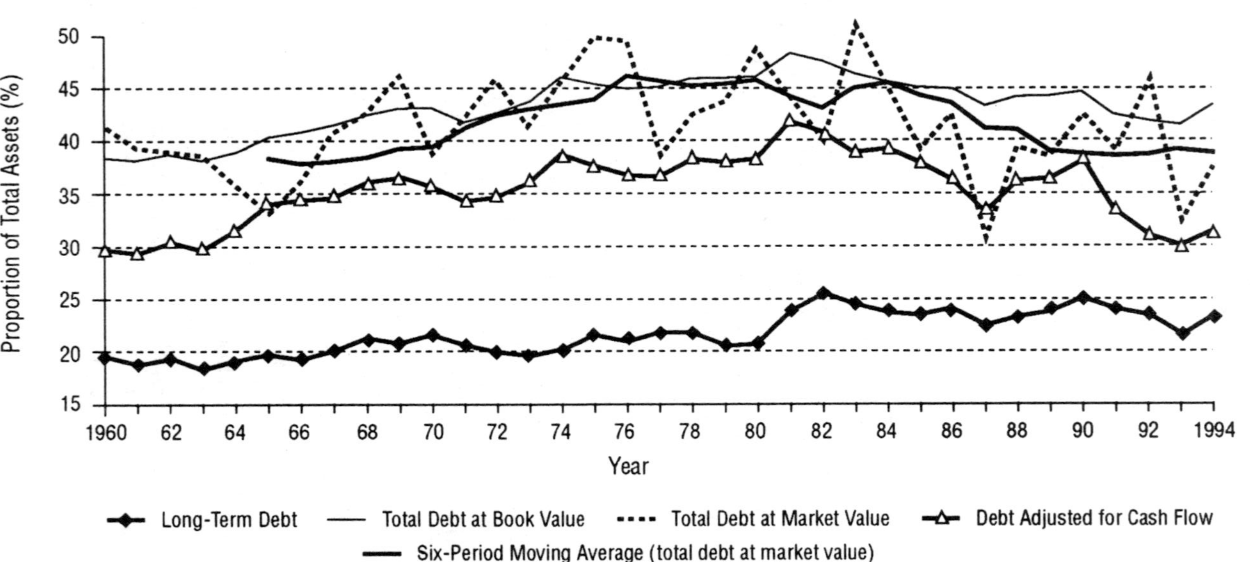

Note: [a] Chart shows average distributions (for a sample of varying composition, drawn from *The Financial Post* and COMPUSTAT data bases) for the following ratios: long-term debt (including debt maturing during the year divided by assets at book value); total debt (short term liabilities plus long-term debt divided by assets at book value); total debt at market value (short-term liabilities plus long-term debt, divided by value of assets minus book value of equity plus market value of equity); adjusted indebtness (ratio of total debt minus cash flow and short-term investment, divided by assets at book value). The moving average is calculated on the last six terms of the series of average ratios of total debt at market value.

TABLE 1

AVERAGE DEBT RATIOS, ALL LARGE CANADIAN FIRMS IN THE SAMPLE, 1960 TO 1994[a]

Year	Long-Term Debt/Assets at Book Value	Total Debt/ Assets at Book Value	Total Debt/ Assets at Quasi-Market Value	Total Debt Adjusted for Cash Flow/Assets at Book Value
1960	0.1965	0.3789	0.4125	0.2975
1961	0.1913	0.3749	0.3941	0.2915
1962	0.1939	0.3824	0.3872	0.3013
1963	0.1821	0.3785	0.3849	0.2968
1964	0.1894	0.3892	0.3641	0.3126
1965	0.1941	0.4028	0.3288	0.3378
1966	0.1897	0.4051	0.3828	0.3460
1967	0.1998	0.4095	0.4077	0.3457
1968	0.2053	0.4240	0.4212	0.3612
1969	0.2022	0.4269	0.4594	0.3648
1970	0.2104	0.4263	0.3808	0.3582
1971	0.2037	0.4150	0.4251	0.3459
1972	0.1987	0.4197	0.4542	0.3494
1973	0.1975	0.4351	0.4150	0.3621
1974	0.1992	0.4537	0.4701	0.3847
1975	0.2086	0.4500	0.4965	0.3755
1976	0.2075	0.4480	0.4941	0.3706
1977	0.2129	0.4493	0.3847	0.3667
1978	0.2122	0.4601	0.4231	0.3778
1979	0.2009	0.4569	0.4417	0.3764
1980	0.2069	0.4602	0.4861	0.3796
1981	0.2351	0.4780	0.4338	0.4195
1982	0.2512	0.4717	0.3970	0.4066
1983	0.2467	0.4626	0.5093	0.3863
1984	0.2383	0.4559	0.4374	0.3882
1985	0.2367	0.4523	0.3927	0.3786
1986	0.2438	0.4506	0.4280	0.3600
1987	0.2244	0.4284	0.3057	0.3316
1988	0.2356	0.4439	0.3926	0.3595
1989	0.2435	0.4452	0.3828	0.3644
1990	0.2502	0.4479	0.4259	0.3798
1991	0.2418	0.4238	0.3940	0.3415
1992	0.2350	0.4214	0.4537	0.3172
1993	0.2209	0.4191	0.3217	0.3016
1994	0.2395	0.4294	0.3738	0.3183

Note: [a] Sample size varies from 222 observations in 1960 to 448 observations in 1993.

Regardless of how it is measured, the debt of Canadian companies does not appear to have increased substantially, in contrast to what occurred in the United States. While short and long-term debt rose until the early 1980s, total debt ratios declined appreciably after that time and long-term debt rose significantly in the early 1980s, then remained relatively stable. Subtracting cash and short-term investments from debt, the total debt-to-assets ratio was virtually the same in 1994 as in 1960, after hitting a peak in the early 1980s. Debt measured at market value also showed no sign of an upward trend. It fell from 41 percent in 1960 to approximately 37 percent in 1994. These observations have a number of implications. First, the behaviour of Canadian firms appears to differ from that of U.S. firms. However, explaining that difference lies outside the scope of our study, despite its obvious interest. These differences in behaviour may be attributable to the ownership structures of firms in the two countries, or to the nature of growth, such as the significant use of debt to finance acquisitions. Second, the capital structure of Canadian companies cannot be considered constant over the study period. Thus, traditional cross-sectional models, which implicitly assume that firms have reached and maintained an optimal target level, are not applicable in the Canadian context. Indeed, the structure of debt used to finance growth has changed over the years and even fluctuated during the period. Accordingly, what is important is financing *decisions*, as reflected in annual changes in liabilities and shareholder equity. These choices likely depend both on overall economic conditions and the characteristics of the firm. In the rest of the study we examine the aggregate financing decisions of firms, followed by a study of decisions at the firm level.

AGGREGATE FINANCING CHOICES IN CANADA: DESCRIPTION AND EXPLANATION

PREVIOUS WORK

MOST STUDIES INVESTIGATING CORPORATE CAPITAL STRUCTURE use models to explain debt levels at a particular point in time,[7] or a series of cross sections to capture some of the dynamics of the process (Homaifar et al., 1994). The general aim of these studies is to explain the level of debt relative to assets or equity. In contrast to this traditional approach, we are interested in how firms finance their growth. This requires a study of financing flows, which entails distinguishing between internal and external flows, whether they arise from debt or equity issues.

Accordingly, the study is in step with the few research projects conducted in the United States on financing decisions of non-financial corporations since World War II (MacKie-Mason, 1990b; Mayer, 1990; Taggart, 1985, 1986; Crabbe et al., 1990). The results of these studies, which are generally consistent, can be summarized as follows: internal financing was used systematically from 1946 to 1987, and earnings before dividends represented 97 percent of total financing. Equity issues covered about 5 percent of total financial requirements until the mid-1970s, but have shown a negative balance since. From 1984 to 1987, stock buy backs accounted for approximately 16 percent of financial requirements (MacKie-Mason, 1990b).

Dividend ratios declined slightly but remained above 20 percent. Financing through public bond issues provided about 10 percent of financing requirements. According to Lintner (1985, p. 75), "The agreement among all series in showing a massive increase in the relative use of debt over the last fifteen or twenty years is simply the most dramatic and best known of the instances of common broad movement." However, aggregate data (taken from the Federal Reserve Flow of Funds Accounts) presented by Taggart differ markedly from those reported by MacKie-Mason, who used the same sources. For example, internal financing represents 52 percent of financing requirements from 1970 to 1979 for Taggart, and about 75 percent for MacKie-Mason. These discrepancies may reflect differences in calculation methods.

Results for long-term trends in indebtedness in Canada derive primarily from comparative studies. Mayer (1990) compared the financing methods used by firms in eight countries between 1970 and 1985 using disaggregated data from the Organization for Economic Co-operation and Development (OECD). He observed that retained earnings were by far the main source of funds, accounting for 76.4 percent of financing in Canada, 85.9 percent in the United States and 102.4 percent in the United Kingdom. Over the same period, equity issues accounted for only 2.5 percent of financial requirements in Canada and 1.1 percent in the United States. Rajan and Zingales (1995) also noted that external financing in Canadian and U.S. firms comes primarily from borrowing, a trend dating back to the early 1980s in the United States and to the mid-1980s in Canada. However, in the early 1980s, a substantial portion of external financing in Canadian firms came apparently from equity issues. Patry and Poitevin (1995) reported aggregate data constructed from OECD statistics for the period 1969 to 1992. The only distinction made in their study was between internal and external funds and the data did not take into account inter-firm financial flows. The Canadian situation is examined in more detail in the remainder of this section.

DATA

UNDERSTANDING CORPORATE FINANCIAL DECISIONS and their determinants requires a study of financing choices. These choices are expressed as percentages of total financial requirements. Since financial requirements may be positive or negative (the latter when assets shrink), the sample should be subdivided on that basis. The latter part of the analysis focuses on cases showing an increase in gross assets.[8] Table 2 reports growth-related financial requirements as a percentage of gross assets at the start of the period, for each year and each category of firm. These values are estimates of the growth rate of gross assets of firms for which data are available for two consecutive years. The inflation rate is also reported in order to assess the real growth rate. On average, annual financial requirements represented 15.75 percent of gross assets, and real average growth was about 10.5 percent. Expanding firms posted an average rate of growth of 17.4 percent, while declining firms showed an average rate of growth of -11.9 percent. The proportion of firms with shrinking assets averaged 6.8 percent from 1960 to 1981. This proportion rose quickly afterward to reach 19.38 percent on average. This substantial gap and the faster rate of

TABLE 2

INFLATION AND GROWTH-RELATED FINANCIAL REQUIREMENTS, LARGE CANADIAN FIRMS, 1960 TO 1994[a]

	All Observations			Growing Firms		Declining Firms	
Year	Inflation Rate	Number of Observations	Inflation Rate	Number of Observations	Growth Rate	Number of Observations	Growth Rate
1960	1.02	222	n.a.	197	n.a.	25	n.a.
1961	1.01	238	13.4	229	13.7	9	-6.1
1962	1.00	245	14.1	231	14.5	14	-5.0
1963	1.98	270	14.8	258	15.3	22	-5.0
1964	1.94	288	15.2	271	15.6	17	-5.2
1965	2.38	300	16.8	293	17.0	7	-2.6
1966	3.72	309	17.5	299	17.8	10	-8.7
1967	3.58	319	16.3	292	17.0	27	-5.3
1968	3.89	336	15.7	316	16.4	20	-8.2
1969	4.58	344	16.3	321	16.7	23	-7.3
1970	3.18	351	16.3	312	17.1	39	-7.7
1971	3.09	403	15.5	360	16.2	43	-5.7
1972	4.87	408	14.6	385	15.0	23	-3.7
1973	7.50	419	18.4	402	18.6	17	-7.3
1974	10.96	415	17.5	388	22.1	27	-4.1
1975	10.77	414	17.2	366	17.8	48	-6.6
1976	7.29	419	14.9	379	15.6	40	-14.3
1977	8.06	410	19.0	374	19.8	36	-6.8
1978	8.85	397	20.9	375	21.7	22	-11.9
1979	9.20	392	21.9	379	22.2	13	-21.2
1980	10.19	388	24.1	367	24.4	21	-13.4

(cont'd)

TABLE 2 (cont'd)

Year	Inflation Rate	All Observations		Growing Firms		Declining Firms	
		Number of Observations	Inflation Rate	Number of Observations	Growth Rate	Number of Observations	Growth Rate
1981	12.45	385	24.2	356	26.5	29	-22.2
1982	10.75	387	12.7	287	16.1	100	-9.1
1983	5.86	385	10.9	314	14.2	71	-15.8
1984	4.32	384	15.7	340	17.6	44	-19.8
1985	4.01	375	16.4	316	18.5	59	-9.5
1986	4.10	362	10.8	274	16.7	88	-12.1
1987	4.42	335	17.5	289	19.9	46	-11.2
1988	4.00	318	17.1	273	19.4	45	-12.4
1989	5.06	303	16.8	250	20.9	53	-14.3
1990	4.71	281	11.3	216	13.8	65	-13.2
1991	5.60	429	8.0	302	11.4	127	-9.4
1992	1.51	450	8.3	349	11.3	101	-9.8
1993	1.86	465	6.3	373	14.1	92	-16.1
1994	0.18	232	15.8	211	16.9	21	-73.0
Average	5.2		15.7		17.4		-11.9

Note: [a] Financial requirements are the increase in the gross value of assets plus paid dividends, for firms for which data were available for two consecutive years, expressed as a percentage of gross assets at the beginning of the period. Gross assets equal assets as per financial statements plus accumulated depreciation.

asset decline since 1980 suggest that a change occurred in the behaviour of Canadian firms. Growth was no longer a certainty, and almost one firm in five experienced a decline in its assets base from one year to the next.

MEASURING FINANCING CHOICES

THE STUDY OF FINANCING DECISIONS INVOLVES MEASURING how companies choose to meet their financial requirements in each period. Theoretically, the information needed to compute these estimates should be available in a firm's statement of change in financial position. However, this statement was made mandatory only in 1985 and appeared in data bases, for all companies, starting in 1988. These data bases do not contain comparable data for previous years. It is also impossible to infer individual statement-of-change items from balance sheet and income statement data for previous years, mainly because of data consolidations.[9]

For this study, we assumed that, in each period, a firm needs financing equal to the gross (before depreciation) growth of its total assets[10] plus dividends. In this case, the financial requirements in year *t* are expressed as:

$$BT_t = (A_t - PM_t) - (A_{t-1} - PM_{t-1}) + Dep_t + DIVI_t - (Enc_t - Enc_{t-1}) \qquad (1)$$

where

BT_t: Total financial requirements in year *t*.
A_t: Total assets in year *t*.
PM_t: Minority interests (from balance sheet).
Dep_t: Depreciation (from income statement) in year *t*.
$DIVI_t$: Dividends on common and preferred equity paid in year *t*.
Enc_t: Cash in year *t*.

The following adjustments were made to changes in net assets. First, minority interests were excluded from assets, which were measured as if only the share of subsidiaries effectively held is consolidated. Second, depreciation was added to the change in net assets to approximate change in gross assets.[11] Third, dividends were added to financing requirements, as in Modigliani and Miller (1963). Net assets are calculated without cash reserves, since the increase in cash does not represent a true financial requirement.

Total financial requirements (funds needed) are obtained from the following sources (SF_t): change in short-term assets (ΔPCT), change in long-term debt (ΔDLT), change in equity capital (ΔCA) and cash flow (ΔFAG).

$$SF_t = BT_t = \Delta PCT_t + \Delta DLT_t + \Delta CA_t + FAG_t \qquad (2)$$

where

ΔPCT: Change in short-term liabilities, excluding the portion of long-term debt maturing during the year. An increase in short-term liabilities can legitimately be considered a source of financing, because total financial requirements are considered, including those associated with an increase in short-term assets.

ΔDLT: Change in long-term debt, including the portion of long-term debt maturing in the year. The change in total debt is denoted $\Delta DTOT$.

ΔCA: Net change in outstanding equity capital. In the descriptive section, common shares and preferred shares are treated separately; in the econometric models, common shares and preferred shares are lumped together.

FAG: Cash flow is separated in two components: the reinvested portion, which comprises change in retained earnings (including deferred taxes) and depreciation, and the distributed portion, which comprises dividends ($DIVI$).

For each firm and for each year, the variables ΔPCT, ΔDLT, ΔCA and FAG (reinvested and distributed portions) were measured against total financial requirements for each firm. As a matter of convenience, the proportions are all expressed in the same way. Average yearly ratios are then calculated. The results are shown in Figure 2 and presented in tables 3, 4 and 5.

Results

Figure 2 shows the results for firms with positive growth. The key role played by internal resources in financing the growth of Canadian firms is apparent. On average, internal resources accounted for 64.7 percent (49.1 percent plus 15.6 percent; see Table 3) of financial requirements as defined in equation (1). However, the importance of this source of funds varies, the lowest values being observed in 1981-1982 and 1988-1989, which coincide approximately with periods of recession. Table 3 presents the proportion of financial requirements provided by the main funding sources, annually, for the entire sample. Tables 4 and 5 present the same information with firms split in two categories: those with positive vs. those with negative asset growth.[12] For expanding companies, reinvested earnings met 47 percent of gross financial requirements, on average, during the 34 years studied, while the proportion paid out as dividends accounted for 14.2 percent of financial requirements. Long-term debt provided 20 percent of funds, compared with 9 percent for short-term borrowings. Issues of common shares represented 8.2 percent of requirements, compared with 1.6 percent for preferred shares. The figures reported in Table 4 for firms with expanding assets differ little, on average, from those for the overall sample. However, Table 5, which reports on firms with negative growth, shows some surprising results.[13] Dividends account for 15.6 percent of the reduction in gross assets, while reinvested funds represent 31.6 percent. These firms even made equity offerings representing 4 percent of the total decrease in assets. Companies experiencing negative growth represent a significant portion of Canadian firms, and would warrant a more in-depth study.

On average, Canadian firms experiencing positive growth behave much like those in other major industrialized countries, particularly the United States. Internal resources are the most important source of funds, while equity issues are seldom used. There are significant variations over time, however. For example, common equity issues represented 19.3 percent of financial requirements in 1983 and 22.1 percent in 1993. Long-term debt financed about 35 percent of requirements from 1987 to 1991. A number of authors have suggested that these variations are linked to business cycle fluctuations and prevailing conditions on financial markets. In the next section, we provide a summary analysis of these hypotheses, to which econometric tests are applied in the final section.

FINANCIAL CHOICES, TAXES AND ECONOMIC CONDITIONS

AS NOTED BY NAKAMURA AND NAKAMURA (1982, note 31), the steady increase in indebtedness in the Unites States can be attributed largely to macro-economic factors. Among the many possible determinants of financing decisions suggested, the most important are probably taxes, inflation and relative financing costs as perceived by managers.

Taxes

In the framework developed by Miller (1977), there is no optimal level of corporate debt, but rather an optimal level of debt for the economy. The tax savings associated with indebtedness are expressed as the quantity G:[14]

$$G = [1 - \frac{(1 - t_{ps})(1 - t_c)}{(1 - t_{pb})}] B \tag{3}$$

where t_{ps} is the individual tax rate on equity income, t_c is the corporate tax rate, and t_{pb} is the individual tax rate on debt income or (in Canada) the personal tax rate, while B represents the market value of debt (after taxes on debt income). At the firm level, G can be negative, positive or nil depending on the tax status of shareholders, a situation that can induce a "clientele effect." Economy-wide tax changes that increase or decrease G should affect financing policies if firms make financing decisions on the basis of tax rules. DeAngelo and Masulis (1980) put forward the notion of non-debt tax shields (NDTS), which they suggested would act as a substitute for debt-related tax savings. In the United States, MacKie-Mason (1990a) and Givoly et al. (1992), who investigated the impact of the 1986 tax reforms, found a weak sensitivity to tax changes among businesses.[15] We have, therefore,

FIGURE 2

AGGREGATE FINANCIAL DECISIONS OF LARGE CANADIAN FIRMS, 1960 TO 1994[a]

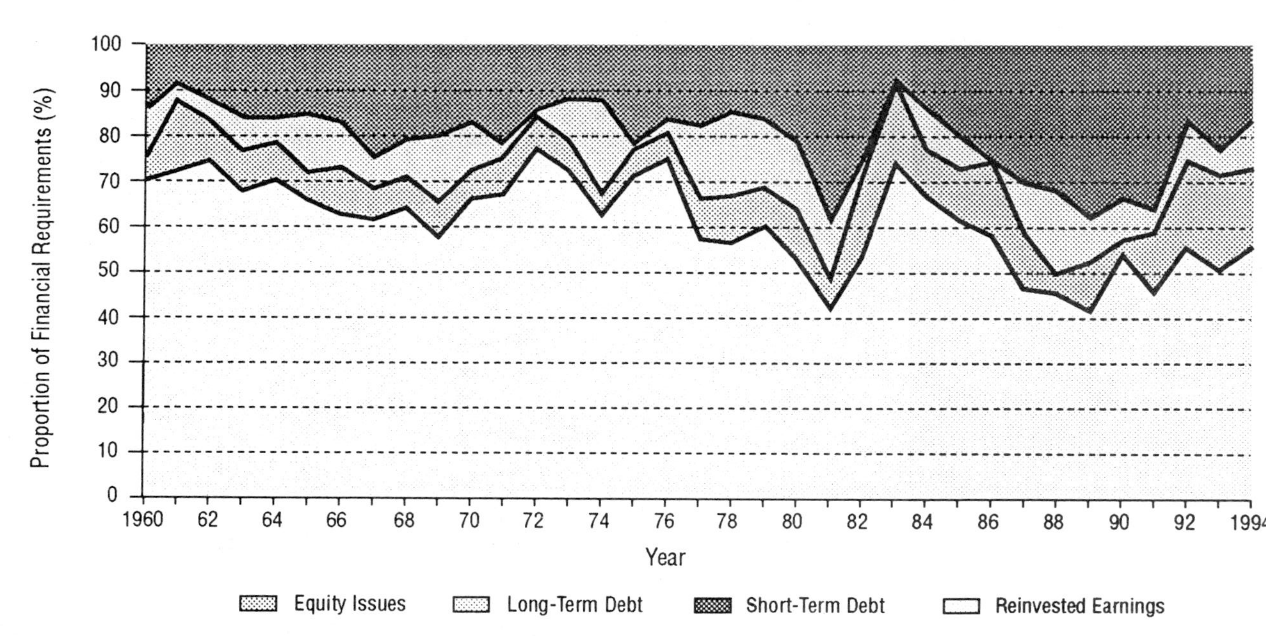

Note: [a] For each year, we computed the ratio of total amount raised from each funding source to total short and long-term financial requirements, including paid dividends. The sample includes all observations available from *The Financial Post* and COMPUSTAT data bases.

TABLE 3

PROPORTION OF GROWTH-RELATED FINANCIAL REQUIREMENTS PROVIDED BY EACH FUNDING SOURCE, ALL CANADIAN FIRMS IN THE SAMPLE, 1960 TO 1994

Year	Proportion of Total Financial Requirements							
	Short-Term Debt	Long-Term Debt	Cash Flow Reinvested	Cash Flow Distributed	Common Stock Issues	Preferred Stock Issues	Total	Number of Observations
1960	0.100	0.136	0.513	0.204	0.036	0.011	1	222
1961	0.029	0.087	0.526	0.207	0.140	0.010	1	238
1962	0.041	0.109	0.555	0.201	0.082	0.012	1	245
1963	0.067	0.115	0.527	0.192	0.078	0.021	1	270
1964	0.048	0.147	0.523	0.192	0.091	-0.002	1	288
1965	0.150	0.136	0.484	0.181	0.035	0.014	1	300
1966	0.105	0.163	0.465	0.171	0.073	0.022	1	309
1967	0.056	0.247	0.443	0.179	0.047	0.028	1	319
1968	0.082	0.196	0.491	0.168	0.047	0.016	1	336
1969	0.140	0.202	0.442	0.154	0.051	0.011	1	344
1970	0.092	0.173	0.491	0.181	0.043	0.020	1	351
1971	0.010	0.221	0.514	0.172	0.060	0.023	1	403
1972	0.005	0.142	0.614	0.172	0.052	0.015	1	408
1973	0.088	0.121	0.596	0.136	0.057	0.002	1	419
1974	0.258	0.053	0.551	0.154	-0.019	0.003	1	415
1975	-0.009	0.226	0.564	0.154	0.051	0.014	1	414
1976	0.029	0.155	0.580	0.171	0.036	0.029	1	419
1977	0.145	0.171	0.460	0.136	0.032	0.055	1	410
1978	0.179	0.132	0.460	0.124	0.062	0.043	1	397
1979	0.148	0.159	0.488	0.122	0.061	0.023	1	392
1980	0.147	0.214	0.436	0.101	0.056	0.046	1	388

(cont'd)

TABLE 3 (cont'd)

Year	Proportion of Total Financial Requirements							
	Short-Term Debt	Long-Term Debt	Cash Flow Reinvested	Cash Flow Distributed	Common Stock Issues	Preferred Stock Issues	Total	Number of Observations
1981	0.094	0.415	0.334	0.090	0.047	0.020	1	385
1982	0.019	0.250	0.408	0.157	0.112	0.053	1	387
1983	-0.073	0.033	0.605	0.180	0.231	0.024	1	385
1984	0.092	0.061	0.590	0.136	0.095	0.026	1	384
1985	0.055	0.166	0.525	0.131	0.096	0.027	1	375
1986	-0.128	0.230	0.505	0.197	0.154	0.042	1	362
1987	0.096	0.277	0.418	0.083	0.144	-0.019	1	335
1988	0.172	0.288	0.369	0.126	0.074	-0.029	1	318
1989	0.068	0.420	0.340	0.092	0.067	0.012	1	303
1990	0.058	0.334	0.433	0.135	0.049	-0.009	1	281
1991	-0.123	0.470	0.282	0.194	0.194	-0.018	1	410
1992	0.094	0.103	0.416	0.158	0.248	-0.019	1	431
1993	-0.072	-0.247	0.712	0.230	0.431	-0.054	1	448
1994	0.077	0.159	0.508	0.088	0.169	-0.001	1	226
Average	0.067	0.179	0.491	0.156	0.094	0.013	1	352

TABLE 4

PROPORTION OF GROWTH-RELATED FINANCIAL REQUIREMENTS PROVIDED BY EACH FUNDING SOURCE, ALL CANADIAN FIRMS WITH POSITIVE GROWTH, 1960 TO 1994

Year	Proportion of Financial Requirements						Total	Number of Observations
	Short-Term Debt	Long-Term Debt	Cash Flow Reinvested	Cash Flow Distributed	Common Stock Issues	Preferred Stock Issues		
1960	0.109	0.144	0.502	0.198	0.036	0.011	1	197
1961	0.039	0.084	0.523	0.205	0.139	0.010	1	229
1962	0.049	0.112	0.547	0.199	0.081	0.012	1	231
1963	0.081	0.144	0.491	0.187	0.076	0.021	1	249
1964	0.066	0.147	0.512	0.187	0.090	-0.002	1	271
1965	0.152	0.138	0.482	0.181	0.034	0.014	1	293
1966	0.107	0.165	0.465	0.168	0.073	0.022	1	299
1967	0.069	0.245	0.438	0.174	0.046	0.028	1	292
1968	0.088	0.207	0.482	0.163	0.044	0.016	1	316
1969	0.150	0.202	0.431	0.153	0.054	0.011	1	321
1970	0.103	0.174	0.484	0.176	0.043	0.019	1	312
1971	0.026	0.218	0.506	0.168	0.058	0.023	1	360
1972	0.009	0.147	0.608	0.170	0.051	0.015	1	385
1973	0.094	0.124	0.589	0.135	0.056	0.003	1	402
1974	0.216	0.124	0.498	0.121	0.024	0.017	1	388
1975	0.013	0.224	0.549	0.150	0.050	0.014	1	366
1976	0.042	0.157	0.572	0.165	0.036	0.028	1	379
1977	0.158	0.172	0.450	0.134	0.030	0.056	1	374
1978	0.187	0.138	0.451	0.122	0.060	0.042	1	375
1979	0.153	0.160	0.482	0.121	0.061	0.022	1	379
1980	0.151	0.214	0.433	0.100	0.055	0.046	1	367

(cont'd)

TABLE 4 (cont'd)

Year	Proportion of Financial Requirements						Total	Number of Observations
	Short-Term Debt	Long-Term Debt	Cash Flow Reinvested	Cash Flow Distributed	Common Stock Issues	Preferred Stock Issues		
1981	0.119	0.392	0.341	0.085	0.044	0.020	1	356
1982	0.042	0.264	0.413	0.135	0.101	0.046	1	287
1983	-0.020	0.079	0.580	0.151	0.193	0.017	1	314
1984	0.098	0.134	0.539	0.126	0.079	0.024	1	340
1985	0.067	0.199	0.502	0.120	0.086	0.026	1	316
1986	0.001	0.259	0.439	0.144	0.131	0.027	1	274
1987	0.112	0.302	0.386	0.077	0.138	-0.015	1	289
1988	0.186	0.314	0.341	0.116	0.068	-0.025	1	273
1989	0.095	0.383	0.338	0.079	0.088	0.017	1	250
1990	0.086	0.337	0.430	0.112	0.043	-0.007	1	216
1991	0.049	0.358	0.323	0.141	0.128	0.001	1	289
1992	0.080	0.168	0.429	0.122	0.194	0.006	1	335
1993	0.070	0.223	0.406	0.102	0.221	-0.021	1	366
1994	0.116	0.165	0.478	0.084	0.160	-0.001	1	206
Average	0.090	0.200	0.470	0.142	0.082	0.016	1	311

TABLE 5

PROPORTION OF GROWTH-RELATED FINANCIAL REQUIREMENTS PROVIDED BY EACH FUNDING SOURCE, ALL CANADIAN FIRMS WITH NEGATIVE GROWTH, 1960 TO 1994

Year	Short-Term Debt	Long-Term Debt	Proportion of Financial Requirements: Cash Flow Reinvested	Cash Flow Distributed	Common Stock Issues	Preferred Stock Issues	Total	Number of Observations
1960	1.715	1.626	-1.447	-0.929	-0.007	0.042	1	25
1961	1.133	-0.356	0.237	-0.056	0.038	0.004	1	9
1962	1.124	0.686	-0.723	-0.053	-0.006	-0.028	1	14
1963	1.578	3.245	-3.321	-0.322	-0.188	0.007	1	21
1964	2.568	0.111	-1.067	-0.603	-0.012	0.002	1	17
1965	0.948	1.218	-1.006	-0.098	-0.063	0.001	1	7
1966	0.395	0.415	0.417	-0.272	-0.001	0.046	1	10
1967	1.475	0.021	-0.046	-0.373	-0.113	0.036	1	27
1968	0.477	0.919	-0.101	-0.169	-0.151	0.025	1	20
1969	1.503	0.200	-1.078	-0.083	0.391	0.067	1	23
1970	0.841	0.234	-0.016	-0.129	0.058	0.012	1	39
1971	1.234	0.043	-0.110	-0.096	-0.079	0.009	1	43
1972	0.646	1.119	-0.539	-0.214	-0.015	0.003	1	23
1973	1.831	0.883	-1.562	-0.126	-0.384	0.358	1	17
1974	0.050	0.405	0.286	-0.008	0.196	0.070	1	27
1975	2.498	-0.023	-1.111	-0.344	-0.033	0.012	1	48
1976	0.596	0.246	0.170	-0.079	0.070	-0.004	1	40
1977	1.396	0.246	-0.483	-0.115	-0.177	0.133	1	36
1978	0.765	0.518	-0.202	-0.015	-0.055	-0.012	1	22
1979	1.073	0.462	-0.467	-0.049	0.032	-0.052	1	13
1980	1.368	0.316	-0.465	-0.173	-0.048	0.002	1	21

(cont'd)

TABLE 5 (cont'd)

Year	Short-Term Debt	Long-Term Debt	Proportion of Financial Requirements: Cash Flow Reinvested	Cash Flow Distributed	Common Stock Issues	Preferred Stock Issues	Total	Number of Observations
1981	0.681	-0.139	0.502	-0.044	-0.023	0.024	1	29
1982	0.271	0.402	0.465	-0.091	-0.020	-0.027	1	100
1983	0.309	0.361	0.424	-0.030	-0.039	-0.025	1	71
1984	0.180	1.238	-0.224	-0.031	-0.158	-0.005	1	44
1985	0.330	0.929	-0.001	-0.131	-0.124	-0.003	1	59
1986	0.558	0.381	0.155	-0.086	0.030	-0.039	1	88
1987	0.425	0.807	-0.250	-0.051	0.010	0.058	1	46
1988	0.465	0.820	-0.209	-0.070	-0.052	0.046	1	45
1989	0.365	0.004	0.318	-0.052	0.297	0.068	1	53
1990	0.343	0.360	0.403	-0.104	-0.013	0.012	1	65
1991	0.958	-0.234	0.540	-0.141	-0.223	0.101	1	121
1992	-0.012	0.611	0.520	-0.123	-0.173	0.176	1	96
1993	0.276	0.907	-0.039	-0.085	-0.085	0.025	1	82
1994	1.958	0.477	-1.016	-0.132	-0.276	-0.008	1	20
Average	0.923	0.556	-0.316	-0.156	-0.040	0.032	1	41

calculated the various tax rates and estimated G for each period. Appendix A, which reports the details of these calculations, shows that the value of G varied widely during the study period, particularly as a result of the 1972 tax reforms. The numerical values are close to those reported by Rajan and Zingales (1995). Two precautionary notes are in order here. First, the capital gains are overestimated because they are assumed to be paid immediately. Since the ownership period and the capital cost are constant, the overvaluation must be constant as well, although this should not adversely affect the estimations. These values are also estimated under the assumption that the marginal investor is an individual. However, when the shareholder is a Canadian corporation with the same marginal tax rate as the subsidiary, the numerical value of G is nil. In these cases, the changes in G are smaller than revealed by the estimations. Lastly, several firms in the study sample are transnational companies that can use transfer prices to move their profits from one jurisdiction to another in order to alleviate the tax burden for the group as a whole. This source of noise – if not outright bias – may skew the statistical estimates of G.[16] A number of adjustments were also made to *NDTS* over the years, but their overall effect on firms is difficult to gauge, and the size of these tax credits varies from firm to firm (Givoly et al., 1992). They are thus introduced in the analysis at the firm level. Figure 3 shows changes in G over time. The maximum rate applicable to corporations is also shown, as well as the proportion of financing provided by short and long-term debt. A weak relationship appears to exist between the value of the gain associated with debt and the share of financing provided by long-term debt. The correlation coefficient between the two variables is -0.032. However, a stronger relationship is observed between total indebtedness and G, with a correlation coefficient of 0.355. Yet 1972, a year that saw a strong increase in debt-related gains, has the lowest incidence of debt financing. A similar phenomenon is apparent for 1982, another year in which G rose. The association between taxes and the financing choices of firms will be examined in greater depth in the section dealing with the financing decisions of individual firms.

Inflation

Several theoretical studies have found a positive link between debt financing and inflation (Modigliani, 1982; Modigliani and Cohn, 1979; Prezas, 1991; Taggart, 1986), but this link generally operates through taxes and agency costs. Taggart (1985) undertook a complete analysis of the interaction between these potential determinants of indebtedness and showed that, in the presence of agency costs, an anticipated increase in inflation triggers the replacement of equity by debt and pushes up the equilibrium debt rate. Some evidence to support this hypothesis is provided by Figure 4, which graphs inflation and the proportion of financial requirements satisfied by total debt and long-term debt. The correlation coefficient between long-term debt and the rate of inflation is 0.2376. When all forms of debt are considered, the correlation coefficient is 0.3312.

FIGURE 3

TAX PARAMETERS AND USE OF DEBT FINANCING, CANADIAN FIRMS WITH POSITIVE GROWTH, 1960 TO 1994[a]

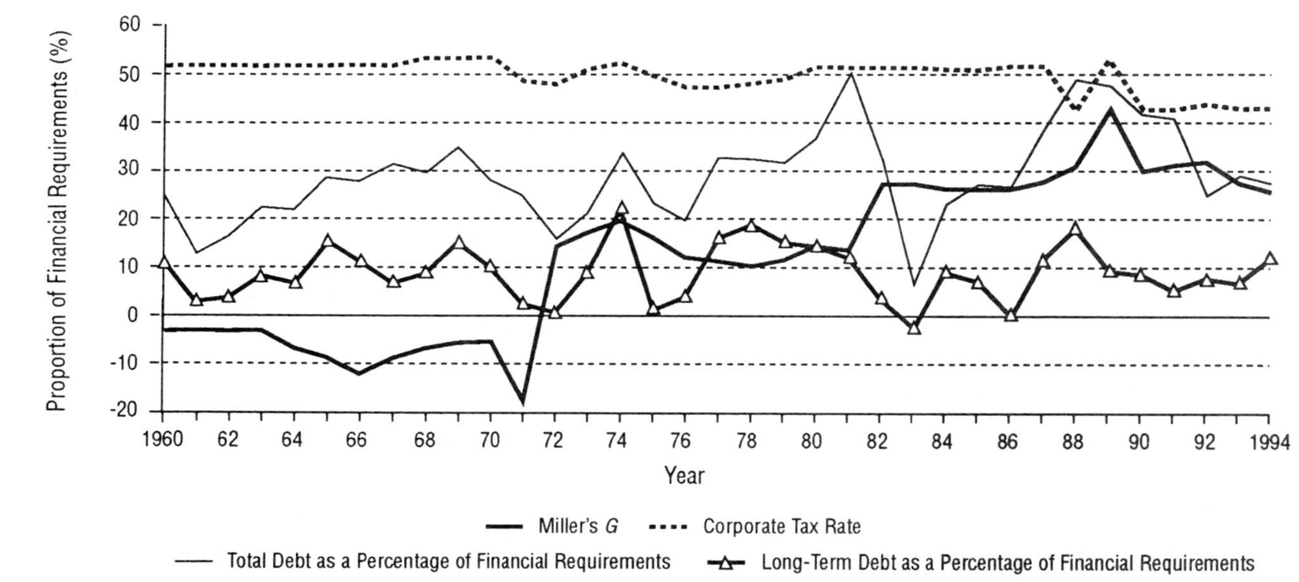

Note: [a] The calculation for Miller's G is explained in Appendix 1. We used the corporate tax rate applicable to an Ontario corporation. The proportion of financial requirements satisfied by the total debt (borrowings) is the ratio of the annual increase in short-term liabilities plus long-term debt, for all firms, to the increase in gross assets plus dividends for the corresponding year. The proportion for long-term debt is calculated in the same way, except that the numerator is the percentage in the long-term debt.

FIGURE 4

INFLATION AND USE OF DEBT FINANCING, CANADIAN FIRMS WITH POSITIVE GROWTH, 1960 TO 1994[a]

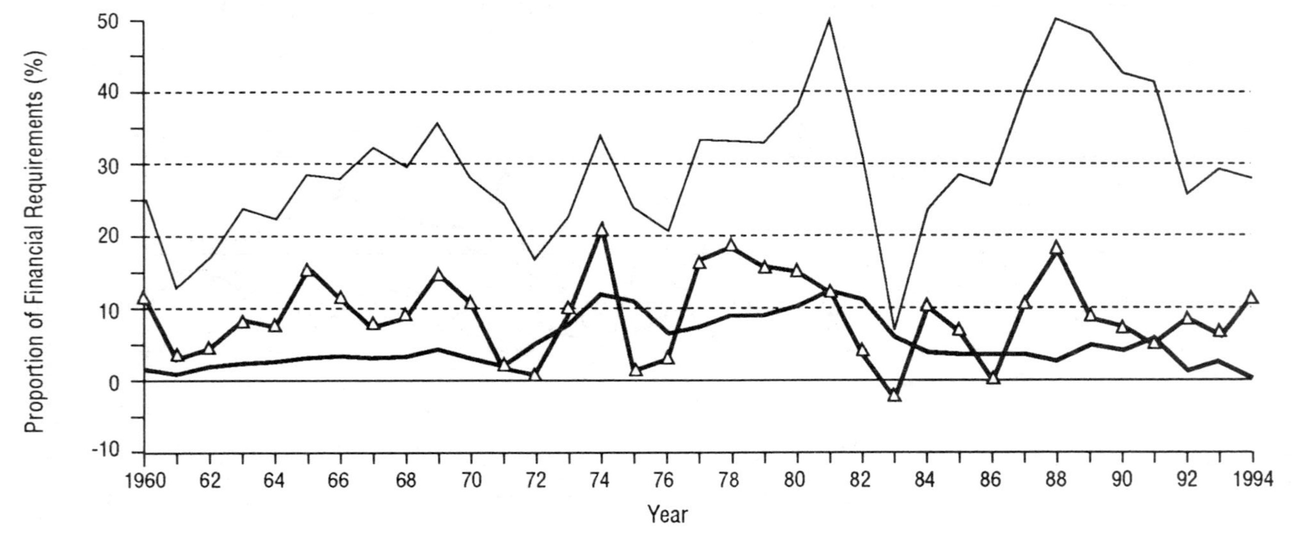

Note: [a] The annual inflation rate is taken from the *Bank of Canada Review*.

Financing Choices and Perceived Financing Costs

The overall condition of the stock market is not usually considered a determinant of firms' financing choices. However, when managers are asked about the factors they take into account when making financing decisions, "capital markets are their primary concern, rather than clients or some market segments" (Norton, 1991, p. 438). In Canada also, the surveyed managers cited general market conditions as a major factor in financing decisions (Cheung et al., 1989). Researchers studying initial public offerings take it for granted that there are favourable periods, which they call "hot issue markets" (Ritter, 1991), during which most issues are made and issuers receive, on average, higher amounts for comparable share offerings.

Some studies have found a link between costs and financing decisions. Viswanath (1993) proposed a modified version of the "pecking order" theory, establishing a link between interest rate expectations and equity issues. According to this theory, equity issues tend to be larger when the term structure of interest rates is falling, which happens most often at business cycle peaks. This phenomenon was identified by Choe et al. (1989). Lastly, various studies on financing choices have underlined the significant role played by variables such as the "book-to-market ratio" (Rajan and Zingales, 1995; Homaifar et al., 1994) and the price/earnings ratio (Chung, 1993). These two ratios, which are considered estimators of the relative importance of future growth prospects, are negatively related to debt. However, these variables are also traditional estimators of financing costs (MacCauley and Zimmer, 1989), and one could argue that the use of external equity capital is more prevalent when these indicators are high, suggesting that equity financing is low cost. This is the view adopted by Singh (1995) who explained that firms in emerging markets derive most of their financing from equity issues because of the relatively low cost of equity financing, which reflects the rapid rise in stock indexes in emerging markets during the 1980s. The high price/earnings ratios seen in many emerging countries prompted firms to make numerous issues. Nakamura and Nakumura (1982) found that long-term debt ratios are positively related to the cost of equity and negatively related to the cost of debt. Accordingly, there would appear to be a link between the relative level of stock indexes and financing choices, as confirmed by Figure 5 which shows changes over time in the average price/earnings ratio of sample firms. The pattern matches fairly well that of the Toronto Stock Exchange, as well as the proportion of financial requirements provided by equity issues. There is a strong relationship between the two series, with correlation reaching 56.6. Thus, it would appear that the general level of stock prices does influence firms' financing choices.

In the same way, if managers take the real cost of debt financing into account, a relative decline in debt financing can be expected when real interest rates are high.[17] Figure 6 shows that there is no such relationship between total debt financing and the real rate of interest. The correlation between these two series is -0.0347. On the other hand, the real long-term bond rate is negatively linked with the use of long-term debt. In the latter case, the correlation is -0.274.

FIGURE 5

AVERAGE PRICE/EARNINGS RATIO AND USE OF EQUITY FINANCING, CANADIAN FIRMS WITH POSITIVE GROWTH, 1960 TO 1994[a]

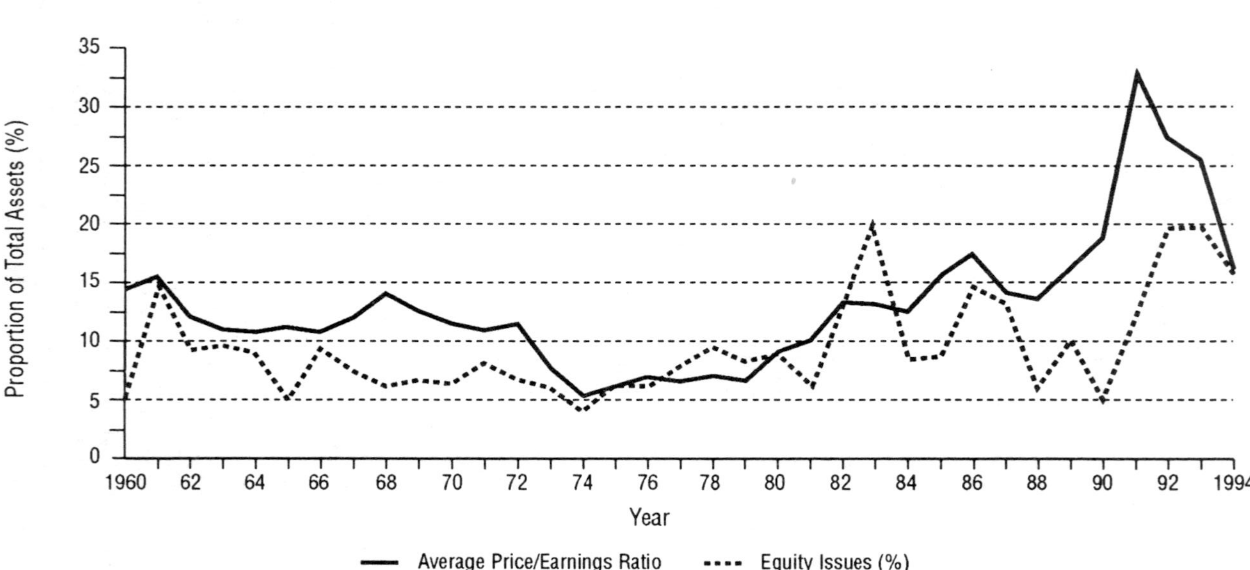

Note: [a] The average price/earnings ratio is the arithmetic mean of the ratios of firms in the sample, calculated from annual earnings and prices at fiscal year-end. The proportion of financial requirements provided by equity issues is the ratio of the annual increase in common and preferred capital stock, for all firms, to the increase in gross assets plus dividends for the corresponding year.

FIGURE 6

REAL LONG-TERM INTEREST RATE AND FINANCING REPRESENTED BY TOTAL DEBT AND LONG-TERM DEBT, CANADIAN FIRMS WITH POSITIVE GROWTH, 1960 TO 1994[a]

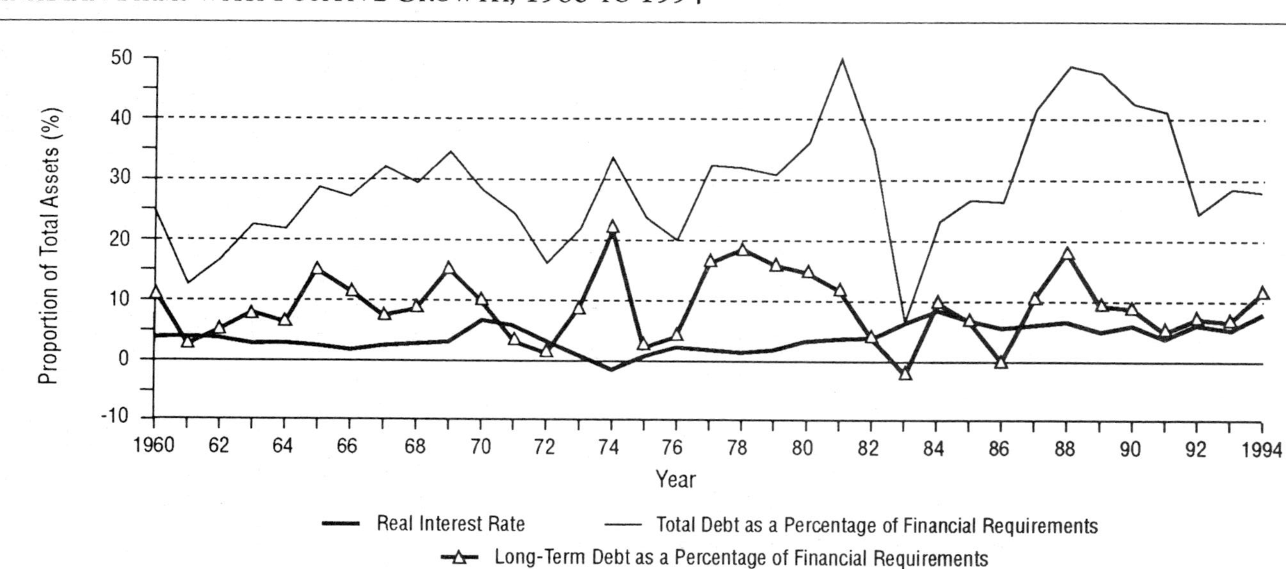

Note: [a] The real interest rate is expressed as $r = ((1 + r_0) / (1 + I) - 1)$, where r_0 is the promised rate on long-term bonds and I is the annual rate of inflation. The promised rate for a given year is the average of promised rates at the end of each month as per the Scotia-McLeod index for industrial bonds. The proportion of financial requirements provided by long-term debt is the ratio of the annual increase in short-term liabilities plus long-term debt, for all firms, to the increase in gross assets plus dividends for the corresponding year. The proportion for long-term debt is calculated in the same way, except that the numerator is the percentage change in long-term debt.

Financing and the Business Cycle

Some studies have linked the financing decisions of firms to the business cycle (Seth, 1992). Taggart (1986, p. 37) suggested that the link between financing decisions and business cycles is negative because there is an inverse relationship between debt financing and the availability of internal funds. He argued that debt financing is likely to be used toward the end of expansionary periods and at the beginning of recessions, when large investment outlays coincide with a drop in cash flow. Figure 7 does not reveal any particularly strong relationship between long-term debt financing and the growth rate of industrial output, which is used here as an indicator of economic growth. The correlation coefficient is 0.12, and positive – contrary to expectations – but not significant. The use of total debt is negatively related to the output growth index, however. A large proportion of financial requirements was satisfied by borrowings during the 1980 to 1982 and the 1986 recessions. The correlation coefficient between the two series is -0.378.

There would thus appear to be strong linkages between the financing choices made by firms and economic and market conditions. This observation is not only intuitive, but is reflected in statements made by corporate managers. The descriptive study presented here is somewhat superficial, however, as it does not take firm-level behavioural differences into account. Moreover, the impact of variables has been considered individually. The remainder of this study is devoted to developing and testing financial decision models incorporating both economic conditions and firm characteristics.

EXPLAINING CORPORATE FINANCING CHOICES

MODELS AND DATA

THE ANALYSES OUTLINED IN THE PREVIOUS SECTIONS showed significant variation over time in how firms use various sources of financing. These variations appear to be partially linked to economic fluctuations. A cross-sectional analysis also reveals significant variation among firms in financing choices made during a given period. In this final section, we try to determine whether these variations are random or whether they can be linked to firm characteristics. We then incorporate market and economic conditions into our analysis.[18]

The econometric models used here serve to determine whether it is possible to explain the financial *decisions* of firms. This study consequently departs from many others that have attempted to explain debt *levels* (Titman and Wessels, 1988). The study closest in approach to ours is that of MacKie-Mason (1990b), carried out in the United States. The author used a nested probit model in which the dependent variables are binary,[19] following the "pecking order" theory, and in which a distinction is made between internal financing (reinvestment and borrowing) and external financing (public debt and equity issues).[20] However, MacKie-Mason acknowledges that the main problem with his model lies in the aggregation of two very different types of internal financing – reinvestments and bank borrowings.

FIGURE 7

GROWTH RATE OF INDUSTRIAL OUTPUT AND FINANCING REPRESENTED BY TOTAL DEBT AND LONG-TERM DEBT, CANADIAN FIRMS WITH POSITIVE GROWTH, 1960 TO 1994[a]

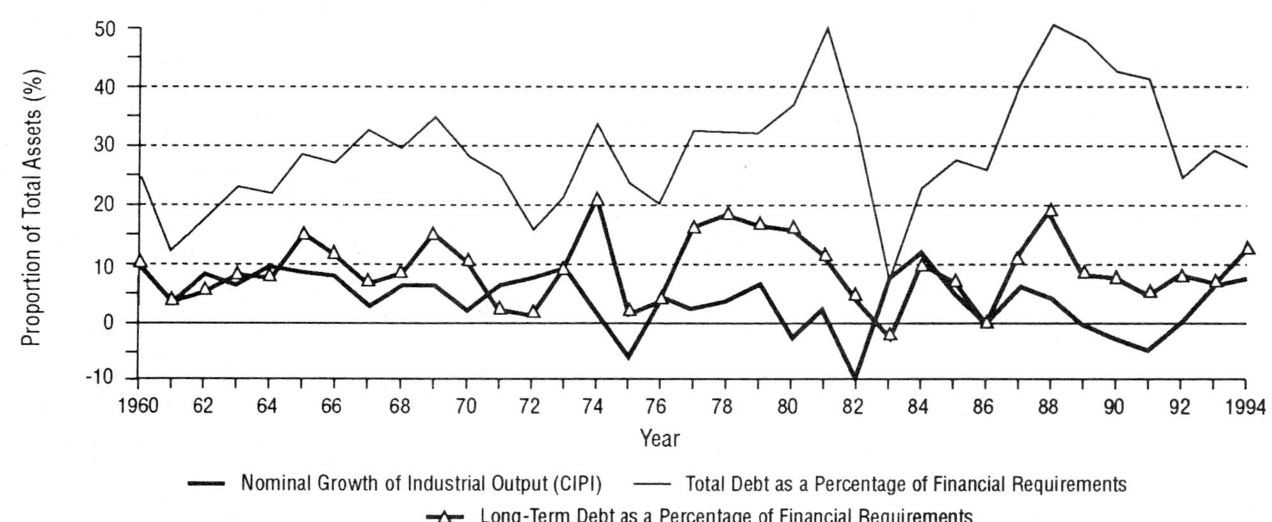

Note: [a] The growth rate is calculated from the successive values of the output index without adjustment for inflation. The proportion of financial requirements provided by total debt is the ratio of the annual increase in short-term liabilities plus long-term debt, for all firms, to the increase in gross assets plus dividends for the corresponding year. The ratio for long-term debt is calculated in the same way, except that the numerator is the percentage change in long-term debt.

That is why we have not used this method. For MacKie-Mason, the determinants of debt financing are taxes, the real costs of bankruptcy and agency costs. The financing decisions of firms can also be analysed with discrete choice models, where the binary dependent variable depends on the decision to issue bonds or shares (Marsh, 1982; Bayless and Diltz, 1994). That method was not used here, for several reasons. First, it considers only external financing, which accounts for only a relatively modest part of total financing requirements. Second, bank loans and private bond issues are excluded from the analysis. Finally, reducing financial choices to a binary variable represents a loss of information, because large issues are treated in the same way as small issues and because years in which both types of issues occur have been excluded. While binary-type methodologies do allow two financing methods to be examined simultaneously, they do not account for the entire range of financing operations at a particular point in time. Accordingly, we opted for a series of models, each of which explains one aspect of financing. In the first round, these models are applied sequentially instead of simultaneously in order to avoid specification problems.[21]

The purpose of this study is not to test any particular theory of corporate behaviour. As Myers (1994) noted, we are still lacking a consistent theory to explain firm behaviour. Our proposed model, like that of Rajan and Zingales (1995), relies on a synthesis of previous research to define variables that could explain financing decisions. We agree with Harris and Raviv (1991, p. 334) that leverage increases with fixed assets, non-debt tax shields, growth opportunities and firm size, and decreases with volatility, advertising expenditures, research and development expenditures, bankruptcy probability, profitability and uniqueness of the product. Rajan and Zingales selected four variables to explain indebtedness: an indicator of asset "tangibility" (ratio of fixed to total assets), a measure of growth expectations (market-to-book ratio), size and profitability (ratio of operating cash flow to book value of assets). The variables used here are slightly different, since we want to explain the use of various debt instruments and not the level of indebtedness. After describing and analysing the impact of firm-specific variables, we introduce into our model the major macro-economic indicators discussed above. Note that each financing method will be analysed separately; in a future study, the coefficients of the various explanatory variables will be estimated using a system of simultaneous equations.

Because of the length of the study period, an important variable in financing decisions – the distribution of voting rights – was excluded. Accordingly, the conclusions apply primarily to large, widely held firms. At the firm level, the concentration of voting rights is relatively high in Canada, and principal shareholders are frequently other taxable Canadian corporations (Gadhoum, 1995). It is logical for these majority shareholders to prefer dividends over capital gains, because the latter are not subject to income tax. Accordingly, these investors will use their influence to limit internal financing. In addition, when the shareholder corporation and its subsidiary or affiliate face the same marginal tax rate, they will have no preference, from a tax standpoint, between debt or equity in intercompany financing operations. When managers are also major shareholders, debt ratios (Friend and Lang, 1988; Firth, 1995) and distribution ratios (Eckbo and Verma, 1994) should be lower than they would be otherwise. This behaviour, too, is logical: in order to retain control, these shareholders hold portfolios that are less diversified and, consequently, riskier. They may seek to offset this non-systematic risk – which diversification could have eliminated – by reducing the financial risk of the firm. In addition, reinvesting earnings allows them to be transformed into capital gains, thereby deferring income tax.[22]

Explaining the Percentage of Financing Requirements Provided by Internal Resources

According to the "pecking order" theory, debt financing will increase with higher profitability and slower growth. Asset growth (*CROIS*) and profitability (*RENT*) are thus the two main variables explaining the proportion of financial requirements met through reinvested earnings. As in the Jensen et al. (1992) model, dividend policy is considered here as an explanatory variable. It is measured by *DIST*, the ratio of paid dividends to earnings available to shareholders during the last three fiscal years. If dividend policy is a constraint, as previous work seems to indicate, the variable *DIST* should have a significant and negative coefficient when explaining the proportion of internal financing. Finally, it seems impossible to treat, in the same fashion, firms that incurred losses and firms that earned profits in previous fiscal years. The former did not really have to make financing choices and the observed relationships might reflect a simple accounting calculus effect.[23] A binary variable *BP* was thus introduced in our model to capture loss. We also incorporated into the model the proportion of fixed assets financed in year t, expressed in relation to financial requirements (*AI*).[24] Since fixed assets are used as collateral, they tend to reduce the potential agency costs of creditors and facilitate access to borrowing.[25] The proportion of internal financing should be negatively linked to this variable.

In light of the aggregate results reported in the previous sections, we agree with Jalilvand and Harris (1984) and Homaifar et al. (1994) that stock market conditions influence financing decisions. However, the stock market yield does not appear to be a good indicator of these conditions, because it can be especially high at the beginning of a bull cycle, when company managers feel their shares are still undervalued by the market. The relative earnings/price ratio (*EPRR*) is used here as an indicator of relative stock prices. To account for changes in this indicator over time and among companies, the ratios were adjusted twice. The first adjustment is made in relation to the market and the second in relation to the historical trend of the adjusted ratio. The resulting figure is commonly used by financial analysts to judge whether a stock is undervalued or not (Melkinof, 1988). A high value for this indicator suggests that the stock is not highly valued by the market. In this case, a firm should rely more heavily on internal financing (and on debt), instead of issuing equity. The model will thus take the following form:

$$\Delta AUTO_{it} = \alpha_0 + \alpha_1 CROIS_{it} + \alpha_2 RENT_{it} + \alpha_3 DIST_{it} + \alpha_4 BP_{it} + \alpha_5 AI_{it} + \alpha_6 EPRR_{it} + e_{1it} \qquad \text{(M1)}$$

where

$\Delta AUTO_{it}$: The share of financial requirements covered by internal financing for firm i in year t. It equals the increase in retained earnings plus depreciation, divided by financial requirements as given by equation (1), including dividends and depreciation.

$CROIS_{it}$: Annual average geometric growth rate of gross assets (book value of assets + accumulated depreciation) during the last three fiscal years for firm i at time t.

$$CROIS_{it} = (ACTIF_{it} / ACTIF_{it-3})^{1/3} - 1 \qquad (4)$$

$RENT_{it}$: Average return on assets before interests and taxes for firm i at time t. It is the average for the last three fiscal years.

$$RENT_{it} = \sum_{s=t-2}^{t} BAIL_{is} / \sum_{s=t-2}^{t} ACTIF_{is} \qquad (5)$$

$DIST_{it}$: Indicator of dividend policy. This is the ratio of paid dividends to earnings available to shareholders for the three fiscal years ending on the date of the analysis. When dividends are paid out in spite of losses, the indicator has a value of 0, and all earnings are considered to have been distributed.

$$DIST_{it} = \frac{\sum_{s=t-2}^{t} dividends_{is}}{\sum_{s=t-2}^{t} net\ earnings_{is}} \quad or\ 0\ if \sum_{s=t-2}^{t} earnings < 0 \qquad (6)$$

BP_{it}: Binary variable that takes a value of 1 when total earnings over the last three fiscal years are negative.

$$BP_{it} = 1\ if \sum_{s=t-2}^{t} earnings < 0\ or\ 0\ otherwise \qquad (7)$$

AI_{it}: Increase in the gross value of fixed assets as a proportion of the total increase in gross assets (financial requirements).

$EPRR_{it}$: Relative earnings/price ratio expressed in terms of its historical average. First, the earnings/price ratio is adjusted by the average distribution of the ratio for year t. The result is the ratio relative to the average, designated EPM_{it}. This first step is necessary in order to handle the ratio's intertemporal fluctuations.

$$EPM_{it} = EP_{it} / EP_{mt} \tag{8}$$

The historical average of the ratio is then calculated for three fiscal years: t, t-1 and t-2. The quantity $EPMH_{it}$ indicates the usual position of the stock's ratio relative to the market, which allows possible size or sector-related effects to be accounted for.

$$EPMH_{it} = \frac{1}{3}\sum_{s=t-2}^{t} EPM_{is} \tag{9}$$

The relative earnings/price ratio is defined by equation (10). It indicates by how much the stock's relative earnings/price ratio is above or below its historical average. This indicator is commonly used by financial analysts to determine whether a stock is over or undervalued.

$$EPRR_{it} = EPM_{it} / EPMH_{it} \tag{10}$$

The macro-economic variables associated with this model are the rate of growth of economic activity (*CIPI*), the aggregate index of relative market value (earnings/market price: *EPM*), the rate of inflation (*INF*) and the long-term interest rate (*OBLIG*).

Explaining the Percentage of Financing Requirements Provided by Debt

Debt is the next option when internal financing possibilities have been exhausted (according to the "pecking order" theory). We have thus incorporated the explanatory variables from the M1 model into the total debt financing model (M2a) and the long-term debt financing model (M2b). Previous work has identified two other variables – taxes and size – that help determine indebtedness levels and likely play a part in explaining annual choices of financing instruments. Taxes exert their influence through non-debt tax shields (*NDTS*). The "Miller" type of tax gain does not come in to play at the individual level since, at any given time, firms are subject to the same tax rate, unless they have accumulated significant losses. In the absence of complete data on stock ownership, we must assume also that shareholders are subject to the same tax rate, which suggests that gains associated with indebtedness vary over time but not among firms. The variable *RDF* (ratio of tax deductions) represents the ratio of *NDTS* available in year t to the average cash flow for the last three fiscal years. The calculation is very similar to that used by Davis (1994), and we expect to see an inverse relationship between debt financing and the variable *RDF*.[26]

Lastly, relative size was entered into the model. In previous work, size generally had a positive link with indebtedness (Harris and Raviv, 1991; Rajan and Zingales, 1995), although no fully satisfactory explanation of this relationship has been offered. The two most frequently cited hypotheses are a negative link between size and bankruptcy costs, and the fact that larger firms have easier access to bond markets.

The models explaining the share of financing provided by total debt (M2a) and long-term debt (M2b) are now as follows:

$$\Delta DT_{it} = \beta_0 + \beta_1 CROIS_{it} + \beta_2 RENT_{it} + \beta_3 DIST_{it} + \beta_4 BP_{it} + \beta_5 AI_{it} + \beta_6 EPRR_{it} + \beta_7 RDF_{it} + \beta_8 Taille_{it} + e_{2it} \quad \text{(M2a)}$$

$$\Delta DLT_{it} = \beta_0 + \beta_1 CROIS_{it} + \beta_2 RENT_{it} + \beta_3 DIST_{it} + \beta_4 BP_{it} + \beta_5 AI_{it} + \beta_6 EPRR_{it} + \beta_7 RDF_{it} + \beta_8 Taille_{it} + e_{2it} \quad \text{(M2b)}$$

where, in addition to the variables previously defined, we have:

ΔDT_{it}: Portion of financial requirements represented by the increase in all types of debt (short-term liabilities + long-term debt)

ΔDLT_{it}: Portion of financial requirements represented by the increase in long-term debt.

RDF_{it}: Ratio of non-debt tax shields. This is the ratio of *NDTS* estimated for year *t* to the average cash flow over the last three years (*CFM*). This expression of relative tax credits is derived from that developed by Davis (1994) for the Canadian tax system. It has been adapted to reflect the limit on the number of balance sheet items available in the data base. Details of the calculations are given in Appendix A.

$$RDF_{it} = NDTS_{it} \,/\, CFM \quad (11)$$

$Taille_{it}$: Total market valuation of equity divided by average market valuation for all observations in year *t*. An adjustment is required because of the length of the study period.[27]

The macro-economic variables associated with this model are the rate of inflation (*INF*), the fixed long-term interest rate (*OBLIG*) and the tax advantage associated with corporate debt (Miller's G).

Explaining the Percentage of Financial Requirements Provided by Equity Issues

The variables used earlier to explain debt financing can also be used (with reverse signs) to explain public equity issues – except for firm size and *NDTS*, which are generally not associated with equity financing. The M3 model takes the following form:

$$\Delta CA_{it} = \gamma_0 + \gamma_1 CROIS_{it} + \gamma_2 RENT_{it} + \gamma_3 DIST_{it} + \gamma_4 BP_{it} + \gamma_5 EPRR_{it} + e_{3it} \qquad \text{(M3)}$$

where

ΔCA_{it}: Portion of financial requirements raised through equity issues.

The macro-economic variables associated with this model are the index of change in economic activity (*CIPI*), inflation (*INF*) and long-term interest rates (*OBLIG*). The first variable is an estimator of the relative cost of financing through equity issues. The other two variables are potential determinants of debt financing. High long-term interest rates should induce firms to issue equity, *ceteris paribus*.[28]

Conclusions

Table 6 summarizes the models discussed and the expected signs of the variables.

Description of Variables

Table 7 summarizes the main distribution characteristics of the variables used in the various models. In order to limit the influence of extreme data in our estimates, values below the first percentile or above the last percentile were adjusted to the value of these percentiles. The average or median data for financing methods differ slightly from the overall averages reported in the first part of the study. This is because the firm-level analysis involves calculating ratio averages, while the aggregate analysis involves the calculation of average ratios.

Dependent Variables

Internal financing represented on average 74.3 percent of the funding sources used by Canadian firms over the last 32 years. However, this distribution is strongly right asymmetrical, with the median at 52 percent. This means that, for one firm in two, internal financing represents less than 52 percent of funding sources. This median value is close to the aggregate value computed earlier (47 percent). These extreme positive values deserve some explanation. They represent situations where cash flow exceeds financial requirements. This situation may arise when slow-growing

TABLE 6 (A MODEL SUMMARY)					
Models		**M1**	**M2a**	**M2b**	**M3**
Dependent Variables as a Proportion of Financial Requirements		*AUTO*	ΔDT	ΔDLT	ΔCA
Code			**Expected Signs**		
Firm-Specific Explanatory Variables					
CROIS	Average growth rate	-	+	+	+
RENT	Average profitability	+	-	-	-
DIST	Distribution ratio	-	+	+	+
BP	Binary variable related to losses	-	+	+	+
RDF	Ratio of non-debt tax shields		-	-	
AI	Change in fixed assets as a proportion of total growth	-	+	+	
EPRR	Earnings/price ratio based on the historical trend in the ratio to market value	+	+	+	-
Taille	Size in terms of market capitalization, expressed in relation to the average size of sample firms		+	+	
Macro-Economic Variables					
CIPI	Rate of change in industrial output	+	-	-	+
INF	Inflation rate	-	+	+	-
OBLIG	Fixed rate of interest on long-term bonds	+	-	-	+
G	Tax gain on corporate debt (Miller's G)		+	+	
EPM	Average earnings/price ratio for market	+			-

firms with strong cash flows use them to pay down debt. It occurred mainly toward the end of the study period. The distribution has a high standard deviation, indicating major differences among firms or over time.

The average share of debt financing (all forms) is negative (-3.9 percent), but the median is positive and close to the aggregate value measured (26.6 percent vs. 29 percent for firms with positive growth, in Table 4). This strong asymmetry is caused by approximately one one-hundredth of observations, for which the value was limited to -12.88. Once again, these are special situations, generally involving firms with modest financing requirements that use large equity issues or earnings to reduce their indebtedness. Long-term debt represents on average 5.31 percent of financial requirements. For almost 3,800 observations, however, there is no variation in long-term debt. Most often, this simply reflects the fact that firms did not use this method of financing, which explains why the median of the distribution is close to zero.

We also assessed dividend payments in relation to total financial requirements. Over the period, they represent 17.3 percent of the total financial requirements of firms, a proportion fairly close to what was observed at the aggregate level. This result confirms that firms paid out more to shareholders than they received through equity issues.

Explanatory Variables

Among the sample firms, growth averaged 16.2 percent. The median lies at 11.6 percent, however, reflecting the influence of a subgroup of observations with extremely strong growth. The picture for rates of return is basically similar: the growth distribution is right asymmetrical, and the return on assets averaged 13.4 percent, while the median was 10.8 percent. The dividend-distribution ratio for the sample was on average 28.6 percent.[29] We noted that 3.5 percent of firms continued to pay dividends even when they suffered losses (on average) over the last three fiscal years, confirming the constraining nature of dividend policies. The average and median for the relative earnings/price ratio are close to unity at 1.031 and 0.99. As well, 7.4 percent of firms experienced losses, leading us to isolate this subgroup and consider a dichotomous variable, *EPN*. On average, the variation in gross fixed assets represents only 27.3 percent of financial requirements. This relatively low percentage reflects both how financing requirements were calculated and the fact that growth occurred through acquisitions in many cases.

Methodology and Results

The financing choice explanatory models are first estimated using a two-stage process. This involves estimating 32 cross-sectional regressions for each year from 1963 to 1994.[30] The average coefficients are then computed.[31] Their dispersion is calculated in order to estimate the *t* values. This technique, used by Fama and French (1992), allows for annual variations in the estimated parameters. However, while this method reveals the temporal instability of the estimated coefficients, it cannot explain the origin of these variations. In the second section, the models (M1 through M3) are estimated in a single step using a "pooling" method. This method offers more degrees of freedom, reduces the collinearity among explanatory variables and, thus, produces more efficient estimates. It also allows us to use more powerful tests and to incorporate macro-economic variables into the models that may have a bearing on corporate financing choices. Introducing these variables also partially corrects for the implicit assumption underlying this type of estimation – that the intercept and slopes associated with the various variables are stable over time.[32] Each of the models, therefore, is estimated using three different methods: the two-stage method, the pooling method with firm-specific variables only and the pooling method with macro-economic variables. The parameters estimated with each of the three methods and for each model are shown in Table 8 (equity models) and Table 9 (debt models).

TABLE 7

MAIN CHARACTERISTICS OF THE DISTRIBUTIONS OF VARIABLES USED IN EXPLANATORY MODELS OF FINANCING DECISIONS[a]

Dependent Variables	Average	Standard Deviation	Maximum	Minimum	Median
Internal financing as a percentage of financial requirements (Δ*AUTO*)	0.743	1.056	7.610	-2.37	0.520
Financing by total debt as a percentage of financial requirements (Δ*DTOT*)	-0.039	1.356	2.450	-12.88	0.266
Financing by long-term debt as a percentage of financial requirements (Δ*DTLT*)	0.053	0.623	3.57	-4.30	0.001
Financing by equity issues as a percentage of financial requirements (Δ*CA*)	0.109	0.521	10.734	-8.583	0.000
Distribution ratio (*DIVI*)	0.173	0.270	1.790	0.000	0.093
Explanatory Variables					
Average return on assets (*RENT*)	0.134	0.388	19.200	-0.290	0.108
Average growth rate of gross assets (*CROIS*)	0.162	0.193	2.267	-0.445	0.116
Dividend distribution as a percentage of net earnings (*DIST*)	0.286	0.426	4.200	0.000	0.185
Market capitalization relative to average size of sample firms (*TAILLE*)	1.102	2.001	26.548	0.005	0.354
Earnings/price ratio relative to the market and to its historical value (*EPRR*)	1.031	0.566	3.000	0.000	0.990
Proportion of financial requirements represented by fixed assets (*AI*)	0.273	0.581	1.450	-5.610	0.331

Note: [a] The sample includes 7,833 annual observations for the period 1963 to 1994.

Model M1: Share of Internal Financing in Total Financing Requirements

The average coefficients and their significance levels for each estimation model appear in the first three columns of Table 8. The results for the annual regressions show that the coefficients have the expected signs for almost all the years studied. The intercept is positive and highly significant, reflecting that internal financing is, on average, one of the more important sources of funding for firms. The average coefficients are also statistically different from 0, with the expected sign.

The use of internal financing is inversely related to growth (the coefficient is -0.884 and positively related to profitability, while the average coefficient is 1.222). These findings are consistent with a system of hierarchical ordering among financing choices. As expected, the coefficient associated with the *DIST* variable, which represents the distribution rate, is negative and significant (-0.493). Given equal profitability and growth, the higher the dividend distribution ratio, the more difficult it is for a firm to rely on internal financing. This result suggests that firms take the payment of dividends as a constraint. According to our data, many firms simultaneously pay dividends and issue equity. The average coefficient associated with the binary variable *BP* is negative and significant (-0.850), as expected. This reflects the fact that a firm incurring losses has limited internal financing capabilities.

The variable *EPRR*, which indicates the degree to which the stock is over or undervalued, has a positive sign. This is in line with expectations. It is only logical to see more reinvestment in periods when the company's stock is low. The coefficient of the variable *AI* is negative and statistically significant, indicating that the use of internal financing tends to increase when growth is not driven by the acquisition of tangible assets.

The pooling estimation produces results that are very similar to the two-stage approach. The slopes associated with the variables explaining the shares of each method of financing firms' growth appear to be relatively stable over the study period. The determination coefficient of the M1 model is 22 percent.

In the last estimation, we introduced four macro-economic variables that presumably influence the share of internal financing. They are economic activity, measured by the variation in the industrial output index (*CIPI*); the annual rate of inflation (*INF*), as reported by Statistics Canada; an aggregate indicator of the level of the stock market, calculated from the arithmetic average of the earnings/price ratios of the sample firms (*EPM*); and the long-run return on industrial bonds, measured by the arithmetic mean of the fixed monthly rates offered (*OBLIG*). Except for the stock market level indicator, all indicators play a significant role in explaining the proportion of internal financing. Internal financing falls in periods of economic growth. The coefficient is -0.008 and is statistically significant. Inflation is also negatively related to internal financing, reflecting the greater attractiveness of debt in inflationary times. Lastly, variations in internal financing levels do not seem related to the earnings/price ratio for the market as a whole.

TABLE 8

COEFFICIENTS AND STATISTICAL TESTS OF TWO-STAGE AND POOLED ESTIMATES FROM THE VARIOUS EXPLANATORY MODELS OF EQUITY-FINANCING DECISIONS

	M1: Internal Financing			M3: Equity Issue		
	Two-Stage	Pooled	Pooled, Macro	Two-Stage	Pooled	Pooled, Macro
Specific Variables						
Intercept	0.730	0.696	0.624	0.112	0.112	0.186
	(13.52)*	(24.20)*	(7.53)*	(4.07)*	(7.15)*	(4.10)*
CROIS	-0.884	-0.831	-0.837	0.392	0.395	0.383
	(-8.89)*	(-12.94)*	(-12.96)*	(7.33)*	(11.56)*	(11.17)*
RENT	1.122	1.285	1.344	-0.325	-0.578	-0.469
	(5.23)*	(9.71)*	(9.93)*	(-1.32)	(-7.95)*	(-6.33)*
DIST	-0.493	-0.472	-0.476	-0.001	0.002	-0.007
	(-13.59)*	(-17.79)*	(-17.77)*	(-0.09)	(0.14)	(-0.53)
BP	-0.850	-0.803	-0.811	0.248	0.298	0.292
	(-12.08)*	(-13.44)*	(-13.56)*	(3.41)*	(9.09)*	(8.19)*
EPRR	0.323	0.345	0.343	-0.012	-0.005	-0.008
	(11.45)*	(18.50)*	(18.38)*	(-0.83)	(-0.58)	(-0.83)
AI	-0.627	-0.629	-0.630			
	(-9.51)*	(-33.34)*	(-33.36)*			
Macro-Economic Variables						
CIPI			-0.008			-0.002
			(-3.22)*			(-1.77)
INF			-0.027			-0.008
			(-3.32)*			(-1.76)
OBL			0.020			0.007
			(2.64)*			(1.68)
EPM			0.848			-1.067
			(1.27)			(-2.92)*
R2		0.220	0.222		0.031	0.039
F		369.519	224.68		51.586	36.64

Note: * Significant at the 5 percent level.

Economic conditions thus appear to have an influence on financing decisions, but the very modest increase in the determination coefficient indicates that the addition of these macro-economic variables brings only minimal improvement to the econometric model.

M3: Share of Equity Issues

The right side of Table 8 shows the coefficients and tests associated with the M3 model. For the two-stage estimation, the coefficients of the *CROIS* variable are positive for 30 of the 31 estimations. Coefficients associated with the *RENT* variable are negative for 28 of the 32 years. On average (Table 8), these coefficients are statistically significant. Financing through equity issues thus tends to increase with rapid growth and with lower profitability. The variable for average dividend distribution policy plays no role, regardless of the estimation method used. However, the binary loss variable has a positive and statistically significant coefficient. Firms that finance a large part of their growth through equity issues are those that had no earnings in previous fiscal years (the binary variable was assigned a value of 1 when the firm incurred a loss). It is not surprising, therefore, to find no relationship between the relative price indicator and the relative size of equity issues. The coefficient associated with *EPRR* is indeed negative, but not significant.

The pooling estimation produces results similar to those obtained with the two-stage method. The only notable change is in the level of significance of the variable *RENT*. None of the macro-economic variables appears to play an explanatory role except for the market-level indicator. The latter is negatively and significantly related to the proportion of financing provided by equity issues. Issues thus increase inversely with the price/earnings ratio, on average. This reflects a positive relationship between the proportion of financing provided by equity and the price/earnings ratio.

All the models used to explain the contribution of equity issues to financing requirements have relatively low explanatory power. The determination coefficient is 3.9 percent in the best case.

Models M2a and M2b: Share of Total Debt and Long-Term Debt

The results of the debt financing models are reported in Table 9. Since they are similar for total debt and long-term debt, only the main differences are discussed.

As expected, the average coefficient associated with the variable *CROIS* is positive and significant (0.486). The coefficient is positive for each of the annual estimates. Also as expected, the average coefficient associated with the variable RENT is negative and significant (-0.532). The coefficient of the variable *DIST* is positive (0.131) and statistically significant. This indicates that, on average, firms with a generous dividend policy make greater use of debt financing than other firms. Dividend policy would thus seem to be a constraint. The binary loss variable also has a positive and significant coefficient. Since a value of 1 is associated with loss, the positive relationship indicates that firms with very low profitability tend to use primarily long-term debt financing.

The indicator of the relative value of non-debt tax shields (*RDF*) plays no role in explaining long-term debt and is linked positively and significantly to the proportion financed by total debt. This result is the opposite of what was expected (DeAngelo and Masulis, 1980). However, the estimation used here, which was developed by Davis, includes tax depreciation, which under Canadian law never expires. This means that the analyses based on U.S. regulations are not necessarily applicable to the Canadian economy and the results presented are plausible.[33]

The variable *EPRR* is negatively and significantly related to the proportion of debt financing, both long-term and total debt. This indicates that debt financing increases in importance as the price of the stock rises relative to its yield (after adjustment). This finding runs counter to intuition, since high share values should encourage more equity issues. It is possible that this result reflects the influence of profitability. By making internal financing easier, higher earnings may reduce the need to resort to debt financing.

As expected, debt financing is associated with larger capital investment (*AI*). Size is positively linked with the use of long-term debt, but shows no relation to total debt. This result is consistent with easier access to the bond market (*TAILLE*) by large firms.

The results are not much affected by the estimation method and by introducing macro-economic variables which marginally improve the models' explanatory power. Inflation is positively and significantly related to debt financing. Turning to the level of long-term interest rates, the coefficient for long-term debt is not significant. The coefficient for total debt, on the other hand, is negative and significant at the 10 percent level. Economic growth is positively associated with an increase in total indebtedness, which may reflect the increase in short-term liabilities during an expansionary period. On the other hand, the link with long-term debt is negative and significant at the 10 percent level.

Lastly, G, which represents the gain associated with the indebtedness of firms, is negatively related to debt financing. The fact that the results are significant but consistently at odds with theory is one of the major findings of this exercise. It is also one of the most puzzling aspects of our study, even taking into account the reservations laid out in the section entitled Financial Choices, Taxes and Economic Conditions.

Conclusion

THIS STUDY HAS EXAMINED THE CAPITAL STRUCTURE of large Canadian firms from 1960 to 1994. It is divided into three parts with the first devoted to trends in indebtedness, the second offering an aggregate analysis of financing choices and the third presenting econometric models to explain corporate financing decisions.

The first part of the study shows that a significant increase in the level of total corporate debt has not been observed in Canada, as has been the case in the United States. Total indebtedness rose from 1960 to 1982, but started declining afterward to reach, in 1994, a level 500 basis points above its 1960 level. If we take into account the market value of equity, however, total indebtedness was actually

TABLE 9

COEFFICIENTS AND STATISTICAL TESTS OF TWO-STAGE AND POOLED ESTIMATES FROM THE VARIOUS EXPLANATORY MODELS OF DEBT-FINANCING DECISIONS

	M2a: Long-Term Debt			M2b: Total Debt		
	Two-Stage	Pooled	Pooled, Macro	Two-Stage	Pooled	Pooled, Macro
Specific Variables						
Intercept	-0.0011	0.0353	0.009	-0.046	-0.058	-0.176
	(-0.02)	(1.67)	(0.24)	(-0.54)	(-1.28)	(-2.02)*
CROIS	0.486	0.436	0.430	0.693	0.548	0.566
	(8.34)*	(11.18)*	(11.01)*	(4.44)*	(6.48)*	(6.70)*
RENT	-0.532	-0.595	-0.653	-1.410	-1.195	-1.385
	(-4.15)*	(-7.11)*	(-7.73)*	(-4.87)*	(-6.59)*	(-7.57)*
DIST	0.131	0.112	0.11	0.309	0.288	0.301
	(5.92)*	(7.00)*	(7.21)*	(9.68)*	(8.29)*	(8.64)*
BP	0.235	0.214	0.22	0.507	0.392	0.413
	(3.67)*	(5.94)*	(6.11)*	(5.46)*	(5.02)*	(5.29)*
RDF	-0.006	-0.006	0.000	0.114	0.137	0.167
	(-0.24)	(-0.35)	(0.02)	(2.58)*	(3.49)*	(4.25)*
EPRR	-0.114	-0.132	-0.12	-0.301	-0.323	-0.314
	(-8.13)*	(-11.60)*	(-11.18)*	(-8.96)*	(-13.1)*	(-12.74)*
AI	0.404	0.408	0.404	0.853	0.925	0.921
	(18.05)*	(35.95)*	(35.71)*	(9.92)*	(37.56)*	(37.55)*
TAILLE	0.009	0.008	0.008	0.005	0.006	0.009
	(3.05)*	(2.57)*	(2.79)*	(1.06)	(0.93)	(1.37)

(cont'd)

TABLE 9 (cont'd)

	M2a: Long-Term Debt			M2b: Total Debt		
	Two-Stage	Pooled	Pooled, Macro	Two-Stage	Pooled	Pooled, Macro
Macro-Economic Variables						
CIPI			-0.002			0.015
			(-1.72)			(4.50)*
INF			0.008			0.041
			(2.80)*			(6.73)*
OBL			0.000			-0.015
			(0.12)			(-1.72)
G			-0.149			-0.327
			(-2.79)*			(-2.82)*
R2		0.196	0.198		0.199	0.206
F		240.186	163		244.403	170.94

Note: * Significant at the 5 percent level.

lower in 1994 than in 1960. The relative stability of total indebtedness is the result of an increase in long-term debt and a decline in corporate short-term liabilities. This means that the concerns expressed by some U.S. authors about the rapid rise in corporate indebtedness are not justified in the Canadian case. Only long-term debt has increased in this country, a phenomenon unrelated to developments in the United States.

The second part of the study investigates the relationship between financing choices and prevailing economic and market conditions. Financing decisions are measured by the proportion of total financial requirements (including depreciation and dividends) provided through various sources of funds. Over the period, cash flow was used to meet 61.2 percent of the financial requirements of growing firms, on average, while long-term debt covered 20 percent of needs. Equity issues accounted for only 9.8 percent of financial requirements, while dividend payments far exceeded the amounts raised through equity. The relatively modest use made of equity is also observed in other industrialized countries, but again the phenomenon is less pronounced in Canada than in the United States, where net issues became negative (because of stock buy backs) according to some recent studies. In Canada, there has been an increase recently in the proportion of financing raised through equity issues (22.1 percent of financial requirements in 1993). The relative importance of the various methods of financing appears to be strongly influenced by economic conditions. Inflation and stock market levels are positively related to debt financing and equity issues, respectively. On the other hand, there appears to be no link between tax changes and the aggregate behaviour of firms. For example, tax changes that made debt financing more attractive did not translate into an increase in indebtedness. The real interest rate is negatively related to long-term debt but does not appear to have any influence over total indebtedness. Lastly, periods of recession generally coincide with debt financing, likely because of lower cash flows. The financing choices of Canadian firms thus largely depend on prevailing economic and financial conditions but do not seem to be significantly affected by tax changes. There are, however, important variations among firms, a subject we examined in the final part of the study.

Four models were used to explain the relative importance of various sources of funds at the firm level, and several estimation methods are applied to a sample containing 7,833 annual observations from 1963 to 1994. The results for profitability and growth are consistent with the behaviour predicted by the "pecking order" theory. Internal financing is positively related to higher profitability and negatively related to growth. Dividend policy is perceived as a constraint. In our debt explanation models, the variable for the relative size of non-debt tax shields has a positive sign, the opposite of what theory predicts. However, the measure used is essentially based on tax depreciation, and since this never expires (as it does in the United States), the results remain plausible. The ratio of fixed to total assets is positively and very significantly related to the choice of debt financing, which confirms the important role of collateral in explaining the use of debt financing. Finally, size is positively related to debt financing. The introduction of macro-economic variables into the models generally confirms the relationships observed at the aggregate level. However, the amount of tax gain associated with indebtedness is significantly and negatively related to debt financing, which runs counter to expectations. One possible explanation for this result is that some of the tax changes coincided with a period of economic slowdown and with changes in the ownership structure of firms.

In conclusion, we did not find any significant change in the level of indebtedness of Canadian companies over the 35 years examined. The only significant development was an increase in debt level in 1981-1982. At the individual firm level, growth and profitability are the two main factors explaining financing choices, while the tax structure does not appear to have any significant impact. This study has a number of limitations, however, which open up several avenues for future research. The main shortcoming is clearly that the ownership structure of firms is not taken into consideration. The type of shareholder appears to influence financing decisions (Israel, 1992; Grier and Zychowicz, 1994), and the tax status of shareholders affects the tax advantage associated with debt financing (Gagnon et al., 1987). While it is difficult to determine precise ownership structures when studying periods of 30 years or more, this aspect will eventually need to be incorporated into the various explanatory models. Second, a number of sectoral factors appear to play a role in financing decisions, such as the nature of assets (Balakrishnan and Fox, 1993; Chung, 1993; Williamson, 1988). The available data for Canada do not permit an accurate assessment of the specificity of particular assets, mainly because of a lack of data on research and development activities. Finally, corporate financing choices cannot be fully predicted at the individual level. Thus it would be useful to do this exercise again using an estimation method based on simultaneous equations. It is an avenue that we intend to pursue in future research.

The results of this study have a number of implications for economic and tax policy. First, the increase in corporate debt levels, which has so alarmed U.S. researchers and authorities, has not been observed in Canada, and so does not require any remedial action. Corporate debt levels rise in difficult economic times or when corporate profits decline. When profitability grows again, indebtedness declines. Second, tax changes that might be expected to affect the behaviour of Canadian firms do not appear to have the expected impact, and so it seems doubtful that the government can influence the financing choices of firms through tax incentives. Third, internal financing is widely used by large Canadian firms, even when they stand to benefit from external financing because of favourable economic conditions, such as a booming stock market. Therefore, there is no sign of dysfunction that might call for government intervention. Finally, the large size of dividend payouts indicates that firms have enjoyed ample cash flows. And despite these dividend distributions, total indebtedness has fallen since 1982. Accordingly, it would seem very difficult to argue that these corporations were under some financing constraint during the study period. However, long-term debt has risen, a phenomenon that is difficult to reconcile with the suggestion that firms experience difficulty using bond markets as a source of funds.

APPENDIX A
ORIGIN AND MEASUREMENT OF TAX PARAMETERS

TWO SETS OF TAX PARAMETERS ARE CALCULATED. The first concerns gains associated with debt as proposed by Miller (1977). This set produces estimates of variables that apply to firms in the aggregate; their values change as tax rules change. The second set of parameters refers to the concept of non-debt tax shields (NDTS). Their values are firm specific.

DEBT-RELATED CREDITS

GIVEN THE COMPLEXITY OF THE CANADIAN TAX SYSTEM and differences among provinces, a number of simplifying assumption were made.[34] An Ontario taxpayer was used as the typical investor and Ontario tax parameters are applied to firms.[35]

Personal Income Tax Rates

The highest combined (federal and provincial) income tax rate for an Ontario resident was used, as supplied by Revenue Canada (tax statistics, various years). The calculation is complicated by the surtaxes linked to certain tax brackets. We used the following equation:

$$t_p = [t_{pf} \times (1 + t_{pp})] (1 + s)$$

where t_p, t_{pf}, t_{pp} and s are, respectively, the combined tax rate of an Ontario resident, the provincial tax as a proportion of the federal tax, the maximum marginal tax rate at the federal level and the maximum surtax. Before 1971, maximum rates went as high as 80 percent for taxpayers with taxable incomes of over $400,000. To avoid distortion, we adjusted incomes for inflation in years before and after 1971, based on a taxable income of $100,000 in that year. The tax rates used are those applicable in each year to that taxable income after indexing.

Tax Treatment of Dividends

Let:

- α: Dividend credit factor, expressed as a percentage of dividends received (for calculation purposes).[36]
- γ: Dividend gross-up, expressed as a percentage of dividends received.
- t_{pf}: Personal federal tax rate.
- t_{pp}: Personal provincial tax for an Ontario taxpayer, expressed as a percentage of the federal tax.
- t_p: Combined personal tax rate.
- t_{pd}: Combined personal tax rate on dividends.

Dn: Net dividends.
D: Gross dividends.

Net dividends are given by:

$$Dn = D - (\gamma D t_{pf} - \alpha_f D) - t_{pp}(\gamma D t_{pf} - \alpha_f D)$$

$$Dn = D[1 - (\gamma t_{pf} + \alpha_f)(1 + t_{pp})]$$

and the tax rate on dividends is given by:

$$t_{pd} = (\gamma t_{pf} + \alpha_f) \times (1 + t_{pp})$$

For example, given a dividend of $1,000, a markup factor of 1.25 and the credit factor prescribed by the federal *Income Tax Act* of two thirds of the markup (i.e., 0.167 of the dividend received), then t_{pp} = 0.5.[37]

Tax Treatment of Capital Gains

The tax rate used is the combined federal and provincial tax rate multiplied by the proportion of taxable capital gains.

Tax Treatment of Investment Income

Because investment income has generally not been taxed at the same rate throughout the study period, the dividend distribution policies of firms must be taken into account. The average payout for each year was estimated by dividing the total amount of dividends paid by all firms, by earnings available to shareholders. The rate applicable to equity income (t_{pa}) is the weighted average of the rates applicable to dividends and to capital gains using the payout ratio as the weighting factor. Thus, our calculation implicitly assumes that the marginal taxpayer is an individual who is indifferent to ownership structure.

Corporate Tax Rate

The corporate tax rate is the maximum rate applicable to income from business activities other than manufacturing. The idea of categorizing firms according to whether they were eligible for the reduced rate on manufacturing income was abandoned, considering that most firms would not fall neatly into one category or the other because they receive income from several sources. Table A1 summarizes the values of the main tax parameters estimated and used in our study for the period 1960 to 1994.

Non-debt Tax Shields

NON-DEBT TAX SHIELDS (NDTS) ARE EXPRESSED AS TOTAL DEDUCTIONS divided by average earnings before deductions. The estimation is complicated by the fact that financial statements report either credits or deductions. We used the following formula:

$$RDF_{it} = \frac{NDTS_{it}}{CFM} = [AMORT_{it} + \frac{IR_{it}}{\tau} + \frac{APR_{it}}{\tau} + \frac{CNR_{it}}{\tau}] / CFM$$

where

RDF: Ratio of non-debt tax deductions.

NDTS: Non-debt tax shields (actually deductions).

CFM: Average cash flow during the last three fiscal years; cash flow is obtained by adding taxes paid, depreciation and interest to net earnings (CF = BNET + taxes paid + interest + depreciation). Average cash flow is calculated for three fiscal years: *t*, *t-1* and *t-2*.

AMORT: Book depreciation according to income statements.

IR: Deferred taxes, primarily resulting from the difference between depreciation for tax purposes and book depreciation. The quantity ($AMORT + IT / \tau$) is thus an estimator of depreciation claimed for tax purposes.

APR: Adjustment to taxes as a result of loss carryover. Dividing this amount by the tax rate yields the amount deducted for loss carryover in the year considered.

CNR: Credits not reported in income statement but mentioned in the notes to financial statements. Dividing them by the tax rate yields an estimate of the amount claimed.

The quantity *RDF* thus represents the ratio of claimed deductions in year *t* to the average cash flow over the three years ending on the estimation date. A value of *RDF* equal to or higher than unity would indicate a situation where the firm is capable of totally eliminating its taxable earnings. This is an imperfect measure. It would be better to have the cumulative amounts for, say, loss carryover. Unfortunately, this is not possible with the data bases used here.

TABLE A1

MAIN TAX PARAMETERS USED TO DETERMINE THE GAIN FROM DEBT[a]

	Dividends Tax Rate	Capital Gains Tax Rate	Personal Income Tax Rate	Corporate Income Tax Rate	Average Dividend Payout	Investment Income Tax Rate	Miller's G
1960	0.520	0.000	0.650	0.520	0.4720	0.245	-0.0348
1961	0.520	0.000	0.650	0.520	0.4720	0.245	-0.0348
1962	0.520	0.000	0.650	0.520	0.4720	0.245	-0.0348
1963	0.520	0.000	0.650	0.520	0.4720	0.245	-0.0348
1964	0.520	0.000	0.650	0.520	0.4252	0.221	-0.0682
1965	0.520	0.000	0.650	0.520	0.3975	0.207	-0.0880
1966	0.520	0.000	0.650	0.520	0.3565	0.185	-0.1172
1967	0.520	0.000	0.650	0.520	0.3919	0.204	-0.0920
1968	0.520	0.000	0.650	0.534	0.3833	0.199	-0.0658
1969	0.520	0.000	0.650	0.534	0.4014	0.209	-0.0533
1970	0.520	0.000	0.650	0.534	0.4014	0.209	-0.0533
1971	0.517	0.000	0.647	0.487	0.3631	0.188	-0.1792
1972	0.470	0.307	0.613	0.485	0.3174	0.358	0.1461
1973	0.470	0.307	0.613	0.510	0.2690	0.351	0.1770
1974	0.470	0.307	0.613	0.526	0.2419	0.346	0.1984
1975	0.470	0.307	0.613	0.502	0.2468	0.347	0.1589
1976	0.470	0.307	0.613	0.480	0.2380	0.345	0.1198
1977	0.466	0.310	0.619	0.480	0.2509	0.349	0.1107
1978	0.389	0.310	0.619	0.490	0.2463	0.329	0.1015
1979	0.389	0.310	0.619	0.500	0.2121	0.326	0.1155
1980	0.389	0.310	0.619	0.518	0.2019	0.326	0.1464

(cont'd)

TABLE A1 (cont'd)

	Dividends Tax Rate	Capital Gains Tax Rate	Personal Income Tax Rate	Corporate Income Tax Rate	Average Dividend Payout	Investment Income Tax Rate	Miller's G
1981	0.394	0.314	0.628	0.518	0.2396	0.333	0.1364
1982	0.252	0.252	0.503	0.518	0.2348	0.252	0.2739
1983	0.252	0.252	0.503	0.518	0.2335	0.252	0.2739
1984	0.252	0.252	0.503	0.510	0.2352	0.252	0.2618
1985	0.252	0.252	0.503	0.510	0.2175	0.252	0.2618
1986	0.255	0.255	0.510	0.515	0.2624	0.255	0.2626
1987	0.347	0.255	0.510	0.515	0.2277	0.276	0.2833
1988	0.312	0.338	0.451	0.435	0.2915	0.331	0.3109
1989	0.314	0.341	0.454	0.535	0.2611	0.334	0.4324
1990	0.320	0.347	0.463	0.435	0.3454	0.338	0.3033
1991	0.316	0.343	0.457	0.435	0.2152	0.337	0.3101
1992	0.316	0.343	0.457	0.443	0.2805	0.335	0.3185
1993	0.374	0.390	0.521	0.435	0.1856	0.387	0.2780
1994	0.395	0.413	0.550	0.435	0.1391	0.410	0.2592

Note: [a] Combined tax rate (provincial and federal) of an Ontario taxpayer whose real income of $100,000 in 1970 remained the same throughout the study period.

Source: The main sources used were Canadian Tax Foundation, *The National Finance*, various years, and C.C.H. Canadian Limited, *Canadian Income Tax Guide*, Don Mills, Ontario, various years.

ENDNOTES

1 Centre interuniversitaire de recherche en analyse des organisations, 2020 University Street, 25th Floor, Montréal (Qc) H3A 2A5; tel. 514-985-4030; e-mail: SURETJ@cirano.umontreal.ca.

2 These models are known as stock models rather than flow models. Analysing financing decisions through models that explain debt *levels* implicitly assumes that firms stay at their target debt level (MacKie-Mason, 1990b, p. 92). The variability of debt levels makes this approach inappropriate for Canada.

3 Rajan and Zingales used firm data from *Global Vantage* and compare them with data derived from OECD aggregated statistics. They found little difference between the two data sources, but pointed out the importance of considering the particular features of accounting systems in order to measure debt correctly. Singh (1995), however, reported significantly different results between "flow-of-funds" data from the OECD and the accounting data of firms. Our study relies on firm-level data. Mayer (1990) discussed the advantages and problems associated with the use of various types of data to study financing choices.

4 Before merging the two data bases, we verified that the amounts reported for the same years, observations and items were roughly the same.

5 Deferred taxes were integrated into equity. Minority interests were deducted from equity but, in order to preserve balance sheet equilibrium, we proportionately reduced all items on the left side of the balance sheet. The values calculated in this way correspond to what would be obtained if the consolidation took into account the proportion of shares actually held and if the subsidiaries' books were structured in essentially the same way as those of the parent company.

6 Trends observed from 1983 to 1989 match exactly those reported by Grant et al. (1990).

7 See Harris and Raviv (1991) for a survey of previous work, and Titman and Wessels (1988) and Rajan and Zingales (1995) for representative studies.

8 Other researchers have simply excluded cases where assets declined (MacKie-Mason, 1990b). Such cases were retained in the first part of our study because they account for a fair share of observations, particularly after 1980, and because the behaviour of these firms has certain interesting characteristics.

9 When a firm acquires a subsidiary and proceeds to a consolidation, the investment reported in the statement of changes corresponds to an increase in all items listed under assets, not simply an increase in capital assets. At best, where a service sector subsidiary is acquired, inventory and accounts receivable items on the parent company's books may increase, while fixed assets will remain unchanged if the subsidiary does not have much in the way of capital assets. The change in accounting method for investments could also change the amount of capital assets without any additional investment. Attempts to reconstruct financial statement items from balance sheets and income statements, where available, have produced discrepancies as high as 100 percent.

10 Contrary to Mayer (1990, p. 329), we do not take net financing flows into account. An investment in a real asset is thus treated in the same way as an investment in a financial asset. If that distinction were made, it would mean accounting for an investment in a subsidiary that is consolidated (with, for example, 51 percent of shares) but not including the same investment if it did not lead to a consolidation (e.g., 49 percent of shares). It is true that taking into account long-term financial investments increases the measure of investment, whereas the use of net flows serves to eliminate cases where financial

investment does not lead to an increase in physical assets. In this study we are ultimately interested in firms' individual behaviour and so treat identically an investment in real assets, the acquisition and consolidation of a subsidiary or the purchase of an interest in another company, all of which are different forms of growth.

11 Treating change in accumulated depreciation as a financial requirement and annual depreciation as a source of financing has a significant impact on the estimation of financing choices. This is probably the reason behind the significant differences observed among studies using this type of data. The accompanying table illustrates these effects. Using the gross flows method, required funds are 200. They are met by an equity issue of 100 and by internal financing (reinvestment of 50 and depreciation over the period of 50). The internal financing ratio is thus 50 percent. Using the net flows method, required funds are 150, which is the change in book assets. The internal financing ratio (retained earnings/required funds) is thus 33 percent.

	Year 1	Year 2	Change
Short-term assets	200	200	0
Gross fixed assets	200	400	200
Net fixed assets	100	250	150
Assets (net value)	300	450	150
Assets (gross value)	400	600	200
Short-term liabilities	100	100	0
Long-term debt	100	100	0
Capital stock	100	200	100
Retained earnings	0	50	50
Equity and liabilities	300	450	150

12 This distinction is important because of the way variables are calculated. A firm that reduces its assets because of a loss will have 100 percent entered into the reinvested earnings column, just like a firm that financed its growth entirely out of earnings. Similar studies usually exclude firms with negative growth. They are retained here because of their relative importance. To be in this group, however, the firm only has to satisfy the following condition in any one year: a decline in assets adjusted for cash greater in absolute value than the sum of depreciation and dividends. Firms may remain in the negative growth category or move from one category to another in different years. This point merits further exploration.

13 Since the denominator has a negative sign, a negative ratio indicates an increase in the use of a financing source.

14 Grier and Strebel (1983) used exactly the same measure, which they called the "net debt incentive ratio," to assess the sensitivity of U.S. firms to changes in tax parameters during the period 1964 to 1976. Their results were ambiguous and only supported in part Miller's hypothesis.

15 The U.S. reforms reduced non-debt tax shields, which made interest deductions more attractive, but simultaneously changed the taxation of corporations and individuals. At the aggregate level, the change in firms' indebtedness was minimal (0.007 according to Givoly et al.), but the adjustments at the firm level confirm the simultaneous impact of individual and corporate taxes on financing decisions.

16 Thanks to J.-M. Gagnon for these comments.

17 Brick and Palmon (1992) established a link between debt and interest rate changes based on the concept of "tax-timing option," which would make debt issues more advantageous when rates are volatile. This variable was not retained here, however.

18 The interaction between economic conditions and the characteristics of firms was not taken into account in the first part of the study.

19 The code "New shares" is given if the firm issues shares, no matter what other financing methods are used; the code "Bonds" is given if the firm is issuing bonds; the code "Private debt" is given if the firm borrows; and the code "Retained earnings" is given in all other cases.

20 In this study, bond issues and external public financing are lumped together. Crabbe et al. (1990) observed that the amount of private bond investments exceeded public investments in 1988 and 1989. These private investments are made directly by institutional investors.

21 See Jensen et al. (1992) for a partial explanatory model of capital structure based on a system of simultaneous equations. Their objective was different from that pursued here, however. Jalilvand and Harris (1984) also used an equation system to explain financing decisions.

22 Thanks to J.-M. Gagnon for these comments.

23 See Allen (1993) for a discussion of these problems. Like him, we avoid them by explaining financing decisions in period *t* by variables measured *ex ante*.

24 Since we are using a model to explain variations, it is the change in the gross value of fixed assets that is related to the total increase in assets in year *t*.

25 It might also be argued that the size of fixed assets is positively related to operating risk, which should in turn be inversely related to financial risk and thus to indebtedness. It is also clear that fixed assets generate non-debt tax shields. Consequently, the size of fixed assets is once again negatively related to debt. See Balakrishnan and Fox (1993) for a discussion of this problem. One likely solution is to measure the specificity of these assets (Balakrishnan and Fox, 1993; Malitz et al., 1989), something that is not possible with the available data.

26 The adjustment of NDTS according to cash flow is necessary because of differences in firm size and the length of the study period.

27 The choice of this measure might be questioned, over alternatives such as assets or sales. Tests were made using these other measures, and the results were essentially the same. While size undoubtedly does not play the same role in all sectors, the growth of fixed assets likely captures part of this sectoral effect.

28 *Ceteris paribus* here means, among other things, that the required stock market rates do not adjust to reflect these high interest rates, leading to a fall in stock prices. Ideally, we should use a measure of the difference between long-term financing costs, similar to that proposed by Fillion (1992). Work is currently under way in this area.

29 This ratio (*DIST*) is calculated with respect to available earnings, while the variable *DIVI* is calculated with respect to financial requirements. This explains the difference in the average level of these two dividend policy indicators.

30 The loss in the first years of the study period stems from the calculation of certain variables, such as the rate of return, over a three-year period. The year 1968 was also omitted from the two-stage estimation because the binary loss variable for that year had only one value different from 0, giving the coefficient an extreme value. The observations for 1968 are included in the pooling estimates, however.

31 The average coefficients are estimated as follows:

$$\bar{\alpha}_k = \frac{1}{32}\sum_{t=1}^{32} \hat{\alpha}_{kt} \textit{ idem for } \beta, \gamma$$

32 Note that the models presented here do not take into account the variability of slopes, but simply the variability of the intercept.

33 Thanks to J.-M. Gagnon for these comments.

34 A detailed analysis of the tax system and its impact on the financing behaviour of Canadian firms falls outside the scope of this study. More in-depth research, including work on various market defects, has been carried out by Bartholdy et al. (1986). See also Davis (1994), Gagnon and Suret (1988) and Suret and Gagnon (1989) for a discussion of the linkages between the tax regime and dividend policies.

35 Davis, 1994.

36 This factor is usually expressed relative to dividends received. To express it in terms of markup, it is divided by (γ-*1*), where γ is the markup factor.

37 This particular example is supplied by Thornton, 1993, p. 106.

ACKNOWLEDGEMENTS

THIS STUDY WAS CARRIED OUT AS PART OF THE PROGRAMME DE RECHERCHE sur le financement des entreprises canadiennes (research program on the financing of Canadian enterprises), with the support of Industry Canada. The authors would like to extend special thanks to Jean-Marie Gagnon for his comments on an earlier draft of the study, Stephan Smith for extensive programming assistance and Isabelle Côté for data verification and processing.

BIBLIOGRAPHY

Allen, D.E. "The Pecking Order Hypothesis: Australian Evidence." *Applied Financial Economics*. 3 (1993): 101-112.

Balakrishnan, S. and I. Fox. "Asset Specificity, Firm Heterogeneity and Capital Structure." *Strategic Management Journal*. 14:3 (1993): 3-16.

Bartholdy, J., G. Fisher and J.M. Mintz. *Taxation and the Firm's Leverage Decision: A Survey of Theoretical Issues*. Discussion Paper 674. Kingston: Department of Economics, Queen's University, October 1986.

——. *An Empirical Study of the Impact of Corporate Taxation on the Debt Policy of Canadian Firms*. Discussion Paper 742. Kingston: Queen's Institute for Economic Research, May 1989.

Bayless, M.E. and J. Diltz. "Security Offering and Capital Structure Theory." *Journal of Business, Finance and Accounting*. 21:1 (January 1994): 77-91.

Bernanke, B. and J.Y. Campbell. "Is There a Corporate Debt Crisis?" *Brookings Paper on Economic Activity*. 1 (1988): 83-125.

Brick, I.E. and O. Palmon. "Interest Rates Fluctuations and the Advantage of Long Term Financing: A Note on the Effects of the Tax-Timing Option." *Financial Review*. 27:3 (1992): 167-174.

Canadian Tax Foundation. *The National Finance*. Toronto: Canadian Tax Foundation, various years.

C.C.H. Canadian Limited. *Canadian Income Tax Guide*. Don Mills, Ontario: C.C.H. Canadian Limited, various years.

Cheung, J.K., S.P. Roy and I. Gordon. "Financing Policies of Large Canadian Corporations." *CMA Magazine*. (May 1989): 26-31.

Choe, H., R. Masulis and V. Nanda. *On the Timing of Seasoned Common Stock Issues: Theory and Evidence*. Working Paper. Southern Methodist University, 1989.

Chung, K.H. "Asset Characteristics and Corporate Debt Policy: An Empirical Test." *Journal of Business, Finance and Accounting*. 20:1 (1993): 83-98.

Crabbe, L.E., M.H. Pickering and S.D. Prowse. "Recent Developments in Corporate Finance." *Federal Reserve Bulletin*. 76:8 (August 1990): 593-603.

Davis, A.H.R. "The Corporate Use of Debt Substitute in Canada: A Test of the DeAngelo-Masulis Substitution Hypothesis." *Canadian Journal of Administrative Sciences*. 11:1 (1994): 105-115.

DeAngelo H. and R. Masulis. "Optimal Capital Structure under Corporate and Personal Taxation." *Journal of Financial Economics*. 8 (March 1980): 3-29.

Eckbo, B.E. and S. Verma. "Managerial Ownership, Voting Power, and Cash Dividend Policy." *Journal of Corporate Finance*. 1:1 (March 1994): 33-62.

Fama, E.F. and K.R. French. "The Cross-Section of Expected Stock Returns." *Journal of Finance*. 46:2 (June 1992): 427-465.

Fillion, J-F. *Un modèle du coût du financement et du ratio d'endettement des entreprises non financières*. Ottawa: Bank of Canada, October 1992.

Firth, M. "The Impact of Institutional Stockholders and Managerial Interests on the Capital Structure of Firms." *Managerial and Decision Economics*. 16:2 (March-April 1995): 167-175.

Friedman, B. "Increasing Indebtedness and Financial Instability in the United States." In *Debt, Financial Stability and Public Policy*. Edited by S.H. Axelrod et al. Kansas City: Federal Reserve Bank of Kansas City, 1986.

Friend, I. and L.H.P. Lang. "An Empirical Test of the Impact of Managerial Self-Interest on Corporate Capital Structure." *The Journal of Finance*. 43:2 (June 1988): 271-281.

Gadhoum, Y. "Concentration de la propriété et décisions de dividendes." Unpublished doctoral dissertation, Université Laval, 1995.

Gagnon, J.-M. and B. Papillon. *Financial Risk, Rate of Return of Canadian Firms, and Implications for Government Intervention*. Ottawa: Economic Council of Canada, 1984.

Gagnon, J.-M. and J.-M. Suret. "Tax Rules and Corporate Financing: A Canadian Perspective." *Canadian Journal of Administrative Sciences*. 5:1 (March 1988): 36-46.

Gagnon, J.-M., J.-M. Suret and J. St-Pierre. "Asymétrie, fiscalité et endettement du Canada." *Finance, revue de l'Association française de finance*. 8:1 (June 1987): 75-103.

Gertler, M. and G.R. Hubbard. "Corporate Financial Policy, Taxation, and Macroeconomic Risk." *Rand Journal of Economics*. 24:2 (Summer 1993): 286-303.

Givoly, D., C. Hayn, A. Ofer and O. Sarig. "Taxes and Capital Structure: Evidence from Firms' Response to the Tax Reform Act of 1986." *The Review of Financial Studies*. 5:2 (1992): 331-355.

Grant, J., M. Webb and P. Hendrick. "Financing Corporate Canada in the 1990's." *Canadian Investment Review*. (Spring 1990): 9-14.

Grier, P. and P. Strebel. "The Empirical Relationship Between Taxation and Capital Structure." *The Financial Review*. 6:2 (1983): 45-57.

Grier, P. and E. Zychowicz. "Institutional Investors, Corporate Discipline and the Role of Debt." *Journal of Economics and Business*. 46:1 (1994): 1-11.

Harris, M. and A. Raviv. "The Theory of Capital Structure." *The Journal of Finance*. 46:1 (March 1991): 297-355.

Homaifar, G., J. Zietz and O. Benkato. "An Empirical Model of Capital Structure: Some New Evidence." *Journal of Business, Finance and Accounting*. 21:1 (January 1994): 1-14.

Israel, R. "Capital and Ownership Structures, and the Market for Corporate Control." *Review of Financial Studies*. 5:2 (1992): 181-198.

Jalilvand, A. and R.S. Harris. "Corporate Behaviour in Adjusting to Capital Structure and Dividend Targets: An Econometric Study." *The Journal of Finance*. 39 (March 1984): 127-146.

Jensen, G.R., D.P. Solberg and T. Zorn. "Simultaneous Determination of Insider Ownership, Debt and Dividend Policies." *Journal of Financial and Quantitative Analysis*. 27:2 (1992): 247-263.

Jensen, M.C. "Agency Costs of Free Cash Flow, Corporate Finance and Takeovers." *American Economic Association Papers and Proceedings*. 76:2 (1986): 323-329.

Lintner, J. "Comment on Secular Patterns in the Financing of U.S. Corporations." In *Corporate Capital Structures in the United States*. Edited by B. Friedman. Chicago: University of Chicago Press, 1985, pp. 75-80.

MacCauley, R. and S. Zimmer. "Explaining International Differences in the Cost of Capital." *Federal Bank of New York Quarterly Review*. (Summer 1989): 7-28.

MacKie-Mason, J.K. "Do Taxes Affect Corporate Financing Decisions?" *The Journal of Finance*. 45 (1990a):1471-1493.

—. "Do Firms Care Who Provide Their Financing?" In *Asymmetric Information, Corporate Finance, and Investment*. Edited by G. Hubbard. National Bureau of Economic Research. Chicago and London: The University of Chicago Press, 1990b, pp. 63-103.

Malitz. I.B., M.S. Long and A.P. Prezas. "The Relative Importance of Operating Risk and Asset Type in the Choice of Capital Structure." Working Paper. FMA Meeting, Boston, October 1989.

Mandron A. "Stabilité de quelques déterminants des structures de capital." *Fineco*. 3:1 (First Semester 1993): 69-94.

Marsh, P. "The Choice Between Debt and Equity: An Empirical Study." *The Journal of Finance*. 37:1 (1982): 121-144.

Mayer, C. "Financial Systems, Corporate Finance, and Economic Development." In *Asymmetric Information, Corporate Finance, and Investment*. Edited by G. Hubbard. National Bureau of Economic Research. Chicago and London: The University of Chicago Press, 1990, pp. 307-332.

Melkinoff, M. "Anomaly Investing." In *The Financial Analysts Handbook*. Edited by M. Levine. Dow-Jones Irwin, 1988, pp. 699-721.

Miller, M. "Debt and Taxes." *The Journal of Finance*. 32 (1977): 261-275.

Modigliani, F. "Debt, Dividend Policy, Taxes, Inflation and Market Valuation." *Journal of Finance*. 37:2 (1982): 255-273.

Modigliani, F. and R.A. Cohn. "Inflation and the Stock Market." *Financial Analysts Journal*. 35:2 (1979): 24-44.

Modigliani, F. and M.H. Miller. "Corporate Income Taxes and the Cost of Capital." *American Economic Review*. (June 1963): 333-348.

Myers, S.C. "Still Searching for Optimal Capital Structure." *Journal of Applied Corporate Finance*. (1994): 4-14.

Nakamura, A. and M. Nakamura. "On the Firm's Production, Capital Structure and Demand for Debt." *The Review of Economics and Statistics*. (1982): 384-393.

Norton, E. "Factors Affecting Capital Structure Decisions." *The Financial Review*. 26:3 (1991): 431-446.

Patry, M. and M. Poitevin. "Pourquoi les investisseurs institutionnels ne sont pas de meilleurs actionnaires?" In *La prise de décision dans les entreprises au Canada*. Edited by R.J. Daniels and R. Mork. Industry Canada Research Document. Calgary: University of Calgary Press, 1995, pp. 401-443.

Prezas, A.P. "Inflation, Investment, and Debt." *Journal of Financial Research*. 14:1 (Spring 1991): 15-26.

Rajan, G.R. and L. Zingales. "What Do We Know About Capital Structure? Some Evidence From International Data." *The Journal of Finance*. 50:5 (December 1995): 1421-1460.

Ritter, J.R. "The Long Run Performance of Initial Public Offerings." *The Journal of Finance* 46:1 (March 1991): 3-28.

Ross, S.A., R.W. Westerfield, J.E. Jaffe and G. Roberts. *Corporate Finance*. First Canadian Edition. Toronto: Irwin, 1995.

Seth, R. "Corporate Leverage and the Business Cycle." *Contemporary Policy Issues*. 10:1 (January 1992): 65-80.

Singh, A. *Corporate Financial Patterns in Industrializing Economies: A Comparative International Study*. IFC Technical Paper No. 2. Washington D.C.: The World Bank, 1995.

Suret, J.-M. and J.-M. Gagnon. "The Canadian Tax Reform and Dividends, A Reexamination." *Finance, revue de l'Association française de finance*. 10:2 (1989): 27-49.

Taggart, R.A. "Secular Patterns in the Financing of U.S. Corporations." In *Corporate Capital Structure in the United-States*. Edited by B. Friedman. Chicago: University of Chicago Press, 1985, pp. 13-75.

——. "Corporate Financing: Too Much Debt?" *Financial Analysts Journal*. (May-June 1986): 35-42.

Thornton, D.R. *Managerial Tax Planning: A Canadian Perspective*. John Wiley and Sons Canada, 1993.

Titman, S. and R. Wessels. "The Determinants of Capital Structure Choice." *The Journal of Finance*. 43 (March 1988): 1-19.

Viswanath, P.V. "Strategic Considerations, the Pecking Order Hypothesis, and Market Reactions to Equity Financing." *The Journal of Financial and Quantitative Analysis*. 26:2 (June 1993): 211-234.

Williamson, O. "Corporate Financing and Corporate Governance." *Journal of Finance*. 43 (1988): 567-591.

Comments on Session IV: Financing Constraints and Large Firms

Seasoned Equity Offerings and the Cost of Equity in the Canadian Market

Comment by Andrew Karolyi
Richard Ivey School of Business
University of Western Ontario

Professor Mittoo presents an interesting perspective on the costs of raising equity capital in the Canadian market. She studies a sample of 108 seasoned equity offerings between 1982 and 1993 by firms in the Toronto Stock Exchange (TSE) 300. Using an event-study methodology, significantly negative abnormal returns arise around the announcement date of these seasoned equity offerings and in second-pass cross-sectional regression tests, several interesting firm-specific characteristics are shown to explain these abnormal returns. Specifically, size is positively related to the negative returns, and a dummy variable related to whether the TSE firm is cross-listed on a U.S. exchange is negatively related to the negative returns. That larger firms, which are not cross-listed in the United States, yield a more adverse reaction to the announcement of a seasoned equity offering likely reflects the limited shareholder base and lower trading volumes experienced in the Canadian market.

This study contributes nicely to the growing literature on the global marketplace for security issuances and highlights factors uniquely featured in the global context: the process of liberalization in financial markets around the world, differences in share ownership and the role of large institutions in monitoring firms. Consider a few examples. Kim and Stulz (1992) showed that the positive stock price reactions earned by American firms around their issuances of dollar-denominated convertible bonds in the off-shore Eurobond market dissipated following 1984 after U.S. tax law changes no longer required withholding 30 percent of interest due to foreign holders of convertible bonds. Also, Kato and Schallheim (1995) and Kang and Stulz (forthcoming) have shown that seasoned equity offerings and equity-linked bond issues by Japanese firms experience a non-negative share price reaction due, in large part, to the ownership presence of banks, which provide an important monitoring and certification role for investors at large. These same factors likely play an important role in explaining the different price reactions to Canadian seasoned equity offerings for the interlisted and purely domestic firms studied by Mittoo. The certification role of the process of listing shares on the major American exchanges with the more intense scrutiny by the disclosure requirements of the Securities and Exchange Commission (SEC) lends some credence to their monitoring role for Canadian capital markets. Similarly, the rapid pace with which Canadian firms are choosing to list in the United States can be associated with regulatory changes, such as changes in the tax treatment of dividends in 1992 and the proposed reconciliation in accounting standards addressed by the Multijurisdicational Disclosure System (MJDS) initiated in 1991. The current study lays the groundwork for investigations that will tighten the link between the interlisting process in Canada and security issuances.

These studies on global security issues test the limits of existing theories based on adverse selection and moral hazard problems (Myers and Majluf, 1984; Lucas and McDonald, 1990) which have been traditionally employed to explain the short and long-run stock price dynamics. Adverse selection models argue that managers with inside information about the long-term prospects for the firm choose to issue the new stock when it is seen as "overvalued," and investors similarly take time to re-evaluate the firm with additional information as it arrives. These theories explain the short and long-term underperformance of equity issues, particularly in relation to preferred and bond issues. Mittoo's study provides an opportuniry to examine, in future work, other stylized facts related to security issues, such as the timing of these programs relative to the business cycle in Canada and the United States (Choe et al., 1993), and the different reactions for preferred stock, convertible bonds and straight bond issues (Korajczyk et al., 1992) with their unique tax treatment in Canada.

Finally, the choice of initiating a seasoned equity offering is identified in many surveys as the primary reason for listing a firm's shares in the United States (Mittoo, 1992). We need to reconcile whether the underperformance of Canadian firms on listing their shares in the United States (Foerster and Karolyi, 1993) is due to the fact that a disproportionately large number of these firms engage in seasoned equity offerings or whether there are unique features due to the segmentation of the two financial markets. It is also possible that the limited scope of the new investor base for purely domestic Canadian seasoned equity offerings uniquely explains the underperformance phenomenon. Disentangling these issues clearly has important implications for corporate policy with regards to measurement of the cost of capital and for regulatory policy with regards to expanding financial information disclosures.

BIBLIOGRAPHY

Choe, H., R. Masulis and V. Nanda. "Common Stock Offerings Across the Business Cycle: Theory and Evidence." *Journal of Empirical Finance*. 1, (1993): 3-32.

Foerster, S. and G.A. Karolyi. "International Listings of Stocks: The Case of Canada and the U.S." *Journal of International Business Studies*. 24, (1993): 763-784.

Kato, K. and J. Schallheim. "Public and Private Placements of Seasoned Equity Issues in Japan." Working paper, University of Utah, 1995.

Kang, J. and R. Stulz, "How Different is Japanese Corporate Finance? An Investigation of the Information Content of New Security Issues." *Review of Financial Studies*. forthcoming.

Kim, Y.C. and R. Stulz. "Is There a Global Market for Convertible Bonds?" *Journal of Business*. 65, (1992): 75-91.

Korajczyk, R., D. Lucas and R. McDonald. "Equity Issues with Time-Varying Asymmetric Information." *Journal of Financial and Quantitative Analysis*. 27, (1992): 397-417.

Lucas, D. and R. McDonald. "Equity Issues and Stock Price Dynamics," *Journal of Finance*. 45, (1990): 75-91.

Mittoo, U. "Managerial Perceptions of the Net Benefits of Foreign Listing: Canadian Evidence." *Journal of International Financial Management and Accounting*. 4, (1992): 40-62.

Myers, S. and N. Majluf. "Corporate Financing and Investment Decisions when Firms Have Information that Investors Do Not Have." *Journal of Financial Economics*. 13, (1984): 187-221.

THE EVOLVING CAPITAL STRUCTURE OF LARGE CANADIAN FIRMS

Comment by Jean-Marie Gagnon
Professor of Financial Management
Université Laval

JEAN-MARC SURET AND JEAN-FRANÇOIS L'HER SET THEMSELVES TWO TASKS. First, they analyse the indebtedness of large Canadian firms and how their capital structures have changed over time. Then, they attempt to develop an empirical framework for explaining corporate financing decisions. At the firm level, they offer a statistical analysis of the relative proportion of capital provided by internal financing, borrowing and equity issues. Their work is far-reaching in scope and represents a valuable contribution to our knowledge of corporate financing decisions.

The first part seems quite comprehensive and methodologically sound. My comments on the second part fall into three categories:

- the impact of the distribution of voting rights among shareholders;
- taxation; and
- the measurement of certain variables.

The Distribution of Voting Rights

This issue, while not addressed by the authors, is not trivial. Empirical studies have suggested two hypotheses in this regard.

First, at the firm level, the concentration of voting rights is relatively high in Canada and the principal shareholder is frequently another taxable Canadian corporation (Gadhoum, 1995). It is logical for these majority shareholders to prefer dividends over capital gains, because the former are not subject to income tax. Therefore, these investors will use their influence to limit internal financing by the corporation. In addition, when the shareholder corporation and its subsidiary or satellite firm face the same marginal tax rate, it will have no preference, from a tax point of view, between intercompany borrowing and equity issues.

Second, when managers are also major stockholders, debt ratios (Friend and Lang, 1988; Firth, 1995) and distribution ratios (Eckbo and Verma, 1994), should be lower than they would be otherwise. This behaviour is logical. In order to retain control, these shareholders hold portfolios that are less diversified and, consequently, riskier. One way to compensate for this non-systematic risk, which diversification would help eliminate, is to reduce the financial risk faced by the firm. In addition, the reinvestment of earnings allows their conversion into capital gains, thereby deferring income tax.

These considerations suggest that it would be difficult to develop a statistical explanation of Canadian corporate capital structures without taking into account the distribution of voting rights. I would therefore suggest that the authors' analysis is only perfectly suited to large, widely held firms.

Taxation

As the authors acknowledge, the fact that Miller's G does not bear the expected sign is puzzling. The figures were carefully estimated, on the basis of reasonable assumptions made at the outset. In addition, the authors' results are very close to those of other researchers (Rajan and Zingales, 1995).

The tax on capital gains is overestimated because it is assumed to be paid immediately. In addition, when the average holding period and the cost of capital remain constant, the overvaluation also remains constant and, consequently, should not influence the estimated values.

On the other hand, when the shareholder is a Canadian corporation facing the same marginal tax rate as the subsidiary or satellite firm, G is nil. In this case, it may not have fluctuated as much as indicated in the authors' estimates. This could explain their results.

It is likely that the authors' observations include several transnational corporations. These firms can use transfer pricing to move profits from one country to another to reduce the overall tax burden of the group. These observations will be a source of noise, or even bias, that could skew the statistical estimates.

It is less surprising to note that non-debt related tax deductions have no significant impact on the results. After all, these factors only sporadically come into play – to be precise, when the probability of not being able to take advantage of them increases significantly. Yet the authors' estimates include primarily the capital cost allowance which, under Canadian tax law, never expires (the situation being different, of course, for commercial losses). In this case, analyses based on the statutes and regulations in force in the United States are not necessarily valid for the Canadian economy. That is why, in my opinion, the results presented here seem plausible.

The Estimation of Certain Variables

I WOULD LIKE TO MAKE A FEW SUGGESTIONS ABOUT THE MEASUREMENT of firm size, dividend distribution policy, the earnings/price ratio and firms in decline. Finally, I will raise some methodological questions.

Firm Size

Firm size is represented here by the total value of the firm's capital stock divided by market value. This choice is no doubt motivated by earlier works on the "size effect," a risk component that may not be captured by the capital assets pricing model (CAPM). Is this the appropriate measure? I do not think so. As defined, the "small enterprise" category includes both large, heavily indebted firms and small businesses with little debt. It is difficult to interpret results based on such heterogeneous observation classes. In my opinion, a less ambiguous measure, such as assets or sales, would make interpretation easier.

I also find it risky to assume that size plays the same role in the primary, secondary and tertiary sectors. For example, the assets of exploration companies or service firms do not lend themselves well to debt financing. Perhaps the authors believe that they have captured this effect in the variable used for fixed-asset growth.

As the title of the study indicates, all the firms selected by the authors are relatively large in size. While the size effect is undoubtedly significant, it cannot be as important as it would be in a broader universe of observations. Hence, we should refrain from extrapolating these results to all Canadian firms.

Dividends

The authors used two measures of the relative magnitude of cash dividends: their relationship to earnings – the distribution ratio (*DIST*) – and their relationship to financing requirements (*DIVI*). The first measure, although frequently used in financial theory and analysis, seems problematic in this case given the volatility of periodic earnings. I would suggest that the ratio of the dividend to the cumulated value of earnings (i.e., adding a constant, to the book value of equity capital) would be a more robust measure that would not require imposing limit values.

Incidentally, with regard to this variable, I would like to point out what appears to be an inversion of the symbols and definitions in the Table 9 summary and in Table 6. This makes it hard to follow the reasoning.

Earnings/Price Ratio

The variable, earnings/price ratio, also needs to be re-examined. It appears to me that, despite the statement to the contrary in the section where the results of the M1 model are explained, the results presented in Table 8 are indeed consistent with the predictions listed in the summary diagram. The text seems to indicate that the authors actually calculated the price/earnings ratio, causing the results to be inverted.

Methodology

The authors quite naturally attempt to explain the proportions of financing coming from each source of funds. The sum is necessarily equal to one. Consequently, in the diagram summarizing the models, should the same explanatory variables not be found in each of the equations, but with opposite signs? Since this is not always the case, an explanation is clearly in order. It is also difficult to go along with the assumption that dividends "explain" internal financing, because earnings are in effect a complement of internal financing and are already included among the explanatory variables. It may have been preferable to use a simultaneous equation system.

Firms with Negative Growth

The authors had the interesting idea to separate growing firms from those in decline. More information on this latter group would be useful. On what basis was membership in the group determined? It would appear that a firm was considered in decline when the decrease in its assets, adjusted for the variation in its cash position, was lower than the sum of book depreciation and dividends. Does this condition have to be satisfied repeatedly? Does a firm have to meet the condition only once in order to move from one category to the other? Are there some more or less "permanent" members of the group? I think that an explanatory paragraph or two would be very helpful to the reader.

Sources of Funds

In the section, Measuring Financing Choices, the estimation of financial requirements is represented by equation (1). In my view, a parallel equation could be used to describe the estimation of funding sources. Then, the proportions appearing in the various tables could be determined using these two accounting equations. This, again, would facilitate the reader's understanding.

Conclusion

I AM SURE THAT THE AUTHORS ALREADY HAVE ANSWERS TO THE QUESTIONS I have raised. I am merely suggesting that they be incorporated into their well-conducted analysis.

BIBLIOGRAPHY

Eckbo, B.E. and S. Verma. "Managerial Ownership, Voting Power, and Cash Dividend Policy." *Journal of Corporate Finance.* 1:1 (March 1994): 33-62.

Firth, M. "The Impact of Institutional Stockholders and Managerial Interests on the Capital Structure of Firms." *Managerial and Decision Economics.* 16:2 (March-April 1995): 167-175.

Friend, I. and L.H.P. Lang. "An Empirical Test of the Impact of Managerial Self-Interest on Corporate Capital Structure." *The Journal of Finance.* 43:2 (June 1988): 271-281.

Gadhoum, Y. "Concentration de la propriété et décisions de dividendes." Unpublished doctoral dissertation. Université Laval, 1995.

Rajan, R.G. and L. Zingales. "What Do We Know About Capital Structure? Some Evidence from International Data." *The Journal of Finance.* 50:5 (December 1995): 1421-1460.

Session V Recent Financing Initiatives

Jean-Marc Suret & Élise Cormier
CIRANO[1] Université Laval

12

The Quebec Stock Savings Plan: Overview and Assessment

SUMMARY

THE FOLLOWING DETAILED ASSESSMENT OF THE QUEBEC STOCK SAVINGS PLAN (QSSP) is based on an evaluation of its various components using different criteria, each corresponding to one of the stated objectives of the program. Originally designed to lower income taxes for high-income individuals and to increase the proportion of savings held in the form of equity capital, the QSSP was revised several times in an effort to channel more funds toward small business. For the purposes of the study, we undertook a detailed survey of the information available on equity issues made by companies with assets of under $1 billion. The performance of these shares and of the issuing companies was tracked up to 1994. The main conclusions of the study are summarized below.

SMALL BUSINESSES

IN THE SHORT RUN, THE QSSP GENERATED A SIGNIFICANT NUMBER of initial issues from small firms, particularly because it coincided with a relaxation in exchange listing requirements. QSSP issues did not suffer from an initial undervaluation, as occurred with Ontario issues during the same period. This suggests that the issue prices of QSSP-eligible shares were adjusted upward. As a general rule, these issues have performed very poorly. The number of issues in the small-business category has fallen sharply since 1987, ending up at more or less the same level as before the QSSP (although the Plan remains in force). A high proportion of small businesses that made initial public offerings under the Plan have now disappeared following a bankruptcy or a takeover. Investors who participated in this aspect of the Plan have been extremely disappointed, and their opportunity loss amounts to several hundreds of millions of dollars.

In addition, the impact on the capitalization of small firms was short-lived. On average, these firms ended up, after two or three years, with the same debt load as before their equity issues. Some are actually deeper in debt, reflecting their stock's relatively poor performance. On average, these companies were significantly less profitable after making equity issues than before.

Our analysis indicates that using fiscal measures to encourage stock listings has, in this case at least, been ineffectual. Moreover, the QSSP has probably been counter-productive by souring many investors on equity markets.

MEDIUM-SIZED BUSINESSES

MEDIUM-SIZED FIRMS MADE EXTENSIVE USE OF THE QSSP, some making several public offerings under the Plan. Several participating companies recorded significant growth. However, it is not clear whether this growth can be attributed to the Plan, for a number of reasons. 1) These firms were often receiving large subsidies at the same time; 2) generally, their cash flow was adequate to finance their expansion needs; and 3) for several firms, a substantial portion of the funds collected under the Plan was paid out as dividends in the same period. Thus, new equity issues were not really needed. On average, the rate of return on the shares of companies in this category was better than that of small firms, but it was not exceptional. In fact, it compared to the rate of return on initial share offerings in Ontario during the same period.

It is possible that the QSSP helped some businesses grow more quickly. However, it is difficult to show that the QSSP was a key factor in this growth, and a number of indicators suggest that it would have happened without this tax initiative.

LARGE BUSINESSES

ORIGINALLY, THE QSSP ALLOWED UNLIMITED ACQUISITION OF SHARES of large firms. Later, the deduction for this type of investment and the authorized amount were reduced. While the amounts of large-firm issues and the associated tax credits were significant, the impact on the capitalization of these firms, most of which had a generous dividend policy, was negligible. Very large firms have an extensive capital base, and it is hard to find an economic rationale for offering them tax incentives for issuing shares. In this case, we considered the Plan's goals of lowering personal income tax rates and increasing stock ownership among investors. The first objective could have been achieved more easily by simply reducing the tax rate. And the economic significance of the second objective has yet to be demonstrated.

The hundreds of millions of tax dollars spent on the Quebec Stock Savings Plan do not appear to have had the expected results, at least in terms of financing small business. While the QSSP may have helped a few medium-sized firms, its overall impact was certainly not major. The part of the Plan aimed at large firms had no perceptible impact other than reducing the taxes paid by participating taxpayers.

THE QUEBEC STOCK SAVINGS PLAN: OVERVIEW AND ASSESSMENT

IN 1979, THE QUEBEC GOVERNMENT LAUNCHED THE QSSP. The Plan had three objectives: reducing the tax burden of high-income taxpayers, encouraging Quebec investors to acquire shares and fostering an increase in the permanent capital base of firms. In the early years, the Plan benefited, almost exclusively, very large firms. Later, the government revised the Plan's rules in an effort to channel a significant portion of the funds invested toward shares issued by medium-sized companies and, subsequently, toward those of small capitalization (small cap) firms. The QSSP became, in part, a business capitalization development program.

Given the significant amounts allowed in tax credits, the virtual disappearance of the Plan after several years of euphoria and the widespread disappointment of investors, a broad assessment of the QSSP is in order. That is the first aim of the present study, which completes and updates the analyses undertaken by SECOR (1986), Lussier and Hawkins (1991) and Suret (1990, 1993). The study is divided into three parts. The first reviews the circumstances surrounding the creation and development of the Plan. It reports issued amounts by category and the total costs of the Plan. A classification of companies is also offered that will be used in the other two parts.

The second part of the study examines the Plan from the standpoint of investors. First, the increase in the share of Quebec household savings held in the form of equity is examined. Next, the pattern of share issues over time is analysed by company size at the time of issue and by relative market performance up to December 31, 1994. A distinction is made between initial issues and subsequent offerings, and the opportunity gains and losses are evaluated for each of the business subgroups.

In the small-business category, the value of issues declined by more than 40 percent. Tax credits partially offset this sharp drop in value, but investors suffered a significant opportunity loss. Few issues in this category produced gains, and more than 44 percent of the shares issued are no longer traded or have extremely low market value. In the medium-sized business category, issues lost about 25 percent of their value, although tax credits allowed investors to recoup a small gain. The overall performance of QSSP issues has been disappointing. The return on small-firm issues has been much poorer than that of corresponding Ontario stocks, while issues of medium-sized businesses have performed roughly the same as initial offerings made in Toronto.

The third part of the study is devoted to the Plan's impact on businesses. First, we examine the overall impact – the definite but temporary increase in the number of first issues and the reduction in the cost of initial public offerings. The impact of the Plan on business financing structure, which became the main objective of the Plan following the 1983 reform, is then assessed for small businesses (assets under $25 million at time of issue) and for medium-sized businesses (assets of $25 million to $250 million). The temporary nature of the reduction in debt load and the steep and lasting decline in the profitability of issuing businesses are then examined. A detailed examination of companies that participated in the Plan on more than three occasions leads to the conclusion that, in most cases, it is difficult to show that the Plan had any significant impact on the growth of these businesses.

THE QSSP AND STOCK ISSUES

THE QSSP

CREATED IN 1979, THE QSSP UNDERWENT SO MANY MODIFICATIONS in terms of both its objectives and its rules that it is hard to regard it as a single program. Its main "constant" provision was that an individual residing in Quebec could claim an income tax deduction for part of the cost of acquiring "eligible shares" of "eligible corporations." To be eligible, a company had to have at least five full-time employees in the year preceding the share issue, and to have its head office in Quebec or pay more than half its wages in Quebec. Portfolio investments could not exceed 50 percent of the assets of an eligible corporation. In addition, the company had to make a public issue of shares conferring at least one voting right. Restricted or subordinate shares were permitted, but the deduction was usually smaller than for common stock. To enjoy the deduction, the investor had to hold the shares for two complete calendar years, although they could be replaced by other eligible shares.

The various rules regarding eligible companies, deduction rates, limits and so on were adjusted so many times that it would be impractical to list them here.[2] Four main periods can be distinguished: program start-up (1979 to 1982), expansion (1983 to 1986), refocusing (1987 to 1988), and attempts at renewal (1989 to 1994).

Start-up

Initially, the QSSP offered the same deduction for all eligible shares, irrespective of the size of the issuing company. Consequently, from 1979 to 1982, investors concentrated their purchases on large companies with dividend reinvestment and stock purchase plans. Most of the tax credits claimed during that period were associated with these plans (Table 1).

Expansion

In his Budget speech of May 10, 1983, the Quebec finance minister reviewed the situation described above. He noted that the QSSP had not been as useful for businesses as it had for individuals, and that 10 or so large firms that did not really need the QSSP to sell their shares accounted for most stock issues, while small and medium-sized firms had not benefited as much from the Plan. Yet, the minister observed, undercapitalization was a more severe problem for the latter than for large banks and holdings such as Canadian Pacific Enterprises.[3] In order to channel funds toward small businesses, firms were divided into categories according to the value of their assets or capital base. Those categories and the type of shares issued dictated the percentage of the acquisition cost that could be deducted; it was as high as 150 percent for developing businesses.[4] The deduction for shares of large corporations – those with assets of over $1 billion – was limited to $1,000 per individual. These changes to the Plan served to refocus investments toward shares of smaller companies.

TABLE 1

AMOUNTS ISSUED UNDER THE QSSP, BY CATEGORY OF BUSINESS AND METHOD OF ISSUE, CATEGORY LIMITS AND DEDUCTION RATES, 1979 TO 1994[a]

Year	Large Firms				Medium-Sized Firms				Developing Firms		Others		Total
	%[b]	Prospectus[c]	Plans[d]	Total	%	Prospectus	Plans	Total	%	$M	%	$M	$M
1979	100	55.41	22.90	78.31	100	17.23	4.05	21.28	100	0.00	100	9.40	109.00
1980	100	0.00	51.43	51.43	100	69.87	10.83	80.70	100	0.67	100	17.61	150.41
1981	100	0.00	157.31	157.31	100	64.68	6.58	71.25	100	9.72	100	9.45	247.73
1982	100	47.08	129.96	177.04	100	27.09	7.91	34.99	100	0.00	100	2.05	214.08
1983	100	173.00	445.38	618.38	100	74.36	9.65	84.01	100	63.15	100	0.00	765.54
1984	75	38.82	475.97	514.79	100	81.58	12.00	93.58	150	106.06	100	2.02	716.45
1985	50	243.94	459.04	702.97	100	267.70	25.00	292.70	150	261.52	100	15.59	1,272.78
1986	50	210.19	192.06	402.26	75	871.08	22.00	893.08	100	449.66	75	1.12	1,746.12
1987	50	24.14	200.28	224.42	75	104.28	21.00	125.28	100	197.03	75	6.44	553.17
1988	50	91.83	n.a.	91.83	75	0.00	n.a.	0.00	100	28.16	n.a.	0.00	119.99
1989	50	24.31	n.a.	24.31	75	1.80	n.a.	1.80	100	21.87	n.a.	0.00	47.98
1990	50	44.22	n.a.	44.22	75	4.12	n.a.	4.12	100	6.00	n.a.	0.00	54.34
1991	50	63.79	n.a.	63.79	75	60.50	n.a.	60.50	100	35.00	n.a.	0.00	159.29
1992	50	209.17	n.a.	209.17	75	115.62	n.a.	115.62	100	40.86	n.a.	0.00	365.65
1993	50	0.00	n.a.	0.00	75	83.35	n.a.	83.35	100	37.98	n.a.	0.00	121.33
1994	50	0.00	n.a.	0.00	75	0.00	n.a.	0.00	100	396.16	n.a.	0.00	396.16
Total		1,225.90		3,360.23		1,843.24		1,962.26		1,653.84		63.68	7,040.02

Notes: [a] Only amounts of shares sold in Quebec are included. Data on amounts issued through dividend reinvestment and stock purchase plans are not available from 1988 on. This table is based on the categories established by the QSSP.
[b] Percentage deduction for common shares in this category.
[c] Total amount of issues offered by prospectus actually sold in Quebec, in millions of dollars.
[d] Amounts obtained through reinvestment and share purchase plans. Because data are not available from 1988 on, the totals shown here are underestimated.

Sources: Martin reports, 1979 and 1987; listing of issues published by the Montreal Exchange subsequently.

As shown in Table 1, the QSSP expanded rapidly over this period. Eligible issues reached $1.27 billion in 1985 and $1.75 billion the following year. Reinvestment plans of large corporations still accounted for the largest portion of deductions claimed during this period. Table 2 shows that the tax cost of the Plan exceeded $156 million in 1985 alone.

Refocusing

Several major changes were made to the Plan in 1986. These can be seen as a response not only to the burgeoning costs of the Plan, but also to some obvious operational problems. First, despite the lower deduction rates, large firms still attracted a substantial part of the funds collected under the Plan during the 1982 to 1986 period. Second, about 15 companies had to cancel their issues, and a number of others had to reduce their issue price or otherwise "sweeten" their offer with warrants. Third, many companies had issued restricted shares. In 1986, 36 issues – 45 percent of the value of QSSP issues sold in Quebec – consisted of restricted shares (Martin, 1987). Finally, several firms had apparently used part of the funds received from QSSP issues to repurchase their outstanding shares.

In late 1986, major changes to the Plan's operating rules were announced in two minister's statements. The most important was a downward adjustment in the dividing line between large and medium-sized firms. Corporations with assets of between $250 million and $1 billion were now considered large businesses, which meant a lower deduction rate for their shares. Most importantly, a limit of $1,000 a year was imposed on the deduction allowed for those shares.[5] From 1987 on, the focus of the Plan shifted to the shares of companies with assets of under $250 million. This was the situation when the October 1987 stock market crash occurred and the value of QSSP shares dropped suddenly, prompting widespread investor disenchantment with the Plan and, subsequently, attempts by the government to revitalize it.

Attempts at Renewal

As shown in Table 2, $487.36 million in deductions were claimed in 1986, while deduction claw backs were $24.24 million.[6] That year, 169,360 taxpayers participated in the Plan. In 1987, deductions amounted to only $181.65 million, while the amounts recovered totalled $60.02 million. This means that 29,760 taxpayers decided not to hold QSSP shares for the required minimum period. The decline continued in 1988, with deductions net of recoveries falling to $90.62 million. The number of issues under the Plan plummeted.

In an effort to stop this trend, changes were adopted to ease the conditions imposed on investors and issuing firms. In 1988, the ceiling of $5,500 was removed, leaving only the limit of 10 percent of total income. Investors also obtained the right to purchase shares in developing companies on the secondary market to replace shares acquired during the two previous tax years with no impact on their allowable tax deduction. Starting in 1989, the shares of developing companies and medium-sized firms obtained on conversion of other securities became eligible for the Plan

TABLE 2

AMOUNTS DEDUCTED, NUMBER OF PARTICIPANTS, AMOUNTS OF TAX RECOVERED AND TAX CREDITS UNDER THE QSSP, 1979 TO 1994

Year	Claimed Deductions			Amounts Recovered[a] on Earlier Deductions		
	Amount ($M)	Taxpayers (thousands)	% of Taxpayers	Amount ($M)	Taxpayers (thousands)	Tax Credits (Cost of Plan) ($M)
1979	49.36	14.35	0.43	n.a.	n.a.	14.66
1980	103.94	28.39	0.83	1.00	0.59	30.68
1981	120.38	33.53	0.90	2.45	1.24	35.50
1982	176.68	44.16	1.19	5.36	2.98	51.74
1983	493.58	108.56	2.89	6.96	3.60	135.28
1984	531.44	121.71	3.15	13.10	6.30	160.41
1985	706.02	155.98	3.98	14.75	8.25	156.54
1986	487.36	169.36	4.27	24.24	13.85	120.87
1987	181.65	102.33	2.50	60.02	29.76	30.41
1988	113.34	80.91	1.96	22.72	15.57	22.66
1989	122.31	60.41	1.43	13.80	12.61	27.13
1990	57.74	43.42	0.99	10.27	8.77	11.87
1991	59.37	33.47	0.74	7.83	6.24	12.88
1992	84.07	19.12	0.42	4.28	4.26	19.95
1993	96.10	18.68	n.a.	4.47	3.42	22.91
1994	53.56	10.69	n.a.	n.a.	n.a.	13.39
Total	3,436.90			191.25		866.88

Note: [a] Average marginal tax rates were calculated by weighting the maximum rates for each tax bracket using the percentage of deductions claimed by taxpayers in the bracket. After 1985, a uniform rate was used because of the levelling of the marginal tax rates for many tax brackets and of a lack of detailed data on the distribution of deductions among taxpayer categories. The tax rates used were as follows: 1979, 29.7%; 1980, 29.8%; 1981, 30.1%; 1982, 30.2%; 1983, 27.8%; 1984, 30.2%; 1985, 27.4%; 1986, 26.1%; and 1987-1994, 25%.

Sources: *Portrait de la fiscalité des particuliers au Québec*, Ministère du Revenu du Québec, 1979-1987; and Martin reports, Commission des valeurs mobilières du Québec, various years. When the two sources differ, the Ministry of Revenue data were used. Deduction amounts for 1988 to 1994 were obtained directly from the Quebec Ministry of Revenue.

at the deduction rate specified for these shares. In 1990, the rules governing QSSP investment funds were also eased. Henceforth, if a fund invested at least 50 percent of the proceeds of its issues in developing businesses, it would enjoy an extra 12 months to invest the balance. In 1991, the deduction for medium-sized businesses was raised to 75 percent, and the $1,000 ceiling on the amount deductible for shares of these corporations was lifted. The deduction limit was raised to $2,500 for large corporations. Lastly, a temporary deduction was instituted for shares that were convertible into QSSP-eligible shares (50 percent for shares of developing companies and 25 percent for shares of medium-sized firms).

These measures seemed to have partially revitalized the Plan. In 1994, the so-called developing corporations issued almost $400 million in eligible shares. However, this amount largely reflects the activities of a handful of firms that made it in this category following the increase in the assets criterion (from $25 million to $250 million). These firms issued, on average, between $30 million and $40 million in shares. Thus, it is hard to conclude that the Plan was revitalized, since it continued to be used primarily by larger firms.

Overview of Share Issues

Table 1 summarizes the amounts issued and the deduction allowed (in percentage) by category, for each year from 1979 to 1994. Over the period, the value of eligible issues invested in Quebec totalled more than $7 billion. Large firms accounted for the largest share – $3.4 billion. Medium-sized firms represented almost $2 billion, while developing and other businesses were responsible for issues totalling $1.72 billion. The deduction percentages vary for each category. To assess more accurately the benefits of the Plan, the value of issues in each category was multiplied by the corresponding deduction rate. The amounts deducted for the three categories work out to $2.35 billion, $1.32 billion and $1.9 billion, respectively, for a total of $5.57 billion. At an average marginal tax rate of 25 percent, this amounts to almost $900 million in tax credits, an amount far in excess of the actual tax credits extended (Table 2). The discrepancy is due to the fact that institutional investors acquired eligible shares but were not allowed to claim the corresponding deduction. Other investors failed to hold the shares for the required two-year period and had to reimburse part of the tax credits they had received. Nevertheless, the main beneficiaries were investors who purchased shares of large corporations, even though the changes made may have altered the distribution of tax credits among categories. Table 1 shows the effect of these successive reforms as well as the impact of the 1987 stock market crash.

From 1979 to 1982, investors purchased mainly shares of large corporations since the tax credit was the same as for small businesses which had very few issues. Large firms accounted for 64 percent of deductions claimed during the initial period.[7] During the next period (1983 to 1986), the percentage of the acquisition cost a taxpayer could deduct depended on the size category in which the firm was classified and on the type of shares issued.[8] In addition, the deduction for large-firm shares was limited to $1,000 per taxpayer. These changes were intended to redirect equity investments toward smaller businesses. Yet, during this period of expansion, a majority of issues were still made by large corporations. The value of eligible issues of large firms accounted for 49.7 percent of the total, compared with 30.3 percent for medium-sized firms and 20 percent for developing businesses. During the reorientation period (1987 to 1988), the share of large-business issues remained fairly stable (47 percent), even though these issues were only eligible for a 50 percent deduction. The value of issues peaked in 1986 at $1.7 billion. By 1989, the total value of eligible issues sold in Quebec was only $47.98 million.

In 1986, the value of developing-business issues exceeded that of large firms. But over the next few years, the total value of issues fell sharply. Although the QSSP seemed to enjoy a recovery after 1989, the growth mainly reflected the activities of large and medium-sized businesses. Developing businesses collected only $103.7 million from 1989 to 1992 – 16.54 percent of the total value of issues, which exceeded $627 million. The QSSP had once again become a program aimed primarily at medium and large capitalization firms.

Table 2 shows the actual tax credits used from 1979 to 1994. The data indicate that the QSSP cost the Quebec Treasury $866.88 million. The tax credits represent the deductions claimed by taxpayers multiplied by the average marginal tax rate faced by taxpayers participating in the Plan. A breakdown of deductions claimed by taxpayer category, from 1979 to 1985 (Martin, various years), made it possible to calculate a weighted average marginal tax rate. Disaggregated data are not available after 1985, and we used an average rate of 25 percent. This is the maximum tax rate for a large portion of taxpayers as a result of the levelling of the tax structure. Martin (1987) used the same estimate. On the basis of the estimates presented in Table 1 and taking into account the differences in deduction rates, the share of tax credits associated with stock issues of very large corporations works out to 47 percent.

Classification of Issues

In the following section of the study, eligible issues are divided into four categories. The QSSP's own classification system was not used for several reasons. First, the boundaries between categories were modified several times. For instance, a corporation with assets of $200 million was considered a medium-sized business until 1988, and a developing business afterward. Second, there appears to be numerous exceptions to the size and asset rules, yet the reasons for these exemptions are not clear.[9] Finally, it is difficult to define fixed-size categories over a long period characterized by relatively high inflation rates. The classification used in the present study is as follows. Small businesses are those with assets of under $25 million (in $1986) at the time of issue; medium-sized businesses are those with assets of between $25 million and $250 million (in $1986); large businesses are those with assets of from $250 million to $1 billion (in $1986); and very large businesses are those with assets of more than $1 billion. The consumer price index was used to adjust these limits on an annual basis.

Table 3 shows the distribution of issues by total assets of issuing companies for each of the groups defined above.

TABLE 3

DISTRIBUTION OF ASSETS OF FIRMS ISSUING QSSP-ELIGIBLE SHARES, BY BUSINESS CATEGORY AS DEFINED IN THE STUDY

Total Assets at Time of Issue ($M)	Small Firms		Medium-Sized Firms		Large Firms		Very Large Firms	
	Number (% of issues)	Amount (% of gross proceeds)	Number (% of issues)	Amount (% of gross proceeds)	Number (% of issues)	Amount (% of gross proceeds)	Number (% of issues)	Amount (% of gross proceeds)
Less than 3.5	41 (22.04%)	153,670 (12.23%)						
3.5 to 7	42 (22.58%)	207,807 (16.54%)						
7 to 14	51 (27.42%)	279,462 (22.24%)						
14 to 25	52 (27.96%)	615,513 (48.99%)						
25 to 50			40 (41.24%)	475,627 (33.07%)				
50 to 100			31 (31.96%)	468,866 (32.60%)				
100 to 250			26 (26.80%)	493,954 (34.34%)				
250 to 500					22 (56.41%)	440,401 (44.41%)		
500 to 1,000					15 (38.46%)	498,452 (50.26%)	1 (4%)	31,388 (3.42%)
1,000 and over					2 (5.13%)	52,856 (5.33%)	24 (96%)	886,123 (96.58%)
Total[a]	186	1,256,452	97	1,438,447	39	991,709	25	917,511

Note: [a] We were unable to obtain information on the amounts representing shares sold in Quebec (gross proceeds) for 10 firms and on assets at time of issue for 34 other firms (for a total of 44 issues with missing data).

THE QSSP AND INVESTORS

THE TWO BASIC AIMS OF THE QSSP WERE TO REDUCE THE TAXES PAID by high-income taxpayers and to increase the proportion of equity shares held in the portfolios of Quebec households. The Plan's success in achieving these goals can be measured. As for the tax objective, the verdict is clear: the tax burden of individuals was reduced by close to $900 million. Breakdowns of this tax concession by taxpayer categories are presented in the various Martin reports and are not repeated here. Changes in the stock ownership rate are examined in the next section. However, the Plan could only induce a permanent change in the behaviour of Quebec households if it is profitable to redirect savings from fixed-income instruments to equity shares. Thus, the gains and losses of QSSP investors need to be examined.[10] This is done in the following sections, first for shares of small businesses and then for medium-sized businesses.

OVERALL IMPACT

AS SHOWN IN TABLE 4, THE PROPORTION OF STOCKS in the total assets of Quebec households rose from 0.8 percent in 1977 to 2.3 percent in 1984. This figure compares with that observed for Canada as a whole. Over the same period, this ratio remained fairly stable in Ontario (rising from 2.6 percent to 2.7 percent). Hence, there is a possible link between the QSSP and the rapid increase in the stock ownership ratio. A similar trend can be seen in the proportion of stocks in financial assets, which rose from 3.8 percent to 9.2 percent in Quebec, while it declined in Ontario. It should be noted that the proportion of funds held in shares increased more in British Columbia than in Quebec, even though that province had no program like the QSSP. The data presented here come from ad hoc surveys undertaken by Statistics Canada. There are no comparable data for more recent periods, and it is not possible to determine to what extent the increase in the proportion of stocks in total savings represents a lasting change.

Table 5 shows the stock ownership rate in Quebec, Ontario, Canada and the United States. In 1977, 4.4 percent of Quebeckers owned shares, compared with 11.4 percent of Ontarians. In 1986 and 1987, the stock ownership rate climbed to 16 percent in Quebec and 20 percent in Ontario, and reached 18 percent for Canada as a whole. Thus, the QSSP coincided with an upsurge in stock ownership in Quebec that closely followed similar developments observed throughout the country. But the share ownership rate dipped in Quebec during the period 1986 to 1988, possibly reflecting investor disenchantment with the QSSP, although this cannot be verified with the data available. In terms of stock ownership, the Plan appears to have had the expected effect.[11]

TABLE 4

PERCENTAGE OF SHARES IN TOTAL ASSETS AND IN TOTAL FINANCIAL HOLDINGS OF HOUSEHOLDS, SELECTED PROVINCES AND CANADA, 1977 AND 1984

Region	Percentage of Shares in Total Assets		Percentage of Shares in Financial Holdings	
	1977	1984	1977	1984
Quebec	0.8	2.3	3.8	9.2
Ontario	2.6	2.7	12.7	11.6
British Columbia	1.5	2.9	5.6	13.8
Canada	1.7	2.2	8.5	10.0

Sources: Statistics Canada, *The Distribution of Wealth in Canada*, 1984; *Income, Assets and Debts of Canadian Families*, 1977.

INVESTORS AND SMALL QSSP BUSINESSES[12]

BUSINESSES IN THIS CATEGORY HAD ASSETS OF UNDER $25 MILLION (in $1986) at the time of issue. This mainly includes firms classified under the Plan as "developing." A few companies below the minimum size requirement of $2 million in assets also issued shares under the Plan in the "other businesses" category. They are included in the small-business category for the purpose of this analysis. Starting in 1984, shares

TABLE 5

STOCK OWNERSHIP RATE IN QUEBEC, ONTARIO, CANADA AND THE UNITED STATES, 1977-1988, VARIOUS YEARS

Region	Percentage of Shares in Total Assets			Percentage of Shares in Financial Holdings		
	1977	1983	1984	1985	1986-87	1988
Quebec	4.4	7.5	9.6	10.0	16.0	15.0
Ontario	11.4	12.3	14.9	n.a.	20.0	n.a.
Canada	8.5	10.0	12.0	12.0	18.0	n.a.
United States	n.a.	18.5	19.6	21.8	n.a.	n.a.

Sources: Statistics Canada, *The Distribution of Wealth in Canada*, 1984; *Income, Assets and Debts of Canadian Families*, 1977; Toronto Stock Exchange, Canadian Shareowners, April 1984 and December 1986; Martin, M., *L'actionnariat au Québec en 1986*, Commission des valeurs mobilières du Québec, August 1985 and May 1986; New York Stock Exchange, *Shareownership Survey 85*, July 1985.

of companies in this group offered a higher deduction than that of large businesses: 100 percent to 150 percent for small firms vs. 75 percent in 1984 and 50 percent subsequently, for large firms. Here, the objective of the Plan was clearly to improve the capitalization of small businesses. It coincided with the Programme d'aide à la capitalisation des entreprises (PAC), which offered subsidies to cover part and sometimes all of the costs associated with initial public offerings.

In most cases, small businesses made their initial public offering under the Plan. These QSSP issues can be divided as follows:

Initial issues accompanied by a stock listing	154
Issues subsequent to an initial QSSP issue	23
Subsequent issues	11
Total number of cases for which information is available[13]	183

Issues: Status and Trend

Small businesses' equity issues that were followed by a stock listing, sold in Quebec,[14] totalled $1.252 billion. At the same time, corporations that remained closely held raised approximately $24.75 million, an amount that we did not include in our analysis (Table 6). The average issue raised $6.84 million. This rather modest value reflects the size of the firms involved. On average, total assets at the time of issue stood at $12.74 million, although this value is strongly influenced by a few issues. Hence, the QSSP prompted very small businesses to undertake public issues. More than half of these issues originated in the service sector. This is a peculiar situation. Small capitalization stocks certainly exist elsewhere – many mining stocks traded on the Vancouver Stock Exchange fall into this category – but what is unique is the listing of a large number of small capitalization stocks associated with sectors that do not generally offer high yields.

Between 1979 and 1994 inclusively, we were able to identify 217 issues in the small-business category, for a total value of $1.277 billion. Only 183 of these issues led to a listing and can be included in our analysis. Information on gross proceeds, issue price and deduction rate for each issue is taken from the lists of the Commission des valeurs mobilières du Québec (Martin reports) and of the Montreal Exchange. The Montreal Exchange's daily newsletter was also consulted to track mergers, bankruptcies, acquisitions and name changes, and to obtain closing prices as of December 31, 1994.

Issues were grouped in a variety of ways, as described in Table 6, to calculate the market value of the increase in equity capital. One group consisted of 35 issues by companies that went bankrupt or whose shares were suspended from trading on the exchange following financial difficulties. These issues accounted for an opportunity loss of $186.87 million, which represents the value of these issues adjusted by the rate of return of the Small Cap Index.

TABLE 6

SUMMARY OF SMALL-BUSINESS ISSUES AS OF DECEMBER 31, 1994[a]

Status of Issue as of December 31, 1994	Number (1)	Gross Proceeds from Issue (2)	Value of Issue at December 31, 1994 (3)	Net Outlay by Investors (4)	Accrued Value of Amount Invested (5)	Opportunity Gain or Loss (3)-(5)
Part A: Small businesses (assets under $25 million)						
Bankrupt	35	170.42	0.00	121.05	186.87	-186.87
Buy back, $ARS > P_{ea}$	11	54.72	132.62	38.18	62.87	69.74
Buy back, $0.20\ Pea > ARS > P_{ea}$	18	95.19	86.13	68.76	105.71	-19.58
Buy back, $ARS < 0.20\ P_{ea}$	5	28.09	5.40	18.64	40.10	-34.70
Traded, $P_m > P_{ea}$	27	243.53	605.25	178.56	234.28	415.36
Traded, $0.20\ P_{ea} > P_m > P_{ea}$	47	372.09	225.94	267.71	371.86	-145.92
Traded, $P_m < 0.20\ P_{ea}$	40	287.99	34.12	215.08	349.81	-315.69
Total, public issues	183	1,252.03	1,089.46	907.98	1,351.50	-217.66
Closely-held corporations	34	24.75	n.a.			
Part B: Initial issues of small businesses (assets under $25 million)						
Bankrupt	28	109.62	0.00	79.88	116.80	-116.80
Buy back, $ARS > P_{ea}$	8	31.51	90.98	21.32	38.23	52.75
Buy back, $0.20\ P_{ea} > ARS > P_{ea}$	17	90.26	82.58	64.76	101.06	-18.48
Buy back, $ARS < 0.20\ P_{ea}$	4	17.29	4.03	12.35	25.64	-21.61
Traded, $P_m > P_{ea}$	24	191.38	585.00	139.50	180.21	404.79
Traded, $0.20\ P_{ea} > P_m > P_{ea}$	42	342.76	208.02	246.00	339.77	-131.74
Traded, $P_m < 0.20\ P_{ea}$	31	185.26	27.15	138.70	208.02	-180.87
Total, public issues	154	968.08	997.76	702.51	1,009.73	-11.96

(cont'd)

TABLE 6 (cont'd)

Notes: [a]Sample of businesses with total assets of under $25 million ($1986) at time of issue (Part A); initial issues only are shown in Part B.

P_m: closing share price on December 31, 1994.

P_{ea}: gross issue price, adjusted for changes in the Small Cap Index from issue date to December 31, 1994, (valuation date).

ARS: amount received by shareholders at merger or acquisition, accrued based on changes in the Small Cap Index.

The classification of shares does not take into account tax credits. Gross proceeds equal the number of shares times the issue price. The value of the issue at December 31, 1994 is zero for companies that have been delisted or gone bankrupt. For shares still traded, it equals the market closing price P_m times the number of shares. In the case of a merger or acquisition, the *ARS* is multiplied by the number of shares. The net outlay from investors is the issue price net of tax credits multiplied by the number of shares. Adjusting this amount with the index's rate of return gives the accrued value, which is the wealth investors would have accumulated by leaving the funds in an indexed portfolio since the issue date. The opportunity loss or gain is the difference between the value of the issue on December 31, 1994 and the accrued value. This calculation does take the tax credit into account.

For corporations which were acquired and whose shares are still traded, an arbitrary classification was established. It is based on the issue price adjusted for changes in the Small Cap Index, or P_{ea}. P_{ea} is calculated using the following formula when the shares were still traded as of December 31, 1994:

$$P_{ea} = P_e \frac{\textit{Small Cap Index as of December 31, 1994}}{\textit{Small Cap Index on the day of issue}}$$

P_{ea} is the accrued value on December 31, 1994 of the gross issue price P_e using the rate of return of the Small Cap Index. The total performance index was used, since no business in this category paid dividends.[15]

When the shares were still being traded, a simple comparison of the market closing price and the P_{ea} of the shares provided an assessment of its performance relative to the index. In cases where the shares were redeemed during the study period, the amount received by shareholders (*ARS*) at the time of the transaction was adjusted by the index's rate of return, on the assumption that shareholders reinvested the proceeds at the market rate associated with that particular risk category. This produces the adjusted *ARS*.

The issue is considered a success if shares were trading higher than P_{ea} or if the *ARS* was higher than P_{ea}. The issue is considered a failure if its closing price on December 31, 1994 (or the *ARS*) was below 20 percent of P_{ea}.[16,17]

In total, 34 share issues made under the QSSP were redeemed, merged or exchanged. In 11 cases, the amount received by shareholders was higher than P_{ea}, and these shareholders made an opportunity gain of $69.74 million. In all other cases, the redemption resulted in an opportunity loss, estimated at $54.28 million.

The 114 issues still being traded on December 31, 1994 include 27 "successes," which together produced an opportunity gain of $415.36 million. However, this amount is heavily weighted by a handful of observations. Cott Beverages ($68.4 million), IAF Biochem ($76.4 million) and Mux Lab ($44.5 million) together generated a gain of $189.3 million for investors – 45.5 percent of the total gains registered. In the redemption category, Aligro alone accounted for $22.3 million of the $69.74 million in gains.

Only 20.7 percent of issues can be considered a success, with returns exceeding the index. As of December 31, 1994, 21.9 percent of QSSP securities were trading at prices below 20 percent of their issue price. Altogether, issues in this category produced opportunity losses estimated at $217.66 million. At the time of our assessment, 45 issues were trading (or had been repurchased) at prices below 20 percent of P_{ea}.

The above analysis does not give an accurate picture of the true performance of the QSSP share issues because it does not account for the tax credit. If the credit is ignored, the opportunity loss amounts to $745.79 million for all issues in this category, with an accrued value of gross receipts equal to $1.894 billion on December 31, 1994. These issues were thus trading at 59.57 percent of their initial value after a period of time ranging from four to twelve months.

Relatively mediocre returns on initial issues during the first three to five years is not a feature restricted to QSSP issues. In several countries, including the United States, portfolios of initial issues have, on average, offered significantly lower returns than portfolios of equivalent stocks (Loughram and Ritter, 1995). Jog and Srivastava (1995) showed that this holds for Canada as well. The return on initial issues listed on the Toronto Stock Exchange (TSE) from 1984 to 1992 was -52.24 percent after four years, while the TSE 300 advanced by 28.05 percent. After 72 months, the cumulated return on initial issues was 14.18 percent, while the index had a total return of 40.71 percent. The excess cumulative return was approximately 24.72 percent after 72 months. QSSP issues, therefore, seem to have performed even worse than similar Ontario issues. However, initial issues must be singled out in order to make a valid comparison.

Initial Issues of Small Businesses

Initial issues have generated average proceeds of \$6.28 million.[18] This is very small by North American standards. In the United States, the 1798 initial issues made from 1983 to 1985 brought in an average of US\$13.94 million (Young and Zaima, 1988). In Ontario, the average value of the 154 initial issues made during the 1984 to 1992 period and examined by Jog and Srivastava (1995) was \$36.9 million.

The results of our analysis of initial issues are presented in Part B of Table 6. It is surprising to note that, on average, initial issues out performed secondary issues of similar size. Altogether, the 154 initial issues produced an opportunity loss of \$11.96 million when the tax credit is factored in. However, if we exclude the tax credit, the opportunity loss reaches \$416.21 million or 43 percent of the gross proceeds of these issues. The excess cumulative return over the period is around -43 percent. Although the indexes and periods used for calculating returns in the two studies do not match perfectly, it appears that returns on new QSSP issues were substantially poorer than returns on similar Ontario issues. The tax credit partially offset this poor performance, but investors still suffered a significant opportunity loss.

Investors and Medium-Sized Businesses

We carried out the same classification for medium-sized businesses. The results are shown in Part A of Table 7. Whether or not the shares were bought or traded at a price higher than the issue price, adjusted for changes in the index was used as the criterion for success. On this basis, 30 of the 93 issues (32 percent) can be considered a success. The group of companies whose shares were being traded at a price higher than P_{ea} produced gains of \$380.98 million. To a large extent, these gains come from a handful of firms: Vidéotron (\$59.3 million), Québécor (\$102.86 million), Mémotec Data (\$36.2 million) and Télé-Capitale (\$33.7 million). These four corporations alone accounted for \$232.06 million in gains. The situation is thus identical to that of small businesses and, again, suggests caution in using or interpreting average values. While, on the whole, issues in this category produced gains estimated at \$116.49 million, no less than two thirds of investors who purchased shares of these corporations sustained opportunity losses.

TABLE 7

SUMMARY OF MEDIUM-SIZED-BUSINESS ISSUES AS OF DECEMBER 31, 1994[a]

Status of Issue as of December 31, 1994	Number (1)	Gross Proceeds from Issue (2)	Value of Issue at December 31, 1994 (3)	Net Outlay by Investors (4)	Accrued Value of Amount Invested (5)	Opportunity Gain or Loss (3)-(5)
Part A: Medium-sized businesses (assets between $25 million and $250 million)						
Bankrupt	7	46.51	0.00	36.27	58.90	-58.90
Buy back, $ARS > P_{ea}$	7	112.93	226.82	87.73	140.09	98.72
Buy back, $0.20\ P_{ea} > ARS > P_{ea}$	10	112.24	123.50	82.74	134.16	-10.66
Buy back, $ARS < 0.20\ P_{ea}$	0	0.00	0.00	0.00	0.00	0.00
Traded, $P_m > P_{ea}$	23	481.11	952.33	391.07	571.35	380.98
Traded, $0.20\ P_{ea} > P_m > P_{ea}$	33	504.71	420.44	383.76	522.12	-101.68
Traded, $P_m < 0.20\ P_{ea}$	13	173.76	32.72	134.91	224.69	-191.97
Total for all issues	93	1,431.26	1,755.81	1,116.48	1,651.31	116.49
Part B: Initial issues of medium-sized businesses (assets between $25 million and $250 million)						
Bankrupt	5	29.63	0.00	26.86	34.78	-34.78
Buy back, $ARS > P_{ea}$	6	90.44	184.30	68.17	111.45	84.84
Buy back, $0.20\ P_{ea} > ARS > P_{ea}$	7	90.07	96.64	66.07	104.09	-7.44
Buy back, $ARS < 0.20\ P_{ea}$	0	0.00	0.00	0.00	0.00	0.00
Traded, $P_m > P_{ea}$	9	225.64	424.92	184.52	267.27	157.65
Traded, $0.20\ P_{ea} > P_m > P_{ea}$	14	201.21	160.70	151.19	206.63	-45.93
Traded, $P_m < 0.20\ P_{ea}$	5	54.91	9.25	44.00	71.91	-62.65
Total for initial issues	46	691.9	875.81	540.81	796.13	91.69

(cont'd)

TABLE 7 (cont'd)

Notes: [a] Sample of firms with total assets of between $25 million and $250 million ($1986) at time of issue (Part A); initial issues only are shown in Part B.

P_m: closing stock price on December 31, 1994.

P_{ea}: gross issue price, adjusted for changes in the Small Cap Index from issue date to December 31, 1994 (valuation date).

ARS: amount received by shareholders at merger or acquisition, accrued based on changes in the Small Cap Index.

The classification of shares does not take into account tax credits. Gross proceeds equal the number of shares times the issue price. The value of the issue at December 31, 1994 is zero for companies that have been delisted or gone bankrupt. For shares still being traded, it equals the market closing price P_m times the number of shares. In the case of a merger or acquisition, the *ARS* is multiplied by the number of shares. The net outlay by investors is the issue price net of tax credits multiplied by the number of shares. Adjusting this amount with the index's rate of return gives the accrued value, which is the wealth investors would have accumulated by leaving the funds in an indexed portfolio since the issue date. The opportunity loss or gain is the difference between the issue value at December 31, 1994 and the accrued value. This calculation does take the tax credit into account.

It should be noted that the gain comes entirely from the tax credit. Excluding the tax credit, the investors' opportunity loss is estimated at $358.61 million, the gross value of issues accrued at the rate of return of the Small Cap Index is $2.131 billion, while the value of issues as of December 31, 1994 was only $1.756 billion. The excess cumulative return on this group of issues is approximately -25 percent, which is fairly close to the return of -24.72 percent measured by Jog and Srivastava (1995).

Here again, the sample includes both initial issues and subsequent public offerings. Part B of Table 7 presents similar information but only for initial issues of medium-sized businesses. These 46 initial issues raised an average amount (in Quebec) of $15.04 million. Overall, they produced an opportunity gain of $91.69 million, taking the tax credit into account. As with small firms, initial issues performed better, on average, than subsequent issues. But when the tax credit is omitted from the assessment of the real performance of these shares, the opportunity loss rises to $141.74 million, or 20.49 percent of the original value. Hence, as a group, these initial issues recorded a slightly better performance than their Ontario counterparts.

Conclusion

Overall, the quality of the shares issued under the QSSP would appear to be poor. Excluding the tax credits received by investors, small-business issues generated losses equal to 59.57 percent of the amounts initially collected, and in the case of issues made by companies with assets of between $25 million and $250 million, the loss was 25 percent. The tax credit partially offset this negative return for small firms, while in the case of medium-sized firms it produced a minimal gain. However, a very small sub-group of firms was responsible for the larger part of these gains, and it is probable that the vast majority of investors attracted by the QSSP, who were unable to diversify adequately their portfolios under the Plan rules, incurred significant losses. These losses probably explain why taxpayers became disenchanted with the Plan, leading to a decline in both the amount claimed in deduction and in the number of eligible issues.

The poor performance of small stock issues is not unique to the QSSP. Loughram and Ritter (1995) showed that initial public offerings in the United States also turned in disappointing returns. Table 1 shows that issues made from 1983 to 1987 have a relative wealth index of 85.5 after three years and 82.1 after five years. The opportunity loss after five years is thus close to 20 percent, while the drop in value of small QSSP issues is around 45 percent.[19]

A number of factors may explain the mediocre quality of small capitalization stocks issued under the Plan. Investors may have been blinded by the tax credit and failed to analyse thoroughly the prospectuses and other available information, paving the way for issues that would never have occurred outside of the Plan. It is also possible that, faced with a strong demand for eligible shares and finding themselves in a position to float issues quickly, investment dealers relaxed their scrutiny. Finally, some companies may have perceived the QSSP as a convenient source of cheap financing, even though they had no viable projects or lacked the management know-how required to handle rapid growth properly.

The QSSP and Businesses

What has gradually emerged from the various statements and program reforms is the goal of business capitalization (i.e., increasing the share of equity capital in the financial structure of corporations). According to Delisle (1985), adequate capitalization is a necessary but not sufficient condition to ensure the growth and restructuring of the Quebec economy, through investments, the integration of new and more efficient technologies, the penetration of new markets and the expansion of businesses. The high cost of capital is responsible for the undercapitalization of small and medium-sized businesses. In the life cycle of a firm, there are two critical stages (aside from start-up) where the high cost of external equity financing may be problematic: the first attempt to attract private capital and the first public equity offering (Budget, 1985-1986, p. A-32). As noted in the 1983-1984 Budget speech, the undercapitalization of the business sector is an endemic problem. It is obvious that businesses must be encouraged to increase their equity capital, and that individuals must be encouraged to purchase equity shares (p. 22).

To achieve this goal, the Quebec government has launched a capitalization assistance program (PAC), which we do not examine here. Its aim is to subsidize equity issues by funding all or part of the direct costs of the issue, including brokers' commissions, prospectuses, etc. The government also created the QSSP, which seeks to lower the rate of return required by investors and, therefore, the cost of funds for businesses.

There are several ways to assess how well the Plan has met its objectives in this regard. One way is to evaluate how much the cost of initial issues was reduced for corporations and how much initial public offerings increased in number and size. That is what we attempt to do in the first section. Another approach would be to measure directly the impact of the Plan on the financial structure of businesses. This aspect is examined in the second section. Finally, case studies could be used to establish a link between the amounts raised under the Plan and the expansion of businesses, which is what we have done in the third and final section.

Overview

Reduction in Issue Costs

One reason mentioned for the introduction of the QSSP was the high cost of initial public offerings. There are three components to this cost: brokers' commissions, incidental costs (analyses, prospectuses, etc.) and the initial undervaluation of the share price. The undervaluation phenomenon has been observed in most countries. It is reflected in the upward adjustment of share prices during the first few weeks of trading and is seen as a cost to the issuing firm, since it does not receive the full value of the shares as determined by the market. Table 8 compares the various components of issue costs for selected initial issues carried out from 1979 to 1985 in Ontario and under the QSSP. The average cost is broken down by firm size, since this variable is an important determinant of the issue cost.[20]

As Table 8 indicates, the QSSP did not have an appreciable impact on commissions or incidental costs, which remain similar in Quebec and Ontario. However, the initial undervaluation disappeared entirely for Quebec issues valued at over $5 million. Moreover, the largest issues appear to have carried a premium of 4 percent to 6 percent. In Ontario, on the other hand, undervaluation persisted. The gap between the two provinces is particularly obvious for issues with a value of between $1 million and $2 million. In Ontario, there was an average undervaluation of 30 percent, which was not observed under the QSSP. On the whole, the undervaluation disappeared in Quebec but stood at around 12.66 percent in Ontario.[21] This situation likely helped increase the number of initial equity offerings.

Increase in the Number of Initial Issues

As Table 9 shows, the QSSP seems to have prompted a temporary, but real, increase in initial issues and exchange listings. Forty new corporations were listed on the Montreal Exchange between 1979 and 1982, while the corresponding figure for the Toronto Stock Exchange over the same period was 175 – a ratio of 23 percent. From 1983 to 1987, when the Plan was expanding, the ratio of new listings in Montreal vs. Toronto rose to 75 percent but, after 1987, fell back to 36 percent. A similar pattern emerges for initial issues, which increased from one or two a year between 1979 and 1982 to 83 in 1986 alone. There were twice as many new issues in Quebec as in Ontario in 1985. However, this flood of new issues was temporary. Only 32 initial public offerings were made under the Plan from 1989 to 1992. One of them was Air Canada's initial issue, and another came from a QSSP investment fund. In terms of increasing equity financing for small businesses, therefore, the QSSP had only a temporary effect. The poor performance of a large number of stock issues in the developing-firm category probably accounts for the current scarcity of new issues.[22]

The Use of Funds

For small and medium-sized businesses, the main and explicit aim of the QSSP was to increase permanent capital. There are two ways to measure its success in meeting this objective: by examining how the net proceeds of an issue were used, as disclosed in the prospectus, and by analysing the characteristics of the firms before and after an issue. Both these methods are used below.

Use of the Proceeds of an Issue

Part of the funds raised under the QSSP went to financial intermediaries. A previous study (Suret et al., 1990) showed that expenses and brokers' commissions absorbed about 10.64 percent of gross issue proceeds.

The average breakdown of net proceeds as reported by issuers is shown below.[23] More than a third of the funds were used to pay off debt. The probable immediate effect was an improvement in capitalization.[24] Only 32.5 percent of the funds were directly invested. If research and development expenditures are included, the figure

TABLE 8

COMPARISON OF ISSUE COSTS IN ONTARIO AND QUEBEC, 1979 TO 1985

Size of issue ($M)	Quebec (QSSP) Number of Observations	Quebec (QSSP) Other Charges (%)	Quebec (QSSP) Fees and Commissions (%)	Quebec (QSSP) Initial Undervaluation (%)	Ontario Number of Observations	Ontario Other Charges (%)	Ontario Fees and Commissions (%)	Ontario Initial Undervaluation (%)
Less than 0.50					3	6.49	11.13	19.93
0.50 to 0.99	1	2.38	10.00	22.57	7	6.76	8.10	28.31
1.00 to 1.99	4	7.19	8.52	-1.98	10	3.76	8.93	30.24
2.00 to 4.99	21	5.32	7.62	6.06	15	4.87	7.47	18.42
5.00 to 9.99	15	2.86	6.84	-0.46	14	2.58	6.94	5.11
10.00 to 19.99	9	1.29	6.55	-6.33	18	2.00	6.32	5.62
20.00 to 49.99	9	1.29	5.98	-4.23	10	0.91	6.05	2.79
50.00 to 99.99					5	0.56	5.80	-3.46
100.00 and over					4	0.20	4.81	-1.63
Average		3.57	7.07	-0.32		3.07	7.11	12.66

Notes: Costs were measured as follows: The initial undervaluation (IUV) is adjusted to take into account market fluctuations between the date on which the price was set and the first days of trading:

$$IUV = \frac{P_m - P_e}{P_e} - \beta_j \frac{M_l - M_0}{M_0}$$

P_m: Observed market price, measured as the average closing price of the first five days of trading.
P_e: Issue price disclosed in the official prospectus.
β_j: Systematic risk of firm j, calculated from weekly returns following the issue, assuming that investors are generally able to accurately assess the systematic risk associated with the share issue from the data available at the time of issue.
M_l: Market index (XXM or TSE) in the first days of trading of stock j.
M_0: Market index on the date of the official prospectus, which is the time at which the issue price was set.
Other charges and brokers' commissions are taken from prospectuses and expressed as a percentage of gross issue proceeds.

TABLE 9

NEW EXCHANGE LISTINGS AND NEW ISSUES, TORONTO AND MONTREAL, 1979 TO 1994

Year	Number of New Listings			Number of First Share Issues on the Exchange		
	Montreal	Toronto	Montreal/Toronto	Montreal	Toronto	Montreal/Toronto
1979	5	29	0.17	0	n.a.	
1980	16	39	0.41	1	6	0.17
1981	13	73	0.18	2	23	0.09
1982	6	34	0.18	1	8	0.13
1983	38	96	0.40	8	48	0.17
1984	52	100	0.52	17	25	0.68
1985	71	73	0.97	41	21	1.95
1986	177	165	1.07	83	70[a]	1.19
1987	123	180	0.68	29	30	0.97
1988	52	87	0.60	30	4	7.50
1989	30	72	0.42	10	10	1.00
1990	17	49	0.35	2	14	0.14
1991	18	35	0.51	11	17	0.65
1992	22	62	0.35	9	27	0.33
1993	38	153	0.25	31	89	0.35
1994	42	143	0.29	17	63	0.27
Total	720	1,390	0.52	292	455	0.64
Analysis by sub-period						
1979-82	40	175	0.23	4	37	0.11
1983-87	461	614	0.75	178	194	0.92
1988-94	219	601	0.36	110	224	0.49

Note: [a] For the period 1986 to 1990, data on Ontario issues are taken from Jog and Srivastava (1995). They do not include complex issues or issues made by investment funds. The total number of issues in Ontario during this period is thus underestimated.

Sources: *Statistiques, recherche et information sur le marché*, Bourse de Montréal, 1986-1992; and *Toronto Stock Exchange Review*, 1986-1994.

TABLE 10

PERCENTAGE BREAKDOWN OF FUNDS RECEIVED BY SMALL BUSINESSES UNDER THE QSSP

Investment	35.24
Research and development	7.65
Loan reimbursement	34.38
Share repurchase	2.48
Working capital	20.45

rises to 42.9 percent. The proportion of funds used to buy back outstanding shares is minimal, which is partly attributable to the fact that this practice was severely limited by the government from 1987 on.

A priori, then, QSSP issues should have translated into a significant improvement in the capitalization of small businesses which had issued equities. What remains to be determined is how permanent this change was.

IMPROVEMENT IN THE CAPITALIZATION OF BUSINESSES

AN EARLIER STUDY (ST-PIERRE AND BEAUDOIN, 1996) EXAMINED DIFFERENCES in the debt structure of Quebec businesses at the time of an initial public offering. It showed that after two years, the debt-to-assets ratio had returned to its previous level. Short-term liabilities also fell at the time of issue and then increased, but did not return to their original level. Overall, the impact of initial issues on the debt structure was small. The same study revealed a significant decrease in average and median profitability ratios after the initial issue. The analysis presented here differs from the that study in several respects. First, we are interested in all QSSP issues, not only initial issues. A firm that made several issues will appear in the sample more than once.[25] Second, the number of observations was kept constant to avoid any survival bias.[26] Third, the follow-up analysis was done four years after the issue to assess the medium-term effects. Finally, we used non-parametric statistical tests to compare the frequency distributions of the main variables before and after the issue.

For each issue, the main accounting data were extracted from prospectuses, financial statements and, for some firms, the CANCORP and Stock Guide data bases.[27] The main items appearing on the balance sheet and the income statement were compiled and standardized. Four ratios were used: the ratio of long-term debt to total assets (long-term debt ratio), the ratio of total debt to total assets (total-debt ratio), the rate of return on shareholders' equity (ROE) and the rate of return on assets (ROA). These ratios were computed for fiscal years -1 to +4, year 1 being the year in which the amounts received from the issue were integrated into the balance sheet. Year 0 is the last fiscal year before the issue. The number of available observations decreases in later years, for several reasons. Many firms are no longer listed on the exchange because of financial difficulties, while others have become privately owned corporations following the repurchase of their shares or an acquisition. Finally, it is impossible to assess medium-term trends for the most recent issues. While the survey included 268 issues, only 147 could be analysed for four consecutive fiscal years, 173 could be studied until fiscal year +3 and 192 could be tracked until year +2. The analysis is essentially based on this latter sample, but comparable results are presented for the two other samples. In fact, it is important to assess the impact on the results of firms whose shares are delisted shortly after a share issue.

Indebtedness

Table 11 shows the main characteristics of the distributions of the four ratios calculated for each of the years surrounding the issue and for each of the samples.[28] Part A presents the results for the largest sample, whose observation period is limited to one year following the year in which the issue appeared in the firm's financial statements. Equity issues clearly helped reduce debt ratios, as the median fell from 0.63 to 0.49. The long-term debt ratio also fell, from 0.17 to 0.14. However, both ratios began to climb in year +2, with the total-debt ratio reaching 0.53 and the long-term debt ratio rising above its pre-issue level.

Part B, which shows the results for the sample of 173 observations tracked over five years, confirms the growing indebtedness following equity issues, at a rate comparable to that observed for initial public offerings by St-Pierre and Beaudoin (1996). The choice of sample does not affect the median or average ratios. Excluding firms that were delisted from the exchange does not appear to have a significant impact on the results.

The ratios presented in Part C confirm the slow but steady growth of average and median indebtedness among issuing firms. In particular, long-term debt is substantially higher after an issue than before. Its median value is 21 percent, compared with 17 percent prior to the issue. The average values are 34 percent and 20 percent respectively. Note that these figures are influenced by a few extreme observations.

The presence of extreme values calls for an analysis of distributions, which is presented in Table 12. It shows changes in the frequency distribution of the total-debt ratio over the six fiscal years surrounding the issue. In year 1, there is a shift in the distribution toward lower values. Then, increased indebtedness pushes the distribution back toward its pre-issue level, although a difference appears to persist between the distributions of year 4 and year 0. A difference test conducted on these two distributions (after combining classes with too few observations) yielded a chi-squared value of 14.17 with nine degrees of freedom. The similarity hypothesis between the two distributions cannot be rejected at the usual 5 percent significance level; it can only be rejected at about the 10 percent level.

Distributions for year 5, which we have not reported here because of the large drop in the number of observations, indicate that by then, any statistical difference between the distributions of the total-debt ratios before and after the issue has disappeared. QSSP issues have therefore had a real, but temporary, impact on the capitalization of small and medium-sized businesses (assets of under $250 million). Three years

TABLE 11

DISTRIBUTION STATISTICS FOR TOTAL-DEBT RATIOS, LONG-TERM DEBT RATIOS, RATE OF RETURN ON EQUITY AND RATE OF RETURN ON ASSETS, BY YEAR, FOR SELECTED SAMPLES OF ISSUES[a]

	Total-Debt/Assets Ratio						Long-term Debt/Assets Ratio					
Year	-1	0	1	2	3	4	-1	0	1	2	3	4
Part A: Sample of 192 observations to fiscal year 2												
Average	0.65	0.62	0.47	0.54			0.21	0.21	0.17	0.21		
Median	0.65	0.63	0.49	0.53			0.17	0.17	0.14	0.18		
STD	0.26	0.24	0.22	0.24			0.24	0.20	0.17	0.17		
Range	2.8	2.3	1.1	1.5			2.6	1.8	1.0	1.0		
Minimum	0.0	0.0	0.0	0.0			0.0	0.0	0.0	0.0		
Maximum	2.8	2.3	1.1	1.5			2.6	1.8	1.0	1.0		
Part B: Sample of 173 observations to fiscal year 3												
Average	0.65	0.62	0.47	0.55	0.70		0.21	0.21	0.17	0.21	0.27	
Median	0.66	0.62	0.49	0.53	0.56		0.17	0.17	0.14	0.19	0.21	
STD	0.27	0.24	0.22	0.24	1.39		0.24	0.20	0.17	0.17	0.39	
Range	2.8	2.3	1.1	1.5	17.9		2.6	1.8	1.0	1.0	4.4	
Minimum	0.0	0.0	0.0	0.0	0.0		0.0	0.0	0.0	0.0	0.0	
Maximum	2.8	2.3	1.1	1.5	17.9		2.6	1.8	1.0	1.0	4.4	
Part C: Sample of 147 observations to fiscal year 4												
Average	0.65	0.62	0.47	0.55	0.58	0.68	0.20	0.20	0.17	0.21	0.25	0.34
Median	0.67	0.62	0.49	0.53	0.55	0.57	0.17	0.17	0.15	0.19	0.21	0.21
STD	0.28	0.25	0.22	0.23	0.47	1.24	0.25	0.20	0.15	0.15	0.39	1.18
Range	2.8	2.3	1.1	1.3	5.5	15.2	2.6	1.8	1.0	0.7	4.4	14.4
Minimum	0.0	0.0	0.0	0.0	0.0	0.0	0.0	0.0	0.0	0.0	0.0	0.0
Maximum	2.8	2.3	1.1	1.3	5.5	15.2	2.6	1.8	1.0	0.7	4.4	14.4

(cont'd)

TABLE 11 (cont'd)

	Rate of Return on Shareholders' Equity						Rate of Return on Assets					
Year	-1	0	1	2	3	4	-1	0	1	2	3	4
Part A: Sample of 192 observations to fiscal year 2												
Average	0.48	0.38	-0.53	-0.42			0.08	0.08	0.03	-0.01		
Median	0.22	0.23	0.11	0.10			0.07	0.07	0.06	0.04		
STD	1.86	1.82	6.11	4.93			0.19	0.15	0.14	0.22		
Range	21.7	27.1	65.4	75.1			2.8	2.4	1.2	2.0		
Minimum	-3.3	-2.0	-64.9	-64.9			-1.7	-1.2	-1.0	-1.7		
Maximum	18.5	25.1	0.5	10.2			1.1	1.1	0.2	0.4		
Part B: Sample of 173 observations to fiscal year 3												
Average	0.50	0.40	-0.60	-0.46	-0.27		0.07	0.08	0.03	-0.01	-0.12	
Median	0.22	0.25	0.12	0.10	0.08		0.07	0.07	0.06	0.04	0.03	
STD	1.96	1.91	6.43	5.19	2.90		0.20	0.16	0.15	0.22	1.04	
Range	21.7	27.1	65.4	75.1	133.4		2.8	2.4	1.2	2.0	17.9	
Minimum	-3.3	-2.0	-64.9	-64.9	-35.0		-1.7	-1.2	-1.0	-1.7	0.0	
Maximum	18.5	25.1	0.5	10.2	356.0		1.1	1.1	0.2	0.4	17.9	
Part C: Sample of 147 observations to fiscal year 4												
Average	0.53	0.42	-0.35	-0.52	0.01	0.01	0.09	0.08	0.04	0.00	-0.07	-0.02
Median	0.24	0.25	0.12	0.11	0.09	0.06	0.07	0.07	0.06	0.05	0.04	0.02
STD	2.10	2.08	5.36	5.60	0.71	1.44	0.16	0.16	0.14	0.19	0.77	0.23
Range	21.7	27.1	65.4	75.1	9.7	22.8	2.4	2.4	1.2	1.2	9.1	2.6
Minimum	-3.3	-2.0	-64.9	-64.9	-6.2	-13.4	-1.2	-1.2	-1.0	-1.0	-8.9	-2.3
Maximum	18.5	25.1	0.5	10.2	356.0	9.4	1.1	1.1	0.2	0.2	0.1	0.3

Note: [a] Sample composition reflects availability of data after issue. Year 0 is the last year before the issue. Shareholders' equity does not include the proceeds from this issue, which does not affect the ratios until year 1.

after an issue, there is no longer any statistical difference (at the usual 5 percent level) between the debt ratios of the 147 available observations.[29] The slow rise in indebtedness likely reflects the poor profitability of firms, a factor we consider in the next section. In Canada, there is a significant inverse relationship between profitability and the amount of debt financing (Suret and L'Her, 1997). While this relationship has been identified primarily in large-firm samples, it also exists for small businesses, as shown by Suret (1984) and Suret and Arnoux (1996). This hypothesis leads us quite naturally to examine the profitability of issuing firms.

Profitability

The most obvious effect of QSSP issues on firms is undoubtedly the significant and lasting reduction in the returns on equity and assets. Looking again at the right side of Table 11 (in Part C), we can see that the median ROE falls from 25 percent in period 0 to 12 percent once the issue is integrated into the firm's financial statements. This is not simply an arithmetic consequence of the increase in equity capital. Indeed, the median ROE continues to decline, reaching 9 percent by year 4. A similar pattern emerges from Part A and Part B, so the drop in the profitability of issuing firms cannot be attributed to the sample. It should be noted that the least profitable firms generally disappear three years after issue. The pattern of ROA values is also quite clear: the median falls from 7 percent prior to issue to 2 percent in year 4.[30]

Part B of Table 12 shows the distribution of ROE values over time. Prior to issue, less than 10 percent of firms had negative rates of return, which would indicate losses. The proportion rises to 28.57 percent by year 4. At the other end of the distribution, the percentage of firms reporting a ROE above 30 percent fell from 40.8 percent prior to issue to 5.4 percent by year 4. Combining distribution categories, we obtain a chi-square value (90.89, with nine degrees of freedom) that allows us to reject the hypothesis of equal distributions in periods -1 and +4 at a confidence level of 1 percent. Clearly, the distribution of rates of return exhibits no sign of a recovery that might indicate a temporary disequilibrium linked to equity issues. The lower leverage may partly explain this decline, but the real reason lies elsewhere. As the reduction in indebtedness is temporary and relatively minor in the medium run, it cannot account for the decline in the ROA. The most likely explanation for the significant and lasting decline in the rate of return is that the projects contemplated by issuing firms did not offer a rate of return higher than the cost of capital. Hence, these firms were not truly facing a financing problem, defined as an inability to fund profitable projects. This is a potentially important finding. It suggests that the QSSP did not channel funds toward profitable activities, but rather toward projects with such low rates of return that they did not warrant financing.

TABLE 12

DISTRIBUTIONS OF ABSOLUTE AND RELATIVE FREQUENCIES OF TOTAL-DEBT RATIOS AND RATES OF RETURN ON EQUITY FOR A CONSTANT SAMPLE OF 142 ISSUES MADE UNDER THE QSSP BY COMPANIES WITH ASSETS OF UNDER $250 MILLION AT TIME OF ISSUE

	Year -1		Year 0		Year 1		Year 2		Year 3		Year 4	
	A[a]	R (%)	A	R (%)	A	R (%)	A	R (%)	A	R (%)	A	R (%)
Part A: Total-debt/assets ratio												
Less than 0.1	4	2.72	2	1.36	5	3.40	5	3.40	3	2.04	4	2.72
0.1 to 0.2	4	2.72	6	4.08	13	8.84	9	6.12	7	4.76	6	4.08
0.2 to 0.3	3	2.04	8	5.44	14	9.52	5	3.40	6	4.08	10	6.80
0.3 to 0.4	8	5.44	7	4.76	23	15.65	19	12.93	21	14.29	13	8.84
0.4 to 0.5	13	8.84	16	10.88	20	13.61	24	16.33	28	19.05	20	13.61
0.5 to 0.6	22	14.97	29	19.73	38	25.85	33	22.45	32	21.77	34	23.13
0.6 to 0.7	31	21.09	28	19.05	20	13.61	21	14.29	17	11.56	24	16.33
0.7 to 0.8	36	24.49	28	19.05	4	2.72	14	9.52	15	10.20	13	8.84
0.8 to 0.9	17	11.56	13	8.84	5	3.40	9	6.12	5	3.40	8	5.44
0.9 to 1.0	4	2.72	7	4.76	2	1.36	5	3.40	7	4.76	5	3.40
1.0 to 1.1	3	2.04	1	0.68	2	1.36	1	0.68	3	2.04	6	4.08
Over 1.1	2	1.36	2	1.36	1	0.68	2	1.36	3	2.04	4	2.72

(cont'd)

TABLE 12 (cont'd)

	Year -1		Year 0		Year 1		Year 2		Year 3		Year 4	
	A[a]	R (%)	A	R (%)	A	R (%)	A	R (%)	A	R (%)	A	R (%)
Part B: Rate of return on equity (ROE)												
Less than -0.1	4	2.72	7	4.76	7	4.76	16	10.88	21	14.29	27	18.37
-0.1 to -0.05	3	2.04	1	0.68	1	0.68	6	4.08	7	4.76	4	2.72
-0.05 to 0	6	4.08	6	4.08	11	7.48	10	6.80	11	7.48	11	7.48
0 to 0.05	3	2.04	5	3.40	14	9.52	12	8.16	14	9.52	23	15.65
0.05 to 0.1	12	8.16	14	9.52	28	19.05	29	19.73	28	19.05	27	18.37
0.1 to 0.15	16	10.88	14	9.52	34	23.13	29	19.73	33	22.45	24	16.33
0.15 to 0.2	16	10.88	17	11.56	32	21.77	21	14.29	15	10.20	12	8.16
0.2 to 0.25	17	11.56	9	6.12	11	7.48	17	11.56	9	6.12	9	6.12
0.25 to 0.3	9	6.12	14	9.52	5	3.40	5	3.40	3	2.04	2	1.36
0.3 to 0.35	15	10.20	18	12.24	2	1.36	0	0.00	2	1.36	0	0.00
0.35 to 0.4	12	8.16	6	4.08	0	0.00	1	0.68	0	0.00	0	0.00
0.4 to 0.45	6	4.08	6	4.08	0	0.00	0	0.00	0	0.00	1	0.68
0.45 to 0.5	3	2.04	9	6.12	1	0.68	0	0.00	0	0.00	0	0.00
0.5 to 0.55	4	2.72	3	2.04	1	0.68	0	0.00	0	0.00	1	0.68
Over 0.55	21	14.29	18	12.24	0	0.00	1	0.68	4	2.72	6	4.08

Note: [a] A: absolute frequency; R: relative frequency.

CASE-BY-CASE ANALYSIS

IN THE FOREGOING ANALYSIS, WE ONLY CONSIDERED FIRMS WITH ASSETS of under $250 million. While the analysis sheds some light on equity issues generally, it conceals important disparities. It is also limited by the fact that, during the study period, several firms crossed the limits arbitrarily set between categories. Also, a separate analysis gets more complicated as firms proceed to three, four or five successive equity issues. These considerations have led us to conduct a case-by-case study of the large and medium-sized businesses that have used the Plan most often. This group consisted of 10 Quebec corporations, listed in Table 13, whose combined assets rose over the period from $1.7 billion to $14.9 billion. The criterion for inclusion was that they issued shares under the QSSP at least three times. These issues totalled more than $1.22 billion, but the amount invested in Quebec was $752 million. Whether the funds collected had a significant impact of the growth of these firms remains to be determined.

The main data on these firms come from their prospectuses and annual reports, and are summarized in Table 13, which shows assets and equity at the beginning and end of the study period, changes in equity and dividends paid on common shares. The ratio of funds obtained through QSSP issues to changes in equity was calculated, as well as the ratio of dividends to funds raised under the Plan.

Table 13 illustrates the wide variety of conditions facing the sample firms, which can be divided into two groups. The first group includes firms that paid out, in dividends, amounts close to or exceeding the funds raised from QSSP issues. These firms are: Donohue, with dividends of 194.38 percent of QSSP funds collected in Quebec, Bombardier (126.21 percent), UAP (121.11 percent), Québécor (78.76 percent), and Mémotec Data-Téléglobe (55.72 percent). Altogether, these companies paid $410.8 million in dividends, while they issued $338 million of tax-credit-eligible shares. Therefore, it seems difficult to suggest that the Plan played a significant role in the growth of these firms. Had the Plan not existed, the funds needed to finance their growth could have been freed up by reducing the amounts paid out in dividends.

In the second group, we find corporations that paid relatively low dividends and seemed to have used the funds raised to strengthen their capital base. They are: Cascades, Gaz Métropolitain, Groupe Transcontinental GTC, Métro-Richelieu and Tembec. The suggestion that the Plan had an impact on the growth of participating firms is only valid for this subsample. This impact can be measured by expressing the funds collected through QSSP issues as a percentage of the net change in equity. This provides an estimate of the relative contribution of QSSP issues to the increase in these companies' capital base. The percentage ranges from 10.37 percent for Québécor to 42.29 percent for Métro-Richelieu.

This brief analysis reveals that the relationship between large businesses and the QSSP varies widely. While it is difficult to draw any general conclusions from this exercise, it seems clear that the Plan was of little use for the majority of firms studied, since they were able to pay shareholders more than they collected in Quebec under the Plan. For three of the firms that paid relatively low dividends on ordinary shares, the funds raised through QSSP issues accounted for 20 percent of

TABLE 13

TOTAL AMOUNTS COLLECTED UNDER THE QSSP, CHANGES IN ASSETS AND SHAREHOLDERS' EQUITY, AND AMOUNTS PAID OUT AS DIVIDENDS BETWEEN THE FIRST QSSP ISSUE AND 1993, MEDIUM-SIZED BUSINESSES THAT MADE AT LEAST THREE ISSUES

	Issues			Total Assets		Equity Capital		Increase in Capital	Dividends	QSSP Funds as % of Increase in Capital	Dividends as % of QSSP Funds
	N[a]	Gross Proceeds		At Time of First Issue (1979-86)	In 1993	At Time of First Issue (1979-86)	In 1993				
		Total	Sold in Quebec								
Bombardier	4	247.2	103.4	277.4	4,270.0	98.3	984.1	885.8	130.5	11.67	126.21
Cascades Inc.	4	65.7	64.1	24.4	1,400.9	6.3	383.7	376.9	0.2	17.01	0.27
Donohue	3	119.2	61.5	570.4	766.2	121.3	379.6	258.3	119.6	23.82	194.38
Gaz Métropolitain[b]	5	170.2	126.4	304.8	1,204.4	107.8	430.6	322.8	39.2	39.15	31.05
Groupe G.T.C.	3	57.3	48.2	32.9	616.1	5.7	247.7	242.0	5.3	19.92	10.97
Mémotec Data (Téléglobe)	5	221.7	120.9	4.5	1,768.2	1.0	701.4	700.4	67.4	17.26	55.72
Métro-Richelieu	3	84.0	84.0	257.5	587.4	43.1	241.6	198.5	0.0	42.29	0.00
Québécor	3	116.7	73.4	75.8	2,986.6	34.5	742.3	707.9	57.8	10.37	78.76
Tembec	4	113.6	40.9	130.4	974.7	35.4	234.2	198.7	0.0	20.58	0.00
U.A.P.	3	31.9	29.3	73.6	306.2	22.8	165.1	142.4	35.5	20.56	121.11
Total	37	1,227.3	752.0	1,751.6	14,880.7	476.2	4,510.3	4,034.1	455.4	18.64	60.56

Notes: [a] Total number of issues made under the Plan, all categories combined.
[b] Data for this company are incomplete. Assets in last fiscal year before buy back of issued shares are for 1991. Data on dividends cover only the period 1979 to 1982. Dividends were paired to the amount of issues placed in Quebec for the corresponding period. Data taken mainly from the CANCORP data base.

the increase in equity. In only one case (Métro-Richelieu) did QSSP funds represent a significant portion of the change in equity capital (42.29 percent). However, the relatively modest increase in equity capital in that case was associated with low profits during the period 1986 to 1990 ($1.69 million a year on average).

Our study of firms that benefited most from the QSSP fails to demonstrate that the Plan provided critical support for financing their growth. While it might have had a significant impact on a few firms, the majority of those examined could have obtained the required funds simply by reducing dividends. These findings are consistent with the results from a questionnaire survey of executives of firms with assets exceeding $25 million undertaken by SECOR (1986). Sixty-seven percent of respondents indicated that without the QSSP their company's growth would have been the same or only slightly different. Only 22 percent of respondents said their firm's growth would have been stalled or seriously hampered.

The case study approach should be pursued further as several questions have not yet been addressed. For instance, it seems that funds raised from QSSP issues may have been used by some firms to finance foreign investments or modernization projects that had no positive impact on employment in Quebec. Another factor to take into account is government intervention in its various forms during this period, for example subsidies and tax credits that were made available to businesses. However, these questions lie outside the scope of our study.

Very Large Businesses

Although they account for a very large part of tax credits offered under the QSSP, we did not pay particular attention to very large firms in this study. The market capitalization of most of these firms exceeded $1 billion toward the middle of the period reviewed.[31] Financing problems cannot be claimed in their case, and trying to assess the impact of the Plan on their indebtedness would have little significance. The only purpose in making their shares eligible for the Plan was to reduce the tax burden of individuals and to increase the proportion of savings held in the form of equity capital. We have already discussed the extent to which these two objectives were met.

Conclusion

Several objectives were pursued through the QSSP and at least one of them was met. That objective was to reduce the tax burden, and taxpayers did receive tax credits estimated at close to $900 million. It could be argued, however, that there are less complicated ways to reduce personal income taxes. Quebeckers' stock ownership also increased, but given the questionable quality of some of the shares issued under the Plan and the losses incurred by a large number of taxpayers, this increase may prove to be temporary, as it was for initial issues. These issues, like new exchange listings, have fallen back to the level (relative to the Toronto Stock Exchange) at which they stood before the Plan was put in place.

Efforts to use tax credits to encourage small firms to list their shares on the stock exchange seemed to have failed. Using a performance superior to the index as a benchmark, only a very small proportion of firms that made equity issues under the Plan were successful. Bankruptcies and large drops in value were particularly common among small businesses, whose issues lost more than 40 percent of their initial value. An analysis of firms' indebtedness shows that the improvement in their capital base was temporary. After three years, the debt-ratio distribution of firms with assets of under $250 million at the time of issue was statistically identical to that observed prior to the issue. The most troubling observation is probably the significant decline in the return on assets and the return on equity of issuing firms, a phenomenon that persists three years after the issue. The most likely explanation is that these firms did not have profitable projects to finance with the funds raised through the QSSP. A detailed study of a few larger firms that used the QSSP on more than one occasion showed that many were able to pay their shareholders dividends equal to or greater than the amounts collected under the Plan.

It would seem difficult to argue that the QSSP had a lasting impact on the capitalization of businesses. Instead, it made it easier for firms to list their shares on the stock exchange without projects offering returns at least equal to their financing costs. Without the Plan, it would have been difficult for these firms to find funds for their projects – and rightly so. It was government intervention that made it possible. The end result is that firms that survived show accounting rates of return that are very low and significantly below pre-issue rates of return. Low returns translate into disappointing market performance for investors.

Of course, there are exceptions. Some small firms may have turned into world-class businesses thanks to the QSSP. As well, some investors made healthy gains. Nonetheless, after examining all the equity issues made by firms with assets of under $1 billion and tracking the performance of all eligible firms after their initial equity issue under the Plan, we find ourselves unable to conclude that the QSSP had a significant impact on the capitalization and growth of Quebec businesses.

APPENDIX 1

MAJOR CHANGES TO THE QUEBEC STOCK SAVINGS PLAN, 1979-94

THE MAIN STAGES IN THE EVOLUTION OF THE QUEBEC STOCK SAVINGS PLAN are described below.

June 22, 1979: Creation of the Quebec Stock Savings Plan.

Budget of May 10, 1983: New direction given to the Quebec Stock Savings Plan to improve access to small and medium-sized businesses.

1) Introduction of the concept of a "developing business," i.e., a firm with assets of between $2 million and $25 million *or* with net shareholders' equity of $750,000 to $10 million. Shares of these corporations eligible to a deduction equal to 150 percent of their acquisition cost.
2) Henceforth, only ordinary shares with full voting rights (or preferred shares convertible into ordinary shares) are eligible.

Minister's statement of May 3, 1994: Restricted shares with voting rights become eligible.

Budget of April 23, 1985

1) Changes to deduction rates effective January 1, 1986:
   Developing businesses: rate lowered from 150 percent to 100 percent for ordinary shares, and from 100 percent to 75 percent for restricted shares.
   Medium-sized businesses: rate lowered from 100 percent to 75 percent for ordinary shares, and from 75 percent to 50 percent for restricted shares.
   Large businesses: rate maintained at 50 percent; maximum annual deduction of $1,000.
2) Maximum annual deduction: the lower of 20 percent of total income or $20,000.
3) Reduction in $20,000 ceiling to $12,000 announced in 1986.
4) Government announces that it will be possible to create QSSP investment corporations and QSSP investment funds (FIR) effective April 24, 1985. A FIR must commit to invest all or part of the funds collected in QSSP-eligible shares, receiving in return deductions comparable to those granted for the direct acquisition of QSSP shares.

Budget of May 1, 1986 and Minister's statement of May 29, 1986: Announcement of measures contained in Bill 120.

November 11, 1986: Tabling of Bill 120 (modifying various tax-related statutory provisions) **and Minister's statement.**

1) Rules to limit share buy back with funds raised through an eligible issue.
2) The deduction ceiling of $1,000 for large-business shares is extended to shares of firms with assets of over $250 million; the minimum asset level for this category is lowered, thereby modifying the deduction rates.
3) The deduction rate for restricted shares is set at 50 percent.

December 11, 1986: Minister's statement

1) Creation of a new type of eligible business: regional venture capital corporations.
2) Listing on exchange: To be eligible for the purposes of the Plan, firms (except regional venture capital corporations) must have their QSSP-eligible shares listed on the Montreal Exchange within 60 days of the issue date.
3) New restrictions imposed on the repurchase of shares with the proceeds of an issue.

1987 Budget: Announcement of a reduction in the allowable deduction from $12,000 to $5,500 effective in 1987.

Budget of May 12, 1988

1) The maximum amount that an individual may deduct in one year is limited to 10 percent of his total income. The ceiling of $5,500 is abolished.
2) The category "developing businesses" is expanded to include firms with assets of between $2 million and $50 million or with a net equity of $750,000 to $20 million.
3) New measures designed to stimulate the secondary market: investors will now be able to purchase shares of developing businesses on the secondary market to replace shares acquired during the previous two tax years without any tax consequences.

Budget of May 16, 1989

To revitalize the QSSP, shares otherwise eligible that are acquired by an individual through the conversion of debentures or convertible preferred shares of corporations with assets of under $250 million (i.e., medium-sized and developing businesses) are made eligible for the purposes of the Plan, at the applicable deduction rate.

Budget of April 26, 1990

Regulations governing FIRs are relaxed. As long as these funds invest at least 50 percent of receipts from their QSSP issues in developing businesses, they have an additional 12 months to invest the balance in QSSP-eligible shares.

Budget of May 1991

1) Change in categories and deduction rates, as follows:
Developing businesses: Assets of between $2 million and $250 million; net equity requirement dropped, deduction rate remains at 100 percent.
Medium-sized businesses: Assets of between $250 million and $1 billion; deduction rate raised to 75 percent, deduction ceiling of $1,000 dropped.
Large businesses: Assets of between $1 billion and $2.5 billion; deduction rate remains at 50 percent, $1,000 ceiling raised to $2,500 for 1991 and 1992.
2) Changes in deduction rate for convertible shares: temporary deduction on convertible shares of 50 percent (developing businesses) and 25 percent (medium-sized businesses); no longer necessary to wait for conversion to use the tax deduction.
3) Following the Montreal Exchange decision to eliminate restricted shares, this category is removed.

1992 Budget: No changes.

TABLE A1

MAJOR CHANGES TO THE QUEBEC STOCK SAVINGS PLAN, 1983 TO 1991

	1983	1984	1985	1986	1987	1988	1989[a]	1990	1991	1992	1993	1994
Large businesses												
Size limit, assets	over $1 billion				over $250 million				$1 to $2.5 billion			
Deduction for ordinary shares (%)	100	75	50	50	50	50	50	50	50	50	50	50
Deduction for restricted shares (%)	n.a.	75	50	50	50	50	50	50	n.a.	n.a.	n.a.	n.a
Medium-sized businesses												
Size limit, assets	$25 million to $1 billion				$25 to $250 million	$50 to $250 million			$250 million to $1 billion			
Deduction for ordinary shares (%)	100	100	100	75	75	75	75	75	75	75	75	75
Deduction for restricted shares (%)	n.a.	75	75	50	50	50	50	50	n.a.	n.a.	n.a.	n.a.
Deduction for convertible shares (%)	n.a.	n.a.	n.a.	n.a.	n.a.	n.a.	n.a.	n.a.	25	25	25	25

(cont'd)

TABLE A1 (cont'd)

	1983	1984	1985	1986	1987	1988	1989[a]	1990	1991	1992	1993	1994
Developing businesses												
Size limit, assets	$2 to $25 million or equity of $750,000 to $1 million				$2 to $25 million or equity of $750,000 to $1 million	$2 to $50 million or equity of $750,000 to $1 million			$2 to $250 million			
Deduction for ordinary shares (%)	150	150	150	100	100	100	100	100	100	100	100	100
Deduction for restricted shares (%)	n.a.	100	100	75	75/50[b]	75/50	75/50	75/50	n.a.	n.a.	n.a.	n.a.
Deduction for convertible shares (%)	n.a.	n.a.	n.a.	n.a.	n.a.	n.a.	n.a.	n.a.	50	50	50	50
Other businesses												
	100	100	100	75	75	75	75	n.a.	n.a.	n.a.	n.a.	n.a.

Notes: [a] As of 1989, shares of developing businesses and medium-sized businesses acquired by conversion are eligible at the applicable deduction rate.
[b] As of 1987, restricted shares of developing businesses are eligible for a 75 percent deduction if they carry more than 1/10 of an ordinary share vote and for a 50 percent deduction if they carry less than 1/10 of an ordinary share vote.

ENDNOTES

1 Centre interuniversitaire de recherche en analyse des organisations, 2020 University Street, 25th floor, Montreal, Quebec H3A 2A5, Tel: (514) 985-4030, e-mail: SURETJ@cirano.umontreal.ca. This study was carried out as part of a research program on the financing of Canadian businesses, undertaken by CIRANO with the support of Industry Canada. We wish to thank Isabelle Côté and Patrick Chamberland for their assistance with the collection and verification of the basic data used in the study.

2 See Lacroix (1987a) for a detailed analysis of the Plan's operation in 1986, and the various Martin reports for details on the adjustments made over the years. A summary of the main changes is presented in Appendix 1.

3 Quebec, Ministry of Finance, Budget Speech, May 10, 1983.

4 There were four categories of businesses: large, medium-sized, developing and other, and two types of shares: ordinary and restricted.

5 See Appendix 1 for a summary of other changes made on this occasion.

6 A tax recovery is imposed on taxpayers who fail to hold the shares for two calendar years after their acquisition.

7 Tables 1 and 2 are based mainly on estimates. There has been no official source of information on the Plan since the Quebec Securities Commission stopped publishing its reports in 1988. Tax statistics provide no details on claimed deductions since 1989. Therefore, the scope and cost of the Plan cannot be established with any accuracy. In particular, estimates of the distribution of tax credits by category of companies are based on the unverifiable assumption that the ratio of investment to deductions is the same for all categories of firm. The percentage of deductions linked to each category was estimated by adjusting the total value of issues for the year by the applicable deduction rate.

8 Information on the limits set to define categories and the applicable deduction rates by year, category of firm and type of shares is presented in Appendix 1.

9 For example, IAF Biochem, with assets of $1.9 million, was classified as a medium-sized business even though the minimum threshold for this category was $25 million. There are six other cases where small firms were assigned to the medium-sized business category. These classifications may reflect certain anti-avoidance rules or special conditions regarding the measurement of equity and assets, but the prospectuses do not make this clear.

10 The concepts of gain and loss were used in the study because reliable stock market data were not available (thus limiting the calculation of rates of return) and because stocks were held for varying periods.

11 Obviously, we cannot judge the merit of this objective, which is based on the assumption that wide ownership of equity shares stimulates economic growth and improves welfare. It could also be argued that wide ownership of risky and low-quality shares reduces the value of savings and discourages investors from future direct participation in business financing.

12 The detailed analysis presented in the remainder of the study is based on an exhaustive survey of the following data: 1) characteristics of issues and firms, taken from prospectuses made available by the Quebec Securities Commission, 2) characteristics of firms after issue, taken from financial statements made available by the firms and the Commission, and in certain cases from the CANCORP data base, 3) percentage of shares actually acquired in Quebec, taken from the Martin and Caisse de dépôt reports, 4) share prices at each year end since issue and the dilution factor, taken from the monthly stock listings published by the Montreal Exchange, 5) changes in the status of the firm from the issue

date to the end of 1994, taken from the official daily bulletins of the Montreal Exchange, the *Survey of Predecessor and Defunct Companies* (Financial Post Datagroup), the *Bulletin de statistiques* of the Quebec Securities Commission and the *Manuel des statistiques* of the Montreal Exchange, as well as *Mergers and Acquisitions in Canada* (Venture Economics Canada Limited) and the central registry of commercial businesses (Office of Quebec's Inspector General of Financial Institutions).

Several sources had to be consulted because there is no consistent compendium of Quebec stock issue data. The compilations of the Régime d'épargne-actions du Québec issues done by Martin do not go beyond 1987. Accounting and financial data of companies listed on the Montreal Exchange are not directly accessible and can only be consulted on-site at the Commission archives. Moreover, we were unable to obtain stock market data earlier than 1989 from the Montreal Exchange.

Data were compiled for 400 issues. There were many instances of discrepancies among sources, as well as with data from previous studies. One of the main differences was between 1) issue proceeds as indicated in the prospectus, 2) the amount actually recorded (lower or higher) and 3) the amount actually invested in Quebec. There are probably still some inaccuracies in the compilations. In particular, we could not determine what had happened to some issues. Nonetheless, this compilation is the result of a systematic survey of all published information on firms that participated in the QSSP.

13 Some issues were not followed by a listing on the exchange, while the information was incomplete in other cases. They were not included in the study. In most cases, the firms involved were very small.

14 The amounts reflect the proportion of shares eligible for the QSSP (if acquired by individuals) actually sold in Quebec. Otherwise, large firm issues would be significantly overrepresented. Firms with assets of under $25 million (small businesses) marketed 99.4 percent (1984) and 91.6 percent (1985) of their eligible shares through the QSSP, while the corresponding values for firms with assets of between $250 million and $1 billion (large businesses) were 84.4 percent (1984) and 82.5 percent (1986). The figures for very large firms were 61.9 percent and 65.5 percent respectively.

15 The Small Cap Index is made up of stocks that account for less than 0.1 percent of the TSE 300 plus the next 300 stocks with the largest capitalization not included in that index. In 1995, the TSE-listed companies with ranks between the 200th and 600th spots had an average capitalization of $141 million. This is equivalent to $55 million in 1985, adjusted for changes in the total return index. The average market value of the equity capital of QSSP firms, including medium-sized businesses, was about $32.7 million, taking into account the proceeds of share issues. Companies that make up the Small Cap Index are thus substantially more capitalized than the firms in our sample, for both the small and medium-sized business categories. While this index does not conform perfectly to the adjusted prices of shares issued under the QSSP, it represents the best possible compromise. In addition, the progression of the index over time does not differ substantially from that of the TSE 300 for the period studied. Therefore, our results show little sensitivity to the choice of the index.

16 Our assessment of performance is based on the premise that the issues under study have the same average risk as the benchmark Small Cap Index. Ideally, the adjustment of prices in response to market fluctuations should take account of the systematic risk of each issue. This risk was calculated for a subgroup of issues and used in our assessment of the initial undervaluation (see the Overview section). However, the beta coefficients were very low (0.76 on average). Accordingly, they were not used in the analysis, especially

since there was no computerized data base on returns for many shares. The low beta values probably reflect the low frequency of transactions, although the usual correction techniques failed to significantly improve the estimated coefficient. Also, the fact that many firms experienced difficulties may have reduced the systematic risk; McEnally and Todd (1993) found evidence of a decrease in systematic risk in cases of financial difficulties.

17 Another method would be to pair issues with other firms of the same size operating in the same sector, as did Loughram and Ritter (1995). This would have been difficult for QSSP issues, because the capitalization of the QSSP firms at issue is generally much lower than that of firms whose shares are traded on the Toronto Stock Exchange. Only 50 percent of QSSP issues could be paired in this way if we set the maximum difference at 100 percent of the capitalization of the QSSP firm.

18 In fact, the total amounts could be slightly higher, since only the amounts invested in Quebec are taken into account. In the case of small firms, the percentage of funds invested in Quebec is generally 100 percent.

19 Loughram and Ritter measured relative wealth by using a pairing technique. The values reported here were obtained by weighting the annual index by the percentage of issues surveyed between 1984 and 1987, the period when the vast majority of QSSP issues occurred. For the 1970 to 1990 period, the relative wealth index was 80 percent on average after three years and 70 percent after five years.

20 See Suret et al. (1990) for a detailed study of the impact of the QSSP on issue costs. However, a recent study by Jog and Srivastava (1995) found that the initial undervaluation declined in Ontario over the 1984 to 1992 period. A more in-depth study would be required to gauge the real impact of the QSSP on this aspect.

21 An earlier study (Suret et al., 1990) used econometric models to detect a statistically significant difference between Ontario issues and Quebec issues made under the QSSP. The binary variable associated with the QSSP was significant in explaining the initial undervaluation of the stock price and the total cost of the issue. The results of this study are not reported here.

22 There is wide dispersion in opportunity gains and losses, and it would be interesting to link stock price movements, which determine values, to the characteristics of issues and to the economic and financial conditions in which they took place. Work is currently under way in this area, but the detailed results are not presented here due to a lack of space. What is clear is that such factors as issue size, firm size, sector of activity and age of the issuing firm can partially explain the observed differences in the behaviour of their shares on the secondary market. However, there appears to be significant interactions among these variables that add to the complexity of the analysis because of the small sample sizes.

23 Tests revealed no systematic difference between the expected and actual use of the funds. The data on expected use are presented here because they were easier to obtain than data on the real use of funds.

24 Financial intermediaries were probably the first to benefit from the Plan, since it facilitated debt repayment and consolidated the position of lenders for remaining loans.

25 The special case of multiple issues is examined in the section on medium-sized businesses, since it primarily concerns those firms.

26 The St-Pierre and Beaudoin study encompassed 106 issues, but only 77 could be tracked two years after issue. The missing issues were likely delisted, usually as a result of financial hardship. Because the omitted firms were probably the most highly indebted, excluding these observations would lead to underestimating the average debt ratio after issue. To

avoid this problem, the following rules were applied: when the company was delisted because of significant financial difficulties or was liquidated, the debt ratio was set to 100 percent and the rate of return to zero. When the circumstances of the issuing company could not be accurately determined or when its shares were repurchased, the observation was dropped altogether from the sample.

27 The CANCORP data base is produced by Disclosure Inc., of Bethesda, Maryland, and distributed in Canada by Société nationale d'information (Montreal). The Stock Guide data base is produced and distributed by Stock Guide Productions Inc., of Williamston, Ontario.

28 It is unclear whether different samples from the one studied here might depict similar behaviour or whether QSSP issues have special characteristics that set them apart from other initial issues. This question could only be answered by a comparative analysis, which lies outside the scope of the present study.

29 The sample examined here includes 12 cases of multiple issues by the same firm during the study period. In these cases, the funds raised in subsequent issues may have influenced the debt structure of the firm. To gauge the importance of this phenomenon, the calculations were redone, this time excluding issues that were followed by a second public offering during the period studied. The results obtained after excluding these 15 issues did not differ substantially and are not reported here. For example, the median of the debt ratio distribution in year +4 for the 147-observation sample rose from 0.55 to 0.577 while the average rose from .068 to 0.698.

30 Note that this is the net rate of return, i.e., calculated on the basis of net profits before extraordinary items. Given the change in financing structure, it would have been more appropriate to use the rate of return before interest and taxes. But because a significant percentage of the firms in the sample did not report interest payments, it was not possible to calculate profits before interest and taxes. It can be assumed, however, that the decline in gross returns was even steeper than that in net returns because of lower debt-servicing costs.

31 The firms that benefited the most from the Plan are (capitalization on December 31, 1987 in billions of dollars): Bell Canada Enterprises (10.5), Canadian Pacific (6.18), Alcan Aluminum (5.9), Royal Bank (4.1), Bank of Montreal (3.1), Consolidated Bathurst (2.03), National Bank (1.36) and Power Financial Corporation (1.3).

BIBLIOGRAPHY

Delisle, A. *Objectifs des propositions budgétaires et fiscales québécoises concernant l'augmentation des fonds propres externes des entreprises québécoises.* Presentation at a seminar on new sources of financing for Quebec businesses, Québec, September 1985.

Jog, V. M. and A. Srivastava. *Perspectives on Canadian Initial Public Offerings: Underpricing, Long-Term Performance and the Process of Going Public.* Working paper, Carleton University, Ottawa, April 1995, p. 39.

Lacroix, D. "Les régimes d'épargne-actions : nouvelles orientations au Québec, premiers pas dans l'Ouest – première partie." *Revue fiscale canadienne*, 35, 2 (1987a): 50-87.

—. "Les régimes d'épargne-actions : nouvelles orientations au Québec, premiers pas dans l'Ouest – deuxième partie." *Revue fiscale canadienne*, 35, 2 (1987b): 314-349.

Loughram, T. and J. R. Ritter. "The New Issues Puzzle." *Journal of Finance*, 50, 1 (1995): 23-51.

Lussier, P. and K. Hawkins. *Analyse de la rentabilité des titres émis dans le cadre du RÉA*. Collection Recherche. Montreal: Caisse de dépôt et placement du Québec, 1991.

Martin, M. *Le Régime d'épargne-actions du Québec – Un programme unique en Amérique du Nord*. Montreal: Commission des valeurs mobilières du Québec, July 1984.

—. *Le Régime d'épargne-actions du Québec – Mise à jour et synthèse des principales données pour les années 1979 à 1984*. Montreal: Commission des valeurs mobilières du Québec, June 1985.

—. *Le Régime d'épargne-actions du Québec – Sept ans plus tard*. Montreal: Commission des valeurs mobilières du Québec, August 1986.

—. *Le Régime d'épargne-actions du Québec – A un tournant*. Montreal: Commission des valeurs mobilières du Québec, August 1987.

McEnally, R. and R. B. Todd. "Systematic Risk Behavior of Financially Distressed Firms." *Quarterly Journal of Business and Economics*, 32, 3 (Summer 1993): 3-19.

Ritter, J. R. "The Long Run Performance of Initial Public Offerings." *Journal of Finance*, (March 1991): 3-27.

SECOR. *L'évaluation du Régime d'épargne-actions du Québec*. Report prepared for the Investment Dealers Association of Canada, the Montreal Exchange and the Montreal Chamber of Commerce, 1986.

St-Pierre, J. and R. Beaudoin. "L'évolution de la structure de financement après un premier appel public à l'épargne : une étude descriptive." *Revue internationale PME*, 1996.

Suret, J.-M. "Une évaluation des dépenses fiscales et des subventions dans le domaine de la capitalisation des entreprises." *L'Actualité économique* (June 1993): 15-38.

—. "Les initiatives québécoises dans le domaine de la capitalisation des entreprises : le point de vue des investisseurs." *Canadian Public Policy/Analyse de politiques*, (September 1990): 121-133.

—. "Facteurs explicatifs des structures financières des PME québécoises." *L'Actualité économique*, 60, 1 (March 1984): 59-71.

Suret, J.-M. and L. Arnoux. "Capitalisation des entreprises québécoises: évolution et état de la situation." *Revue internationale PME*, 1996.

Suret, J.-M. and J.-F. L'Her. "The Evolving Capital Structure of Large Canadian Firms." In *Financing Growth in Canada*. Edited by Paul Halpern. Industry Canada Research Series, 1997, pp. 457-514.

Suret, J.-M., É. Cormier and B. Lemay. "Le RÉAQ et la sous-évaluation initiale du prix des titres." *Revue canadienne des sciences de l'administration*, 7, 3 (1990): 47-56.

Young, J. E. and J. K. Zaima. "The After Market Performance of Small Firm Initial Public Offerings." *Journal of Business Venturing*, 3 (1988): 77-87.

Young, J. E. and J. K. Zaima. "Does It 'Pay' to Invest in Small Business IPOs?" *Journal of Small Business Management*, 24 (1986): 39-50.

François Vaillancourt
Département de sciences économiques and
Centre de recherche et développement en économique
Université de Montréal

with the assistance of Ariane Brûlé, Miodrag Jovanovic and Julie Trottier

13

Labour-Sponsored Venture Capital Funds in Canada: Institutional Aspects, Tax Expenditures and Employment Creation

THIS PAPER EXAMINES THE MAIN ECONOMIC DIMENSIONS of labour-sponsored venture capital funds (LSVCFs) in Canada. This topic is of interest since the supply, cost and impact on economic activity of venture capital is important for policy makers. In particular, the paper draws on the Quebec evidence to assess the costs to government and their contribution to the use of LSVCFs. The paper is divided into four parts. In the first, we present LSVCFs. We then examine the tax expenditures associated with them and the impact of LSVCFs on employment in Quebec. In the last section, we address policy issues.

LSVCFs: INSTITUTIONAL ASPECTS

WE FIRST EXAMINE THE IMPORTANCE OF LSVCFs in the venture capital market and present information on their mandates and governance.

IMPORTANCE

THERE IS NO OFFICIAL (I.E., BANK OF CANADA OR STATISTICS CANADA[1]) estimate of the size of the venture capital market in Canada. Table 1 presents the most commonly used data – those produced by Macdonald & Associates Limited. The table shows an increase in the stock of venture capital in Canada from 1991 to 1994 (last available year at the time of writing) from $3 billion to $5 billion. It also shows that the share of LSVCFs has doubled over that period, and 60 percent ($1.2 billion of $2 billion) of the increase in venture capital is associated with LSVCFs. Part of this is the result of the association between private venture capital firms and labour unions: the private firms provide management expertise while the labour unions give access to tax credits. Finally, Macdonald & Associates Limited estimates that $1.9 billion of venture capital was available in 1994, broken down as follows: Quebec 45 percent, Ontario 31 percent, Prairies 16 percent and British Columbia 8 percent. Thus, venture capital was most easily available in the two provinces with the largest LSVCFs (see Table 3).

TABLE 1

STOCK OF VENTURE CAPITAL BY TYPE OF SUPPLIER IN CANADA, 1989, 1991, 1993 AND 1994 (IN $ BILLIONS)

Suppliers	1989 (%)	1991 (%)	1993 (%)	1994 (%)
Private funds				
Private independent firms	45	47	41	35
Corporate subsidiaries	31	20	9	11
Others	9	10	7	10
Subtotal	85	77	57	56
Public funds*				
Labour-sponsored funds	8	17	31	34
Government	7	6	12	10
Subtotal	15	23	43	44
Total %	100	100	100	100
$ Billions	3.4	3.0	4.0	5.0

Note: * A public fund is either a fund financed by the government or a fund which benefits from tax incentives.

Sources: 1989 and 1993: Canadian Labour Market and Productivity Centre, (1995) p. 24, Figure 4. 1991 and 1994: Macdonald & Associates Limited, private communication.

STRUCTURE

LSVCFS ARE ONE MECHANISM TO INCREASE FINANCIAL PARTICIPATION by unions in the ownership of capital. As such, their roots can be traced back to 19th century British social ideals (Matthews, 1989). In Canada, LSVCFs were started in Quebec in 1983 and became much more common in the early 1990s.

History of LSVCFs

The first LSVCF, Le Fond de solidarité des travailleurs du Quebec (FSTQ), was created by a Quebec law adopted on June 23, 1983. It began to collect funds on February 3, 1984, and became truly active in 1986 (three investments in 1985 and 10 in 1986). It had been put forward in 1982 as one tool to help the Quebec economy recover from the recession of 1981 and 1982 at a time when the Parti Québécois was in power. Having just imposed a clawback on wage increases granted to public sector employees in 1979, the government was interested in regaining some union support albeit from a mainly private sector union (Fédération des travailleurs du Quebec [FTQ]) rather than from the mainly public sector union (Confédération des syndicats nationaux [CSN]). It can be seen as one more innovative tool, along with the Québec Stock Savings Plan or the Caisse de dépôt et placement, used in Québec to raise capital.

In 1988, the Working Ventures Canadian Fund sponsored by the Canadian Federation of Labour was established. It attracts provincial tax credits in Prince Edward Island, New Brunswick, Nova Scotia, Ontario and Saskatchewan. In Newfoundland and Alberta, no funds receive such credits. In Quebec, the FSTQ was already active and, in British Columbia and Manitoba, single provincial funds were established in 1991 and 1992 respectively. Finally, a significant number of funds were established in Ontario in 1994, a provincial fund was established in New Brunswick in 1995 and a second fund (Fondaction of the CSN) was established in Quebec in January 1996.

At the end of 1995, the market structure of LSVCFs in Canada was as follows.

- Newfoundland and Alberta saw little fund activity.
- Quebec, Manitoba and British Columbia had one provincial LSVCF benefiting from a *de jure* monopoly position (Quebec, in 1996, moved to a duopoly with the creation of Fondaction).
- In Prince Edward Island, Nova Scotia and Saskatchewan, the Working Ventures Canadian Fund was dominant with no provincial funds.
- In New Brunswick, a provincial fund was being set up, but the Working Ventures Canadian Fund was active in that province.
- Ontario had several LSVCFs, some of which were closely associated with private venture capital firms, such as the Canadian Medical Discoveries Fund, MDS Ventures, Trillium Growth Capital Inc. and Canadian Corporate Funding. Some became active in other provinces, and a few now receive tax credits in provinces outside Ontario.

Objectives of LSVCFs

The goals of LSVCFs are set out in the relevant provincial legislation and are broader than the maximization of profits, the goal of private venture capital firms. Table 2 presents the goals of LSVCFs, as set out in provincial law in five provinces. It also indicates the type of firms targeted by LSVCFs and their governance provisions. Because of federal tax regulations, all LSVCFs must invest at least 60 percent of their funds (more in some provinces) in eligible firms after a few start-up years. Table 2 shows that the goals of the funds vary across provinces. For example, the Quebec, Ontario and Manitoba LSVCFs have, as an explicit goal, the provision of employment while the British Columbia LSVCF does not. While Quebec and British Columbia have the education of workers to facilitate their involvement in the management of economic matters as one goal, only Manitoba explicitly promotes worker involvement in governance. It also has additional goals, such as workplace safety and environmental suitability, not found elsewhere.

Table 2 also shows that restrictions put on businesses eligible for LSVCF investment always use provincial employment (wages) and size to target small/medium firms doing business mainly in the province where the LSVCF operates. The tax treatment of LSVCF shares (see below) is a strong inducement to invest in

TABLE 2

INVESTMENT GOALS, ELIGIBLE FIRMS AND GOVERNANCE OF LSVCFs

	Quebec	Ontario	Manitoba	British Columbia	New Brunswick
Investment goals	• Invest in Quebec firms to create/maintain/save jobs • Educate workers in economic matters • Stimulate Quebec's economy by strategic investment • Favour growth of Quebec firms	Assist the development of eligible businesses by creating/maintaining/ saving jobs through provision of advice and capital	• Capital retention/ economic/stability • Employee ownership/ governance • Job creation/retention • Ownership by Manitobans of Manitoba economy • Ethical employment practices, workplace safety, environmental suitability	• Make an investment • Provide expertise • Educate employees in economic matters	Promote capital formation and local ownership by: • Fund earning income • Promoting/maintaining capital retention • Favouring job creation and retention • Increasing awareness and involvement of workers in economic matters
Eligible firms	• Majority of employees reside in Quebec • Gross assets < $50 million Net assets < $20 million	• > 50% of wages found in Ontario • > 50% of employees reside in Ontario • Assets < $50 million • Employees ≤ 500	• > 50% of employees in Manitoba • Assets < $50 million	• > 50% of wages in British Columbia • Assets < $35 million • Engage in manufacturing/ processing, research and development tourism, aquaculture or prescribed activity	Not stated
Governance	17-member board • 10 named by FTQ • 2 elected by shareholders • 4 named by the board • president	Depend on by-laws of a specific fund	• 1 Manitoba government nominee • 1 elected by shareholders • 3 named by Manitoba Federation of Labour • 0, 1 or 2 by holders of special (corporate) shares with matching (0, 1, 2) members named by Manitoba Federation of Labour	10 members • 6 members of various unions • 4 government nominees	New Brunswick Federation of Labour – details not stated

Source: Provincial statutes.

TABLE 3
LSVCFs, CANADA, 1995

Name	Year Created	Number of Shareholders/ Investments	Assets/ Portfolio ($000,000)	Provincial Tax Credit
Fond de solidarité des travailleurs du Québec Inc. (FSTQ)	1983	239,000/131	1,300/641	Québec
Working Ventures Canadian Fund Inc.	1988	91,000/52	498/133	Ontario New Brunswick Prince Edward Island Nova Scotia Saskatchewan
Working Opportunity Fund (EVCC) Ltd.	1991	15,000/15	82.7/20.6	British Columbia
Crocus Investment Fund Inc.	1992	6,600/7	26.2/9	Manitoba
Integrated Growth Fund Inc.	1993	3,900/6	15.3/3.1	Ontario
DGC Entertainment Ventures Corporation Inc.	1993	1,100/3	4.3/0.8	Ontario
Active Communications Growth Fund Inc.[a]	1994	n/a	n/a	Ontario
Canadian Medical Discoveries Fund Inc.	1994	4,400/5	17.3/5.3	Ontario New Brunswick Prince Edward Island Nova Scotia
Capital Alliance Ventures Inc.	1994	1,500/2	5.8/1.0	Ontario
CI-CPA Business Ventures Fund Inc./ Covington	1994	4,100/3	16.5/4.5	Ontario

(cont'd)

TABLE 3 (cont'd)

Name	Year Created	Number of Shareholders/ Investments	Assets/ Portfolio ($000,000)	Provincial Tax Credit
FESA Enterprise Venture Capital Fund of Canada Ltd.	1994	800/n/a	3.3/n/a	Ontario
First Ontario Labour-Sponsored Investment Fund Inc.	1994	650/n/a	2.1/n/a	Ontario
Sports Fund Inc.	1994	850/n/a	3.5/n/a	Ontario
TCU Development Fund Inc.[a]	1994	n/a	n/a	Ontario
Trillium Growth Capital Inc.	1994	1,500/1	4.7/0.3	Ontario
Vengrowth Investment Fund Inc.	1994	7,900/3	32.8/4	Ontario
Worker's Investment Fund Inc.[a]	1994	n/a	n/a	New Brunswick
Retrocom Growth Fund Inc.	1995	n/a	22.5/n/a	Ontario

Notes: n/a: not applicable
[a] No funds raised yet

Source: Canadian Labour Market and Productivity Centre (1995) Figure 2, pp. 8-9.

an LSVCF. To retain these funds, LSVCFs have a minimum holding period imposed by federal tax regulations that can only be waved in the case of death, terminal illness or disability. In addition, these are fund-specific provisions. For example, the FSTQ normal holding period is until age 65 or retirement (if it occurs between the ages of 60 and 64). As a result, early redemption must be applied for and is often permitted, e.g., in case of death, disability, return to school, unemployment or departure from Quebec. The normal holding period is eight years for the Working Ventures Canadian Fund and Working Opportunity Fund (British Columbia) and seven for the Crocus Investment Fund (Manitoba).

Table 3 provides a list of LSVCFs for 1995. It shows that the FSTQ accounts for 65 percent of all LSVCF assets followed by the Working Ventures Canadian Fund at 25 percent. These two funds are also the largest providers of venture capital in Canada and, with the Working Opportunity Fund and the Crocus Investment Fund, account for 95 percent of all LSVCF assets.

Tax Rules

From 1985 to 1988, an LSVCF was not eligible for a federal tax credit unless set up by a provincial law. Thus, only the shares in the FSTQ were eligible for a 20 percent provincial and a 20 percent federal tax credit and could be held in a registered retirement savings plan (RRSP). In 1988, the federal tax rules were amended to allow for a national LSVCF. Such a fund had first been discussed in the May 1985 budget: its views were to encourage long-term investment of individuals and to maintain or create jobs or stimulate the economy. From 1988 to 1996, the federal tax credit had a maximum of 20 percent of the value of the shares purchased, but was 0 percent if the provincial credit for a provincial fund was not 20 percent. If the provincial credit was above 20 percent, the federal credit was reduced to ensure a maximum combined credit of 40 percent. The maximum federal/credit amount was raised from $700 to $1,000 from 1992 until 1996. Thus, in 1995, a $1,000 investment in an LSVCF held in an RRSP could, in most provinces, cost as little as $45, if one faced the highest marginal personal income tax rate.

The Financing of LSVCFs: Tax Expenditures

As indicated in the preceding section, LSVCF shares could yield, in most provinces, personal income tax credits of 20 percent of the investment, at both the federal and provincial levels, with the maximum admissible investment increasing in 1992 from $3,500 to $5,000 until the March 6, 1996 federal budget. In that budget, the federal tax credit was reduced to a maximum of 15 percent and a minimum of 10 percent. The maximum admissible amount returned to $3,500 and the minimum holding period increased from five years to eight years. The minimum credit applies where there is no matching provincial tax credit. Should the matching provincial tax credit be between 10 percent and 15 percent, the federal credit rate would be set equal to the provincial credit rate. In addition, those selling LSVCF shares in a given year will not be able to claim a tax credit for new shares purchased that year or in the following two years. Provincial governments in Nova Scotia, Quebec, Ontario and Manitoba took similar action, reducing the maximum investment and the tax credit to the same values as those of the federal budget (Perry and Treff, 1996). LSVCF shares remain eligible investments for RRSPs: the amount purchased can be deducted in the computation of taxable income. Thus, the purchase of LSVCF shares will reduce the tax revenue of governments.

TABLE 4

LSVCF FEDERAL TAX CREDITS, DISTRIBUTION BY INCOME GROUP, CANADA, 1993

Income Groups ($000s)	Number of Tax Filers		Amount		
	Number	Percentage	Total ($000s)	Mean ($)	Percentage
	(1)	(2)	(3)	(4)	(5)
0-5	0	0	0	0	0
5-10	460	0.3	50	109	0.09
10-15	2,520	1.8	468	186	0.8
15-20	5,390	3.8	1,182	231	3.1
20-25	8,890	6.3	2,072	233	3.6
25-30	12,890	9.2	3,357	260	5.8
30-35	13,960	10.0	4,351	312	7.6
35-40	15,300	10.9	5,396	353	9.4
40-45	15,240	10.9	5,728	376	10.0
45-50	13,480	9.6	5,517	409	9.6
50-100	47,160	33.6	25,490	541	44.4
100+	4,820	3.4	3,833	795	6.7
Total	140,110	100.0	57,444	410	100.0

Source: Special tabulation from Revenue Canada and calculations made by the author.

The reduction in government revenue that result from a specific disposition in the income tax law is referred to as a tax expenditure by economists. This term was first put forward in the United States by Surrey (1973) to draw attention to the fact that the government could achieve a given objective by either spending a given amount or not collecting the same amount as taxes, but only the first choice would appear in the standard budget document.

THE EXISTING LITERATURE

THE MAIN STUDIES OF LSVCF-RELATED TAX EXPENDITURES are those by Suret (1990, 1993, 1994 and forthcoming) which examine the costs and returns of various tax saving schemes offered by the Quebec government, including the FSTQ. These studies all use a similar methodology but update the data as time goes by. Since Suret's 1994 study is the most complete for our purposes, its analysis of the FSTQ is outlined below.

Suret (1994) first described the history of the FSTQ and its relationship with other capitalization schemes, such as the QSSP. He then carried out a cost benefit analysis based on the following assumptions.

TABLE 5

INCIDENCE OF LSVCF CREDIT (1993) AND TAX EXPENDITURES (1991), CANADA

Income Groups ($000s)	LSVCF Indices (1993) TE/Taxpayers (1)	TE/Income Assessed (2)	TE/Federal Tax (3)	All Credits (1991) TE/Income Assessed (4)	TE/Federal Tax (5)
0-10	0.0	0.0	0.3		
10-15	0.1	0.1	0.4	1.6	4.4
15-20	0.3	0.4	0.8	1.6	2.7
20-25	0.4	0.5	0.6	1.3	1.8
25-30	0.7	0.7	0.8	1.2	1.5
30-35	1.2	0.9	1.0	1.1	1.2
35-40	1.8	1.2	1.2	1.0	1.0
40-45	2.4	1.4	1.3	0.9	0.8
45-50	2.9	1.6	1.3	0.9	0.7
50-100	4.7	1.9	1.4	0.7	0.0
100+	4.7	0.6	0.4	0.5	0.03

Notes: Numbers are ratios of percentage.
TE: tax expenditure

Sources: Columns 1, 2 and 3 calculated using data from Table 4 and *Taxation Statistics 1995*, Revenue Canada, Table 2.

Columns 4 and 5 are an interpolation using data from St-Hilaire (1995, Table 5).

- FSTQ investors receive a tax break of 80 percent since they hold their FSTQ shares (40 percent credit) in their RRSPs (40 percent deduction). As of October 31, 1994, the cumulative estimated cost of these tax breaks was $563.5 million (Suret, forthcoming, Table 5).
- Under the assumption of a 25-year holding period (assuming the mean age of an FSTQ shareholder at first purchase is 40 years and he or she retires at 65) and given the observed returns to the FSTQ (5.4 percent) and the stock market (12 percent), $1 of investment will be worth $37 for the FSTQ shareholder and $34 for an ordinary shareholder at the end of the 25 years.

This analysis is, as Suret noted (forthcoming, p. 27), laden with difficulties, since it requires making projections of fund returns and the tax system. For example, the abolition of the lifetime capital gains exemption in 1994 modifies these calculations. Overall, Suret concluded that the difference in rates of returns that slightly favours the FSTQ does not compensate for the lack of diversity or liquidity.

TABLE 6

LSVCF FEDERAL TAX CREDIT, DISTRIBUTION BY PROVINCE, CANADA, 1993

Provinces	Number of Tax Filers		Amount			Percentage of Tax Filers by Province
	Number	Percentage	Total ($000)	Mean	Percentage	
Newfoundland	0	0	0	0	0	0
Prince Edward Island	480	0.3	311	648	0.5	0.5
Nova Scotia	20	0.01	10	500	0.02	0.003
New Brunswick	730	0.5	547	749	0.9	0.1
Quebec	92,540	66.0	22,837	247	39.6	1.9
Ontario	32,400	23.1	25,069	774	43.6	0.4
Manitoba	2,320	1.7	1,153	497	2.0	0.3
Saskatchewan	5,890	4.2	3,367	572	5.9	0.9
Alberta	40	0.03	21	525	0.04	0.002
British Columbia	5,670	4.0	4,122	727	7.2	0.2
Yukon, Northwest Territories	0	0	0	0	0	0
Total	140,110	100.0	57,444	410	100.0	0.7

Source: Special tabulation from Revenue Canada and calculations made by the author.

Allen (1994) used a similar methodology but different assumptions and concluded that the FSTQ is a better private investment than Suret had argued. He also commented that Suret overestimated the tax expenditure associated with an FSTQ investment by overestimating the RRSP component, and he neglected the benefits of job creation and associated government revenues. Jackson and Lamontagne (1995) also examined the fiscal costs and benefits of LSVCFs and the payback period to governments. We do not attempt to arbitrate between the various authors, since we are incapable of assessing the best projections for the rates of returns, tax rates and revenues over 25 years, or of establishing the net contribution of LSVCFs to output, employment and government revenues.

In our opinion, the tax expenditure associated with LSVCFs and the FSTQ is the result of the federal and provincial tax credits and was equal, in most provinces, to 40 percent of the value of the share purchase up to $2,000 per year, from 1992 to 1996. Since LSVCF shares are one potential RRSP investment, such an additional tax expenditure is RRSP driven and not caused by the LSVCF.

Therefore, we limit ourselves to a traditional tax expenditure analysis (Bruce, 1990) similar to the one recently carried out for Canada (St-Hilaire, 1995). Such an analysis is not a cost-benefit analysis but rather a simple evaluation of the amount and distribution of the tax expenditure.

Tax Expenditures for LSVCFs: Canada, 1993 and Quebec, 1986 to 1993

In this section, we first present evidence for Canada for 1993. We then turn to evidence for Quebec from 1986 to 1993. We do this for two reasons. First, since there are no published figures for Canada, we had to obtain a special tabulation from Revenue Canada for 1993. Second, given the age of the various LSVCFs, it is only for Quebec that a time series is meaningful.

Table 4 presents the federal tax credit by income groups. The amounts claimed average about $400, increase as income increases (column 4) and are more heavily concentrated in the $50,000+ groups (51.1 percent) (which represents only 37 percent of the claimants). This could indicate a regressive tax expenditure, i.e., one whose value increases faster than income, thus benefiting better off individuals. To establish this more formally, we use three indices, first put forward by St-Hilaire (1995). These are the ratios for each income group of:

- the tax expenditure percentage to the number of filers;
- the tax expenditure percentage to the assessed income; and
- the tax expenditure percentage to the federal tax.

The ratios indicate if a tax expenditure is concentrated in a given income range. Concentration in the high-income range indicates regressivity and, as Table 5 clearly shows, the LSVCF tax credit is regressive over the $15,000 to $100,000 income range. When compared to all non-refundable tax credits for 1991, using

TABLE 7

QUEBEC FSTQ TAX CREDIT, EVOLUTION OF TAKE-UP RATE AND AMOUNT, 1986 TO 1994

Year	Number of Tax Filers		Amount	
	Number	Percentage of All Tax Filers	Total ($000s)	Mean
1986	30,899	0.78	8,715	282
1987	not available			
1988	48,864	1.18	13,268	272
1989	52,675	1.25	13,303	253
1990	53,473	1.22	13,887	260
1991	79,639	1.76	24,448	307
1992	110,816	2.41	40,105	362
1993	92,924	1.98	23,518	253

Source: Ministère du revenu du Québec, *Statistiques fiscales des particuliers*, Table 2, various years.

income assessed or federal tax payable, the LSVCF tax credit is more regressive than all non-refundable tax credits.

The distribution across provinces is also interesting. Table 6 shows that two thirds of LSVCF tax credit claimants are from Quebec, but they account for only 40 percent of the amounts obtained. The mean claim in Quebec is the lowest in Canada, reflecting, in part, the high take-up rate of about 2 percent by Quebec tax filers: it is equal to one third of the mean claim in Ontario or British Columbia. The second lowest mean claim is in Manitoba. Several factors may explain the interprovincial differences found in Table 6:

- the differences in provincial tax credits between provinces;
- the fact that the FSTQ has been established longer than other funds, i.e., it is a better-known savings vehicle; and
- perhaps most important, the differences in marketing techniques among the provinces. In Quebec, sales of FSTQ shares are made by a network of union-based representatives with no sales by investment dealers or brokers, and with payroll deduction plans in 2,245 collective agreements. On the other hand, sales of shares of the Working Ventures Canadian Fund (Ontario) are made by investment dealers and brokers with only 20 payroll deduction plans. In British Columbia, the Working Opportunity Fund uses only investment dealers and brokers, but in Manitoba, both union representatives, and investment dealers and brokers sell shares of the Crocus Investment Fund.

Table 7 allows us to explore the impact of time on the Quebec tax credit take-up rate. Two years after its inception, the take-up rate was already 0.78 percent. Five years after, it was 1.25 percent and, by 1992, it had grown to 2.41 percent. Its drop from 1992 to 1993 was mainly the result of a cap on the total amount of tax credit which could have been claimed in 1993 that was introduced in the provincial budget of 1993. It limited the amount of shares that could have been issued without a special 20 percent tax to 97 million in 1993-1994 and 75 million in 1994-1995. This tax was abolished by the new government in the fall of 1994.

Table 8 shows the distribution of FSTQ tax credits for the 15 nominal income groups for which the information is reported in Quebec's tax statistics. It indicates a shift to higher income categories.

This shift may be illusory in that it may result from inflation. To allow for this, we constructed an inflation-adjusted distribution by:

- increasing the midpoint income (1986) of each income interval by the relevant inflation rate; and
- redistributing the relevant percentage points around the inflated midpoint in the appropriate income interval assuming a uniform distribution around the midpoint. Such an assumption is probably quite reasonable for the first 11 ($50,000 or less) income intervals and acceptable for the remainder.

The results are found in Table 9. When compared to those of Table 8, they show an increase in the share of the tax expenditures claimed by higher-income groups ($60,000+) relative to what could have been projected for 1993.

How does the distribution of the LSVCF tax credit in Quebec compare to the one in Ontario? Table 10 shows a greater concentration among the $50,000 income groups in Ontario than in Quebec. This agrees with the higher mean credit reported in Table 6.

The Impact of the FSTQ on Employment

As indicated above, one of the two key differences between LSVCFs and private venture capital is that the objectives of LSVCFs are usually employment oriented. Thus, it is appropriate to examine if the tax expenditures consented to by society have had an impact on employment. This issue is examined for the FSTQ, since it is the only LSVCF with a long enough investment period to allow for an impact on employment. This is done by estimating an econometric model of labour demand for the manufacturing sector and for six specific manufacturing subsectors for the 1970 to 1994 period. First, existing literature on the determinants of employment in the manufacturing sector is reviewed followed by a discussion of the results.

TABLE 8

FSTQ TAX CREDIT BY INCOME GROUP AND DISTRIBUTION OF TAX EXPENDITURES RELATIVE TO THE NUMBER OF TAXPAYERS, QUEBEC, 1986 AND 1993

Year	1986 Amount FSTQ Tax Credit			1986 Returns			1993 Amount FSTQ Tax Credit			1993 Returns	
Income Range ($000s)	($000s)	Average ($)	% by Income Class	Number	% by Income Range	Income Range ($000s)	($000s)	Average ($)	% by Income Class	Number	% by Income Class
0-5	0	0	0.0	0	0.0	0-5	0	0	0.0	0	0.0
5-10	38	64	0.4	592	1.9	5-10	26	74	0.1	353	0.4
10-15	256	178	2.9	1,438	4.7	10-15	251	130	1.1	1,932	2.1
15-20	591	220	6.8	2,687	8.7	15-20	584	149	2.5	3,918	4.2
20-25	930	244	10.7	3,819	12.4	20-25	1,084	159	4.6	6,804	7.3
25-30	1,235	271	14.2	4,560	14.8	25-30	1,837	181	7.8	10,175	11.0
30-35	1,519	293	17.4	5,188	16.8	30-35	2,262	212	9.6	10,677	11.5
35-37.5	683	301	7.8	2,268	7.3	35-40	2,638	237	11.2	11,145	12.0
37.5-40	630	176	7.2	2,046	6.6	40-45	2,837	257	12.1	11,031	11.9
40-45	1,037	315	12.0	3,296	10.7	45-50	2,521	271	10.7	9,313	10.0
45-50	711	333	8.2	2,135	6.9	50-60	4,252	302	18.1	14,064	15.1
50-60	646	351	7.4	1,840	5.9	60-70	2,407	344	10.2	6,997	7.5
60-100	381	414	4.4	921	3.0	70-100	2,162	414	9.2	5,218	5.6
100-200	51	510	0.6	100	0.3	100-200	587	497	2.5	1,182	1.3
200+	0	0	0.0	0	0.0	200+	70	609	0.3	115	0.1
Total	8,708	282	100.0	30,890	100.0	Total	23,518	253	100.0	92,924	100.0

Note: The calculations are from the author.

Source: Ministère du revenu du Québec, *Portrait de la fiscalité des particuliers au Québec*, various years.

TABLE 9

INFLATION CORRECTED INCOME CLASS DISTRIBUTION, QUEBEC, PROJECTION OF 1986 TO 1993, FSTQ TAX CREDIT

Income Range ($000s)	1993 Percentage by Income Class	1993 Cumulative Distribution (%)
0-5	0.0	0.0
5-10	0.2	0.2
10-15	0.8	1.0
15-20	6.4	7.4
20-25	11.3	18.7
25-30	2.1	20.8
30-35	3.0	23.8
35-40	18.3	42.1
40-45	22.4	64.5
45-50	15.0	79.5
50-60	16.0	95.5
60-100	4.0	99.5
100-200	0.2	99.7
200+	0.003	100.0
Total	100.0	

Note: The calculations are from the author.

Source: *Canadian Economic Observer: Historical Statistics Supplement*, Statistics Canada, 1995, Table 12 (CPI all items).

THE LITERATURE

THE FIRST ECONOMETRIC STUDY OF THE DETERMINANTS of employment in the manufacturing sector appears to be the work of Brechling (1965). It was followed by studies by Ball and Saint-Cyr (1966), Brechling and O'Brien (1969) and Ireland and Smyth (1970). These studies focus on the adjustment between the desired (E^*) and observed (E) demand for labour. Cohen-Skalli and Laskar (1980) reviewed this literature and used the Ball and Saint-Cyr specifications in their exposition. They showed that using a Cobb-Douglas production function, a standard cost function and a partial employment adjustment process, results in the following speed of adjustment model:

$$\ln E_t = B_0 + B_1 t + B_2 \ln Q_t + B_3 \ln E_{t-1} \qquad (1)$$

TABLE 10

DISTRIBUTION OF TAX EXPENDITURES RELATIVE TO INCOME, QUEBEC AND ONTARIO, 1993

Income Range ($000s)	FSTQ Tax Credit	Average ($)	Percent by Income Class	Ontario LSVCF Tax Credit	Average ($)	Percent by Income Class
0-5	0	0	0.0	0	0	0.0
5-10	27	79	0.1	16	229	0.1
10-15	228	126	1.0	147	350	0.6
15-20	563	140	2.5	380	494	1.5
20-25	1,061	149	4.6	644	631	2.5
25-30	1,819	174	8.0	1,028	681	4.1
30-35	2,226	208	9.7	1,427	706	5.7
35-40	2,596	231	11.4	1,854	739	7.4
40-45	2,788	252	12.2	1,998	751	8.0
45-50	2,454	268	10.7	2,075	757	8.3
50-100	8,493	333	37.2	12,857	815	51.3
100+	583	503	2.6	2,642	908	10.5
Total	22,838	247	100.0	25,068	774	100.0

Note: The calculations are made from the author.

Source: Special tabulation from Revenue Canada, Statistical Services Division, 1995.

where E is employment, Q is output (value added) and t is a time trend for technical progress with capital assumed constant. Following this first group of studies, additional work was carried out in the 1970s and 1980s. In particular, a series of studies examined the wage elasticity of the demand for labour. Hamermesh (1986) and Dormont (1994) reviewed this literature with the latter indicating that the best equation is:

$$\ln E_t = B_0 + B_1 t + B_2 \ln Q_t + B_3 \frac{W}{P} + B_4 \frac{K_p}{P} \qquad (2)$$

where W is the labour cost per unit of work, P is the price of output and K_p is the price of capital.

There are also various studies along the line of the speed of adjustment literature. The most recent appears to be by Lesueur (1992) who estimated the following:

$$\ln \left(\frac{E_t}{E_{t-1}}\right) = B_0 + B_1 t + B_2 \ln \left(\frac{Q_t}{E_{t-1}}\right) + B_3 \ln LMT_t \qquad (3)$$

where *LMT* is labour market tension, i.e., demand minus supply of labour. Overall, employment at time *t* is in all cases, explained by output at time *t*, employment at time *t-1* and a time trend.

Our study uses the following model:

$$\ln E_t = B_0 + B_1 t + B_2 LQL + B_3 \ln E_{t-1} + B_4 FSTQ + B_5 NAFTA \quad (4)$$

to examine the determinant of annual employment in the manufacturing sector as a whole and in six two-digit sectors from 1970 to 1994 in Quebec. This model was selected using equation (1), since it is less constrained than equation (3). Data is not good for labour market tension by sector, and an econometric estimation of equation (3), with or without unemployment as a proxy for labour market tension, yielded similar results for the variable of interest, *FSTQ*.

FSTQ is a spline variable. It aims at measuring the impact of FSTQ investment on employment. It takes the following values: 1970 to 1985: 0, 1986: 0.05, 1987 and 1988: 0.1, 1989: 0.2, 1990: 0.3, 1991: 0.5, 1992: 0.6, 1993: 0.8 and 1994: 1.0. It gives greater weight to years in which the FSTQ was more active.

The North American Free Trade Agreement *NAFTA* variable takes the following values 1970 to 1988: 0, 1989: 0.1, 1990: 0.2, 1991: 0.3, 1992: 0.4, 1993: 0.5 and 1994: 0.6 to account for the gradual implementation of free trade.

The Results for Quebec

The sectors were selected following Lamonde et al. (1994) who argued that the FSTQ was responsible for maintaining and creating jobs by helping enterprises which had financial problems and even saving enterprises which were about to close down. They stated that the largest positive impacts of these investments occurred in rubber and plastic, furniture, wood and wood products, printing and publishing, paper, chemical products and other manufacturing sectors.

The results found in Table 11 indicate that our model explains fairly well the evolution of employment in Quebec's manufacturing sector and the selected subsector with a high R-squared. No autocorrelation was detected. The time trend is significant ($t > 2.1$) and negative six out of seven times indicating that technical or managerial progress reduces employment. Output and past employment both have a positive impact on current employment, but it is not always significant. The free trade variable is usually negative, but not significant. The *FSTQ* variable has no significant impact on employment in the sectors studied. This does not mean that it may not have been helpful in maintaining employment at the firm level, but that this had no sector impact, perhaps because of interfirm shifts in employment.

TABLE 11

IMPACT OF FSTQ ON EMPLOYMENT, ALL MANUFACTURING SECTORS AND SIX INDUSTRIES, QUEBEC, 1970 TO 1994, ORDINARY LEAST SQUARES ESTIMATES

Variable	All Manufacturing	Wood Products	Furniture	Printing/ Publishing	Papers	Chemicals	Petroleum Products
Constant	1.03	-1.13	-2.69	0.42	1.46	4.53	2.71
	(0.74)	(-0.3)	(-2.22)	(0.12)	(0.57)	(1.95)	(1.65)
$ln\ t$	-0.013	-0.024	-0.009	0.002	-0.004	0.0009	-0.020
	(-7.09)	(-3.79)	(-3.40)	(0.23)	(-2.30)	(0.29)	(-2.09)
$ln\ Q_t$	0.62	0.74	0.94	0.35	0.20	0.08	0.025
	(6.73)	(5.75)	(7.78)	(1.39)	(2.06)	(0.96)	(0.25)
$ln\ E_{t-1}$	0.17	0.20	0.11	0.49	0.60	0.41	0.62
	(1.77)	(1.86)	(1.22)	(2.74)	(3.39)	(2.01)	(3.59)
FSTQ	0.16	0.30	0.76	0.69	-0.038	-0.21	0.055
	(0.90)	(0.80)	(1.96)	(1.34)	(-0.14)	(-0.78)	(0.05)
NAFTA	-0.46	-0.43	-1.42	-1.19	-0.091	0.11	-0.016
	(-1.71)	(-0.69)	(-2.40)	(1.62)	(-0.22)	(0.26)	(0.009)
R-squared	0.95	0.91	0.93	0.90	0.93	0.65	0.92

POLICY ISSUES AND CONCLUSION

IN THIS LAST PART OF THE PAPER, we examine policy issues related to four key features of LSVCFs.

- LSVCFs are an important source of venture capital in Canada.
- LSVCFs have goals other than profit maximization, such as employment, but evidence from Quebec does not show that they add to net employment.
- There is no single Canadian LSVCF market: there are 10 provincial markets characterized by discouraged entry, monopoly, duopoly or a small number of funds.
- LSVCFs are one of the most tax-favoured investments in Canada.

Let us relate these features to three policy issues.

DO WE NEED LSVCFS?

Venture Capital Supply

This study did not determine formally if there was an under or oversupply of venture capital in Canada before and after the appearance of LSVCFs, since the required data on the demand, supply and price of venture capital were not available. Suret (1994) argued that, even before the generalization of LSVCFs in Canada, there was no evidence of a lack of venture capital. Even if he was wrong, we could find no evidence that requiring venture capital to be channelled through LSVCFs is the best way to increase its supply or to allocate it efficiently.

Employment

The only LSVCF for which the impact on employment was examined, the FSTQ, did not, according to the model we used, have an impact on overall employment. This does not mean that it did not help specific employers but that such help had no positive sectoral impact. Will other LSVCFs have a positive impact on employment in their province or industry? We do not know. Given, however, the results for the FSTQ, an LSVCF's role in job creation may not be the best argument for its existence and tax status.

Given the above, one may wonder why LSVCFs are promoted. The Canadian Labour Market and Productivity Centre (CLMPC) (1995) has identified 10 salient qualities of LSVCFs. They have been regrouped here under four goals:

1. **Increased Supply of Venture Capital** This regroups four qualities: responsiveness to public policy concerns, interest in Canadian private equity markets geared to risk, interest in addressing capital supply barriers to firms in certain sectors and capital resource mobilization on a provincial basis.

2. **Increased Employment** This regroups two qualities: the responsiveness to public policy concerns (mentioned above), along with mandates that guide investments according to economic and social goals.
3. **Better Investment Vehicle** This regroups two qualities: participation by a broad base of average working people and a commitment to provide market returns to shareholders.
4. **Increased Labour Involvement** This regroups three qualities: organization and direction by a legitimate labour body with involvement of workers and unions in enterprise-based decisions, and facilitation of co-operation between business and labour.

The first two goals have been addressed already. Under the third goal, one should note that the evidence on the tax credit by income group (tables 4, 5, 8 and 10) does not support the view of LSVCFs as a broadly based savings vehicle, at least outside Quebec.

This leaves the fourth goal of increased labour involvement in the economy, in general, and in the management of firms, in particular. The CLMPC (1995, p. 56) stated that "research argues that employee involvement in company management and ownership improves overall economic efficiency." While this may be true, this does not show the need for a special tax treatment.

Thus, from a policy perspective, the need for a special treatment of LSVCFs relative to other venture capital funds has not been firmly established. Therefore, we question a need for the existing tax credit. That said, let us assume it exists when addressing the following two points.

Is the LSVCF Market Correctly Structured?

The current structure of the LSVCF market makes it difficult for individual investors to diversify their portfolio regionally or by type of investment in a tax-effective way. It also puts the small firms of a province with a monopoly fund in a weaker bargaining position than they would be in in a multifund province. Finally, the supply of venture capital may not be optimally distributed across regions, sectors and firms due to tax-induced distortions. To correct this, LSVCF investors in a province should be entitled to the federal tax credit only if that province allows unrestricted access to all LSVCFs, both as sellers of shares and investors. This would strengthen the Canadian capital market.

Is the Tax Treatment Appropriate?

Given the goals of LSVCFs, it may be necessary to give the owners tax credits. That said, the appropriate credit rate is not obvious. The reduction from 20 percent to 15 percent in the March 1996 federal budget probably moves closer to that rate, and the minimum federal rate of 10 percent is probably appropriate with a matching provincial credit. However, if the rate is suitably set, there should be no blackout period for using the tax credit following the sale of LSVCF shares. Finally, one cannot justify allowing the deductibility, for RRSP purposes, of the LSVCF shares gross of the credits. It is only the net of credit amount that should be eligible for RRSP deductibility.

To conclude, LSVCFs are an important source of venture capital in Canada that received, until 1996, an extremely favourable tax treatment and still receive a very favourable tax treatment. Given the available evidence, less tax payer generosity could be appropriate.

ENDNOTE

1 The assets of venture capital funds are regrouped with those of various institutions under the heading "Other Financial Institution" in the national balance sheet tables. On inquiry, we were informed that data on venture capital could not, at this time, be broken out.

ACKNOWLEDGEMENTS

THANKS TO P. HALPERN, M. POITEVIN AND B. SMITH for useful comments on a first draft of this paper, and M. Macdonald and K. Falconer for useful information.

BIBLIOGRAPHY

Allen, D. "Revue d'une analyse du FSTQ preparé pour l'Institut Fraser par Jean-Marc Suret, Université Laval." mimeo, 1994.

Ball, R.J. and E.B.A. Saint-Cyr. "Short Term Employment Functions in British Manufacturing Industries." *Review of Economic Studies*. (July 1966): 179-207.

Brechling, F. "The Relationship between Output and Employment in British Manufacturing Industries." *Review of Economic Studies*. (July 1965): 187-216.

Brechling, F. and P. O'Brien. "Short-Run Employment Functions in Manufacturing Industries: An International Comparison." *Review of Economics and Statistics*. (August 1969): 277-287.

Bruce, N. "Pathways to Tax Expenditures." In *Tax Expenditures and Government Policies*. Edited by N. Bruce. Kingston: John Deutsch Institute for Economic Research, Queen's University, 1990, pp. 2-61.

Canadian Labour Market and Productivity Centre. *The Role and Performance of Labour-Sponsored Investment Funds in the Canadian Economy. An Institutional Profile*. November 1995.

Cohen-Skalli, B. and D. Laskar. "Fonction d'emploi à court terme et cycles de productivité : un essai de synthèse." *Annales de l'INSEE*. (1980): 123-151.

Dormont, B. "Quelle est l'influence du coût du travail sur l'emploi." *Revue économique*. (1994): 399-414.

Hamermesh, O. "The Demand for Labor in the Long Run." In *Handbook of Labor Economics*. Volume 1. Edited by O. Ashenfelter and R. Layard. Amsterdam: North Holland, 1986.

Ireland, N.J. and D.J. Smyth. "The Specification of Short-Run Employment Models." *The Review of Economic Studies*. (April 1970).

Jackson, E.T. and F. Lamontagne. *Adding Volume: The Economic and Social Impacts of Labour-Sponsored Venture Capital Corporations on Their Investee Firms*. Ottawa: Canadian Labour Market and Productivity Centre, 1995.

Lamonde, P., Y. Martineau and D. Allen. "Impact économique et fiscal des investissements du Fonds de solidarité des travailleurs du Québec (FSTQ), 1984-1993." Mimeo, October 1994.

Lesueur, J.-Y. "Relation d'efficience, structures de marché et ajustement de l'emploi." *Revue d'économie industrielle*. 61, (1992): 68-85.

Matthews, J. "The Democratization of Capital." *Economic and Industrial Democracy*. 10, (1989): 165-193.

Ministère du revenu du Québec. *Statistiques fiscales des particuliers*.

——. *Portrait de la fiscalité des particuliers au Québec*.

Perry, P. And K. Treff. "Provincial Budget Roundup 1996." *Canadian Tax Journal*. 44 (3), (1996): 760-778.

Revenue Canada. *Taxation Statistics 1995*. Ottawa: Revenue Canada.

St-Hilaire, F. "Les finances publiques: à qui profitent les avantages fiscaux?" *IRPP Choix*. 1 (5), (1995): 1-51.

Statistics Canada. *Canadian Economic Observer: Historical Statistics Supplement*. Cat. 11-210,

Suret, J.-M. "Les initiatives québécoises dans le domaine de la capitalisation des entreprises le point de vue des investisseurs." *Canadian Public Policy*. 16 (3), (1990): 239-251.

——. "Une évaluation des dépenses fiscales et des subventions dans le domaine de la capitalisation des entreprises." *L'Actualité économique*. 69 (2), (1993): 17-40.

——. "Le gouvernement du Québec et le financement des entreprises : les mauvaises réponses à un faux problème." In *l'État interventionniste*. Edited by P. Palda. The Fraser Institute, 1994, pp.113-168.

——. "Analyse et bilan de deux programmes d'encadrement financier du développement : le RÉAQ et le FSTQ." *Actes du congrès de l'ASDEQ, 1995*. 1-13 (forthcoming).

Surrey, S.S. *Pathways for Tax Reform*. Cambridge: Harvard University Press. 1973.

Michael J. Robinson
Faculty of Management
University of Calgary

14

Raising Equity Capital for Small and Medium-Sized Enterprises Using Canada's Public Equity Markets

INTRODUCTION

CONTINUED ECONOMIC DEVELOPMENT IN A COUNTRY OR REGION depends on the emergence and growth of new economic entities. New firms increase the level of competition in existing industries and develop many of the technological innovations that fuel economic growth. One barrier to the creation and growth of new firms is that raising seed and secondary capital for such ventures is difficult.

Entrepreneurs have trouble raising debt capital because they often lack the proven cash flows or collateral required by lenders. This means that, until a firm has grown to a certain size, the owner must search for equity capital. Unfortunately, raising equity capital can be just as difficult. Venture capital firms provide limited support for start-ups because they prefer to invest in a few selected businesses in which they can take a substantial equity interest and exert control over management (see Barry et al., 1990; Sahlman, 1990). A more important source of equity capital for start-ups is investment angels (see Wetzel, 1983; Riding et al., 1993). Riding et al. found that, in Canada, angels provide almost twice as much equity for small firms as formal venture capitalists.

There have been a number of recent studies which examine the problems of raising equity financing for small and medium-sized enterprises (SMEs). The definition of an SME varies from study to study, and the Ontario Securities Commission (OSC) Task Force on Small Business Financing adopted the definition that any firm with annual sales of less than $10 million should be considered an SME. The Task Force (OSC, 1994, p. 6) noted that a major problem for these SMEs is "...the relative scarcity of equity capital financing deals at the low end of the market, generally in the range from $50,000 or $100,000 to $1,000,000."

The regulatory and institutional barriers for firms attempting to arrange private equity financing of this amount in Canada are discussed in MacIntosh (1994a, b). The OSC Task Force also analysed this problem and provided a number of recommendations for reducing the cost and regulatory burden placed on issuers of private placements in Ontario.

The OSC Task Force (OSC, 1994, p. 6) considered the roadblocks experienced by SMEs in accessing public equity financing. One major problem they noted was "...the lack of a developed distribution network in the Canadian marketplace for offerings of less than $10 million." The Task Force provided a number of recommendations to lower the cost and regulatory burden associated with the raising of public equity by SMEs. Their recommendations included the establishment of a simplified "small business prospectus form," a simplification and liberalization of the escrow requirements of these issuers and an elimination of the requirement to involve an underwriter in public offerings by SMEs.

The purpose of this study is to examine whether the public equity markets in Canada currently provide a viable alternative source of equity financing for SMEs. It focuses on whether the public markets are suitable for raising small amounts of equity, in the range of $50,000 to $1,000,000, and discusses the role of these markets in raising larger equity amounts. The next section examines the costs of publicly listing a security in Canada to see if these costs impose a major obstacle to SMEs. The listing requirements of Canadian exchanges are then examined to see if they restrict the ability of SMEs to raise equity capital. This is followed by a consideration of other institutional issues which may restrict the availability of equity capital to SMEs. Programs which have been initiated in Canada and other countries to increase the ability of SMEs to seek public sources of equity are reviewed, the results of the study are summarized and recommendations of how to improve the access of SMEs to the public equity markets are provided.

Costs of Raising Capital Through an Initial Public Offering

There are two major cost components associated with an initial public offering (IPO). The first is the cash expenses the firm must pay to have its equity distributed to the public. This component has two elements: a regulatory cost and the underwriter's commission. The regulatory cost includes legal fees, accounting and auditing fees, listing fees and printing costs associated with the preparation of the IPO prospectus and with satisfying the regulators and a stock exchange. The underwriter's commission typically has two components: a direct fee, usually based on a fixed percentage of the issue, and warrants issued to the underwriter with an exercise price equal to the issue price.

The second major cost component of an IPO is the discount at which the firm must offer its shares to the public to ensure that the issue will be sold.

Cash Expenses of an IPO

Before a firm can issue its shares to the public using an IPO, it must pass a number of hurdles. The first is to locate an underwriter willing to distribute the shares. Underwriting firms are concerned about their reputation and want to ensure that a firm's shares will have value to investors. The underwriting firm will conduct a due diligence examination of the firm and incur expenses which will be charged to the IPO firm. Once the underwriter is satisfied, the IPO firm must be approved by the appropriate securities regulator and exchange officials. In order to receive this approval, the IPO firm will incur legal expenses, accounting and auditing expenses, and may be required to have an independent evaluation of its business plans prepared. Following the approval of the securities commission and the exchange, the IPO firm must incur the expense of printing the prospectus to be distributed to potential investors.

The above regulatory costs are direct cash expenditures which are over and above any costs the firm itself must bear, e.g., the opportunity cost of management in planning the IPO and searching for an underwriter. The length of the period from inception of the IPO to the listing of the security on an exchange can vary from case to case. In general, the more established the firm and the higher its earning potential, the shorter the listing time.

These regulatory costs are in place to protect the investing public. The intention of securities regulators and stock exchange officials is to impose a minimum level of information disclosure to the investing public. These regulators also attempt to ensure that the information presented is a factual representation of the situation facing the IPO firm. The continued confidence of the investing public is necessary to ensure that equity markets function effectively and that investors will be willing to purchase additional IPO securities in the future.

Many regulatory expenses are fixed, e.g., legal fees and exchange listing fees, and economies of scale in the distribution of shares to the public are expected. Thus, the percentage cost of an IPO's regulatory expenses should be a decreasing function of the amount of capital raised.

A brokerage firm will also charge the IPO firm a fee for conducting the underwriting. There are two predominant methods of underwriting a security issue. In a best-efforts underwriting, the investment dealer attempts to sell as many shares as possible at an agreed upon selling price. In this case, the investment dealer does not guarantee the amount of capital which will be raised for the IPO firm. Therefore, the risk of the share offering being undersubscribed is borne by the IPO issuer. With a firm-commitment share offering, the underwriting firm guarantees the proceeds of the issue to the IPO firm. In this instance, the underwriter bears the risk of an undersubscription. In general, best-efforts underwriting is used by smaller more risky companies in which the underwriter is unwilling to guarantee the amount of proceeds received from the issue, or the cost of the guarantee to the issuing firm is too high.

As compensation for its efforts, the underwriting firm charges the IPO firm a commission based on the amount of capital raised. This commission takes the form of a percentage of the proceeds of the issue and is deducted from the issue proceeds which are forwarded to the IPO issuer. Generally, the commission is higher for firm-commitment underwriting than for best-efforts underwriting. For the smaller equity issues, the underwriter may also take share warrants with an exercise price equal to the IPO price.

An Examination of the Cash Costs of U.S. IPOs

Ritter (1987), in a study of 1,028 IPOs between 1977 and 1982, found evidence that there are economies of scale in the cash expenses of an underwriting, and determined that the cash expense can be estimated as $250,000 plus 7 percent of

TABLE 1

AVERAGE ISSUE COSTS FOR U.S. IPOs BETWEEN 1977 AND 1987

Panel A: Average Dollar Costs of Issue

Type and Size of IPO	Regulatory Expenses ($000s)	Underwriter Commission ($000s)	Average Issue Size ($000s)
Best-efforts			
Group 1	108.51	193.86	1,897.05
Group 2	175.46	384.69	3,918.21
Firm-commitment			
Group 1	148.72	217.51	2,188.44
Group 2	288.59	493.72	5,723.35
Group 3	406.30	1,031.66	13,434.32
Group 4	522.17	2,573.60	38,838.00

Panel B: Average Percentage Costs (of Issue Proceeds)

Type and Size of IPO	Regulatory Expenses (%)	Underwriter Commission (%)	Total Cash Expenses (%)
Best-efforts			
Group 1	5.87	10.25	16.12
Group 2	4.72	9.88	14.60
Firm-commitment			
Group 1	7.03	9.99	17.01
Group 2	5.29	8.83	14.12
Group 3	3.09	7.81	10.90
Group 4	1.58	6.84	8.42

Notes: Based on a sample of 1,852 IPOs (1,556 firm-commitment and 296 best-efforts) between 1977 and 1987. The groups are categorized by the amount of capital raised (in thousands of dollars).
Amount raised:
Group 1: less than $3,000
Group 2: $3,000 to $9,530
Group 3: $9,531 to $18,924
Group 4: $18,925 and over.

Source: Aggarwal and Rivoli (1991), Table 2.

the gross proceeds of the underwriting. In a study of 1,852 IPOs between 1977 and 1987, Aggarwal and Rivoli (1991) also found economies of scale in the cost of an IPO, and determined that the average regulatory cost of a best-efforts IPO of less than $3 million is $108,510, and the average underwriter commission is $193,860 for a total cash cost of $302,370 (see Table 1, panel A). This table also shows that the average cost of an IPO is higher for firm-commitment IPOs than for comparable best-efforts IPOs. This result is expected due to the higher risk borne by the underwriter of a firm-commitment IPO. The magnitude of these underwriting costs suggests that it would be uneconomic for a U.S. firm to conduct an underwriting of less than $1 million.

On a percentage basis, Ritter found that, for best-efforts IPOs between $1 million and $2 million, the regulatory and underwriter commission expenses are 9.52 percent and 10.63 percent of the issue proceeds, for a total cash cost of 20.15 percent (see Table 2). This table also provides a good illustration of the economies of scale in the costs of IPOs as the percentage cost of an IPO is steadily decreasing as a function of issue size. Aggarwal and Rivoli (1991) reported similar results (see Table 1, panel B). In their sample, small best-efforts IPOs, under $3 million, have average regulatory and commission expenses of 5.87 percent and 10.25 percent respectively, for a total cash cost of 16.12 percent. Note that the percentage regulatory cost reported by Aggarwal and Rivoli for offerings of less than $4 million are much lower than the values reported by Ritter which suggests that the regulatory costs have decreased over time in the United States.

An Examination of the Cash Costs of Canadian IPOs

The cost of issuing securities in Canada will depend on the type of underwriting and the province in which the underwriting is being conducted. According to industry participants, the least expensive jurisdiction for an underwriting is Alberta. In the Alberta Stock Exchange (ASE) (1994) publication *Going Public*, the ASE estimated the regulatory costs of an IPO as ranging from $28,000 up to $105,000, with average underwriting costs of between 5 percent and 20 percent of the issue proceeds. The low end of the fixed cost range involves Junior Capital Pool (JCP) IPOs. The details of this special type of IPO are discussed in subsequent sections.

To conduct a regular IPO in Alberta usually costs a firm between $65,000 and $150,000 in regulatory expenses. The underwriter's commission would be an additional 7.5 percent to 10 percent of the capital raised. In Alberta, it is possible to use the Exchange Offer Prospectus (EOP) program to lower regulatory expenses to the range of $40,000 to $75,000, but it restricts the security to being listed only on the ASE. As an illustration, the EOP underwriting for Vicom Multimedia in November 1994 had a regulatory cost of $70,000 and an agent's commission of 7.5 percent. Thus, the total cost of issue would have been $257,500 for the minimum underwriting of $2.5 million, and $370,000 for the maximum underwriting of $4 million.

As mentioned above, the lowest dollar cost form of underwriting in Alberta is the JCP program. Table 3, panel A illustrates that the average regulatory cost of a JCP IPO has been less than $25,000 since the program's inception in 1986 and,

TABLE 2

AVERAGE ISSUE COSTS FOR U.S. IPOS BETWEEN 1977 AND 1982

Type and Size of IPO	Regulatory Expenses (%)	Underwriter Commission (%)	Total Cash Expenses (%)
Best-efforts			
Group 1	9.52	10.63	20.15
Group 2	6.21	10.00	16.21
Group 3	3.71	9.86	13.57
Group 4	3.42	9.80	13.22
Group 5	2.40	8.03	10.43
Firm-commitment			
Group 1	9.64	9.84	19.48
Group 2	7.60	9.83	17.43
Group 3	5.67	9.10	14.77
Group 4	4.31	8.03	12.34
Group 5	2.10	7.24	9.34

Notes: Based on a sample of 1,028 IPOs (664 firm-commitment and 364 best-efforts) between 1977 and 1982. The groups are categorized by the amount of capital raised (in thousands of dollars).
Amount raised:
Group 1: $1,000 to $1,999
Group 2: $2,000 to $3,999
Group 3: $4,000 to $5,999
Group 4: $6,000 to $9,999
Group 5: $10,000 to $120,174.

Source: Ritter (1987), Table 3.

although the underwriter's commission has been increasing in recent years, it is still less than $15,000. Thus, the average total cost of a JCP IPO between 1986 and 1992 was less than $40,000. In percentage terms, the average total IPO costs never exceeded 18 percent of the issue proceeds and were usually less than 16 percent (see Table 3, panel B). Thus, the percentage costs of small JCP IPOs on the ASE are comparable with the percentage costs of small issues in the United States contained in Table 1, panel B and Table 2. Table 3 also illustrates that the average size of a JCP IPO has been steadily increasing over time.

To issue securities on the Vancouver Stock Exchange (VSE) in British Columbia would increase the cost of an underwriting by approximately $20,000 to $30,000 over the cost of a similar issue in Alberta. The reason for this increase is the requirement to have an independent evaluation of the business as specified in

TABLE 3

AVERAGE ISSUE COSTS FOR CANADIAN JCP IPOS BETWEEN 1986 AND 1992

Panel A: Average Dollar Costs of Issue

Year	Regulatory Expenses ($000s)	Underwriter Commission ($000s)	Average Issue Size ($000s)
1986	11.97	0.78	97.93
1987	15.30	1.87	136.13
1988	18.86	4.63	154.38
1989	19.55	8.26	181.05
1990	24.94	6.34	195.81
1991	22.67	14.08	204.42
1992	18.38	12.57	224.22

Panel B: Average Percentage Costs (of Issue Proceeds)

Year	Regulatory Expenses (%)	Underwriter Commission (%)	Total Cash Expenses (%)
1986	12.23	0.80	13.03
1987	11.24	1.38	12.62
1988	12.45	3.10	15.55
1989	10.80	4.56	15.36
1990	12.74	3.24	15.98
1991	11.09	6.89	17.98
1992	8.20	5.61	13.81

Source: Alberta Stock Exchange public files.

Local Interim Policy Statement 317. This policy statement also has the effect of increasing the length of time required to conduct the underwriting in British Columbia vs. Alberta.

In Ontario and Quebec, the minimum regulatory cost of an IPO is between $100,000 and $150,000. Jog (this volume) estimates average total TSE issue costs at $300,000 to $400,000 plus 6 percent to 7 percent of issue proceeds. Due to the larger size of IPOs on exchanges in these provinces, however, the percentage cost of an IPO is lower than in Alberta or British Columbia. Using a sample of 46 IPOs on the TSE between 1991 and 1993, MacIntosh (1994a) estimated the average regulatory costs of an IPO of less than $5 million at 5.6 percent of the issue proceeds, and the average underwriting cost at 17 percent (although this was skewed by an underwriting with a commission of 40 percent), for a total cash cost of 22.6 percent. He found evidence of economies of scale in TSE IPO expenses, as average percentage cash costs decrease with issue size. For example, average total costs for IPOs between $5 million and $10 million are around 12 percent.

This evidence suggests that the dollar cost of publicly listing a security is lower in Canada than in the United States. Thus, it is possible, economically, to raise an amount ranging from several hundred thousand dollars for an ASE JCP firm, to more than a million dollars for a regular IPO on the major exchanges. For a firm attempting to raise several hundred thousand dollars of equity financing using the public equity markets in Canada, the ASE's JCP program is the only economical alternative. Medium-sized enterprises could use either the ASE or VSE to raise a minimum amount of approximately $1 million. According to the OSC Task Force report (1994), Ontario investment dealers prefer to issue equity offerings of $10 million or more. Investment dealers in Quebec are expected to have minimum offer sizes greater than Alberta and Vancouver, but lower than Ontario.

Underpricing of IPOs

The second major cost of an IPO underwriting is indirect and is borne by the issuing firm. This cost results from the underwriters' habit of setting the IPO price at a level below the equilibrium value of a firm's shares. This empirical phenomena has been noted in many countries including Canada, and a number of explanations have been put forth.

Baron (1982) developed a theory for the demand for investment banking advisory services in which the advisor is better informed about the capital markets than the issuing firm. In this situation, the issuer contracts with the investment dealer for the provision of both advisory and distribution services, and dealers use their superior information to establish an issue price below the first-best offer price. This results in IPOs being initially underpriced when they are first issued. Baron's theory was directly tested by Muscarella and Vetsuypens (1989). They examined the IPOs for a set of investment banks which went public between 1970 and 1987. Since in these cases the investment dealer company is acting as its own advisor and distributor of shares, there is no asymmetry in the information between the issuer and the advisor. Muscarella and Vetsuypens found that, contrary to Baron's theory, these self-marketed IPOs experienced underpricing which was significantly higher than other IPOs. Using a sample of IPOs for Canadian brokerage firms, Cheung and Krinsky (1994) were also unable to find support for Baron's hypothesis.

Rock (1986) and Beatty and Ritter (1986) developed alternative models to explain IPO underpricing. In their models, there are two classes of investors: informed investors and uninformed investors. The informed investors are able to determine the investment quality of a particular IPO and will attempt to purchase a large amount of the underpriced IPOs and a lesser amount of the overpriced IPOs. The uninformed investors are unable to differentiate between the types of IPOs and will wind up purchasing a higher percentage of the overpriced IPOs (thereby incurring the winner's curse) and a lower percentage of the underpriced IPOs. To entice the uninformed investors to purchase IPOs, all IPOs must be sufficiently underpriced to allow uninformed investors to cover their losses on the overpriced IPOs. Beatty and Ritter contended that underwriters will enforce the IPO underpricing to maintain their reputation, and provided weak evidence that investment firms which price IPOs incorrectly lose market share in subsequent periods. A direct test of this hypothesis was conducted, using data from Singapore, by Koh and Walter (1989). Due to the institutional arrangements in that country, it was possible to gather information on the rationing of IPO securities. Using this data, the authors found that, when the rationing associated with new issues was accounted for, the underpricing of new issues disappeared.

Other authors have tried to determine what elements of information will reduce the level of investor uncertainty about a particular security, and thus lower the extent of the underpricing of the new issue. In Canada, Jog and Riding (1987) found that IPO underpricing was significantly related to the firm's industry group and the use of the proceeds of the issue. Clarkson and Merkley (1994) found that the younger the firm and the lower the level of pre-issue annual sales, the higher the underpricing. As well, firms in the extractive industries had higher levels of underpricing than firms in the retail trade, services, financial and consumer products sectors. The authors also identified a number of management choice variables which explained cross-sectional differences in IPO underpricing. Underpricing was lower for firms which used a "Big Eight" accounting firm, was lower for high-prestige than lower-prestige underwriting firms and was lower if the managers included an earnings forecast in the prospectus. Finally, they found that the underpricing was lower if the proceeds of the issue were to be used for financing as opposed to operational or investment purposes.

Tinic (1988) developed and tested the hypothesis that the underpricing of IPOs occurs because investment dealers are protecting their firm against the legal liabilities of an overpriced issue and want to minimize the damage an overpriced issue will do to the firm's reputation. Keloharju (1993) found high initial IPO returns in a study of Finnish IPOs and noted a much lower probability of shareholder lawsuits in Finland than in the United States. Thus, the legal liability hypothesis was not a likely explanation for the underpricing of Finnish IPOs.

More recently, Allen and Faulhaber (1989), Chemmanur (1993), Grinblatt and Hwang (1989) and Welch (1989) developed signalling models which explained new issue underpricing. Under these models, issuers have better information than underwriters or investors about the value of a firm. The high-quality firms view the IPO as the first stage of their financing program, and intend to raise additional capital through a secondary offering in the future. To signal that their firm is high quality and to sell their stock at a higher price in secondary offerings, these high-quality firms choose to underprice their IPO. Thus, the high-quality firms will incur the higher underpricing cost in the initial market to realize a higher selling price in the secondary market. Lower-quality firms which do not intend to return to the market with a secondary offering will have no incentive to underprice their IPO deliberately. Thus, the high-quality firms' behaviour will not be mimicked by the lower-quality firms. Empirical examinations of this hypothesis by Jegadeesh et al. (1993) and Jog (this volume) found weak evidence in support of this hypothesis.

U.S. empirical evidence from Aggarwal and Rivoli (1990) and Ritter (1991), and Canadian evidence from Cheung and Krinsky (1994) suggests that IPO underpricing is a short-run phenomena. Ruud (1993) and Hanley et al. (1993) proposed an alternative explanation for the underpricing of IPOs based on stabilization activities by the underwriters of IPOs which effectively put a floor on the losses of IPOs and thus truncate the left tail of IPO return distributions. Since most studies of IPO underpricing measure underpricing from the initial issue price to the closing price at the end of the first trading day, these truncated distributions would result in a higher average day 1 return than would be the case if the stabilization activity did not occur. Both Ruud and Hanley et al. pointed out that this stabilization is acknowledged by the Securities and Exchange Commission (SEC) to be a form of price manipulation, but the SEC argues that firms which engage in stabilization for the purposes of manipulation will suffer a loss in reputation which will lower their ability to sell securities in the future. Using data from firm commitment underwritings, Ruud demonstrated that the distribution of one-day stock returns was positively skewed and inordinately peaked at a zero return. She also demonstrated that most securities with a day 1 return of zero subsequently fell in price. This is consistent with the evidence that IPO underpricing is a short-run phenomena. A more recent paper by Schultz and Zaman (1994) supported this dealer stabilization hypothesis by reporting that underwriters, on average, repurchase over 20 percent of the shares issued in an IPO during the first three days following the stock's listing.

Empirical Evidence of the Underpricing of IPO Securities

Early U.S. studies that document high returns immediately after issue for IPO securities include Reilly and Hatfield (1969), Stoll and Curly (1970) and Ibbotson (1975). Ibbotson reported that this return, measured over the first month of trading for a security, averages 11.4 percent. A summary of IPO underpricing in many countries around the world is presented in Kunz and Aggarwal (1994, Table 1).

Ibbotson and Jaffe (1975) examined the existence of "hot issue" markets for U.S. IPOs and found that IPO returns in the immediate after-market vary over time. They also found that a time series of IPO returns exhibited serial dependence and that "hot issue" markets persist over time. Ritter (1984) demonstrated the extent of this phenomena when he noted that over the 15 months beginning January 1980, U.S. IPO securities experienced a gain of 48.4 percent on the first day of trading. This return was significantly higher than the average return of 16.3 percent earned during the rest of the six-year period he studied (1977 to 1982). Ritter found that the "hot issue" phenomena was restricted to natural resource securities.

Ritter (1987) provided evidence that the underpricing of an IPO security depended on whether the issue was distributed on a best-efforts basis, or as a firm-commitment offer (see Table 4). Using a firm-commitment issue will send a signal to investors that the underwriting firm has confidence in the issue price. Therefore,

TABLE 4

AVERAGE UNDERPRICING AND TOTAL ISSUE COSTS FOR U.S. IPOS IN PERCENTAGE TERMS BETWEEN 1977 AND 1982

Type and Size of IPO	Average Cash Expenses (%)	Average Underpricing (%)	Total Average Issue Costs (%)[a]
Best-efforts			
Group 1	20.15	39.62	31.89
Group 2	16.21	63.41	36.28
Group 3	13.57	26.82	14.49
Group 4	13.22	40.79	25.97
Group 5	10.43	-5.42	-0.17
Firm-commitment			
Group 1	19.48	26.92	31.73
Group 2	17.43	20.70	24.93
Group 3	14.77	12.57	20.90
Group 4	12.34	8.99	17.85
Group 5	9.34	10.32	16.27

Notes: Based on a sample of 1,028 IPOs (664 firm-commitment and 364 best-efforts) between 1977 and 1982. The groups are categorized by the amount of capital raised (in thousands of dollars).
Amount raised:
Group 1: $1,000 to $1,999
Group 2: $2,000 to $3,999
Group 3: $4,000 to $5,999
Group 4: $6,000 to $9,999
Group 5: $10,000 to $120,174.

[a] Total issue costs are computed as 100 percent minus the net proceeds of the issue as a percentage of the closing price on the first day of trading. Thus, it is not simply the sum of cash expenses and underpricing.

Source: Ritter (1987), Table 4.

the results show a much lower degree of underpricing for the firm-commitment issues. The table also illustrates the total cost of underwriting an IPO, including both the cash costs and the underpricing. For best-efforts and firm-commitment issues under $2 million, the total issue costs are 32 percent. For the most part, the total average issue costs are a decreasing function of issue size.

In a more recent study, Aggarwal and Rivoli (1991) reported higher underpricing for best-efforts issues, but lower underpricing for firm-commitment issues compared to Ritter's 1987 study (see Table 5). For best-efforts underwritings under $3 million, they found average underpricing of 65 percent and total average issue

TABLE 5

AVERAGE UNDERPRICING AND TOTAL ISSUE COSTS FOR U.S. IPOS IN PERCENTAGE TERMS BETWEEN 1977 AND 1987

Type and Size of IPO	Average Cash Expenses (%)	Average Underpricing (%)	Average Total Issue Costs (%)[a]
Best-efforts			
Group 1	16.13	65.32	49.27
Group 2	14.60	40.74	39.32
Firm-commitment			
Group 1	17.01	23.17	32.62
Group 2	14.12	10.16	22.04
Group 3	10.90	6.01	15.95
Group 4	8.42	7.08	14.48

Notes: Based on a sample of 1,852 IPOs (1,556 firm-commitment and 296 best-efforts) between 1977 and 1987. The groups are categorized by the amount of capital raised (in thousands of dollars).
Amount raised:
Group 1: less than $3,000
Group 2: $3,000 to $9,530
Group 3: $9,531 to $18,924
Group 4: $18,925 and over.

[a] Total issue costs are computed as 100 percent minus the net proceeds of the issue as a percentage of the closing price on the first day of trading. Thus, it is not simply the sum of cash expenses and underpricing.

Source: Aggarwal and Rivoli (1991), Table 2.

costs of almost 50 percent, while for firm-commitment issues of similar size they found average underpricing of 23 percent and total issue costs of 33 percent. Consistent with the Ritter results, Aggarwal and Rivoli found that firm-commitment issues had lower underpricing and total costs than best-efforts issues, and that underpricing and issue costs decreased with issue size.

Canadian studies of IPOs that report underpricing include Jog and Riding (1987), Krinsky and Rotenberg (1989), Falk and Thornton (1992) and Jog (this volume). Jog and Riding reported that short-term returns following the initial listing of a security averaged 9 percent to 11.5 percent between 1971 and 1983. However, Jog (this volume) has found lower returns after 1983. Over the period 1983 to 1988, Falk and Thornton reported average returns, adjusted for market returns, of 19 percent for TSE IPOs, 25 percent for Montreal Exchange (ME) IPOs and 307 percent for ASE IPOs. Their sample of ASE securities included both regularly listed ASE and JCP securities. The large difference between the returns reported by Jog and Riding and Falk and Thornton suggests that "hot issue" markets exist in Canada.

The underpricing and total issue costs of ASE JCP securities are illustrated in Table 6. The first time period includes only blind pools listed before the establishment of the JCP program. In a blind pool stock offering, the prospective shareholder invests in a company with no earnings history and receives little indication of how the money being raised will be spent. Some of these blind pools were subject to fraudulent trading and, thus, the results in this time period are biased upward. These illegal trading activities resulted in the establishment of JCP guidelines in late November 1986. Thus, only the last three time periods in Table 6 include true JCP securities. The results indicate a high degree of underpricing in the early days of the JCP program, but a dramatic reduction in this underpricing as investors became accustomed to the characteristics of the securities, e.g., risk and return. Since the minimum issue price was raised to $0.10, the degree of underpricing of JCP securities is very similar to the underpricing of small U.S. securities. Thus, the total percentage costs of a JCP issue are currently similar to those of small U.S. firms.

Table 6

Average Underpricing and Total Issue Costs for ASE JCP IPOs in Percentage Terms between 1986 and 1992

Time Period	Average Cash Expenses (%)	Average Underpricing (%)	Average Total Issue Costs (%)[a]
04/18/86-10/31/86	13.03	864.00	90.98
12/01/86-10/16/87	12.62	529.00	86.11
10/19/87-07/19/88	15.55	248.00	75.73
07/20/88-12/31/92	15.78	62.00	48.01

Notes: The time periods were chosen to correspond to dates in which major changes were made to the JCP program, or to investor confidence. The first period starts when the first blind pool offering was made and ends when a moratorium was placed on new blind pool registrations. The second period begins when the moratorium was lifted and the JCP program was officially started. JCP regulations include a requirement for a minimum number of shareholders, escrow requirements, etc. The second period ends on the day before the stock market crash on October 19, 1987. The third time period begins with the stock market crash of 1987 and ends on the day that the last $0.05 stock offering was first listed. In the last period, only stocks with an initial price of $0.10 are included. (Although the Alberta Securities Commission raised the minimum share offering price to $0.10 in late 1987, it was several months before the last $0.05 stock offering actually became listed on the Alberta Stock Exchange.) The average cash expenses for the first three periods were the costs in 1986, 1987 and 1988 respectively. The average cash expense in the last period was the average of the cash expenses in 1989, 1990, 1991 and 1992.

[a] Total issue costs are computed as 100 percent minus the net proceeds of the issue as a percentage of the closing price on the first day of trading. Thus, it is not simply the sum of cash expenses and underpricing.

Source: Alberta Stock Exchange data records.

SUMMARY OF THE LITERATURE CONCERNING THE ISSUE COSTS OF AN IPO

THE CASH EXPENSES ASSOCIATED WITH AN IPO consist of fixed regulatory expenses, plus a commission expense which varies with the issue size. In Canada, these costs make it uneconomical to conduct an IPO with a value of much less than $1 million on the Toronto, Montreal or Vancouver stock exchanges. On the Alberta exchange it is possible to conduct an IPO of only a few hundred thousand dollars using the JCP program.

A large component of the cost of an IPO is the fact that the securities are issued to the public at an initial price that is lower than the security's equilibrium price. Recent evidence suggests that some of the underpricing is due to the support activities of an IPO's underwriters after issue. Nonetheless, it does appear that underwriters do set the issue price of an IPO at less than the equilibrium price. The most commonly accepted explanation for this phenomena is the asymmetry in information which exists between issuers and uninformed investors. Uninformed investors will reduce the price they are willing to pay for a firm's IPO to offset the winner's curse, suffered from purchasing proportionately too many overvalued IPOs. Further research has identified IPO characteristics, some of which are under management control, which can lower the extent of the information asymmetry and of the underpricing. Some researchers use these findings to suggest that there may be an optimal strategy for deciding when and how to conduct an IPO. For example, Aggarwal and Rivoli (1991) suggested that firms can seek to minimize their total costs of an IPO by waiting until the firm has a strong history of earnings, can justify an issue size approaching $10 million and can convince a prestigious underwriting firm to conduct the IPO. They concluded that "the entrepreneur is likely to pay dearly in going public prematurely" (p. 360).

This advice ignores the important question of how a firm raises equity before it is optimal to go public. Implicit in the recommendations is the belief that it is less costly to use private equity financing than public equity financing for small equity issues. In Canada, MacIntosh (1994a, b) and the Ontario Securities Commission (1994) presented evidence that significant regulatory and institutional barriers exist which make it difficult for small firms to access private equity financing. Discussions with brokerage industry participants in Alberta have indicated that it is much more difficult to raise seed capital from individual investors for a company which intends to stay private, than for a private company which intends to conduct a public offering in the near term. The fact that there are economies of scale in the issuing of IPOs does not mean that using the public equity markets is impractical for small equity issuers.

LISTING REQUIREMENTS OF CANADIAN STOCK EXCHANGES

THE LISTING REQUIREMENTS OF THE ASE, ME, TSE AND VSE for the different industry types are presented in Appendix A. The TSE, which dramatically tightened its requirements in 1992, has the toughest standards. Since 1992, the required public share float of all new companies has been $2 million, up from the previous level of $1 million. As well, any industrial firms with annual profits of less than $100,000 are required to have at least $5 million in tangible assets, an increase from the previous $1 million level. These changes effectively limit the TSE to the larger IPO issues of several million dollars. Thus, smaller Ontario firms which want to access public equity markets are forced to consider listing on the Ontario over-the-counter (OTC) market, the Canadian Dealer Network (CDN) or on one of the Canadian junior stock exchanges.

The ME has significantly lower listing requirements than the TSE. An ME industrial firm requires only $1 million in public equity, provided it has adequate assets and income. Similarly, the minimum public equity for mining firms is $500,000, and the minimum public equity for oil and gas exploration firms is $750,000. These resource industry firms must also have strong assets and earning potential to be able to list with the minimum amount of equity.

Regular listing on the VSE requires a minimum public equity level of $1.8 million for industrial firms and non-oil resource firms, and $1 million for oil and gas firms. A listing category also exists for venture companies with lower minimum listing requirements than for a regular listing. Resource companies need a minimum of $450,000 in equity, while non-resource companies need a minimum of $850,000.

The lowest listing requirements in the country are on the ASE. For example, it is possible to list an industrial firm with a minimum asset base of $400,000, as long as a minimum of 500,000 shares are held by at least 300 public shareholders. Using the JCP program, it is possible for entrepreneurs with at least $100,000 in seed capital to raise up to several hundred thousand dollars from public investors. In the first years of the JCP program, entrepreneurs did not need a clear idea of the purpose for which the funds were being raised; however, in recent years underwriting firms have been unwilling to take a JCP issue public unless the entrepreneur has a strong business track record and a good idea of how the funds will be invested.

Many authors like to discuss how the U.S. OTC markets, the National Association of Securities Dealers Automated Quotations/National Market System (NASDAQ/NMS) and the regular NASDAQ market, have allowed the listing of many small start-up companies in the United States. It should be noted that the listing requirements of these exchanges are higher than for most Canadian exchanges. For example, the pre-eminent market, the NASDAQ/NMS requires a minimum equity float of $3 million which is higher than even the TSE (see Schwartz, 1991, p. 51). Even the second-tier market, the regular NASDAQ, requires a firm to have a minimum of $2 million in assets, $1 million in capital and retained earnings, but has no minimum market float value. Clearly, the listing requirements of the major U.S. OTC markets are more stringent than those of the smaller Canadian exchanges.

To summarize, it is clear that the potential exists to raise equity capital of less than $1 million for venture firms using the ASE and VSE, and for resource issues on the ME. Due to the costs of listing, for practical purposes, most of the regular IPOs on these exchanges will not be much below the $1 million level. The TSE remains reserved for medium and large firms requiring equity of over $2 million. Although there is an OTC market in Ontario, it appears that there is a gap in the availability of public equity of less than $1 million in that province. Small Ontario firms can seek to list on the ASE or VSE; however, the underwriters and regulators of these exchanges have difficulty with listing applications from other jurisdictions. One of the reasons for the success of the ASE's JCP program, discussed in the next section, is that the majority of the issues were Calgary firms. This allowed the underwriters and regulators to obtain a great deal of information about the JCP principals. As well, since only Alberta residents were able to purchase IPO shares in a JCP firm, it allowed the principals to identify investors, called "President's List" investors, for the public offering. In many cases, JCP principals of Alberta companies were able to go to the underwriter of the JCP offering with almost the entire issue placed with their friends and business associates.

Other Constraints to Public Listing of SME Equity

The two major reasons why junior firms will choose to list their shares on a stock exchange are to allow the seed equity investors the opportunity to cash in their investment in full or partially, or to allow the firm the opportunity to re-enter the equity market with a secondary offering to raise additional equity capital. In either case, it is vitally important that an active secondary market for the firm's shares develops after the initial listing. Without this secondary market, the firm's share price will drift lower after issue, making it harder for the firm to issue a secondary offering and for investors to sell their shares.

MacIntosh (1994a) noted that a "catch-22" exists in the development of a market for junior equities. Primary offerings in such a market are not likely to be successful unless there is some assurance that there will be an active secondary market following the initial listing. Unfortunately, an active secondary market for such securities cannot develop until there have been successful primary offerings in the market.

Further exacerbating the liquidity issue is the fact that large underwriting firms are unlikely to be interested in participating in the issuance of junior equity issues. MacIntosh (1994a, p. 140) stated, "The national investment dealers have shown very little interest in servicing the IPO market for offerings of less than $25 million." In the United States, Wolfe et al. (1994) found that prestigious underwriters avoid the smaller riskier new issues.

Large underwriting firms avoid the smaller firms for three main reasons. First, they are concerned about the reputation of their firm being affected if they begin to participate in the underwriting of smaller firms. Second, as noted earlier, the underwriting commission is typically a function of the issue size. Thus, the larger firms have an incentive to participate in only the larger issues because of the overhead associated with maintaining their position as a prestigious firm. Finally, as Rasch (1994) noted, the low turnover of the small firms makes it unprofitable for brokerage firms to research the companies because the costs associated with collecting and processing the company information will not be recovered by brokerage commissions.

In studying the development and decline of special stock market segments for small firms on European exchanges, Rasch noted that when there is a decline in trading for these types of firms a "vicious circle" of illiquidity develops. There are two elements to this circle: the flow of information and the flow of funds. Within the flow of information circle, a lack of stock exchange turnover leads to a low demand for research about the companies and low incentive for brokerage firms to generate the research. Without the research, however, there is low investor interest in the securities and a low level of stock turnover. Within the flow of funds circle, low stock turnover creates an illiquid secondary market for these securities which increases transaction costs in this market. The higher transaction costs reduce the incentive of investors to trade in these securities and leads to low investor interest and low levels of trading.

Rasch (1994) also observed that a low liquidity in the secondary market for the equity of junior firms will have a significant impact on the issuing firms. He stated, "In order to attract investors, these companies have to offer a higher expected return than blue chips. This, however, raises their cost of equity and puts them at a disadvantage against large companies in terms of competitiveness" (p. 24).

Thus, the successful development of an active primary market for junior equity issues requires the establishment of a viable secondary market for these securities. Unfortunately, the evidence from Canada, the United States and Europe indicates that the large prestigious national brokerage firms avoid underwriting and supporting junior equities. Thus, the development of a market for this type of equity security requires strong regional and boutique investment dealers. In Canada, MacIntosh (1994a, p. 140) noted, "The development of a regional dealer network in Canada has greatly lagged that in the United States." One reason for the lack of these dealers in Canada is that economies of scale exist in the investment industry, and Canada's capital markets are not large enough to support specialized investment dealers. MacIntosh also pointed out that limits on the underwriting compensation of small issues in Ontario, due to Ontario Policy Statement 5.2, have hampered the activities of investment dealers in the junior market.

In Alberta, a number of regional brokerage firms have taken advantage of the JCP program to carve out a profitable underwriting and trading niche. The compensation to these dealers for an underwriting consists of a cash commission, plus stock warrants equal to 10 percent of the issued shares. In the early years of the JCP program, the underwriters kept the cash commissions low in order to build the program but, recently, the cash commissions have been increasing. The client base for the JCP program is predominately retail, although a number of JCP firms are able to arrange private placements soon after issue from institutional investors.

A regional brokerage firm in Ontario indicated that there is a market for underwriting small equity issues, but the majority of these issues are listed on the OTC market. The disadvantage of this form of listing for junior equities is the lack of liquidity for firms listed on the CDN. As discussed above, an active secondary market is essential before the primary market for these securities can fully develop. The regional firm indicated that, for slightly larger firms, it is possible to take the firm public by conducting a reverse takeover of a TSE shell. MacIntosh (1994a) pointed out that the price of a TSE shell is approximately $200,000 to $250,000. After acquiring a shell, a firm would incur additional regulatory and underwriting expenses when raising additional equity capital.

History of Junior Equity Issues

In this section, the history of junior stock programs in a number of countries are examined. In the United States, blind pool programs were implemented in the 1980s to assist start-up firms in raising equity. Unfortunately, the experience of U.S. investors with blind pools has been poor. Out of a sample of 68 U.S. blind pools in existence in 1986, only 23 (33.8 percent) were trading at a price above the initial subscription price, and one blind pool underwriter estimated that only 2 percent of these pools were successful (see Stern and Bornstein, 1986). One problem with these programs is that dishonest promoters use the fact that securities regulations, especially for small stock offerings in certain states, are inadequate or supervision is lax to defraud investors of millions of dollars (see Holdman, 1984; Stern et al., 1989). Stern and Bornstein (1986, p. 41) reported, "One state securities director says the SEC regularly brushes aside complaints involving securities fraud under $1 million as too small for them to look into." States with relatively lax regulations, such as Utah, attracted criminals interested in fraudulent stock trading (see Holdman, 1984). These lax states have attempted to improve their legislation and enforcement to combat the fraud. As well, recent rule changes by the SEC have been instituted to combat fraud in the trading of low-priced U.S. stocks (see Reuter, 1992).

During the 1980s, a number of major European stock exchanges established special stock market segments for trading the shares of small firms (see Rasch, 1994). The first special segments included the Unlisted Securities Market (USM) of the London Stock Exchange, the Official Parallel Market (OPM) of the Amsterdam Stock Exchange, the Mercatto Ristretto in Italy, and the Second Marché in Paris. The Geregelter (regulated) Market was established in Germany in 1987. These exchanges were introduced to combat the low number of new equity listings on European stock exchanges. Rasch (1994, p. 2.) stated, "By the end of the 1970s the European stock exchanges had lost their role as an important source of finance."

These special market segments were introduced to be an intermediate market between the existing major stock exchanges and the OTC markets. The admission and disclosure requirements were set at a lower level than for the major stock markets. For example, in the junior markets a firm had to offer a minimum of only 10 percent of its equity to the general public to qualify for listing, while the requirement was a minimum of 25 percent on the major exchanges. These special market segments were designed as transition markets to allow firms to grow to a size where they could be listed on a major exchange.

During the first years of their development, many of these exchanges experienced great success in primary offerings and secondary market trading. For example, the USM of the London Stock Exchange began in 1980 and, by 1988, more than 780 securities had been listed on it. In January 1987, the London Stock Exchange opened a third market specifically designed to appeal to even smaller firms which could not satisfy the USM listing requirements. This third market did not develop strong investor interest and, in the face of declining interest, was closed in 1990 with about half of the listed companies being transferred to the USM. Since secondary market trading and only seven new companies were listed in 1992. One reason for the decline was the lowering of listing requirements for regular London Stock Exchange firms and an increase in the costs of issue of USM firms to a level close to the costs of a regular listing. The London Stock Exchange decided to close the USM in 1992, but postponed the implementation date to 1996.

Similar experiences have been observed for the French Second Marché, Amsterdam's OPM (closed in 1992), Italy's Mercatto Ristretto and Germany's Geregelter Market. These markets were significantly affected by the stock market decline in October 1987; however, structural problems with these markets also existed. Since the exchanges were regarded as transitory, the strong firms would grow into regularly listed firms and only the weaker firms would be left on the junior exchanges. When the supply of new listings dried up in the early 1990s, these exchanges acquired a reputation of containing inferior securities. This affected secondary market trading and the willingness of new firms to seek listings on these markets. As well, there was inadequate differentiation between the junior markets and the regular markets in some countries so, as regulations and costs associated with listing on the major exchanges were lowered, there was little incentive for firms to list on the junior markets.

A final problem is that the growth in importance of institutional investors in Europe increased the demand for large, heavily traded, European securities at the expense of the junior securities. Many of these institutions adopted passive investment strategies which entailed duplicating stock market indices based on blue-chip securities only. As discussed above, this lack of demand for junior securities meant that many brokerage firms did not research or support the trading of the juniors, and the liquidity of these securities declined.

Alberta's Junior Capital Pool Program

THE JCP PROGRAM WAS INITIATED IN NOVEMBER 1986, after public hearings examined the performance of a series of blind pools which had been introduced in Alberta earlier in the year. The stated objective of the JCP program is as follows (see Alberta Stock Exchange Circular No. 7, 1990, p. 7-1):

> The Junior Capital Pool concept is designed to provide junior start up companies with an enhanced opportunity to become listed on The Alberta Stock Exchange thereby providing a viable and efficient mechanism to enable junior companies to raise further equity capital from the investing public. The Exchange recognizes however that as the listing and prospectus disclosure requirements for Junior Capital Pool Companies are substantially less than what is required for other companies, additional requirements are necessary to provide the market with sufficient disclosure and to limit abuse of this system.

To set up a JCP firm, a group of inside investors (promoters) raise seed capital by issuing themselves shares in exchange for cash. The amount of seed capital required before an offering can be made to outside shareholders has been changed four times: $30,000, to $50,000, to $75,000 and recently to $100,000. The firm raises additional equity capital through a JCP IPO to outside shareholders with a minimum share value of at least $0.10. The current JCP regulations require that the share value for seed capital can be no less than 50 percent of the price of the shares offered to the public through the IPO. The prospectus requirements for a JCP IPO are much less onerous than those of a regular IPO, and include a requirement to identify all seed capital purchasers and provide an idea of the line of business in which the JCP firm will be pursuing asset acquisitions. As noted in Appendix A, a JCP firm can have no significant operating assets, nor agreements in place to acquire assets, before being listed on the ASE.

Thus, investors in a JCP IPO are at a severe information disadvantage with respect to the promoters of the firm. There are, however, a number of regulations designed to protect JCP IPO investors against this information asymmetry. First, all JCP stock offerings must be conducted by registered investment dealers who are bound by "know your client" rules. These brokerage firms must ensure that any investors in a JCP firm fully understand the investment characteristics, including the risk, of their investment. Brokerage firms are also concerned with maintaining their reputation and will only underwrite JCP issues which they believe have a high probability of success. In order to have a JCP issue accepted by a brokerage firm, the promoters must have a proven track record in the industry they have identified for the firm, must have a clean record with the Alberta Securities Commission (ASC) and the ASE, and should have experience on the board of a public company.

A JCP listing is transitory because once listed on the ASE the JCP firm has 18 months in which to complete a major transaction – an asset acquisition – which will change the company from a JCP firm to a regularly listed ASE firm. The major transaction must be large enough (over $400,000) for the JCP firm to qualify for regular listing on the ASE. To minimize the possibility of investor funds being misappropriated, only Canadian assets are eligible for major transactions. Failure to complete a major transaction within the allowed period may result in the JCP firm being delisted by the ASE. To further protect outside investors in a JCP firm, inside investors are required to provide full disclosure regarding the details of a major transaction prior to its implementation, and the majority of the outside shareholders must approve the transaction before it can be completed. It is possible that this 18-month period may force some outside shareholders to make suboptimal investment decisions near the end of the period if they are concerned about their shares being delisted. The ASE has tried to combat this potential problem by allowing JCP firms to become reinstated if they complete a major transaction after the 18-month period.

The JCP rules have been tightened to provide further protection for investors. For example, in late 1987 the minimum price of a JCP share was raised to $0.10 from $0.05 and, more recently, the minimum price of seed capital was set at 50 percent of the public offer price. The net result has been to increase the level of protection afforded to outside shareholders in a JCP company; however, they have also increased the cost of listing a JCP company. Alberta regulators were attempting to make the appropriate trade-off between ensuring full disclosure and fair treatment for minority shareholders, and the cost of publicly listing a company.

One agency problem with all junior equities, including JCP equities, is that the market float is relatively low making it easier for the price of securities to be manipulated by the firm's promoters. Some enforcement experts maintain that fraud in the junior Canadian markets is widespread (see Mathias 1994a, p. 10) and the odds of transgressors being caught and convicted very low (see Mathias 1994a, b and c). To overcome this agency problem, the JCP program has very strict escrow requirements. One hundred percent of the shares of inside shareholders (the seed capital providers) must be held in escrow at the time of the initial listing of the security. One third of the securities in escrow are released on each of the first, second and third anniversaries of the firm's major transaction. The regulations seek to overcome the agency problem by ensuring that inside shareholders will benefit from a JCP issue only if the firm succeeds in building shareholder value over a long period.

Another problem with junior equity markets, discussed by MacIntosh (1994a) and Rasch (1994), is that there may be a problem with low liquidity of securities after an IPO. The JCP program has been structured to help overcome that problem by requiring that each JCP firm must have at least 300 public shareholders owning an aggregate total of at least 500,000 shares. As well, to prevent initial share holdings in the public market from being too concentrated, the maximum percentage any one outside shareholder can purchase of an IPO is 2 percent of the shares issued. It is felt that these regulations will provide for an active secondary market for JCP securities. Also helping the secondary market is the posting of public bids and asks for a JCP firm by the brokerage company underwriting the issue.

The JCP program was very successful in the late 1980s in increasing the number of firms that were publicly listed in Alberta. Table 7 illustrates that between 1986 and 1992, 405 companies were listed as JCP firms (or were converted to JCP firms) and over $77 million was raised in initial JCP offerings (including seed capital and IPO proceeds). Although the number of JCP issues declined significantly in the early 1990s, the number of new JCP listings reached 56 in 1993 and 99 in 1994.

A major objective of the JCP program was to allow small start-up companies to become listed in Alberta, making it easier for them to access equity capital markets to finance their expansion. To determine the success of the JCP program in meeting this objective, two issues were examined: how many JCP firms completed major transactions and became regularly listed ASE firms, and how successful were JCP companies in raising capital in the secondary markets, both equity and debt, to finance their growth.

Table 8 illustrates that of the 384 JCP firms that went public between 1986 and 1992, 324 or 86 percent had completed a major transaction by the end of 1992. By excluding the 15 JCP firms listed in the 18 months prior to the end of 1992,

TABLE 7

INITIAL CAPITAL RAISED BY JCP COMPANIES

Year	Number Listed	Seed Capital ($)	JCP IPO Capital ($)
Pre-JCP	21	752,500	2,094,500
		(35,833)	(99,738)
1986	1	10,000	60,000
		(10,000)	(60,000)
1987	172	6,527,949	23,414,849
		(37,953)	(136,133)
1988	156	6,268,106	24,083,711
		(40,180)	(154,383)
1989	24	1,027,322	4,345,222
		(42,805)	(181,051)
1990	8	456,500	1,566,500
		(57,063)	(195,813)
1991	6	306,495	1,226,495
		(51,083)	(204,416)
1992	17	991,750	3,811,750
		(58,338)	(224,221)
Total	405	16,340,622	60,603,027
		(40,347)	(149,637)

Note: This table illustrates the total equity raised. The average amount is displayed in parentheses, for each year of the JCP program.

which were actively searching for a major transaction, the success rate increased to 88 percent. In Table 8, firms are assigned to industry categories based on the investment intentions outlined in their initial prospectus. These intentions were not binding on the promoters of the security but, in most cases, the promoters did complete a major transaction in the indicated industry. Note that in the majority of cases, the promoters had no clear idea of how they would invest the proceeds of the IPO. When the success of JCP firms in completing major transactions is considered as a function of the industry category, in 210 of 213 cases (excluding 12 JCP firms recently listed and still searching for a major transaction) (99 percent) where the promoters of a JCP issue indicated the industry in which they would invest, the firm completed a major transaction. When the promoters did not have a clear purpose for the funds, only 120 of 156 (excluding three JCP firms recently listed and still searching for a major transaction) (77 percent) firms completed a major transaction.

Table 8 also shows how many JCP companies were still listed on the ASE at the end of 1992. The fact that a firm is no longer listed on the ASE does not necessarily mean that it has gone bankrupt. Some firms are taken over or move to more senior

TABLE 8

REVIEW OF HOW MANY ASE JCP IPOS BECAME VIABLE BUSINESSES

Industry[a]	Number Listed since Program Was Initiated	Number of Major Transactions Completed	Number of[b] Firms Delisted by December 31, 1992	Number of Firms Delisted Due to a Takeover	Number of Firms Delisted Due to a Move to the TSE
Oil and gas	96	90	23	12	8
Manufacturing	17	17	3	0	0
Service	49	42	17	1	1
Real estate	24	24	5	1	0
Mining	33	31	9	2	0
Financial services	6	6	1	0	0
Other[c]	159	120	73	6	1
Total JCP	384	330	131	22	10
Pre-JCP	21	16	11	0	0

Notes: [a] Firms were assigned to industries based on the stated investment intentions of the firm at the time of the JCP IPO.
[b] Two possible reasons for delisting are presented in the following two columns.
[c] Business was specified as an investment or holding company, or was unspecified.

Source: Alberta Stock Exchange data records.

exchanges, while others stop paying ASE listing fees and, in essence, become private companies. Overall, 131 of the original 384 firms were delisted, but 32 of these firms were either taken over or moved to another exchange. Thus, the number of failures is 99 of 384 firms, or 26 percent. Examining the failure rate by industry, shows that it was just 3 percent for oil and gas firms, around 17 percent for manufacturing, real estate and financial services firms, 21 percent for mining firms and 31 percent for firms in the service industry. The failure rate was a much higher 42 percent for JCP firms where the promoters had no stated industry. The survival rate with an industry listed compares favourably with the success rate of U.S. venture capital investments. A study of 383 such investments from 1969 to 1985 found that 35 percent of the investments had decreased in value, and 12 percent had lost all their value (see Venture Economics, 1988). As the JCP firms listed in recent years all had a specified industry, and raised a larger amount of initial capital, it is expected that the survival rate has increased over time.

For JCP companies to grow and become viable businesses they are required to access sources of capital following the IPO. From an initial capital base of just under $77 million, JCP companies (including pre-JCP firms) have raised an additional $475 million in equity since the JCP program was initiated (see Table 9). Over half of this amount came from share-for-asset exchanges; however, a significant amount of cash, almost $215 million, has been raised by the selling of shares for cash. JCP firms have also been successful in raising capital by using preferred share and debt financing. Since the program's inception, over $19 million of preferred shares have been issued, and $165 million of debt financing arranged. While some of the debt was issued to sellers of assets to JCP firms, $34 million represents bank loans.

The above results show that the JCP program has been successful in helping entrepreneurs use the public equity markets to raise the initial capital for their businesses. They have been able to grow their businesses by accessing secondary financing. A summary of survey results gathered from interviews with JCP principals, underwriters and regulators is contained in Hopkins and Robinson (1994). These results suggested that participants have been happy with how the JCP program has developed and view it as a viable program for financing small Canadian firms. The program reduces the regulatory cost and burden of accessing the public equity markets, yet it is still monitored and regulated at a high level.

Summarizing the above information provides some insights into the success of the JCP program and suggests some ideas for adopting a similar program in other jurisdictions. The JCP program evolved as a regional program to meet the needs of issuers and investors in Alberta, particularly Calgary. Before its establishment, the ASE had strong membership from regional brokerage firms which were in the business of listing junior firms and had a client base of retail investors who wished to invest in these types of securities. The JCP program was just an evolution for the exchange, not a dramatic change in focus.

The program's success in its early years was in the listing of oil and gas firms. The introduction of the JCP program coincided with the downsizing of the major oil firms in Calgary, which put many highly trained oil professionals on the street with generous severance packages. The JCP program allowed these individuals to

TABLE 9

SECONDARY EQUITY FINANCING BY JCP FIRMS BY INDUSTRY

Industry	Private Placements ($)	Options and Warrants ($)	Acquisitions[a] ($)
Oil and gas	82,872,065	3,822,286	64,361,609
Manufacturing	4,023,535	1,175,056	6,505,694
Services	35,701,097	1,842,083	53,073,595
Real estate	5,820,645	894,083	17,233,622
Mining	15,396,849	1,707,802	17,322,577
Financial services	1,110,640	137,500	1,012,951
Other	50,529,532	3,238,970	72,125,943
Total JCP	195,454,363	12,817,870	231,636,031
Pre-JCP	19,532,900	894,820	15,136,403

Note: [a] Shares were issued by the JCP firm to either acquire assets or to take over an existing private, or public, company.

Source: Alberta Stock Exchange public files and data records.

gather a pool of capital to use to purchase the properties which the major oil and gas firms were selling because they were not economically viable for a large company; however, the junior companies had much lower overhead and were able to manage these properties economically. Over time, the JCP program has diversified its listings to include the manufacturing, services and high-technology sectors.

From the start, the JCP program was transitory. JCP firms had a limit of 18 months in which to complete their major transaction or they were delisted by the ASE. This time limit imposed discipline on JCP issuers and removed the weak firms from the program so a reputation of only having poor quality firms did not develop. As well, the restrictive escrow requirements ensured that the JCP issuer would only be able to benefit if the firm actually turned into a regularly listed ASE firm.

Finally, as mentioned above, the JCP program began as, and still remains, essentially a local program. This allows underwriters and regulators to learn a great deal about prospective JCP issuers before approving the firm's listing. This close monitoring has helped ensure that any JCP firms which come to market have a strong management team and a good chance of success.

The JCP program has created a viable second-tier market for small equity listings in Alberta. What are the implications of the success of the JCP program for other jurisdictions in Canada? As stated above, the program was developed during the late 1980s when there was a need for a financing program to allow the formation of small firms to pursue opportunities in the oil and gas industry. It was built by regional brokerage firms with an established base of retail investors used to investing in small higher-risk firms. Without this combination of factors in place, it is questionable whether the JCP model could be replicated in other Canadian provinces. Any attempt to create a second-tier equity market would require a close examination of existing programs, the stock exchange and over-the-counter market, to determine how a new program could fill an equity financing gap. An alternative could be the modification, or enhancement, of existing programs. In the context of junior equity issues, a promising alternative could be the development of a more liquid over-the-counter market.

Summary and Recommendations

The future growth of an economy depends on the development of new economic entities. However, financing SMEs is difficult in many countries because of regulatory and institutional restrictions, or an unwillingness by investors to provide equity for these firms. An element of this investor unwillingness is the fact that most investments in SMEs are illiquid.

This report considered whether it is possible for SMEs to provide liquidity to potential investors by listing their equity on a public stock exchange. It examined the costs of publicly listing in Canada, and the United States, and found a lower limit on equity financing of approximately $1 million for the ME and the VSE. Thus, these exchanges will not be a source of financing for small Canadian firms, but are suitable for listing medium-sized firms. The ASE's JCP program does allow the listing of small firms on a public equity exchange. For seed capital of only $100,000 an entrepreneur, or group of entrepreneurs, with a strong business opportunity and an unblemished record can raise an additional several hundred thousand dollars to pursue an opportunity. The costs of listing on the TSE make it suitable for equity issues of an amount over $1 million. This report notes that the dollar costs of public listing in Canada are lower than the cost of listing on a U.S. exchange and finds that the percentage cost of listing in Canada for SMEs is similar to the cost in the United States.

This report also examined the listing requirements of the Canadian exchanges to see if these requirements imposed a restriction on the availability of equity financing to SMEs. The TSE has significantly increased its listing requirements and is now suitable for only well-established medium-sized firms. This has created a gap in the financing of smaller firms in Ontario, which is only partially filled by the OTC market and the other Canadian regional exchanges. Regular listing on the VSE and the ME is available for only medium-sized firms requiring over $1 million in equity capital, although there are less-stringent requirements for resource firms on the ME, and venture firms on the VSE. The ASE listing requirements are much lower than those on the other exchanges, and an industrial firm can be listed with a minimum asset base of $400,000. In addition, the ASE's JCP program allows the public listing of equity with a market capitalization of several hundred thousand dollars.

This report also discussed the experience of a number of countries in the development of special programs to allow the listing of SMEs on public equity markets. It notes that there is a potential problem with market manipulation in junior equity markets, and regulators have to develop strong regulations and enforcement practices to combat this problem. The report also found that a significant problem in the development of a program for the listing of junior equities is the need to ensure a liquid secondary market for these securities following issuance. Failure to develop a strong secondary market will doom the primary market to failure.

Examining the JCP program on the ASE provided some insights into how a program for the listing of junior Canadian equities can be developed. It is important to note that the JCP program was an evolutionary, not a revolutionary, change for the ASE. The ASE already had a well-established regional dealer network and a strong retail following for junior equity issues. Thus, any attempt to add a second tier of equity trading to a larger senior exchange can be difficult. In Europe, the large prestigious brokerage firms trading on the senior exchanges did not find it economical to underwrite and research the smaller equity issues of the junior exchanges. The current trend in Europe is to establish new markets for smaller companies which are independent of the existing stock exchanges.

The JCP program also succeeded because it began as a local program geared to the needs of Alberta. When it began, there was a dramatic change in the employment and activities of the senior oil companies in Alberta which generated great opportunities for junior oil companies. Thus, the program satisfied a local need for capital formation. (In other regions, the needs of firms and investors may necessitate a different type of junior program.) Finally, the JCP program has had strong regulations from its inception, including strict escrow requirements which require the JCP principals to build a successful company before being able to sell their shares.

Overall, the results provide evidence that it is possible to establish a system for financing small equity ventures using public stock exchanges as long as there are strict regulations governing the program and careful monitoring once it is established. In the first year of its existence, Alberta's JCP program experienced some of the problems that have plagued similar programs in the United States, but Alberta regulators reacted quickly to these events and minimized the damage to Alberta's investing public and to the reputation of the program.

The implications for other Canadian provinces are less clear. While the development of a viable second-tier equity market in these jurisdictions would help fill a financing gap for equity amounts in the range of $50,000 to $1,000,000, it is unclear whether the JCP program would be the best model outside Alberta. In provinces with an established OTC market, increasing the liquidity and profile of this market may prove a better alternative.

Appendix A
Exchange Listing Requirements

Alberta Stock Exchange (ASE), Minimum Listing Requirements
Requirements
There are different requirements for companies to obtain a listing depending on classification. The ASE may exercise its discretion to list companies that may not meet the specified requirements. The staff of the Exchange should be consulted by the company at an early stage as this may alleviate technical problems arising at the time of formal listing. All companies, except Junior Capital Pool companies, must have a minimum of 500,000 shares held by at least 300 public shareholders (other than principals and promoters), each holding a board lot (normally 500 shares) or more. In addition, at least 20 percent of the issued and outstanding shares must be free-trading and held by public shareholders. Specific requirements for companies (in industry sectors) are:
Industrial Company: • Net tangible assets of $400,000. • Adequate working capital to carry on business. • History of profitable operations. • Where there is no record of earnings, the company must have a working commercial prototype of its product. A minimum of $250,000 in development expenses must have been spent in the previous five years, and the company must have a feasibility study prepared by an independent qualified consultant which demonstrates the economic viability of the company's product or service, together with a management plan for at least one year.
Real Estate Company: • Net tangible assets of $1,500,000 if the company has a record of earnings or $2,000,000 if there is no record of earnings. • Adequate working capital to carry on business. • History of profitable operations. • If the company has no history of earnings, each application will be considered based on its own merits.
Investment Company: • Net tangible assets of $1,500,000 if the company has a record of earnings or $2,000,000 if there is no record of earnings. • Adequate working capital to carry on business. • History of profitable operations in cases where the company has a history of earnings. • Stated investment guidelines and restrictions. (cont'd)

ALBERTA STOCK EXCHANGE (ASE), MINIMUM LISTING REQUIREMENTS (cont'd)

Mining:

- An interest in a resource property with geological merit.
- A minimum of $200,000 in exploration and development costs must have been expended on the property in the previous five years.
- Exploration or development program of a minimum of $200,000.
- Net working capital sufficient to carry out the work program with an additional $100,000 in unallocated funds.
- An up-to-date report on the property by an independent engineer or geologist.

Oil and Gas:

- For producing companies – $50,000 cash flow and proved producing reserves of $500,000 discounted at 15 percent.
- For development companies – sufficient working capital to carry out an identified work program, a minimum of $100,000 in unallocated funds, proven and probable reserves of $500,000 discounted at 15 percent and probable reserves discounted a further 50 percent. Proven producing reserves must account for at least $250,000 of the above stated value.
- For exploration companies – sufficient net working capital to carry out an identified work program of a minimum of $500,000 consisting of at least a four-well drilling program and an additional $100,000 in unallocated funds.
- An up-do-date independent petroleum engineer's or geologist's report.

Research and Development:

- A minimum of $500,000 in research and development expenses in the last five years.
- Independent technical assessment of previous research which recommends a further research program of at least $500,000.
- Net working capital sufficient to carry out the research program together with an additional $100,000 in unallocated funds.

Junior Capital Pool:

- The founders of the applicant company are required to inject a minimum of $100,000 into the company at a price not less than 50 percent of the public offer price.
- A maximum of $500,000 may be raised before listing, including funds raised prior to the public offering and the proceeds of the public offering.
- Only companies which do not have significant operating assets, other than cash, nor agreements in place to acquire operating assets would be eligible to apply for listing under the Junior Capital Pool program.
- The minimum offering price is $0.10 per share, and the maximum purchase by any subscriber under the prospectus is 2 percent of the number of shares distributed to the public.
- A minimum of 500,000 shares held by at least 300 public shareholders each holding a board lot.

Source: Alberta Stock Exchange, *Policy and Procedures Manual*, 1995.

Montreal Exchange (ME), Industrial, Financial and Real Estate Companies, Minimum Listing Requirements	
Requirements	**Requirements for Exemption**[a]
(a) Minimum tangible net worth of $1,000,000.	(a) Minimum tangible net worth of $3,500,000.
(b) Net income of at least $100,000 before taxes in the fiscal year immediately preceding the filing of the listing application, and a minimum of two of the last three years must have been profitable.	(b) Net income of at least $200,000 before taxes in the last fiscal year. (c) Pre-tax cash flow of $500,000 in the last fiscal year.
(c) Adequate working capital and capitalization to carry on its business.	(d) Adequate working capital and capitalization to carry on its business.
(d) A minimum market value of $1,000,000 of publicly held shares which must be free of any trading restrictions.	
(e) A minimum of 1,000,000 publicly held securities which must be free of any trading restrictions.	
(f) If the applicant company is a financial company, the Exchange may apply reduced prior earnings requirements to the extent appropriate for its nature of business and long-term growth policy.	
(g) If the applicant is a financial investment company, the Exchange must be satisfied as to the independence and qualifications of the investment manager and as to the trustee which will be holding the securities.	

Note: [a] Requirements for exemption from the provision of paragraph (b) of article 9153 of the Rules of the Montreal Exchange for Industrial, Financial and Real Estate Companies.

Source: CCH Canadian Limited, *Canadian Securities Law Reporter*, 1995.

MONTREAL EXCHANGE, MINING EXPLORATION COMPANIES, MINIMUM LISTING REQUIREMENTS

Requirements	Requirements for Exemption[a]
(a) Definition: A mining exploration company is a company principally engaged in the exploration and development of mineral properties. The company must hold at least one mineral property of demonstrable merit which must be satisfactory to the Exchange.	(a) Definition: A mining company is a company principally engaged in developing mineral properties and bringing them into production. (b) Proven reserves of ore: The company must have proven reserves of ore sufficient to yield a mine life of at least three years as evidenced by an independent feasibility study which must be satisfactory to the Exchange.
(b) Seed capital and previous work: A company which is making an initial public offering or which is being revived after a long period of inactivity, must have raised by way of the sale of common shares, net proceeds of a minimum total amount of $100,000 and must have expended during the last 12 months a minimum amount of $50,000 in exploration or development work on its properties.	(c) Financial requirements: (i) pre-tax profitability in the last fiscal year; (ii) pre-tax cash flow of $350,000 in the last fiscal year; (iii) an average pre-tax cash flow of $300,000 for the last two fiscal years; and (iv) adequate working capital and capitalization to carry on its business.
(c) Exploration program: The company shall submit a report prepared by an independent mining expert which must include recommendations for a program of exploration or development for a minimum amount of $300,000.	(d) Market value of publicly held shares: The market value of publicly held shares free of any trading restrictions must be at least equal to $1,000,000.
(d) Additional reports: When the company is scheduling a significant program (more than $100,000) on one or more additional properties within the next two years, using funds on hand at the time of listing, the Exchange may require the submission of additional reports recommending such programs.	(e) Publicly held securities: A minimum of 1,000,000 publicly held securities which must be free of any trading restrictions.

(cont'd)

Montreal Exchange, Mining Exploration Companies, Minimum Listing Requirements (cont'd)

Requirements	Requirements for Exemption[a]
(e) Working capital: The company shall have adequate working capital to carry out the recommended program of exploration or development on its mineral properties for the current year with a minimum of $400,000, including a minimum of $100,000 of unallocated funds. This amount is net of funds required to keep important property options in good standing in the next 12 months.	
(f) Capitalization: The capitalization of the company must be adequate to carry on its business.	
(g) Market value of publicly held shares: The market value of publicly held shares free of any trading restrictions must be at least equal to $500,000.	
(h) Publicly held securities: A minimum of 500,000 publicly held securities which must be free of any trading restrictions.	

Note: [a] Requirements for exemption from the provision of paragraph (b) of article 9153 of the Rules of the Montreal Exchange for Mining Companies.

Source: CCH Canadian Limited, *Canadian Securities Law Reporter*, 1995.

Montreal Exchange, Oil and Gas Exploration Companies, Minimum Listing Requirements

Requirements	Requirements for Exemption[a]
(a) Definition: An oil and gas exploration company is a company principally engaged, directly or indirectly, in the exploration and development of oil or gas properties.	(a) Definition: An oil or gas company is a company principally engaged, directly or indirectly, in developing oil or gas properties and bringing them into production.
(b) Program to increase reserves: The company shall submit a program, not limited to proposed acquisitions of undeveloped acreage, satisfactory to the Exchange, which can reasonably be expected to increase reserves.	(b) Proven reserves: The company must have proven reserves of recoverable oil or gas having a value of at least $5,000,000 (based on the discount rate generally used by the industry) as evidenced by an independent study which must be satisfactory to the Exchange.
(c) Reserves: The company must have proven reserves of recoverable oil or gas of $2,000,000 (based on the discount rate generally used in the industry).	(c) Financial requirements:
(d) Working capital: The company shall have adequate working capital to execute its program and to carry on its business, with a minimum of $400,000.	(i) pre-tax profitability in the last fiscal year; (ii) pre-tax cash flow of $500,000 in the last fiscal year; (iii) an average annual pre-tax cash flow of $400,000 for the last two fiscal years; and (iv) adequate working capital and capitalization to carry on its business.
(e) Capitalization: The capitalization of the company must be adequate to carry on its business.	
(f) Market value of publicly held shares: The market value of publicly held shares, free of any trading restrictions, must be at least equal to $750,000.	(d) Market value of publicly held shares: The market value of publicly held shares, free of any trading restrictions, must be at least equal to $1,000,000.
(g) Publicly held securities: A minimum of 750,000 publicly held securities which must be free of any trading restrictions.	(e) Publicly held securities: A minimum of 1,000,000 publicly held securities which must be free of any trading restrictions.

Note: [a] Requirements for exemption from the provision of paragraph (b) of article 9153 of the Rules of the Montreal Exchange for Oil and Gas Companies.

Source: CCH Canadian Limited, *Canadian Securities Law Reporter*, 1995.

Toronto Stock Exchange (TSE), Industrial Companies, Minimum Listing Requirements

Requirements	Requirements for Exemption[a]
(a) (i) net tangible assets of $1,000,000; (ii) earnings of at least $100,000, before taxes and extraordinary items, in the fiscal year immediately preceding the filing of the listing application; (iii) pre-tax cash flow of $400,000 in the fiscal year immediately preceding the filing of the listing application; and (iv) adequate working capital and capitalization to carry on the business. OR (b) (i) net tangible assets of $5,000,000; (ii) evidence, satisfactory to the Exchange, indicating a reasonable likelihood of future profitability; and (iii) adequate working capital and capitalization to carry on the business. OR (c) (i) earnings of at least $200,000, before taxes and extraordinary items, in the fiscal year immediately preceding the filing of the listing application; (ii) pre-tax cash flow of $500,000 in the fiscal year immediately preceding the filing of the listing application; and (iii) adequate working capital and capitalization to carry on the business.	(i) net tangible assets of $5,000,000; (ii) earnings of at least $200,000, before taxes and extraordinary items, in the fiscal year immediately preceding the filing of the listing application; (iii) pre-tax cash flow of $500,000 in the fiscal year immediately preceding the filing of the listing application; and (iv) adequate working capital and capitalization to carry on the business.
Public distribution of at least 1,000,000 shares that can be freely traded with an aggregate market value of $2,000,000.	
At least 300 public shareholders each owning at least one board lot.	

Note: [a] Requirements for eligibility for exemption from section 19.09 of the Toronto Stock Exchange General By-Law.

Source: Toronto Stock Exchange, *Members' Manual*, 1995.

Toronto Stock Exchange (TSE), Mining Companies, Minimum Listing Requirements

Requirements	Requirements for Exemption[a]
(a) (i) proven reserves to provide a mine life of at least three years, calculated by a qualified and independent technical authority; (ii) evidence, satisfactory to the Exchange, indicating a reasonable likelihood of future profitability; and (iii) adequate working capital and capitalization to carry on the business. OR (b) (i) net tangible assets of $2,000,000; (ii) a program of exploration and/or development, satisfactory to the Exchange, on an advanced property, and prepared by a qualified and independent technical authority; (iii) sufficient funds (at least $500,000) to complete at least the next phase of the recommended exploration and/or development program on the company's properties; (iv) sufficient funds to meet estimated general, administrative and capital expenditures for a reasonable period of time (at least 18 months); and (v) adequate capitalization to carry on the business.	(i) net tangible assets of $5,000,000; (ii) pre-tax profitability in the fiscal year immediately preceding the filing of the listing application; (iii) pre-tax cash flow of $350,000 in the fiscal year immediately preceding the filing of the listing application and an average pre-tax cash flow of $300,000 for the two fiscal years immediately preceding the filing of the listing application; (iv) proven reserves to provide a mine life of at least three years, calculated by a qualified and independent technical authority; and (v) adequate working capital and capitalization to carry on the business.
Public distribution of at least 1,000,000 shares that can be freely traded with an aggregate market value of $2,000,000.	
At least 300 public shareholders each owning at least one board lot.	

Note: [a] Requirements for eligibility for exemption from section 19.09 of the Toronto Stock Exchange General By-Law.

Source: Toronto Stock Exchange, *Members' Manual*, 1995.

TORONTO STOCK EXCHANGE (TSE), OIL AND GAS COMPANIES, MINIMUM LISTING REQUIREMENTS	
Requirements	**Requirements for Exemption**[a]
(a) (i) proven developed reserves of \$2,000,000 based on the discount rate prescribed by the Exchange; (ii) a definitive program, satisfactory to the Exchange, which can reasonably be expected to increase reserves, and sufficient funds available to execute the program; (iii) adequate working capital to carry on the business with a minimum of \$500,000; and (iv) adequate capitalization to carry on the business. OR (b) (i) proven developed reserves of \$5,000,000 based on the discount rate prescribed by the Exchange; (ii) a definitive program satisfactory to the Exchange, which can be reasonably expected to increase reserves, and sufficient funds to execute the program; (iii) minimum annual pre-tax cash flow of \$200,000; and (iv) adequate working capital and capitalization to carry on the business.	(i) proven developed reserves of \$5,000,000 based on the discount rate prescribed by the Exchange; (ii) pre-tax profitability in the fiscal year immediately following the filing of the listing application; (iii) pre-tax cash flow of \$500,000 in the fiscal year immediately preceding the filing of the listing application and an average annual pre-tax cash flow of \$400,000 for the two fiscal years immediately preceding the filing of the listing application; and (iv) adequate working capital and capitalization to carry on the business.
Public distribution of at least 1,000,000 shares that can be freely traded with an aggregate market value of at least \$2,000,000.	
At least 300 public shareholders each owning at least one board lot.	
Notes: [a] Requirements for eligibility for exemption from section 19.09 of the Toronto Stock Exchange General By-Law. Source: Toronto Stock Exchange, *Members' Manual*, 1995.	

Vancouver Stock Exchange (VSE), Commercial/Industrial Companies, Minimum Listing Requirements

Commercial/Industrial Company Listing Requirements	Without History of Earnings	With a History of Earnings
Public distribution and market capitalization	At least 1,000,000 shares without resale restrictions having an aggregate market value of $1,800,000, held by at least 300 shareholders, each holding one board lot or more.	
Assets	$3,000,000 net tangible assets.	$900,000 net tangible assets.
Profitability	Evidence indicating a reasonable likelihood of profitability.	At least $100,000, before income taxes and extraordinary items, in the immediately preceding fiscal year.
Working capital and financial resources	Adequate to carry on the business.	

Source: Vancouver Stock Exchange, *Listing Policy and Procedure Manual*, 1995.

Vancouver Stock Exchange (VSE), Resource Company (Other than Oil and Gas), Minimum Listing Requirements

Company Listing Requirements	With Proven Reserves or Exploration and/or Development of Industrial Mineral Properties	In the Exploration and/or Development Stage
Public float and market capitalization	At least 1,000,000 shares without resale restrictions, having an aggregate market value of $1,800,000 held by at least 300 shareholders (exclusive of insiders), each holding one board lot or more.	
Assets	Interest in a mineral property with proven reserves for a three-year mine life.	$1,800,000 net tangible assets.
Profitability or development program	Evidence indicating a reasonable likelihood of future profitability.	A program of exploration and/or development on an advanced property.
Working capital and financial resources	Adequate to carry on the business.	Sufficient funds, at least $450,000, to complete the next phase of recommended exploration and/or development.
		Sufficient funds to meet estimated general, administrative and capital expenditures for at least 18 months.

Source: Vancouver Stock Exchange, *Listing Policy and Procedure Manual*, 1995.

Vancouver Stock Exchange (VSE) Oil and Gas Resource Company, Minimum Listing Requirements

Public float and market capitalization	At least 1,000,000 shares without resale restrictions, having an aggregate market value of $1,000,000 held by at least 300 shareholders (exclusive of insiders), each holding one board lot or more.
Assets	$1,800,000 proven developed reserves.
Profitability or development program	A definite program which can reasonably be expected to increase reserves.
Working capital and financial reserves	Financial resources to carry on the business with a minimum of $300,000.
	Sufficient funds to meet estimated general, administrative and capital expenditures for at least 18 months.

Source: Vancouver Stock Exchange, *Listing Policy and Procedures Manual*, 1995.

Vancouver Stock Exchange (VSE), Venture Companies, Minimum Listing Requirements

Initial Listings Requirements	Natural Resource Company	Non-Resource Company
Seed capital price per share	$0.25	$0.25
Net seed capital proceeds	$175,000	$400,000
Minimum prospectus price per share or unit (net)	$0.30/share $0.40/unit	$0.30/share $0.40/unit
Combined net proceeds from seed capital and first public distribution by prospectus	$450,000	$850,000
Minimum number of shares sold under prospectus	500,000	600,000
Minimum number of shares in public float	300,000	300,000
Number of public shareholders holding at least a purchase lot	300	300
Prior expenditures on properties or business to be funded by prospectus	$100,000	$300,000
Minimum funds allotted for exploration in prospectus	$100,000 in first phase	not applicable
Unallocated working capital on full listing	$100,000	$100,000

Source: Vancouver Stock Exchange, *Listing Policy and Procedure Manual*, 1995.

Vancouver Stock Exchange (VSE), Exempt Companies, Minimum Listing Requirements

Exempt Company Listing Requirements	Resource Companies Other than Oil and Gas	Oil and Gas Resource Companies	Commercial/Industrial Companies
Public float	At least 300,000 shares which are beneficially owned by 300 shareholders, exclusive of insiders, each of whom must beneficially own one or more board lots which are free of resale restrictions.		
Assets	$5,000,000 in net tangible assets.	$5,000,000 in proven developed reserves.	$5,000,000 in net tangible assets.
	Proven reserves to provide a mine life of at least three years.		
Profitability	Pre-tax profitability in the immediately preceding fiscal year.		At least $200,000 in pre-tax profitability in the immediately preceding fiscal year.
Working capital and financial resources	Average annual pre-tax cash flow of $300,000 in the immediately preceding fiscal year.	Pre-tax cash flow of $5,000,000 in the immediately preceding fiscal year.	
	Average annual pre-tax cash flow of $300,000 for the two immediately preceding fiscal years.	Average annual pre-tax cash flow of $400,000 for the two immediately preceding fiscal years.	
	Adequate working capital and financial resources to carry on the business.		

Source: Vancouver Stock Exchange, *Listing Policy and Procedure Manual*, 1995.

ACKNOWLEDGEMENTS

THE AUTHOR WOULD LIKE TO ACKNOWLEDGE FINANCIAL SUPPORT received from Industry Canada, the Social Sciences and Humanities Research Council of Canada and the University of Calgary Future Fund. The author would also like to thank the Alberta Stock Exchange for providing the data used in this study.

BIBLIOGRAPHY

Aggarwal, Reena and Pietra Rivoli. "Fads in the Initial Public Offering Market?" *Financial Management*. 19, (1990): 45-57.

—. "Evaluating the Costs of Raising Capital Through an Initial Public Offering." *Journal of Business Venturing*. 6, (1991): 351-361.

Alberta Securities Commission. *An Analysis of the Results of Junior Capital Pool Financing (1986-1990)*. Confidential report of the Alberta Securities Commission Agency, June 17, 1991.

Alberta Stock Exchange. Circular No. 7, Calgary, Alberta, June 1990.

—. *Going Public*. Calgary, Alberta, January 1994.

—. *Policy and Procedures Manual*. Calgary, Alberta, June 1995.

Allen, Franklin and Gerald R. Faulhaber. "Signalling by Underpricing in the IPO Market." *Journal of Financial Economics*. 23, (1989): 303-323.

Baron, David P. "A Model of the Demand for Investment Banking Advising and Distribution Services for New Issues." *Journal of Finance*. 37, (1982): 955-976.

Barry, C.B., C.J. Muscarella, J.W. Peavy III and M.R. Vetsuypens. "The Role of Venture Capital in the Creation of Public Companies." *Journal of Financial Economics*. 29, (1990): 447-471.

Beatty, Randolph P. and Jay R. Ritter. "Investment Banking, Reputation, and the Underpricing of Initial Public Offerings." *Journal of Financial Economics*. 15, (1986): 213-232.

CCH Canadian Limited. *Canadian Securities Law Reporter*. North York, Ontario, 1995.

Chemmanur, Thomas J. "The Pricing of Initial Public Offerings: A Dynamic Model with Information Production." *Journal of Finance*. 48, (1993): 285-304.

Cheung, C. Sherman and Itzhak Krinsky. "Information Asymmetry and the Underpricing of Initial Public Offerings: Further Empirical Evidence." *Journal of Business Finance & Accounting*. 21, (1994): 739-747.

Clarkson, Peter M. and Jack Merkley. "Ex Ante Uncertainty and the Underpricing of Initial Public Offerings: Further Canadian Evidence." *Canadian Journal of Administrative Sciences*. 11, (1994): 54-67.

Falk, Haim and Daniel B. Thornton. "The Canadian Market for Initial Public Offerings: Evidence from the Toronto, Montreal and Alberta Stock Exchanges." Unpublished working paper, 1992.

Grinblatt, Mark and Chaun Y. Hwang. "Signalling and the Pricing of Unseasoned New Issues." *Journal of Finance*. 44, (1989): 393-420.

Hanley, Kathleen Weiss, A. Arun Kumar and Paul J. Seguin. "Price Stabilization in the Market for New Issues." *Journal of Financial Economics*. 34, (1993): 177-197.

Holdman, William F. "The 'Stock Fraud Capital' Tries to Clean up its Act." *Business Week.* (February 6, 1984): 76.

Hopkins, Darrin and Michael J. Robinson. "Using Alberta's Junior Capital Pool Program to Raise Start-up Equity Capital." Working Paper #94-31, Faculty of Management, The University of Calgary, Calgary, 1994.

Ibbotson, Roger G. "Price Performance of Common Stock New Issues." *Journal of Financial Economics.* 2, (1975): 235-272.

Ibbotson, Roger G. and Jeffrey J. Jaffe. "'Hot Issue' Markets." *Journal of Finance.* 30, (1975): 1027-1042.

Jegadeesh, Narasimhan, Mark Weinstein and Ivo Welch. "An Empirical Investigation of IPO Returns and Subsequent Equity Offerings." *Journal of Financial Economics.* 34, (1993): 153-175.

Jog, Vijay M. and Allan L. Riding. "Underpricing in Canadian IPO's." *Financial Analysts Journal.* 43, (1987): 48-55.

Keloharju, Matti., "The Winner's Curse, Legal Liability, and the Long-Run Price Performance of Initial Public Offerings in Finland." *Journal of Financial Economics.* 34, (1993): 251-277.

Koh, F. and T. Walter. "A Direct Test of Rock's Model of the Pricing of Unseasoned Issues." *Journal of Financial Economics.* 23, (1989): 251-272.

Krinsky, I. and Wendy Rotenberg. "Signalling and the Valuation of Unseasoned New Issues Revisited." *Journal of Financial and Quantitative Analysis.* 24, (1989): 257-265.

Kunz, Roger M. and Reena Aggarwal. "Why Initial Public Offerings are Underpriced: Evidence from Switzerland." *Journal of Banking and Finance.* 18, (1994): 705-723.

MacIntosh, Jeffrey G. "Legal and Institutional Barriers to Financing Innovative Enterprise in Canada." Discussion paper, Government and Competitiveness Project, School of Policy Studies, Queen's University, Kingston, 1994a.

—. "Regulatory Barriers to Raising Capital for Small Firms." *Canadian Financial Services Alert.* 6, (1994b): 57-64.

Mathias, Phillip. "Police, Regulators Losing the Fight as Stock Fraud Runs Rampant." *The Financial Post.* October 1, 1994a, pp. 10-11.

—. "Stock Fraud: Pity the Poor Prosecutors." *The Financial Post.* October 15, 1994b, p. 9.

—. "Stock Fraud: Finding Better Ways to Catch the Thieves." *The Financial Post.* October 22, 1994c, p. 9.

Muscarella, Chris J. and Michael R. Vetsuypens. "A Simple Test of Baron's Model of IPO Underpricing." *Journal of Financial Economics.* 24, (1989): 125-135.

Ontario Securities Commission. "Task Force on Small Business Financing." Preliminary report submitted to the Ontario Securities Commission, June 21, 1994.

Rasch, Sebastian. "Special Stock Market Segments for Small Company Shares in Europe – What Went Wrong?" Discussion Paper No. 94-13, Centre for European Economic Research (ZEW), Mannheim, Germany, 1994.

Reilly, Frank K. and Kenneth Hatfield. "Investor Experience With New Stock Issues." *Financial Analysts Journal.* 25, (1969): 73-80.

Reuter. "Curbing Penny Stock Fraud." *The Financial Post.* April 13, 1992, p. 17.

Riding, A., P. Dalcin, L. Duxbury, G. Haines and R. Safrita. "Informal Investors in Canada: The Identification of Salient Characteristics." Report submitted to the Department of Industry, Science and Technology (Canada) and to the Ministry of Economic Development and Trade (Ontario), May 23, 1993.

Ritter, Jay R. "The 'Hot Issue' Market of 1980." *Journal of Business.* 57, (1984): 215-240.

——. "The Costs of Going Public." *Journal of Financial Economics*. 19, (1987): 269-281.

——. "The Long-Run Underperformance of Initial Public Offerings." *Journal of Finance*. 46, (1991): 3-27.

Rock, Kevin. "Why New Issues are Underpriced." *Journal of Financial Economics*. 15, (1986): 187-212.

Ruud, Judith S. "Underwriter Price Support and the IPO Underpricing Puzzle." *Journal of Financial Economics*. 34, (1993): 135-151.

Sahlman, W.A. "The Structure and Governance of Venture-Capital Organizations." *Journal of Financial Economics*. 29, (1990): 473-521.

Schultz, Paul H. and Mir A. Zaman. "Aftermarket Support and Underpricing of Initial Public Offerings." *Journal of Financial Economics*. 35, (1994): 199-219.

Schwartz, Robert A. *Reshaping the Equity Markets*. Harper Business, Harper Collins Publishers, 1991.

Stern, Richard L. and Paul Bornstein. "Why new issues are lousy investment." *Forbes*. (December 2, 1985): 152-190.

——. "Ethereal Equities." *Forbes*. (March 24, 1986): 40-42.

Stern, Richard L., Matthew Schifrin and Claire Poole. "Never, but Never, Give a Sucker an Even Break." *Forbes*. (January 9, 1989): 46-50.

Stoll, Hans R. and Anthony J. Curley. "Small Business and the New Issues Market for Equities." *Journal of Financial and Quantitative Analysis*. 5, (1970): 309-322.

Tinic, Seha. "Anatomy of Initial Public Offerings of Common Stock." *Journal of Finance*. 43, (1988): 789-822.

Toronto Stock Exchange. *Members' Manual*. Toronto, Ontario, 1995.

Venture Economics. *Venture Capital Performance: Review of the Financial Performance of Venture Capital Partnerships*. Needham, MA: Venture Economics, 1988.

Welch, Ivo. "Seasoned Offerings, Imitation Costs and the Underpricing of Initial Public Offerings." *Journal of Finance*. 44, (1989): 421-449.

Wetzel, W.E. "Angels and Informal Risk Capital." *Sloan Management Review*. (Summer, 1983): 23-34.

Wolfe, Glenn A., Elizabeth S. Cooperman and Stephen P. Ferris. "An Analysis of the Underwriter Selection Process for Initial Public Offerings." *Journal of Financial Research*. 17, (1994): 77-90.

Vancouver Stock Exchange. *Listing Policy and Procedure Manual*. Vancouver, British Columbia, 1995.

Allan L. Riding
School of Business
Carleton University

15

On the Care and Nurture of Loan Guarantee Programs

INTRODUCTION

IT IS OFTEN ASSUMED THAT SMALLER FIRMS ARE LESS ABLE TO OBTAIN DEBT CAPITAL than larger firms. This premise forms the basis for the provision of loan guarantees by governments and other institutions. Although implemented differently, governments of Canada, the United Kingdom, United States, Japan and those of most European Union countries provide loan guarantee schemes for small firms. This paper reports on three issues pertaining to the provision of loan guarantees to small firms. It:

- draws on economic theory to examine the case for loan guarantee programs;
- reviews the development and experience of the Canadian *Small Business Loans Act* (SBLA) and addresses design issues using agency theory; and
- examines loan guarantee schemes in other nations and extracts lessons from their experience.

The structure of loan guarantee programs is similar internationally. The common stated objective of all such schemes is to redress a perceived flaw in the credit markets whereby small firms are unable to access debt capital. In all cases, the process is initiated when a small or medium-sized enterprise (SME) approaches a lender institution for a loan. If the borrower is eligible and in need of a guarantee, the guarantee is invoked with differing degrees of guarantor involvement. On approval, a proportion of the loan is guaranteed, and the borrower and lender risk the balance. Borrowers pay a fee for the guarantee, and lenders charge interest and require security. In the event of a default, the guarantor makes good on the guaranteed portion, and the lender often takes a loss on the balance.

Without exception, the loan guarantee schemes of most countries are intended to provide access to capital for small businesses. Also, without exception, there is controversy surrounding these programs. The tenor of the debate may be understood from the following comments, both made before the U.S. Congress House

Committee on Small Business. On the one hand, advocates of the loan guarantee programs argue along the lines of B.H. Brown, vice-president of Allied Lending Corporation when he said that the "loan guarantee program is a vital source of long term capital for this country's small business community. It is a program which generates revenues in excess of its costs to the government and is an excellent partnership between the public and private sectors."[1]

Conversely, the arguments of opponents' follow along the lines of D. Stockman, Director, Office of Management and Budget, when he remarked that the loan guarantee program "serves no rigorously-defined public purpose at all...[and] may inflict unfair private economic harm to the 99 percent of non-SBA borrowers who must compete with government-fostered and subsidized competitors."[2]

While these comments reflect the tenor of the debate in the United States, similar comments may be heard in the halls of various governments, including those of Canada. The pressure on such programs is all the greater given national deficits and the contingent liability associated with honouring loan guarantees. In part, the debate flourishes because both proponents and opponents have lost sight of the intention of loan guarantee programs. Debates surround the economic benefits of supporting risky firms and the programs' potential to guide investment to disadvantaged business owners. Proponents of this approach argue that there are social welfare benefits that accrue due to risk-taking behaviour. However, even if such benefits do occur, tax-funded mediation in the credit market is not implied. MacIntosh points out that Canadian SMEs tend to be highly levered and that further debt is often inappropriate. Indeed, risk investments are traditionally best financed by equity.

In no case, however, have such objectives of risk subsidization or social targeting been articulated for loan guarantee schemes. The single objective expressed in all loan guarantee schemes is the same as that of Canada's *Small Business Loans Act*: "to increase the availability of loans for the purpose of the establishment, expansion, modernization and improvement of small business enterprises" (SBLA, 1991, p. 2). The objective is to assist small firms, *not* to subsidize risky firms. At any firm size, a distribution of risk is associated with the borrower. It is the task of credit markets to discriminate according to the quality of the borrower. It is the objective of the loan guarantee scheme to facilitate capital formation for small firms.

This paper reports on an analysis of issues that pertain to the provision of loan guarantees to small firms. It proceeds by drawing on economic theory to justify loan guarantee programs. Next, it provides a review of the history and experience of the Canadian SBLA program. Issues in program design are identified. These are addressed by invoking agency theory. Government, as the principal, wants private sector lenders to deliver the program. The lenders, as government's agents, have their own objectives of profit maximization. Alignment of the goals provides useful and practical guidelines for program design. The generic features of loan guarantee programs of the United States, Japan, Germany and the United Kingdom are described, and the paper closes with a summary of the issues and recommendations.

Economic Theory of Loan Guarantee Programs: A Case for Intervention

The Premise of Loan Guarantee Programs

THE UNDERLYING PREMISE OF LOAN GUARANTEE PROGRAMS is that small firms cannot obtain proportionally as much credit (or credit on such good terms) as larger firms of *equal credit risk*. To illustrate this point, it is instructive to review the stated goals of loan guarantee programs enacted in various countries. These are listed in Table 1.

Table 1

Stated Objectives of Loan Guarantee Programs

Country	Objective
Canada	"...to encourage lenders in the private sector to increase the availability of loans for the purpose of the establishment, modernization and improvement of small business enterprises" (SBLA, p. 2).
Japan	"...to facilitate loans from financial institutions to smaller enterprises for business needs by extending insurance coverage to guarantee liabilities...for loans to smaller enterprises made by financial institutions" (Small Business Credit, 1976, p. 6).
United Kingdom	to provide "government-backed guarantees to support viable propositions from small business owners who have insufficient resources [due to lack of security or track record] to obtain conventional loans" (Pieda plc, 1992, p. 6).
United States	"...an attempt to increase access of small- and medium-sized enterprises to credit and in so doing to stimulate growth in the small business sector" (Rhyne, 1988, p. 11).

Without exception, the goals of the various programs relate to correction of a perceived flaw in the credit market: that *small* firms have disproportionately less access to credit than larger firms of equivalent credit risk. The goal statements do not ordain that firms whose debt has been guaranteed should be any *riskier* than other firms. Proper design of loan guarantee programs must bear in mind that there is a distinction between size and risk. It may be true that, on average, smaller firms are riskier;[3] however, within a size category, there is always a distribution of risk.

The goals listed previously are the stated principles behind the programs. There are, in addition, a variety of other potential and real objectives of loan guarantee schemes. Resolution of the debates requires assessment of the extent to which existing programs are meeting their stated objectives. Improvements to program designs must align program objectives with those of the agent lenders who implement the initiatives.

Alternative Objectives of Loan Guarantee Programs

Rhyne (1988, chapter 5) identified three categories of objectives for loan guarantee programs: credit market imperfections, externality benefits associated with small firms and distributional aims.

Mitigation of credit market imperfections includes three different objectives that may be attributable to loan guarantee plans. First, overcome a credit gap due to equilibrium quality credit rationing. Second, protect against credit tightening during recessions. Third, allow small businesses access to credit. The U.K. loan guarantee scheme also views its program as a means of "training" lenders to deal with small firms.

The issue of quality credit rationing is discussed at length in subsequent sections; however, the findings of those sections may be succinctly summarized. First, it is not clear from either theory or empirical evidence what form, if any, credit rationing takes. Second, credit rationing is not necessarily a problem if the role of credit markets is to discriminate on the basis of quality and if such discrimination is not a binding constraint to the growth of those firms that contribute to economic development. It is true that small firms account for most growth in employment and that small firms often have difficulty raising expansion capital. However, it is the growth of a minority of such firms (estimated at 4 percent of the total) that drives economic development. If this minority is not rationed, credit rationing of the other is not a constraint.

The objective of preventing recession-related so-called "credit crunches" was also identified by Rhyne (1988). However, lending ceilings are normally based on demand or legislation, and none of the loan guarantee schemes reviewed for this research is designed to include a countercyclical element. Thus, the "market flaw" rationale reduces to the third possibility: that small firms, with attendant small borrowing balances, fall below a threshold that lenders find economically viable to consider. According to this rationale, the flaw is related to the financial system vis-à-vis the size of the firm, not its quality.

The second category of objectives that Rhyne (1988) noted are those related to the external social welfare benefits associated with SMEs: job creation, support for technological innovation, promotion of competition, etc. Indeed, the study that recommended formation of the U.K. loan guarantee scheme, the Wilson Committee (1979, p. 26) noted explicitly that the promotion of a guarantee program could be justified if "the public return from the activities of small firms was greater than the private benefit because, for example, of their importance to job creation. In the latter case it would also follow that some public subsidy was justified."

If this rationale is accepted, the issue becomes one of comparing the cost of the implied subsidy with the value of external benefits necessary to justify it. The value of social welfare benefits accruing to loan guarantee programs has not been satisfactorily evaluated. To perform such a study with the necessary rigour requires a longitudinal comparison of guarantee-assisted borrowers[4] vis-à-vis a valid benchmark sample of borrowers who did not use a guarantee. No such study has been performed. In general, studies of the impact of loan guarantee programs have been simplistic. As a result, hard evidence concerning external benefits of loan guarantees is lacking. This is surprising in view of the significant amount of government funds at stake.

Distributional aims are mentioned as a third set of objectives for guarantee programs. Arguably, loan guarantees assist disadvantaged borrowers. However, with some minor exceptions, the design of most loan guarantee initiatives does not provide lender agents with any explicit targeting directives.

The problems of program design, justification and political defence are vested in the objective(s) of the initiative. The goals of loan guarantee programs are invariably stated in terms of the first of these categories: to address the flaw in credit markets whereby small firms are thought to be unable to access capital to the same extent as large firms. If size is the issue, there ought to be no subsidy and the only firms to receive loan guarantees would be less risky ones within the small-firm universe.

For the balance of this study, the operating premise is taken as the stated objective: loan guarantee programs are intended to facilitate access to capital for small but viable firms. As Thornton (1996, p. 1) pointed out, this is a public policy issue because it is widely believed that many of the small businesses that would otherwise be denied credit do not contribute significantly to Canadian society nor are they able to enhance significantly Canada's competitive position internationally. The thrust of what follows is directed toward the design of loan guarantee schemes that accomplish this objective. To succeed, such programs need to align, in an explicit way, the objectives of the program with those of the agent lenders. Accordingly, a review of the operation of credit markets is in order.

The Research Literature on Credit Markets

The Bank-SME Interface

Hanson (1983) argued that the availability of expansion capital is *the* central issue in economic development:

> Access to capital is the central issue.... Entrepreneurial talent is not the prerogative of the wealthy, but is broadly distributed throughout the population as a whole. Without reasonable access to financing, many of our countries' most talented and aggressive entrepreneurs will be cut out of the economic system. Innovation and business development will become a luxury reserved for the wealthy, and the economy as a whole will suffer.

Therefore, the decision to grant credit is critical, not just to the entrepreneur whose particular request is being considered, but also to society. Justification of loan guarantee initiatives is often based, by invocation of the literature, on credit rationing (see, for example, the works of Berger and Udell, 1990; Chan and Kanatas, 1985; deMeza and Webb, 1987, 1992; Besanko and Thakor, 1987; and Stiglitz and Weiss, 1981). Cressy (1995) argued convincingly that access to capital is not a barrier in the credit rationing sense. Rather, he made a strong case for human capital as the more essential ingredient to survival. Growth, however, does require capital. To the extent that smaller firms suffer disproportionately less access, availability of capital is a public policy issue. The basis of government intervention in financial marketplaces is an understanding that, because of the way markets operate, smaller firms face proportionately greater difficulty raising credit than larger firms, other factors (including risk) being equal.

In Canada, the demand side of the marketplace for small business debt capital comprises approximately 900,000 small businesses. On the supply side, banks are the primary, indeed almost exclusive, suppliers of debt capital to small business. The supply side of the market comprises six national multibranch banks, several smaller regional lenders and (in some provinces) small co-operative lending institutions.

The relationship between banks and small business borrowers has been turbulent. Wynant and Hatch (1990), Orser et al. (1993) and others revealed dissatisfaction among a high proportion of SME clients. In the spirit of Cressy (1995), bankers argue that the poor management skills of some small business owners are problematic. Banks' fiduciary responsibilities to their depositors mitigate against lending to firms that do not present fiscally responsible management.[5]

Smaller firms, in particular, seem less able to obtain debt capital from banks. M.J. Grant and Co. Ltd. (1988) reported that banks turned down newer smaller companies most frequently, a finding confirmed by Orser et al. (1993). Further, Wynant and Hatch (1990) and Riding and Haines (1994) found that (unlike in the United States and other countries) the margins on bank loans to Canadian SMEs are almost universally less than 3 percent above prime. Riskier firms tend to be turned down in attempts to arrange bank financing. This finding is consistent with credit rationing based on quality.

Credit rationing carries implications for credit markets. Foremost is that, under credit rationing, there remains an excess of demand for credit over supply. With credit rationing, lenders are unwilling to provide, at current market rates, the loans SMEs seek. Lenders ration credit to control the quality of their loan portfolios. It follows that the so-called laws of supply and demand and of single price do not hold. This restricts the application of conventional methods of economic theory development. Moreover, and most important, the level of investment may be at variance with that which is socially optimal (Stiglitz and Weiss, 1981; and deMeza and Webb, 1987).

It is worth reviewing the literature on credit rationing because it is often invoked as a justification for loan guarantee programs (for example, Pieda plc, 1992). The literature on credit rationing does not address directly the role of firm size as it pertains to access to credit; it focuses on risk. Nonetheless, the literature does provide a template for considering the issue of size.

The Literature on Credit Rationing

In their seminal work, Stiglitz and Weiss (1981) identified severe informational asymmetries as a potential cause of equilibrium quantity credit rationing. They distinguished low-risk from high-risk firms according to the relative variances of the (mean preserving) probability distributions of business owners' projects and assumed, *inter alia*, that banks control the price and quantity of credit and that borrowers have access only to banks. Stiglitz and Weiss argued that the interest rate set by lenders affects the riskiness of loans in the marketplace in two ways. First, because of adverse selection,[6] borrowers willing to pay high rates may, on average, be poor risks. Second, as the interest rates rise, borrowers who had been good risks are increasingly encouraged to present moral hazard[7] by undertaking projects with higher returns but a lower likelihood of success. Stiglitz and Weiss contended that an optimal interest rate may exist on loans beyond which profits to banks decrease because additional defaults from riskier borrowers offset the increase in profits.[8] As an additional result, they argued that entrepreneurs will prefer debt as the financing source of choice.[9]

deMeza and Webb (1987) challenged the findings of Stiglitz and Weiss. They relaxed the assumption of mean-preserving distributions of project risk and, as a result, arrived at findings contradictory to those of Stiglitz and Weiss: that asymmetric information leads good projects to draw in bad risks. They concluded that one consequence of informational asymmetry is more investment than is socially efficient and that business owners prefer debt to equity as a means of financing.

In their 1992 study, deMeza and Webb again reviewed the Stiglitz and Weiss result under the assumption that entrepreneurs can vary in their ability such that the assumption of mean-preserving distributions of project returns is replaced by the assumption of first-order stochastic dominance between projects. deMeza and Webb concluded that "this payoff structure implies equity rather than debt...although if equity contracts are costly...debt emerges [and] even under risk neutrality investment will be socially too low" (p. 214). Thus, the credit rationing issue has implications that go beyond the market for debt capital and spill over into the demand for equity funds by entrepreneurs.

Besanko and Thakor (1987) addressed the role of collateral in the context of asymmetric information between lenders and borrowers. Their analysis modelled collateral as being costly to liquidate, leading them to conclude that, in a monopolistic market, lenders would not seek collateral as it was "an inefficient tool for extracting borrower surplus" (p. 675).

The Stiglitz and Weiss (1981) study and those of deMeza and Webb (1987, 1992) and Besanko and Thakor (1987) differ with respect to certain key assumptions about the nature of the marketplace, assumptions that lead to divergent findings. The crucial assumption appears to relate to the parameters of the distributions of entrepreneurial returns. Thus, implications of economic theory with regard to credit rationing and the role of collateral are seen to depend on the researchers' assumptions about the underlying distributions of the returns on projects undertaken by borrowers.

Regardless of the result, equilibrium quality credit rationing is not necessarily a flaw: credit markets are *supposed* to discriminate on the basis of credit risk. At issue is whether or not credit markets discriminate on the basis of size. The literature on credit rationing explains why *riskier* firms have difficulty accessing bank loans; however, it does not explain why *smaller* firms are necessarily accorded reduced access to debt. This is because studies of credit rationing have not explicitly allowed for firm size as a variable. Usually, interpretations of these studies have tacitly assumed that risk and size are related. Alternatively, they proceed on a marginal basis and consider only the incremental dollar of debt financing.

LENDERS' RESPONSE TO SIZE OF LOAN: A CASE FOR INTERVENTION

Lending in the Absence of a Loan Guarantee

An analysis of lenders' response to size of loan is carried out in this section by adapting the approaches deMeza and Webb (1987, 1992) and Besanko and Thakor (1987) employed to investigate lenders' response to risk. Their paradigms are amended to three ways.

1. A scale dimension is explicitly introduced by incorporating variables that reflect the size of the loan and fixed and variable dimensions of the lenders' costs of due diligence and monitoring.
2. A constraint that represents lenders' upper limit on bad debt losses is articulated.
3. Risk is expressed as a probability of default, but does not differ across firms.

Under these assumptions, a loan is considered to be declined if the borrower is unable to meet the lender's requirements for collateral.

Using notation consistent with that of Besanko and Thakor (1987), it is supposed that the business owner faces an investment that will return r (r = 1+ rate of return) with probability $(1-\delta)$. The investment, therefore, has a probability of failure of δ, in which event the firm will be unable to pay the loan and the lender will claim the collateral. The lender requires collateral of c percent of the loan. The investment requires $\$K$ (loan principal), an amount that will be raised entirely by borrowing at a rate i (i = 1+ prime + risk premium over prime). The borrower's opportunity cost of funds is b percent.[10] The business owner will decide to invest if the expected net return exceeds the opportunity return:

$$(1-\delta)(r-i)K - \delta cK > bK \qquad (1)$$

that is:

$$r > i + \delta(1-\delta)^{-1}c + b(1-\delta)^{-1} \qquad (2)$$

It is assumed that the lender makes decisions on the basis of profit maximization and specifies a maximum bad debt loss of d percent of the loan portfolio. Lenders discriminate on the basis of risk. In advancing a loan, they face their internal cost of funds (k = 1 + cost of funds), a variable and a fixed cost of due diligence (v, F). Thus, the bank's margin on the loan is $\alpha(\alpha = 1 + i - k)$. It is supposed that banks realize β percent of the value of the collateral in the event of default. Thus, the bank wants to maximize profits subject to a constraint on bad debts, and expects a return on the project in excess of its opportunity cost. That is, they want to maximize:

$$(1-\delta)\alpha K + \delta\beta cK - vK - F \qquad (3)$$

subject to:

$$(1-\delta)(r-i)K - \delta cK > bK \qquad (4)$$

$$\delta(kK + vK + F) - \delta\beta cK < dK \qquad (5)$$

The quantities are now those that are characteristic of bank portfolios. The bank's credit policy is given by i and c. Solving for these quantities yields:

$$i = k + r - \delta(1-\delta)^{-1}c - b(1-\delta)^{-1} \qquad (6)$$

$$c = [k + v - d\delta^{-1} + FK^{-1}]\beta^{-1} \qquad (7)$$

This solution reveals that the lender's collateral requirement has a bank-specific component k, v, d and F, a risk component δ and a size element K^{-1}. The impact of size results from the requirement for a minimum element of due diligence regardless of size or quality of loan. The liquidity of the collateral β is seen as a moderating variable. The lender sets the collateral requirement such that the fixed costs of due diligence are warranted; firms unable to meet the collateral requirement would not be advanced credit. Since $c \geq 0$, equation (7) implies that a minimum loan size depends jointly on the lenders costs and bad debt limit, and on the risk of the investment.

In the spirit of Besanko and Thakor (1987), the amount of collateral available to the business owner is the owner's initial endowment W, augmented by the value of the assets that comprise the investment, i.e., K. Thus:

$$cK < W + K$$

or

$$K < (\beta W - F)/(k + v - d\delta^{-1} - \beta)$$

The size of the loan is governed by availability and liquidity of collateral, and the bank's internal costs and policies. Firms that lack sufficient liquid security would not receive loans. The interest rate has four components: the lender's internal cost of funds, the profitability of the investment, a term that expresses the interaction of risk and collateral protection, and a firm-specific risk term. These theory-based predictions require empirical validation before further analysis is warranted.

Empirical Tests of Predictions

To test equations (6) and (7), secondary data analysis was conducted using a sample of data extracted from bank loan files. Details of the data and the collection procedures may be found in Riding and Haines (1994). The data represented 1,393 case histories of bank lending to SMEs drawn randomly from the six major bank lenders, nationally, according to bank market share and geographic distribution of SMEs.

Equation (7) predicts that the collateral-to-loan ratio is jointly determined by the risk of the borrower, the size of the loan and a bank-specific component. The latter was modelled by a vector of dummy variables that identified each of the banks.[11] The data collected from the bank files included each bank's risk rating of the borrower. However, each bank used a different means of scoring risk. Therefore, the borrowers of each bank were ranked by internal risk ranking. The borrowers in the quartile with the highest risk rating were identified as high-risk firms and identified with a dummy variable. Equation (7) specifies that collateral-to-loan ratios depend on the reciprocal of loan size. However, both the distributions of collateral-to-loan and of the reciprocal of loan size were skewed. Accordingly, natural logarithms of both were taken. In addition, the denominators of the dependent variable (collateral-to-loan ratio) and the independent variable (reciprocal of loan size) are common. To avoid simultaneous equations bias, the latter variable was ranked and the ranks of loan size used in the regression. The results are listed in Table 2.

Table 3 reports the ordinary least squares estimation of the predictions of equation (6). Here, the natural logarithm of the interest rate on term loans was the dependent variable. Independent variables included a vector of six dummy variables that identified the firm's banker, a dummy variable equal to one for those firms ranked in the highest-risk quartile of each bank's clients and the natural logarithm of the collateral-to-loan ratio.

Tables 2 and 3 provide partial support to the predictions of equations (6) and (7). The effect of individual bank costs and policies appears to be supported by the data. The collateral requirement is highly correlated with the size of the loan and in the manner predicted. Risk is not a strong determinant of collateral, but is

TABLE 2

REGRESSION RESULTS: ESTIMATION OF EQUATION (7)

Variable	Estimated Coefficient	t-value	Significance Level
Risk	0.1220	0.81	0.424
Rank of loan size	0.0098	19.68	0.000
Vector of bank identifiers	f(6,237) = 5.04		<0.05

correlated significantly to interest rates and in the manner predicted. Interest rates are also dependent on the collateral-to-loan ratio. However, the direction of the relationship is not as predicted, probably due to the interaction with risk predicted by equation (6). Further empirical work is required.

Lending in the Presence of a Loan Guarantee

With a loan guarantee, the borrower pays a fee of f percent of the loan, and g percent of the loan is guaranteed. In this setting, the owner decides to invest in the opportunity if:

$$(1-\omega)(r-i-f)K - \omega cK > bK \tag{8}$$

that is, the owner's required return is:

$$r > i + f + \omega(1-\omega)^{-1}c + b(1-\omega)^{-1} \tag{9}$$

Thus, in the presence of a costly loan guarantee, the owner will require a higher rate of return to compensate for the cost of the guarantee. Increasing the fees acts as a disincentive to business owners to invest.

From the lender's perspective, profits are as for the case of no loan guarantee with the guarantee replacing part of the collateral. However, under the terms of the SBLA the loan must also be secured by either a first fixed charge on the assets required, or by a *pari passu* fixed charge with the other sources of financing provided

TABLE 3

REGRESSION RESULTS: ESTIMATION OF EQUATION (7)

Variable	Estimated Coefficient	t-value	Significance Level
Risk	0.212	3.445	0.0007
Log of collateral to loan ratio	0.040	1.913	0.0569
Vector of bank identifiers	f(6,237) = 5.04		<0.05

for the project by the SBLA lender. The bank's lending policy i and c depend on the profit maximization problem modified for the presence of the guarantee by maximizing:[12]

$$(1-\omega)\alpha K + \omega g K + \omega\beta c K - \upsilon K - f \quad (10)$$

subject to:

$$(1-\omega)(r - i - f)K - \omega c K > bK \quad (11)$$

$$\omega(kK + \upsilon K + F) - \omega g K - \omega\beta c K < dK \quad (12)$$

Solving this for the credit policy yields:

$$i = k + r - f - \omega(1-\omega)^{-1}c - b(1-\omega)^{-1} \quad (13)$$

$$c = [k + \upsilon - g + FK^{-1} - d\omega^{-1}]\,\beta^{-1} \quad (14)$$

Given initial endowment W, the maximum loan in the presence of a loan guarantee is:

$$K < (\beta W - F)/(k + \upsilon - g - d\omega^{-1} - \beta)$$

The effect of the loan guarantee is twofold. First, the guarantee reduces the lender's demand for collateral, making debt more generally accessible to firms, particularly small firms, that lack the resources to pledge for security. Moreover, the lender assesses a lower rate of interest, recognizing that the business owner's return on investment is reduced by the amount of the fees. As a result, higher fees not only discourage owners from investing, they reduce the profits to the lender, discouraging their involvement.

SUMMARY

THE OBJECTIVE OF LOAN GUARANTEE SCHEMES IS TO FACILITATE capital for small viable firms. The stated goals do not include (except as side benefits) economic development, countercyclical or distributional aims. Loan size, a close proxy for firm size, appears to be a natural barrier to capital formation given the profit maximization motives of institutional lenders. It has been shown that the introduction of a loan guarantee scheme ameliorates the size problem and provides incentive for lenders to make larger loans to small businesses. What remains is the provision of guidance for program design. This will be advanced following a review of the SBLA, a consideration of the agency relationship between guarantor and lender, and an examination of international experience.

THE SBLA PROGRAM

AS NOTED IN THE PRECEDING SECTION, the role of loan guarantees as a means of ensuring that SMEs have adequate access to financing is an important public policy issue. This is especially true for the Canadian federal government – a government elected in 1993 on a platform that stressed economic recovery through support for small businesses. Since financial markets do not provide appropriate access to capital for small loans, government intervention is warranted. Loan guarantee programs are a primary means by which national governments of our international competitors facilitate access to debt capital for small businesses.

Small businesses are particularly reliant on debt financing. For small firms, it is estimated that the annual investment rate of equity in Canada is less than $500 million. This comprises approximately $100 million to $200 million from institutional venture capital firms (ACVCC, 1993) and $200 million to $300 million from private informal investors (DalCin et al., 1993). Only a minority of businesses have access to equity through organized stock exchanges. By contrast, bank lending under the terms of the SBLA alone exceeded $4 billion in 1994. Operating loans, commercial mortgages and non-guaranteed term loans were additional to this amount. Loan guarantee programs are intended to ensure that debt capital is, in principle, available to the smallest of firms.

Governments face a predicament with respect to loan guarantee initiatives. On the one hand, access to capital is, indeed, a significant barrier to SME growth and the attendant economic development. On the other hand, it is argued that firms that must avail themselves of loan guarantees are subject to rates of default that exceed those of banks' other borrowers. The costs of default can be significant for governments that face material budgetary deficits. At a more basic level, should the public underwrite SME borrowing? Conversely, loan guarantee programs that accomplish the objectives without cost to the public are feasible. This study seeks to address these issues.

BACKGROUND, HISTORY AND GOALS OF THE PROGRAM

SINCE ITS INCEPTION IN 1961, THE SBLA HAS PROVIDED for federally guaranteed term loans through approved lenders. The relationship between the government and the approved lenders is an application of agency theory. The government, acting as the principal, has objectives for the loan guarantee program that it would like its agents (the lenders) to fulfill. The lenders have their own objectives, ones that need not coincide with the aims of the government. In the setting of agency theory, the design of the contract between agent and principal must be based on a clear articulation of the objectives of each party. Program design must align the goals of the principal with those of the delivery agents.

To obtain an SBLA-guaranteed loan, borrowers obtain a loan from an approved lender. Approved lenders include the six multibranch national chartered banks as well as other institutions. Within the terms of eligibility, the loan guarantee decision rests in the hands of the lender and borrower. Lenders have full discretion

FIGURE 1

TAKE-UP OF SBLA LOANS: 1970 TO 1993

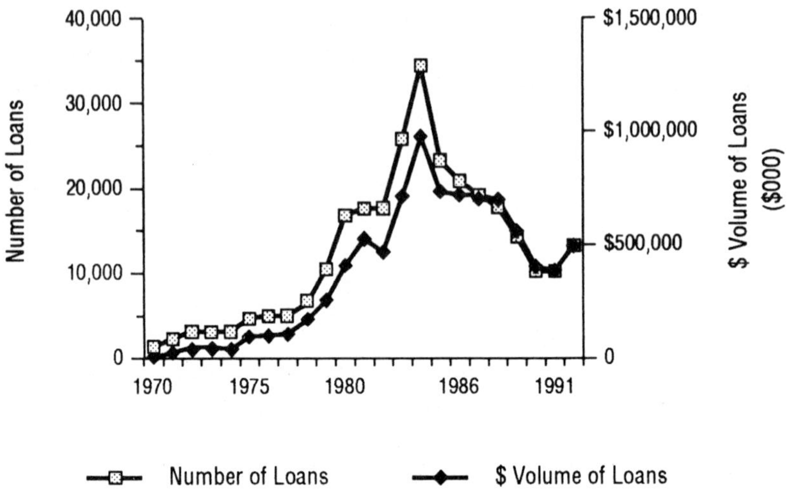

regarding the loan decision. The SBLA Administration Branch is responsible primarily for maintaining registration of the loans and, in the event of default, the Administration Branch honours the guarantee. Unlike loan guarantee schemes in the United States and United Kingdom, the role of the Canadian government is passive. Figure 1 shows the take-up of the program in terms of loan and dollar volume from 1970 to 1993.

The SBLA program provides exclusively for guarantees of term loans where the proceeds are used to finance land, premises, equipment and certain other items. Proceeds may not be used to finance working capital, share acquisition, refinancing and intangibles (including franchise and operating permits).

In April 1993, the Canadian federal government amended the SBLA. These changes included:

- increasing the level of the guarantee temporarily from 85 percent of loan loss to 90 percent;
- widening eligibility to firms with annual revenues of up to $5 million (the previous limit was set at $2 million);
- increasing the maximum loan size from $100,000 to $250,000;
- widening eligibility to firms in sectors such as finance, insurance, mining and the professions; and

- providing for a higher interest rate spread to 1.75 percent over prime on floating-rate term loans and allowing for interest rates as high as 1.75 percent over the residential mortgage rate on fixed-rate term loans.

As a partial result of these changes, lending volume under the terms of the SBLA increased dramatically. From a dollar volume of approximately $500,000 in 1993, SBLA lending approached $3.5 billion during 1994. Cumulative lending under the SBLA surpassed the $4 billion legislated ceiling, prompting significant concerns related to issues of:

- the economic impact of SBLA lending;
- the risk and exposure of the government; and
- incrementality.

Economic Impacts of SBLA Borrowing

Assessing the impact of loan guarantee schemes is not straightforward. As yet, no rigorous and comprehensive analysis appears to have been conducted of any loan guarantee program in the United States, United Kingdom or Canada. To conduct this analysis, such evaluations need to be done frequently, ideally using longitudinal data. Such data, according to Rhyne (1988) would need to encompass:

- change(s) in firm performance before and after the loan;
- a compilation of credit experience subsequent to the loan, including the development of a customer relationship with the lender;
- a compilation of alternatives to loan guarantees;
- the measurement of attributes and credit experience with reference to a control group; and
- the measurement, from the lenders' perspectives, of the performance of lenders' portfolios of guaranteed loans including long-run default and charge-off rates and returns to lenders.

In short, without comprehensive longitudinal data, it is virtually impossible to assess the level of external benefits accruing from the loan guarantee program. Any evaluation of such benefits are beyond the scope of this study.

Nonetheless, several attempts to estimate external benefits have been reported. According to the SBLA (1991, p. 12), the cost per job is of the order of $656 to $1,113. Moreover, between 1990 and 1993, the additional employment associated with SBLA lending was in excess of 100,000 new jobs.

These findings are suspect for at least two reasons. First, they are based on firms' self-reports of expected job creation at the time of application for the loan guarantee. Accordingly, they likely overstate the level of external benefit. Second, they do not consider incrementality in that some proportion of the loans (and the resultant jobs) would have been advanced if the SBLA were not available.

There is an additional concern regarding the evaluation of economic impacts. Implicit in such an investigation is a cost-benefit analysis. Some costs are clear: program administration and obligations to honour loans in default. Such costs constitute an implicit subsidy to risky firms if not offset by fee incomes. The implicit benefits of job creation, etc. ought to be weighed against the implicit subsidy. This analysis has not been conducted.

Issues of Incrementality

One concern raised recently with respect to the SBLA is that of incrementality. Incrementality involves two aspects. One relates to the 1993 revisions to the eligibility criteria which made firms, with sales of $2 million to $5 million, eligible borrowers. Firms in particular industrial sectors also became eligible. In this sense, some borrowers are incremental in that they would not have been eligible before April 1993. In terms of this definition of incrementality, 8.6 percent of borrowers reported sales in excess of $2 million per year and are incremental in the first sense. In terms of the new sectoral criteria, 8 percent of borrowers are in the professions; another 4 percent are in the finance, insurance and real estate sector (Haines and Riding, 1994).

The second aspect of incrementality relates to the "bankability" of the firm. The question has arisen as to whether or not firms that have borrowed under the SBLA would have qualified for a term loan without the need for a government guarantee. That is, "what proportion of SBLA lending is really incremental, in the sense that the loans would not have been made without the program?"[13]

Evaluation of incrementality in the "bankability" sense is less straightforward. One means of investigating incrementality is to examine the banks' treatment of SBLA clients with respect to terms of credit on operating loans and non-SBLA term loans. For example, in the sample of 1,393 bank loan files, 254 firms had borrowed under the terms of the SBLA and *also* maintained an operating loan facility with the same lender. Likewise, 326 firms had a term loan under the SBLA as well as one or more term loans that were not guaranteed. Table 4 presents the distributions (and cumulative distributions) of interest rates on operating loans held by SBLA and non-SBLA term loan borrowers. Table 5 presents distributions of rates on non-SBLA term loans for borrowers who also held an SBLA loan and for term loan borrowers who did not report an SBLA loan.

The median rate on operating loans paid by non-SBLA borrowers is 125 basis points above prime. In finance theory and according to stated bank practice, the interest rates charged by lenders reflects the lenders' assessments of client riskiness. As Table 4 shows, 30.3 percent of SBLA borrowers have been assessed an operating loan interest rate that reflects a ranking that lies in the *lower* half of rates assessed to operating loan clients. Even though SBLA borrowers are, on average, smaller and younger, and have fewer assets, 30.3 percent of these firms do not seem to have been regarded by the lender as among the riskier firms. Likewise, in Table 5, 39.4 percent of SBLA borrowers paid lower than median rates (150 basis points above prime) on non-SBLA term loans from the same lender from whom an SBLA loan had been advanced.

TABLE 4

DISTRIBUTIONS OF INTEREST RATES ON OPERATING LOANS

Interest Rate Ranges Above Prime	SBLA Borrowers (%)	SBLA Borrowers (Cumulative %)	Non-SBLA Borrowers (%)	Non-SBLA Borrowers (Cumulative %)
0 to 0.25	1.6		7.4	
0.251 to 0.5	3.9	5.5	10.5	17.9
0.501 to 0.75	2.4	7.9	6.6	24.5
0.751 to 1.00	17.3	25.2	21.0	45.5
1.001 to 1.25	5.1	30.3	5.5	51.0
1.251 to 1.5	24.0	54.3	16.3	67.3
1.501 to 1.75	4.3	58.7	2.9	70.2
1.751 to 2.0	21.3	79.9	17.3	87.4
Greater than 2.0	20.0	100.0	12.6	100.0

Source: 1994 Carleton University survey of bank loan files.

These results indicate that from 30 percent to 40 percent of SBLA loans were to firms that are among the *least* risky in the lenders' portfolios. Perhaps as many borrowers again were assessed interest rates commensurate with rates that banks charge borrowers who do not use the program. Incrementality, however, is a multi-faceted concept. On the one hand, extension of loans to less risky SMEs is good news for the government: each firm pays a 2 percent fee but the likelihood of default is low. Moreover, lenders have been subject to considerable pressure to increase lending to SMEs. The SBLA is a useful vehicle for accomplishing this goal. On the other hand, non-incremental loans are dead weight that uses up part of the limit on the portfolio of guarantees available under the terms of the SBLA.

The program objectives relate primarily to size, not risk. Ideally, incrementality ought to be viewed on the domain of size. However, the result is not very different. Of the SBLA loans outstanding in 1994, an estimated 36 percent were to firms that had been in business for less than three years. This compares with 12.5 percent of non-SBLA term loans outstanding at the same time. Approximately one quarter of SBLA loans were incremental. Fifty-three percent of SBLA term loans were made to firms with sales of less than $500,000, compared to 45 percent of non-SBLA term loans.

The Canadian experience with respect to incrementality is not unique. According to Pletcher and Tootelion (1992), the extent of incrementality of the SBLA program is estimated to be one third. Pieda plc (1992) estimated a 68 percent level of incrementality for the U.K. Loan Guarantee Scheme (LGS). Such estimates are inherently ball-park in nature; it is heroic to attempt to measure what would have happened in the absence of the guarantee program.

TABLE 5

DISTRIBUTIONS OF INTEREST RATES ON TERM LOANS

Interest Rate Ranges Above Prime	SBLA Borrowers (%)	SBLA Borrowers (Cumulative %)	Non-SBLA Borrowers (%)	Non-SBLA Borrowers (Cumulative %)
0 to 0.25	1.8		2.5	
.251 to 0.5	0.0	1.8	4.0	6.5
.501 to 0.75	1.8	3.6	4.6	11.0
.751 to 1.00	12.5	16.1	17.2	28.2
1.001 to 1.125	5.4	21.5	4.3	32.5
1.126 to 1.5	17.9	39.4	19.9	52.5
1.501 to 1.75	8.9	48.3	4.3	56.7
1.751 to 2.0	31.3	79.6	24.8	81.6
Greater than 2.0	20.5	100.0	18.4	100.0

Source: 1994 Carleton University survey of bank loan files.

With the high take-up rate, increased absolute dollar costs should be expected from additional loan losses due to defaults and higher program administration costs due to the volume of program-related responsibilities. Estimating these costs is not straightforward.

DEFAULT RATES

DEFAULT RATES OF SBLA LOANS WERE ANALYSED BY GOSS GILROY INC. (1994) using an event history approach. According to the Gilroy findings, the long-term mean default rates on SBLA loans are 4.8 percent to 6.7 percent. Between 1970 and 1991, $8.1 billion of loans under the SBLA resulted in losses of $307 million, a 3.8 percent loss rate. These estimates are not inconsistent. The Goss Gilroy estimates represent the number of loans that default. Most defaults occur during the third and fourth years of the loan term, part of the loan having been repaid. (Figure 2 illustrates the chronology of defaults and plots the proportion of defaulted loans that occur in each year of the term.) Therefore, dollar value losses, as a proportion of dollar loan volume, are likely to be less than the proportion of loans that default.

These findings are instructive. On an international scale, the default rates are extremely low for a loan guarantee program. Also, the agency relationship between the government and the private sector program delivery agents necessarily implies a somewhat higher default rate than the lenders would accept in the absence of a loan guarantee program.

Very few defaults (less than 10 percent) occur within the first two years. This is strong evidence that lenders have been appropriately screening loan applicants for risk. In the absence of such screening, high *initial* default rates would be expected. The experience of U.S. and U.K. loan guarantee programs is quite different in this respect.

FIGURE 2

CHRONOLOGY OF DEFAULTS: SBLA LOANS

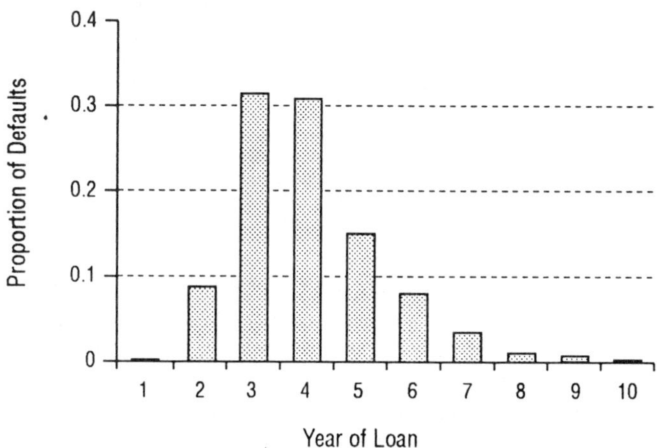

ISSUES IN THE DESIGN OF THE SBLA: FEES, DEFAULT RATES AND THE GUARANTEE LEVEL

THE SINGLE OBJECTIVE OF THE SBLA IS TO FACILITATE ACCESS to capital for small firms. In the face of government budget deficits, it would be desirable to accomplish this objective with no fiscal impact on government. The primary source of income for a fiscally self-sufficient SBLA is fee income. Thus, the objective is to ensure that fee income covers the costs of default and administration.[14] A small amount of income comes from recoveries of defaulted loans.[15] However, for the SBLA, the cost of administration is offset by the income from recoveries. Hence, to a very close approximation, fees must cover defaults. Mathematically, this is expressed as:

$$f = \omega g \qquad (15)$$

where f is the fee income expressed as a percentage of the loan principal, g is the level of the guarantee set by the guarantor and ω is the rate of default in the portfolio of guaranteed loans.

For the program to be delivered by the lending institution agents, the lenders must have incentives to do so. Among potential incentives are reductions in administration costs for the lenders (reduced costs of due diligence and monitoring given the presence of the guarantee), customer development and the guaranteed loans' contribution to profits. Clearly, it is not in the interests of the guarantor to set the guarantee level so high that banks fail to carry out adequate due diligence and monitoring. Thus, the task is to set the level of the guarantee such that the profit to lenders is at least equivalent (after allowing for defaults and recoveries) to the profits from non-guaranteed loans to SMEs.

Lenders' incomes have two components: the receipt of the amortized principal and interest from loans that do not default and the value of collateral realized from firms that do default. Their costs arise from the internal cost of the invested capital and the variable and fixed costs of due diligence and monitoring. These components can be expressed mathematically as profits to lenders. For non-guaranteed loans to SMEs, lenders' profits may be expressed as:

$$(1-\delta)\,\alpha K + \delta\beta c K - vK - F \tag{16}$$

where δ is the relative frequency of defaults in the portfolio of non-guaranteed loans, α is one plus the spread between the interest rate and the lender's cost of funds, β is the proportion of the value of collateral that the lender can realize in the event of default, c is the ratio of collateral to loan, K is the amount of the loan, and v and F are the variable and fixed costs, respectively, of due diligence and monitoring. In the presence of a loan guarantee, the level of defaults in the portfolio may change. If the relative frequency of defaults in the portfolio of guaranteed loans is given by ω, the lender's profit function is given by:

$$(1-\omega)\alpha K + \omega g K + \omega\beta c K - vK - F \tag{17}$$

The proceeds of the guarantee supplement the realized value of collateral in the event of default. Since the program objective remains to facilitate capital for small firms (and not to subsidize risky firms), differential risk is not an issue except to the extent that lenders adjust the quality of their portfolio to retain profitability. Equating (16) with (17) yields the following relationship between default rates δ and ω and the level of the guarantee g:

$$\omega = \frac{\alpha - \beta c}{\alpha - \beta c - g}\,\delta \tag{18}$$

This result shows that the frequency of defaults in the portfolio of guaranteed loans is extremely sensitive to the level of guarantee set by the guarantor body. Recourse to Canadian experience allows this generic expression to be simplified. First, as shown in tables 4 and 5, interest rates on loans to SMEs rarely exceed the prime rate plus 3 percent. Moreover, the rates to SBLA and non-SBLA borrowers are not significantly different from each other. Hence, α is of the order of 1.02 to 1.05. Second, recall that recoveries under the SBLA between 1970 and 1991 totalled \$7.5 million on claims of \$307 million. This implies $\beta c \approx 0.024$. As a good approximation, then, equation (18) may be written:

$$\omega \approx \frac{1}{1 - g}\delta \tag{18a}$$

This equation may be used to predict the default rate as a function of the loan guarantee. In Canada, bank lenders target a maximum bad debt loss δ of less than 1 percent. This is typically 0.6 percent to 0.8 percent. Based on these data, equation (18a) predicts SBLA default rates of 4.0 percent to 5.3 percent. These estimates are consistent with the Goss Gilroy Inc. (1994) analysis of Canadian experience. Note also that in 1993 the level of guarantee was temporarily raised from 85 percent to 90 percent. Based on equation (18a), this change would lead to an increase in the default rate of 50 percent.[16]

The sensitivity of the default rate to the level of guarantee is underscored by expressing the rate of change of the default rate with respect to the level of guarantee mathematically:

$$\frac{\partial\omega}{\partial g} = -(1 - g)^{-2}\delta \tag{19}$$

Substituting equation (18a) into equation (15) and minimizing the level of defaults suggests that the level of guarantee is 50 percent. While this rate minimizes defaults, it may not be optimum in a social welfare sense. Nor are the effects on take-up rates sufficiently well understood that such a change in the program parameters is advised. However, higher levels of guarantee imply both higher default rates, a concomitant need for higher fee income and greater bank profits from their portfolios of guaranteed loans. Yet, setting the level of guarantee too low removes the incentive for delivery agent lenders to participate in the program. Table 6 lists the implied default rates and fee rates, based on a bad debt loss on non-guaranteed loans of 0.7 percent and equations (18a) and (15), respectively, for a range of guarantee levels.

In general, the higher the level of the guarantee, the greater the proportion of poor quality loans that lenders can tolerate in their portfolio. On the other hand, if the guarantee is too low, lenders lose incentive to deliver the program. For the current Canadian situation, it seems likely that bank lenders may earn more from their portfolio of guaranteed loans than from their portfolio of non-guaranteed loans to SMEs.

It is instructive to examine the experience of loan guarantee programs in other countries to further investigate how their experiences are affected by the parameters of the relationship.

TABLE 6

SIMULATED DEFAULT RATES AND FEE REQUIREMENTS BY LEVEL OF GUARANTEE

Level of Guarantee (g)	Implicit Default Rate (%) (ω)	Implicit Fee Requirement (f)
0.50	1.40	0.70
0.55	1.56	0.86
0.60	1.75	1.05
0.65	2.00	1.30
0.70	2.33	1.63
0.75	2.80	2.10
0.80	3.50	2.80
0.85	4.67	3.97
0.90	7.00	6.30
0.95	14.00	13.30

SMALL BUSINESS LOAN GUARANTEE PROGRAMS: AN INTERNATIONAL PERSPECTIVE

THE U.S. SMALL BUSINESS ADMINISTRATION LOAN GUARANTEE PROGRAM

THE SMALL BUSINESS ADMINISTRATION (SBA) WAS CREATED IN 1953 to make direct loans and loans in partnership with banks, and to provide loan guarantees. The premise of the SBA was that banks were too risk averse to lend to small firms, yet there were plenty of "good" small businesses that were worthy of credit. At its inception, it was intended that the SBA would not compete with bank lenders. Accordingly, over time, the SBA has moved away from direct lending toward loan guarantees.[17] Such guarantees were intended for borrowers who, because of their small size, did not meet bank credit standards.

Historically, a borrower seeking a loan that a lender was unwilling to provide could apply, through the lender, to the SBA for a guarantee. The application was reviewed by SBA staff and, if approved, a guarantee of up to 90 percent of loans up to $155,000 could be advanced. The guarantee could be triggered when the borrower was 60 days in arrears of monthly amortization requirements. Then, on demand from the lender, the SBA would purchase the outstanding principal and interest under the terms of the guarantee. The SBA then became responsible for further collection.

To be eligible, the borrower must be a small business (the definition of which varies by industry), and the lender must certify that the business does not qualify for credit without the guarantee, but the likelihood of repayment is sound. The loan must be secured to the extent that tangible assets are available and the chief executive's personal guarantee is required. Personal assets of owners may also be required as collateral. Interest rates are negotiated between the borrower and lender subject to the SBA maximums of 2.75 percent above prime for maturities of seven years or more and 2.25 percent over prime for shorter maturities.

Recently, the SBA moved away from approval of all loan applications to place more responsibility on the lenders. The SBA identifies several categories of SBA lenders. Approximately two thirds of U.S. banks act as lenders under the SBA program, yet there is considerable variation in the extent to which various lenders actually participate. Rhyne (1988) identified four categories of SBA lenders.

1. **Non-users** These tend to be small, rural, conservative institutions with low loan-to-equity ratios. They constitute approximately 28 percent of bank lenders.
2. **Infrequent Users** These include banks that carry fewer than 10 SBA loans. Making up 54 percent of the SBA lender population, infrequent users extend about one third of SBA loan guarantees, usually on an ad hoc basis.
3. **Active Users** These are defined as users that carry more than 10 SBA loans, but the SBA portfolio comprises less than 20 percent of their commercial and industrial lending. This includes large and moderate-sized banks. These banks tend to have staff devoted to the SBA.
4. **Intensive Users** These banks have more than 10 SBA loans that comprise more than 20 percent of their commercial lending. This category accounts for only 5 percent of all banks. These lenders are usually small but with relatively large lending portfolios. They tend to be highly leveraged and aggressive, often using SBA loans to promote the growth of the bank.

In 1982, the SBA established its Preferred Lender Program. Preferred lenders were banks that were accorded the ability to authorize SBA loans without prior SBA approval. Lenders qualify for this status through their track records of SBA lending. The intention of the Program was to increase the level of SBA guarantees. An additional benefit is the attendant reduction in SBA staff costs. The level of guarantee, however, is only 75 percent of the loan, compared with 90 percent for traditional SBA loan guarantees.

Experience with the Preferred Lender Program has been sufficiently good that the SBA has continued to move in this direction. The Program has put more SBA loans into the hands of lenders that are committed to the SBA program, has reduced costs both to lenders and the SBA, has approached the true market-perfecting aim of the loan guarantee scheme and has reduced default rates. As noted by Rhyne (1988), the raw purchase rate of defaulted loans under the preferred lender program was 2.6 percent, a rate that compares with the 14 percent for non-certified lenders.[18]

The average size of SBA-backed loans is considerably higher than that of Canadian SBLA-guaranteed loans. In 1982, the average SBA loan was $109,000 and by 1986 this had increased to $155,000. Both values exceed the average size of non-guaranteed commercial bank loans. Moreover, according to Rhyne's (1988) findings, SBA borrowers tend to have received larger loans than they might otherwise have obtained and for longer maturities, in accordance with the predictions set out earlier in this paper.

As noted, the SBA has had considerable praise, but has also been subject to intense criticism. Among the major causes of concern are the high costs of program administration and the purchase of loans in default. The operating budget of the SBA is about $70 million per year (Rhyne, 1988) and estimates of long-run default rates range from 16.4 percent (SBA, 1983) to 23.5 percent (Rhyne, 1988). Both of these costs compare badly with those of the Canadian SBLA (administration cost of approximately $1.3 million per year with long-run default rates of the order of 4 percent to 6 percent), even though the level of outstanding loan guarantees does not differ materially between the Canadian SBLA and the U.S. SBA program.

The U.K. Loan Guarantee Scheme

The Loan Guarantee Scheme (LGS) was introduced in 1981 by the U.K. Department of Trade and Industry (DTI) following the recommendations of the Wilson Committee (1979) that "competition between banks...was insufficiently effective to ensure that viable small businesses always had the necessary access to sufficient funds on reasonable terms." While the Wilson Committee recognized the disproportionate public benefits stemming from the expansion of small firms, it is clear that the primary objective of the LGS is to remedy the market for small *viable* firms. This remediation is reflected in two aims of the LGS:

- to facilitate the supply of debt capital to viable small businesses that are unable to obtain conventional loans due to a lack of security; and
- to provide lenders with experience in lending to businesses that are viable but do not satisfy traditional lending criteria.

DTI restricts loan guarantees to firms that have tried and failed to obtain a loan. The scheme is a joint venture between the DTI and lenders. Lenders must satisfy themselves that they would have offered conventional loans but for the lack of collateral or a track record, and that all available personal assets have been used for conventional loans.

The small firm's application to a lender for credit initiates the process. If the lender decides that the applicant has a viable business proposal but there is insufficient security to justify the loan, the lender applies to the DTI. On acceptance, the DTI provides the lender with a guarantee for 85 percent of the total loan. In return for government backing, the borrower must pay the DTI an annual premium.[19] In addition, the lender may require a pledge of real assets as security and will usually take a fixed or floating charge on such assets. The security applies to the whole loan, and the borrower remains liable for the full debt. Lenders seek recovery, possibly through liquidation, in the event of default. LGS loans may not exceed a term of seven years.

Originally the loan guarantee was set at 80 percent, and a 3 percent premium of the guaranteed amount was payable. Since then, the program has been altered on several occasions with variations in the size of the guarantee and the amount of the premium.[20] These had a significant impact on the take-up rate of the program and, according to Cowling and Clay (1995), are the two primary determinants of the take-up rate.

The scheme differentiates between new and established businesses. Established businesses are those that have been trading for two years or more. For established firms, the guarantee and the maximum loan size are higher. The loan guarantee may be obtained, up to the maximum amount only once by any one individual.

Fees are relatively high and represent annual payments to the guarantor, reducing the cost of the program by reducing default risk. To the extent that DTI approval is involved, the program is not fully delivered by the private sector. Moreover, the program is somewhat restrictive and unwieldy, and requires lenders to undertake the expense of the due diligence process. Nonetheless, the program provided at least £1 billion in loans to more than 33,000 SMEs between 1981 and 1993.

The four major trading banks in the United Kingdom account for 80 percent of LGS lending. Most LGS loans are extended to firms in the distribution, manufacturing and service sectors. Unlike the Canadian SBLA process, proceeds of the loan can be used to finance working capital (as happens in approximately 40 percent of the cases). As noted by Pieda plc (1992, Appendix 5), defaults were more common among those firms that used the guarantee to finance working capital. This result is to be expected: the use of long-term obligations to finance short-term assets contravenes long-standing financial wisdom.

As noted in Pieda plc (1992), the default rates of LGS loans are substantial. A long-run default rate of approximately 40 percent has been experienced for loans granted from June 1981 through March 1984, with the majority of defaults occurring within the first two years. Also according to Pieda plc, the U.K. Department of Employment reported that 30 percent of loans granted from October 1988 through September 1989 defaulted within the first two years.

Default Rates: United States, United Kingdom and Canada

Figure 3 charts the cumulative default rates for the Canadian SBLA, the U.S. SBA program and the U.K. LGS for seven-year maturity loans. This figure is revealing in that the high default rates during the initial years of the U.K., and to a lesser extent, the U.S. approaches imply that loans have been advanced to non-viable businesses, in contravention of the explicit objectives of the two programs. Three differences in program design may be pertinent to this finding.

FIGURE 3

CUMULATIVE DEFAULT RATES: U.S., U.K., CANADIAN LOAN GUARANTEE PROGRAMS

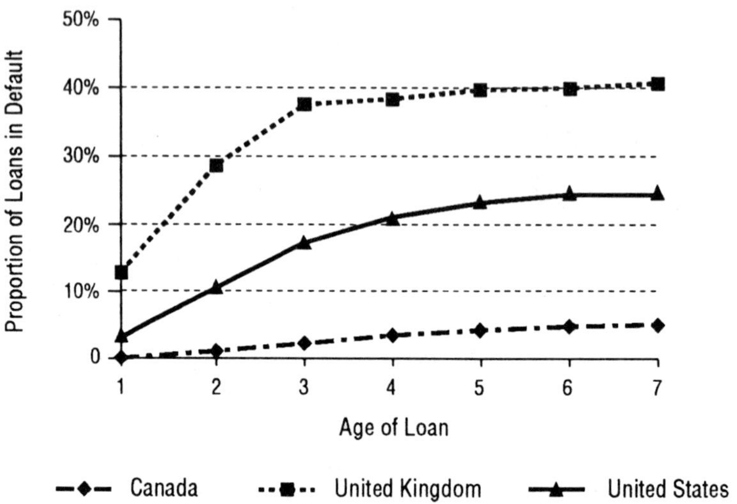

First, both the U.K. and U.S. approaches have traditionally involved the guarantor in the loan approval step, at least in name. This is time consuming, costly and at variance with the idea that commercial lenders are best equipped to make credit decisions. In Canada, the decision is left exclusively to the lender, relying to a greater extent on the expertise that the banking sector can contribute. Second, the level of guarantee has a dramatic impact on default rates. For the period during which the default rates in the United States were measured, the level of the guarantee had been set at 90 percent. This implies (Table 6) somewhat higher default rates, although not to the extent seen above. Third, the level of fees can also affect the quality of borrower drawn to the program. If the fees are too high, good quality borrowers will not use the program, and the cycle of market deterioration described by Akerlof (1970) can result: the only users of the program, in the context of high fees, would be poor credit risks. The analogy from life insurance is that when life insurance is extremely costly, the only customers would be those who are extremely ill.

Higher default rates are not, of themselves, negative indications. What is important is the degree to which social welfare benefits exceed the subsidy implicit in the costs of the program. In Canada, with recoveries taking care of the administrative component, the subsidy is equivalent to loan losses – about 4 percent. In the United States, this subsidy has been estimated at 11 percent to 13 percent (Rhyne, 1988) and, in the United Kingdom, the subsidy exceeds 30 percent (Cowling and

Clay, 1995). Since no rigorous assessment of social welfare benefits has been conducted in either the United States, United Kingdom or Canada, no statement about the relative effectiveness of the programs can be rendered. However, it is clear that the hurdles to positive assessments are greater in the United Kingdom and United States than in Canada.

OTHER APPROACHES TO LOAN GUARANTEE SYSTEMS

MOST DEVELOPED COUNTRIES HAVE SCHEMES DESIGNED to facilitate SME financing. In the Netherlands and Germany, governments provide guarantees for all or part of business loans. Organizations external to government issue loan guarantees on behalf of the governments in Belgium, Luxembourg, Ireland, France, Portugal and Greece. Loan guarantee associations are formed in Spain to guarantee loans for their members. The operating policies and details of the various programs differ considerably across jurisdictions. To illustrate the gamut of such programs and, because they each display interesting attributes, the loan guarantee programs of Japan and Germany are described.

Japan: the Credit Supplementation System

The Credit Supplementation System was founded in Japan in 1958. It comprises two levels of operation. The Credit Guarantee Corporations (CGCs) (of which there were 52 in 1993) provide lenders with guarantees for their loans to SMEs. When a small firm applies for a loan, the prospective lender may ask the CGC to act as guarantor. If, after investigation, the CGC agrees, the lender extends credit to the business and the business pays a guarantee fee to the CGC. As a rule, the guarantee is then automatically insured by the second component of the Credit Supplementation System: the national Credit Insurance Corporation (CIC). The CGC pays an insurance premium to the CIC.

In the event of default, the CGC repays the remaining principal to the original lender. The CGC then applies to the CIC under the terms of the insurance and, normally, the CIC would pay the CGC 70 percent to 80 percent of the original capital. The CGC takes the remaining 20 percent to 30 percent as a loss, pending recoveries. The CGCs must make "the utmost efforts" to recover the outstanding debt directly from the business. From recoveries, 70 percent to 80 percent must be refunded to the CIC.

The CGCs obtain their capital from contributions by banks and local governments, and they borrow their operating funds from local governments and the CIC. The CIC was initially endowed with a capital fund by the national government. From 1987 through 1991, the CIC's insurance payouts were less than incomes received from insurance premiums and recovered moneys. The 1992 recession resulted in a deficit.

This clearly meets the goal of enabling small firms to overcome financial disadvantages. It also removes from the lender much of the onus for due diligence and efforts toward recoveries. Moreover, the CIC's impact on the national budget is minimal: from 1987 through 1991 revenues from recoveries and fees exceeded insurance payouts by more than ¥325 billion (approximately C$3.5 billion).

Germany: the Burgschaftsbank[21]

The German credit guarantee system is one part of a support system for SMEs in Germany. The system includes direct cash subsidies related to particular interest and research and development expenses, and large direct lending programs. A system of loan guarantees has been established in Germany since 1954. The credit guarantee system is decentralized and bears a similarity to that of Japan in that a reinsurance step is involved and the guarantor body is self-financing.

Potential business borrowers (including professionals) approach their banks for credit. If they lack traditional security for the loan, they may apply for a loan guarantee to the Burgschaftsbank in their state. (One Burgschaftsbank is to be established for each of the 16 states of the united Germany.) The purpose of the Burgschaftsbank is to provide guarantees for SMEs so trading banks can advance debt capital. The application entails a business plan and documentation of professional affiliations, and is reviewed by several levels: the firm's original banker, the management of the Burgschaftsbank and the applications committee of the Burgschaftsbank. This latter committee comprises industry representatives and is elected. The proposal must survive each level of appraisal. According to Dr. Georg Licht, of the Zentrum für Europäische, Mannheim, Germany, this appraisal process results in a lower take-up rate and low default rates.[22]

Borrowers must pay both an initial premium of 1 percent of the guaranteed portion of the loan as well as an annual fee of 0.5 percent to 1 percent of the outstanding debt. Loans can be for any amount, but the maximum guarantee is DM 1 million. Loans may not be used for refinancing. Interest rates are determined between the borrower and the original banker.

Originally endowed with capital raised from government and participating organizations, the Burgschaftsbanks act as the initial guarantors of loans. If the Burgschaftsbank approves the application, it issues a guarantee for up to 80 percent of the funds. In turn, the Burgschaftsbank receives reinsurance of 60 percent of the loan from the state and federal governments and a further 12.5 percent guarantee from the European Recovery Program. The Burgschaftsbanks appear to operate autonomously and are financially self-sufficient. Their sources of income include the initial guarantee fees, annual fees and interest on invested capital.

The long-run default rate does not appear to be public information. However, defaults in 1990 amounted to about 4 percent of the guarantees extended that year (Licht, personal interview).

Summary

The fact that most of Canada's primary international competitors use loan guarantee programs is a compelling reason to argue that Canada's SMEs also require this form of support. Loan guarantee systems that boast high rates of default, such as those in the United Kingdom and the United States, are essentially government-based subsidies for risky firms – not merely a means of remedying a flaw in the credit market. Such a subsidy potentially places Canadian SMEs in a vulnerable position.

The Canadian SBLA scheme has much to recommend it. Among its attractive features are its extraordinarily low administrative cost and the low costs associated with honouring guarantees. Administration costs and the costs of default associated with any of the other national approaches are many times greater that those of the SBLA. Moreover, the U.K. and German schemes are considerably more expensive for borrowers who must pay fees annually. The German and Japanese experience, however, demonstrate that loan guarantees can be provided by a financially self-sufficient intermediary.

Whether or not the programs accomplish their primary objective (remediation of the credit markets for small firms), they do appear to provide societal benefits. In general, the programs provide indirect benefits to governments in the form of tax payments, reductions in welfare payments, etc. Mandel (1992) noted that evidence to the U.S. House of Representatives suggests an internal rate of return in the order of 26 percent on the government's investment in SBA-guaranteed loans when these corollary benefits are accounted for. These estimates, however, lack the rigour that would be achieved if proper longitudinal tests of social welfare benefits were to be conducted.

There are other attributes of foreign approaches that may be of benefit. The U.K. distinction between established and un-established firms may be useful in terms of program design. The U.K. rule that an individual may avail himself or herself of a guarantee only once might be a useful means of combating misuse of the program.

At the heart of all programs is the agent-principal relationship between the government guarantor and the lenders. The relationship requires careful nurturing and adjustment if the program objectives are to be fulfilled and if costs to the public are to be minimized, or even eliminated. To do so, requires a clear understanding of the objectives of the program.

SUMMARY, IMPLICATIONS AND FUTURE RESEARCH

THIS PAPER REPORTED ON ISSUES THAT PERTAIN TO LOAN GUARANTEE PROGRAMS for small firms. A review of the development and experience of the Canadian *Small Business Loans Act* identified issues of program design. The primary, indeed, virtually exclusive, objective of loan guarantee programs is to ease access to debt capital for small businesses, i.e., to redress a perceived flaw in the credit market, to "level the playing field."

This investigation argues that lenders will demand disproportionately more collateral from firms seeking smaller loans. This disproportionate demand for collateral is not temporary: it is a normal result of the operation of the credit market. To the extent that small firms are unable to provide the requisite security, their access to capital is restricted. It is argued that the presence of a loan guarantee mitigates the lenders' collateral demand, thereby expanding access to capital for small firms. The need for ongoing loan guarantees targeted to SMEs is implied.

Given the need for ongoing intervention, the issue becomes one of program design. The relationship between guarantor and the lender-delivery agents dictates a default rate that is necessarily higher than with lenders' portfolios of non-guaranteed loans. This implies a subsidy, both to the lender-delivery agents and to the riskier firms that obtain loan guarantees. Because of the absence of rigorous longitudinal evaluation, the extent to which the economic benefits compensate for the subsidy remains unknown.

The agency relationship is such that the guarantor controls the level of the guarantee and the level of fees. Lenders control the quality of the loan portfolio. This separation of responsibilities makes sense. The central task of the guarantor, then, is to set the level of the guarantee sufficiently high that lenders have economic incentive to deliver the program yet not so high that lenders lose incentive to discriminate on the basis of borrower quality. The level of the guarantee and the fee level need to be established in conjunction with each other. The guarantee rate implies the default rate and thereby the loan loss rate. The level of fees must offset the loan losses yet remain low enough that poor quality risks do not drive out the high quality borrowers whose success subsidizes the failures.

Analytically, defaults are reduced if the guarantee level declines toward 50 percent. This implies both low fees and the need for lenders to exercise full due diligence. Under such conditions, the following are likely outcomes.

1. The level of fees would be low enough and the rate of guarantee sufficiently high that owners of SMEs would find the terms of the guarantee attractive.
2. Delivery agent lenders would have economic incentive to deliver the scheme broadly, to manage carefully the quality of the portfolio and to carry out sufficient due diligence to control defaults.
3. Income from fees would at least offset the contingent liabilities of the guarantees.
4. Good credit risks would not abandon the market to risky firms, yet the level of guarantee, being lower, would reduce dead weight.

Previous research suggested considerable dead weight. This lack of incrementality was occasioned by two factors: the low fees and the high level of the guarantee. In the context of loan guarantees, as in the context of insurance, dead weight is not necessarily a problem. Fees paid by the majority of firms that will not default partially or even completely offset the guarantor's liabilities resulting from the defaults of the minority of firms.

Default rates associated with the Canadian SBLA are of the order of 4 percent to 6 percent, part of which is covered by fee income. By international standards, this is low. Agency theory implies that the level of defaults is sensitive to the guarantee level. Higher guarantee levels allow lenders to tolerate higher proportions of defaults without any reduction in profits. The agency relationship predicted default rates for the SBLA and the U.S. SBA program that are consistent with experience. Moreover, according to the agency argument, the temporary increase in the SBLA guarantee level from 85 percent to 90 percent in 1993 could lead to a material increase in the level of defaults.

Historically, the U.S. SBA program has experienced default rates in the order of 20 percent. Moreover, the operating budget of the SBA program is far higher than that for the SBLA even though the absolute levels of activity of both programs are comparable. In part, the higher default rate in the United States could be attributed to a higher guarantee level of 90 percent. More recently, the SBA has been evolving toward lower levels of guarantee and less guarantor involvement, steps likely to result in better quality portfolios and lower administration costs. The early experience with this change in strategy has been encouraging (Rhyne, 1988) and Mandel (1992).

The default level associated with the LGS in the United Kingdom is in the order of 40 percent, the highest of all countries examined. In part, this is attributable to both self selection due to the high fees and to suspect screening practices. Nonetheless, there are some attractive features of the LGS:

- the distinction between established and new firms;
- provisions for targeting loan guarantees geographically and according to particular government priorities; and
- the stipulation that an individual qualifies only once under the terms of the LGS. The governments of Germany and Japan have, in effect, privatized their loan guarantee schemes. In Japan, one-off funding of the Credit Insurance Corporation has provided for a re-insurance process. In Germany, the role of the Burgschaftsbanks and their re-insurance from the states, the federal government and the European Recovery Commission provide for a similar situation. While the default rates in Germany are very low, the extensive and demanding selection process may defeat widespread program delivery.

Loan guarantee programs form the cornerstone of small business finance support for many of Canada's most important international competitors. Currently, the SBLA provides Canada with competitive advantage through several attractive attributes:

- the ease of access attendant on passive government involvement;
- low administration costs; and
- low default rates compared to those experienced in the United Kingdom and United States.

Revisions should take the form of small reductions in the level of guarantee and fee levels. Before doing so, econometric analysis of the determinants of take-up rates, in the manner that Cowling and Clay (1995) conducted for the U.K. LGS, should be undertaken.

Finally, program delivery implies economic incentive to lenders and a small degree of subsidization of the riskier firms in the portfolio. A rigorous longitudinal analysis of the social welfare benefits accruing to firms that have received loan guarantees must be undertaken. Without such an analysis, decisions about program continuance and design ought not to be taken.[23]

Endnotes

1 Statement to the U.S. Congress House Committee of Small Business, 99th Congress, Second Session, 1987, as noted in Rhyne (1988, p. 6).

2 Ibid.

3 Conversely, there is some evidence that particularly small firms are less likely to default or exceed limits on operating loans than mid-sized firms (Orser et al., 1993). As Storey (1994) observed, during the normal course of firm development, the ability of the owner-entrepreneur to manage and control effectively is outstripped, and professional management must be installed. In the interim, the firm is, arguably, particularly vulnerable.

4 Such a study would require time series information, changes in firm performance before and after the loan, subsequent credit experience, evaluation of relationships with lenders, a sense of the degree to which the guaranteed loan was incremental and a taxonomy of firm attributes. As noted by Thornton (1981), such a study would necessarily have to control for all intervening variables.

5 Thornton (1981) added some empirical substance to these contentions. Thornton used discriminant analysis to study several aspects of the financial management of Canadian small businesses. One dependent grouping was whether or not the small-firm owner respondent had been turned down for financing in the last three years. Fifty-two of 289 respondents reported loan turndowns. Thornton found that significant variables associated with the turndown decision included sector, financial management ability and the size of the firm.

6 Adverse selection can follow if lenders are unable to distinguish good credit risks from poor risks. As originally noted by Ackerlof (1970), the lender will charge all borrowers fees and interest rates that reflect the average level of risk in the marketplace. As a result, good risk borrowers would be overcharged and would be subsidizing poor credit risks. Consequently, the argument maintains that good risk borrowers drop out of the market. This worsens the mix and initiates a cycle that ultimately results in a marketplace in which only high risk borrowers remain as they are the only ones willing to pay the higher rates. The market degenerates. It can be argued that such asymmetry of information reflects the reality of the Canadian marketplace. Wynant and Hatch (1990) reported that bank loan account managers typically manage of the order of 100 accounts. Given training, administrative duties, vacation, etc., this leaves the account manager with approximately one working day per year per client. Moreover, the rate of account

manager turnover is non-trivial. It may be argued, therefore, that loan account managers do not, in the Canadian setting, have sufficient time to perform the due diligence necessary to distinguish good from poor risks.

7 Once a loan is advanced, the lender must ensure that the borrower does not act contrary to the lender's interests, a problem known as moral hazard. Clearly, moral hazard can arise from self-serving behaviours, such as diversion of perquisites, fraud, misrepresentation, etc. However, moral hazard can also arise from simple inconsistencies between the wealth-maximizing objectives of the lender and the borrower. In particular, the debt contract fixes the repayment from borrower to lender. Benefits of success are skewed in favour of the borrower. However, the lender stands to lose the entire loan capital in the event of failure while the borrower is protected by limited liability. This yields incentive for the borrower to undertake high-risk projects. Losses fall to the lender and gains (less fixed interest and principal repayment) fall to the borrower. Moreover, the potential for moral hazard is greatest when the owner has little to lose (e.g., low levels of equity on the balance sheet).

8 Again, the Canadian setting is consistent with these predictions. Wyant and Hatch (1990), Riding and Haines (1994) and others found that very few bank loans to SME customers are priced at more than 3 percent above prime rate. Storey (1994) contended that when a lender is concerned about a particular borrower, the lender is likely to apply quantity rationing to future lending rather than credit limits, signalling a loss of bank confidence.

9 Mankiw (1986) noted that, in the event of credit rationing as described by Stiglitz and Weiss, a sharp exogenous rise in interest rates could trigger a general collapse of the marketplace. Mankiw argued that monetary tightening leads to additional adverse selection as good risks increasingly refuse to pay higher rates. Adverse selection is exacerbated because the effect of the shock makes it more difficult for lenders to screen borrowers. Moreover, shock-related decreases in the value of collateral further reduce lender confidence. Finally, shock-related decreases in the values of borrowers' assets induce a greater likelihood of moral-hazard-type borrower activities. The result is a general decline in borrowing, a decline that has its largest impact on borrowers whose credit quality is difficult to determine.

10 All quantities are net of taxes.

11 The confidentiality agreement under which the bank file data were collected prohibits reporting of bank-specific results. The f-statistic reported here tests the contribution, to the reduction of the sum of squared errors, of the addition of the vector of six bank-specific dummy variables. Four of the six dummy variables were positive and significant at the 1 percent level.

12 The symbol ω, as used here, denotes the probability of failure/default which can differ systematically between guaranteed and non-guaranteed loans. Thus, δ can be viewed as the rate of default in the portfolio of non-guaranteed loans and ω as the default rate among guaranteed loans. The relationship between δ and ω is discussed in the section on issues in the design of the SBLA, later in this paper.

13 Internal memorandum, ESBO, Industry Canada, April 1994.

14 For the SBLA, the annual operating budget in 1994 was $1.3 million. This compares rather favourably with the annual budget of the U.S. Small Business Administration (SBA) loan guarantee program which, in 1984, was $68.5 million. Both programs administer a comparable quantity of guaranteed lending.

15 For 1991, recoveries from defaulted SBLA loans were $1.7 million, more than offsetting administration expenses. Recoveries of prior years' claims from 1970 through 1991 amounted to $7.5 million on loans of $8.1 billion and claims of $307 million over the same period (SBLA, 1991, tables 1 and 3, pp.13 and 15).

16 The default rate implied from equations (18) and (18a) is consistent with actual default experience of the SBLA (Goss Gilroy Inc., 1994). A further increase in the level of guarantee to 95 percent (as for the U.S. SBA program during the 1980s) implies a default rate of 11.5 percent. According to Rhyne (1988) actual default experience in the United States was between 17 percent and 25 percent.

17 Rhyne (1988) reported that in 1986 the SBA had $160 million in direct loans outstanding and $2.8 million in loan guarantees extended.

18 However, it was also found that clients may already have been "bankable" under the Preferred Lender Program. Accordingly, a fee of 2 percent was instituted in 1986.

19 As of June 1993, this premium was 2.5 percent per year on the guaranteed portion of the loan or 1.5 percent on the whole loan for variable-rate loans.

20 According to Cowling and Clay (1995), the loan guarantee was reduced to 70 percent from June 1984 through July 1993, when it was increased to 85 percent. The premium, originally 3 percent, was increased to 5 percent in June 1984 and reduced to 2.5 percent in May 1986.

21 This section is based on Pieda plc (1992, Annex A), *Economic Incentives in Germany's New Federal States* (Federal Ministry of Economics, 1994), and interviews with Prof. B. Harrison, Associate Professor of Economics, Humboldt University, L. Neu, Manager of Corporate Relations, Deutsche Handelsbank, and Dr. Peter Wieczorek, Bundesministerium für Wirtschaft.

22 Personal Interview, September 13, 1995.

23 The discussant of this paper argues convincingly that research to assess the effects of "turning the dials" of the SBLA on social welfare benefits is unlikely to be fruitful. This is probably true. However, the purpose of the longitudinal analysis recommended here is far more modest: to assess whether or not the value of social welfare benefits of the SBLA, as currently constituted, exceed the cost of the subsidy implicit in the program expenses. This obviates concerns about self-selection bias as long as the degree of incrementality can be estimated.

BIBLIOGRAPHY

ACVCC, Association of Canadian Venture Capital Companies. *Annual report for 1992*. Toronto, Ontario, 1993.

Akerlof, G. "The Market for Lemons: Qualitative Uncertainty and the Market Mechanism." *Quarterly Journal of Economics*. 84, (1970): 488-500.

Berger, A. and G. Udell. "Collateral, Loan Quality, and Bank Risk." *Journal of Monetary Economics*. 25, (1990): 21-42.

Besanko, D. and A. V. Thakor. "Collateral and Rationing: Sorting Equilibria in Monopolistic and Competitive Credit Markets." *International Economic Review*. 28, (1987): 671-683.

Chan, Y-S. and G. Kanatas. "Asymmetric Valuations and the Role of Collateral in Loan Agreements." *Journal of Money, Credit, and Banking*. 17, (1985): 84-95.

Cowling, M. and N. Clay. "Factors Influencing Take-Up Rates on the Loan Guarantee Scheme." *Small Business Economics*. 7, (1995): 141-152.

Cressy, R. "Are Business Startups Debt-Rationed?" Working paper, Small and Medium Sized Enterprises Centre, University of Warwick, 1995.

DalCin, P., G. Haines, A. Riding and R. Safrata. *Salient Characteristics of Informal Investors*. Carleton University, Ottawa, 1993.

deMeza, D. and D.C. Webb. "Too Much Investment: A Problem of Asymmetric Information." *Quarterly Journal of Economics*. 102, (1987): 281-292.

—. "Efficient Credit Rationing." *European Economic Review*. 36 (1992): 1277-1290.

Federal Ministry of Economics. *Economic Incentives in Germany's New Federal States*. Germany, 1994.

Goss Gilroy Inc. *Study and Forecast of Claims Activity Under the Small Business Loans Act*. Ottawa: Small Business Loans Administration, Industry Canada, 1994.

Haines, G., A. Riding and R. Thomas. "Changing Bankers: An Empirical Analysis of Factors Leading Small Businesses to Switch." In *Proceedings, ASAC Finance Division*. Edited by Trevor Chamberlain. Whistler, BC: Administrative Sciences Association of Canada – Finance Division, 1990, pp. 109-118.

Haines, G.H. Jr., A. Riding and R. Thomas. "The Bank-Small Business Relationship: A Model and Some Canadian Experience." *Entrepreneurship: Theory and Practice*. 1994.

Hanson, D. "Introduction." In *Financing State and Local Economic Development, Part IV*. Edited by Michael Barber. Durham, North Carolina: Duke University Press, 1983, pp. 359-473.

Jankowicz, A.D. and R.D. Hisrich. "Intuition in Small Business Lending Decisions." *Journal of Small Business Management*. 25, (1987).

Mandel, A.S. "Small Business, Banks and Loan Guarantees: Comment." *Small Business Economics*. 4: (1992): 169-170.

Mankiw, N.G. "The Allocation of Credit and Financial Collapse." *Quarterly Journal of Economics*. 101 (3) (August 1986).

M.J. Grant and Co. Ltd. *Small Business Views the Banks: The Bottom Line*. Canadian Federation of Independent Business, 1988.

Orser, B., A. Riding and C. Swift. "Banking Experiences of Canadian Micro-Businesses." *Journal of Enterprising Culture*. 1, (1993).

Pieda plc. *Evaluation of the Loan Guarantee Scheme*. London, U.K.: Department of Employment, Government of the United Kingdom, 1992.

Pletcher, D.D., and D.H. Tootelion. "SBA Loans Recipients Societal Benefits – A Comparison with National Averages." Working paper, School of Business Administration, California State University, Sacramento as noted in Pieda plc. *Evaluation of the Loan Guarantee Scheme*. London, U.K.: Department of Employment, Government of the United Kingdom, 1992.

Rhyne, E.H. *Small Business, Banks, and SBA Loan Guarantees: Subsidizing the Weak or Bridging a Credit Gap*. Westport, CT: Quorum Books, 1988.

Riding, A., and G. Haines. "Empirical Findings from Survey Data." *Access to Credit: Lending Priorities and SMEs*. Volume II, Carleton University, Ottawa, 1994.

Small Business Credit Insurance Corporation. *Outline of Small Business Credit Insurance Corporation*. Research Department, Tokyo, Japan, October 1976.

SBLA, (1992). *Small Business Loans Act, Annual Report on Operations* for the 12-month period ended March 31, 1991.

Standing Committee on Industry. *Taking Care of Small Business*, Second Report. Ottawa: Government of Canada, 1994.

Stiglitz, J. and A. Weiss. "Credit Rationing in Markets with Imperfect Information." *American Economic Review*. 81, (1981): 393-410.

Storey, D.J. "New Firm Growth and Bank Financing." *Small Business Economics*. 6 (2) (April 1994).

Thornton, D. "Small Business Financing Policies and Practices: An Interview Survey of Managers." *Small Business Financing and Non-Bank Financial Institutions*. Toronto: Facsym Research Limited, 1981.

Wilson Committee. *The Financing of Small Firms*. HMSO, Command Paper 7503, Department of Employment, Government of the United Kingdom, London, 1979.

Wynant, L. and J. Hatch. *Banks and Small Business Borrowers*. London, Ontario: The Western Business School, University of Western Ontario, 1990.

Comments on Session V: Recent Financing Initiatives

THE QUEBEC STOCK SAVINGS PLAN: OVERVIEW AND ASSESSMENT

Comment by Simon Lalancette
Département de sciences économiques
Université du Québec à Montréal

THIS STUDY IS ORGANIZED IN THREE PARTS. In the first, the authors describe how the Quebec Stock Savings Plan (QSSP) works; in the second, they analyse the performance of the QSSP from the investor's point of view; and in the third, they assess the performance of the Plan from the standpoint of businesses.

Tables 6 and 7 of the study report on the performance of the QSSP from an investor's point of view. The authors consider a share issue a success if its market price at the end of 1994 was higher than the issue price, which is capitalized using the rate of return of the Small Cap Index. If the market price was lower at that point in time, the issue is considered a failure. This approach is not precise enough and does not allow us to draw conclusions about the success of an issue. Three elements come into play when assessing the performance of a stock: the inherent risk of the stock, the market behaviour during the evaluation period, and a statistical or econometric analysis of the results. The authors consider only the second factor, and then only partially.

The composition of the Small Cap Index needs to be defined more precisely, for two reasons. First, in Table 7 the authors capitalize the prices of small-firm issues using the rate of return on this index. This approach seems hardly logical, because the small businesses that *seem* to make up the Small Cap Index are more likely to behave differently over time than medium-sized firms. Second, a descriptive assessment of the return on this index would, in my opinion, greatly enhance the study's results.

The methodology used in Table 8 is also deficient because it is applied in a more deterministic and less robust way than the econometric techniques used to make empirical measurements in financial analysis. Moreover, I have some difficulty understanding the methodology underlying tables 6 and 7 and footnote 10, because the authors estimate systematic risk coefficients using the mathematical expression shown at the end of Table 8. Some clarification of this point is in order.

To draw valid conclusions, the analysis of the ratios presented in Table 10 should include a comparison with a sample of firms from outside Quebec. Given the specific nature of the Plan, it is quite possible that there are common systematic factors at play for QSSP firms.

In my opinion, the relationship between the tax credits offered to investors and the returns on QSSP issues, particularly small issues, is a complex one and goes beyond the simple incorporation of tax credits into monetary losses or gains in order to calculate the net gain made by investors. In particular, the excess demand for small issues and the resulting overvaluation of issue prices are considerations that lead us to believe that the tax credits received by investors are a systematic factor compensated by the market that has a direct impact on the average return generated by small stock issues.

My last two comments are editorial in nature. First, in tables 6 and 7, the inequality $0.20\ P_{ea} > ARS > P_{ea}$ should, in my view, be expressed as $P_{ea} > ARS > 0.20\ P_{ea}$. Second, the mathematical expression appearing at the bottom of Table 8 should have a minus sign.

Labour-Sponsored Venture Capital Funds in Canada: Institutional Aspects, Tax Expenditures and Employment Creation

Comment by Brian F. Smith
School of Business and Economics
Wilfrid Laurier University

The paper by Professor Vaillancourt briefly describes the labour-sponsored venture capital funds (LSVCFs) in Canada and their policy objectives. It goes on to examine the tax expenditures associated with them and the employment effects associated with Le Fond de solidarité des travailleurs du Québec (FSTQ). The paper concludes that the tax expenditures are regressive and that the FSTQ did not lead to a significant increase in employment in manufacturing in Quebec. The author concludes that the social objectives of the LSVCFs are not being achieved.

In describing LSVCFs, Vaillancourt argues that the supply of venture capital in Canada is adequate as of 1995. Given that the ratio of venture capital to the gross national product (GNP) did not shift significantly from 1990 to 1994 (0.53 percent to 0.60 percent), an argument could be made that the supply of venture capital was also adequate in 1990 and that the expansion of LSVCFs has resulted in a shift away from private funds. It is interesting to note that the recently founded Canadian Medical Discoveries Fund has the active involvement of MDS Health Group which previously had an extensive venture capital subsidiary in the medical field. Thus, it is likely that the MDS Health Group will funnel venture capital projects through the LSVCF rather than fund them directly.

Among the arguments raised to address the issue of the adequacy of supply of venture capital in Canada, Vaillancourt asserts that LSVCFs do not invest most of their funds as they obtain them. It would be helpful if the paper provided some evidence on the amount of funds that are invested on a long-term basis in companies and the amount invested in short-term marketable securities such as t-bills. This would be especially useful for the FSTQ because of its much longer history. The author also mentions the limited penetration by American venture capital funds into Canada. However, given the need for close monitoring of an investment, the distance probably serves as a natural barrier to entry to foreign firms. But, what are the barriers to entry for local venture capital firms?

Venture capital is often segmented by type of investment, such as early stage or restructuring. Is there any evidence of a shortage in particular segments of venture capital? Evidence on the realized rate of return would also be helpful. The 10-year compound rate of return of the FSTQ as of December 1995 was only 5.4 percent vs. 8.0 percent for three-month Canadian t-bills. For the five-year period ended December 1995, the Working Ventures Canadian Fund and the FSTQ earned only 4.2 percent and 6.1 percent vs. 6.3 percent for three month Canadian t-bills. (Of course, on an after-tax basis, to the investor, the returns would be considerably larger for the LSVCF.) The limited evidence on the realized return of other funds does not suggest that their realized returns are excessive. Since the realized rate of return of venture capital in Canada does not exceed the expected risk-adjusted rate, this would suggest that the supply of venture capital is adequate.

The paper should more clearly contrast the policy objectives and corporate governance of the public tax-sponsored funds in Canada vs. those of private venture capital funds. To what extent will a public tax-sponsored fund in Canada accept a lower rate of return, in order to meet political objectives? To understand the role of government, it would be useful to document the influence, if any, that governments have on the election of directors of the funds. Do governments retain a block of the units of the LSVCFs? Did the government appoint the original board and senior management of the LSVCF? It is my understanding that an LSVCF is restricted to certain types of investments to be eligible for the special tax status. For example, the recently founded Triax Growth Fund can invest in any company with fewer than 500 employees, less than $50 million in assets and resident in Ontario. It is permitted to invest in private companies as well as in secondary offerings in public companies. Are there job creation requirements associated with each investment? What influence do unions, as fund sponsors, have on the decisions of LSVCFs? Do the fund prospectuses specify objectives beyond that of trying to earn the maximum risk-adjusted return? All this information is available and should be documented.

The paper analyses the distribution of tax benefits from LSVCFs across income levels and provides convincing evidence that initial FSTQ tax credits are concentrated among the middle and upper middle class in Quebec and at higher incomes in Ontario. Given the finding that the tax expenditures are regressive, the author should then comment on whether this is a serious concern. Does it violate the mandate of the LSVCFs?

The final section of the paper investigates whether there is a link between employment in one of six manufacturing sectors in Quebec and the presence of the FSTQ. The approach in measuring the impact on employment in the whole industry is superior to that of Lamonde et al. (1994) who argued that jobs were saved based on the fact that specific companies were given an opportunity to continue with FSTQ funding. Vaillancourt should discuss why it is important to examine employment at other companies in the industry which did not receive FSTQ funding. In doing so, he should also explain why there may be no impact from FSTQ funding on aggregate employment.

For example, let's assume an industry has excess capacity, and the least-efficient industry member experiences financial distress. If the company receives FSTQ funding, then jobs are likely preserved at that company. If the company does not receive FSTQ funding, then jobs will likely be lost at that company. However, production and employment at other companies will likely increase as they move in to fill the bankrupt company's market share. In addition, the higher profits at these other companies from greater capacity utilization will lead to higher operating cash flows which, in turn, will allow companies to increase productivity-enhancing capital expenditures. This will strengthen the industry relative to foreign competitors which will ensure employment in the industry on a longer term. In addition, if the company was just poorly managed, FSTQ funding would merely protect inefficient management. Without FSTQ funding, such companies might be bankrupt but the operations would likely be reorganized and refinanced through private funding arrangements with new shareholders and senior managers taking control. Thus, overall employment may be unaffected. One could even argue that aggregate employment may be lower because FSTQ is subsidizing capital which is often a substitute for labour, i.e., the FSTQ funds could be used to invest in labour-saving equipment.

Another argument to consider as to why there may be no link between the LSVCFs and employment levels is that the tax benefits of the LSVCFs are not passed along to companies. There is evidence that management expenses of LSVCFs are significantly higher than other funds. In addition, evidence suggests that the supply of venture capital has not significantly increased relative to GNP and there has been a shift to LSVCFs from other venture capital sources. In other words, the same level of venture capital financing is occurring but LSVCF fund managers, distributors and tax-paying unitholders are benefiting at the expense of other taxpayers.

The regression model used in the analysis needs to be respecified. First, the underlying production function from which the model is derived should be discussed. The production function should make explicit the substitutability of capital and labour. This is important as the key impact of an LSVCF is to reduce the cost of capital for a subset of firms in an industry. In addition, assumptions about the competitiveness of the industry and the price elasticity of aggregate demand are important as they will determine whether output prices fall and output increases. Adding the FSTQ variable to the regression (as shown in the paper as an independent variable) will likely lead to multicollinearity given its significant positive correlation with output.

Finally, the FSTQ variable could be respecified as the percentage of the capital provided by FSTQ of all capital in the industrial sector. This would be a better measure of the impact of the FSTQ on the cost of capital for a sector. In addition, the time trend crudely accounts only for the technological changes that have occurred in the manufacturing sector during the 1980s. It may be better to account for these changes by examining the level of employment in an industry sector in Quebec relative to the rest of Canada.

As a final comment on the tests of whether the FSTQ program has increased employment, one should assess whether there are other social objectives, such as enhancing the competitiveness of an industry, that are equally important. For example, one could examine whether a Quebec industrial sector has been able to expand its market share in Canada as a whole as a result of the FSTQ. However, if it has, is the FSTQ a type of subsidy that is in contravention of recent initiatives to reduce interprovincial trade barriers?

In its conclusion, the paper asserts that social solidarity or Canadian/Quebec ownership may be the rationale for these funds. I am unsure why the author asserts that LSVCFs would increase social solidarity. I believe that the actions of LSVCFs may, in fact, be socially divisive. Employment in one company in an industry is maintained while employment at other companies in an industry is lower than otherwise. Given the labour union orientation of the original sponsors of some of the provincial funds, unionized employees may be favoured to the detriment of non-unionized employees. The regressiveness of the tax expenditures is also socially divisive. In addition, are there not sufficient other means such as the foreign content rules on registered pension plans and the Quebec Stock Savings Plan to promote Canadian/Quebec ownership? I suggest that the author considers other explicit and implicit policy objectives.

BIBLIOGRAPHY

Lamonde, P., Y. Martineau and D. Allen. "Impact économique et fiscal des investissements du Fonds de solidarité des travailleurs du Québec (FSTQ), 1984-1993." Mimeo, October 1994.

Raising Equity Capital for Small and Medium-Sized Enterprises Using Canada's Public Equity Markets

Comment by Eric Kirzner
Faculty of Management
University of Toronto

IRONICALLY, AS I WAS PREPARING MY COMMENTS, two events provided a practical spin on Professor Robinson's paper. The local media were avidly reporting the fortunes of a Waterloo, Ontario company, Open Text, which had just completed its primary distribution in the United States with a listing on the National Association of Securities Dealers Automated Quotations (NASDAQ), the U.S. electronic bill-board trading system. The shares, which were issued at $15 each, traded as high as $26.50 in the first day after-market, representing a 77 percent premium (or under-pricing depending on how you look at it). As one reporter stated, "On the [Toronto Stock Exchange] TSE, the underwriter is guilty of underestimating investor demand. This is called leaving money on the table, and it gets an underwriter fired."[1]

Meanwhile, the president of the Montreal Exchange, apparently representing his Board of Governor's views, had some interesting comments about the future of markets in Canada and suggested a restructuring and rationalization of Canadian exchanges with each exchange specializing in specific areas. For example, Toronto would operate the large capitalization equity market and Montreal the derivatives market. Listings for junior and natural resource companies would be allocated to Vancouver and Calgary.

It was interesting to read Professor Robinson's paper against the backdrop of these events, particularly as the structure and nature of our capital markets is under review by a number of regulatory bodies within the context of disclosure, fair treatment, fragmentation, costs and availability of capital.

Robinson examines and discusses the primary issue equity market for Canadian-based small and medium-sized enterprises (SMEs).[2] I found three useful features in this paper. First, there is an insightful review of the literature on the pricing of IPOs in Canada and the United States. Second, the characteristics and structure of the Alberta Stock Exchange's Junior Capital Pool (JCP) program is thoroughly described. And finally, the paper underscores the controversial question of second-tier equity markets, namely, whose interests they should serve and how, and if they should even be encouraged, operated and regulated. I support the idea of a second-tier market, although I am not convinced that the JCP program is the prototype.

I'm going to briefly review Robinson's paper, following his structure, and then discuss the pros and cons of following his suggested route for SME financing.

Raising Capital through an Initial Public Offering

Professor Robinson identifies two major costs associated with initial public offerings (IPOs): cash expenses (including regulatory cost and underwriter's commission) and the pervasive underwriter discount.

He finds that the cash expenses vary considerably by type of underwriting (firm-commitment vs. best-efforts) and by province. Not surprisingly, there is strong evidence of economies of scale – per unit cash expense costs are higher for small firms. He concludes, "For a firm attempting to raise several hundred thousand dollars of equity financing using the public equity markets in Canada, the ASE's [Alberta Stock Exchange's] JCP program is the only economical alternative."

Robinson then provides a review and discussion of the literature on underpricing of IPOs. He discusses a number of theorems[3] and concludes that the strongest empirical evidence supports the uninformed buyers hypothesis. (In a "market for lemons" argument, uninformed buyers secure a disproportionate number of overpriced IPOs – the winner's curse. Accordingly, all IPOs must be underpriced to entice the uninformed to continue buying in the primary market.)

It might be interesting to examine an additional hypothesis. Could the underpricing reflect some type of "neglected stock" or "dual research" methodology effect? Are valuation methods different for SMEs than non-SMEs? SMEs are marketed to a smaller audience, and the pre-issue period when the underwriter surveys the market is, accordingly, subject to a smaller information feedback loop. Possibly, underwriters of SMEs don't search for the same market information since many institutions are either uninterested or prohibited from participating. Robinson points out that large underwriting firms in Canada are unlikely to be interested in participating in new junior equity issues.[4]

Listing Requirements

Robinson then provides an examination of listing requirements on Canadian stock exchanges and concludes that there is a limited opportunity to raise small amounts of equity capital for venture firms on the Vancouver and Alberta exchanges, and for resource issues on the Montreal Exchange but, due to economies of scale, most of the regular IPOs are not much below $1 million. He concludes that there is a financing gap in Ontario.

Other Constraints

Robinson goes on to deal with secondary market liquidity and why an active primary market for junior equities requires a viable secondary market for these securities. The identified restraints on Canada's development include the aforementioned economies of scale in the investment industry, the small size of Canada's capital markets and limits in Ontario on underwriting compensation on small issues.

Junior Equity Issues

Robinson examines the history of junior stock or second-tier market programs in various countries and then discusses the Alberta JCP program. Based on data as well as interview results, he concludes that the JCP program is successful and could serve as a prototype for second-tier exchanges elsewhere.[5] He points out that the JCP program was evolutionary, building from an established regional dealer network and a strong retail following.[6]

Conclusions

The central issue of Robinson's paper is how small and medium-sized firms should obtain financing. The idea of a junior or second-tier market is the focus.

Second-tier markets are designed for junior companies that cannot, or choose not to, meet listing requirements on the primary market. Some of the second-tier markets introduced as adjuncts to major exchanges include the Amsterdam Stock Exchange's Official Parallel Market and the Unlisted Securities Market of the London Stock Exchange. One second-tier market had a brief history. The American Stock Exchange's (AMEX) Emerging Company Marketplace,[7] opened in 1992 and closed in 1995 after a series of scandals related to both market manipulation and the failure of the AMEX listing department to supervise the companies properly. I also note that order flow is shrinking on all the existing second-tier markets.

The second-tier market is at the very core of venture capital. It raises the issues of central exchanges, whose interests they should serve and how small start-up companies should obtain seed and development capital. Is public equity the appropriate approach and should such companies have exchange listings? But what are the potential benefits and the potential problems with second-tier markets, and is the Alberta JCP program a suitable prototype?

The Benefits of Second-Tier Markets

There are some benefits to a second-tier market. From an issuer standpoint, there is obviously access to a market otherwise restricted by stringent listing requirements, high listing costs or government indifference.

From a regulatory/protection point of view, there are some particularly strong benefits. If smaller companies are more volatile, less liquid and easier to manipulate than their larger counterparts (as appears to be the evidence), the public is probably better served if such shares are listed on a regulated, active and visible auction exchange as compared to an over-the-counter (OTC) dealer market. The surveillance is more thorough because of the major role played by the self-regulatory body – the stock exchange. For example, the Toronto Stock Exchange (TSE) has a highly advanced artificial intelligence system for detecting market manipulation, high trading techniques and other irregularities that can undermine market integrity.[8]

Furthermore, an enforceable set of primary and secondary priority trading rules, as imposed in an auction-style rather than a dealer-style market, provides a more transparent and equitable trading system.

Investors who want to hold shares in small venture-type companies have a trading vehicle. And obviously, the public interest is served by any channel that supports seed or venture capital financing.

For these reasons, I support the concept of a second-tier market as an adjunct to a regulated exchange.

The Problems with Second-Tier Markets

However, the encouragement of second-tier markets as a policy has to be viewed in the context of overall market impact. A high failure rate of second-tier-listed companies, as measured by suspension or delisting due to poor earnings results or a poor trading record, could reflect on the entire listing and surveillance functions. The spillover may in fact be country wide. For example, do problems on the Vancouver Stock Exchange have negative implications for foreign investors looking at the Toronto or Alberta exchanges?

If the rules are too strict, junior start-up companies may fail to get financing or may look to other markets with the resulting loss to the local market.

Do retail investors, who are often the active participants on second-tier markets, always know what they are buying? Will they understand they are buying shares in companies subject to less-stringent listing requirements? Is enforcement of a "know your client" rule more difficult on a second-tier market? There may be a "halo" effect – a notion that listing implies a minimum level of perceived value that may be more apparent than real.

The real problem is how do you create a market that is imbued with the desired attributes of a responsive central auction, namely a market that offers liquidity, so there are sufficient orders on both the buy and sell side; a market that creates sufficient information flow to support a robust price discovery process, that minimizes trading costs,[9] that offers speed of execution and maintains integrity (minimizing trading abuses and providing reasonable visibility)? That's the problem with second-tier markets: they are normally deficient in some or all of these areas.

As for the JCP program as a model, I have some severe reservations. Has the JCP worked because of restrictive rules, the regional club atmosphere and the unique conditions that existed at that time?[10] Might its success be idiosyncratic to the conditions prevailing in Alberta? Another concern is whether the special rules designed to offset the reduced listing requirements may, in themselves, be detrimental. For example, under the JCP program does the 18-month rule lead to suboptimal decision making on the part of management? Might they be influenced by an approaching deadline for a major transaction?

An alternative model is that of the Canadian Dealer Network (CDN), a dealer market operated by the TSE. The CDN, which could be called a third-tier market, is a unique case in Canada, as it is essentially an OTC market operated by a recognized exchange. There are no listing requirements although the market is subject to some market surveillance. The CDN model represents an interesting contrast to the Alberta JCP program.

Another related issue is that of the labour-sponsored funds. There are now some 16 government-supported labour-sponsored investment funds which are supposed to provide venture capital funding to small enterprises. There is over $2 billion invested in the funds. Curiously, about 75 percent of labour fund capital is currently in cash. If these funds start investing more aggressively, might this create a major source of financing in itself? Do labour-sponsored funds represent a better or more promising outlook? Why aren't they doing what they are supposed to do? Does this reflect a lack of suitable venture capital opportunities or a lack of effort on the part of the fund managers or advisors? It's difficult to separate the issue of fostering the development of second-tier markets from the future of labour-sponsored funds without knowing whether the funds' lack of activity reflects management lassitude or a lack of good prospects?

In conclusion, I found this to be an interesting paper in terms of its literature review and the issues it raises. Its primary application is in describing a model for equity financing of small and medium-sized businesses in Canada using Alberta's JCP model. I have reservations, however, about its applicability outside the Alberta market.

ENDNOTES

1 I'm not sure if he really meant fired or successfully sued.
2 SMEs were defined by the Ontario Securities Commission (1994) task force as firms with annual sales of under $10 million. Open Text's $10 million in sales qualified it for the SME definition.
3 These include: (i) asymmetric information (the advisor knows more than the issuer), (ii) uncertainty premium (the industry and use of proceeds influence the degree of underpricing, (iii) underwriters support hypothesis (suggesting the possibility of illusory underpricing), (iv) legal lawsuit hypothesis (the underwriter is protecting against lawsuits and loss of reputation associated with overpriced issue), (v) the signalling model (issuers know more than underwriters and investors, and underprice as an indication that a secondary offering will occur in the future. To signal that their firm is high quality they underprice the issue.)
4 Large underwriters avoid smaller firms for three reasons. First, there is the risk to their reputation. Second, underwriting commissions are too low since they are a function of issue size and presumably they cannot capture the fixed reputation cost component. And most compelling, the low trading turnover associated with small firms makes it unprofitable for brokerage firms to research the companies. Underwriter's profits are not limited to those earned in the primary market distribution. Many of the underwriter's clients will be holding the shares and the underwriter will capture a portion (sometimes substantial) of short and long-term secondary market turnover.
5 The discriminating factors he examines include: the number of listings, the number of failures (delistings that were not taken over or moved to another exchange), the number of JCP firms completing major transactions and moving to a regular listing and how successful JCPs have been in raising debt and equity capital.

6 He concludes that the JCP program's success provides evidence that a system for financing small equity ventures using public stock exchanges can work as long as there are strict regulations and careful monitoring of the program once established.
7 For example, this market opened on March 18, 1992 with 22 companies listed for trading. The companies were previously traded on over-the-counter markets or other stock exchanges including the Vancouver Stock Exchange. Initial listing requirements included a net worth requirement of $2 million for IPOs and $41 million for publicly traded companies. The companies were subject to a screening process by an expert panel. The shares were listed and shown separately in the quotations, and denoted by the letters EC after the ticker symbol.
8 See for example, Olivari (1996), p. 51.
9 These are measured by facility, dealer market and market impact costs.
10 For example, the downsizing of oil companies.

BIBLIOGRAPHY

Olivari, Nick. "TSE steps up investment in market surveillance." *Investment Executive.* (February 1996).

Ontario Securities Commission. "Task Force on Small Business Financing." Preliminary report submitted to the Ontario Securities Commission, June 21, 1994.

ON THE CARE AND NURTURE OF LOAN GUARANTEE PROGRAMS

Comment by Daniel B. Thornton
School of Business
Queen's University

ACCORDING TO STIGLITZ AND WEISS (1981) AND PROFESSOR RIDING, the fact that small businesses are risky cannot, by itself, explain why banks deny them credit. In principle, banks could set interest rates high enough to compensate for risk. Moral hazard and adverse selection are to blame, say the authors. Canadian evidence also suggests that banks turn down some applicants because they lack expertise in financial management (Thornton, 1981). This is a public policy issue because it is widely believed that many of the small businesses that were denied credit lost their chances to contribute significantly to Canadian society and to enhance Canada's competitive position in world markets.

Professor Riding focuses on the private gains from trade that could be affected by mitigating agency costs in the market for small business loans. From a bank's perspective, as the promised rate of interest on the loans increases, the shortfall between the promised and expected rates of return increases for two reasons.

1. The more creditworthy borrowers tend to drop out, since the going interest rate is higher than the rate they would pay, if they could convince the bank they were "above average."[1] This leaves a less able group of loan applicants – lemons – which have a higher probability of default.
2. Increasingly, borrowers tend to take on projects that are riskier than the bank anticipated when it granted the loan.[2]

To mitigate such effects, banks could institute costly *screening* procedures to assess the creditworthiness of the applicants. Screening costs are largely fixed, however, so they are high in proportion to the value of the loans to small businesses. Unless applicants bear the screening costs themselves by promising to pay higher interest rates, the bank prefers larger borrowers. It rations credit in the small business sector.

Another way of mitigating the lemons effect is for the applicants to *signal* their credit worthiness, by hiring prestigious auditors. But such auditors command a fee premium, and small businesses cannot generally afford the luxury of retaining them (Chung and Lindsay, 1988; Thornton and Moore, 1993). Or, the borrowers could assign the role of "hostage" to some of their equity shares, placing them in escrow, as a guarantee against moral hazard. But many applicants are unable or unwilling to bear such signalling and screening costs.

To alleviate credit rationing, the federal government revised the parameters of the *Small Business Loans Act* (SBLA) in April 1993. Under this Act, the government guarantees banks' loans to small firms, up to 90 percent of their face value, as long as the interest rate is less than a "maximum amount," normally prime plus 1.75 percent. In theory, the low promised interest rate mitigates adverse selection because it encourages the more creditworthy borrowers to stay in the game and be screened. Because they have a competitive advantage over the less creditworthy applicants in paying the fees, the fee becomes a credible signalling mechanism.

During the two months before the announced amendments to the SBLA took effect in 1993, Canada's "Big-Six" banks advertised the new loans on television, on radio and in newspapers. "The Bank of Montreal has set aside a billion dollars for small businesses. I could use some of that," said a veterinarian as she returned a puppy to its master in one commercial. "This is a great [interest] rate and I think people will choke at matching it," said Warren Walker, Scotiabank's vice-president of Canadian commercial banking.[3] Thus, the new law seemed a good way of solving the credit rationing dilemma posed by Stiglitz and Weiss (1981).

Turning the Dials

Table 1 lists the outputs that might be affected by "turning the dials" in a loan guarantee program. The dials turned in 1993 included the percent of the loan guaranteed (up), insurance fee (down or constant), ceiling interest rate (down) and total volume allowed (up). The changes in outputs were the volume of loans granted, the default rate, administrative costs and, most important, a social welfare function that includes the private and social value of successes vs. the costs of failure.

Table 1

Variables Influencing the Effectiveness of Loan Guarantee Programs

	Inputs		
	Policy Variables	**Intervening Variables**	
Loan guarantee	Percentage guaranteed and "insurance fee" Ceiling interest rate (prime + 1.75 percent) Constraints on total volume; who lends	Management	Moral hazard (and adverse selection) Competence (1981 questionnaire study)
Tax system	Small business deduction ($t \approx 20$ percent)	Signalling	Auditor quality; escrowed shares
	Carry forward period for losses		
	Capital cost allowances (CCA) rates (interacts with above)	Screening	Lender expertise and effort
	Allowable business investment losses (ABIL) legislation (spurs equity investors)	Monitoring	Reward system for loan officers

Outputs

Volume of loans
Default rate
Administrative costs and dead weight
Most important, private and social value of successes vs. costs of failures (probably asymmetric)

Professor Riding's paper shows that the volume of SBLA lending increased by 700 percent in 1993. The default rate and the administrative costs remained low by international standards.

The increase in social welfare, however, is difficult if not impossible to measure and Riding did not attempt to do so. Agency theory suggests that a major benefit would be that some deserving entrepreneurs would stay in the pool of applicants instead of dropping out. At the margin, however, to encourage one good applicant to stay in, might entail granting three bad loans. Until the benefit function has been identified, it is impossible to measure the desirability of the outputs. Moreover, the effect of the inputs on the observed outputs is only speculation. The reason is that the inputs that were manipulated interact with certain other inputs that were not controlled in producing those outputs.

In Table 1, the loan guarantee program is only one policy variable affecting the outputs. The tax system is another major way in which the government assists small business and it undoubtedly mediates or interacts with the guarantee program. Several other "intervening variables" would also affect the outputs. Without controlling for these other variables, it is not meaningful to compare Canada's loan guarantee program with those of other countries.

Policy Variables

Canada's tax system is quite favourable to Canadian-controlled private corporations (CCPCs). CCPCs all get a small business deduction that lowers their corporate tax rate to the range of 18 percent to 23 percent, depending on the province where they reside. Business losses for tax purposes can be carried back three years and forward seven. At first, this may seem less generous than the carryover periods allowed in the United States. But U.S. firms must take the full amount of capital cost allowances (CCA) each year, increasing their loss carryovers and possibly pushing them beyond the carryforward period. Canadian companies, in contrast, can take any amount of CCA they like, up to the maximum. In effect, they have valuable flexibility that ensures they will be able to write off their start-up losses, should they eventually be profitable.

When Canadians invest in small businesses that carry on an active business in Canada, they can deduct allowable business investment losses (ABIL) from other taxable income if the businesses become insolvent. For example, if you bought some of a CCPC's debt or equity securities for $10,000 and the company became insolvent, you could write off that loss against employment income (Thornton 1993, chapter 3).[4] If you had experienced the same loss from investing in the shares or bonds of a public corporation, you would have had a capital loss for tax purposes. Capital losses can be deducted only from capital gains, and they are only three-quarters deductible. Thus, all else being equal, the ABIL legislation already gives investors strong tax incentives to invest in small business instead of large public corporations.

Intervening Variables

Of course, economic and cultural conditions vary widely across countries and over time. Any assessment of the take-up rate and the default rate would have to take such variations into account. In Japan, for instance, it seems that cultural norms make it less likely that moral hazard would be a problem, and more likely that a bank would delay calling a loan that was technically in default.

In assessing the impact of a guarantee program, one would also need to control for the extent of private signalling by the borrowers. As already mentioned, some borrowers might retain higher quality auditors whose "deep pockets" would assuage lenders' concerns about the possibility of being misled by financial statement information. The degree of lender expertise and effort would also determine who got credit and how well they were monitored. The reward system for loan officers is a salient determinant of this. Are they rewarded on the basis of the number or percentage of defaults? The dollar value of defaults? The volume of loans granted?

Finally, the degree of financial expertise probably varies widely in the pool of small business applicants. Rather than just screening applicants out on the basis of their present qualifications, the government could consider mounting education and training programs or providing financial consulting to small businesses before encouraging them to apply for guaranteed loans.

Empirical Research

Is it possible to do empirical research that would tell us whether the dials had been turned in the right direction? To assess the effectiveness of a change in a loan guarantee program, one would first have to specify the dependent variable, a social welfare function. It would include the volume of lending and the incidence of defaults but, clearly, the optimal number of defaults would not be the minimum. It would have to refer to more than just the explicit costs and benefits of the lenders, the borrowers and the government.

Professor Riding's paper gives us much useful information concerning some of the observable effects of the change in SBLA parameters. It does not, however, tell us whether the changes were unequivocally good; and there is no assurance that the results would hold if some of the other policy or intervening variables were different. Since the policy and intervening variables differ in other countries, comparing the default rates and observable outputs across countries is interesting but hazardous.

Finally, I doubt that the "controlled experiment" suggested in the closing pages of the paper would bear fruit. Professor Riding suggests comparing a group of firms that obtained guaranteed loans with a "control group" that didn't apply at all. If Stiglitz and Weiss (1981) and the author are right – if adverse selection is really the culprit that needs to be apprehended – this experiment would not work because the firms would already have self-selected. One would need to select a random sample of, say, 1,000 small firms. For each firm, one would flip a coin: heads you get a guaranteed loan, tails you don't. Only then would we be able to assess the impact of the program using the longitudinal study that the author recommends. Even then, the problem of what to measure would remain. And what about the "good" credit risks in the 500 that were randomly turned down?

Conclusion

In sum, I think Professor Riding's paper is an excellent descriptive study of the nature of loan guarantees both domestic and international. It asks the right questions. It provides useful data. It takes a solid step toward developing a more comprehensive theory of loan guarantees.[5] But where public policy is concerned, it is always hard to jump from theory and data to prescriptions. The paper gives regulators a lot to think about; but it doesn't tell them what they should do.

Endnotes

1 Some bide their time, hoping interest rates will come down. Others try to raise equity capital, perhaps migrating to the wrong financing clientele. The cost of being in the wrong clientele can be viewed as an agency cost.
2 For example, a company borrows $100,000 to finance business expansion. It is not going to be the kind of expansion the bank lending officer envisages, however. The directors of the firm will go to a gambling casino and bet the entire $100,000 on "red 11" at the roulette wheel. If red 11 comes up, they will repay the bank and take early retirement. If red 11 does not come up, the firm will default on the loan and declare bankruptcy.
3 *Calgary Sun*, March 24, 1993.
4 The maximum write-off is $500,000.
5 The theory might be extended using option pricing theory. The government essentially takes a 90 percent share of a put option held by the borrower, in which the whole firm can be put to the bank and the government at a striking price equal to the face value of the loan. One might ask how the value of this put option is affected by turning the dials in the loan guarantee program.

Bibliography

Calgary Sun. March 24, 1993.

Chung, D. and W. Lindsay. "The Pricing of Audit Services: The Canadian Perspective." *Contemporary Accounting Research*. (Fall 1988): 19-46

Stiglitz, J. and L. Weiss. "Credit Rationing in Markets with Imperfect Information." *American Economic Review*. 81, (1981): 393-410.

Thornton, D. *Managerial Tax Planning: A Canadian Perspective*. Toronto: John Wiley & Sons, 1993.

Thornton, D. "Small Business Financing Policies and Practices: An Interview Survey of Managers." In *Small Business Financing and Non-Bank Financial Institutions*. Edited by J. Poapst. Toronto: Facsym Research Limited, 1981.

Thornton, D. and G. Moore. "Auditor Choice and Audit Fee Determinants." *Journal of Business Finance and Accounting*. 20 (3), (April 1993): 333-349.

Session VI Summary and Policy Perspectives

Donald J.S. Brean
Faculty of Management
University of Toronto

Conference Report

INTRODUCTION

LET'S GO BACK TO THE BEGINNING. Denis Gauthier indicated that this group – academics, policy analysts and representatives of the financial sector – are assembled as part of Industry Canada's continuing effort to assist business in the promotion of enriching jobs and productive investment. The objectives of the conference are to explore issues in capital markets that have implications for investment, competitiveness and economic growth. The intention – or the hope – is to enhance our knowledge of the cost of capital for Canadian industry, to document the sources and composition of business finance and, especially, to examine questions of access (or impediments to access) to financial markets. Ultimately, the purpose is to inform the policy process.

Gauthier suggested that we are especially concerned with whether investment suffers due to a "financial gap." Are good projects, good investments going wanting because of a lack of funds for such investment?

Paul Halpern, the conference organizer, then outlined the way in which the conference is designed to address economic, financial, institutional and policy dimensions of capital markets. To put the agenda in sharp relief, Halpern rhetorically asked whether the cost of capital is important. The answer depends, to a large extent, on the size of the elasticity of investment with respect to the cost of capital. If that elasticity is low, inefficiencies and distortions in capital markets that could cause the cost of capital to be higher than it would otherwise be are relatively unimportant. If the elasticity of investment with respect to the cost of capital is high *and* if institutional inefficiencies, market failures and/or the weight of inappropriate public policy, such as taxation, regulation or interventionist policies, are responsible for adding any number of basis points to the cost of capital, then the cost of capital is crucially important. Thus, it is important, as per the mission of this conference, to understand more fully the factors that determine the cost of capital including the influences of institutional inefficiencies, market failures and the weight of current public policy.

Halpern then sketched the way that the various topics and themes of the conference are linked. By design, the conference juxtaposes macro and micro-economic perspectives, viewpoints that represent both finance and economics, theoretical approaches balanced by empirical analysis, and public policy as well as the practitioner's view.

The macro-economic perspective is concerned with the role of capital markets in determining the aggregate level of investment, economic growth and employment. The implications of the international integration of capital markets for the cost of capital in any one country, e.g., Canada, or international comparisons of the cost of capital are within the purview of macro-economics.

The micro-economic perspective, on the other hand, focuses on the efficiency of market mechanisms *per se*. Here, with respect to the signals and incentives that govern the flow of finance from savers to investors and allocate investment among a variety of investments of differing risk, maturity and prospective return, the question is whether the market mechanism produces socially optimal results. If financial markets do not meet the test of efficiency in the funding of investment – a point which itself is difficult to discern – then there is a *prima facie* case of market failure reflected as a "financial gap" as suggested by Gauthier. High transaction costs in financial dealings, including costs that decline with volume due to a fixed cost component, represent an impediment to the flow of savings to investment but not necessarily a market failure. However, if systematic and irresolvable differences in information between financiers and investors cause the former to be wary of the latter, then financial markets can be said to fail. Good projects would go wanting because of a lack of funds. Moreover, an adverse selection process may emerge in which less worthy projects are funded ahead of the more worthy.

SESSION I COST OF CAPITAL

THE USER COST OF CAPITAL AND INVESTMENT SPENDING: IMPLICATIONS FOR CANADIAN FIRMS

ROBERT CHIRINKO AND ANDREW MEYER ARE CONCERNED with the mechanism by which policy can induce investment spending. How, and by how much, can policy induce investment? Policy aimed at investment has two links:

- the effectiveness of the policy instrument in changing the incentive; and
- the sensitivity of the target (investment) to the incentive.

Policy instruments are typically taxes, and reductions thereof, or subsidies. The incentive is the after-tax (or after-subsidy) return on investment. The target, of course, is investment.

Chirinko and Meyer focus on the elasticity of investment with respect to the user cost of capital. Their concern is measurement. Their approach is to apply the Jorgenson neoclassical model of investment and the user cost of capital. In this model, the firm maximizes the discounted after-tax flow of profits over an infinite horizon. Capital depreciates at a geometric rate. Delivery lags, adjustment costs and vintage effects are absent.

Before turning to their own empirical work, Chirinko and Meyer present a useful critique of the evolution of the theory and empirical application of neoclassical models of investment and the user cost of capital. Serious theoretical shortcomings of the model in the basic formulation that dates back to Jorgenson include the failure to incorporate investors' expectations, no recognition of the influence of technology and disregard of adjustment costs. Assumptions concerning expectations, technology and adjustment costs are implicit (or naively suppressed) in the simple model of the user cost of capital. Attempts to represent these important considerations explicitly, such as the Brainard-Tobin Q, the Euler equation or direct forecasting models, have met with mixed success. Unfortunately, although implicit models are conceptually deficient they nevertheless perform much better than the theoretically more complete explicit models. Implicit models explain a reasonable amount of the variation in aggregate investment and, apart from the user cost of capital, they usually produce estimated coefficients that have the theoretically correct sign and statistical significance. Moreover, Chirinko and Meyer suggest that, despite the availability of many alternative specifications of investment models, implicit models containing output, user cost and liquidity as explanatory variables continue to be the model of choice of forecasters and policy analysts.

Approaching their empirical work with the objective of estimating the sensitivity of Canadian investment spending with respect to the user cost of capital, Chirinko and Meyer encountered a formidable obstacle – the lack of appropriate data. Proper estimation of the user cost of capital requires time series data at the firm level. The necessary data include series on relative prices of capital goods, the financial costs of capital, asset mixes and detailed information on firm-specific tax circumstances including tax rates, depreciation rates and how firms specifically handle tax losses through carry back and carry forward.

To finesse the problem of the lack of data, Chirinko and Meyer select a panel of U.S. companies for which data are available, choosing firms that provide reasonable representation of Canadian industry. The sectors they examine, defined by Standard Industrial Classification (SIC) categories, are information, health, aerospace, manufacturing, forestry, plastics, services, chemicals, transportation, fashion and automobiles. The investment elasticity with respect to the user cost of capital is found to vary widely across the 11 sectors studied. Despite the variance, imprecision in the estimates of the elasticity forces the conclusion that we do not have a clear sense of the likely response of investment spending to variation in investment incentives.

Chirinko and Meyer indicate that corporate cash flow appears to be an important element in the investment equation. They suggest that it would be useful to gain further understanding of whether the significant role of cash flow is related to finance constraints or is merely a proxy for current and future demand.

Ideally, if the data would allow, one would want to obtain a broad cross-sectoral set of elasticities of investment with respect to the user cost of capital and then proceed to an analysis that focuses on the factors (production relations, sector-specific tax influences, investment irreversibility, etc.) that explain the sectoral variation in the elasticity of investment with respect to the user cost of capital. Why would that be useful? For one thing, it would take us closer to understanding the potential bang for the policy buck, including tax expenditures.

Perhaps such considerations underlie the Chirinko and Meyer remark that "substantial changes in the user cost are necessary but not sufficient for effective policy." While variation in the user cost is useful to analyse incentive effects and to explain why different sectors respond to a common incentive differently, a common elasticity of investment with respect to the user cost of capital would not preclude effective policy. It would imply that a given policy (something that reduces marginal effective tax rates [METRs], for example) would have the same effect on all sectors.

In his comments on the Chirinko and Meyer paper, Serge Nadeau expressed a general frustration with the lack of reliable empirical findings concerning an important relationship – the elasticity of investment spending with respect to the user cost of capital – that theory and common sense hold to be true. We know that the elasticity must be significantly negative, but we are having a devil of a time observing it.

Regardless, Nadeau believes that the merit of the Chirinko and Meyer paper is the use of micro firm-level data for analysis. Inasmuch as investment is carried out at the firm level, it is a chronic source of concern in policy analysis that heretofore so much of this type of empirical work involves highly aggregated data. Alas, in Chirinko and Meyer's work, the high standard errors on the estimated coefficients – so high that in almost all sectors they cannot reject the hypothesis that the estimate is zero – suggest missing variables. What are those missing variables? It seems necessary to return to a more complete specification of the capital expenditure decisions of firms.

Nadeau indicated he is uncomfortable with the way that cash flow is modelled. He would like more understanding as to why current cash flow is important for investment.

In fact, in a recent piece published in the *Journal of Money, Credit and Banking* entitled "Why Does Liquidity Matter in Investment Equations?" Chirinko and Schaller reported the results of an analysis of a sample of 212 Canadian firms. They provided evidence of the existence, sources and economic importance of internal finance constraints. Potential sources of finance constraints include both asymmetric information and transactions costs, which Chirinko and Schaller attempted to disentangle with interpretations that are germane to this conference. Asymmetric information is the leading theoretical explanation for finance constraints on firms. However, even if asymmetric information problems are unimportant, transaction costs in the form of shelf registration fees, underwriters' spreads and other administrative costs associated with new issues of stocks or bonds could create a wedge between the costs of internal and external finance. While these two sources of finance constraints are not mutually exclusive, the associated policy implications do differ. For example, if asymmetric information problems loom large, reducing disclosure requirements and streamlining procedures for new share issues may not be especially helpful in easing finance constraints. On the other hand, since firms that are in a weak information position depend heavily on bank credit, easing access to such institutional credit could have substantial effects on investment spending.

Cost of Capital for the United States, Japan and Canada

The paper by Albert Ando, John Hancock and Gary Sawchuk extends a line of research developed by Ando and Auerbach comparing the cost of capital in the United States and Japan. The paper is updated and extended to include Canada.

The user cost of capital is the amount of money a firm pays to use one dollar's worth of capital for a period of time, say one year. In the absence of taxes, and assuming perfect capital markets, this cost must be equal to the real rate of return in the market plus the economic rate of depreciation. When using this approach, one must allow for corporate taxes, inflation and market imperfections.

Over a reasonable length of time and based on a sufficiently large number of firms, the cost of capital can be expressed as the ratio of capital payments to capital stock. This is an *ex post* return on capital which, by averaging over time and firms, represents an approximation of the economically relevant *ex ante* perspective. Capital payments include interest, dividends, retained earnings with an inventory valuation adjustment and capital consumption allowance and taxes. Capital stock is the value of capital employed. Alternative means of recording capital stock are a micro or market measure based on the value of corporate equity plus the value of debt (generally augmented by adjustments to accounting figures in corporate balance sheets) or a macro national accounts measure based on aggregate data. If the alternative measures of the cost of capital are reasonably similar, the corroboration of one by the other is evidence of proper empirical specification.

The national accounting and market measures of the cost of capital tend to track each other closely in the United States. Japan, however, exhibits a curious and strongly negative correlation between the two measures throughout the 1985 to 1994 period, characterized as a boom from 1985 to 1989 and a bust from 1990 to 1995.

The main empirical finding of the analysis by Ando, Hancock and Sawchuk is that the before tax cost of capital in Japan is some 5 to 6 percentage points lower than that for the United States over the full period 1967 to 1994. This result is on the basis of the market valuation measure. Caution is advised in accepting this result since, if the national accounting numbers are used in Japan, the cost of capital would be *higher* in Japan by 1 or 2 percentage points.

Which to choose? In discussion, Ando expressed serious distrust of the Japanese national accounts. As a result, he is more inclined to trust results based on an aggregation of micro data, simply because he knows how the data are generated. On this basis he concludes that Japan has a substantially lower cost of capital than the United States.

For Canada, Ando, Hancock and Sawchuk confess that they cannot make much sense out of the erratic estimates of the cost of capital generated by available data. They suggest that the limits on their sample for Canada, both in terms of the length of the period (from 1976 to 1993) and the number of firms (100 before 1983, 160 to 240 thereafter) is the main reason for the disappointing result.

With respect to deviations in the cost of capital between the United States and Japan, Ando, Hancock and Sawchuk suggest some considerations beyond the more commonly cited reasons – different risk premiums and different fiscal systems. First, short-term interest rates in the the two countries may differ due to the volatility of expectations of exchange rate movements. Second, the capitalization rate that relates short-term rates to long-term rates need not necessarily reflect similar expectations in the two countries. These factors, Ando, Hancock and Sawchuk assert, are capable of creating substantial differences in the cost of capital between or among countries, and they suggest that market forces would not necessarily serve to eliminate the differences as long as the underlying causes persist.

Japanese depreciation, especially after the adjustments for inflation, may be over-estimated. The reported depreciation rate for Japanese corporations is 2 or 3 percentage points higher than that in the United States. If these depreciation rates reflect the reality of the two countries, then there is no problem. However, if the true rate of depreciation is the same while the reported rate is higher for Japan than for the United States, then this may cause the reported rate of return in the United States to be higher than that for Japan.

The debt-to-equity ratio for Japanese corporations is twice as large as that of U.S. corporations. Given the tax treatment of interest payments on the one hand and the cost of equity on the other, this Japan/United States debt-to-equity differential would make the total before-tax rate of return greater in the United States than in Japan. Ando, Hancock and Sawchuk report that in the late 1980s this potential distortion seemed to dissipate as the debt-to-equity ratio (measured at market values for equity) was observed to fall. This effect, they argue, ought to be dismissed as due largely to the stock market bubble of the late 1980s. As the price of equity shares declined in more recent years, the Japanese debt-to-equity ratio rose more or less to the earlier levels. A high level of the debt-to-equity ratio cannot fail to make the total cost of capital somewhat smaller in the way Ando, Hancock and Sawchuk choose to measure it.

In discussion, Ando also suggested that the huge bubble in Japanese land prices together with the substantial value of land in Japanese corporate balance sheets contribute to the observed lower Japanese cost of capital since increases in land value increase the denominator of the ratio used to measure the cost of capital. In other words, most Japanese firms, especially large established corporations, acquired their land before the price of land in Japan had become so much higher than land in other countries. Since accounting does not effectively recognize the replacement value of land, companies treat the cost of land as a sunk cost. Nevertheless, the market for equity recognizes the appreciation of corporate land holdings and, as this is priced in the equity, the price-to-earnings ratio appears high and, hence, the implied cost of capital is low. Thus the extraordinarily high price of land is reflected in the value of Japanese corporate shares but not in the costs of production and output prices. If this hypothesis is correct, the conventionally calculated cost of capital in Japan is low while the cost of capital for new firms forced to purchase land at market prices is exceptionally high, thus inhibiting the formation of new firms and making the penetration of the Japanese market difficult for foreign firms.

In his comments as discussant, Jack Mintz expressed concern regarding the empirically convenient average rate of return on capital and whether it is an appropriate proxy for the economically relevant marginal rate of return. In Canada, perhaps more than elsewhere, the presence of oligopoly, fixed factors of production (e.g., in the capital-intensive resource sectors) and government regulation are likely to leave the average return chronically, and substantially, above the marginal return. Tax incentives that target investment are likely to widen the average/marginal differential.

Mintz also rhetorically asked why we are interested in international comparisons of rates of return on capital in the first place. The empirical exercise has relevance for investment, Mintz maintains, only insofar as the observed return on capital is a measure of the cost of capital. He also expressed concern about the implications of observed international differentials in cost of capital that do not seem to be eroded by the arbitrage processes of international financial markets. The issue represents a challenge to the standard assumptions of highly integrated international capital markets and the relevance of the so-called "world rate of interest" generally invoked in most empirical models of cost of capital and investment. Mintz also stressed the importance, and the difficulty, of full and accurate representation of all components of the cost of capital, including the cost of finance, the cost of depreciation and tax influences inclusive of property taxes, capital and sales taxes as well as the corporate tax.

THE IMPACT OF TAXATION ON CAPITAL MARKETS AND COMPETITIVENESS

IN THE OUTLINE OF THE FIRST SESSION we indicated that the mechanism through which policy induces investment spending has two links:

- the effectiveness of the policy instrument in changing the incentive; and
- the sensitivity of the target to the incentive.

Policy instruments are typically related to taxes or subsidies. Incentives take the form of an increase in the after-tax (or after-subsidy) return on investment. The target, of course, is investment spending.

Chirinko and Meyer focused on the second link, the elasticity of investment with respect to the user cost of capital.

In this session, Duanjie Chen and Kenneth McKenzie provide information crucial to the first link in policy transmission – tax distortions of the user cost of capital. They apply the empirical methodology for estimating METRs. In concept, METRs are consistent with the user cost of capital in its neoclassical formulation à la Jorgenson. As a tool of policy analysis, METRs provide a summary measure of the source of economic distortion – the wedge between the pre-tax and after-tax rate of return relative to the pre-tax rate of return. Empirical estimation of METRs requires careful representation of the detail of the full weight of tax on corporate income inclusive of depreciation (capital cost allowance in Canada), corporate-personal tax integration, and a variety of non-income taxes such as property and capital tax. In addition, the analysis requires estimates of various bits of real economic data such as the financial cost of capital, the economic rate of depreciation, the nominal rate of return on capital and the expected rate of inflation.

Chen and McKenzie begin with an overview of the empirical methodology of computing METRs with special attention to how the model is modified to incorporate risk and the METR-raising impact of irreversibility in corporate investment. To the extent that a METR is the economically relevant index of tax-induced distortion, METR-calculations offer insight into the potential impact of taxation on capital accumulation and economic growth. Moreover, while METRs are essentially simulations, a set of METRs in industrial or regional cross section provides a consistent summary of biases and policy preferences embedded in the tax structure.

Chen and McKenzie report two sets of METR estimates. The first involves an international comparison of METRs in the G7 industrial nations plus Mexico and Hong Kong, while the second is an intersectoral and interprovincial analysis of METRs on non-financial industry in Canada. In presenting the paper, McKenzie stressed how sensitive the results can be to the assumed values of the economic parameters, especially expected inflation and risk premium or industrial characteristics such as financial structure of the investment mix of buildings, machinery and inventory. The call for caution in interpreting METRs is especially pertinent when two (or more) estimates are examined for differences, for example industry A versus industry B or country X versus country Y. Real differences of course drive distortions, yet differences in point estimates are less likely to pass a test of statistical significance the greater the uncertainty of the data inputs to the estimating model.

In a straightforward comparison of taxes affecting domestic investment in a cross-section of nine countries, Canada's METR for manufacturing appears in the international mid-range and at the high end for services. In the always important United States-Canada bilateral context, our manufacturing METR is 4 points higher than in the United States while our rate for services is a whopping 11 points higher than in the United States.

The detailed analytic effort to estimate METRs seems worth the candle if, as Chen and McKenzie suggest, we learn that Canada's METR on manufacturing is indeed higher than in the United States – by 4 points – despite the fact that our statutory rate on this sector is 4 points *lower*. Factors that account for the difference include less generous depreciation allowances in Canada especially with respect to buildings, Canada's relatively harsh tax treatment of inventories by mandatory use of FIFO and less than full relief of provincial sales taxes on manufacturing equipment.

Substantially more complex international considerations arise when estimating METRs on outward and inward-bound foreign direct investment. In this situation, the analysis must entertain complicated international financial structures, the meshing of at least two tax systems inclusive of so-called foreign tax relief arrangements and cross-border capital payments. Chen and McKenzie observe a small tax differential in favour of Canadian investment abroad versus domestic investment, which one might view as merely an offset to the well-known capital-export bias favouring U.S. investment abroad that Canada has enjoyed for many years.

Within Canada, there appears to be substantial intersectoral and interprovincial variation in METRs. Mining, services and communications sectors, for example, are favoured in virtually every province, while oil and gas, construction and trade tend to face higher rates. Manufacturing endures a relatively high METR in spite of its low statutory rate, a finding that Chen and McKenzie ascribe to the observed low debt-to-asset ratio in this sector. One could also argue that the low statutory rate results in a relatively high after-tax cost of debt and, thus, the debt-to-asset ratio and the METR are determined simultaneously.

The within-sector cross-provincial METR variance is remarkably high. It is a matter for concern if the structure of taxation in Canada has significant influence on investment location decisions. However, as a tax influence, the distortion may be more apparent than real. In Canada, the interprovincial statutory corporate tax rate variance is quite small (especially in the non-resource sectors). Federal-provincial tax collection agreements provide a high degree of uniformity in the corporate tax base, and interest rates and inflation are common. As a result, the variance of METRs within industrial sectors but across provinces is perhaps driven by the variance of pre-tax profitability and subsidies as opposed to interprovincial structural tax differences.

In his comments on the analysis and the results, Michael Daly acknowledged the practical difficulty in such empirical work. Referring first to the estimation of (sectoral and provincial) marginal effective tax rates within Canada, Daly acknowledged the relevance of the intersectoral and interprovincial differences in METRS and agreed that such differences represent a potential influence on the allocation of capital within Canada. When Daly turned attention to the reported international METR differentials, he vigorously challenged the reliability of the exercise, illustrating the uncertainty by comparing results of structurally similar earlier analyses that produced strikingly different results. Daly used the conflict to caution the conference with respect to the sensitivity of the results to underlying structural assumptions and parameter values, stressing, in particular, the importance of detailed understanding of the workings of national tax systems and the scope for international tax planning by multinational enterprises.

In discussion, Donald Brean asked whether differentials in METRs might correspond to different levels of publicly provided services that are valuable to industry. McKenzie replied that other empirical work suggests that the corporate tax does not have the character of a benefits tax. Brean acknowledged that such conclusions are generally drawn from cross-sectional studies within nations where public provision of services is relatively uniform, whereas in an international cross section – where both taxation and publicly provided services each have greater variance – there is potential merit in examining the correlation.

INVESTING IN CANADA: ESTIMATION OF THE SECTORAL COST OF CAPITAL IN CANADA AND CASE STUDIES FOR INTERNATIONAL COMPARISON

THIS PAPER TAKES A DECIDEDLY BUSINESS APPROACH to defining and estimating the cost of capital. In motivating the work, Vijay Jog suggests that the economist's user cost of capital and its policy derivative, METRs, have little relevance for corporate investment decisions since such computations naively assume identical capital structure for all sectors as well as identical costs of debt and equity. This is despite substantial differences in underlying business risk, debt-to-equity ratios and component costs of equity and debt.

The business approach to estimating the cost of capital, invariably on an after-tax basis, takes explicit account of the composition of finance (the debt-to-equity ratio), the opportunity cost of each component of financial or capital structure (debt and equity), with special attention to risk premiums associated with the particular business of a firm.

The history of modern corporate finance is marked by competing theories of the corporate cost of capital. At higher levels of abstraction, the debate continues as to how markets value risky assets and how, in the process, capital markets assign project-specific risk-adjusted opportunity costs to risky investments. At an empirical level, the most tractable and generally accepted approach postulates a weighted average cost of capital (WACC) that incorporates the cost of debt and equity (common and preferred), with each component weighted by its proportion in the overall financing of the firm. Crucially, the weights on components of finance are recorded at market (not book) values. The return to equity is net of interest and taxes, whereas debt has the concession of tax deductibility of interest payments.

To take explicit account of risky equity, Jog first introduces the standard measure of risk – beta as derived via regression of sector returns on returns on a market index. With sector-specific indices of risk at hand, Jog generates sector-specific risk-adjusted required returns on equity by applying beta to estimates of the riskless rate of return and the average risk premium in the equities market. In fact, Jog simulates the impact of alternative values of the market risk premium on the WACC.

Jog computes the WACC for 714 Canadian firms grouped into 22 industrial sectors. The estimates are based on measures of risk, equity returns, interest costs and capital structures from 1988 to 1994. The reported real WACC for the average of all 22 sectors in the study – a rough index of WACC for Canadian industry – wavered between 7.73 percent and 9.33 percent between 1988 and 1993, and rose sharply to 11.69 percent in 1994. The cross-sectional rank ordering of sector WACCs was remarkably steady throughout the seven-year period.

Following the Canadian sectoral WACC analysis, Jog addresses a number of more specific issues, including differences in the risk-free rate between Canada and the United States, foreign exchange exposure and company-specific risk in a particular sector (forestry), case studies of the cost of capital for a Canadian and a U.S. firm in telecommunications and, finally, a comparison of the cost of capital for the Canadian pulp and paper sector with the same industry in Finland. Overall, this compendium of empirical studies of WACC illustrates the methodological and empirical challenges in using the business approach to estimating the cost of capital in an international cross section. Conclusions, tentative as they are, suggest that the United States enjoys an advantage vis-à-vis other countries in the form of a lower cost of capital due, in large part, to a low country-risk premium. Indeed, the United States represents the base – with other countries enduring premiums (WACC penalties) relative to the United States. The cost of capital disadvantage for a typical Canadian firm is almost 2 percentage points. If Jog's estimates are accurate, one might reasonably ask whether the relative tax disadvantage suffered by Canadian industry, as suggested earlier by Chen and McKenzie, is a contributing factor.

In his comments as discussant, Louis Calvet draws critical attention to several explicit and implicit assumptions underlying Jog's analysis, especially with regard to the international financial equilibrating mechanisms that govern, for example, the international interest differentials. Calvet takes serious exception to how Jog decomposes the United States-Canada short-term interest rate differential in order to estimate exchange rate and country risk premiums. Jog's estimate of the latter, as noted above, is an important factor in the higher cost of capital in Canada vis-à-vis the United States. Calvet outlined a more complex Frankel-type decomposition of the differential to take account of the bias in the forward exchange rate, the effect of which is to suggest that Jog's estimates of the international interest rate differential and, hence, the cost of capital differential, are too high.

Session II Financing Constraints and Small Firms

Venture Capital Financing of Entrepreneurship in Canada

Entrepreneurial firms are increasingly important in Canada. The annual rate of new business registrations, to cite a rough index, doubled between 1979 and 1989.

Entrepreneurship appears to be closely related to innovation and technological progress. The small and emerging businesses sector is often touted as the most effective generator of jobs. However, despite the observed growth of this sector, entrepreneurial activity in Canada may not be as focused nor as vigorous as it might be. In particular, as per the theme of this conference, concerns have been raised about possible gaps or failures in the flow of finance to business in its vulnerable developmental stages.

Venture capital, defined as equity and so-called "mixed finance" to young privately held firms, is a crucial form of finance for the entrepreneurial sector. Unfortunately, relatively little is known about the structure, strategy and performance of the venture capital industry in Canada. The primary objective of the paper by Raphael Amit, James Brander and Christoph Zott is to address this lack of information by providing an empirical overview of venture capital financing in Canada. They rely on a comprehensive micro-level data base of Canadian venture capital investments, data drawn from both sides of entrepreneurial finance – recipients of venture capital as well as venture capital firms.

From these data, Amit, Brander and Zott observe a number of structural characteristics of the Canadian venture capital industry. For instance, the geographical pattern of venture capital activity in Canada fails to match the geographical pattern of economic activity. The level of venture capitalism is relatively high in Quebec and relatively low in Ontario and Atlantic Canada. High-tech industries make up a disproportionately large share of venture capital investments. While this is not surprising, a more puzzling fact is that spending on research and development by firms funded by venture capital is no higher than the Canadian industrial average – approximately 3 percent of revenues.

The average venture capital equity (or ownership) share in an investee firm is about 35 percent. The majority of Canadian venture capital investments are not syndicated as each round of investment is provided by a single venture capitalist and, in about half the time, fledgling firms get only one round of venture capital. Syndication is much less common in Canada than, for instance, in the United States. While venture capital investments may include both debt and equity, about two thirds of Canadian investments are pure equity.

For Amit, Brander and Zott, the performance record of venture capital investments is especially telling. Most investments do not do particularly well, generating returns that are lower than alternative risk-free investments. However, in the jargon of performance, the poor batting average of the majority is offset by a small number of "hits" that do very well. This general pattern is reflected in revenue and employment growth, where, in both cases, the average is much higher than the median – indicative of skewing. Most investee firms grow slowly if at all, while an exceptional few grow very rapidly.

Exit behaviour is intriguing. In more than 37 percent of cases, firms sever their ties with venture capital via management or corporate buyouts: insiders buy out the venture capitalist. A substantial share, 13 percent, end with third-party acquisitions, and these tend to be successful investments. A further 16 percent progress to more permanent capital through initial public offerings (IPOs) of stock. About 18 percent of venture-capital-supported investments fail and are written off: the venture capitalist loses the entire investment.

From this information, Amit, Brander and Zott identify four empirical regularities that, they suggest, a theory of venture capitalism must accommodate. First, a theory must provide a reason for the existence of a specialized venture capital industry. Second, it must explain the emphasis on development and expansion rather than start-up. Third, it must account for the observed pattern of exit from venture capital and, finally, the theory must be consistent with the skewed pattern of returns.

The concepts that integrate the theory of venture capital are information, asymmetric information in particular, and limited liability with low collateral. Informational asymmetry, where the investor knows less about the probability of the project's success than the investee, leads to market failure. There is understandably less money available for pigs in pokes. Investors are wary of both adverse selection and moral hazard and, when they cannot reliably discriminate among untried projects, underinvestment is a consequence of the gaps in information. However, there is obviously potential gain from obtaining the information necessary to make informed investment decisions. Venture capitalists exist because they can reduce information-based failures through careful selection, monitoring and other means. As venture capitalists become more skilled in reducing these sources of market failure, the venture capital sector functions more efficiently.

Amit, Brander and Zott develop a theoretical model of venture capital contracts, financial structure and entrepreneurial effort. They bring the model to data using taxes paid as a proxy for profit. Their empirical results suggest that the venture capitalists' share in finance is negatively related to performance. Firms with a relatively low level of venture capital ownership tend to do better. While this explains only a small portion of total variance in performance, the effect is consistent with the existence of both moral hazard and adverse selection.

In his comments on the Amit, Brander and Zott paper, Ralph Winter began by challenging the proposition that asymmetric information is necessary to explain each of the stylized facts of the venture capital market. For example, in Winter's view, the specialized venture capital market is a reflection of costly information regarding young projects and the efficient accommodation of financial markets to the costly search for such information and, thus, the existence *per se* of the market is not necessarily due to investee-investor informational asymmetry. Likewise, the skewed pattern of returns, with a very few highly successful projects in the right tail of the distribution, can be explained without reliance on asymmetrical information. Indeed, Winter argues, if insiders (the investors) have superior information concerning the probability of commercial success, they would be disinclined to seek venture capital for projects they (asymmetrically) know to have exceptionally high promise, for this would mean an unnecessary sharing of the rewards. Consequently, the right tail of the distribution of returns should be *thinner* and the more important is the informational asymmetry.

In an especially insightful extension of the Amit, Brander and Zott paper – and among the more creative points raised at the conference – Winter begins with the observation that insider buyouts dominate among alternative exit devices from venture capital. This fact does accord with the hypothesis of superior insider information. It also has profound implications for the optimal response to the type of agency problem that Amit, Brander and Zott analyse in their paper – limited liability with hidden action. An optimal contract between the principal and the agent (investor and investee) is a contract that is compatible with the incentives of both. The contract must draw finance to the risky project, encourage performance commitment on the part of the investor, while leaving no benefit to a strategy that hides information. Winter suggests that an option would be all-round incentive compatible. In contrast to straight equity, an option held by the venture capitalist increases the venture capitalist's share of the residual claim (the marginal profit) under successful outcomes. Options come into the money at higher levels of profit. The efficiency and incentive compatibility of an option contract stems from the fact that while the rewards to *both* principal and agent increase as the project is more successful, the proportion of the rewards captured by the agent (the venture capitalist) increases at the margin of profitability.

In his closing comment, Winter notes that the framework developed by Amit, Brander and Zott does not address the normative economic issue of whether the equilibrium in the venture capital market under imperfect information can be improved by policy intervention, for example by a government agency in pursuit of economic efficiency. Whether asymmetric information is sufficient to warrant intervention in the form of government action through, for example, subsidies or guaranteed financing, is an issue that Winter suggests deserves further research.

Venture Capital Market Exits in Canada and the United States

Jeffery MacIntosh focuses on venture capital exits – the means by which suppliers of high-risk capital dispose of their investments. The exit perspective generally receives less attention than the (entry) decision to fund or not to fund fledgling firms, an uneven balance of emphasis that may reflect misplaced assumptions concerning the strategy of suppliers of risk capital. MacIntosh makes a convincing case that the entry and exit decisions are interrelated. *Ex ante*, financiers feel that being stuck is not an option.

Exit is an important factor in establishing both explicit and implicit contractual relations between the suppliers and users of venture capital.

MacIntosh argues that effective exit mechanisms tend to lower the cost of capital. Alternative exit routes include IPOs, private sale, company buy back (whereby the firm buys out the venture capitalist), secondary sale of the venture capital, liquidation and write-off. Insofar as exit is integral to the full life cycle of venture capital, understanding exits, theoretically and empirically, is fundamental to understanding the role, if any, for constructive intervention in the process. Financial market failures or inefficiencies that constrain or distort alternatives to unwind will likewise constrain or distort the general supply of venture capital.

Exit alternatives are shaped *inter alia* by regulatory factors, capital market depth and sophistication, and taxation.

MacIntosh deals directly with the operational efficiency of the venture capital market, drawing on data from the United States and Canada to glean insight into exit strategies, economies of scale in the venture capital transaction, and specialization in venture capital services. In his view, U.S. venture capitalists are substantially more specialized, with firms that deal exclusively in computer software or electronics or biotechnology, etc., whereas Canadian firms are more likely to be generalists. The relevance of the difference between specialists and generalists hinges on the fact that services provided by venture capitalists, including investment screening, structuring the deal to establish entrepreneurial incentives, engaging in operational monitoring and advice, securing additional sources of capital *and* choosing the timing and means of exit, all have a bearing on the long-run commercial viability of the venture. If specialists provide superior service, then a venture capital market populated by specialists is likely to be more efficient.

The IPO market is an important exit mechanism from venture capital, although somewhat less so in Canada than in the United States. Buy backs predominate in Canada. Alas, write-offs are also more likely in Canada than in the United States, with 32 percent (vs. 21 percent) ending in the dustbin. In both Canada and the United States, the most spectacularly successful venture capital investments move to market via initial public offerings of equity. As the exit of choice, however, the IPO route may underlie subtle inefficiencies in venture capitalism. IPOs tend to be oversubscribed and underpriced in the short term. IPOs also tend to cluster around peaks in the equities markets, followed by protracted underperformance. The downward slide indicates fundamentally overpriced IPOs. Overpriced IPOs represent excessive rewards to venture capital (at the expense of both the funded firm and the new financiers) an allocative inefficiency in financial markets. On these matters, the evidence in Canada is slim but suggestive.

Tax influences on the supply of venture capital are substantial in both the United States and Canada. When the *Employment Retirement Income Security Act* (1974) in the United States allowed pension funds to channel capital to commercial adventures, the result was an explosion of financial activity. In Canada, labour-sponsored venture capital funds are tax driven, as are provincial (e.g., Quebec) stock savings plans. The structure of tax incentives for venture capitalism may influence the efficiency with which such funds are used. For example, pension funds are institutional sources of capital whereas labour-sponsored plans draw funds from individuals. This difference, MacIntosh suggests, may help explain why labour-sponsored funds are only 17 percent invested in risky ventures, while giving reason to question whether the tax expenditures are being well spent.

In his comments on MacIntosh's paper, Michel Poitevin likens ease of exit to liquidity. Poitevin also points out that exit strategy depends on the nature and degree of informational asymmetry between the venture capitalist and those who replenish the young firm's finances. To give empirical content to the role of asymmetric information, Poitevin recommends examining the relation between share of the firm withheld by the venture capitalist at the time of exit and the subsequent profitability of the firm following the refinancing.

THE CLIMATE FOR INITIAL PUBLIC OFFERINGS IN CANADA

IPOs OCCUPY A PLACE OF IMPORTANCE AT THIS CONFERENCE. MacIntosh noted the importance of the IPO as an exit route from venture capital, especially for those firms that are most successful in their early development phase. Amit, Brander and Zott drew a similar conclusion from their analysis of venture capital financing. Michael Robinson described a particular institutional arrangement to accommodate IPOs, the Alberta Junior Capital Pool. It appears that a strong and efficient market for IPOs is crucial for the provision of long-term finance to firms with demonstrated substantial commercial viability and growth potential that is otherwise constrained by debt limits and a shortage of built-up capital. Investment requires a new infusion of equity.

An IPO represents a major financial transaction at a crucial juncture in the life of a firm. An IPO involves an infusion of equity and restructured ownership along with the new discipline of market scrutiny of corporate performance. The fact that equity, as opposed to debt, is the financial vehicle of choice for young, growing firms is all the more important as Canada shifts from its traditional reliance on resource and manufacturing toward services and knowledge-based industry. Debt is a relatively low-cost, accessible form of finance, when it is secured by tangible assets such as machinery and equipment. Knowledge-based industry, in contrast, derives value from commercial ideas, patents and intangible prospects that traditional creditors, such as banks or bondholders, are less willing to finance. So-called "soft assets" are difficult to appraise and virtually impossible to salvage. Although there is no empirical evidence on the potential difficulty of raising funds for knowledge-based firms, it would seem that a strong IPO market is a necessary financial market condition for the industrial shift toward a knowledge-based economy.

In his paper, Vijay Jog examines the climate for IPOs in Canada. Jog provides evidence on the at-issue underpricing of IPOs, longer-term price performance of IPOs and the financial performance of firms in the post-IPO phase. He also summarizes results of a selective survey of managerial strategies and attitudes toward the IPO decision and the process of going public.

IPOs are new, unseasoned and relatively unknown equity issues. As a result, the general uncertainty of future profitability as well as the asymmetry of information between issuer and investor are much greater than for conventional issues by listed firms. Consequently, without reference to similar securities trading in the secondary market, the at-issue price of an IPO is problematic for the underwriter. The share price of an IPO typically moves up or down substantially immediately following the release of the issue. Jog, in earlier work with Srivastava (1994, 1995), documented the substantial at-issue underpricing of Canadian IPOs. In other words, the trading price of an IPO tends to jump abruptly above the issue price. Jog reports that the phenomenon of underpricing of IPOs persists through recent data, but to a degree that has significantly diminished.

Post-IPO performance, as measured by the holding return on such shares, is systematically disappointing. In a sample of 254 IPOs on the Toronto Stock Exchange (TSE) from 1971 to 1992, IPOs significantly underperformed the TSE

300 index for at least six years following the IPO listing. On a market-adjusted basis, investors who buy an "average" IPO incur a loss of 40 percent in four years. The underperformance is observed regardless of whether the stock was originally overpriced or underpriced at issue, although overpriced stocks perform significantly worse than underpriced stocks over the first four years.

At-issue IPO underpricing represents a transfer of wealth from the existing shareholders to the new investors. Thereafter, the persistent poor stock price performance suggests that young firms chronically fail to generate returns equal to their cost of capital. As a result, original shareholders, as well as those who purchased the IPO, suffer losses of wealth. Evidence of poor post-IPO economic performance might appear in accounting data – applying standard measures of corporate production efficiency and profitability. Jog reports that a number of performance indices deteriorate post-IPO. These findings are consistent with active earnings management pre-IPO, intended no doubt to enhance the perception of earnings potential and productivity.

Despite the underpricing and the generally disappointing post-IPO corporate performance, Jog suggests that "Canadian capital markets are doing a good job in allocating risk capital to entrepreneurs." Acknowledging that, from the investors' point of view, the results are disappointing, Jog nevertheless believes that the Canadian IPO environment is attractive for the entrepreneur. On the evidence, these conclusions are unconvincing. Although random wealth redistributions in the process of financing investment are not inconsistent with capital market efficiency, the persistent losses to investors that Jog documents are likely to be a factor that inhibits the flow of equity capital to neophyte firms. The fact that he does not have a counterfactual, i.e, the volume and cost of IPO capital if persistent losses were not the norm, renders Jog's strong, positive conclusions questionable.

Elizabeth Maynes, in formal comments on Jog's paper, begins by questioning whether the data – exclusively successful IPOs on the TSE – accurately depict the market for IPOs in a broader Canadian context. Maynes' point, while reason for pause in a general way, is perhaps more a challenge than a criticism since, on specific empirical issues, Jog purports to say no more than what his data indicate.

In his findings, Jog shows that IPOs come in waves. IPO waves, he suggests, are driven by the ebb and flow of the tides of the broader market. Maynes feels that this relation between IPO activity and market conditions deserves more attention.

Maynes is especially perplexed about the negative post-IPO performance of both stock price and corporate performance. Indeed, it is unfortunate that Jog identifies no causal link between IPOs and subsequent corporate performance (per accounting data), with extension to the relative performance of stock returns. Equally important, given the persistent nature of these relations, does this "information" condition the general pricing of IPOs? As mentioned above, one can be properly sceptical of the view that the IPO market in Canada is "good."

The persistent erosion of the post-IPO return to equity, if true, is a puzzle. The observation itself may be distorted by the application of inappropriate benchmarks, a point that Andrew Karolyi raised with respect to Usha Mittoo's analysis.

If the evidence can withstand scrutiny, however, the result is either an indictment of capital market efficiency or a financial asset pricing phenomenon that is not fully captured by conventional equity valuation models. For example, an IPO is likely to have the skewed risk characteristics of an option (at the money or simply near the money) as opposed to the characteristics of seasoned equity. The time value of the option would be greatest at (IPO) issue, and the return structure would be more skewed than at any other time. Thus, the time value of the option would dissipate as surviving firms move into the money and the risk structure becomes more symmetrical.[1] This explanation of an evolving risk structure for equity also suggests that the cost of equity capital for emerging firms is higher than for established firms because of the embedded option in the equity of the former.

Session IV Financing Constraints and Large Firms

Canada-United States Market Segmentation and The Cost of Equity Capital

The integration of international capital markets has important implications for the cost of capital of industry in small open economies. The greater the degree of international integration, the more elastic is the supply of financial capital to industry regardless of the size of the domestic capital market. Moreover, risks that are idiosyncratic but less than fully diversifiable in a small capital market are likely to be diversifiable internationally and, thus, have less relevance for the cost of capital if, of course, the small economy's capital market is integrated with markets abroad.

Usha Mittoo examines the extent to which the relatively small Canadian market for publicly issued equities is segmented from the much larger U.S. market. The focus is the after-issue price performance of Canadian seasoned equity issues. Capital market integration is addressed through a comparison of the after-issue price performance of interlisted (Toronto-New York) shares vs. non-interlisted shares. The data set consists of seasoned equity issues by TSE 300 firms from 1982 until 1993.

The empirical approach adopted by Mittoo, referred to as event study methodology, normalizes the risk-adjusted daily return movements of each new issue around its announcement date, computes the daily average of such returns for all issuances for each of several days before and after the event of the announcement, and then records cumulative average abnormal returns relative to the zero-dated time of the event. The time pattern of returns relative to the event lends itself to interpretation in terms of the event itself.

Mittoo reports that the stock markets react negatively to announcements of seasoned equity issues. On average, the announcement of an issue triggers a 1.75 percent drop in share price in the two-day period surrounding the announcement date. Cross-sectional analysis reveals that larger firms experience a more pronounced negative reaction than is the case for smaller firms. With respect to the primary focus of the study – whether Canadian and U.S. equity markets are integrated and, if so, whether or not such integration matters – interlisting indeed seems to provide (or perhaps as a proxy) superior access to equity capital. The two-day drop in share price for the interlisted firms is only 0.87 percent vs. 2.33 percent for non-interlisted firms.

In a second analytic step intended to identify firm-specific characteristics that govern how efficiently seasoned equity issues are absorbed in the market, Mittoo conducts a cross-sectional analysis of firm-specific cumulative abnormal returns (indexed to days relative to issuance announcement) with explanatory variables that include size, turnover, ownership structure, dividend payout, issue size and, with a dummy variable, whether or not the firm's shares are interlisted in Toronto and New York. Of the explanatory variables that exhibit some statistical significance in their regression coefficients, size is decidedly negative, which indicates that larger firms take a larger hit on new issues, whereas international interlisting appears to result in a generally lower cost of new equity finance.

Mittoo suggests these results confirm that the Canadian equities market is segmented from the U.S. market. Interlisting appears to be a means for individual firms to overcome the barriers. Otherwise, large Canadian firms that are not interlisted face a higher cost of equity capital than their U.S. counterparts.

According to Mittoo, effective action to lower the direct cost of international interlisting, to mitigate the home bias in international equity holdings, to improve international liquidity in traded equities and, generally, to enhance information available to potential offshore purchasers of Canadian equities would lower the cost of capital for Canadian industry.

Mittoo's conclusion is consistent with the results of a recent study by Kang and Stulz (1995) dealing with Japan. Kang and Stulz found that the large fixed costs of establishing an information access network for foreign securities represent the major barrier to international portfolio investment. With less information than domestic investors, foreigners simply stay away. In another recent study, Cooper and Kaplanis (1995) suggested additional reasons for the home bias, including the hedge against (domestic) inflation, withholding taxes and transactions costs, and a more nebulous foreign risk premium that, theory would predict, ought to be eroded by efficient international portfolio management. Regardless of the reasons, the home bias is a substantial fact, evidenced by Cooper and Kaplanis' data presented in Table 1.

Karolyi, in his remarks, stresses that Mittoo's work is first and foremost an analysis of the at-announcement price behaviour of seasoned equity offerings. The second stage of her work, involving cross-sectional analysis of firm and issue characteristics crucial to conclusions concerning capital market integration, rests entirely on the first stage results. Karolyi feels that the first stage results – the negative impact on a firm's return following its announcement of a new issue – suggest a limited scope for expansion of the Canadian investor base for seasoned equity offerings. The negative announcement impact has been observed elsewhere and over longer periods. Karolyi's overriding concern is with the methodology for measuring performance, especially the choice of benchmark and risk adjustments. If the (first

TABLE 1

THE HOME BIAS IN EQUITY PORTFOLIOS

Country	Market Capitalization (% of total) (1)	Percent of Equity in Domestic Stocks (2)	Home Bias (2)-(1)
Canada	3	84	81
France	4	92	88
Germany	3	78	75
Italy	2	92	90
Japan	33	92	59
Netherlands	1	51	50
Switzerland	2	66	64
United Kingdom	10	69	59
United States	42	95	53
	100		

Source: Cooper and Kaplanis (1995) Table 2.

stage) negative performance is mis-specified or overestimated, the (second stage) conclusions concerning the merits of international interlisting are likewise overstated.

Karolyi points to evidence suggesting that Canadian equity yields tend to underperform following international interlisting. Does this mean that Canadian equities enter the United States with a super risk premium due to information deficiency, he asks. This raises the question of why firms choose to interlist. What does this mean for the supposed benefits of an expanded investor base? The issue warrants an event study of interlisting to understand better the basis of the negative hit on prices of newly interlisted stocks.

Karolyi acknowledges that Mittoo's paper highlights the importance of understanding the effects of market deregulation and dismantling formal barriers (e.g., legal and tax) to international securities ownership. In a closing remark, Karolyi indicated that it is important for Canada to continue to lobby the U.S. Securities and Exchange Commission to secure fast-track approval of qualified foreign listings, i.e., without the delay involved in verifying compliance with U.S. Generally Accepted Accounting Principles (GAAP).

THE QUEBEC STOCK SAVINGS PLAN: PANACEA OR BANE?

THE QUEBEC STOCK SAVINGS PLAN (QSSP) WAS LAUNCHED IN 1979. According to Jean-Marc Suret and Elise Cormier, the Quebec government had two objectives for the QSSP. First, it was designed to reduce effectively and constructively the burden of the individual income tax. Second, with a view to channelling the reduced tax payments into Quebec investment, the Plan would encourage Quebecers to hold equity securities issued by Quebec industries by offering personal income tax credits for purchases of eligible shares.

Suret and Cormier discuss the design and multiple redesign of the QSSP, with attention to the effectiveness of the Plan in meeting its objectives.

In its early stage, from 1979 to 1983, the QSSP did not differentiate eligibility between shares of large and small firms. Inasmuch as shares of larger firms are more familiar, more liquid and less risky, the QSSP was dominated by issues and purchases of shares of large firms. Large firms, however, typically do not face serious problems in raising capital whereas Quebec's small firms, which are more likely to have difficulty raising equity, appeared unable to take advantage of the QSSP.

In 1986, the balance of the benefits of the Plan was tilted toward small companies by altering the terms of QSSP eligibility. Small and medium-sized industries in Quebec responded enthusiastically by issuing shares in large volume.

In October 1987, equity markets crashed. Along with shareholders in general, the new shareholders attracted by the QSSP suffered significant losses. The number of QSSP shareholders declined considerably thereafter.

Suret and Cormier estimate that the Quebec tax system absorbed approximately $1 billion in tax losses. On this account, they point out, with some cynicism, that the goal of reducing the personal tax burden was achieved. In view of the $1 billion tax expenditure, however, what were the real effects of the QSSP?

In terms of numbers, the market listings of small and even very small Quebec businesses increased substantially and significantly as more Quebecers held shares. From the investors' perspective, many QSSP shares had poor gross-of-tax yields. On the other hand, three or four firms had exceptionally good returns, accounting for more than half of all gains. Suret and Cormier liken QSSP-eligible investments to a lottery – a small chance of large gains counterbalanced by a large chance of loss. The one sure payoff to the investor was captured up front in the form of the tax credit.

From the firms' perspective, the QSSP pushed up the share prices of QSSP-eligible firms and lowered the cost of capital. This explains, in part, the spectacular interest in IPOs on the Montreal Exchange. The ratio of IPOs in Montreal to IPOs in Toronto illustrates the effect. From 1979 to 1982 the ratio was 0.23; from 1983 to 1986, 0.76; and 1987 and after, 0.33.

The QSSP was designed to improve capitalization permanently, to lower the cost of funds for Quebec firms and to foster productive investment. Suret and Cormier report, however, that only 25 percent of fresh funds supported by the QSSP went into new investment. A great deal of the funds, at least 33 percent, was used to reduce the debt of QSSP-eligible firms. There is also evidence, especially for those firms that were successful, that their dividend payout increased, representing a flow through of QSSP-supported funds.

In general, the rate of return on equity tended to fall, in some cases dramatically, after an issue of QSSP-eligible shares. This suggests that many firms had no cost-effective plans for investment. The investors' financial incentive to contribute funds to industry did not correspond to an enhanced set of investment opportunities for firms.

In deriving their results, Suret and Cormier compare returns on QSSP-funded firms with a small capitalization index. This choice of index, including its arbitrary representation of risk, is disconcerting to Simon Lalancette, the discussant. Indeed, most questions in discussion addressed empirical methodology, especially with respect to the treatment of risk and dividends. Robert Chirinko pointed out, for example, that when ascribing corporate financial effects to the QSSP (or, indeed, *ex post* for any structural intervention in capital markets), it is difficult to have confidence in the counterfactual. General business and financial conditions of the time, rather than the QSSP *per se*, may have prompted the observed increase in dividend payout. Suret replied that small and medium-sized firms – growing enterprises – are expected to maintain low dividend payout. Any increase in dividend payout subsequent to access to QSSP funds can be reasonably interpreted as a flow through.

Labour-Sponsored Venture Capital Funds in Canada: Institutional Aspects, Tax Expenditures and Employment Creation

François Vallaincourt asks whether tax-based labour-sponsored venture capital funds (LSVCFs) represent good tax policy. He concludes, based largely on evidence from Quebec, that they do not. Above all, he argues, LSVCFs fail to finance the investment that ought to generate the employment that represents the policy raison d'être. Moreover, the direct tax benefits of LSVCFs – the tax relief to contributors – are unevenly distributed in favour of higher income groups.

Vaillancourt begins with a synoptic overview of the objectives, structure, governance and size of the various federal and provincial LSVCFs. The programs have strong similarity of purpose, including investment, employment and local industrial favouritism. There is also a general bias toward providing funds for small and medium-sized firms.

The essence of an LSVCF is a generous tax concession to contributors. In 1995, for example, a \$1,000 investment in an LSVCF held in a Registered Retirement Savings Plan (RRSP) could, in most provinces, cost as little as \$45 for an investor facing the highest marginal personal income tax rate. The tax relief stems from a combination of federal and provincial tax credits for the venture capital fund contributions together with the pre-tax status of RRSP investments.

Despite the tax advantages, LSVCFs in Quebec have never attracted more than 2.5 percent of tax filers. Within this relatively small group, Vaillancourt observes that the distribution of tax credits is skewed toward higher income groups. He does not concern himself with the reasons for, or consequences of, this pattern, noting only that it represents an uneven distribution of the tax expenditure. One might suggest that the distribution is consistent with the fact that tax incentives are most attractive to those in higher tax brackets (and, therefore, higher income brackets), especially as LSVCF credits are coupled with RRSP contributions, and that upper income groups generally tend to save/invest more.

LSVCFs' focus on employment is often touted as differentiating such programs from private venture capitalism. If an infusion of venture capital, LSVCF or private, effectively provides funds to firms that are otherwise denied finance, the resulting new investment ought to have positive employment effects. Vaillancourt attempts to measure this by introducing a spline variable representing LSVCFs into a conventional model of sector-specific employment. The spline variable, essentially a time-varying index of participation in the Fonds de solidarité des travailleurs du Québec, fails to have explanatory power. Vaillancourt interprets this as failure of the policy to meet its objective. However, the relationship between finance and employment – dependent, as it is, on investment – seems unlikely to be adequately captured by the augmented employment function. Earlier in the conference, in an exercise focused exclusively on the elasticity of investment with respect to the cost of capital, Chirinko and Meyer could not report conclusive results. The chances of observing a significant relationship, if such a relationship should exist, are even slimmer in Vaillancourt's specification, since the finance/investment/employment effects with which he is concerned involve the investment:cost-of-capital elasticity *plus* the relationship between investment and employment.

In his comments on this paper, Brian Smith suggests that labour-sponsored venture capital funds likely affect the composition of venture capital funds in Canada, but not necessarily the total volume of such funds.

Smith takes issue with Vaillancourt's analysis of employment effects of LSVCFs. He warns of a problem in failing to distinguish potentially significant substitution effects from gross effects. The focus on sectoral aggregate employment effects, for example, is unlikely to expose LSVCF funding of firms that might otherwise fail. Scarce financial resources in that case are diverted from their most useful purpose.

Flagging a criticism often, and legitimately, directed at programs ostensibly aimed at increasing employment by subsidizing capital, Smith reminds the conference that any program that lowers the cost of capital relative to the cost of labour is likely to induce investment in labour-saving production capital, subverting the employment objective.

Raising Equity Capital for Small and Medium-Sized Enterprises Using Canada's Public Equity Markets

The question addressed by Michael Robinson is whether Canadian equity markets provide an effective means for small and medium-sized enterprises to raise equity capital.

In the first part of his paper, Robinson analyses the cost of raising equity capital via IPOs in Canada. He confirms the general impression that the cost of raising equity capital is inversely related to the size of the issue, a finding consistent with the cost structure for raising debt as suggested by Riding. Robinson also reports that the dollar cost of public listing in Canada is generally lower than the cost of listing on a U.S. exchange, while the percentage cost of listing in Canada for small and medium-sized firms, in particular, is similar to the cost in the United States.

Cash costs of bringing an equity issue to market are typically in excess of $100,000 for regular listings on the major markets – Toronto, Montreal and Vancouver – and substantially less on the Alberta Stock Exchange. A useful distinction is drawn between cash expenses, including legal and underwriting fees, and the implicit cost due to the typically substantial discount at which primary issues enter the market. These fixed costs make it expensive for firms to consider equity issues of less than $1 million on the major exchanges.

A large part of the cost of an IPO is due to underpricing the issue. The conventional explanation for this phenomenon is the information asymmetry between issuers and the uninformed investors, an asymmetry that is likely to be especially large for initial issues of small new business. Uninformed investors, wary of the winner's curse, tend to reduce the price they are willing to pay for a firm's IPO.

Robinson directs most of his attention to the Junior Capital Pool of the Alberta Stock Exchange. Information on cash costs, listing requirements and regulations in the major equity markets provide a backdrop for a more detailed discussion of the club-like market in Alberta. In Alberta, less onerous listing requirements allow firms to go public through the Junior Capital Pool for as little as $40,000, with market capitalization as low as several hundred thousand dollars.

Robinson concludes that it is possible to establish a stock exchange program that allows small and medium-sized enterprises to raise equity capital through IPOs as well as secondary financings. To achieve these efficiencies, however, the program must be regionally based and built on an existing financial infrastructure such as regional brokerage firms, a strong local retail investor base and reputable entrepreneurs. To avoid the wrath of Gresham's Law applied to finance, the market mechanism that Robinson advocates requires close surveillance by regulatory authorities to ensure that low-quality issues do not drive out the good ones. An efficient and liquid secondary market is crucial. Finally, firms must be given strong incentive to grow and leave the junior market or face delisting although, unfortunately, Robinson does not indicate explicitly what such incentives might be.

Robinson's insistence on good institutional governance, surveillance and the building of reputation in all aspects of junior capital pools is driven by his observation of the negative experience in many other countries. Lax regulation, fraudulent stock trading, inadequate differentiation between junior and regular markets together with a lack of institutional interest (especially in Europe) in junior issues are discouraging and must be confronted for the successful development of junior stock programs.

In his comments on Robinson's paper, Eric Kirzner insists that second-tier markets are the very core of venture capital, challenging Robinson's pessimism for this institutional structure. Indeed, in Kirzner's opinion, the Alberta Junior Capital Pool is a particular example of a second-tier market, although perhaps not the best one. Second-tier markets, in general, are designed for junior companies that cannot, or choose not to, meet the listing requirements on the senior market. From the perspective of the issuer, second-tier markets provide access to an equity market that would otherwise be restricted due to stringent listing requirements and high listing costs. Second-tier markets provide especially strong benefits in terms of investor protection that are integral to the supply of finance. Since small and relatively unknown companies seeking equity tend to be more volatile, less liquid and more vulnerable to manipulation than larger more established listed firms, the public interest is better served, Kirzner argues, if such shares are listed on a regulated active and visible auction market as opposed to an over-the-counter dealer market. Surveillance is more thorough on an auction market than on the less regulated over-the-counter market because of the major role and reputation of the self-regulating body – the stock exchange. An enforceable set of primary and secondary priority trading rules in the auction format fosters transparent and equitable trading.

Turning to Robinson's endorsement of the Junior Capital Pool as a specific prototype for institutional development for a more accessible equities market, Kirzner expresses reservation. He points to the regional "club" atmosphere and the possibility of idiosyncratic conditions in Alberta. Kirzner sees a promising alternative in the Canadian Dealing Network (CDN), a dealer market operated by the TSE. The CDN, essentially a third tier, is an over-the-counter market operated by a recognized exchange. There are no listing requirements although the market is subject to some market surveillance.

On The Care and Nurture of Loan Guarantee Programs

Loan guarantee programs are designed to redress an apparent flaw in credit markets, viz., that small firms face systemic barriers to debt capital.

In his paper, Allan Riding reviews the theory underlying the perceived failure of debt markets to serve the needs of small business. He interprets the bias against small loans as a function of fixed costs of credit administration, in particular, the average cost of lending is inversely related to loan size. The need for a minimum degree of due diligence in a profit-maximizing lending strategy involves fixed costs that loom relatively large for small loans. Exacerbating the cost bias against small loans, in Riding's model, lenders set collateral requirements as a function of the fixed cost of due diligence, which likewise makes the required collateral (percent of loan) inversely related to the size of the loan.

Governments in virtually all industrialized countries, and many developing countries as well, underwrite loan guarantee programs for small business. In practice, loan guarantee programs are characterized by a combination of lax lending to bad credit risks and, thus, defaults, and subsidized loans to low-risk free-riders. In view of these chronic operational difficulties, Riding suggests that the primary responsibility of the guarantor is to set an optimal level of loan guarantee, enhancing the lenders' incentive to lend without unduly undermining the lenders' responsibility to discriminate on the basis of borrower quality.

Taking a position on policy, Riding prefers loan guarantee programs to be self-financing and quasi-commercial. He advocates a central role for fees levied on those who receive guaranteed loans. Fees, according to Riding, are also the means to address the problem of incrementality (wherein borrowers who do not need the guarantee take it anyway – free-riders). Perhaps more important to his view of a properly designed program, "fees must offset the loan losses."

In his focus on fees, Riding loses sight of the main problem of capital market failure. For example, referring to the Loan Guarantee Scheme in the United Kingdom, Riding indicates that "fees ... represent annual payments to the guarantor, *reducing the cost of the program by reducing default risk*" (emphasis added). Just how fees reduce or screen for default risk is not clear, and the proposition is especially puzzling in view of Riding's finding that the U.K. Loan Guarantee Program (that requires fees) has the highest default rate among all countries examined.

Rather than viewing fees as a constructive component of program design, one might argue that fees on guaranteed loans are thinly disguised and ill-advised taxes. First of all, fees are suspect in programs intended to rectify a distortionary (loan) cost structure. As Riding acknowledges elsewhere, fees establish a deterrent to access to loan guarantee programs. As fees deter applicants, program costs are reduced only because they reduce the size of the program. Riding does not present a case for fees as efficient credit quality screens, i.e., that fees reduce adverse selection or address the problem of free-riding.

Furthermore, fees are fiscal revenues. Thus, questions arise as to the efficiency of this particular form of taxation. More fundamentally, should loan guarantee programs be self-funding, shouldering their own cost through a form of "earmarked" taxation? Second-best arguments aside, there is no obvious reason to develop a revenue-generating mechanism specific to, and built within, this particular program. If the problem is one of genuine capital market failure, fees represent an inappropriate application of the benefit or user-pay principle of taxation.

If, for whatever reason, fees are to be applied, then to minimize both inefficiency and deterrence, fees should not be imposed unconditionally *ex ante*. Fees should be assessed *ex post* on successful investments but not, contrary to Riding, to subsidize losses. *Ex post* conditional fees may be construed as calls (held by the guarantor) on the earnings of all firms that borrow. If a firm is successful and survives, the call expires "in the money," whereas the call expires with zero value if a firm fails. Fees based strictly on *ex post* positive performance (which is bound to include some economic rent) would mitigate some of the deterrence effect that would otherwise arise with unconditional *ex ante* fees. This is roughly the idea behind forgivable loans. Nevertheless, it is well recognized in corporate finance that securities with embedded options are a relatively costly means of finance. In this respect, the conditional fee as call is fortunately a "limited call" with maximum value (or cost to the firm) equal to the required fee.

Given the relative importance of debt finance for start-up business, the issues addressed in Riding's paper are among the most important of the conference. Evidence to the effect that Canada's policy intervention – via the *Small Business*

Loans Act – has fewer defaults than comparable schemes elsewhere is not necessarily encouraging in terms of the ostensible goals of the program. Nor does Riding demonstrate that the low default rate reflects operational efficiencies.

To focus his argument concerning the failure of credit markets to provide undifferentiated access for small and large firms, Riding coins the term "equivalent credit risk." He goes on to suggest that small and large firms of equivalent credit risk do not have equivalent access to debt. This concept seems vacuous for standardizing risk in order to address the effects of size differences. Credit risk is notoriously difficult to define, let alone measure directly and compare. From the lender's perspective, and that is really the only perspective that counts in this case, credit risk involves a combination of the probability of default, the credit at stake, as well as portfolio effects in the loan portfolio. Lenders have substantial difficulty in obtaining reliable information, or proxies for information, on firms without a track record. Firms that are established and have been around for a while *ipso facto* are less risky because they have demonstrated that they are capable of business and finance decisions that prove to be successful. Survival is an index. Since firms grow, their age and size are correlated. Implicit within this, is another (inverse) relation between size and risk. Such fundamental considerations are absent in Riding's formulation of lending criteria and strategy.

In his comments on Riding's paper, Daniel Thornton underscores the importance of providing empirical content to the concepts outlined by Riding, especially the sensitivity of the policy objective (improved access to credit by small firms) to each of the policy variables: percent of loan guaranteed, fee, ceiling interest rate and maximum guaranteed loan. Thornton also expresses caution with respect to intervention in view of the fact that we do not know the extent of hindered access that small firms face in credit markets.

From the floor, Basil Kalymon strongly challenged Riding's interpretation of the application of regulations governing loan guarantees under the *Small Business Loans Act* as amended in April 1993. Kalymon pointed out that as a bank manages its portfolio of guaranteed loans, *Small Business Loans Act* constraints on the structure of that portfolio severely limit the amount of the guarantee. At the margin of their loan portfolio, Kalymon suggests that banks may realize as little as 10 percent guarantee.

James Brander asked if Riding had an objective function in mind that might govern the purpose as well as the form and extent of policy intervention.

Overview: Pulling It All Together

THIS CONFERENCE ADDRESSED ISSUES IN CAPITAL MARKETS that have implications for investment, competiveness and economic growth. The papers and discussions were organized around four interrelated themes:

- the cost of capital;
- financing constraints on small firms;
- financing constraints on medium and large firms; and
- initiatives to facilitate access to capital markets.

The test of the success of this conference is whether we reached a deeper understanding of Canadian capital markets with particular reference to the efficiency and effectiveness by which those markets channel funds to industry. A specific end point was defined at the outset, viz., could we arrive at a conclusive view concerning the existence and significance of a financial gap that inhibits real investment and economic growth?

A financial gap, if one exists, is unlikely to be observed via direct measurement of, for instance, volumes of financial flows or new investment. Indicators of capital market distortions or inefficiencies take the form of differentials – between countries, industries, risk categories or firms according to size – in the cost of capital and/or the required return on (financial) investment. The reference point, or counterfactual, is a first-best world of costless, efficient capital markets.

Finance is intermediary. Capital markets serve to allocate finance from savers to investors. If this process is operationally and informationally efficient, then capital markets allocate savings to investment by assigning an appropriate price for risk that is mutually acceptable to the savers who bear the risk and the investors who pay for it. On the other hand, if the process linking savings to investment is defective or distorted, real costs ensue in the form of investment left wanting for finance, reduced economic growth and lower-quality jobs. The orientation of the conference is predominantly institutional, in view of the challenge to determine whether the relevant financial institutions and markets in Canada provide properly priced access to capital across the spectrum of risk. The contributions to the conference, collectively and on occasion within individual presentations, combine the theory of finance with empirical methods to produce results that suggest that the answer to the guiding question concerning a financial gap is neither conclusive nor simple.

A Selective Point-by-Point Summary

The following paraphrased excerpts from individual papers provide a selective set of findings, considered positions and implications germane to the theme of the conference.

On the Elasticity of Investment with Respect to the Cost of Capital

There is too much imprecision in sectoral estimates of the elasticity to reach firm conclusions about the likely response of investment spending to investment incentives (Chirinko and Meyer).

On the International Difference in Return on Capital

In a trilateral estimation, the erratic pattern of results for Canada precludes any conclusion with respect to the rate of return on capital in Canada vs. the United States and Japan (Ando, Hancock and Sawchuk).

On the International Difference in Weighted Average Cost of Capital (WACC)

The Canada-United States differential in WACC, to the disadvantage of Canadian industry, is conservatively estimated to be 2 percentage points (Jog).

On International Capital Market Segmentation

The Canadian equities market is segmented from the U.S. market, although the segmentation is less severe for interlisted stocks. Most firms attempting to raise new equity in Canada face a more costly, less elastic supply of capital than their U.S. counterparts (Mittoo).

On Taxation as a Source of Distortion

Taxation appears to be responsible for relatively little distortion of investment in the international context, i.e., in terms of favouring investment to or from Canada. However, within Canada, substantial interprovincial and intersectoral variance in marginal effective tax rates suggest potentially serious distortionary influences (Chen and McKenzie).

On the Importance of Exit from Venture Finance

Entry and exit are inextricably linked. Effective exit mechanisms tend to lower the early stage cost of capital, while ineffective mechanisms have the contrary effect. Understanding exit options is vital to understanding the venture capital process (MacIntosh).

On Venture Capitalism and Information

Asymmetric information and limited liability (with low collateral) are the central features of venture capital investment. Venture capitalists exist because they can reduce information-based market failures through careful selection, monitoring and other means (Amit, Brander and Zott).

On Venture Capital in the Life Cycle of Finance

Venture capital activity in Canada is targeted to the expansion and growth of industry rather than start-up (Amit, Brander and Zott).

On Small Firms' Access to Equity

Regulations on major Canadian stock exchanges effectively favour medium-sized and larger firms. This represents a gap in financing alternatives for small firms which is only partially filled by the over-the-counter market and regional exchanges (Robinson).

On Small Firms' Access to Debt

Access to debt capital is biased against small firms since the collateral requirement is inversely related to loan size. This is a capital market failure that justifies loan guarantee programs (Riding).

On Internal Finance

Cash flow appears to be an important element in the investment equation. This represents a financial advantage for mature firms (Chirinko and Meyer).

On Corporate Finance and Industrial Growth

Retention of profit is crucial for financing expansion. A clear pecking order of finance is observed in Canada: (1) retained earnings, (2) debt and (3) stock issue (Suret and L'Her).

On Labour-Sponsored Venture Capital Funds (LSVCFs)

Venture capital activity is characterized by discouraged entry and monopoly finance. The generous tax preference for labour-sponsored venture capital, ostensibly to encourage investment *and* employment, has resulted in no net employment in Quebec (Vaillancourt).

On the Quebec Stock Savings Plan

The QSSP created a tax expenditure of $1 billion. Only 25 percent of fresh funds supported by the QSSP went into new investment. The return on equity tended to fall after issue of QSSP-eligible shares, suggesting that many firms had no plans for investment (Suret and Cormier).

The foregoing points are informative in the particular as well as in their diversity. The conference obviously encountered difficulty in reaching consensus concerning the existence, let alone the significance, of financial gaps that thwart real investment in Canada.

Central Issues to the Conference

The following remarks address a number of issues that proved to be central to the conference. These issues sparked significant discussion and include the cost of capital, asymmetric information, international competitiveness, economies of scale in capital markets and the policy research agenda.

Cost of Capital

Perhaps the most frequently used expression at this conference has been "cost of capital." From the outset, we were made aware that anything that raises the cost of capital penalizes investment. We learned that cost of capital is difficult to measure. We heard suggestions of international and intersectoral differences in the cost of capital.

Throughout, there has been serious ambiguity in the use of the term "cost of capital." This ambiguity highlights the difference between the economic and financial perspectives on the issues addressed at this conference. In a less flattering light, the ambiguity in the use of the cost of capital weakens any argument that makes use of a variant of the term without regard for the alternatives.

There are at least three variants.

Let me begin with what is generally called the corporate cost of capital. This concept is well known in the business literature. At this conference, it was invoked explicitly by Jog in his analysis of sectoral cost of capital. The corporate cost of capital is essentially the cost of finance, expressed as a weighted average of the costs of debt and equity on an after-tax basis. It is exclusively a private cost of capital. The substantial contribution of the business finance literature to this issue, a contribution that distinguishes finance from economics, is to incorporate risk explicitly into the cost of finance – the capital asset pricing model (CAPM) and all that. Since much of what we are concerned with at this conference is the idea of risk, and how risk affects the flow of savings to risky investments, the corporate cost of capital represents a useful perspective. In the investment decision, the corporate cost of capital finesses problems introduced by inflation since expected inflation is incorporated into both the (nominal) cost of capital and the nominal rate of return on investment (or future cash flows in the computation of net present value). The main shortcomings of the corporate cost of capital include the fact that it is an average rather than a marginal concept, and its relevance to economic efficiency is limited due to its private perspective.

An important component of the corporate cost of capital is the cost of equity. This is an opportunity cost, interpreted as the return on equity required to maintain the market value of equity. Mittoo's analysis of IPOs and international interlisting involves a direct application of standard empirical methodology premised on this interpretation of the cost of equity. Likewise, Robinson's assessment of institutional barriers to access to equity finance faced by small firms, while not a direct estimation of the size of such barriers, nevertheless suggests that they raise the cost of equity capital.

In contrast to the corporate cost of capital, the user cost of capital is an approach developed from neoclassical investment theory à la Jorgenson. User cost of capital is, arguably, a more economically complete concept. It is generally more complex than the weighted average corporate cost of capital. For instance, the user cost of capital takes explicit account of economic depreciation of physical capital as well as the relative price of capital goods although, unfortunately, these factors are notoriously difficult to measure. In estimating user cost of capital, the corporate cost of capital is but one component. The conceptual advantage of the user cost of capital is that it is measured at the margin of investment, i.e., for the last dollar of investment.

In this conference, the user cost of capital was defined and estimated by Chirinko and Meyer with results that were unfortunately, or perhaps tellingly, inconclusive. Furthermore, the marginal effective tax calculations by Chen and McKenzie apply a methodology with a genesis firmly planted in the Jorgenson neo-classical framework. The empirical work in this area is one of the more important developments in policy analysis. However, insofar as the user cost of capital handles risk only in the most arbitrary fashion, finance people are nonplussed. Worse, the user cost of capital gives short shrift to financial adjustments that business uses to mitigate the impact of tax on the corporate cost of capital. Debt-to-equity ratios and dividend payouts, for example, are invariably fixed in user cost of capital and marginal effective tax computations, often over a range of considered taxes, whereas the corporate cost of capital approach explicitly accounts for after-tax (corporate) cost of capital minimization.

A third use of the term cost of capital is illustrated in the presentation by Ando, Hancock and Sawchuk in their international comparison of the United States, Japan and Canada. In an effort to measure the opportunity cost of capital in a steady state, and to do so in a manner that is internationally comparable, Ando, Hancock and Sawchuk compute a ratio of the flow of all payments for the use of capital (in a highly aggregated fashion) – interest, dividends, retained earnings – to the capital employed. In this sense, the cost of capital is a highly aggregated macroeconomic concept derived from the national accounts (or similar). The degree of aggregation is unlikely to reveal sources of distortion underlying capital market imperfections.

The differences in the variants of cost of capital are more than differences in computational methods. The corporate cost of capital constructs a hurdle rate for investment from the components of after-tax cash costs of debt (interest) plus the opportunity cost of equity. The user cost of capital, on the other hand, in computation focuses on technological considerations such as the economic depreciation of capital, the relative price of capital and (as presented at this conference) cash flow and sales generated by the invested capital. The user cost of capital has little to contribute to our understanding of the efficiency by which savings are channelled to investment since it is not designed to decompose industrial finance into its components and their respective costs. For the immediate purpose of exploring industrial access to sources of financial capital, therefore, it would seem that the more direct approach underlying the corporate cost of capital is more useful than the user cost approach. Perhaps that explains why the papers in the conference that take the corporate cost approach (Jog, Mittoo, Robinson, Riding, Suret and L'Her, for example) are conclusive and explicit in identifying sources of inefficiency and distortion in financial markets. Regardless, it would be helpful, and in keeping with the theme of the conference, to know (1) the correlation between the corporate and the user costs of capital, (2) whether the alternative specifications respond in the same way to structural, parameter and policy changes, and (3) in a head-to-head race, which specification better explains investment spending.

Asymmetric Information

The cost of capital – debt or equity – increases directly with risk. Risk is defined in terms of the probability distribution of outcomes of the investment. At any level of risk, capital is allocated efficiently as long as users and suppliers of capital hold similar views of the distribution of risky outcomes, allowing them to agree on a price (interest on debt, or yield on equity) commensurate with that risk. Competition in financial markets in most cases is expected to generate this efficient result. A serious problem for the allocation of capital arises, however, when suppliers and prospective users of capital cannot agree on the risk and return characteristics of particular investments. Suppliers of capital, understandably suspicious, tend to view the users' assessment of risk, or at least the users' declaration of risk, as unduly optimistic if not strategically understated. Suppliers of capital are generally not in a position to specify fully and to assess the risks to which their capital could be exposed, an informational disadvantage vis-à-vis users of capital. In the face of such asymmetry of crucial information, the price of capital (the expected rate of return) that is acceptable to suppliers rises above what the user is willing to pay. Without agreement, there can be no transaction. Capital markets fail. These problems are especially prevalent for fledgling firms, the sort that seek venture capital.

Asymmetric information, its causes and consequences, properly received a great deal of attention at this conference. Perhaps the most detailed commentary came from Amit, Brander and Zott who outlined a theory of venture capital with explicit reference to the specific pathology of moral hazard and adverse selection. Firms looking for venture capital must make a credible case concerning the worth and the risk of their proposal and, likewise, provide assurance that they will not take the money and run – that they will remain fully committed to the project *after* it is financed. On the other hand, while financiers strive to distinguish good projects from bad ones, the process itself may entice them to do the opposite if better projects find the impositions too onerous and bad projects accept funding at any cost.

MacIntosh deals with asymmetric information in the context of exit from venture capital. In this case the insiders (the management of firms currently funded with venture capital) have information on returns and risk that is superior to information available to prospective long-term financiers. The information gap raises the cost of exit and, hence, stymies the transformation to finance that is appropriate to more mature firms. Equally distressing, as MacIntosh argues with some force, if the way out is blocked, then initial entrance into the venture capital market is discouraged. These problems underlie the failure of financial markets to match finance and investment efficiently to firms at various stages in a life cycle of risky investment.

Riding on loan guarantee programs, Robinson on public equity markets and Jog on IPOs all had reason to refer to the effects of asymmetric information on the costs of finance and the efficiency by which financial markets channel savings to investment. Mittoo was concerned with international informational asymmetry that tends to be to the disadvantage of small countries. Despite different institutional factors in which these various analyses are set, they have a common concern with innovations in finance – either through institutional development or market behaviour – that address capital market inefficiencies through effective signalling, performance monitoring and the design of incentive-compatible contracts.

Competitiveness

An overworked and potentially misleading expression frequently invoked at this conference is competitiveness. Paul Krugman is right to insist that nations do not compete, companies do. Given the concern for the cost of capital, it is constructive to consider the difference between a general reduction in the cost of capital for Canada vis-à-vis the world – as addressed in analyses by Ando, Hancock and Sawchuk, Chen and McKenzie, and Jog – as opposed to improved access to capital for specific Canadian industrial sectors. A general reduction in the Canadian cost of capital, as per reductions in the differential (if such exists) between Canadian and world interest rates, or between Canadian and foreign risk-adjusted required returns on equity across the full spectrum of risk must, in the first instance, reflect improved productivity of capital employed in Canada. Such an improvement in productivity in the industrial world's most capital-intensive country would no doubt produce substantial economic gains. In the process, the exchange rate would strengthen and our terms of trade would improve, the capital-to-labour ratio would rise even further, and Canadian real wage rates would inevitably increase. Moreover, as a result of the higher real exchange rate, there would be an incentive for Canada to shift production away from non-traded goods toward traded goods. (Therein lies what one might construe as a true improvement in competitiveness, although the root cause is the improved capital productivity).

On the other hand, much of this conference has been concerned with sectoral access to capital, especially for small and medium-sized industry in early and risky stages of development. If market failure and transaction costs inhibit financial market access, and raise the cost of capital, the potential economic effects of improved access to capital would include expanded risk taking and more innovative industry in the heretofore restricted sectors. Such industry-specific expansionary effects differ from the macro-economic measures noted above. In particular, more investment does not necessarily mean more *productive* investment. Indeed, unleashed innovation could well be targeted to non-traded goods such as construction, infrastructure or services with relatively little direct consequence for international trade or so-called competitiveness. A substantially more complex set of questions, involving investment in research and development and the links between capital spending and productivity, must be considered in a proper assessment of the connection between improved capital market access and structural change in Canada's international trade position. Industry Canada is exploring these issues in depth in a science and technology research program.

Economies of Scale

At various points in the conference, authors referred to economies of scale in financial issues (for example, Riding with respect to debt or Robinson and, implicitly, Mittoo with respect to equity) which are attributed explicitly to the fixed costs of issuance, i.e., average issue costs are inversely related to issue size. However, this average cost-to-size relation is not what is generally understood by economies of scale. Economies of scale refer to an inverse relation between marginal cost and scale. In other words, in reference to real production, but with some relevance to finance, true economies of scale reflect efficiencies that depend on scale as opposed to a simple spreading out of fixed costs. This distinction is more than a definitional quibble. It has profound implications for the relevant type of intervention appropriate to problems of limited access – high average cost – facing small firms that bring small financial issues to market. For example, if the real impediment is relatively high fixed costs of issuance, then the target for subsidy, assistance or support is fixed costs *per se*, and such support should *not* be a function of issue size. On the other hand, in the face of true economies of scale whereby, for example, large issues attract lower yields, the proper policy prescription is aimed at the margin, which implies that any subsidy, assistance or support ought to be proportional to the total size of the issue.

A Policy Agenda? No! A Policy Research Agenda

It is inevitable that intense discussion of a complex issue will raise more questions than it answers. It is indicative of a properly focused format that the sessions close with enthusiasm to pursue new ideas raised at the conference.

In Canada, we accept that because of our natural circumstances we must pay more for heat. Is it equally imperative, perhaps because of unique industrial and financial circumstances, that our industry must also pay more for capital? Is the cost of capital for Canadian industry systematically higher than elsewhere? Are our small firms at a disadvantage vis-à-vis larger firms when it comes to raising capital? Is more venture capital the panacea? Have targeted policies, such as LSVCFs or stock savings plans, been worth the effort and the fiscal cost? Is our tax system unduly burdensome on industry? Is Canada benefiting from international financial integration? Are our financial markets deficient in some fundamental yet correctible way? Are there recognizable ways in which our capital markets fail to perform efficiently and effectively, at significant economic cost, in view of which prescriptive policies follow immediately?

Market failure justifies policy intervention. If markets cannot provide the optimal level of national defence, research or whatever, then policy calls for direct public sector provision or incentives to overcome private sector disinclination. As far as industry is concerned, the tradition of public policy varies from tax incentives, subsidies and government procurement as well as financially oriented schemes with which we have been concerned. The more direct, targeted incentives smack of industrial policy that, in most circles, is out of favour (although the so-called new growth theory and strategic trade policy is perhaps new wine in old bottles). Policy intervention to correct capital market failures is more in the realm of infrastructural development. But how to proceed?

Two general categories of factors contribute to financial market failure – failure that is reflected in limited access to capital and a cost of capital that is higher than it might otherwise be, given the level of risk. First, there are those factors that are likely to fade as financial markets expand and become broader, deeper and more complex. Increasing financial market efficiency, enhanced by volume as well as by communications technology, international financial integration and financial engineering, is driven largely by the profit opportunities afforded by existing imperfections. The unimpeded process of market development leads to market efficiency. This is the way of markets, this is Schumpeterian. On the other hand, there are aspects of market inefficiency that are more entrenched and slower to erode because incentives and rewards from the inefficiency are perversely protected by the institutions positioned to profit from the inefficiency.

At this conference, a strong sentiment emerged that policy intervention, if called for at all, ought to concern itself with encouraging a first-best solution of correcting the market – removing distortions and allowing the capital market to become more efficient – as opposed to direct public sector provision of, for example, loan capital.

Is there an endogenous development process in financial markets? It seems likely that there is. Even the toughest nut to crack, asymmetric information which, according to evidence presented at this conference, stymies some transactions and creates adverse selection in others, may have an endogenous, efficiency-enhancing market solution. For example, we heard on several occasions that venture capitalists are a form of specialized labour – expert in surveillance, effective in monitoring, pricing and risk allocation – functions that serve to lessen informational asymmetries. If market dynamics are teleologically consistent with the first-best solution of efficient markets, as most researchers in finance would hold, then the role for interventionist policy is limited. When in doubt, a strong presumption in favour of markets seems wise.

We also heard evidence, rooted largely in Quebec, that policy can dramatically induce activity in venture capitalism through labour-sponsored venture capital funds and subsidized equity investment via the QSSP. Among the verifiable results, it appears that in Quebec a substantial amount of finance was deflected from its intended goal of real investment, especially in ventures. This wrenching of the financial structure of Quebec industry, with questionable economic payoff in terms of either investment or employment, came with a substantially more certain fiscal cost of at least $1 billion of tax expenditure. Even if net investment and employment were essentially unaffected by these programs, the induced reallocation of investment and employment is likely to have introduced inefficiency on the production side.

This conference did not produce a policy agenda. Perhaps it was not expected to. However, the analysis and discussion frequently forced consideration of the alternatives of intervention vs. a more hands-off approach to finance. Most discussion focused on one form of intervention or another, or the merits of non-intervention. The case for intervention in response to market failure requires not only that the failure is damaging but also that government policy can do something about it.

In his thoughtful remarks to the conference, Edward Neufeld alluded to the constructively organic forces in finance. For example, the famous four pillars of institutional finance – banks, trusts, investment dealers and insurance – began to crumble as the relevance of the distinctions among them began to fade. This reflects institutional adaption and regulatory adjustment in the evolution of the financial system in Canada. The market mechanism, it seems, will inevitably render regulators redundant. It is crucial to recognize and encourage self-regulation in finance.

Finally, with a nod to an especially exciting area of modern finance, our understanding and interpretation of financial incentives – the cost of capital to industry or the structure of payoffs to financiers in the face of risk – is enhanced considerably by an understanding of options, contingent claims and derivative securities. Many of the issues raised at this conference involve complex option-like risk-to-return structures that could accurately be depicted as contingent claims, especially for unseasoned and unknown securities issued by young firms in novel lines of business activity. Perhaps the debilitating financial gaps with which we have been most concerned could be better understood and appropriate financial instruments and institutional policies more effectively designed through a deeper appreciation of options.

ENDNOTE

1 Equity in conjunction with debt can always be construed as an option. However, well-seasoned equities are generally deep in the money (vis-à-vis their debt, the present value of which represents the "exercise price") with risk characteristics defined by symmetrical lognormal returns.

Jack M. Mintz
Faculty of Management
University of Toronto

17

Policy Perspectives on Capital Market Issues

INTRODUCTION

THE AIM OF THIS PAPER IS TO PROVIDE POLICY PERSPECTIVES on capital market issues drawn from a body of economic and finance research prepared for a conference held by Industry Canada on capital market issues in Canada. The research is wide ranging including measurements of the cost of capital for Canadian businesses, an analysis of the impact of taxation on capital investments, an examination of venture capital markets, initial public offerings and financing structures of businesses, and an evaluation of public policies used to address capital market issues such as stock savings plans, tax-assisted venture capital funds and loan guarantee programs.

The focus of the conference was on corporate financing obtained from investors through stock and bond markets rather than through financial intermediaries. Thus, this paper primarily limits itself to an analysis of capital markets in relation to stock and bond financing of companies and only briefly touches on the role of financial intermediaries.

A body of research that provides new perspectives on the functioning of capital markets immediately raises a number of interesting policy issues for federal and provincial governments in Canada. The approach taken to analyze public policy in this paper is based on a familiar approach taken in public economics literature. First, it is important to identify how markets behave using economic analysis. Second, analysis should consider whether markets achieve a socially optimal allocation of resources in the economy or whether some "market failure" exists that results in a less than socially desirable outcome. Third, one can then consider how public policies could be designed to correct market failures.

For policy makers, three important questions come to mind:

- What are the economic and finance issues that affect capital markets?
- What causes inefficiency in capital markets?

- What, if any, role should governments have that would successfully assist the efficient functioning of capital markets?

Any analysis that provides answers to the above questions is very welcome. However, research often leads to more questions rather than providing solutions to the most significant problems. The research prepared for Industry Canada does not provide quick and easy answers for all questions. However, there are some interesting results that are important for policy makers. The most important conclusions can be summed up in two statements which will be developed in more detail below.

1. There are economic and public policy variables that affect the functioning of capital markets. Thus, there seems to be some role for governments to improve the efficiency of capital markets, either by eliminating public policies that impair efficiency or using public policies to overcome capital market "failures." (The theory for determining when governments should be involved with capital markets will be elaborated on below.)
2. Given the experience of Canadian governments in trying to promote efficient markets, such as stock savings plans, labour-sponsored venture capital funds and loan guarantee programs, one comes to the conclusion that public policies intended to promote more efficient markets have not always been prudent. In part, the quality of the public program depends on how well it is designed. When conditions of government programs are not sufficiently stringent, too many non-profitable borrowers take up loans with a high revenue cost for the government.

This survey which draws from the research prepared for Industry Canada is divided in four parts. First, we examine how capital market issues affect the economy. This discussion is based on a definition and understanding of how capital market variables affect the cost of capital faced by businesses. Next, we look at how government policies affect the functioning of capital markets, and then consider the role of the government in fostering economic growth by improving the efficiency of capital markets.

THE ROLE OF CAPITAL MARKETS AND THE COST OF CAPITAL

WHY ARE CAPITAL MARKETS IMPORTANT?[1] They provide the most efficient mechanism to ensure that individuals with savings may lend money to borrowers at the lowest cost. By reducing the costs of financial transactions, capital investment and savings are encouraged. In this section, two particular issues are discussed: how do capital markets contribute to the efficiency of financial transactions and how do the activities of capital markets affect investment decisions in the economy?

The Role of Capital Markets

In capital markets, funds are exchanged under contractual arrangements through institutions such as investment houses and financial institutions. The activities in capital markets enhance the efficiency of the financial transactions in three ways.

First, financial markets allow individuals to diversify risks by selling claims in some projects in favour of other assets to minimize the riskiness of their investments. Risk imposes a cost on investors in that they would be willing to pay to avoid such risks or accept an investment with a lower rate of return. For an individual to hold an asset, the return, net of the cost of risk, would have to be equal to the "safe" rate of return on an asset. Economists like to think of two types of risk diversification: risk-pooling and risk-spreading. Risk-pooling (Vickrey, 1960) is achieved by investors holding investments that have returns that are uncorrelated or offset each other (e.g., hedging) so risks are reduced if not altogether eliminated. Risk-spreading arises by selling assets to a large number of individuals so each person's share of the asset's risk, independent of other risks, becomes negligible (Arrow and Lind, 1970). One might think of a person's investment in a financial institution as a similar case in which risks are spread over a large number of bond and stock owners.

The second is that financial markets reduce search costs of matching lenders and borrowers. Stock, bond, commodity, option and foreign exchanges facilitate transactions at a low cost for lenders and borrowers by efficiently handling market transactions. Without these markets, individuals seeking funds would have to spend significantly more time and resources finding other investors in informal markets.

Third, financial traders and institutions in markets minimize informational costs faced by savers seeking new investments. There are two costs associated with informational asymmetries: adverse selection (Akerlof, 1970) and moral hazard (Arrow, 1965). Adverse selection arises from the lack of knowledge that outside investors might have about the quality of investments which is better known by an insider who is borrowing the funds. Moral hazard arises from insiders taking actions that are of non-pecuniary value to them and that reduce the expected amount of profits paid to outside investors. To overcome informational asymmetries, investors expend resources in developing financial contracts that minimize the effects of informational asymmetries on markets (e.g., bond covenants) or better monitor firms. An important role of financial markets is to allow financial transactions to be completed with reduced monitoring, signalling and screening costs.[2] Financial markets and institutions provide mechanisms that help reduce information costs, including research departments of investment houses and information regarding the quality of borrowers.

Capital Markets, the Cost of Capital and Investment

The above discussion points to the importance of capital markets in providing an efficient mechanism for the exchange of funds among borrowers and lenders. This efficiency translates into lower finance costs. What effect, therefore, does the cost of finance have on the economy? The efficiency of capital markets has two important impacts.

First, savers who lend money are able to do so at lower cost, resulting in a higher rate of return on assets. With a higher rate of return on savings, investors are willing to postpone their current consumption for future purposes such as providing income for retirement and contingencies. Increased savings also result in more Canadian ownership of assets, thereby reducing international indebtedness and interest rates (a significant issue for Canada which is highly reliant on foreign capital to fund both private and public debt).

Second, borrowers face a lower cost of funds as a result of efficiency in capital markets. A lower cost of funds results in a lower cost of capital which can encourage more investments. Investment, in turn, increases the productive capacity of the economy and its ability to achieve economic growth.

The research prepared for the Industry Canada conference concentrates on capital market issues related primarily to investment and the financing of firms. The role of government policy in affecting savings and portfolio investment decisions of individuals is not a focus for discussion below. However, it is useful to remember that efficiency in capital markets is not only beneficial to businesses but also to individuals.

Economic evidence regarding the impact of the cost of capital on investment and economic growth is mixed. Recent research using panel data sets of individual firms over time has tended to show larger impacts of the cost of capital on investment as in the case of the paper by Chirinko and Meyer prepared for this volume.

It would be appropriate, at this point, to define more carefully the cost of capital. The cost of capital is of special interest since firms will invest in capital until the rate of return is equal to the cost of holding the last (marginal) unit of capital. The cost of capital term plays an important part in policy discussions since it is related to investment and long-run economic growth.

Economists, beginning with Jorgenson (1963) have linked investment expenditure to the *user cost of capital* which is the cost of capital gross of depreciation, financing, risk and tax costs. The user cost of capital can be broadly defined to include four components.

- **Economic Depreciation:** Economic depreciation is the cost of replacing capital due to wear and tear net of the anticipated real capital gains arising from holding assets. More formally, economic depreciation is the difference between the value of an asset in the previous period less the value of the asset in the current period. Under this definition, assets such as land also "depreciate" since land prices may be uncertain.

- **Cost of Financing Capital:** This is the weighted average cost of debt and equity finance obtained from capital markets.[3] The cost of debt is interest expense, adjusted for inflation. The cost of debt finance is also adjusted to take taxation into account (discussed further below). The cost of equity finance is the opportunity cost of shareholder funds that could be invested in a riskless alternative asset (risk is an additional cost discussed below). The cost of finance, in principle, will also be affected by informational asymmetries, transaction costs and the cost of bankruptcy that will affect the interest rates and the opportunity cost of debt finance. Moreover, if firms are constrained from borrowing in markets, the effective cost of finance may be greater than the observed cost.

- **The Cost of Risk:** The cost of risk is the pecuniary measure of uncertainty faced by capital owners of the firm. An investor will hold both risky and riskless assets if the risk-adjusted rate of return on both assets are equal. Thus, to invest in a risky asset, the asset must offer a higher expected rate of return than a riskless asset; the difference between the expected rate of return on the risky asset and the rate of return on the riskless asset is the monetary compensation for risk as determined by markets.

  The cost of risk depends on its source and affects the user cost of capital in different ways.[4] Capital risk is related to uncertainty in capital good prices and depreciation (Bulow and Summers, 1984); income risk is related to uncertainty with respect to gross income earned on investments; financial risk is associated with uncertainties related to debt liabilities; irreversibility risk (Dixit and Pindyck, 1994; and McKenzie, 1994) arises from the effects on uncertainty on the value of capital that cannot be sold off in secondary markets (sunk capital); and political risk is related to uncertainty in public policies such as monetary and tax policies.

  Some types of risk, such as income and capital risk, are easily observed so investors can engage in financial transactions in markets to avoid risk (e.g., hedging). Other types of risk, such as irreversibility and political risk, are more difficult to measure and therefore less diversifiable in financial markets.

- **Tax Policy Variables:** Taxes affect the cost of capital in a number of ways.[5] The corporate income tax is assessed as a rate multiplied by a base. The amount of tax payable is reduced by corporate income tax credits. The base is equal to gross income net of salaries and wages, material expenses, capital cost allowances (tax depreciation), investment allowances, inventory expenses, interest expenses and the application of prior years' losses.[6] Corporate income tax credits include investment tax credits (a percentage of gross investment expenditure is deducted from tax paid) and research and development tax credits. Effectively, the corporate income tax falls on the operating income (gross of economic depreciation), thereby increasing the user cost of capital. The corporate income tax will, however, reduce the effective cost of purchasing capital goods by the tax value of capital consumption allowances, investment allowances and investment tax credits. Corporate income taxes also reduce the cost of debt finance since interest, unadjusted for inflation, is deductible as an expense from income.

In addition to the corporate income tax, other taxes will affect the cost of capital. Personal income taxes on capital gains, dividends and interest income may increase the cost of financing although this depends on the degree to which firms borrow from international capital markets. If Canadian firms obtain their financing at the margin from international markets, then Canadian personal taxes may have none or a limited impact on the cost of finance. Instead, the relevant personal tax rates that affect the Canadian cost of capital may be those of some international investor. Annual capital taxes on gross assets, property taxes and excise or sales on capital goods will increase the effective purchasing cost of capital. Minimum taxes, withholding taxes and foreign taxes (as they interact with Canadian taxes) will also affect the cost of capital. On the other hand, government subsidies associated with infrastructure, loan guarantee programs and capital subsidies will lower the cost of capital.

As mentioned above, the user cost of capital is measured gross of depreciation and risk costs which is appropriate for determining how investments are affected by the various economic variables (as in Chirinko and Meyer's paper). Conceptually, firms will invest in different types of capital projects until the net of tax return on investment, after adjusting for depreciation and risk, is equal to the riskless after-tax cost of finance. In other situations, the cost of capital is measured as the user cost of capital net of depreciation but gross of risk and taxes. This is sensible if one wishes to consider explicitly how risk as well as finance and taxes comparatively affect investment decisions across industries or countries facing differential risk (e.g., the Ando, Hancock and Sawchuk, and Jog papers in this volume). However, if one only wishes to compare the effects of taxes on investments (by measuring the effective tax rate on capital), then only the rate of return on capital, net of risk and depreciation but gross of taxes, would be compared across assets (Chen and McKenzie's paper in this volume).

The first several papers prepared for this conference provide information on the cost of capital for Canada. Although the results are somewhat tentative due to data limitations, the Chirinko and Meyer paper suggests that investment decisions are relatively sensitive to the user cost of capital, sales growth and cash flow of firms. Their results are not inconsistent with recent empirical work in the United States and United Kingdom which finds that the user cost of capital and taxes affect investment decisions (Mintz, 1995). Higher user costs of capital are found to reduce investment, sales growth increases the demand for investment and the cash flow of a firm is suggested to be a cheap source of finance that allows for more investment. (Of course, the latter might suggest some inefficiency in capital markets due to asymmetric information.) The user cost of capital is found to have a significant effect on investment (in a statistical sense) for most industries. The cash flow of firms also affects capital investment while sales growth, which is correlated with cash flow, has a smaller impact on investment.

Comparisons of the cost of capital are made by the Ando, Hancock and Sawchuk, and Jog papers. The Ando, Hancock and Sawchuk paper actually measures the before tax rate of return on capital, adjusted for inflation. In principle, the rate of return on capital should be equal to the cost of capital at the margin. However, the approach of measuring the average rate of return on capital may not provide the same answer as measuring the marginal rate of return on capital (the latter is equal to the cost of capital once a firm has chosen its optimal capital stock). One suspects that average rates of return on capital may not be equal to the marginal return if firms earn above normal rates of return on capital ("economic rents" as in the case of resource industries) or the tax paid for marginal investments differs from the average tax rate. The Ando, Hancock and Sawchuk comparison of Canada, Japan and the United States suggests the before tax rate of return on capital is lowest in Japan while roughly comparable in the United States and Canada in recent years.

The Jog paper on the sectoral cost of capital uses a different approach by measuring the gross of risk cost of financing capital (net of the tax savings associated with interest deductions for debt finance). This measure is only one part of the user cost of capital as explained above (the cost of finance plus risk). Only one part of the tax system is included in the measure (taxes saved by interest deductibility) so the measure provides a rather strange conclusion that countries with higher statutory tax rates have lower costs of capital, with all else equal.[7] Nonetheless, the measure is still helpful since it does help capture the financial cost of capital, including risk.

Jog's conclusions are that some industries, particularly utilities and real estate, have the highest financial cost of capital; the financial cost of capital has increased somewhat since 1989 but especially in 1994; and Canada has a higher financial cost of capital than the United States primarily due to risk. The high cost of capital for utilities is somewhat surprising since these industries are often regulated so they are guaranteed a certain rate of return on capital (thereby being riskless in this sense). However, in terms of variability of the stock relative to the market, these industries are relatively risky. The higher risk for Canadian industries compared to U.S. industries may reflect political risk, but Jog is not in a position to determine the source of risk in Canada.

The third set of results is found in the Chen and McKenzie paper on effective tax rates on capital. To compute these rates, the researcher must empirically measure the user cost of capital for all components, including taxes, risk and depreciation. Chen and McKenzie examine the effective tax rate on different types of investment in provinces and across countries, using alternative assumptions regarding financial arbitrage, risk, foreign ownership and irreversibility of investment. The most important conclusion is that Canada's effective tax rate on capital in 1995 is higher than in the United States (somewhat comparable for manufacturing). This is consistent with earlier years when Canada's effective tax rate on capital was higher as calculated by the Organization for Economic Co-operation and Development (OECD, 1991) and McKenzie and Mintz (1992).

Effective tax rates have declined slightly in recent years for two reasons: much lower inflation rates that have contributed to a lower effective tax rate on inventories and a decline in corporate income tax rates for manufacturing. There are still substantial variations of effective tax rates across industries in Canada: mining industries enjoy negative effective tax rates (negative rates imply firms have tax losses to shelter other sources of income from taxes) and the oil and gas industry is highly taxed (due to the royalty system). Small firms are less highly taxed than large firms primarily due to the small business deduction. Firms facing capital risk due to uncertain economic depreciation are taxed much more highly than firms that do not face such uncertainty.

One can cautiously derive several conclusions from the above research prepared for Industry Canada. There is some evidence that the cost of capital does affect investment in a substantial way. Some industries, such as mining, face greater risk in terms of irreversibilities of investment, yet the Chen and McKenzie results suggest that these industries are least-taxed. It seems that Canada's cost of capital is higher than in the United States as found by Jog, but the effective tax rate on capital may now be lower than in the United States. However, none of these approaches is brought together to provide an overall measure of the cost of capital, properly including taxes and risk to see if Canadian investments are facing a major disadvantage relative to investment made abroad.

One point that is not well articulated in any of these papers is the impact of political uncertainty on the cost of capital. Yet, political uncertainty associated with government fiscal deficits and the Quebec question may result in a cost imposed on Canadian investment expenditures. The cost goes beyond the measure of interest rates on Canada's debt. It includes, for example, the "option" cost associated with the irreversibility of investment, as discussed in the Chen and McKenzie paper: firms may wait to determine how Canada resolves its fiscal and political problems before making risky investments. Unfortunately, uncertainties due to government decisions are not easy to capture without a more formal understanding of the impact of political decisions on variables such as rates of tax, inflation and interest rates.

The Efficiency of Capital Markets

To understand the role of government policy, one has to consider first whether capital markets are inefficient. As discussed in the previous section, market efficiency depends on various costs that can affect the financing and investment decisions of firms. These costs include transaction costs, informational asymmetries and government policies themselves such as taxes and financial regulations. For now, we only consider inefficiencies related to "market failure" rather than government policy (the latter is considered in the next section).

The inefficiency of capital markets has been subject to considerable debate in the literature. Originally, many analysts took the view that markets were efficient in that investors could fully diversify portfolio risks in a costless world with information revealed through the prices of assets. In later years, with a large body of literature devoted to the analysis of taxes, transaction costs and informational asymmetries, it was recognized that capital markets may not be fully efficient. Nonetheless, although market failures may arise (further discussed below), there is no reason to expect that economies could ever do better in the presence of such inefficiencies. Thus, economists have developed the notion of "constrained" efficiency which implies that certain barriers, such as transaction and information costs, cannot be avoided so efficiency must be evaluated in relation to such imperfections.

There are several "market failures" that could result in imperfections in capital markets. First, transaction costs, especially of a fixed nature, may be sufficiently large that some segments of capital markets cannot obtain financing from institutional and individual lenders. Second, according to one view, there may be substantial economies of scale in banking and other financial intermediary activity leading to too few lenders with "market power" in certain parts of the capital market where entry might be restricted (e.g., lending to small businesses). Third, certain private activities may benefit or harm other persons or firms who are not responsible for the activity but cannot be excluded from its effects. Economists refer to these cases as "externalities." When there are positive externalities, too little activity is undertaken (since the originator is not compensated for benefits accruing to others) and, when there are negative externalities, too much activity is carried out as the originator does not bear the cost imposed on others. Fourth, informational asymmetries might result in some markets breaking down entirely (e.g., venture capital markets) or informational barriers that are prohibitive resulting in segmented capital markets. In particular, some firms, such as smaller companies, may have difficulty obtaining equity and debt financing for assets of a unique nature that are not traded in capital markets and are, hence, illiquid. A more detailed discussion of these "market failures" in relation to capital market issues is provided below.

Fixed transaction costs are a matter of technology. Given recent innovations, many transactions, once considered too costly to make, have been achievable. This point particularly applies to foreign asset transactions. As discussed by Edey and Hviding (1995), cross-border financial transactions have increased sevenfold as a percentage of GDP from 1980 to 1990, largely reflecting improved technology. Although, as pointed out by French and Poterba (1991), most equity is owned domestically rather than by foreigners, transactions of foreign equities have increased dramatically, particularly through mutual funds. Of course, mutual funds are an institutional response to the transaction costs that are inherent with financial transactions.

The existence of imperfect competition in financial markets has been subject to a long debate in Canada going back to discussions preceding various decennial *Bank Act* reviews. Canada has always had a limited number of chartered banks that have serviced business lending, consumer lending, mortgage, deposit taking and foreign exchange markets although the opening of Canadian markets to foreign entry has improved competition especially in wholesale markets. It has been largely accepted that large borrowers and lenders face very competitive markets since they have access to various types of financial intermediaries in Canada and abroad. Economies of scale in the provision of capital to large firms are not a significant factor. Whether there is sufficient competition in small business lending and retail deposit markets has been subject to much more controversial debate. Past studies have supported different views regarding the state of competition in small business lending and retail deposit markets.[8] Although it might be argued that there is insufficient competition in small business and retail markets, many analysts have argued that this may be more a result of government regulatory policy than of economies of scale in banking. (The Economic Council of Canada [1976] argued for the expansion of powers for all types of financial intermediaries and the entry of foreign banks to promote competition.)

Externalities, such as those associated with information acquisition and research and development, suggest that firms may undertake too little activity leading to market inefficiencies. Externalities can be "internalized" in the private sector if firms or individuals create a "price" system that ensures that firms bearing the cost are properly compensated by others who benefit from the activity. However, without contracts that are costly to put into effect, firms, on their own may not internalize the externalities. Thus, it is often suggested that governments should provide subsidies or regulate industries to ensure that externalities are internalized. In terms of the financial sector, information gathered on companies provides a service to investors which may not be appropriated by the firms through the sale of such information. Thus, the firm may try to keep such information "private." The size of the financial firm obtaining the information may reduce the costs of acquisition and internalize externalities. The desire to internalize externalities provides incentives for financial institutions to share information or simply become larger.

The presence of information asymmetries is perhaps the most important issue that has been raised as a cause of inefficiencies in capital markets. As discussed earlier, the existence of adverse selection or moral hazard may cause some parts of capital markets to fail. Beginning with Akerlof's lemon problem (1970), it has been argued that "bad" firms may chase out "good" firms from markets in the case of adverse selection. For example, suppose that owners know whether their own firm is a good or a bad prospect for investment but outsiders only know the distribution of types of investments. If prices of assets are determined by the average quality of investments, then only the bad investments would issue securities since the good investments would be vastly underpriced. Markets would fail in that investors would know that only bad firms would issue securities. Thus, as discussed by Myers and Majluf (1984), new equity and risky debt markets could break down with firms investing capital up to the amount of cash flow available to them.

As later pointed out in the literature, markets may overcome the lemons problem in two ways. Borrowers may use signals to indicate quality (e.g., the share of the insider's investment to total investment, dividend policy or the debt-equity ratio) or lenders may screen different types of firms to determine their true types (e.g., requiring certain conditions as part of contracts such as bond covenants or the payment of non-interest fees as well as interest). Myers and Majluf, for example, argue that those firms that issue more costly new equity will be considered to be of poorer quality, and Miller and Rock (1985) suggest that firms that issue dividends that are costly (for tax and other reasons) will be considered to be of higher quality.

One of the important results of the asymmetric information literature in the presence of signalling and screening is that markets will at best be "constrained" efficient. The existence of bad firms will impose a cost on good firms. For example, in the Akerlof-type problem, a good firm will try to separate itself from a bad firm by issuing a costly signal. For signalling to be successful, the cost of the signal must be greater for the bad firm compared to the good firm (otherwise the bad firm can duplicate what the good firm does and look like a good firm). In what is called a "separating equilibrium," a good firm will issue more of the signal than the bad firm to indicate higher quality (Spence, 1973; and Rothschild and Stiglitz, 1976). But, the good firms lose profits by relying on a costly signal to indicate quality. For example, good firms may issue more highly taxed dividends (Battacharya, 1979) or debt that increases the probability of bankruptcy (Ross, 1977).

Several of the research papers prepared for Industry Canada deal specifically with the issue of imperfections in capital markets. Two of the papers, one by Amit, Brander and Zott, and the other by MacIntosh, explicitly consider the effects of imperfections in venture capital markets. Jog examines initial public offerings (IPOs); Mittoo examines segmentation in U.S. and Canadian capital markets; and Suret and L'Her examine the determinants of financing decisions of Canadian companies from 1963 to 1993.

The Amit, Brander and Zott, and MacIntosh papers provide some analysis of interesting data recently collected on venture capital firms in Canada. These firms have been of particular interest lately for several reasons. First, they tend to be innovative and engaged in research and development. Thus, it is argued that there are important research and development externalities associated with venture capital investments: policies should be used to encourage research and development beyond what would be achieved by the market. Second, venture capital firms tend to be small firms first created by an entrepreneur who needs both financial capital and business organizational skills. However, given the lack of knowledge outsiders would have with respect to the success of a project and their ability to monitor the firm, entrepreneurs may have difficulty finding sympathetic lenders. Third, new inventions tend to be very risky since there is a great deal of uncertainty as to whether a project will be successful or not.

The overall conclusion reached by the Amit, Brander and Zott and MacIntosh studies is that venture capital investments are highly risky: they involve very high returns (major "hits") and a large number of failures. Thus, if any market should be subject to informational asymmetries, it would involve the venture capital market. The two papers also indicate that venture capital lending comes from one or a few partners who are specialists that help organize the firm after initial start-up as a private company. Most of the financing is in the form of equity although debt may be relied on in later stages. Also, Canadian venture capitalists tend to exit through management or company buyouts rather than IPOs or third party acquisitions.

Do these observations confirm the existence of substantial informational asymmetries? Amit, Brander and Zott provide some evidence of the importance of moral hazard – the greater the share of the entrepreneur's ownership of the firm (and the lower the venture capitalist's) the more likely it is that that firm will perform better in terms of profits.[9] The large number of company and management buyouts by participating partners and fewer IPOs as forms of exit for venture capitalists might suggest that informational costs are reduced by this form of exit. However, the low number of IPOs compared to the United States is a puzzle. No conclusions are provided although it is well known that the tax system in Canada has a number of features that discourage companies from going public.[10]

Jog's paper on IPOs examines the pricing of new securities at the time when a company first becomes public. Consistent with many studies, Jog finds that IPOs are found to be underpriced although the degree of underpricing in Canada is not that much different from in the United States and is lower in recent years compared to the past. The underpricing of IPOs is linked to informational asymmetries. The entrepreneurs know the quality of the firm but outside investors do not; thus, as predicted by Myers and Majluf, prices of new equities are bid down as a result of outside investors believing that only the poorer quality firms go to the market. This informational asymmetry imposes a cost on IPOs as a source of finance. This is in addition to Jog's reported underwriting cost of 6 percent to 7 percent of IPO market value. More intriguing, however, is Jog's conclusion that IPOs long-run performance (relative to past performance and the rest of the market) has been poor. There is no easy explanation given. One possibility is that IPOs tend to be "lemon" type companies with poorer prospects compared to firms that stay private. As Jog reports, the main reason firms go public is a result of liquidity shortages. In a "separating" equilibrium that is exactly what one would predict, poorer quality firms would issue more new equity while cash-flow-rich firms would be less willing to go public. However, if this is the case, then security prices of IPOs should be well underpriced compared to the average firm in the market, and the long-run performance should be similar to the market. However, there could be other factors explaining the long-run poor performance of IPOs, including tax factors referred to above.

The paper by Mittoo provides additional evidence using seasoned equity issues (for the period 1982 to 1993) that there appears to be some segmentation between Canadian and U.S. equity markets. When new issues are made and the investment level is fixed, one expects share prices to fall as a result of the "dilution" effect whereby new equity issues reduce the earnings per share of existing owners. Although shares of companies listed on both U.S. and Canadian stock exchanges have similar experiences (as one would expect for non-segmented markets), companies that list only on Canadian markets have a different experience compared to companies in the United States. It seems that the price of equities falls more dramatically for Canadian companies which suggests that the cost of new equity finance is higher in Canada. Mittoo's conclusion regarding segmentation is based on the size of the Canadian market: share prices in the presence of new issues fall more for those companies that only rely on Canadian market absorption. This raises two questions. First, firms could easily avoid the smallness of the Canadian market by listing in the United States – so why not do so? Second, if there are profits to be had, why should there not be more foreign participation in Canadian markets? Perhaps, smaller firms that do not list in U.S. markets are too small to satisfy requirements for listing or more subject to the "lemons" problem discussed above so their share prices fall more. Alternatively, as speculated by Mittoo, government regulatory and tax policies may interfere with equity markets and cause segmentation. This point will be further discussed below.

The paper by Suret and L'Her deals with debt financing by Canadian companies and provides two interesting conclusions. The first is that Canadian debt-equity ratios did not rise during the 1980s unlike in the United States where, during the same period, firms became less capitalized with the tremendous surge in leveraged buyouts. Thus, Canadian companies during the 1980s did not become more risky in terms of undercapitalization. The second result is that debt decisions are particularly affected by growth and pre-tax profits (gross of interest expense) as shown in many recent empirical studies. Growth creates more demand for debt relative to retained earnings and new equity (which is less desirable to issue), and pre-tax profits reduce the amount of debt finance. Both these observations are partly consistent with the asymmetric information stories: cash flow of firms reduces the need to seek outside sources of finance, and growth requires firms to obtain more outside finance. However, there is still an issue as to why risky debt is more preferable than new equity finance since the lack of information of outside investors affects the pricing of both risky debt and equity finance. One usually argues that risky debt may be preferred given the deductibility of interest expense for corporate tax purposes, but the authors suggest that taxes do not influence debt decisions. There are problems, however, with their measure of the tax variables that would likely result in the lack of correlation between taxes and debt decisions.[11]

The overwhelming conclusion one derives from these five studies prepared for Industry Canada is the importance of informational asymmetries between inside and outside investors in determining financial decisions and the pricing of securities. Thus, one can conclude that there is a "market failure" in that poor quality firms cause good quality firms to choose suboptimal or costly financial and investment strategies that reduce profitability.

Even with investment houses and financial institutions, it may not be possible to overcome informational asymmetries altogether. However, as noted above, "market failures" arising from imperfect information can be "constrained efficient" in that no other institutional response could achieve a better allocation of resources.

Note that the studies discussed in Section I of the conference on the user cost of capital are unrelated to the studies discussed in Section II on the efficiency of capital markets. The reason for this is that few if any studies have considered how informational asymmetries empirically affect the user cost of capital. We know that informational asymmetries result in firms giving up investment projects that would otherwise be profitable. However, the theory used to measure the cost of capital of firms ignores the possibility that informational asymmetries might cause the cost of capital to be greater.

The question that is critical for policy analysts is the following. Even if there are "market failures," what should the government do about them? The notion of "constrained" efficiency comes back to haunt us at this point – it might be that governments cannot achieve anything at all to improve the performance of capital markets. This is discussion left to the next section.

The Role of Government Policy

There are two general views that might be taken with respect to the role of government in enhancing the efficiency of capital markets. The first is that government intervention is needed in capital markets to overcome "market failures" (thus there are "good" government policies). The success of public policy ultimately depends on the information and policy instruments available to governments to improve efficiency in capital markets. The second view is that capital markets are efficient in a "constrained" sense: the role of public policy is to avoid impairing the efficiency of capital markets. Given this view, one wishes to avoid "bad" policy that interferes with the efficiency of capital markets so reform would result in fewer barriers to efficiency in capital markets.

This section initially concentrates on the first issue: what is the role, if any, of government policy in the presence of market failures? If government policy is unsuccessful, then the second view – eliminating public policy barriers to efficiency – is more clear. In this second case, the role of government policy is to eliminate, as much as possible, unjustified policies that hinder the efficiency of capital markets.

As discussed in the previous section, potential "market failures" are associated with information asymmetries and transaction costs that might result in inefficient transactions or, in some cases, the breakdown of markets. The most significant result predicted by various theories, as well as the evidence supporting them, is that firms, particularly with good prospects, will underinvest in capital due to financing constraints. Thus, the lack of venture capital, IPOs and cross-national equity transactions and the overreliance on debt financing are "ills" that result in too little investment. Government policy, as the argument goes, can be used to correct for underinvestment by subsidizing those financial transactions that are undersupplied.

It should first be noted that private markets have created institutions that have tried to minimize or eliminate altogether any potential imperfections, sanctioned by law. For example, licensing requirements for members of a profession, stock exchange, etc. are used to exclude poor quality firms from entering the market. However, a group of members that restricts membership has two objectives: create confidence in its products or services and earn profits. When members restrict entry, they may choose qualifications that are too onerous in order to limit competition. A public body, however, would, in principle, be interested in economic welfare. Thus, public control over conditions for entry into an industry may allow for more competition while still limiting free entry.

Governments use several types of policy instruments to overcome the underinvestment problem.

- **Regulation of Securities Markets and Financial Intermediaries:** To encourage investors to provide capital to firms, especially those with good prospects, governments may require firms to satisfy certain qualifications in order to limit the entry of poor quality and, even worse, fraudulent firms. These regulations include restrictions on the types of firms that list on stock exchanges, qualifications for firms to operate as financial institutions and the development of consumer protection laws to encourage confidence in the market. Regulations may require that firms have a certain minimum level of equity investment and a historical record of profitability to issue stocks, provide full disclosure regarding assets and income and satisfy a certain degree of capitalization (as in the case of financial and insurance institutions). Some regulations may actually be used to force financial lenders to hold certain types of assets in the interest of certain public policy objectives (e.g., foreign content rules for pension plans have been in place on equity investments in Canadian companies).

- **Taxes and Subsidies:** Instead of governments regulating industries, they may choose to provide subsidies or tax incentives to encourage more investment or equity financing. Subsidies or investment tax credits (e.g., research and development) may be given for capital expenditures as in the case of regional development programs. Alternatively, grants or tax incentives may be provided for the purchase of equity (such as stock savings plans, venture capital funds and flow-through shares).
- **Favourable Interest Lending:** Alternatively, governments have improved access to financing by making interest rates on loans more favourable to borrowers. Lower interest costs are achieved by direct subsidies through public lending programs, loan guarantee programs and tax preferences (e.g., exempting interest on loans to small business).

As a result of informational asymmetries, good quality firms will underinvest in capital since the cost of finance is driven up by the existence of bad quality firms. The question is whether the above public policies that are used to correct for market imperfections can improve the efficiency of capital markets. Although governments may pave the road with good intentions, they may lead the economy down the wrong road. This view of public policy may be stated unfairly but does emphasize the problems that arise when governments intervene in capital markets to correct for underinvestment in the presence of informational asymmetries.

To illustrate this point,[12] consider a group of firms that are facing constraints or higher costs when seeking financing from outside investors. As a result of underinvestment, a government might wish to subsidize firms in the industry. However, governments, as outsiders, are likely to have less information than private lenders in determining which type of borrower is of good or bad quality. If governments did have perfect information, they could clearly separate the good from the bad quality firms and only provide subsidies to the best firms.[13] The best governments can do is to use whatever information is available to them to determine the degree of, and conditions for, subsidization. In many cases, the government is likely unable to discriminate good from poor quality borrowers.

Now suppose the government does wish to subsidize investments or financing to overcome the underinvestment problem. The availability of the subsidy will promote more investment and/or financing by good quality firms which would invest in more assets, closer to a socially optimal amount of capital. However, the presence of the subsidy would encourage low quality firms to invest in too much capital[14] or result in the entry of new firms that are also of low quality. Thus, the subsidy, while beneficial to the high quality firms, could result in too much investment in poor quality projects. Governments could minimize the social cost of subsidies by using certain qualifications that exclude poor quality firms (e.g., minimum capital size or history of profits). However, satisfaction of these conditions could result in some firms of relatively good quality being excluded from public programs.

A more difficult question is to determine which type of subsidy is best to use. The best public policy is one that is directed at a particular market failure. In the case of informational asymmetries, the issue is whether the market failure is underinvestment or insufficient funding from outside investors. Governments could subsidize investments (e.g., an investment tax credit) or subsidize new equity or risky debt finance (e.g., flow-through shares or stock savings plans, loan guarantee programs, etc.). Which subsidy would be better: an investment or external financing subsidy?

The answer is somewhat complicated. If good firms separate from bad firms by a costly "signal" (e.g., the share of internal resources as a percentage of investment), an investment subsidy increases the internal cash flow of good and poor quality firms, reducing their need to issue equity or debt to outside investors. The investment subsidy allows higher quality firms to expand investment and reduce their reliance on issuing costly securities (if these are issued at all) to outside investors. Thus, the higher quality firms are able to separate themselves at less cost from the low quality firms. On the other hand, an external financing incentive reduces the cost of issuing securities to outside investors for both high and low quality firms. Low quality firms rely more on external finance so they benefit more from the equity subsidy compared to the high quality firms. But, underinvestment is more severe for high quality firms. Thus, the equity incentive is less efficient than the investment subsidy in mitigating the underinvestment problem. Given this theory, an investment tax credit is better than a subsidy for equity finance.

Policy Prescription No. 1: In the face of informational asymmetries between outside and inside investors, the optimal policy is to subsidize the activity that is not being sufficiently undertaken and tax the costly signal being used to indicate quality.

As an example, the issue of new equity may be a signal of quality. To improve the allocation of resources, governments should provide an investment tax credit that is financed by a tax on new equity issues. This policy prescription is opposite to what is often the case. For example, Canadian governments have provided tax incentives to issue equity (e.g., flow-through shares) to encourage investments by smaller companies but at the cost of increasing the tax on the investment.

It is important to remember that government tax incentives and subsidies may be given without sufficient monitoring of investments. Thus, the incentives could encourage inappropriate behaviour by firms (moral hazard), which would result in other inefficiencies besides the signalling issues discussed above.

The application of information asymmetry theories to public policy issues in capital markets and empirical work is virgin territory for public policy analysts. Therefore, several of the research papers prepared for Industry Canada provide very useful contributions in terms of specifying the success or failure of public policies used to improve efficiency in capital markets in the presence of asymmetric information.

The intriguing paper by Suret and Cormier on Quebec Stock Saving Plans (QSSPs) provides a perspective on the problem of savings incentives as a means of providing more financial capital to small and medium-sized businesses. Initially, the Quebec government provided credits for the purchase of equities issued by Quebec-based companies for firms of all sizes. Most savings were then directed at large public companies with access to Canadian and international markets rather than at smaller companies. It seems that the large companies did not invest more; instead, dividend payments increased. Later rules restricted the QSSP program to smaller-sized and undercapitalized businesses. After all, it is the financing of new public and under-capitalized companies that would be most subject to problems associated with informational asymmetries. As Suret and Cormier suggest, the experience investors had with these investments was disappointing in terms of profitability. One could surmise from this experience that the QSSP encouraged too many "losers" to expand or start up even though it assisted some winners to develop.

A similar story could perhaps be told with Labour-Sponsored Venture Capital Funds (LSVCFs). As discussed at the conference by Vaillancourt, Brûlé, Jovanovic and Trottier, federal and provincial governments have provided tax credits of up to 40 percent of the cost of the securities issued by a federal or provincially regulated LSVCF to individual investors in Quebec (the recent federal budget has reduced the federal credit from 20 percent to 15 percent). Shares must be held for a minimum number of years for the taxpayer to maintain the tax benefit. As a result of LSVCFs, a substantial pool of savings has developed for venture capital (see the papers on venture capital in this volume). The question is how successful these funds have been since many funds are seeking venture capital opportunities (a significant portion of new funds is held as treasury bills). Vaillancourt et al. suggest that employment effects have been small, largely reflecting the fact that LSVCFs, which are relatively new, have not invested their funds fully in venture capital investments. However, the experience of LSVCFs (Quebec-based funds began in 1984 but the federal credit only began in the early 1990s) is perhaps too early to determine since it could take up to 10 years before the profits from venture capital funds are earned.

Policy Prescription No. 2: Governments should avoid subsidizing equity investments. Instead, the policy should be directed at encouraging real investment activity.

Robinson's paper on the Alberta Stock Exchange provides some documentation on how listing requirements can affect the performance of stock markets. The Alberta Stock Exchange has the least stringent listing requirements in Canada. A Junior Capital Pool (JCP) program allows entrepreneurs with a minimum $100,000 to obtain $400,000 in funds from outside investors. The firm must undertake an asset acquisition within 18 months to become a regularly listed firm on the exchange. Therefore, one would expect that informational asymmetries associated with equity financing by newly created public companies to be particularly important in these markets. Robinson found that almost all JCP firms became listed members (therefore, an asset acquisition was made) but the failure rate (eventual delisting due to bankruptcy) was 25.8 percent. Although this failure rate is not out of line with the U.S. experience for venture capital firms, it is unclear, without more data, whether the JCP firms provided returns to investors to compensate them fully for the risk involved with their investments. However, the experience of JCP programs suggests that regulations can have an important effect on markets.

Policy Prescriptions No. 3: Regulations can play an important role in building confidence by investors in financial markets. Attempts should be made to differentiate markets according to quality.

Riding examines loan guarantee programs for small businesses. Under these programs, the government provides a guarantee on loans made by banks to small businesses. A 2 percent fee as a percentage of the loan principal is paid by firms and is collected by the government to cover the default costs of the program. As the government picks up the default cost of the guarantee, there is an issue as to whether the program results in default rates that are excessive by attracting too many firms of poor quality. The Canadian program has a relatively low default rate (4 percent to 6 percent) by international standards, largely as a result of the contractual arrangements made under the program. The government guarantees 90 percent of the cost of the loan as long as the interest rate charged by the lender is no more than prime plus 1.75 percent. Thus, lenders have some incentive to choose borrowers that are less likely to go bankrupt. A higher interest rate on loans or a greater percentage of the amounts guaranteed would increase defaults significantly. Therefore, the design of a program can mitigate the revenue cost faced by the government although fewer firms would have access to funding.

Policy Prescription No. 4: Any government policy that interferes in markets should be designed to minimize inefficiencies. For example, insurance premiums should be related to experience so beneficiaries of insurance will pay for some of the cost imposed by their own actions.

Government policies, however, often create barriers for capital markets rather than improving economic performance. Examples of barriers that reduce the efficiency of capital markets are plentifold. They include restrictions on pension and registered retirement savings plans to hold foreign assets; restrictions on foreign ownership of certain industries; taxes that discourage savings and investments in industries; premium-based deposit insurance that is unrelated to risks; and limitations to entry in particular parts of financial markets (insurance, banking, etc.). Governments could improve the efficiency of markets by changing regulations and tax structures. Sometimes these regulations and taxes are desirable for other social objectives although the reasons for adopting such policies may become less important now compared to when they were initially put into place (such as increasing Canadian ownership of industry).

Policy Prescription No. 5: Governments should review regulatory and tax policies with the aim of determining which policies impede the efficiency of markets and could be eliminated since they no longer serve a useful purpose.

The above papers exemplify the issues involved with the public programs that try to overcome the informational problems that are so characteristic of capital markets. The overall conclusions reached by the research undertaken for Industry Canada is that public policies should be very carefully designed to minimize the costs associated with any programs designed to improve the efficiency of markets. Otherwise, the cure may be worse than the illness. When policies are poorly designed, governments may create barriers for achieving capital market efficiency rather than enhancing performance.

CONCLUSIONS

THE ABOVE REVIEW PROVIDES SOME OVERRIDING CONCLUSIONS regarding the role of governments in capital markets. Clearly, governments affect capital markets through taxation and regulatory policies. Whether these policies are necessary to change the performance of capital markets is a more debatable issue. The research undertaken for Industry Canada provides several general conclusions.

- Public policies do affect the cost of capital and investment decisions of firms.
- The tax system affects the user cost of capital in an important way.
- Canada's cost of capital seems higher than in the United States primarily due to risk. However, risk is measured using fluctuations in the returns on assets held by owners rather than riskiness associated with specific economic and political variables. Thus, it is not clear that the risk faced by Canadian firms is a matter for public policy to address although one could at least say that public policies, such as uncertain tax and fiscal policies, could create additional risk for firms.

- If governments were to intervene in capital markets, it is largely with the aim of improving efficiency by eliminating government policies that are a barrier to good performance (e.g., taxation and regulations) or to compensate for "market failures" primarily those associated with informational asymmetries.
- Informational asymmetry issues are especially important in those parts of capital markets where lenders do not have sufficient information about the characteristics of the borrower: venture capital, initial public offerings and smaller Canadian companies.
- Governments have used various public policies to assist capital markets in improving their performance. However, public policies that have subsidized financing of firms have not been altogether successful as failure rates have been too high or profitability too low. Moreover, it is unclear whether policies directed at financing are superior to policies directed at the investments made by businesses.

There are many more problems for Canadian researchers to address that go beyond the discussion in this survey. It is too difficult to list all the issues that public policy experts still have not answered. One could say, however, that the integration of imperfect information in the cost of capital measurements and analysis of investment is a good place to start.

ENDNOTES

1 As discussed above, capital markets include all forms of financing businesses, including financial intermediation. However, the focus of the Industry Canada conference was primarily on the financing through markets rather than intermediaries.

2 Johnson and Neave (1995) distinguish between Type S (Standard) and Type N (Nonstandard) transactions. The former involve relatively liquid assets while the latter are non-liquid assets. The Type S transactions require resources to determine the initial value of assets (by investors screening borrowers or by borrowers signalling their characteristics) with little cost associated with monitoring and control after the deal is made. Type N transactions may be more expensive to hold since monitoring and control are often required after the deal is made. This classification is useful to bear in mind for later discussion.

3 There is no presumption as to how the weights are determined. There are two general models used to explain the financing of investments. The first is the static-tradeoff model whereby firms issue securities until the marginal benefit is equal to the marginal cost of issuing each type of security. The second is the "pecking order" model whereby firms first use internal sources of finance followed by external finance (debt and equity). The pecking order model would result in no dividends being issued by the firm (a somewhat disturbing feature of the model). However, the pecking order model does predict that firms would underinvest in capital since the existing shareholders would prefer to give up an investment project rather than issue new securities to outside investors who place less value on the firms' shares.

4 For a discussion of different types of risk and the cost of capital, see Mintz (1995).

5 There is a fairly large literature on the taxation of capital. See Auerbach (1983), King and Fullerton (1984) and Boadway et al. (1984) for original papers on the cost of capital and effective tax rates. The large literature incorporating different aspects of the tax system in the cost of capital is summarized in Mintz (1995). A good application of these results is found in the paper by Chen and McKenzie in this volume. The user cost capital including taxes is derived as a formula which is the following:

$c = (r+\delta+h^*)(1-A)/(1-u)+h$

with

$r = \beta i(1-u)+\beta\rho$

and

β = debt/asset ratio

i = interest rate on debt

u = corporate income tax rate

ρ = risk-free cost of equity finance

δ = rate of economic depreciation

h^* = cost of capital risk

A = present value of annual depreciation allowances, investment tax credit, etc.

h = cost of income risk.

The effective tax rate on capital is derived by subtracting depreciation and risk from the user cost of capital which is equal to the before-tax risk-adjusted marginal rate of return on capital. The effective tax rate is then estimated as the difference between the risk-adjusted before-tax rate of return and after-tax rate of return (all tax variables are equal to zero) divided by the risk-adjusted before-tax rate of return to capital.

6 When the tax base is negative, governments do not refund the loss by sending a cheque to the firm equal to the tax rate times the loss. Instead, governments in most countries will allow losses to be carried back for a limited period for a refund based on prior years' taxes or carried forward, at no rate of interest, against future income. Most losses in Canada are carried forward and written off over time (see Glenday and Mintz, 1991). Thus, there can be a tax penalty imposed on risky or start-up firms since the government fails to share profits and losses fully. If, however, governments provide full refundability, companies might take actions that increase the size of the loss (such as by loading debt in Canada that finances investments elsewhere). Thus, governments limit the amount of loss refundability in the tax system. The actual impact of tax losses on investment is more complicated since previous years' losses could shelter existing income on assets from taxation, thereby encouraging investments in the current period (see Mintz, 1995 for a fuller discussion of these points).

7 This approach was used in 1990 by the National Advisory Board on Science and Technology to measure the cost of capital in Canada compared to other countries in order to determine whether the federal government should change its economic policies. However, before any real policy conclusions are derived from this approach, one should try to measure the whole user cost of capital rather than only one part of it, the financial cost of capital.

8 For a recent discussion of competition in financial markets, see Booth (1995) who provides evidence that neither confirms nor denies market power in financial markets.

9 Amit, Brander and Zott use taxes paid as a proxy of profits. The problem with the use of this variable is that the amount of taxes paid may depend on the type of project. For example, high-technology projects might have more research and development expenses that qualify for the research and development credit.

10 This includes the small business income deduction and certain other tax benefits that are only available to Canadian-controlled private corporations.

11 Suret and L'Her use two tax variables, one which takes into account both corporate income and personal income tax effects on debt decisions and the other which accounts for the effect of corporate tax losses generated by incentives on the value of interest deductions. Neither variable succeeds likely due to mismeasurement. The authors assume that the companies are owned by Ontario residents who, in an open economy, would not be the marginal source of finance. Also, corporate income tax rates should be carefully measured to take into account provincial and industry variations. The use of deferred tax liabilities to measure tax incentives that give rise to losses are affected by Canadian law that allows companies to deduct depreciation, exploration and development expenses on a discretionary basis (companies that do not deduct expenses have less deferred tax liability even though they are expecting not to pay taxes for quite some time). In Bartholdy et al. (1987), the corporate tax rate variable was found to cause the debt ratio to increase, as predicted by theory. They also found that non-taxpaying companies have lower debt ratios. See also Shum (1995).

12 The discussion below is based on unpublished work by Marchand and Mintz.

13 Note that if separation of good and bad firms is possible for governments, it would also be possible for the private sector.

14 In a separating equilibrium such as Myers and Majluf (1984), poor quality firms do not underinvest in capital even though good quality firms do. Bad quality firms issue securities to outside investors in the interest of maximizing profits as best as possible. Good quality firms, by issuing securities to outside investors, lose value as they are viewed by markets to be bad quality firms. Unless the good quality firm has sufficient internal resources to cover all profitable investments, the good quality firm will give up some investments to avoid being viewed as a bad quality firm. Thus, a general subsidy for either investment or financing would encourage poor quality firms to invest in too much capital.

ACKNOWLEDGEMENTS

THE AUTHOR IS INDEBTED TO AN ANONYMOUS REFEREE for helpful comments on this paper.

BIBLIOGRAPHY

Akerlof, G. "The market for 'lemons': quality and the market mechanism." *Quarterly Journal of Economics*. 84, (1970): 488-500.

Arrow, K.J. *Aspects of the Theory of Risk-Bearing*. Helsinki: Yrjo Jahnssonin Saatio: 1965.

Arrow, K. J. and R.C. Lind. "Uncertainty and the evaluation of public investment decisions." *American Economic Review*. 60, (1970): 364-378.

Auerbach, A. J. "Corporate taxation in the United States." *Brookings Papers on Economic Activity*. 2, (1983): 451-505.

Bartholdy, J., G. Fisher and J. Mintz. "Taxation and financial policy of firms theory and empirical application to Canada." Economic Council of Canada Discussion Paper No. 324, 1987.

Battacharya, S. "Imperfect information, dividend policy, and the 'bird in the hand' fallacy." *Bell Journal of Economics*. 10, (1979): 259-270.

Boadway, R., N. Bruce and J. Mintz. "Taxation, inflation and the effective marginal tax rate in Canada." *Canadian Journal of Economics*. 27, (1984): 286-299.

Booth, L. "Competition and Profitability in the Financial Services Industry." *Competition and Regulation of the Financial Service Industry*. Edited by J. Mintz and J. Pesando. C.D. Howe Institute, forthcoming.

Bulow, J. and L. Summers. "The taxation of risky assets." *Journal of Political Economy*, 92, (1984): 20-39.

Dixit, A. and R. Pindyck. *Investment under Uncertainty*. Princeton, New Jersey: Princeton University Press, 1993.

Economic Council of Canada. *The Regulation of Deposit-Taking Institutions in Canada*. Ottawa: Queen's Printers, 1976.

Edey, M. and K. Hviding. "An assessment of financial reform in OECD countries." Organization for Economic Co-operation and Development, Economics Department, Working Paper No. 154, 1995.

French, K. and J. Poterba. "Investor diversification and international equity markets." National Bureau of Economic Research, Working Paper No. 3609, 1991.

Glenday, G. and J. Mintz. "The sources and magnitude of tax losses in Canada." *The Tax Treatment of Losses in Canada*, Clarkson Gordon Foundation, 1991.

Johnson, Lewis D. and Edwin H. Neave. "Corporate governance and supervision of the financial system." In *Corporate Decision-Making in Canada*. Edited by Ronald J. Daniels and Randall Morck. Calgary: University of Calgary Press, 1995.

Jorgenson, D. "Capital theory and investment behavior." *American Economic Review*. 53, (1963): 247-259.

King, M.A. and D. Fullerton (eds.). *The Taxation of Income from Capital*. Chicago: University of Chicago Press, 1984.

McKenzie, K. "The implications of risk and irreversibility for the measurement of marginal tax rates on capital." *Canadian Journal of Economics*. 27, (1994): 604-619.

McKenzie, K. and J. Mintz. "Tax effects and the cost of capital: a Canada-U.S. comparison." In *Canada-U.S. Tax Comparisons*. Edited by J. Shoven and J. Whalley. Chicago: University of Chicago Press, 1992.

Miller, M. and K. Rock. "Dividend policy under asymmetric information." *Journal of Finance*. 40, (1985): 1031-1051.

Mintz, J. "The corporation tax: a survey." *Fiscal Studies*. 16, (1995): 23-68.

Myers, S. and N. Majluf. "Corporate financing and investment decisions: when firms have information that investors do not have." *Journal of Financial Economics*. 13, (1984): 187-221.

OECD (Organization for Economic Co-operation and Development). *Taxing Profits in a Global Economy: Domestic and International Issues*. Paris: OECD, 1991.

Ross, S. "The determination of financial structure: the incentive signalling approach." *Bell Journal of Economics*. 8, (1977): 23-40.

Rothschild, M. and J. Stiglitz. "Equilibrium in competitive insurance markets." *Quarterly Journal of Economics*. 90, (1976): 629-650.

Shum, Pauline. "Tax Asymmetry and Intertemporal Corporate Decisions." Unpublished Ph.D. dissertation, University of Toronto, 1995.

Spence, M. "Job market signalling." *Quarterly Journal of Economics*. 83, (1973): 355-379.

Vickrey, W. "Utility, strategy and social decision rules." *Quarterly Journal of Economics*. 74, (1960): 507-535.

About the Contributors

Raphael (Raffi) Amit is the Peter Wall Distinguished Professor at the Faculty of Commerce and Business Administration, University of British Columbia (UBC). He is the founding Director of the W. Maurice Young Entrepreneurship and Venture Capital Research Centre. Trained as a business economist, he received a Ph.D. in management from Northwestern University. Before joining UBC, he served on the faculty of the J.L. Kellogg Graduate School of Management, Northwestern University, where he has been the recipient of the J.L. Kellogg Research Professorship and the Richard M. Paget Research Chair in Business Policy. His research interests focus on entrepreneurship in independent and corporate settings and on strategic management.

Albert Ando is Professor of Economics and Finance at the University of Pennsylvania. He has his Ph.D. in mathematical economics from the Carnegie Institute of Technology. Throughout his long and distinguished career, he has been associated with the Massachusetts Institute of Technology, the International Monetary Fund, the University of Bonn and the University of Stockholm, among others. He continues as a consultant to the Bank of Italy and as a research associate at the National Bureau of Economic Research. He is the author or co-author of several books and articles. Current studies include the cost of capital in the United States and Japan, and the definition of the cost of capital for investment under inflation when corporate profit tax is present.

James Brander is the Asia-Pacific Professor of International Business and Public Policy in the Faculty of Commerce and Business Administration at the University of British Columbia (UBC). He is also a research co-ordinator in the Entrepreneurship and Venture Capital Research Centre at UBC. He completed his master's degree and Ph.D. in economics at Stanford University, and taught at Queen's University before joining UBC. He has published widely in academic journals, particularly in the areas of international trade policy, industrial organization and financial economics. He is a research associate of the National Bureau of Economic Research. His major current research interests are trade in renewable resources and financing and performance of new firms.

Donald J.S. Brean is Associate Professor of Finance and Economics, Faculty of Management, University of Toronto. He is a member of the International Panel of Tax Experts of the International Monetary Fund and has advised numerous international agencies, including the World Bank, the European Community and the Canadian government. He has published extensively in the areas of international finance and investment, taxation, industrial organization and economic policy.

A. Louis Calvet is Professor of Finance in the Faculty of Administration at the University of Ottawa. Dr. Calvet received his Ph.D. from the Massachusetts Institute of Technology. His research interests are in the areas of stock market volatility, asset pricing models and the management of foreign exchange risk. He is the author of numerous articles and co-author of a book published in 1995 entitled *Financial Instruments: A Guide for Financial Managers*. He has been a consultant for the Department of Finance and the Treasury Board of Canada, and a regular instructor for the Institute of Canadian Bankers.

Duanjie Chen is a Research Associate at the Institute for Policy Analysis and the International Centre for Tax Studies at the University of Toronto. She was awarded her doctorate in philosophy and economics from Wuhan University in China and has been a Fulbright Visiting Scholar at Yale University. She has co-authored (with J. Mintz) a research study of the 1995 Canadian federal budget's tax policy.

Robert Chirinko is an Associate Professor of Economics at Emory University (Atlanta, Georgia) and Visiting Scholar at the Federal Reserve Bank of Kansas City (Missouri). He earned his Ph.D. in economics from Northwestern University. His research examines business behaviour with a special focus on investment spending, credit conditions and tax policy. He has published several papers on the determinants of investment. Current projects include examining whether "bubbles" exist in the United States and Japanese equity markets, and using investment data to test hypotheses about "short-termism" by Canadian firms.

Élise Cormier is Assistant Professor with the Consumer Affairs Department at the Université Laval. She holds an M.B.A. in finance from Laval and has submitted a doctoral thesis to the university on the evaluation of initial share offerings. Her research work centres on the problem small businesses have in becoming listed on the stock market and the relationship between accounting data and the value of securities.

Michael Daly works as a counsellor for the Trade Policies Review Division of the World Trade Organization. He previously was with the Organization for Economic Co-operation and Development, involved in matters related to the negotiation of a Multilateral Agreement on Investment, and with the European Commission, where, as Advisor and Secretary to the Ruding Committee, he was responsible for preparing the Committee's 1992 report on company taxation in the European

Union. Prior to this, he was a Chief in the Tax Policy Branch of the Department of Finance in Ottawa. His main research interests include taxation and trade. He received his Ph.D. in Economics from Queen's University.

Jean-Marie Gagnon is Professor of Financial Management at Université Laval. He holds an M.Sc. from Université Laval and a Ph.D. in Business from the University of Chicago. His research interests are in corporate governance and the effects of income taxes on capital markets, and he has published articles in these areas in several national and international academic journals.

Paul Halpern is Professor of Finance at the Faculty of Management, University of Toronto, Chair of the Advisory Board of the *Canadian Investment Review* and Chair of the Research Committee of the Financial Research Foundation of Canada. He has also served as a consultant to governments, regulatory authorities and corporations in the areas of corporate finance, capital markets and securities. Professor Halpern holds a Ph.D. in finance from the University of Chicago and has published research and applied papers for both academic and practitioner journals. His research interests are in mergers and acquisitions, corporate restructuring and corporate governance.

John Hancock is finishing his doctoral studies at the University of Pennsylvania. His dissertation is on the taxation of income from capital. He received a master's degree from Georgetown University with a specialization in international finance. In addition to his research in capital markets, he has co-authored four publications for the World Bank on the macro-economic impact of AIDS in developing countries.

Vijay M. Jog is Professor of Finance at the School of Business, Carleton University. He is a chemical engineer with graduate degrees in management and finance from McGill University and specializes in corporate finance, value creation, taxation and business financing. He has published extensively on these subjects in leading international financial journals. His current research interests include value creation and corporate performance, executive compensation, financial planning and analysis, and activity-based management and costing.

Andrew G. Karolyi is Associate Professor in the Finance Area Group of the Ivey (Western) School of Business at the University of Western Ontario. Professor Karolyi received his Ph.D. and M.B.A. degrees in finance from the University of Chicago. He also holds a master's degree in economics from the University of Ottawa. Previously, he was an Associate Professor of Finance at the Fisher College of Business, Ohio State University and spent several years as an Economist in the Research Department of the Bank of Canada. He has also taught executive education courses in finance in the United States, Europe and Australia. Professor Karolyi has published in various academic journals. His research program focuses on the study of investment management issues.

Eric Kirzner is an adjunct Associate Professor of Finance at the Faculty of Management, University of Toronto. His primary teaching and research interests are in the areas of investment and risk management applications with derivative products, market micro-structures (market trading rules, surveillance and integrity), product innovation and asset allocation strategies. Professor Kirzner is the Chairman of the Toronto Stock Exchange (TSE) Issuers and Investors Advisory Committee and serves on the TSE's Toronto Index Participation Unit discretion committee. He serves as a Public Governor of the Toronto Futures Exchange and as Public Director of the Canadian Derivatives Clearing Corporation. He is co-author of a number of books.

Jean-François L'Her is Assistant Professor of Finance at the École des Hautes Études Commerciales (HEC) in Montréal. He has a Ph.D. in finance from Université Laval. A specialist in corporate finance, financial analysis and capital markets theory, his current research activities concern financial market efficiency and irrationality, the heterogeneity of expectations and of transaction volumes and prices, the effect of market regulation and micro-structure on the value of securities, and financial decisions made by businesses. He directs the Groupe de Recherche en Finance, and is a researcher at the HEC's Centre d'étude en administration internationale and at the Centre Interuniversitaire de Recherche en Analyse des Organisations in Montréal.

Simon Lalancette is a professor at the École des Hautes Études Commerciales. He previously was a professor with the Département de sciences économiques, Université du Québec à Montréal. He has an M.Sc. from the Université de Sherbrooke and a Ph.D. from Concordia University. His areas of research are financial assets evaluation models, portfolio performance evaluation, econometrics as applied to financial problems, and capital markets. He is the co-author of several articles published in specialized publications.

Jeffrey G. MacIntosh is Professor of Law at the Faculty of Law, University of Toronto. His main teaching interests are in the areas of corporate and securities law, and in law and economics. He has also taught contract and commercial law. Professor MacIntosh has published extensively in the area of corporate and securities law on such topics as shareholders' rights, the legal relationship between majority and minority shareholders, corporate takeovers, poison pills, the statutory oppression remedy, appraisal rights, the role of institutional and retail investors in Canadian capital markets, and directors' fiduciary duties. His current research deals with the special problems of financing high-technology enterprise in Canada.

Elizabeth Maynes is Associate Professor, Finance, Schulich School of Business, York University. She obtained her Ph.D. in economics from Queen's University. She has focused her teaching and research activities in the area of advanced corporate finance, including an analysis of takeover rights, the origins and evolution of restricted shares in Canada and the performance of Canadian initial public offerings.

Kenneth J. McKenzie is an Associate Professor of Economics at the University of Calgary. He has his doctorate in economics from Queen's University. His areas of specialization include taxation, investment under certainty, resource economics, financial economics and micro-economic theory. He began his career as an economist with the Saskatchewan Economic Development Corporation and subsequently joined the Tax Policy Branch of the Department of Finance. He is the author/co-author of numerous studies and articles for scholarly journals examining the impact of changes in tax policy on various sectors of the economy and on the cost of capital. Current research involves an empirical investigation of the Alberta deficit elimination program.

Andrew P. Meyer is an Associate Economist in the Banking Supervision and Regulation Department at the Federal Reserve Bank of St. Louis. He is finishing his doctoral studies at Washington University in St. Louis. His dissertation examines the effect of the cost of capital on U.S. investment. His main areas of interest are investment and bank regulation.

Jack M. Mintz is the Arthur Anderson Professor of Taxation, Faculty of Management, University of Toronto. He is also the Clifford Clark Visiting Economist at the Department of Finance. He has published widely in the field of public finance and fiscal federalism. He has been a Special Advisor to the Assistant Deputy Minister, Tax Policy Branch, Department of Finance, and served on the Working Group on the Corporate Minimum Tax. He has also consulted widely with the World Bank, the International Monetary Fund, the Organization for Economic Co-operation and Development, the governments of Canada, Alberta, Ontario and Saskatchewan, and the Royal Commission on National Passenger Transportation. He is the Editor-in-Chief of *International Tax and Public Finance* and is Associate Dean (Academic), Faculty of Management, University of Toronto.

Usha Mittoo is an Associate Professor of Finance, Faculty of Management, University of Manitoba. She holds a Ph.D. in finance from the University of British Columbia and an M.B.A. from the University of Manitoba. Dr. Mittoo's research interests are in international capital markets and corporate finance, and the relationship between industrial structure and cross-country stock returns and the effect of foreign listing on firm value. She is also investigating the determinants of gains to Canadian bidders in U.S. acquisitions. Her research has been published in a number of scholarly journals.

Serge Nadeau is Director, Micro-Economic Analysis, Industry Canada. He received his Ph.D. in public policy from Carnegie-Mellon University. Before joining Industry Canada, he was Chief, Economic Development, Business Income Tax Division, at the Department of Finance and Assistant Professor of Economics at the University of Victoria. He has published in the areas of taxation theory and policy, and in applied economics.

Edward P. Neufeld is Visiting Senior Research Fellow at the Centre for International Studies, University of Toronto. He is retired as Vice-President, Economic and Corporate Affairs at the Royal Bank of Canada and is a former Professor of Economics at the University of Toronto. He is also a former Assistant Deputy Minister of the Department of Finance where he was in charge of the development of policies and amendments relating to the tax system. He obtained his Ph.D. from the London School of Economics and Political Science.

Michel Poitevin is Associate Professor in the Department of Economics at the Université de Montréal. He is also a researcher at the Centre de recherche en développement économique. He holds a Ph.D. in economics from the University of British Columbia. As a specialist in financial and information economics at the firm level, Dr. Poitevin has conducted research in the areas of financial decision making and production choices, as well as on the economic consequences of asymmetric information and its effects on contracts and investment decisions.

Allan L. Riding is Professor of Finance at the Carleton University School of Business. He obtained his Ph.D. from McGill University. Primary research interests include small business finance and capital market efficiency. His research findings have been published in numerous academic journals. He has been engaged by the public and private sectors as an advisor and consultant. Studies have included an analysis of the *Small Business Loans Act*, banking priorities regarding small businesses and the market for informal equity finance.

Michael J. Robinson is an Associate Professor, Faculty of Management, University of Calgary. He has also been a faculty member at the University of Western Ontario and Wilfrid Laurier University. Dr. Robinson received his M.B.A. and Ph.D. from the University of Western Ontario. His research interests are in the areas of investments, market microstructure, market efficiency and initial public offerings. He has written several articles examining capital markets in Canada and is co-author of *Investment Management in Canada*. Over the years, he has acted as a consultant to a number of Canadian firms.

Gary Sawchuk is a research economist with the Micro-Economic Policy Analysis group at Industry Canada. He holds a Ph.D. from the University of Manitoba and an M.P.A. from Harvard University. He recently co-authored a study on the financing costs of small firms.

Brian F. Smith is Associate Professor of Finance at Wilfrid Laurier University and Director of the Mutual Group Financial Services Research Centre at that University's School of Business and Economics. Dr. Smith has researched extensively in the areas of financial institutions, mergers and acquisitions, and corporate governance. His research has been widely published. He is co-editor of a book on Canadian capital markets and co-author of a paper on stock prices, ordinary dividends and cash flow to shareholders. The Financial Services Research Centre promotes applied research on Canadian financial institutions and markets.

Jean-Marc Suret is a Full Professor at the Finance and Insurance Department of the faculty of Administration at Université Laval. He is the Director of Research at the Centre interuniversitaire de recherche en analyse des organisations in Montréal. He holds a Ph.D. in administration from Laval. His research work is in corporate financing and share price determination mechanisms. His corporate finance research is directed mainly at the policies relating to finance and dividends and at the impact of government intervention on the way businesses manage these areas. His work concerns the way agents with varying expectations determine share prices based on essential data. The subjects studied include the effect of the arrival of information on the market, the impact of different accounting systems and the efficiency of stock markets outside North America.

Daniel B. Thornton is Professor and Chair of the Ph.D. program of the School of Business at Queen's University. Previously, he held the Chartered Accountants' Professorship in Accounting at the University of Calgary, following appointments as Professor at the University of Toronto and Distinguished Visiting Professor at Concordia University. He has consulted with professional organizations and business corporations and has appeared as an expert accounting witness for the federal government. He has published several books including *Managerial Tax Planning: A Canadian Perspective*, *Introduction to Financial Accounting* and *Accounting Literature: Research for Users*. Current research explores the interplay between tax planning and financial reporting, the disclosure of environmental liabilities in a market-game setting, and the effect of continual accounting disclosures on firm valuation.

François Vaillancourt is a Professor, Department of Economics and Research Fellow, Centre de recherche et développement en économique, Université de Montréal and Fellow of the Institute for Research on Public Policy. He teaches, conducts research and has published extensively in the area of public finance and the economics of language. He has conducted research and acted as a consultant for organizations such as the Canadian Tax Foundation, the Conseil de la langue française, the Department of Finance, the Economic Council of Canada, Statistics Canada and the World Bank. Professor Vaillancourt holds a Ph.D. from Queen's University.

Ralph A. Winter is a Professor at the University of Toronto. He teaches theory of contracts and organizations in the Department of Economics, finance in the Faculty of Management, and the law and economics of competition policy in the Faculty of Law at the University. Professor Winter has his Ph.D. in economics from the University of California at Berkeley. He has also had positions as a National Fellow at the Hoover Institution at Stanford and as an Olin Fellow in Law and Economics at Yale. His research interests include the application of contract theory to issues in competition policy, especially the distinction between efficient and anticompetitive contracts or arrangements; the interaction between tort law and the liability insurance markets in influencing incentives as well as insurance market performance; and the design of contracts to control agency problems.

Christoph Zott is a Ph.D. candidate at the Faculty of Commerce and Business Administration, University of British Columbia (UBC). He holds a graduate degree in industrial engineering from the Universität Karlsrihe in Germany and from the Institut National Polytechnique de Grenoble in France. Before joining UBC, he worked as a management consultant in Germany. His main area of research interest is entrepreneurship and strategic management.